Knowledge Representation

Knowledge Representation

Logical, Philosophical, and Computational Foundations

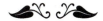

JOHN F. SOWA

Brooks/Cole
Thomson Learning™

Pacific Grove • Albany • Belmont • Boston • Cincinnati • Johannesburg • London • Madrid • Melbourne
Mexico City • New York • Scottsdale • Singapore • Tokyo • Toronto

Sponsoring Editor: *Kallie Swanson and Mike Sugarman*	Interior Design: *Sandra Rigney*
Senior Marketing Manager: *Nathan Wilbur*	Cover Design: *Laurie Albrecht*
Marketing Assistant: *Christina DeVeto*	Interior Illustration: *Northeastern Graphic Services*
Editorial Assistant: *Grace Fujimoto*	Print Buyer: *Vena Dyer*
Production Editor: *Kirk Bomont*	Typesetting: *Northeastern Graphic Services*
Production Service: *Northeastern Graphic Services*	Cover Printing: *Phoenix Color Corporation*
Manuscript Editor: *Sarah Zobel*	Printing and Binding: *R.R. Donnelley, Crawfordsville*

Cover illustration. The diagram on the cover is the tree of nature and logic by the thirteenth century Spanish poet, philosopher, and missionary Ramon Lull. The main trunk supports a version of the *tree of Porphyry*, which illustrates Aristotle's categories. The ten leaves on the right represent ten types of questions, and the ten leaves on the left are keyed to a system of rotating disks for generating answers. Such diagrams and disks comprise Lull's *Ars Magna* [Great Art], which was the first attempt to develop mechanical aids to reasoning. It served as an inspiration to the pioneer in symbolic logic, Gottfried Wilhelm Leibniz.

For more information, contact:
BROOKS/COLE
511 Forest Lodge Road
Pacific Grove, CA 93950 USA
www.brookscole.com

For permission to use material from this work, contact us by
Web: www. thomsonrights.com
fax: 1-800-730-2215
phone: 1-800-730-2214

Printed in the United States of America

10 9 8 7 6 5 4 3 2 1

Library of Congress Cataloging-in-Publication Data

Sowa, John F.
  Knowledge representation: logical, philosophical, and
computational foundations / John F. Sowa.
        p.   cm.
Includes bibliographical references and index.
  ISBN 0 534-94965-7
  1. Knowledge representation (Information theory) I. Title.
Q387.S68 2000   98-5070
003'.54 — dc21

Dedication

To the spirits of the great knowledge engineers,

Aristotle, Leibniz, Kant, Peirce, and Whitehead.

Contents

Preface

Socrates said he was the midwife to his listeners, i.e., he made them reflect better concerning that which they already knew and become better conscious of it. If we only knew what we know, namely, in the use of certain words and concepts that are so subtle in application, we would be astonished at the treasures contained in our knowledge.
IMMANUEL KANT, *"Vienna Logic"*

Like Socrates, knowledge engineers and systems analysts play the role of midwife in bringing knowledge forth and making it explicit. They display the implicit knowledge about a subject in a form that programmers can encode in algorithms and data structures. In the programs themselves, the link to the original knowledge is only mentioned in comments, which the computer cannot understand. To make the hidden knowledge accessible to the computer, knowledge-based systems and object-oriented systems are built around declarative languages whose form of expression is closer to human languages. Such systems help the programmers and knowledge engineers reflect on "the treasures contained in the knowledge" and express it in a form that both the humans and the computers can understand.

Knowledge representation developed as a branch of *artificial intelligence* — the science of designing computer systems to perform tasks that would normally require human intelligence. But today, advanced systems everywhere are performing tasks that used to require human intelligence: information retrieval, stock-market trading, resource allocation, circuit design, virtual reality, speech recognition, and machine translation. As a result, the AI design techniques have converged with techniques from other fields, especially database and object-oriented systems. This book is a general textbook of knowledge-base analysis and design, intended for anyone whose job is to analyze knowledge about the real world and map it to a computable form.

LOGIC, ONTOLOGY, AND COMPUTATION. Knowledge representation is a multidisciplinary subject that applies theories and techniques from three other fields:

1. *Logic* provides the formal structure and rules of inference.
2. *Ontology* defines the kinds of things that exist in the application domain.

3. *Computation* supports the applications that distinguish knowledge representation from pure philosophy.

Without logic, a knowledge representation is vague, with no criteria for determining whether statements are redundant or contradictory. Without ontology, the terms and symbols are ill-defined, confused, and confusing. And without computable models, the logic and ontology cannot be implemented in computer programs. Knowledge representation is the application of logic and ontology to the task of constructing computable models for some domain.

The readers of this book should have some experience in analyzing a problem, identifying the kinds of things that have to be represented, and mapping them to a computable form. This level of experience can be expected of computer science students. Yet because of the interdisciplinary nature of the subject, the book contains considerable material on philosophy and linguistics. Therefore, it is also suitable for philosophy and linguistics students who have some background in artificial intelligence or computer programming. While writing the book, I have used early drafts in graduate-level courses in computer science at Polytechnic University and in the program on Philosophy and Computers and Cognitive Science at Binghamton University.

EXERCISES. At the end of each chapter, the exercises introduce topics that illustrate, supplement, and extend the main presentation. Instead of emphasizing symbol manipulation, the exercises address the problems of analyzing informal specifications and selecting an appropriate ontology for representing them. In effect, the "word problems," which usually give high-school algebra students the most difficulty, are closer to the central issues of knowledge representation than the purely technical problems of manipulating symbols. Answers and hints for a representative sample of the exercises are included at the end of the book.

All of the major knowledge representations are discussed, analyzed, and related to logic: rules, frames, semantic networks, object-oriented languages, Prolog, Java, SQL, Petri nets, and the Knowledge Interchange Format (KIF). The two basic notations used for logic are predicate calculus and conceptual graphs. Predicate calculus is the traditional logic notation that students must know in order to read the literature of AI and computer science. Conceptual graphs are a two-dimensional form of logic that is based on the semantic networks of AI and the logical graphs of C. S. Peirce. Both notations are exactly equivalent in their semantics, and instructors may choose to use either or both in lectures and exercises.

Examples in this book are illustrated in several languages, but no prior knowledge of any of them is expected. The emphasis is on the semantic principles underlying all languages rather than the syntactic details of particular languages. Although computer exercises can help to show how the theory is applied, this book can be used without any special computer accompaniment.

ORGANIZATION.   Chapter 1 introduces logic through a historical survey, ranging from Aristotle's syllogisms to the modern graphic and algebraic systems. The details of the predicate calculus and conceptual graph notations are summarized in Appendix A. For students who have little or no background in logic, the instructor can spend extra time on Chapter 1 and Appendix A to use this book as an introduction to logic. For more advanced students, the instructor can cover Chapter 1 quickly and spend more time on the topics in later chapters.

Chapter 2, which is the most philosophical in the book, introduces *ontology*, the study of existence. Ontology defines the categories of things that are expressed in the predicates of predicate logic, the slots in frames, the tables of a database, or the classes of an object-oriented system. Logic is pure form, and ontology provides the content that is expressed in that form. Depending on the interests of students and the instructor, this chapter can be surveyed briefly or covered in depth.

Chapter 3 introduces the principles of knowledge representation and their role in adapting logic and ontology to the task of constructing computable models of an application domain. It shows how logic and ontology are embodied in a variety of computational languages. This chapter is central to computer applications, but it can be surveyed for students of linguistics or philosophy.

Chapter 4 presents methods for representing dynamically changing processes and events. Petri nets and dataflow graphs are introduced as supplementary notations, which can be translated either to conventional programming languages or to logic in the predicate calculus or conceptual graph notations. Petri nets serve as a bridge between the procedural programming techniques and the declarative logic-based approach that is emphasized in the other chapters.

Chapter 5 shows how purpose and context affect knowledge representation and the various theories of modal and intentional logic. These theories are applied to the encapsulated objects of 0-0 systems and to the design of interacting agents. This chapter has the most detailed logical development, but much of it can be skipped for students whose background in logic is weak.

Chapter 6, on "knowledge soup," stresses the limitations of logic. It discusses the vague, uncertain, unanalyzed, and often inconsistent mix of facts, opinions, and rules of thumb that people have in their heads. It presents the techniques for reconciling logic to the unpredictable, continuously variable aspects of reality. These techniques are not rejections of logic, but methods for adapting logic to the complexities of the real world.

Chapter 7 discusses the problems of knowledge sharing and the ongoing efforts related to the ANSI and ISO projects on ontology and conceptual schemes. It illustrates critical issues in using logic-based techniques to facilitate communication and interoperability of heterogeneous computer systems.

The first section of every chapter is more introductory and less technical than the remaining sections, and the first paragraph of every section gives a quick overview of the rest. Therefore, readers can survey any chapter by reading just the first section and the first paragraph of each remaining section. While skimming through a chapter, readers should glance at the illustrations to get an overview of the topics that are covered.

CAST OF CHARACTERS. Science is a human subject, developed by people who step on each other's toes at least as often as they stand on each other's shoulders. The five philosophers to whom this book is dedicated have been admired and trampled more than most. Their theories and practices are among the best available examples of how logic and ontology can be applied to the representation of knowledge in science, business, and everyday life. For a testimonial to their influence, note the references to them in the index of this book.

As Peirce said, every scientist is deeply indebted to a "community of inquirers" whose contributions, criticisms, and collaboration are essential to the development of the science. While writing this book, I benefited enormously from the overlapping communities in which I participated. Among them are my students and colleagues at SUNY Binghamton and Polytechnic University; the members of the ANSI and ISO working groups on conceptual schemas, ontologies, and the CG and KIF standards, which were chaired by Sandra Perez, Tony Sarris, John Sharp, and Baba Piprani; and the FANTA project at IBM, which included Fan Hsu, Bob Spillers, and Martin van den Berg.

My greatest debt is to the community of the conceptual graph workshops and the International Conferences on Conceptual Structures. Since I don't have the space to list all the participants, I'll just list the organizers of the conferences and the editors of the proceedings: Michel Chein, Walling Cyre, Harry Delugach, Judy Dick, Peter Eklund, Gerard Ellis, John Esch, Jean Fargues, Mary Keeler, Bob Levinson, Dickson Lukose, Guy Mineau, Bernard Moulin, Marie-Laure Mugnier, Tim Nagle, Heather Pfeiffer, Bill Rich, Leroy Searle, Bill Tepfenhart, Eileen Way, and Rudolf Wille. I gratefully thank them and everyone mentioned in the proceedings they edited, which are listed in the bibliography of this book.

My community also includes many people whose contributions are not adequately represented in the above lists: Jaime Carbonell, Norman Foo, Benjamin Grosof, Mike Genesereth, Nicola Guarino, Ed Hovy, Fritz Lehmann, John McCarthy, Michael McCord, Robert Meersman, Julius Moravcsik, Mary Neff, Paula Newman, Paul Rosenbloom, Peter Simons, Doug Skuce, Cora Sowa, and Wlodek Zadrozny. Finally, I thank the editors and staff of Brooks/Cole for their patience in waiting for this book to be finished in December for more Decembers than I would like to admit.

John F. Sowa
Croton-on-Hudson, New York

CHAPTER ONE

Logic

❧ ❧

The very first lesson that we have a right to demand that logic shall teach us is, how to make our ideas clear; and a most important one it is, depreciated only by minds who stand in need of it. To know what we think, to be masters of our own meaning, will make a solid foundation for great and weighty thought.

CHARLES SANDERS PEIRCE, *"How to Make Our Ideas Clear"*

1.1 Historical Background

The words *knowledge* and *representation* have provoked philosophical controversies for over two and a half millennia. In the fifth century B.C., Socrates stirred up some of the deepest controversies by claiming to know very little, if anything. By his relentless questioning, he destroyed the smug self-satisfaction of people who claimed to have knowledge of fundamental subjects like Truth, Beauty, Virtue, and Justice. By recreating Socrates' dialectical process of questioning, his student Plato established the subject of *epistemology* — the study of the nature of knowledge and its justification. Epistemology, in those days, was literally a matter of life and death. For his alleged impiety in questioning cherished beliefs, Socrates was condemned to death as a corrupter of the morals of Athenian youth.

TERMINOLOGY. Plato's student Aristotle shifted the emphasis of philosophy from the nature of knowledge to the less controversial, but more practical problem of representing knowledge. His monumental life's work resulted in an encyclopedic compilation of the knowledge of his day. But before he could compile that knowledge, Aristotle had to invent the words for representing it. He established the initial terminology and defined the scope of logic, physics, metaphysics, biology, psychology, linguistics, politics, ethics, rhetoric, and economics. For all those fields, the terms that he either coined or adopted have become the core of today's international technical vocabulary. Some of them, such as *category, metaphor,* and *hypothesis,* are direct borrowings from Aristotle's Greek. Others, such as *quantity, quality, genus,*

I

species, noun, verb, subject, and *predicate,* are borrowings of Latin words that were coined for the purpose of translating the Greek. The English word *quality,* for example, comes from Cicero's word *qualitas.* Cicero explained that he coined the word as a translation of the Greek *poiotēs* (what-kind-ness), which "among the Greeks is not a word of the common people, but of the philosophers" (*Academicae Quaestiones* 1, 6, 24). Today Aristotle's words have been so thoroughly absorbed into English that *category* is a common term on TV quiz shows and *quality* is more often used by salesmen than by philosophers.

SYLLOGISMS.   Besides his systematic terminology for representing knowledge, Aristotle developed logic as a precise method for reasoning about knowledge. He invented the *syllogism* as a three-part pattern for representing a logical deduction. Following is an example of a syllogism taken from Aristotle's *Posterior Analytics* (98b5):

> If all broad-leafed plants are deciduous,
> and all vines are broad-leafed plants,
> then all vines are deciduous.

The basic pattern of a syllogism combines two premises to derive a conclusion. In this example, "all broad-leafed plants are deciduous" is called the *major premise;* "all vines are broad-leafed plants" is called the *minor premise;* and "all vines are deciduous" is the conclusion. Although this example uses words in a natural language, Aristotle presented most of his syllogisms in a highly formalized style, as in the following quotation from the *Prior Analytics* (25b38):

> For if A is predicated of every B and B of every C, it is necessary for A to be predicated of every C (for it was stated earlier what we mean by the words *of every* [*kata pantos*]). Similarly, if A is predicated of no B, and B of every C, it is necessary that A will apply to no C.

With his patterns for syllogisms, Aristotle introduced the first use of variables in history. But he did much more than give a few examples. He presented many pages of systematic analyses with formal *rules of inference* — rules for converting one pattern into another while preserving truth. In the above quotation, Aristotle used terms like *kata pantos* in a technical sense, which he had to explain even for native speakers. Modern symbolic logic uses symbols like $\forall$ instead of words like *kata pantos,* but many programming languages and rule-based expert systems still follow Aristotle's practice of using stylized natural language with variables.

SCHOLASTIC LOGIC.   The medieval Scholastics named and classified Aristotle's syllogisms to make them easier to remember. They assigned the vowels A, I, E, and O to the four basic types of propositions:

A: *Universal affirmative.* All *a* is *b*.

I: *Particular affirmative.* Some *a* is *b*.

E: *Universal negative.* No *a* is *b*.

O: *Particular negative.* Some *a* is not *b*.

The letters A and I come from the first two vowels of the Latin word *affirmo* (I affirm), and the letters E and O come from the word *nego* (I deny). These letters form the beginning of an elaborate scheme of mnemonics for the valid patterns of syllogisms. The first pattern is named *Barbara*, since the three A's in "Barbara" indicate three universal affirmative propositions:

A: All broad-leafed plants are deciduous.

A: All vines are broad-leafed plants.

A: Therefore, all vines are deciduous.

The pattern *Celarent* has the vowels E, A, E:

E: Nothing absent minded is an elephant.

A: All professors are absent minded.

E: Therefore, no professor is an elephant.

The pattern *Darii* has the vowels A, I, I:

A: All trailer trucks are eighteen wheelers.

I: Some Peterbilt is a trailer truck.

I: Therefore, some Peterbilt is an eighteen wheeler.

And the pattern *Ferio* has the vowels E, I, O:

E: No Corvette is a truck.

I: Some Chevrolet is a Corvette.

O: Therefore, some Chevrolet is not a truck.

Barbara, Celarent, Darii, and Ferio are the four basic patterns, which make up the *first figure*. Another fifteen patterns are derived from them by rules of *conversion*, which change the order of the terms or the types of statements. The patterns Barbara and Darii are the basis for the modern rule of inheritance: by Barbara, the property of being deciduous is *inherited* from the supertype BroadLeafedPlant to the subtype Vine; by Darii, the property of being an EighteenWheeler is inherited from the type TrailerTruck to some instance of a Peterbilt. In the patterns Celarent and Ferio, a negative universal proposition implies that two categories are mutually exclusive, such as Corvette and Truck or AbsentMinded and Elephant. By the conclusion of Celarent, the types Professor and Elephant must also be mutually exclusive. By Ferio, the type Chevrolet cannot be a subtype of Truck, although there could be some overlap: some, but not all Chevrolets may be trucks. The rules Celarent and Ferio are used to check for inconsistencies in a type hierarchy.

The most popular textbook in the Middle Ages, which presented all the rules and mnemonics, was the *Summulae Logicales* by Peter of Spain, who later became Pope John XXI. But the Scholastics did much more than summarize and codify Aristotle's logic. They introduced many innovations in the application of logic to language, and their work on *modal* and *temporal* logic contains insights that have only recently been rediscovered. During the Renaissance, however, the study of logic became unfashionable, and being a logician was no longer a promising career path for a future pope.

SEMANTIC NETWORKS.   Besides the linear notations for logic, researchers in artificial intelligence have developed graphic notations called *semantic networks*. The first semantic network appeared in the margin of a commentary, *On Aristotle's Categories*, by the philosopher Porphyry in the third century A.D. It was a small tree with Aristotle's categories arranged by *genus* (supertype) and *species* (subtype). The medieval logicians developed it into a more detailed hierarchy, which they called the *Tree of Porphyry* (Figure 1.1). Following is Porphyry's description of the hierarchy:

> Substance, for instance, is the single highest genus of substances, for no other genus can be found that is prior to substance. Human is a mere species, for after it come the individuals, the particular humans. The genera that come after substance, but before the mere species human, those that are found between substance and human, are species of the genera prior to them, but are genera of what comes after them.

The features that distinguish different species of the same genus are called *differentiae*. Substance with the differentia material is Body and with the differentia immaterial is Spirit. The technique of *inheritance*, which is used in AI and object-oriented systems, is the process of merging all the differentiae along the path above any category: LivingThing is defined as animate material Substance, and Human is rational sensitive animate material Substance. Aristotle's method of defining new categories by *genus* and *differentiae* is fundamental to AI systems, to object-oriented systems, and to every dictionary from the earliest days to the present.

AUTOMATED REASONING.   In the thirteenth century, the Spanish poet, philosopher, and missionary Ramon Lull invented the first mechanical devices for automated reasoning. At that time, logic and theology were flourishing, and Lull sought to combine both of them in a system he called the *Ars Magna* (Great Art). In the book *De Nova Logica*, Lull illustrated his art with the tree of nature and logic, which is reprinted on the cover of this book. The trunk of the tree supports a version of the tree of Porphyry, extended with Ens (Being) as the supertype of Substance.

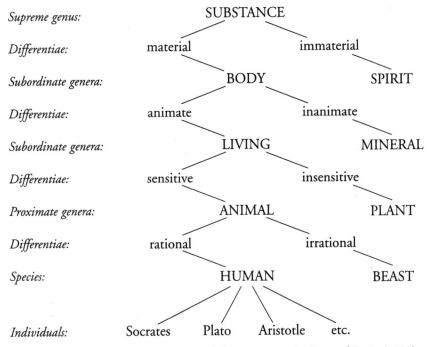

FIGURE I.I Tree of Porphyry, translated from a version by Peter of Spain (1239)

The ten leaves on the right are labeled with ten types of questions that may be asked: *Whether? What? From what? Why? How much? What kind? When? Where? How?* and *With what?* To answer the questions, the leaves on the left are labeled with letters of the alphabet, which are keyed to sectors on disks with rotating circles. Figure 1.2 shows one of his disks with three concentric circles. The outer circle is labeled with the letters B through K; the next circle is labeled with nine attributes of God — Goodness, Magnitude, Duration, Power, Wisdom, Will, Strength, Truth, and Glory; and the inner circle is labeled with the corresponding adjectives.

The circles of Lull's disks were made of metal or parchment that could be rotated to *generate* all possible combinations of the attributes. The alignment in Figure 1.2, for example, indicates that God's goodness (*Bonitas*) is good (*Bonum*), magnitude is great, duration is lasting, and so on. If the circle of attributes were rotated one sector clockwise, the new alignment would indicate that God's goodness is great, magnitude is lasting, and duration is powerful. In one of his books, Lull presented a hundred sermons based on combinations he generated with his rotating circles. Besides theology, which was "closest to his heart," he constructed disks for philosophy, law, medicine, and the four elements (fire, air, water, and earth).

To supplement the disks, Lull added tables, trees, and other diagrams based on

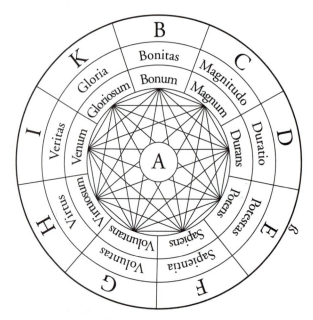

FIGURE 1.2 One of Ramon Lull's disks with rotating circles

Aristotle's categories and syllogisms. To link the circles and diagrams, he used letters of the alphabet for cross-references. As he rotated the circles to generate combinations, Lull checked the diagrams to test whether each combination was logically permissible. In effect, Lull anticipated the most basic and inefficient AI algorithm: *Generate and Test*. With only two or three circles, the number of combinations is manageable. But Lull's largest disk, his *Figura Universalis*, had 14 concentric circles with 16 sectors each. Since the number of possible combinations increases exponentially, Lull must have encountered one of the first combinatorial explosions in history: 16^{14} is over 72 quadrillion.

MATHEMATICAL LOGIC. In the seventeenth century, Gottfried Wilhelm Leibniz served as a diplomat for the elector of Mainz and the duke of Brunswick, but he is best known for his highly creative innovations in mathematics, logic, and philosophy. In mathematics, he and Isaac Newton independently invented the differential calculus, but the modern notation follows Leibniz rather than Newton. In technology, Leibniz designed and built the first mechanical calculator that could do multiplication and division. In logic, he used mathematics to formalize the patterns of syllogistic reasoning. He was also inspired by the binary patterns in the Chinese *I Ching* (*Book of Changes*), which he adapted to form the first system of binary arithmetic. In philosophy, he introduced the notion of possible world and used it to clarify the concepts of modality, identity, and continuity. His definition of modality in terms of possible worlds is still used today in the semantics for *modal logic*, which adds operators for possibility and necessity to the basic logic.

Leibniz was intrigued by the combinatorial possibilities in Lull's *Ars Magna*, but he wanted to establish a better mathematical foundation. For his *Universal Characteristic*, Leibniz assigned prime numbers to the primitive concepts and multiplied them to derive the numbers for each composite concept. As an example, let 2, the first prime number, be assigned to the supreme genus Substance. Then assign the following primes to each of the differentiae in Figure 1.1:

```
material = 3        immaterial = 5
animate = 7         inanimate = 11
sensitive = 13      insensitive = 17
rational = 19       irrational = 23
```

Since Body is material Substance, its number would be 6, the product of 2 for Substance times 3 for material. Similarly, the number for Mineral would be 2×3×11, or 66, and the number for Human would be 2×3×7×13×19, or 10,374. Besides representing the categories, Leibniz also defined operations for reasoning about them. To test whether category A is a subtype of B, Leibniz would divide B by A: since 10,374 for Human is exactly divisible by 6 for Body, every human must be a body; but since 10,374 for Human is not divisible by 66 for Mineral, no human is a mineral.

Leibniz's encoding works best for syllogisms of type Barbara, with their three universal affirmative (type A) statements. In the syllogism about vines, the three statements could be verified by the following computations:

The number for "broad-leafed plant" is divisible by the number for "deciduous."
The number for "vine" is divisible by the number for "broad-leafed plant."
Therefore, the number for "vine" is divisible by the number for "deciduous."

By applying this technique to particular affirmative (type I) statements, Leibniz could also represent the pattern Darii. But this encoding has a serious limitation: multiplication can only represent conjunction; it cannot represent negation, disjunction, or implication. Leibniz later replaced his single numbers with a pair of positive and negative numbers for each concept, but he never found a way to represent all the logical operators and rules of inference.

T-BOX AND A-BOX. Leibniz's partial success was still impressive: even without a complete system for making assertions, he had discovered a powerful method for defining terms. For modern AI systems, Ron Brachman and his colleagues (1983) made a distinction between the *terminological reasoner* (T-box) for defining terms and the *assertional reasoner* (A-box) for making assertions about those terms. As a T-box, Leibniz's products of primes formed a kind of hierarchy called a *lattice*. The two syllogisms that he supported, Barbara and Darii, are the basic rules of inheritance in a terminological hierarchy. His lattice of numbers even supports *multiple inheritance*, which allows a term to inherit properties from more than one supertype. Today, lattices with multiple inheritance are widely used in AI and object-oriented systems.

Leibniz's goal was to reduce reasoning to mathematical computation. But as these examples illustrate, the numbers quickly become rather large. With only 4 differentiae, the number for Human is 10,374 and for Beast 12,558. A more detailed subdivision of categories would lead to much longer numbers and tedious, error-prone calculations. Leibniz, however, was equal to the task since his mechanical calculator could do multiplication and division. A few years earlier, the philosopher Blaise Pascal had invented a mechanical calculator to do addition and subtraction. Pascal's motivation was to help his father with accounting problems in business, but Leibniz saw that accounting machines could also be used for mechanical reasoning — an insight that should entitle him to be called the grandfather of artificial intelligence.

BOOLEAN ALGEBRA. A major breakthrough in formalizing assertional logic was the *Investigation into the Laws of Thought* by George Boole (1854). Like Leibniz, Boole used arithmetic as a model for logical operations. But unlike Leibniz, Boole used numbers to represent *truth values* rather than categories. Instead of large numbers like 546 for the category Animal or 10,374 for Human, Boole needed only two small numbers, 0 for false and 1 for true. Besides multiplication for representing the conjunction *and*, Boole used addition for the disjunction *or* and minus for the negation *not*. As an example, let p represent the proposition *The sun is shining* and let q represent *It is raining*. Then the logical combinations of those propositions would be represented by arithmetic:

- $p \times q$ represents *The sun is shining, and it is raining.*
- $p + q$ represents *The sun is shining, or it is raining.*
- $-p$ represents *The sun is not shining.*

The operator $\times$ behaves like multiplication restricted to the two values 0 and 1: if both conjuncts are true, 1×1 is also 1; if either or both are false, 0×0, 1×0, and 0×1 are all false or 0. For the definition of $+$ and $-$, Boole had to modify the usual arithmetic definitions in order to avoid results less than 0 or greater than 1. Therefore, he defined $-1 = 0$ and $-0 = 1$. For disjunction, he chose the *exclusive or*, for which $1 + 1 = 0$. The logical sum $p + q$ would mean *Either the sun is shining or it is raining, but not both at the same time.*

TRUTH TABLES. The American philosopher Charles Sanders Peirce made a number of extensions and modifications to Boolean algebra. He organized the

And			Or			Not		If-then		
×	0	1	+	0	1	−		≺	0	1
0	0	0	0	0	1	0	1	0	1	1
1	0	1	1	1	1	1	0	1	0	1

FIGURE 1.3 Peirce's truth tables for Boolean algebra

operators in *truth tables*, such as Figure 1.3, which shows the results for logical *and*, *or*, *not*, and *if-then*. The four tables in Figure 1.3 may be read in the same way as the addition and multiplication tables for ordinary arithmetic: the values 0 and 1 along the left of each table represent the possible values of the first operand; the values along the top represent the values of the second operand. Since *not* is a *monadic* operator, it takes one operand; all the others are *dyadic* operators, which take two.

Peirce's multiplication table for *and* is the same as Boole's: for any two propositions p and q, $p \times q$ can only be true when both p and q are true; in all the other combinations, $p \times q$ is false. The addition table, however, differs in the lower right corner. Instead of Boole's *exclusive or*, Peirce chose the *inclusive or*, which is true if either p or q or both are true: $1 + 1 = 1$. The not operator in the third table is the same as Boole's: $-1 = 0$ and $-0 = 1$.

The if-then operator in the fourth table is another of Peirce's innovations. He observed that if p implies q, then the *consequent* q is true whenever the *antecedent* p is true, but q might also be true for other reasons independent of p. Therefore, the truth value of p must always be less than or equal to the truth value of q. Figure 1.3 shows that the truth table for the if-then operator, also called *material implication*, is the same as the table for the ≤ operator: $0 \leq 0$, $0 \leq 1$, and $1 \leq 1$ are all true; but $1 \leq 0$ is false. As the symbol for implication, Peirce preferred to write ≺ instead of ≤. His main reason was that the symbol ≤ suggests a compound of the < and = operators, but the connected symbol ≺ suggests a single, indivisible operation.

FREGE'S *Begriffsschrift.* Instead of following Aristotle in basing logic on language, the German philosopher Gottlob Frege (1879) set out "to break the domination of the word over the human spirit by laying bare the misconceptions that through the use of language often almost unavoidably arise concerning the relations between concepts." With his *Begriffsschrift* (concept writing), Frege developed the first system of *predicate calculus* or *predicate logic*. Figure 1.4 shows the four primitives in Frege's notation: assertion, negation (not), implication (if-then), and universal quantification (for every).

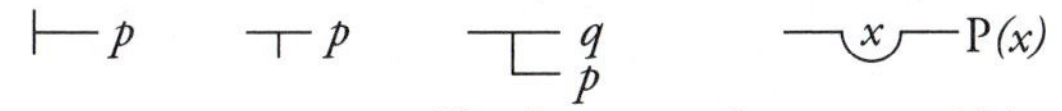

$$\vdash p \qquad \top p \qquad \quad \begin{array}{c} q \\ \rule{0.8em}{0.4pt} \\ p \end{array} \qquad \rule{1em}{0.4pt}(x)\rule{0.8em}{0.4pt}P(x)$$

assert p not p If p then q for every x, $P(x)$

FIGURE 1.4 Four primitives in Frege's *Begriffsschrift*

Although Frege used his *Begriffsschrift* to make pioneering contributions to the foundations of mathematics and logic, no one else ever adopted it. One of its main drawbacks was the awkward mapping to natural language. Before the following sample sentences can be mapped to Frege's notation, they must be paraphrased in a form that uses only the primitives of Figure 1.4:

1. *Every ball is red.*
   For every x, if x is a ball, then x is red.
2. *Some ball is red.*
   It is false that for every x, if x is a ball, then x is not red.
3. *Every cat is on a mat.*
   For every x, if x is a cat, it is false that for all y, if y is a mat, then x is not on y.

The three paraphrased sentences can then be mapped to the diagrams in Figure 1.5. The first paraphrase is commonly used in predicate logic, but the other two contortions are unreadable. Frege chose implication as the primary connective in order to simplify his rules of inference, but that choice made most of the other representations more complex — a typical trade-off between ease of computation and ease of representation.

ALGEBRAIC NOTATION.   Modern systems of predicate calculus are based on the algebraic notation developed by C. S. Peirce in 1883. Unlike Frege, who used only the cup symbol as a quantifier, Peirce started with two distinct symbols: Σ for repeated *or* (logical sum); and Π for repeated *and* (logical product). Peirce called these two symbols *quantifiers*. He observed that the logical sum $\Sigma_x P_x$ is 1 if *there exists* at least one true P_x and that the logical product $\Pi_x P_x$ is 1 only if *every* P_x is true. Therefore, Peirce called Σ the *existential quantifier* and Π the *universal quantifier*. In Peirce's notation, the three sentences of Figure 1.5 can be stated more simply:

1. *For every x, if x is a ball, then x is red:*
   $\Pi_x(\text{ball}_x \!-\!\!<\! \text{red}_x)$.
2. *There exists an x, where x is a ball and x is red:*
   $\Sigma_x(\text{ball}_x \!\cdot\! \text{red}_x)$.
3. *For every x, if x is a cat, then there exists a y which is a mat and x is on y:*
   $\Pi_x(\text{cat}_x \!-\!\!<\! \Pi_y(\text{mat}_y \!\cdot\! \text{on}_{xy}))$.

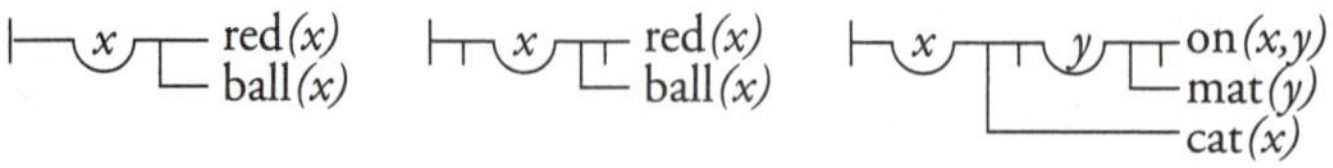

Every ball is red.   *Some ball is red.*   *Every cat is on a mat.*

FIGURE 1.5 Representing three sentences in *Begriffsschrift*

Frege's compatriot Ernst Schröder was aware of the *Begriffsschrift*, but he didn't like the notation. Instead, he adopted Peirce's notation for his three-volume *Vorlesungen über die Algebra der Logik*. Later the Italian mathematician Giuseppe Peano adopted the notation from Schröder, but he changed the symbols, since he wanted to mix mathematical and logical symbols in the same formulas. Peano began the practice of turning letters upside-down or backward to represent the logical symbols:

- *Existential quantifier.* The letter E for existence turned backward becomes ∃ for *there exists.*
- *Implication.* The letter C for consequence turned backward becomes ⊃ for *if-then.*
- *Disjunction.* The letter v from the Latin *vel* becomes ∨ for *or.*
- *Conjunction.* The v turned upside down becomes ∧ for *and.*
- *Negation.* The tilde ~ or curly minus sign is used for *not.*
- *Equivalence.* The equal sign = with an extra line becomes ≡ for *if and only if.*

With these symbols, Peano's notation has exactly the same form as Peirce's notation of 1883. Following are the three sentences of Figure 1.5 in Peano's form:

1. *For every x, if x is a ball, then x is red:*
   $(x)(\text{ball}(x) \supset \text{red}(x))$.
2. *There exists an x, where x is a ball and x is red:*
   $(\exists x)(\text{ball}(x) \wedge \text{red}(x))$.
3. *For every x, if x is a cat, then there exists a y which is a mat and x is on y:*
   $(x)(\text{cat}(x) \supset (\exists y)(\text{mat}(y) \wedge \text{on}(x,y)))$.

Bertrand Russell adopted this notation from Peano for the *Principia Mathematica* (Whitehead & Russell 1910), which became the basis for most work on logic up to the present. Note that Peano enclosed universally quantified variables in parentheses without marking them with a special symbol. He couldn't do much with the letter O for *omnis*, but the German logicians later took the A for *alle* and turned it upside down to form the universal quantifier ∀.

Appendix A.1 presents a survey of predicate calculus. Readers who have not had a course in logic or who would like a quick review should read that section. Exercises 1.1 through 1.6 can be done now.

1.2 Representing Knowledge in Logic

In his work on logic, Leibniz tried to invent a universal language based on mathematical principles. His goal was to make it precise enough to "rectify our reasonings" and general enough to represent and settle all "disputes among persons." Although Leibniz never reached that goal himself, the modern versions of logic are capable of representing any factual information that can be stated precisely in any language, natural or artificial. Natural languages display the widest range of knowledge that can be expressed, and logic enables the precisely formulated subset to be expressed in a computable form. Perhaps there are some kinds of knowledge that cannot be expressed in logic. But if such knowledge exists, it cannot be represented or manipulated on any digital computer in any other notation. The expressive power of logic includes every kind of information that can be stored or programmed on any digital computer.

PROPOSITIONAL LOGIC. As an illustration of the issues in translating language to logic, consider a sample sentence in English that could be mapped to various notations for logic:

Every trailer truck has 18 wheels.

The simplest knowledge representation language is *propositional logic*, which is a modern variation of Boolean algebra. In propositional logic, the sentence about trailer trucks can be represented by a single letter:

p.

This is the simplest possible way of representing the sentence, but it cannot represent any details about the trailer truck, the wheels, the number 18, or their interrelationships. That loss of detail may be an advantage in some applications where the main concern is not the internal structure of propositions, but the patterns of implications between them. For those applications, the absence of distracting detail makes propositional logic an attractive choice of representation.

SUBJECT AND PREDICATE. To show the internal structure of a proposition, the sentence must be broken down into smaller parts that can be represented separately. For his syllogisms, Aristotle divided the sentence into two parts: the *subject* and the *predicate*. In the example of Darii from Section 1.1, the trailer truck sentence could be used as the major premise:

A: All trailer trucks are eighteen wheelers.
I: Some Peterbilt is a trailer truck.
I: Therefore, some Peterbilt is an eighteen wheeler.

In each statement, the phrase before the verb, such as "all trailer trucks," is the subject; the rest of the sentence, which includes the verb and its object, is the predicate. The connection between the two premises is established by having the term *trailer truck*, which is called the *middle term*, appear in the subject of one premise and the predicate of the other premise. Then the conclusion is derived by combining the two remaining terms, called the *extremes*.

Before the premises and conclusion of the syllogism can be translated to predicate logic, their syntactic form must be rearranged. One of the peculiarities of predicate logic is that the linking verb *is* or *are* must be represented differently in statements of type A and statements of type I. The universal quantifier $\forall$ is used with the implication $\supset$, but the existential quantifier $\exists$ is used with the conjunction $\wedge$:

A: For every x, if x is a trailer truck, then x is an eighteen wheeler.

$(\forall x)(\text{trailerTruck}(x) \supset \text{eighteenWheeler}(x))$.

I: There exists an x which is a Peterbilt and a trailer truck.

$(\exists x)(\text{Peterbilt}(x) \wedge \text{trailerTruck}(x))$.

I: There exists an x which is a Peterbilt and an eighteen wheeler.

$(\exists x)(\text{Peterbilt}(x) \wedge \text{eighteenWheeler}(x))$.

The syntactic difference between predicate logic and natural language has long been a point of contention among philosophers. Some, such as Frege and Russell, have had a low opinion of ordinary language. Frege believed that predicate logic lays bare the "misconceptions" that arise through the use of language. Others, however, believe that language has its own inherent logic. Hans Kamp, for example, has developed *discourse representation structures*, which support a more direct mapping between natural languages and logic.

Besides the issues of human factors, which are notoriously difficult to quantify, different knowledge representations may support different *rules of inference*, whose performance is easier to measure in a computer implementation. With the syllogism, the conclusion can be derived from the premises in one step. But with predicate logic, the corresponding proof takes six steps. To improve performance for such inferences, many AI systems implement *inheritance* as a special rule of inference that can derive the conclusion of a syllogism in just one step.

CHOICE OF PREDICATES. The division of a sentence into subject and predicate is an important step, but more detail is needed to show how the wheels are related to the truck and how the number 18 is related to the wheels. An important advantage of predicate logic over Aristotle's syllogisms is the ability to support the analysis and representation of a proposition at any level of detail. Any feature of a sentence that happens to be significant can be emphasized by an appropriate choice of predicates. The number 18, for example, could be shown explicitly by replacing the predicate eighteenWheeler(x) with a dyadic or two-place predicate that relates a vehicle x to a number n:

numberOfWheels(x,n)   The number of wheels of x is n.

With this replacement, the first premise of the syllogism becomes

$(\forall x)(\text{trailerTruck}(x) \supset \text{numberOfWheels}(x,18))$.

The complete formula may be read *For every x, if x is a trailer truck, then the number of wheels of x is 18.*

In the predicate numberOfWheels(x,n), the variable x refers to a truck, n refers to a number, but no variable refers to the wheels. Inside the predicate name, the character string "Wheels" is a helpful mnemonic for the human reader, but it has no more meaning than a cryptic abbreviation like W. Similarly, the string "Truck" in the predicate trailerTruck(x) has no meaning of its own, and there is no way to relate trailer trucks to dump trucks or any other kind of trucks. If such distinctions are important for some application, a more detailed selection of predicates is necessary:

truck(x)	x is a truck.
trailer(x)	x is a trailer.
wheel(x)	x is a wheel.
part(x,y)	x has y as part.
set(s)	s is a set.
count(s,n)	The count of elements in s is n.
member(x,s)	x is a member of the set s.

With this choice of predicates, the trailer-truck formula becomes

$(\forall x)((\text{truck}(x) \wedge (\exists y)(\text{trailer}(y) \wedge \text{part}(x,y)))$
$\supset (\exists s)(\text{set}(s) \wedge \text{count}(s,18)$
$\wedge (\forall w)(\text{member}(w,s) \supset (\text{wheel}(w) \wedge \text{part}(x,w)))$)).

This formula may be read *For every x, if x is a truck and there exists a y where y is a trailer and x has y as part, then there exists an s where s is a set and the count of s is 18 and for every w, if w is a member of s, then w is a wheel and x has w as part.*

LOGIC AND ONTOLOGY. The amount of detail implicit in the trailer-truck sentence illustrates Kant's observation that "we would be astonished at the treasures contained in our knowledge." But almost any sentence taken from a daily newspaper, when analyzed in detail, would lead to as many subtle issues. The analysis suggests several points about logic and ontology:

1. Predicate logic is harder to read than the original English *Every trailer truck has 18 wheels.* The difficulty is partly caused by the greater amount of detail, since the English reading of the formula is just as bad.

2. Much of the distracting detail comes from the variables that link various parts of the formula. For the phrase *18 wheels*, the variables s and w associate the

quantifiers $(\exists s)$ and $(\forall w)$ with the predicates set(s), count(s,18), member(w,s), wheel(w), and part(x,w).

3. Logic itself is a simple language with only a half-dozen basic symbols. The level of detail depends on the choice of predicates, which, strictly speaking, do not belong to logic. Instead, they represent an *ontology* of all the relevant things that exist in the subject matter or application. Different choices of predicates represent different *ontological commitments*.

4. The predicates in an ontology may be divided in two classes: the *domain-dependent* predicates such as truck(x), trailer(x), and wheel(x), which are specific to a particular application; and the more general *domain-independent* predicates such as part(x,y), set(s), count(s,n), and member(x,s), which may be used in many different applications.

These issues are relevant to every knowledge representation language. The distinction between logic and ontology is especially important. Some notations blur the distinction by incorporating some predicates as built-in features of the language itself, often with special symbols such as $x \in s$ for member(x,s) or $s@n$ for count(s,n).

REPRESENTING MUSIC.   Although logic is the most precise and the most fundamental of all declarative languages, it is by no means the only one. New notations, both graphic and linear, are constantly being invented in every field of science, engineering, business, and art. Musical notation, for example, has a history as long as logic. The mathematical relationships between the notes and scales were discovered by Pythagoras and his followers in ancient Greece. The modern notation with notes, staves, and clefs was developed by medieval monks working next door to the ones who were busily copying the textbooks on logic. Yet musical notation and other specialized notations are not competitors, but supplements to logic. Each of them represents a subset of logic with a built-in ontology tailored to a particular domain of interest.

As an example, Figure 1.6 shows a sample melody, called "Frère Jacques" in French or "Brother John" in English. At the beginning of the first line, the *key signature* indicates one sharp for the key of G; the *time signature* 4/4 indicates 4 beats per *measure* with the quarter note having a duration of one time unit. The

FIGURE 1.6 A sample melody to be represented in predicate logic

vertical bars divide the melody in 8 measures, with a total of 32 notes. The vertical position of each note on the staff indicates a *tone*, designated by a letter from A through G (the letter may be qualified by a sharp or flat sign or by a number that indicates the octave). The shape of the note indicates duration: one time unit or *beat* for a quarter note; two units for a half note; or half a unit for an eighth note. The horizontal position of each note indicates that it is sounded after the one on the left and before the one on the right. These features, which represent the elements of an ontology for music, can be translated to logic supplemented with three predicates:

      $\text{tone}(x,t)$ Note x has tone t.
      $\text{dur}(x,d)$ Note x has duration d.
      $\text{next}(x,y)$ The next note after x is y.

To represent all 32 notes in the melody, the corresponding formula in predicate logic would require 32 variables, each with an existential quantifier. For each note, there would be three predicates to indicate its tone, duration, and successor. Following are the beginning and ending lines of the formula that represents the information in Figure 1.6:

$(\exists x_1)(\exists x_2)(\exists x_3)\ldots(\exists x_{32})$
    $(\text{tone}(x_1,\text{G}) \wedge \text{dur}(x_1,1) \wedge \text{next}(x_1,x_2) \wedge$
    $\text{tone}(x_2,\text{A}) \wedge \text{dur}(x_2,1) \wedge \text{next}(x_2,x_3) \wedge$
    $\text{tone}(x_3,\text{B}) \wedge \text{dur}(x_3,1) \wedge \text{next}(x_3,x_4)$
    $\wedge \ldots \wedge \text{tone}(x_{32},\text{G}) \wedge \text{dur}(x_{32},2)).$

The complete formula would start with 32 existential quantifiers and continue with 32 lines of predicates. The last line is shorter than the others because the last note does not have a successor.

     Any musician would prefer to read music in the familiar notation of Figure 1.6 than in the translation to predicate calculus. But a translation to logic is a step toward implementing a program for analyzing the music or synthesizing it digitally. Logic is an *ontologically neutral* notation that can be adapted to any subject by adding one or more domain-dependent predicates. The full musical notation has many more features than those shown in Figure 1.6. Loudness, for example, is usually represented by abbreviations like *mf* for *mezzoforte* (medium loud). That feature could be represented by a predicate $\text{mf}(t_1,t_2)$, which indicates that a mezzoforte passage extends from time t_1 to t_2. But loudness is a continuously varying feature that is only roughly approximated by an abbreviation *mf* or predicate $\text{mf}(t_1,t_2)$. Subtle gradations in volume, timing, and phrasing make all the difference between a performance by Jascha Heifetz and the kid next door practicing the violin. Neither the musical score nor the logical formula represents those differences; each captures or omits exactly the same information.

EXISTENTIAL-CONJUNCTIVE LOGIC.   Another observation about the translation gets to the essence of what logic can contribute: the only logical operators used in the formula are the existential quantifier ∃ and the conjunction ∧. As a musical score becomes more detailed and complex, new kinds of predicates like $mf(t_1,t_2)$ may be needed, but the universal quantifier ∀ and the other Boolean operators are never used. The subset of logic with only ∃ and ∧ is called *existential-conjunctive* or EC logic. It is a common subset for translating, relating, and analyzing the specialized notations of many different fields. It is also the subset used to represent all the information stored in commercial database systems, both relational and object-oriented. EC logic is therefore an extremely important subset, but it has one serious limitation: it cannot represent any generalizations, negations, implications, or alternatives. For that, the operators ∀, ~, ⊃, and ∨ are necessary.

An example of a useful generalization is the principle that certain intervals are difficult to sing and should be avoided. In particular, the interval of three whole tones, called a *tritone*, is considered so dissonant that it was called the *diabolus in musica* in the Middle Ages. In the key of C, the tritone is the interval from B to F or from F to B; in the key of G, it is the interval from F# to C or from C to F#. The next formula rules out the transition from B to F:

$$(\forall x)(\forall y)((\text{tone}(x,B) \land \text{next}(x,y)) \supset \sim\text{tone}(y,F)).$$

This formula says that for every x and y, if the tone of x is B and the next note after x is y, then the tone of y is not F. More rules like this would be needed to rule out the transition from F to B, from C to F#, and so on. A more general rule could be stated in terms of another predicate called *tritone*.

tritone(x,y)   Tone x and tone y form a tritone.

Then only one formula is needed to rule out all of the combinations:

$$(\forall x)(\forall y)(\forall z)(\forall w)$$
$$((\text{next}(x,y) \land \text{tone}(x,z) \land \text{tone}(y,w))$$
$$\supset \sim\text{tritone}(z,w)).$$

This formula says that for every x, y, z, and w, if the next note after x is y, the tone of x is z, and the tone of y is w, then z and w do not form a tritone. Rules like this cannot be stated in traditional musical notation because they use the operators ∀, ⊃, and ~.

DEFINITIONS.   The song "Frère Jacques" is intended to be sung as a *round*, in which a second voice begins the melody when the first voice reaches measure 3. With three voices, the third would begin the melody when the first reaches measure 5 and the second reaches measure 3. The resulting 96 notes would require a very long formula in logic. To reduce the size of the formula, it is possible to define a predicate Frere(x), which represents the 32-note melody:

$$\text{Frere}(x) = (\exists x_2)(\exists x_3) \ldots (\exists x_{32})$$
$$(\text{tone}(x,G) \wedge \text{dur}(x_1,1) \wedge \text{next}(x_1,x_2) \wedge$$
$$\text{tone}(x_2,A) \wedge \text{dur}(x_2,1) \wedge \text{next}(x_2,x_3) \wedge$$
$$\text{tone}(x_3,B) \wedge \text{dur}(x_3,1) \wedge \text{next}(x_3,x_4)$$
$$\wedge \ldots \wedge \text{tone}(x_{32},G) \wedge \text{dur}(x_{32},2)).$$

This definition corresponds to a subroutine or a macro in programming languages. The variable x, which is not governed by a quantifier in the body of the definition, is called the *formal parameter*. The other 31 variables correspond to local variables in a subroutine. With this predicate, the three-voice round can be represented by the following formula:

$$(\exists x)(\exists y)(\exists z)(\text{start}(x,0) \wedge \text{Frere}(x) \wedge$$
$$\text{start}(y,8) \wedge \text{Frere}(y) \wedge \text{start}(z,12) \wedge \text{Frere}(z)).$$

This formula uses a new predicate start(x,t), which would be defined to mean that note x starts at time t. The formula may be read *There exist an* x, *a* y, *and a* z, *where* x *starts at time 0 and Frere(*x*),* y *starts at time 8 and Frere(*y*), and* z *starts at time 12 and Frere(*z*).*

The three variables x, y, and z, which are governed by quantifiers at the beginning of the formula, correspond to *global variables* in programming languages. Each occurrence of the Frere predicate has 31 local variables that are governed by quantifiers inside the definition. When the definitions are expanded, the local variables must be renamed to avoid duplications. The variables in the expansion of Frere(y) could be renamed $y_2, \ldots, y_{32}$, and those in Frere(z) could be renamed $z_2, \ldots, z_{32}$. The methods of renaming variables when a definition is expanded are analogous to the programming techniques used for expanding *in-line* subroutines or macros.

1.3 Varieties of Logic

The version of predicate calculus described in Sections 1.1 and 1.2 is usually called *classical first-order logic*. It is by far the most widely used, studied, and implemented version of logic. What is remarkable about classical FOL is that its inventors, Frege and Peirce, started from widely divergent assumptions with very different notations, but they converged on systems that were semantically identical and could derive exactly the same theorems. Despite the differences, the notations are logically equivalent: any statement in one of them can be mapped to a statement in the other that is true or false under the same circumstances. Yet not all systems of logic are equivalent. At large AI conferences, many sessions are devoted to a variety of systems called logics that vary from classical FOL along six possible dimensions:

1. *Syntax.* The most obvious, but in some respects the least important way that logics differ is in notation. Some variations are as trivial as the replacement of Peirce's symbols Σ and ⚊< with Peano's symbols ∃ and ⊃ or with character strings like "exists" and "implies." Others change the entire structure, such as Frege's *Begriffsschrift* in comparison to the Peirce-Peano algebraic notation. For humans, such differences can have a major impact on readability, learnability, and usability. For computers, they may affect the complexity and efficiency of the theorem provers. For natural language parsers, they may simplify the mapping between language and logic. But in terms of expressive power, the syntactic differences are irrelevant: Frege's *Begriffsschrift*, Peirce-Peano algebra, and many versions of semantic networks in AI can express the same propositions in logically equivalent ways.

2. *Subsets.* More fundamental than the notational variations are constraints on permissible operators or combinations of operators. Aristotle's syllogisms, for example, are limited to four basic statement types (A, I, E, and O), which can express only a small subset of the possible statements in full first-order logic. Propositional logic, which includes Boolean operators but no quantifiers, expresses a different subset of FOL. By adding more operators for combining Aristotle's statement types, the Scholastics developed a somewhat larger but still limited subset.

   Whereas the medieval logicians started with a limited subset and did their best to increase its expressive power, many modern logicians deliberately limit the expressive power of FOL to a more easily computable subset. The Prolog language, for example, is based on the *Horn-clause* subset of FOL, which does not permit disjunctions in the conclusion of an implication. That restriction makes Prolog fast enough to be a practical programming language. Other restrictions improve the performance of *terminological logics* or *definitional logics*, which are used for defining and classifying concepts in a *generalization hierarchy*.

3. *Proof theory.* Instead of restricting the permissible combinations of operators, some versions of logic restrict or extend the permissible proofs. *Intuitionistic logic* and *relevance logic* rule out proofs that might introduce extraneous information, such as the principle that any proposition whatever can be derived from a contradiction. *Nonmonotonic logics* allow the proof procedures to introduce default assumptions if they are consistent with what is currently known. *Access-limited logics* restrict the number of times a proposition can be used in a proof; the most common version, called *linear logic*, allows a proposition to be

used only once. Some natural language parsers use linear logic as a heuristic device for ensuring that every piece of information in a sentence is used once and only once. One version of linear logic is equivalent in expressive power to Petri nets, which are discussed in Chapter 4.

4. *Model theory.* Instead of modifying the notation, operators, or proofs, some versions of logic modify the *denotation* or *truth value* of a statement in terms of some model of the world. Classical FOL is a *two-valued logic* with the truth values 1 and 0 or *true* and *false*. A *three-valued logic* includes an intermediate value *unknown* for statements whose denotation cannot be determined. One of the most popular versions of *multivalued logic* is *fuzzy logic*, which uses the same notation as classical FOL, but with an infinite range of *certainty factors* from 1.0 for certainly true to 0.0 for certainly false. Strictly speaking, the truth values and certainty factors are not part of the logic itself, but of the *model theory* that relates the logic to the world.

5. *Ontology.* An *uninterpreted logic* has no predefined predicates for representing any subject; its only symbols are quantifiers, Boolean operators, and variables. A person who starts with an uninterpreted logic has complete freedom, but also total responsibility for defining all the predicates and axioms for representing everything that exists in the application domain. To provide building blocks for defining the domain-dependent entities, some versions of logic supplement FOL with an ontology of built-in predicates and axioms. Mathematicians usually adopt the ontology of *set theory* as a basis for defining the foundations of mathematics. Time is another fundamental entity, whose ontology is built into the notation and rules of *temporal logics* and *dynamic logics*.

6. *Metalanguage.* Language about language is called *metalanguage*. Classical FOL can be used as a metalanguage for defining, modifying, or extending any version of logic, including itself. A *context-free grammar*, for example, is a version of Horn-clause logic used as a metalanguage for defining the syntax of languages. In general, every grammar is equivalent to some subset of FOL used as a metalanguage. In all of computer science, metalanguages are used as design languages, specification languages, debugging languages, and help facilities. Every one of them can be defined as some subset of logic.

These six dimensions of variation can be mixed in any combination. A version of fuzzy Prolog could be defined as a restriction of FOL to the Horn-clause subset with a modified proof theory and model theory and with metalanguage for expressing certainty factors.

TYPED LOGIC. Predicate calculus has been widely criticized as unreadable, but some *notational engineering* can be done to improve it. A common improvement is to replace most of the monadic or one-place predicates by labels on the variables. Instead of the predicate trailerTruck(x), for example, a *type label* or *sort label* would be appended to the variable x in the quantifier ($\forall x$:TrailerTruck), which may be read *for every x of type trailer truck* or simply *for every trailer truck x.* Following is the syllogism Darii expressed in typed predicate logic:

A: For every trailer truck x, x is an eighteen wheeler.

   $\forall x$:TrailerTruck)eighteenWheeler(x).

I: There exists a Peterbilt x, which is a trailer truck.

   ($\exists x$:Peterbilt)trailerTruck(x).

I: There exists a Peterbilt x, which is an eighteen wheeler.

   ($\exists x$:Peterbilt)eighteenWheeler(x).

This version is more concise because it avoids the extra implications that accompany every universal quantifier. Those implications are still present in the equivalence rules for translations between the typed and untyped versions of logic. Let t be any type label that corresponds to a monadic predicate $t(x)$, and let $P(x)$ be any predicate or expression that contains a free variable x. Then the following typed and untyped formulas are defined to be equivalent:

- *Universal.* $(\forall x{:}t)P(x) \equiv (\forall x)(t(x) \supset P(x))$.
- *Existential.* $(\exists x{:}t)P(x) \equiv (\exists x)(t(x) \land P(x))$.

Typed logic helps reduce the chance of errors by including the implication in the universal quantifier $(\forall x{:}t)$. Forgetting that implication is a common mistake by novices, but even people who know better sometimes omit it.

When the formula contains multiple quantifiers, the advantage of typed logic becomes more pronounced. For the 18 wheels, the quantifier ($\exists s$:Set) specifies the set s of wheels. For the members of the set, the operator ϵ can also be included in the quantifier ($\forall w{\in}s$), which may be read *for every w in the set s.* With these features, the formula would become

$(\forall x$:TrailerTruck$)(\exists s$:Set$)(s@18 \land (\forall w{\in}s)($wheel$(w) \land$ part$(x,w)))$.

This formula may be read *For every trailer truck x, there exists a set s, where the count of s is 18, and for every w in s, w is a wheel and x has w as part.*

The option of defining new types can also enhance readability. A frequently used type or predicate such as trailerTruck may be defined by an equation like the following:

TrailerTruck(x) = truck(x) $\land$ ($\exists y$:Trailer)part(x,y).

In English, *A trailer truck x* is a truck for which there exists a trailer *y* and *x* has as part *y*.

LAMBDA CALCULUS.   Besides the basic operators and quantifiers, a system of logic requires some method for defining new relations. The traditional method, which was used in the previous example, is to write an equation with the name on the left and the defining expression on the right:

NewName(*x*) = DefiningExpression(*x*).

The left side of the equation specifies the name of a predicate or type such as trailerTruck, and the right side is an expression that defines it. The variable *x*, which links the two sides, is called the *formal parameter*. Such equations are convenient for defining named types or predicates, but they cannot be used to define types that have no names. Unnamed types and predicates are especially useful for the intermediate expressions that are generated by macro expansions and translations from one language to another.

As a systematic method for defining and evaluating functions and relations, the logician Alonzo Church (1941) invented the *lambda calculus*. In Church's notation, the name could be written by itself on one side of an equation; on the other side, the Greek letter λ would be used to mark the formal parameter:

TrailerTruck = (λx)(truck(*x*) $\wedge$ ($\exists y$:Trailer)part(*x,y*)).

With this notation, the name is completely separated from the defining expression, which could be used in any position where the name is used. In particular, a lambda expression could be used as the type label of a quantified variable:

$(\forall z: (\lambda x)$(truck(*x*) $\wedge$ ($\exists y$:Trailer)part(*x,y*)))eighteenWheeler(*z*).

This formula may be read *Every truck z for which there exists a trailer* y *and has* y *as part is an eighteen wheeler*. An equivalent, but more natural reading is *Every truck that has a trailer as part is an eighteen wheeler*. Both of these English readings translate the lambda expression to a *restrictive relative clause*. In fact, lambda expressions are often used as a systematic representation for relative clauses in natural language.

To support the lambda notation, Church defined rules of *lambda conversion* for expanding and contracting the expressions. One of the central results of the lambda calculus is the *Church-Rosser theorem*, which says that a nest of multiple lambda expressions may be expanded or contracted in any order and the results will always be equivalent. In effect, the lambda calculus treats functions and relations as *first-class data types*, which can be manipulated and processed like any other kind of data.

Logically, type labels may be considered a more readable way of writing monadic predicates. They also support special rules of inference that can simplify proof procedures. The rule of *inheritance*, which is a *derived rule of inference* for

FIGURE 1.7 Conceptual graph for "Every trailer truck has as part 18 wheels."

typed logic, allows subtypes to inherit all the properties of their supertypes. By simplifying the notation, typed logic improves readability for humans; by the rule of inheritance, it improves performance for computers; and by providing a translation for relative clauses, typed logic with lambda calculus simplifies the mapping to natural languages.

CONCEPTUAL GRAPHS. Although typed variables can simplify formulas, the variables themselves are part of the problem. The original English sentence *Every trailer truck has 18 wheels* has no variables, but the typed or untyped formula has three variables x, s, and w. A graph notation can eliminate variables by showing connections directly. The first and simplest graph logic is the system of *existential graphs* developed by C. S. Peirce, who had also invented the algebraic notation for predicate logic. The system of *conceptual graphs* (Sowa 1984) is a combination of Peirce's logic with the semantic networks used in AI and computational linguistics. The conceptual graph in Figure 1.7 shows how the graph notation preserves the connectivity of the original English sentence.

In a conceptual graph, the boxes are called *concepts*, and the circles are called *conceptual relations*. On the left of each concept box is a *type field*, which contains a *type label* like TrailerTruck or Wheel. On the right is a *referent field*, which may contain a name, a quantifier like ∀, or a plural specification like {*}@18. Conceptual relations show how the referents of the concepts are related. In Figure 1.7, the concept [TrailerTruck: ∀] represents the phrase *every trailer truck*; the concept [Wheel: {*}@18] represents *18 wheels*; and the relation (Part) represents *has as part*. Altogether, the graph may be read *Every trailer truck has as part 18 wheels*.

The type label TrailerTruck is not a primitive, and it can be defined separately, as in Figure 1.8. The symbol *x relates the newly defined type TrailerTruck to its *genus* or *supertype* Truck, which is the type label of the concept marked by the symbol ?x. The *differentia* or *defining graph* says how a trailer truck differs from any other kind of truck. In Figure 1.8, it says that TrailerTruck is a subtype of Truck that has as part a trailer.

Besides the graph notation, there is an equivalent linear notation for conceptual graphs that takes less space on the page. In the linear form, the boxes are represented

type TrailerTruck(*x) **is**

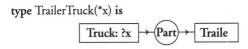

FIGURE 1.8 Definition of the type label TrailerTruck

by square brackets, and the circles are represented by parentheses. Following is the linear form of Figure 1.7:

```
[TrailerTruck: ∀]→(Part)→[Wheel: {*}@18].
```

Since conceptual graphs are a version of typed logic, lambda expressions can also be used to define type labels. The following equation is logically equivalent to the type definition in Figure 1.8:

```
TrailerTruck = [Truck: λ]→(Part)→[Trailer].
```

The symbol λ in the referent field of a concept designates that concept as the formal parameter; the type label Truck is the supertype of the newly defined type Trailer-Truck. As in typed predicate logic, the lambda expression may be used in place of a type label:

```
[[Truck: λ]→(Part)→[Trailer]: ∀]→(Part)→[Wheel: {*}@18].
```

This graph may be read *Every truck that has a trailer has 18 wheels*. As before, lambda expressions in the type field map to restrictive relative clauses in English.

Like the English sentence, the conceptual graph does not represent the variables *x*, *w*, and *s* explicitly, but they are implied by the structure of the graph. When the graph is translated to predicate logic, each concept is assigned a variable whose type is specified by the type label of the concept. The conceptual relations map to predicates with one argument for each arc attached to the circle. Figure 1.7 would map to the formula in typed predicate logic:

$$(\forall x{:}\text{TrailerTruck})(\exists s{:}\text{Set})(s@18 \wedge (\forall w{\in}s)(\text{wheel}(w) \wedge \text{part}(x,w))).$$

The information in the concept [TrailerTruck: ∀] is encoded in the quantifier $(\forall x{:}\text{TrailerTruck})$. The plural form in [Wheel: {*}@18] requires two variables: a variable *s* in $(\exists s{:}\text{Set})$, which represents the set of wheels as a whole; and a variable *w* in $(\forall w{\in}s)$, which ranges over each wheel in the set *s*. The qualifier @18 maps to $s@18$. Finally, the relation Part becomes the predicate $\text{part}(x,w)$. The scope of quantifiers in the graph determines the nesting of the predicates.

Conceptual graphs also simplify the mapping from the English statement of the syllogisms. Following is the syllogism Darii in conceptual graphs:

A: Every trailer truck is an eighteen wheeler.

```
[TrailerTruck: ∀]- - -[EighteenWheeler].
```

I: Some Peterbilt is a trailer truck.

```
[Peterbilt]- - -[TrailerTruck].
```

I: Some Peterbilt is an eighteen wheeler.

```
[Peterbilt]- - -[EighteenWheeler].
```

The dotted line is a *coreference link*, which corresponds to the English word *is*. By the CG rules of inference, which are discussed in Chapter 5, a concept with a universal quantifier can be joined to any existentially quantified concept of the same type; after the join, the ∀ symbol is erased. Therefore, the first two premises can be joined to produce

```
[Peterbilt]- - -[TrailerTruck]- - -[EighteenWheeler].
```

The dotted lines indicate that all three of these concepts are *coreferent*: they refer to exactly the same entity. The corresponding graph may be read *Some Peterbilt is a trailer truck, which is an eighteen wheeler.* By the rules of inference, the middle concept can be erased to form the conclusion:

```
[Peterbilt]- - -[EighteenWheeler].
```

Conceptual graphs were originally designed to simplify the mapping to and from natural languages, but they have also been implemented in efficient theorem provers and search engines.

KIF. The *Knowledge Interchange Format* (KIF) is a version of typed predicate logic that was designed by Michael Genesereth, Richard Fikes, and their colleagues. Its primary purpose is to serve as an interchange language between heterogeneous knowledge bases and databases. Unlike conceptual graphs, which were designed for a direct mapping to and from natural languages, KIF was designed for ease of mapping to and from computer languages. To accommodate the limitations of various implementations, KIF uses a restricted character set without special symbols like ∀ or ∧. Following is the trailer truck sentence in KIF:

```
(forall (?x trailer_truck)
  (exists (?s set)
    (and (count ?s 18)
      (forall (?w in ?s) (and (wheel ?w) (part ?x ?w))) )))
```

This statement may be read *For all x of type trailer truck, there exists a set s, where the count of s is 18, and for all w in s, w is a wheel and x has w as part.* Since KIF does not distinguish upper- and lowercase letters, the two parts of the type label Trailer-Truck are separated by an underscore in the KIF form trailer_truck.

ANSI standards for conceptual graphs and KIF have been defined by the NCITS T2 committee on Information Interchange and Interpretation (NCITS 1998a,b). The two standards have been developed in parallel so that any information represented in one can be automatically translated to the other. The two languages, however, have different strengths that make them suitable for different applications: to make it easy to parse by computer, KIF has a simplified syntax and restricted character set; conceptual graphs have a more readable notation for humans and a more direct mapping to and from natural languages. Chapter 7 discusses the use of KIF and CGs in knowledge sharing; Appendix A summarizes their syntax, as presented in the ANSI standards.

MODAL LOGIC.   Aristotle designed his original syllogisms to represent facts about the current state of the world, but he later extended the syllogisms to accommodate a class of verbs called *modal auxiliaries*. Those verbs are not used to talk about the way the world *is*, but about the way it *may, can, must, should, would,* or *could* be. Aristotle assumed two basic modes: *necessity*, typically expressed by the verb *must* or by the adverb *necessarily*; and *possibility*, expressed by the verb *can* or by the adverb *possibly*. For symbolic logic, Peirce (1906) combined Aristotle's two modes with existential graphs to form the first modern version of quantified modal logic.

The philosopher Clarence Irving Lewis (1918), who was strongly influenced by Peirce, introduced the diamond symbol $\Diamond$ for representing possibility in the algebraic notation. If p is any proposition, then $\Diamond p$ means p is possibly true. For necessity, a box $\Box p$ is used to mean p is necessarily true. Either symbol, $\Diamond$ or $\Box$, can be taken as a primitive, and the other can be defined in terms of it:

- A statement is necessarily true if and only if it is not possibly false:

  $\Box p \equiv \sim\!\Diamond\!\sim\!p.$

- A statement is possibly true if and only if it is not necessarily false:

  $\Diamond p \equiv \sim\!\Box\!\sim\!p.$

Besides these definitions, many other axioms have been discussed since the time of Aristotle and the Scholastics. Three basic axioms form a version of modal logic called *System T*:

- Anything that is provable is necessarily true: if p is a theorem, then $\Box p$.
- Anything that is necessarily true is true: $\Box p \supset p$.
- If it is necessarily true that p implies q, then if p is necessary, q is also necessary: $\Box(p \supset q) \supset (\Box p \supset \Box q)$.

An important theorem of System T is that anything true is possible: $p \supset \Diamond p$. This theorem, like the axioms, are patterns or *schemata* for deriving an arbitrary number of new axioms and theorems by substituting any formula for the variable p.

System T does not include axioms for *iterated modalities*, such as $\Diamond\Box\Diamond p$, which says that p is possibly necessarily possible. Such mind-boggling combinations seldom occur in English, but they may arise in the intermediate stages of a proof. To relate iterated modalities to simple modalities and to one another, Lewis and Langford (1932) defined two additional axioms, called S4 and S5, which may be added to System T:

- S4. If p is necessary, then p is necessarily necessary: $\Box p \supset \Box\Box p$.
- S5. If p is possible, then p is necessarily possible: $\Diamond p \supset \Box\Diamond p$.

For quantified modal logic, Ruth Barcan Marcus proposed the following axiom, which has become known as the *Barcan formula*:

- BF. If for every x, P(x) is necessarily true, then it is necessary that for every x, P(x): .br $(\forall x)\Box P(x) \supset \Box(\forall x)P(x)$.

For different applications, various combinations of axioms may be assumed. A version with fewer axioms is said to be *weaker*, and a version with more axioms is said to be *stronger*. System T combined with axioms S4, S5, and BF is one of the strongest versions of modal logic, but it is often too strong. Exercise 1.16 discusses a version called *deontic logic*, which is weaker than System T.

In database theory, modal logic is important for distinguishing *constraints* from *contingent facts*. Any statement that is stored in a database, either relational or object-oriented, is assumed to be true. But it is only contingently true, because it could just as well be false. An example of a contingent fact is *Alice is the mother of Bob*. Before Bob was born, that statement was not true, but its absence did not create any inconsistencies in the database. A constraint, however, is a necessarily true statement, such as *Every person has a mother*. As soon as Bob is entered in the database, that constraint, together with the axiom $\Box p \supset p$, would require that space be reserved for mentioning Bob's mother. Even if her name were unknown, her existence would be implied.

Unlike classical FOL, for which all the major variations are exactly equivalent in expressive power, there is an open-ended number of modal logics. They have been designed to express the nuances of verbs like *need, ought, hope, fear, wish, believe, know, expect,* and *intend*. For reasoning about time, temporal logic can be considered a kind of modal logic by interpreting the $\Box$ symbol as *always*, and $\Diamond$ as *sometimes*. Without $\Box$ or $\Diamond$, a temporal statement p is assumed true at the current time *now*. The axiom $\Box p \supset p$ would mean *If p is always true, then p is true now*. The theorem $p \supset \Diamond p$ would mean *If p is true now, then it is sometimes true*. Another version of temporal logic represents the time t explicitly: *always* is represented by a universal quantifier ($\forall t$:Time); and *sometimes* is represented by an existential ($\exists t$:Time). In a courtroom, lawyers often use an explicit representation for time. Instead of asking a witness *Did you see the suspect?* they will say *Did there come a time when you saw the suspect?*

HIGHER-ORDER LOGIC.   The medieval Scholastics distinguished two kinds of logical terms: *first intentions* include words that refer to concrete things, and *second intentions* refer to linguistic entities like properties and propositions. Peirce (1885) adopted the Scholastic terminology when he introduced quantifiers in predicate calculus: *first-intentional logic* restricts the quantifiers to concrete individuals; *second-intentional logic* allows the quantifiers to range over relations and propositions. Later, Ernst Schröder replaced Peirce's word *intention* with the German *Ordnung*, which Whitehead and Russell translated back into English for the modern terms *first-order* and *second-order* logic.

The basic version of logic that has been described in this chapter is first-order because the quantified variables have been restricted to nonlinguistic or first-intentional entities. Typed and untyped predicate calculus, conceptual graphs, and KIF are equivalent ways of representing classical FOL. These notations can be extended to *higher-order logic* (HOL) by allowing the quantifiers to range over relations or predicates as well as simple individuals. As an example of second-order logic, the following formula represents the *axiom of induction* for arithmetic:

- For every predicate P, if P is true of 0, and for every integer n, P(n) implies P($n+1$), then P is true for every integer:

$$(\forall P{:}\text{Predicate})((P(0) \wedge (\forall n{:}\text{Integer})(P(n) \supset P(n+1)) \supset (\forall n{:}\text{Integer})P(n)).$$

This formula is second order because the quantifier $\forall P$ ranges over predicates rather than simple individuals. It is the only axiom for arithmetic that requires more power than first-order logic. Higher-order logic may be defined as a metalanguage extension to FOL supplemented with an ontology for relations: second-order logic includes an ontology for all possible relations among simple individuals; third-order logic includes an ontology for all relations of relations; and an ontology for arbitrary HOL would include all possible relations of relations of relations.

METALANGUAGE.   In textbooks, natural language supplemented with variables is used to define, describe, and explain every branch of logic, mathematics, and computer science. To distinguish the describing language or *metalanguage* from the described language or *object language*, some convention is necessary to mark the two levels. Quotation marks are the primary sign that language is being used as metalanguage, but the following words about language also indicate metalanguage:

- Nouns: *word, phrase, sentence, statement, symbol, variable, expression, formula, concept, idea, notion*
- Verbs: *define, describe, represent, mean, prove, translate*
- Adjectives: *true, false, uncertain, correct, provable, equivalent*

Any sentence that uses one or more of these words is a metastatement about some language. As an example, consider the following sentence:

The sentence "It is true that Tom is tall" means the same as "Tom is tall."

The quotation marks indicate metalanguage, but the word *true* in the first quoted sentence indicates that it is also a metastatement. Therefore, the containing sentence must be *metametalanguage*. This paragraph, which discusses a metametastatement, would therefore be *metametametalanguage*. There is no limit to the number of levels of language about language or logic about logic.

Textbooks of mathematics distinguish the metalevel from the object level by using two syntactically different languages: a natural language like English for the metalanguage and an algebraic notation for the object language. In logic, however, the same syntax can be used at both levels as long as some convention is adopted to mark the levels. In conceptual graphs, the two levels are separated by a concept box called a *context*. In predicate calculus, the object-level formula is enclosed in an argument of some predicate, such as the *description predicate* dscr(x,p), which says that the entity x is described by the proposition p. Robert Kowalski (1979, 1994, 1995), one of the pioneers in logic programming, has repeatedly demonstrated that such a two-level combination of first-order logic at the object level and the metalevel provides a powerful and elegant solution to a wide range of problems.

1.4   Names, Types, and Measures

When logic is applied to mathematics, the constants are *numerals*, which serve as the names of numbers. But when logic is applied to a broader range of topics, many more data types are needed: the constants may be names of people and things, names of types of things, or names of the measures of things. Many errors in knowledge representation result from confusing names, types, and measures with the things themselves. The following syllogism illustrates a confusion of names and types:

> Clyde is an elephant.
> Elephant is a species.
> Therefore, Clyde is a species.

In classical terms, this syllogism is fallacious because of a *nondistributed middle term*. In the first premise, the term *an elephant* refers to a particular individual named Clyde. In the second premise, the word *elephant* refers to the entire species or type.

Actors and basketball players who are in a position "to name their own salary" are not likely to choose a proper name like Fred. They are more likely to select a measure like 20 million dollars. People in such enviable positions clearly distinguish names and measures, but more literal-minded computers may make mistakes:

> Every salary is distributed in a paycheck.
> Tom and Sue receive the same salary.
> Therefore, Tom and Sue receive the same paycheck.

A statement that two people earn the same salary should mean that the measures or amounts are the same, but each of them receives a separate paycheck. A failure to observe this distinction is a common source of bugs in computer programs. For this example, Tom and Sue would probably notice the problem quite soon, but sometimes the implications of such bugs spread quietly and corrupt an entire database.

NAMES AND TYPES.   When learning logic, students usually represent the sentence *Tom likes Sue* by the formula like(Tom,Sue). Then they generalize that technique to represent the sentence *Cats like fish* by the formula like(cats,fish). The error in this generalization is caused by the difference between proper names, which denote particular individuals, and common nouns, which denote types. The common nouns *cat* and *fish* must be represented by type labels in typed logic or by monadic predicates in untyped logic. In typed logic, the sentence *Cats like fish* would become

$(\forall x{:}\text{Cat})(\forall y{:}\text{Fish})\text{like}(x,y).$

This formula may be read *For every cat x and fish y, x likes y.*

The rule that proper names map to constants while common nouns map to types or predicates works fairly well for most applications. But it imposes some restrictions: in first-order logic, the variables can only refer to individual entities; they cannot represent types or predicates. One way to ease that restriction is to introduce Type as a second-order type. Then any variable of type Type could refer to types as its value. To relate an entity x to its type t, a dyadic predicate kind(x,t) could be used. Then the sentence about cats and fish would become,

$(\forall x)(\forall y)((\text{kind}(x,\text{Cat}) \land \text{kind}(y,\text{Fish})) \supset \text{like}(x,y)).$

This formula says that for every x and y, if x is a kind of cat and y is a kind of fish, then x likes y. In this example, the kind predicate relates x and y to the *type constants* Cat and Fish. With a *type variable t*, the next formula states the further generalization that cats like every instance of any subtype of fish:

$(\forall x{:}\text{Cat})(\forall y{:}\text{Entity})(\forall t{:}\text{Type})$
$((t{<}\text{Fish} \land \text{kind}(y,t)) \supset \text{like}(x,y)).$

This formula may be read *For every cat x, every entity y, and every type t, if t is a subtype of fish and y is a kind of t, then x likes y.*

HIGHER-ORDER TYPES.   The distinction between names and types provides a way of solving the puzzle about Clyde the elephant. In the sentence *Clyde is an elephant,* the absence of an article preceding the word *Clyde* suggests a proper name, which is placed in the referent field of a concept. Since Clyde's type is not specified, the default type ⊤, which is the top of the type hierarchy, may be used. The result is the concept [⊤: Clyde]. The indefinite article in the phrase *an elephant* indicates some individual of type Elephant, which would be represented by the concept [Elephant]. The word *is* corresponds to a coreference link between the two concepts:

[⊤: Clyde]- - -[Elephant].

The coreference link that connects the two concepts shows that they both refer to the same individual. The first concept says there exists something named Clyde, the second one says there also exists an elephant, and the dotted line indicates that the two individuals are the same. In predicate calculus, coreference is represented by an equal sign:

(∃x:Elephant)x=Clyde.

Without an article, the common noun *elephant* does not refer to a single individual. In the sentence *Elephant is a species*, it is used as a name of the type:

Type: Elephant]- - -[Species].

This graph, which may be read *The type Elephant is a species*, is a higher-order statement about types. The types Type and Species are second-order types whose instances are first-order types like Elephant, whose instances are ordinary individuals like Clyde. The CG maps to the following formula:

(∃x:Species)(type(Elephant) ∧ x=Elephant).

These CGs and the formulas derived from them capture the meaning of the English sentences without permitting the incorrect inference that Clyde is a species.

The distinction between names and types arises in many areas of database and knowledge base design. An important example is the representation of colors, shapes, and sizes. Figure 1.9 shows three conceptual graphs for representing the English phrase *a red ball*. In the first one, the monadic conceptual relation (Red) is attached directly to the concept [Ball]. It corresponds to the following formula:

(∃x:Ball)red(x).

This formula says that there exists a ball *x*, which is red. Although this representation is simple, it is awkward for both database design and natural language semantics.

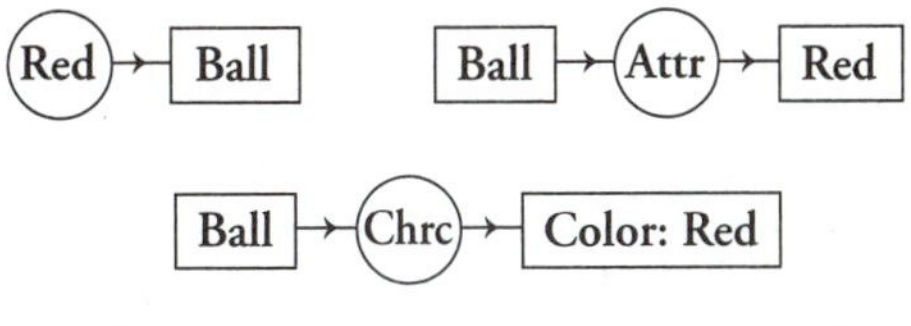

FIGURE 1.9 Three possible ways of representing "a red ball"

The second graph shows a more systematic way of representing natural language sentences: all content words — nouns, verbs, adjectives, and adverbs — are represented by separate concepts. The noun *ball* maps to the concept [Ball], the adjective *red* maps to the concept [Red], and the relationship between them maps to the attribute relation (Attr). When translated to typed logic, both concept nodes map to existential quantifiers and the Attr relation becomes a dyadic predicate:

$(\exists x{:}\text{Ball})(\exists y{:}\text{Red})\text{attr}(x,y).$

This formula says that there exist a ball x and an instance of redness y where the attr predicate relates x to y.

For database design, the third graph is the most convenient. The characteristic relation (Chrc) links the concept of a ball to the concept [Color: Red], whose type label is a second-order type Color, and whose referent is a first-order type Red. That graph maps to the following formula:

$(\exists x{:}\text{Ball})(\text{color}(\text{Red}) \wedge \text{chrc}(x,\text{Red})).$

This formula says that there exists a ball x, Red is a color, and x has Red as a characteristic. In general, Attr relates an entity to a first-order attribute, such as red, large, or heavy; Chrc relates an entity to a second-order characteristic like color, size, or weight. In English, attributes are usually represented by adjectives and characteristics by nouns.

Higher-order types occur in every system of classification. For cars, Make and Model are second-order types, whose instances are first-order types like Ford and Mustang, whose instances are particular cars. Other second-order types include the biological ranks from Species to Kingdom. Their instances are first-order types: [Kingdom: Animal], [Order: Mammal], [Genus: Felis], and [Species: FelisCatus]. The types Rank and Characteristic are third-order types, whose instances are second-order types like Species and Color:

First order:	*The ball is red.*	*Yojo is a felis catus.*
Second order:	*Red is a color.*	*Felis catus is a species.*
Third order:	*Color is a characteristic.*	*Species is a rank.*

Beyond third order, the common English words become scarce, but new technical terms can be invented indefinitely, as in the concepts [ThirdOrderType: Rank] and [FourthOrderType: ThirdOrderType]. Chapter 7 shows how lambda expressions can be used to translate between knowledge representations that use types of different order.

SURROGATES.   The rule of substituting equals for equals, which is commonly used in mathematics, creates problems with names, since one entity may have multiple names or *aliases*, and multiple entities may have the same name. Following is a typical paradox:

Sam believes that Dr. Jekyll is a gentleman.
Dr. Jekyll is Mr. Hyde.
Sam does not believe that Mr. Hyde is a gentleman.

By the principle of substituting equals for equals, the character string "Dr. Jekyll" might be substituted for "Mr. Hyde" in the third sentence. But that would lead to the contradiction that Sam both believes and does not believe that Dr. Jekyll is a gentleman.

In database systems and object-oriented systems, aliases are avoided by using special identifiers called *surrogates*, which uniquely designate the external objects. For the U.S. government, the official surrogate for a person is a social security number. In the Lisp language, the function called GENSYM is guaranteed to generate a unique symbol whenever it is called. Many AI systems use it to generate surrogates for entities that exist outside the computer system.

If surrogates are considered the primary identifiers, names are demoted to the status of characteristics that are no more fundamental than weight or hair color. To relate a surrogate s to a name n, a dyadic predicate hasName(s,n) may be used:

believe(Sam, ($\exists s$)(hasName($s,$"Dr. Jekyll") $\land$ gentleman(s))).
($\exists s$)(hasName($s,$"Dr. Jekyll") $\land$ hasName($s,$"Mr. Hyde")).
~believe(Sam, ($\exists s$)(hasName($s,$"Mr. Hyde") $\land$ gentleman(s))).

The paradox no longer exists because there is no rule of inference that allows the strings "Dr. Jekyll" and "Mr. Hyde" to be substituted for one another. In his personal computer, Sam may have two different surrogates associated with the same person; but when the scandal about Dr. Jekyll appears in the morning newspaper, Sam can update the database to correct his earlier mistake. The temporary mismatch between the database and the real world may cause some misunderstandings, but it doesn't create any logical paradoxes.

UNIQUE NAMING CONVENTION.   For theorem provers, a *unique naming convention* is often adopted to simplify the proof procedures: if two constants a and b have a different spelling, then $a \neq b$ is assumed. KIF has two kinds of constants: for one kind, uniqueness is assumed; for the other kind, either $a = b$ or $a \neq b$ is possible. In conceptual graphs, ordinary names are not assumed to be unique, but special symbols called *individual markers*, which are written with the symbol # followed by an integer, are assumed to be unique. Individual markers serve as surrogates that uniquely identify the individuals that are cataloged in a conceptual system. The

following graph says that the person cataloged as individual #5395 has a characteristic name "Dr. Jekyll":

```
[Person: #5395]→(Chrc)→[Name: "Dr. Jekyll"].
```

By the process of *name contraction*, this graph may be abbreviated by a single
concept [Person: Dr. Jekyll #5395]. If an individual is only mentioned once, it
might not be cataloged. The following graph says that there exists someone (not
otherwise identified) who has the name Dr. Jekyll:

```
[Person]→(Chrc)→[Name: "Dr. Jekyll"].
```

By name contraction, this graph could be abbreviated [Person: Dr. Jekyll]. Before
Sam hears about the scandal in the morning news, his database might contain the
following graphs:

```
[Person: #5395]→(Chrc)→[Name: "Dr. Jekyll"] [Gentleman: #5395].
[Person: #16432]→(Chrc)→[Name: "Mr. Hyde"] ^[ [Gentleman: #16432]].
```

The first graph says that the person cataloged as #5395, whose name is Dr. Jekyll,
is a gentleman. The second says that the person cataloged as #16432, whose name
is Mr. Hyde, is not a gentleman. When Sam hears the news, he can update the
database to cause the separately cataloged information to be merged. At that point,
the system would discover a contradiction about the individual #5395. Sam would
then reevaluate his opinions about Dr. Jekyll, and the assertion [Gentleman: #5395]
would be deleted.

Since surrogates are unique only within a particular computer system, communication between systems still depends on printable names with their potential
ambiguities. For convenience in finding data across the World Wide Web, computer systems depend on *Universal Resource Locators* (URLs), which are recognized
by all the computers connected to the Internet. But those identifiers only designate
resources that can be stored and accessed by computers. There are no URLs for
things that cannot be flattened out and stored on a computer disk, such as dogs,
trees, and people. For such things, the surrogates serve as local substitutes within a
database. But the task of matching the surrogates to the physical objects cannot be
done wholly within a computer or even a network of computers. There must be
some sense organs — human or robotic — that can relate the internal identifiers to
the physical world.

REPRESENTING MEASURES.   Measures are even more ambiguous than names.
Two rods may have the same length even though they occupy different locations;
two rooms may have the same temperature even though they contain different
molecules of air; two jars may have the same volume even though they enclose
distinct regions of space; and two people may earn the same amount even though

they receive different paychecks. The following graph says that Tom and Sue each earn a salary whose amount is $30,000:

```
[Person: Tom]←(Agnt)←[Earn]→(Thme)→[Salary: @ $30,000];
[Person: Sue]←(Agnt)←[Earn]→(Thme)→[Salary: @ $30,000].
```

The first line says that the person Tom is the agent of earn, which has a theme (Thme), which is a salary whose amount is $30,000. The second line says that Sue also earns a salary of $30,000. The symbol @ in the referent field of a concept indicates that the following symbol is a measure of the referent, not its name or surrogate. In predicate calculus, that graph would become

$(\exists x,y{:}\text{Earn})(\exists z,w{:}\text{Salary})$
  $(\text{Person}(\text{Tom}) \wedge \text{Person}(\text{Sue}) \wedge$
  $\text{agnt}(x,\text{Tom}) \wedge \text{thme}(x,z) \wedge \text{hasAmount}(z,\$30{,}000) \wedge$
  $\text{agnt}(y,\text{Sue}) \wedge \text{thme}(y,w) \wedge \text{hasAmount}(w,\$30{,}000))$.

The graph and the formula assign separate concepts or variables to Tom's salary and Sue's salary, but both salaries happen to be measured by the same amount.

Neither the graph nor the formula makes it clear that the two salaries are distinct. To avoid any misunderstanding, the expression $z \neq w$ could be added to the formula, or a relation ($\neq$) could be drawn between the corresponding concepts. Another way to show distinct salaries is to put different individual markers in their referent fields:

```
[Person: Tom]←(Agnt)←[Earn]→(Thme)→[Salary: #78902 @ $30,000];
[Person: Sue]←(Agnt)←[Earn]→(Thme)→[Salary: #41337 @ $30,000].
```

Tom's salary and Sue's salary are identified by different individual markers, #78902 and #41337, but their amounts are the same. In predicate calculus, the unique naming convention could be expressed in the principle that two distinct constants beginning with the symbol # must refer to distinct individuals. That principle would imply the inequality #78902 $\neq$ #41337.

The symbol @ in the referent field of a concept is not a primitive. It is derived by the method of *measure contraction* from a graph that represents the amount in a separate concept linked by the +amount relation (Amt):

```
[Salary: @ $30,000]
   ≡ [Salary]→(Amt)→[Measure: <30000, dollar>].
```

The expanded graph represents the measure $30,000 as an ordered pair of the number 30000 and the unit *dollar*. Such graphs can also be used to say that Tom and Sue earn the same amount of salary without stating how much:

```
[Person: Tom]←(Agnt)←[Earn]→(Thme)→[Salary]→(Amt)→[Measure]←
   (Amt)←[Salary]←(Thme)←[Earn]→(Agnt)→[Person: Sue].
```

This graph may be read *Tom earns a salary whose amount is the same as the salary earned by Sue*. In predicate calculus, the unknown measure can be expressed by a variable *s*:

(∃*x,y*:Earn)(∃*z,w*:Salary)(∃*s*:Measure)
(Person(Tom) ∧ Person(Sue) ∧
agnt(*x*,Tom) ∧ thme(*x,z*) ∧ hasAmount(*z,s*) ∧
agnt(*y*,Sue) ∧ thme(*y,w*) ∧ hasAmount(*w,s*)).

The predicate hasAmounts, which relates some entity to its measure, corresponds to the Amt +relation in conceptual graphs.

Macro expansions allow conceptual graphs to express various features of natural languages in a concise form without changing the semantics of the underlying logic. In the trailer-truck example, the concept for representing *eighteen wheels* uses two macros: {*} for the set and @ for the count of elements in the set:

```
[Wheel: {*}@18] ≡
  [Set: *s]→(Chrc)→[Count: 18]
  [ [[λ]→(ε)→[?s]: ∀]- - -[Wheel] ].
```

The expanded form can then be translated to the following formula in predicate calculus:

(∃*s*:Set)(count(18) ∧ *s*@18 ∧
(∀*w*:(λ*x*)*x*∈*s*)wheel(*w*)).

When the @ symbol is followed by a single number such as 18, it expands to a concept of type Count with just the number in the referent field. But when it is followed by a number with a unit, such as $30,000 or 43.7 m, it expands to a concept of type Measure with the measure represented by an ordered pair <30000, dollar> or <43.7, meter>.

REPRESENTING MUSICAL ENTITIES. The potential confusions that arise with names of people and elephants become more subtle, but even more pervasive with invisible entities like tones, intervals, and durations. To illustrate those features, Figure 1.10 shows a conceptual graph that represents the third measure of "Frère Jacques" with two voices singing in harmony. Each of the seven notes in the measure is represented by a separate concept [Note]. Each note is attached to conceptual relations that correspond to the tone, next, and dur predicates: the Tone relation links the concept of the note to a concept that indicates the type of tone; the Next relation links to the concept of the next note; and the Dur relation links to a concept of a time interval of the specified duration. Two notes that are sounded simultaneously are linked to the same concept. But at the end of the measure, the upper voice is a half note that lasts as long as the two quarter notes in the lower

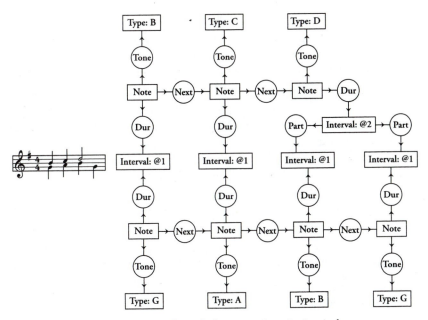

FIGURE 1.10 Conceptual graph for two voices singing in harmony

voice. Therefore, the interval for the half note is linked by two Part relations to the intervals for each of the quarter notes. of "Frère Jacques" with two voices singing in harmony.

Each concept box in Figure 1.10 represents something that exists: a note, an interval, or a type of tone. When the CG is translated to predicate calculus, the corresponding existential quantifiers must be shown explicitly:

$(\exists x_1,x_2,x_3,x_4,x_5,x_6,x_7:$Note$)$
$(\exists y_1,y_2,y_3,y_4,y_5:$Interval$)$
$(\text{tone}(x_1,B) \wedge \text{dur}(x_1,y_1) \wedge \text{hasAmount}(y_1,1\text{beat}) \wedge \text{next}(x_1,x_2) \wedge$
$\text{tone}(x_2,C) \wedge \text{dur}(x_2,y_2) \wedge \text{hasAmount}(y_2,1\text{beat}) \wedge \text{next}(x_2,x_3) \wedge$
$\text{tone}(x_3,D) \wedge \text{dur}(x_3,y_3) \wedge \text{hasAmount}(y_3,2\text{beats}) \wedge$
$\text{tone}(x_4,G) \wedge \text{dur}(x_4,y_1) \wedge \text{next}(x_4,x_5) \wedge$
$\text{tone}(x_5,A) \wedge \text{dur}(x_5,y_2) \wedge \text{next}(x_5,x_6) \wedge$
$\text{tone}(x_6,B) \wedge \text{dur}(x_6,y_4) \wedge \text{hasAmount}(y_4,1\text{beat}) \wedge \text{next}(x_6,x_7) \wedge$
$\text{tone}(x_7,G) \wedge \text{dur}(x_7,y_5) \wedge \text{hasAmount}(y_5,1\text{beat}) \wedge$
$\text{part}(y_3,y_4) \wedge \text{part}(y_3,y_5)$).

The quantifiers at the beginning of this formula specify x_1 through x_7 as notes and y_1 through y_5 as intervals. What makes the formula difficult to read is not the quantifiers, but the proliferation of variables. In the graph, all the information about an entity is localized — either inside the concept box itself or in the relations attached directly to the box. But when the graph is mapped to a linear string, there is no way to preserve the locality of information: the variables that represent the links tend to get scattered throughout the formula.

Since Figure 1.10 is a direct translation from a musical score, it uses only the existential-conjunctive subset of logic. But logic, in both the graphic and linear notations, has much more expressive power for stating rules and generalizations about music. As an example, Figure 1.11 uses conceptual graphs as a metalanguage for stating the definition of a new relation called Simul, which states that two notes are sounded simultaneously. The graph may be read *The relation Simul has a definition (Def), which is a lambda expression that relates a note λ_1 to a note λ_2, in which both notes occur during the same interval.*

The definition of simultaneity in Figure 1.11 shows why it is important to distinguish the interval from its duration. Six of the seven notes in Figure 1.10 have the same duration, but only two pairs are sounded exactly simultaneously. In predicate calculus, Figure 1.11 corresponds to the following definition:

$$\text{simul} = (\lambda x, y : \text{Note})(\exists z : \text{Interval})$$
$$(\text{dur}(x, z) \wedge \text{dur}(y, z)).$$

The Simul relation can be used to state a rule for the harmonious resolution of a dissonance. If two notes sounded together happen to form a dissonant tritone, they can be resolved by having their successors move to a harmonious interval. In the key of G, the tritone of F# and C would be followed by the major third of G and B. In the key of C, the tritone of B and F would be followed by C and E. To avoid having to state a separate rule for every key, those rules can all be summarized by using the relative names for the types of tones: Do, Re, Mi, Fa, So, La, and Ti. Figure 1.12 shows a CG that says that if a note *x* of tone Ti is sounded simultaneously with a note *y* of tone Fa, then the next note after *x* has tone Do and the next note after *y* has tone Mi.

This rule illustrates another feature of music: context-dependent aliases for the names of the tones. If the current key signature indicates a key of G, then Do is an

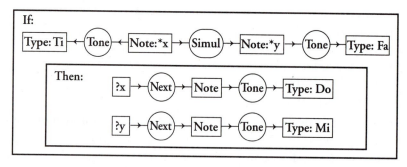

FIGURE I.II Definition of the Simul relation between two notes

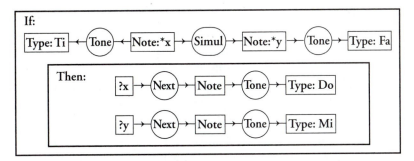

FIGURE 1.12 Rule for the harmonious resolution of a dissonance

alias for G and Mi is an alias for B. But if the current key is C, then Do and Mi are aliases for C and E. Such context dependencies, which often occur in knowledge representations, will be discussed further in Chapter 4. Following is the formula that corresponds to Figure 1.12:

$$(\forall x,y{:}\text{Note})((\text{simul}(x,y) \wedge \text{tone}(x,\text{Ti}) \wedge \text{tone}(y,\text{Fa})) \supset$$
$$(\exists z,w{:}\text{Note})(\text{next}(x,z) \wedge \text{tone}(z,\text{Do}) \wedge \text{next}(y,w) \wedge \text{tone}(w,\text{Mi}))).$$

This formula may be read *For every note x and y, if x and y are simultaneous, the tone of x is Ti, and the tone of y is Fa, then there exist notes z and w, where the next note after x is z, whose tone is Do, and the next note after y is w, whose tone is Mi.*

1.5 Unity Amidst Diversity

As this survey shows, many notations for logic have been invented over the years. But logic is much more than notation. To be a logic, a knowledge representation language must have four essential features:

- *Vocabulary.* A logic must have a collection of symbols, which could be represented as characters, words, icons, diagrams, or even sounds. The symbols may be divided in four groups: the domain-independent *logical symbols* like ∀ or ∧; the domain-dependent *constants*, which identify individuals, properties, or relations in the application domain or *universe of discourse*; the *variables*, whose range of application is governed by quantifiers; and the *punctuation* like commas and parentheses that separate or group the other symbols.

- *Syntax.* A logic must also have grammar rules or *formation rules* that determine how the symbols are combined to form the grammatical or *well-formed* sentences. The rules could be stated in a conventional linear grammar, a graph grammar, or an *abstract syntax* that is independent of any concrete notation.

- *Semantics.* To make meaningful statements, the logic must have a *theory of reference* that determines how the constants and variables are associated with things in the universe of discourse. It must also have a *theory of truth* that is able to distinguish true statements from false statements. In his famous paper "The Concept of Truth in Formalized Languages," Alfred Tarski (1935) introduced formal *models* for representing the semantics of logic. But Aristotle and the Scholastic logicians developed informal theories of truth and reference that made similar distinctions, although not in as precisely stated terms.

- *Rules of inference.* To be more than a notation, a logic must include rules that determine how one pattern can be inferred from another. If the logic is *sound,* the rules of inference must preserve truth as determined by the semantics. However, nonmonotonic logics for plausible or default reasoning have rules that preserve consistency, but not necessarily truth.

These four criteria are general enough to include many different notations for logic. Besides the versions surveyed in this chapter, modern computer systems support logic-based programming languages like Prolog and diverse notations such as the frames and semantic networks of AI, the database query language SQL, and the Express language for describing engineering structures. Even though SQL and Express are not usually called logics, they have the semantics and expressive power of first-order logic.

SEMANTICS OF PROPOSITIONAL LOGIC. The theory of truth tables defines the semantics of propositional logic. As an example, the following truth table shows that $p \land q$ is equivalent to its definition in terms of Frege's primitives $\sim(p \supset \sim q)$. Each of the four rows represents a possible pair of truth values for the variables p and q. Then the truth values of each of the two expressions are computed in terms of the truth values for p and q. For each row, the table shows that the expression $p \land q$ has the same truth value as $\sim(p \supset \sim q)$.

p	q	$p \land q$	$\sim(p \supset \sim q)$
0	0	0	0
0	1	0	0
1	0	0	0
1	1	1	1

The two expressions on the right side of the table are true for some combinations and false for others. An expression such as $p \lor \sim p$, which is true for every possible combination of truth values, is called a *tautology.*

Although truth tables support a systematic method for showing that two formulas are equivalent, their computational time grows exponentially with the number of variables. With two variables p and q, this table has 2^2 or 4 rows. With 5 variables, a table would have 2^5 or 32 rows, and with 20 variables, it would have over a million rows. Many practical problems require hundreds or even thousands of propositional variables. To verify the correctness of VLSI chips, which contain millions of transistors, would require formulas with millions of variables. A network of all the computers in the world computing for the lifetime of the universe could never compute the full truth tables for such problems.

General proof procedures also require exponential amounts of time in the worst case. However, the worst cases for proof procedures are usually different from the worst cases for truth tables. For truth tables, the computing time grows exponentially with the number of variables, but only linearly with the complexity of the formulas. For proof procedures, the time depends on the complexity of the formulas, but not the number of variables. In many special cases, which are implemented in Prolog and rule-based expert systems, the proof procedures take polynomial time. VLSI chips can be described with highly regular formulas, even though the number of variables in the formulas is very large. Many such chips have been successfully analyzed and verified with proof procedures.

STATUS OF FOL.   Among all the varieties of logic, classical first-order logic has a privileged status. It has enough expressive power to define all of mathematics, every digital computer that has ever been built, and the semantics of every version of logic, including itself. Fuzzy logic, modal logic, neural networks, and even higher-order logic can be defined in FOL. Every textbook of mathematics or computer science attests to that fact. They all use a natural language as the metalanguage, but in a form that can be translated to two-valued first-order logic with just the quantifiers $\forall$ and $\exists$ and the basic Boolean operators. Since textbooks use natural language to define everything in mathematics, the FOL translations of natural language must also be sufficient to define all of mathematics.

Although Whitehead and Russell adopted higher-order logic for the *Principia Mathematica*, one of Whitehead's students, Willard Van Orman Quine (1937), demonstrated that first-order logic plus the membership operator ϵ provides enough power to define all of set theory and the foundations of mathematics. Besides expressive power, first-order logic has the best-defined, least problematic model theory and proof theory, and it can be defined in terms of a bare minimum of primitives: just one quantifier (either $\forall$ or $\exists$) and one or two Boolean operators. Even subsets, such as Horn-clause logic or Aristotelian syllogisms, are more complicated, in the sense that more detailed definitions are needed to specify what cannot be said in those subsets than to specify everything that can be said in full FOL.

Since first-order logic has such great power, many philosophers and logicians such as Quine have argued strongly that classical FOL is in some sense the "one true logic" and that the other versions are redundant, unnecessary, or ill-conceived. Some leaders in artificial intelligence, such as John McCarthy, have also argued for first-order logic as the primary, if not the only, system of logic for knowledge representation. Besides discussing the philosophical issues, logicians have worked out the details for translating other logics to FOL. Tamás Gergely and László Úry (1991), for example, show that FOL with explicit quantifiers over time is simpler and more expressive than most versions of temporal and dynamic logic. María Manzano (1996) shows how FOL can serve as the unifying language for defining and supporting an open-ended variety of extended logics. She gives explicit translations of second-order logic, modal logic, and dynamic logic to typed first-order logic.

RELATING VARIOUS LOGICS.   The power of FOL and the prestige of its adherents have not deterred philosophers, logicians, and computer scientists from developing other logics. In response to Quine, his longtime friend and equally eminent philosopher Rudolph Carnap (1947) wrote a book in defense of modal logic and its applications. For various purposes, modal logics, higher-order logics, and other extended logics have some desirable properties:

- *Fewer axioms.* The axiom of induction, with its quantifier ($\forall$P:Predicate), can only be eliminated by brute force — by replacing the variable P with a separate first-order axiom for every predicate that P might represent. Since there are infinitely many possible predicates, that strategy replaces one second-order axiom with an infinity of first-order axioms. Many logicians find an infinity of axioms to be more distasteful than the complexity of higher-order logic.

- *More natural translations.* Without modal logic, an English sentence like *It may rain* would be translated to an awkward paraphrase: *Of all the states of affairs in the set of causal successors of the present, there exists at least one in which it rains.* In modal logic, the lengthy preamble about states of affairs would be replaced by a single symbol, $\Diamond$.

- *More efficient computation.* By incorporating features of the ontology or metalanguage into special operators, such as the modal symbols $\Box$ and $\Diamond$, a complex logic can sometimes simplify knowledge representation. With this technique, much of the computation is transferred from the axioms to the rules of inference. This transfer may speed up deduction, since the rules of inference are more likely to be compiled, but the axioms are more likely to be interpreted.

To computer scientists, these arguments sound like familiar trade-offs: specialized high-level languages versus general-purpose low-level languages, or efficient compilers versus flexible interpreters. For different applications, different versions of logic may vary in readability, efficiency, and expressive power. The knowledge engineers should have the option of using logical notations that are tailored to the applications, while the implementers can decide to compile them to other versions of logic or process them interpretively.

EXERCISES

While doing the following exercises, use Appendices A.1 and A.2 as a summary of the predicate calculus and conceptual graph notations. At the back of the book are answers and hints for some, but not all, of the exercises.

1. Develop the Tree of Porphyry further by adding more differentiae and sub-categories for various kinds of minerals, plants, and animals. Assign a distinct prime number to each differentia and compute the number for each composite concept. Note that some differentiae may be reused in different branches of the tree: some plants and animals may both have scales, and some plants and minerals may both be green.

2. Leibniz's representation with prime numbers for differentiae led him to de-velop a calculator that could speed up the operations of multiplication and division. On modern computers, Boolean ANDs and ORs of bit strings may be faster than multiplication and division. Design an alternate encoding for the Tree of Porphyry with bit strings instead of integers. For each differentia, assign a bit string with a single 1 and all the rest 0. How would you compute the bit strings for each of the composite concepts? What operations on the bit strings would test whether one concept was a subtype or subcategory of another? How would you compute the lowest common supertype of two concepts? Or the highest common subtype of two concepts?

3. Show that your encoding of categories as bit strings in Exercise 1.2 is *isomorphic* to the encoding with products of primes in Exercise 1.1; i.e., show that the corresponding operations on the two different encodings always lead to the same supertypes, subtypes, lowest common supertypes, and highest common sub-types.

4. With N differentiae, each concept could be represented by a string of N bits. How many bits would be needed for the concepts represented in the hierarchy you developed for Exercise 1.1? If the concepts were represented as products of primes, how many bits would be needed for each concept? How would differences in the hierarchy affect the amount of storage space needed?

5. Translate the three *Begriffsschrift* diagrams in Figure 1.5 (page 10) to the equivalent algebraic formulas using only Frege's choice of operators ~, ⊃, and ∀. Then use the definitions of ∧ and ∃ in terms of Frege's operators to show that the formulas are equivalent to the Peirce-Peano versions given in Section

1.1. In doing the conversions, you may assume that any statement p is equivalent to its *double negation* $\sim\sim p$; i.e., two negations cancel each other out. See Appendix A.1 for further discussion of methods for showing that two formulas are equivalent.

6. Frege said that new symbols and abbreviations could be added to the *Begriffsschrift* in order to simplify the notation. Extend Frege's notation by defining three new symbols for representing ∧, ∨, and ∃ in a style compatible with the *Begriffsschrift*. Define those symbols as combinations of the basic primitives of Figure 1.4. Then using your new symbols, redraw the examples in Figure 1.5.

7. Add a predicate tractor(x) meaning "x is a tractor" to the ontology discussed in Section 1.2. Besides variables, use constants like #77, as in part(x,#77) for "x has #77 as part." Use the equality $x=y$ to say that x and y are the same. As an example, the following formula represents the sentence *Tractor #77 is part of one trailer truck, and trailer #238 is part of a different trailer truck*:

$(\exists x)(\exists y)($trailerTruck$(x) \wedge$ tractor$(\#77) \wedge$ part$(x,\#77)$
$\wedge$ trailerTruck$(y) \wedge$ trailer$(\#238) \wedge$ part$(y,\#238) \wedge \sim(x=y))$.

In typed predicate calculus, the formula would be

$(\exists x,y{:}$TrailerTruck$)($tractor$(\#77) \wedge$ part$(x,\#77)$
$\wedge$ trailer$(\#238) \wedge$ part$(y,\#238) \wedge \sim(x=y))$.

Express the following English sentences in both typed and untyped predicate calculus:

a. *Some trailer truck does not have tractor #77 as part.*

b. *There is no trailer truck that is composed of tractor #77 and trailer #238.*

c. *Tractor #77 is not attached to trailer #238.*

d. *It is false that there's a trailer truck with tractor #42 and not trailer #908.*

e. *No trailer truck has two different tractors.*

NOTE: Do not introduce new predicates for words like *composed* or *attached*; use only the predicates described in Section 1.2 and the new ones mentioned in this exercise. In some cases, you may have to rephrase the English sentence in order to map it to predicate calculus; e.g., the last sentence could be expressed *It is false that there exists a trailer truck that has tractors x and y that are not the same.*

8. Translate the five sentences in Exercise 1.7 to conceptual graphs. In the linear CG notation, the sample sentence would become

```
[Tractor: #77]←(Part)←[TrailerTruck]-(≠)-[TrailerTruck]-
  (Part)→[Trailer: #238].
```

Since the ≠ relation is symmetric, the arrows that distinguish the two arcs of the conceptual relation may be omitted; in Appendix B, the relations Dffr and ≠ are defined as synonyms. The hyphen at the end of the first line indicates a continuation on the next line.

9. Select a melody from some music book and translate it to predicate logic and conceptual graphs according to the method used in Sections 1.2 and 1.4.

10. Translate the following statements to modal predicate logic:

    a. *It is necessary that every truck has wheels.*

    b. *Some trailer truck can have 16 wheels.*

    c. *If some trailer truck can have two trailers, then it is possible that it does not have 18 wheels.*

11. Translate the three sentences in Exercise 1.10 to conceptual graphs. To represent $\Diamond p$, use a CG of the following form:

    ```
    (Psbl)→[Proposition: (translation of p to a CG)].
    ```

    The monadic Psbl relation represents possibility and the concept of type Situation represents a situation described by the nested CG, which is generated by translating p. For necessity, use the monadic Necs relation instead of Psbl.

12. Show that $\sim\Diamond p$ (impossible) is equivalent to $\Box\sim p$ (necessarily false) and that $\Diamond\sim p$ (possibly false) is equivalent to $\sim\Box p$ (not necessary). Use only the equivalences for relating possibility and necessity given in Section 1.3 and the principle that a double negation $\sim\sim$ may be inserted or erased in front of any proposition or subproposition.

13. Using the rules of inference of Appendix A.1, show that the formula $p\supset\Diamond p$ is a theorem of System T; i.e., it can be derived from the axioms and definitions.

14. Axioms S4 and S5 are not theorems of System T, but their converses are. From the axioms and definitions of System T, prove that $\Box\Box p\supset\Box p$ and $\Box\Diamond p\supset\Diamond p$.

15. In System S5, which includes System T plus axioms S4 and S5, all the iterated modalities can be replaced by single modalities. Prove that fact by showing that any iterated modality consisting of a sequence of $\Box$ and $\Diamond$ symbols is equivalent to just a single $\Box$ or $\Diamond$.

16. In a version of modal logic called *deontic logic*, $\Box p$ is interpreted *p is obligatory*, and $\Diamond p$ is interpreted *p is permissible*. In a perfect world, all the axioms of System T would be true. But since people are sinners, some axioms and theorems of

System T cannot be assumed. Which one is violated by a sin of omission? Which is violated by a sin of commission?

17. Assume a version of temporal logic with the symbol □ read *always* and ◊ read *sometimes*. Then translate the axioms of System T and the axioms S4, S5, and B to English sentences.

18. Tractors and trailers are long-lasting objects, but trailer trucks only come into existence when a tractor and a trailer are hitched together. Express the following English sentences in temporal logic with the symbol □ for *always* and ◊ for *sometimes*:

   a. *Sometimes, tractor #77 and trailer #238 are part of the same trailer truck.*

   b. *Sometimes, tractor #77 and trailer #238 are each part of different trailer trucks.*

   c. *Tractor #42 and trailer #908 are always part of the same trailer truck.*

   d. *Whenever tractor #42 is part of a trailer truck, the trailer is #908.*

   NOTE: To represent *whenever*, use a combination of □ and ⊃.

19. First-order logic with the typed quantifiers (∀*t*:Time) for *always* and (∃*t*:Time) for *sometimes* is more expressive than temporal logic with the □ and ◊ symbols (Gergely & Úry 1991). Revise the ontology by adding an argument for time to the predicate part(x,y):

   part(x,y,t) x has y as part at time t.

   Then express the next five sentences in FOL with Time as a type:

   a. *Sometimes, tractor #77 and trailer #238 are part of the same trailer truck.*

   b. *Sometimes, tractor #77 and trailer #238 are each part of different trailer trucks.*

   c. *Whenever tractor #42 is part of a trailer truck, the trailer is #908.*

   d. *No tractor is part of two different trailer trucks at the same time.*

   e. *Some tractor is part of two different trailer trucks at different times.*

   As stated, Sentences (d) and (e) cannot be expressed with the symbols □ and ◊ because they explicitly mention time. Find English paraphrases of those two sentences that can be translated to temporal logic with □ and ◊. Find another English sentence that can be represented in FOL with Time as a type, but not in temporal logic with just □ and ◊.

20. Translate the five sentences in Exercise 1.19 to conceptual graphs. To represent ◊*p* for *sometimes*, use a CG of the following form:

```
[Time: {*}]←(PTim)←[Situation: /* Translation of p to a CG */].
```

This graph says that there exist some times, represented by the generic plural {*}, which are the points in time (PTim) of the situation represented by the translation of p to a CG. To represent *always*, insert $\forall$ in the referent field, as in [Time: $\forall$]. To represent two situations that occur at different times, use a graph of the following form:

```
[Situation]←(PTim)←[Time]-(≠)-[Time]→(PTim)→[Situation].
```

21. In Section 1.5, a truth table was used to verify the definition of $\wedge$ in terms of Frege's primitives $\sim$ and $\supset$. Use that technique to show that $p \vee q$ is equivalent to $(\sim p) \supset q$. Truth tables can be used to verify all the equivalences for propositional logic stated in Appendix A.1.

22. The dyadic Boolean operators, which take two truth values as inputs and generate one truth value as output, can be specified by the four possible outputs in their truth tables. In Figure 1.3 (page 000), for example, *and* is specified by 0001, *or* by 0111, and *if-then* by 1101. Following is a list of the 16 possible combinations and the corresponding operator symbols:

0000 Constantly false, F	1000 Nor or Sheffer-stroke, $\curlyvee$ or |
0001 Conjunction, $\wedge$	1001 Equivalence, $\equiv$
0010 Greater-than, $>$	1010 Not-rightside, $\cancel{R}$
0011 Leftside, L	1011 Reverse implication, $\leftarrow$ or $\geq$
0100 Less-than, $<$	1100 Not-leftside, $\cancel{L}$
0101 Rightside, R	1101 Implication, $\supset$ or $\leq$
0110 Exclusive-or, $\veebar$ or $\neq$	1110 Nand, $\curlywedge$
0111 Disjunction, $\vee$	1111 Constantly true, T

Show that all 16 of these operators can be defined in terms of $\sim$ and $\wedge$; for example, $p \supset q$ can be defined as $\sim(p \wedge \sim q)$. For 6 of these operators, one of the inputs can be ignored; for example, pRq can be defined as $p \wedge p$, and pFq as $p \wedge \sim p$ or $q \wedge \sim q$.

23. In computer circuits, the two Boolean operators *nand* and *nor* are often used because they happen to be easy to implement in transistors. In 1880, Peirce showed that either $\curlywedge$ or $\curlyvee$ by itself could be used to define all 16 dyadic Boolean operators. For example, $p \vee q$ can be defined as $(p \curlyvee q) \curlyvee (p \curlyvee q)$. Give the definitions of all 16 operators in terms of $\curlyvee$. Then give the definitions of all 16 in terms of $\curlywedge$.

24. Use the method of truth tables to show that the following formulas are tautologies:

   a. $((p \supset q) \wedge (q \supset r)) \supset (p \supset r)$.
   b. $(p \supset (q \supset r)) \equiv ((p \wedge q) \supset r)$.
   c. $((p \supset r) \wedge (q \supset s)) \supset ((p \wedge q) \supset (r \wedge s))$.

Since formulas a and b have three variables (p, q, and r), their truth tables must have 8 rows. Formula c, which Leibniz called the *Praeclarum Theorema* (splendid theorem), would have 16 rows. Modern theorem-proving techniques can show that formula c is a tautology in about seven or eight steps, each of which is simpler than one line of the truth table.

25. Select some universally quantified sentences from the hotel reservation example in Appendix C, and form syllogisms with each of those sentences as the first or major premise. For example, the following syllogism of type Darii has a major premise taken from the hotel reservation example and a minor premise that might be derived from a question asked by a guest:

A: All guests in rooms that charge a primary room \must check out when the guests in the primary room check out.
I: Some children are guests in rooms that charge a primary room.
I: Therefore, some children must check out when the guests in the primary room check out.

Write at least one syllogism in each of the four patterns, Barbara, Celarent, Darii, and Ferio. Sometimes it may be necessary to rephrase the original sentence to make it fit the syntactic pattern of the syllogism.

26. The four statement types (A, I, E, and O) can only represent one quantifier per sentence. Statements with two or more quantifiers or with dyadic relations such as part(x,y) can be expressed in predicate logic, but not in those four statement types. Following is a typical inference that cannot be expressed in an Aristotelian syllogism because it uses a dyadic relation and requires more than one quantifier.

• Every horse is an animal.
   ($\forall x$:Horse)animal(x).
• Therefore, every part of a horse is part of an animal.
   ($\forall x$:Horse)($\exists y$:Animal)($\forall z$:Entity)
   (part(z,x) $\supset$ part(z,y)).

The conclusion may be read *For every horse x, there exists an animal y, such that for every entity z, if x has z as part, then y has z as part.* Translate these two formulas in typed logic to untyped logic. Then translate them to conceptual graphs. In the CG form, be sure to show the scope of quantifiers correctly.

27. Find some sentences in the hotel reservation example (Appendix C) that cannot be expressed as type A, I, E, or O statements because they require more than one quantifier or more than one argument on a predicate. Translate those sentences to predicate calculus or conceptual graphs.

28. Section 1.3 included a list of nouns, verbs, and adjectives that typically occur in metalanguage about languages, natural or artificial. Find six sentences in this chapter that contain one or more of those words. Find six more sentences containing those words in other sources, such as newspapers, magazines, novels, poetry, advertising, and computer manuals. Are all of those sentences metalanguage statements about an aspect of some language? What other words might be added to the list of terms that signal metalanguage?

29. Review the discussion of higher-order types in Section 1.4. Then find other second-order types that are instances of Characteristic. Do any fourth-order or higher types occur in natural languages? Feel free to consider two- or three-word terms, as well as single words.

30. Represent the following English phrases as single concepts; then expand the concepts to graphs of two concepts linked by the Chrc relation: *person Sue, 25 centiliters of wine, 5 books, a cup of sugar, philosopher Aristotle, three cats.* Then translate the expanded graphs to predicate calculus.

31. Draw a conceptual graph to represent the sentence *Some box has a length of 5 inches, which is the same as 12.7 centimeters.* Then translate the graph to predicate calculus.

32. A sentence like *Bill earns twice as much as Tom* leaves many concepts and relations implicit. To represent it as a CG, assume that it means the same as the sentence *Bill earns a salary whose amount is twice the amount of the salary that Tom earns.* Use a dyadic relation Twice, whose first arc is attached to a concept whose referent is either a number or a pair, such as <30000, dollar>, and whose second arc is attached to another concept whose number part is twice as large as the first. Then translate the CG for that sentence to predicate calculus.

33. Words like *cup* can be used either to describe a particular physical object or to specify a unit of measure. As a measure, the following CG represents the sentence *Sue drank a cup of coffee:*

```
(Past)→[ [Person: Sue]←(Agnt)←[Drink]-
  (Ptnt)→[Coffee: @ 1 cup]].
```

In this graph, the monadic relation Past marks the past tense, the dyadic relations Agnt and Ptnt mark the agent and patient of drinking, and *@ 1 cup* represents the measure of coffee, not its container. As a physical object, the next CG represents *Sue drank the coffee in the cup:*

```
(Past)→[ [Person: Sue]←(Agnt)←[Drink]-
  (Ptnt)→[Coffee: #]→(In)→[Cup: #]].
```

The symbol # in the referent field of a concept represents the definite article *the*. Modify these graphs to represent the next three sentences:

a. *Sue drank half a cup of coffee.*

b. *Sue drank half as much coffee as there was in the cup.*

c. *Sue drank half of the coffee in the cup.*

Assume that the measure *half* can be represented by the fraction 1/2 and that computational *half* can be represented by a dyadic relation Half.

NOTE: the past tense and the definite article *the* are context-dependent features that cannot be translated directly to predicate calculus. They are discussed further in Chapters 4 and 5.

34. The linguist Barbara Partee observed that the following sentence seems to imply that ninety is rising: *The temperature is ninety, and it is rising.* Represent that sentence as a conceptual graph using measure contraction; then draw the expanded graph. As in Exercise 1.33, use the symbol # in the referent field of a concept to represent the article *the*. Does the expanded graph imply that the amount 90° is rising? Why or why not?

35. The following sentence is an example of English used as a metalanguage to talk about logic: *Two distinct individual markers denote distinct entities.* Translate that sentence to typed predicate logic using the types Entity and IndividualMarker and the dyadic predicate denote(m,x), where m is of type IndividualMarker and x is of type Entity.

36. The metalevel statement in Exercise 1.36 is a common assumption used to simplify the representation in databases and knowledge bases. Suppose a database contains information about a thousand distinct entities, each denoted by a distinct surrogate or individual marker. Without that metalevel assumption, how many first-order statements would be needed to ensure that all the entities are distinct? If you happen to know a particular database or knowledge base language such as SQL, how would you state that assumption in that language?

CHAPTER TWO

Ontology

*Find a scientific man who proposes to get along without any
metaphysics . . . and you have found one whose doctrines are thoroughly
vitiated by the crude and uncriticized metaphysics with which they are
packed. We must philosophize, said the great naturalist Aristotle — if only
to avoid philosophizing. Every man of us has a metaphysics, and has to
have one; and it will influence his life greatly. Far better, then, that that
metaphysics should be criticized and not be allowed to run loose.*

CHARLES SANDERS PEIRCE, *"Notes on Scientific Philosophy,"* CP 1.129

2.1 Ontological Categories

In logic, the existential quantifier ∃ is a notation for asserting that something exists.
But logic itself has no vocabulary for describing the things that exist. Ontology fills
that gap: it is the study of existence, of all the kinds of entities — abstract and
concrete — that make up the world. It supplies the predicates of predicate calculus
and the labels that fill the boxes and circles of conceptual graphs. The two sources of
ontological categories are observation and reasoning. Observation provides knowledge of the physical world, and reasoning makes sense of observation by generating
a framework of abstractions called *metaphysics*.

A choice of ontological categories is the first step in designing a database, a
knowledge base, or an object-oriented system. In database theory the categories are
usually called *domains*, in AI they are called *types*, in object-oriented systems they
are called *classes*, and in logic they are called *types* or *sorts*. Whatever they are called,
the selection of categories determines everything that can be represented in a
computer application or an entire family of applications. Any incompleteness,
distortions, or restrictions in the framework of categories must inevitably limit the
generality of every program and database that uses those categories.

QUINE'S CRITERION.   The philosopher Willard Van Orman Quine observed
that the fundamental question of ontology can be expressed in three words: "What
is there?" It can be answered in just one word: "Everything." Yet that answer, as

comprehensive as it is, lacks detail. As a test for determining what kinds of things constitute that all-inclusive "everything," Quine proposed his most famous slogan: "To be is to be the value of a quantified variable." That slogan is a criterion for distinguishing the ontological categories that are implicit in a knowledge representation:

> So I have insisted down the years that to be is to be the value of a variable. More precisely, what one takes there to be are what one admits as values of one's bound variables. The point has been recognized as obvious and trivial, but it has also been deemed unacceptable, even by readers who share my general philosophical outlook. Let me sort out some of the considerations.
>
> The artificial notation '∃x' of existential quantification is explained merely as a symbolic rendering of the words 'there is something x such that'. So, whatever more one may care to say about being or existence, what there are taken to be are assuredly just what are taken to qualify as values of 'x' in quantifications. The point is thus trivial and obvious.
>
> It has been objected that what there is is a question of fact and not of language. True enough. Saying or implying what there is, however, is a matter of language; and this is the place of the bound variables. (Quine 1992)

As Quine's critics have noted, his criterion says nothing about what actually exists; it can only uncover the implicit assumptions in a statement that has already been made. Those who object to it would prefer some guidelines for the kinds of statements that should be made. For the purpose of this chapter, Quine's criterion can be used as a test to determine the ontological commitments in a particular representation. But further analysis is necessary to give the knowledge engineer some guidelines about what to say and how to say it.

MICROWORLDS. Philosophers usually build their ontologies from the top down. They start with grand conceptions about everything in heaven and earth. Programmers, however, tend to work from the bottom up. For their database and AI systems, they start with limited ontologies or *microworlds*, which have a small number of concepts that are tailored for a single application. The *blocks world*, with its ontology of blocks and pyramids, has been popular for prototypes in robotics, planning, machine vision, and machine learning. David Warren and Fernando Pereira (1982) designed a somewhat larger, but still highly simplified microworld of geographical concepts for the Chat-80 question-answering system. The hierarchy in Figure 2.1 shows the Chat-80 categories, which were used for several related purposes: for reasoning, they support inheritance of properties from supertypes to subtypes; for queries, they map to the fields and domains in the database; and for language analysis, they determine the constraints on permissible combinations of nouns, verbs, and adjectives. Yet Figure 2.1 is specialized for a single application:

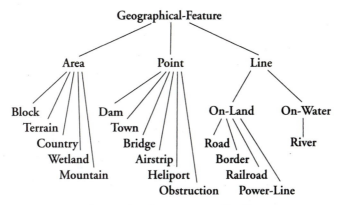

FIGURE 2.1 Geographical categories in the Chat-80 system

rivers and roads are considered subtypes of lines; bridges, towns, and airstrips are treated as single points.

For Chat-80, the restrictions illustrated in Figure 2.1 simplified both the analyzer that interpreted English questions and the inference engine that computed the answers. But the simplifying assumptions that were convenient for Chat-80 would obscure or eliminate details that might be essential for other applications. Reducing entire towns to single points, for example, would make the database unusable for land-use planning. For an airstrip, a pilot would need to know the length and orientation before landing a plane. For steering a ship, the captain must think of a river in three dimensions, since its depth at various distances from the bank is critical. Different applications may classify the same objects in very different ways, and an ontology that is ideally optimized for one application may make knowledge sharing and reuse difficult or impossible.

The Chat-80 ontology represents a typical microworld designed for a single application. Such specialized domains have often been used in successful programs, both in research prototypes and in commercial database systems. The principal advantage of a limited domain is ease of analysis, design, and implementation. Its weakness, however, is the difficulty of sharing and reusing data and programs in other applications. An ontology of parts for an inventory program, for example, might omit all the detail that is needed for designing and using the parts. Recent emphasis on *enterprise integration* (Petrie 1992) requires shared ontologies that can support applications across all areas of a business, including engineering, manufacturing, accounting, and sales. Limited ontologies will always be useful for single applications in highly specialized domains. But to share knowledge with other applications, an ontology must be embedded within a more general framework. Philosophy provides that framework: its guidelines and top-level categories form the superstructure that can relate the details of the lower-level projects.

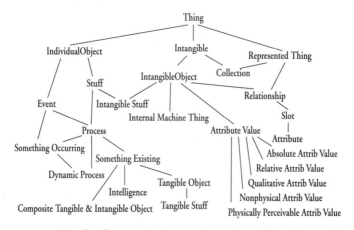

FIGURE 2.2 Top-level categories in an early version of the Cyc ontology

CYC CATEGORIES.   To overcome the limitations of small domains, Doug Lenat and his colleagues have been developing the Cyc system, whose ultimate goal is to accommodate all of human knowledge. Its very name is taken from the stressed syllable of the word *encyclopedia.* Figure 2.2 shows two dozen of the most general categories at the top of the Cyc hierarchy. Beneath the top levels are all the concept types used in the rules and facts of the Cyc knowledge base.

Figure 2.2 is a snapshot of an early stage in the evolution of the Cyc knowledge base (Lenat & Guha 1990). Since then, the knowledge engineers have extended the Cyc hierarchy to over 100,000 concept types with about a million facts and axioms. Although Figure 2.2 is no longer a definitive statement of the current stage of Cyc, it illustrates the kind of logical, philosophical, and computational questions that are discussed throughout this book:

- The most general category called Thing has no properties of its own, and whether it is called Thing, Entity, or ⊤ is a matter of taste. The first significant question concerns the differentiae that distinguish the next three categories under Thing: IndividualObject, Intangible, and RepresentedThing. By what criteria could any given concept be placed under one of those three branches? How would a knowledge engineer use those criteria in system design?

- In discussing their categories, Lenat and Guha explained that Represented-Thing is the complement of InternalMachineThing; i.e., it includes Individual-Object and all intangibles other than the things internal to the machine that Cyc is running on. In later revisions, Guha (1991) added contexts and metalevels, which have enabled Cyc to reflect on its own representations. As a result, the category RepresentedThing has become coextensive with Thing. The issues concerning contexts and metalevels are discussed further in Chapter 5 of this book.

- In treating collections as intangible, the authors explained "We can't conceive of a collection having mass, so every TangibleObject must also be an Individual-Object." As an example, they distinguish TheSetOfPartsOfFredsCar, which is "intangible, imperceivable," from TheStructuredIndividualThatIsFredsCar, which is tangible and perceptible. Yet one can see a flock of birds flying across the sky. Why should a flock be perceptible, but a set imperceptible? This example raises questions about different kinds of collections, which are discussed further in Section 2.6.

- As an example of the category CompositeTangible&IntangibleObject, the authors mention the person GeorgeBush as a composite of a tangible object GeorgeBushsBody and an intangible object GeorgeBushsMind. Another example is a videotape, whose tangible part is a strip of coated plastic and whose intangible part is the information it contains. These issues, which were debated by Plato and Aristotle, are central to the encoding of abstract information in physical entities.

- Process is under IndividualObject, and TangibleObject is under Process. In Cyc, the objects Fred and GeorgeBush are classified as processes with a starting point at birth and a stopping point at death. But are Process and Object coextensive? If not, what differentiates them? These issues concern the representation of processes, events, change, causality, and every kind of time dependency.

Questions like these have been asked about every ontology that has been proposed by anyone from Aristotle to the present. More questions can be asked about Cyc than about most other systems because the Cyc project is so ambitious that the developers have been forced to address every issue of knowledge representation. To facilitate collaboration with other research and development groups, they keep the current version of their top several thousand categories on the World Wide Web (http://www.cyc.com).

2.2 Philosophical Background

The Cyc distinction between tangible objects and intangible information structures is one of the oldest in the history of philosophy. In the sixth century B.C., the Greek philosopher Heraclitus maintained that all things flow (*panta rhei*), as in his famous saying, "One cannot step twice into the same river." But Heraclitus also emphasized the intangible *logos* — translated variously as *word, speech,* or *reason*: "all things (*panta*) come into being according to this logos." The Greek concept of *logos*, which can also be translated *account, reckoning,* or even *computation,* is broad enough to encompass all the abstractions of mathematics and metaphysics. A few centuries after Heraclitus, St. John the Evangelist wrote "In the beginning was the *logos*, and the *logos* was with God, and God was the *logos*. It was in the beginning with God. All things (*panta*) came into being through it, and without it nothing that has come to be came into being" (1,1-3). St. John and Heraclitus used the same words *logos, panta,* and *gignomai* (come to be). What they meant by those words, however, has been a matter of debate for centuries.

The fragments of Heraclitus are as cryptic as those of his contemporaries in India and China: Gautama Buddha, Confucius, and Lao-Tzu. In fact, some of the statements of Lao-Tzu about the Tao (usually translated as *the Way*) bear a striking resemblance to what Heraclitus and St. John said about the *logos*. Following is the beginning of Chapter 42 of the *Book of the Tao*:

> The Tao gave birth to the One;
> The One gave birth to the Two;
> The Two gave birth to the Three;
> And the Three gave birth to the ten thousand things.

Those early insights, as puzzling as they may be, have had a major influence on the history of philosophy in both east and west. A century later, Plato adopted Heraclitus's distinction between the ever-changing flow of all things and the intangible *logos* that determines that flow. In analyzing the concepts underlying the *logos*, Plato proposed the intangible, unchanging mathematical *forms* or *ideas* as the true reality, which is reflected in the changeable, illusory flow of physical things.

ARISTOTLE'S CATEGORIES. Aristotle accepted Plato's distinction, but reversed the emphasis: he considered the physical world to be the ultimate reality and treated the forms as abstractions derived from sensory experience. In the *Categories*, the first treatise in his collected works, he presented ten basic categories for classifying anything that may be said or *predicated* about anything: Substance (*ousia*), Quality (*poion*), Quantity (*poson*), Relation (*pros ti*), Activity (*poiein*), Passivity (*paschein*), Having (*echein*), Situatedness (*keisthai*), Spatiality (*pou*), and Temporality (*pote*). The Tree of Porphyry (Figure 1.1), which was the first attempt to organize Aristotle's categories in a hierarchy, shows only the subtypes under Substance. The Viennese philosopher Franz Brentano (1862) organized all ten categories as the leaves of a single tree (Figure 2.3) whose branches are labeled with other terms taken from Aristotle's works: Being (*to on*), Accident (*symbebēkos*), Property (*pathos*), Inherence (*enyparchonta*), Directedness (*pros tode*), Containment (*ta en tini*), Movement (*kinēsis*), and Intermediacy (*metaxy on*).

For the category labels in Figure 2.3, most of the Greek terms have several possible translations. In choosing labels, Aristotle took advantage of a feature of

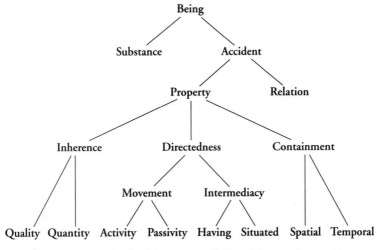

FIGURE 2.3 Brentano's tree of Aristotle's categories

Greek, which allows any word or phrase to be used as a noun when the definite article *the* (*to*) is placed in front. Since most other languages lack that flexibility, some of the translations are barbarisms like *situatedness* or words like *containment*, which could more literally be expressed as *the in-something-ness*. The English terms in Figure 2.3 are a compromise among a literal expression of Aristotle's Greek, the traditional Latin-based translations, and the current terminology in logic, philosophy, and linguistics. The choice of labels, however, is less important than the distinctions that Aristotle discovered and that Brentano organized more systematically than most other commentators. Those underlying distinctions are fundamental to all versions of knowledge representation.

KANT'S CATEGORIES. In the *Critique of Pure Reason*, Immanuel Kant (1787) presented the first major challenge to Aristotle's system of categories. In devising his categories, Kant started with the logically possible ways of combining relationships in a proposition or *judgment*:

> There arise exactly the same number of pure concepts of the understanding which apply *a priori* to objects of intuition in general, as there are logical functions in all possible judgments, because those functions completely specify the understanding and determine all its faculties. Following Aristotle, we shall call these concepts *categories*, for our primary purpose is the same as his, notwithstanding the great difference in manner of execution. (A:79, B:105)

Kant organized his table of categories, like his table of judgments, in four groups of three:

QUANTITY	QUALITY	RELATION	MODALITY
Unity	Reality	Inherence	Possibility
Plurality	Negation	Causality	Existence
Totality	Limitation	Community	Necessity

Kant considered this table a principled framework for organizing the categories, not a rejection of all the work that had been done within Aristotle's framework:

> If one has the original and primitive concepts, it is easy to add the derivative and subsidiary, and thus give a complete picture of the family tree of the pure understanding. Since at present, I am concerned not with the completeness of the system, but only with the principles to be followed, I leave this supplementary work for another occasion. It can easily be carried out with the aid of the ontological manuals, for instance, by placing under the category of causality the predicables of force, activity, passivity; under the category of community the predicables of presence, resistance; among the categories of modality the predicables of origin, extinction, change, etc. (A:82, B:108)

In continuing this discussion, Kant seriously underestimated the amount of effort required to complete his tree of concepts: "From the little I have said, it will be obvious that a dictionary of pure concepts with all the requisite explanations, is not only possible, but easy to complete" (A:83, B:109). Whenever a philosopher or mathematician uses words like "easy" and "obvious," that is a sure sign of difficulty. Kant used those words several times in the course of a page or two; after two hundred years, his easy task is still unfinished.

TRIADS.   The symmetry of Kant's table with four groups of three categories could have been the result of chance, of his esthetic preference, or of some deeper principle. Kant believed that the triadic pattern resulted from something more fundamental than chance or taste:

> In every group, the number of categories is always the same, namely, three. That is remarkable because elsewhere all *a priori* division of concepts must be by dichotomy. Furthermore, the third category always arises from a combination (Verbindung) of the second category with the first. Thus totality is plurality considered as unity; limitation is reality combined with negation; community is the causality of substances reciprocally determining one another; finally, necessity is the existence that is given by possibility itself. It must not be supposed, however, that the third category is merely a derivative, and not a primary concept of the pure understanding. For the combination of the first

and second categories in order to produce the third requires a special act of the understanding, which is not identical with those which produce the first and second. (B:110)

This brief comment raises more questions than it answers. For each of the four triads, Kant suggested a different "act of the understanding" for combining the first and second categories to produce the third. If the act is different in every case, then the symmetry of the categorial system is flawed. But if there is some deeper principle common to all four triads, then that principle is more fundamental than the categories themselves.

The German philosophers who followed Kant searched for a deeper explanation of the triadic patterns. Some of them applied the word *thesis* to the first category, *antithesis* to the second, and *synthesis* to the third. Those Greek words sound impressive, but the word *synthesis* is no more explicit than Kant's word *Verbindung*, which has several meanings ranging from connection to combination. In chemistry, both words *synthesis* and *Verbindung* are used to describe how two substances combine in a chemical reaction. Different molecules combine in different ways, but in each case, the theories of chemistry predict the method of combination from the internal structure of the molecules themselves. A complete theory of categories should likewise show how the internal structure of the concepts determines their method of combination.

The most ambitious development of the triadic approach was by Georg Wilhelm Friedrich Hegel (1831), who wrote a mammoth tome divided and subdivided in patterns of three. In explaining his method of deriving the third from the first and second, Hegel used the verb *aufheben*, which literally means to raise up, but with the further implication that the third supersedes the first two:

Aufheben has a twofold meaning in the language: on the one hand it means to preserve, to maintain, and equally it also means to cause to cease, to put an end to. Even *preserve* includes a negative element, namely, that something is removed from its immediacy and so from an existence which is open to external tendencies, in order to preserve it. Thus what is *aufgehoben* is at the same time preserved; it has only lost its immediacy, but is not on that account annihilated.

In continuing this discussion, Hegel took delight in finding ambiguous words, which "have in themselves a speculative meaning." Throughout his book, he emphasized the contradictions he found among his categories and considered them the basis for generating new categories to replace or "aufheben" the old ones.

Unfortunately, Hegel chose to call his book *The Science of Logic*. That title invited scathing criticism from logicians, who seized upon the contradictions to point out how far from logic it had strayed. At the end of a 16-page discussion of Hegel, Bertrand Russell (1945) concluded "the worse your logic, the more interesting the consequences to which it gives rise." Despite its flaws, what makes Hegel's book interesting is its wealth of categories based on triads. As a generative principle, however, his verb *aufheben* is even more problematic than *combine* or *synthesize*.

PEIRCE'S CATEGORIES. Like most logicians, Peirce found Hegel's logic repugnant, but he was just as intrigued by the patterns of triads in the categories of Kant and Hegel. In his lectures of 1898, he said that in his youth he had been "a passionate devotee of Kant":

> I believed more implicitly in the two tables of the Functions of Judgment and the Categories than if they had been brought down from Sinai. . . . But Kant, as you may remember, calls attention to sundry relations between one category and another. I detected some additional relations between those categories, *all but* forming a regular system, yet not quite so. Those relations seemed to point to some larger list of conceptions in which they might form a regular system of relationship. After puzzling over these matters very diligently for about two years, I rose at length from the problem certain that there was something wrong with Kant's formal logic.

After extensive analysis, Peirce had concluded that some, but not all of Kant's triads reflected three more basic categories, which he called Firstness, Secondness, and Thirdness:

> First is the conception of being or existing independent of anything else. Second is the conception of being relative to, the conception of reaction with, something else. Third is the conception of mediation, whereby a first and a second are brought into relation. (1891)

In distinguishing his triads from Hegel's, Peirce emphasized the equal status of all three categories and rejected the idea that "Firstness and Secondness must somehow be *aufgehoben*" (CP 5.91).

In Kant's system, the clearest illustration of Peirce's principle is the triad under the heading Relation, which corresponds to the three categories under Property in Brentano's tree of Figure 2.3:

1. Inherence characterizes entities by their intrinsic qualities, independent of anything else. In Brentano's tree, it includes qualities such as shape and color and quantities such as size, length, and mass.

2. Causality is represented by dyadic relations between cause and effect. Brentano's category of Directedness is more general than causality, since it also includes dependencies that are not usually considered causal.

3. Community (*Gemeinschaft*), according to Kant, is the "reciprocity between agent and patient" (*Wechselwirkung zwischen dem Handelnden und Leidenden*).

In Peirce's terms, it is the mediation "whereby a first and a second are brought into relation." Under Containment or *in-something-ness*, Brentano put Spatiality and Temporality, which are the two kinds of "something" in which a community is contained.

As Kant observed, most concepts are subdivided by dichotomy. It is therefore significant that Brentano's only triad corresponds to the Kantian triad that most clearly illustrates Peirce's principle.

Peirce's principle is a metalevel distinction for generating new categories by viewing entities from different perspectives. A category of Firstness is determined by qualities inherent in something, Secondness by a relation or reaction directed toward something else, and Thirdness by some mediation that brings multiple entities into relationship. Formally, the three kinds of categories are characterized by the minimum number of entities that must be involved in their definition. The first can be defined by a monadic predicate $P(x)$, which describes an entity x by its inherent qualities, independent of anything external to x. The second requires a dyadic relation $R(x,y)$, which describes some reaction between an entity x and an independent entity y. The third requires an irreducible triadic relation $M(x,y,z)$, which describes how an entity x mediates two entities y and z. Peirce maintained that it is not necessary to go beyond three, because Fourthness, Fifthness, and higher-order relations can be defined in terms of triads.

As an example, the type Animal can be defined by qualities inherent in the individual. The type Pet, however, is defined in relation to some human being. What makes an animal into a pet is a mediating relationship that resembles a contract. As the fox said to Saint-Exupéry's Little Prince, "You become responsible, forever, for what you have tamed." The responsibility on the human's part and the trust on the animal's part constitute the mediating contract that binds them together. Aspects of the three categories appear in the vocabulary of every domain:

1. An individual can be recognized as a human being or as a subtype, such as man or woman, by sensory impressions (Firstness), independent of any external relationships. The type label Woman characterizes an individual by properties that can be recognized without regard to any relationships to other entities.

2. The same individual could be classified relative to many other things, as in the concept types Mother, Attorney, Wife, Pilot, Employee, or Pedestrian. A classification by any of those types depends on an external relationship (Secondness) to some other entity, such as a child, client, husband, airplane, employer, or traffic.

3. Thirdness focuses on the mediation that brings the first and second into relation. Motherhood, which comprises the act of giving birth and the subsequent period

of nurturing, relates the mother and the child. The legal system gives rise to the roles of attorney and client. Marriage relates the wife and the husband. Aviation relates the pilot to the airplane. The business enterprise relates the employee to the employer. And the activity of walking on a street that is dominated by vehicles relates the pedestrian to the ongoing traffic.

Peirce's principle is used throughout this book to generate triads of categories: in Section 2.4, it is used to classify three ways that adjectives can modify nouns; in Section 2.7, to distinguish three kinds of *granularity* in describing or measuring objects; in Section 5.4, to classify contexts as actual, modal, or intentional; and in Section 6.6, to classify signs in nine categories generated by the product of two triads.

HUSSERL'S CATEGORIES.   Like Peirce, Franz Brentano had made a deep study of Aristotelian and Scholastic philosophy. He broadened the Scholastic notion of *intentionality* to a concept that was close to Peirce's mental mediation or Thirdness. Under Brentano's influence, Edmund Husserl, a mathematician who turned to philosophy, brought intentionality to the forefront of ontology:

- Husserl's *Logical Investigations* (1900) could more properly be called *Ontological Investigations*. He criticized Schröder's treatment of logic as a mere calculus without any content. Instead, Husserl developed a "logic of ideal content" in the six parts of his investigations: meaning and expression; genus and species; parts and wholes; the role of grammar in combining meanings; intentional experiences and their contents; and knowledge in terms of meaning intention and meaning fulfillment. The topics of these studies are central to knowledge representation in AI and natural language semantics.

- In *Ideas* (1913), Husserl developed *phenomenology* as a branch of philosophy that emphasizes intentionality as the mechanism that directs attention to the object of perception. Although he never used the terms, Husserl came tantalizingly close to Peirce's distinction of Firstness, Secondness, and Thirdness. For Firstness, he adopted the Greek word *noēma* (thought, concept, or percept), which is the abstract content or meaning (*Sinn*) of a perception. Through an analysis and description of the *noēmata*, Husserl said "we acquire a definite system of predicates . . . and these predicates in their modified conceptual sense determine the content of the object-nucleus of the *noēma* in question" (Section 130). His term for Secondness is *noēsis*, which is the process of recognizing an object according to some *noēma*. His Thirdness is *intentionality*, which is the mental mediation that directs the noēma to its object in the process of *noēsis*. Formally, the recognition of an object x by a *noēma* N is the application of a predicate $P(x)$, which implies $N(x)$.

Husserl also distinguished *independent* or self-sufficient (*selbständig*) entities from *dependent* entities whose existence depends on some other entity. As an example, a rose is independent because it continues to exist when detached from the rosebush. The rose petals are also independent since they continue to exist when detached from the flower. But the rose's shape, color, size, and weight are dependent entities that cannot exist apart from the flower. This distinction is related to Peirce's triad: Firstness is independent, Secondness depends on one other entity, and Thirdness depends on a multiplicity of entities, among which it serves as a mediator. The last clause is crucial: the mediator creates new relationships among the entities it depends on.

WHITEHEAD'S CATEGORIES.   After collaborating with Bertrand Russell on logic, Alfred North Whitehead developed an ontology that combined the insights of some of the greatest philosophers, both ancient and modern. In the book *Process and Reality*, he agreed with Heraclitus that "the flux of things is one ultimate generalization around which we must weave our philosophical system." But he considered the other ultimate generalization to be the "permanences amid the inescapable flux," which Plato tried to capture in his eternal, unchanging Platonic forms:

> Plato found his permanences in a static, spiritual heaven, and his flux in the entanglements of his forms amid the fluent imperfections of the physical world. . . . Aristotle corrected his Platonism into a somewhat different balance. He was the apostle of "substance and attribute," and of the classificatory logic which this notion suggests. But on the other side, he makes a masterly analysis of "generation." Aristotle in his own person expressed a useful protest against the Platonic tendency to separate a static spiritual world from a fluent world of superficial experience. (p. 209)

Although Whitehead never mentioned Peirce, his eight "categories of existence" constitute two Peircean triads, supplemented with two extra categories for generating combinations. To classify "the ultimate facts of immediate actual experience," Whitehead defined categories for *actual entities, prehensions,* and *nexūs,* which make up a triad of physical Firstness, Secondness, and Thirdness:

1. For Firstness, Whitehead used the term *actual entities* for objects and processes that can exist independent of anything else. They "are the final real things of which the world is made up. There is no going behind actual entities to find anything more real. They differ among themselves: God is an actual entity, and so is the most trivial puff of existence in far-off, empty space." (p. 18)

2. For Secondness, he used the term *prehension* for "concrete fact of relatedness." He explained "that every prehension consists of three factors: (a) the *subject*

which is prehending, namely, the actual entity in which that prehension is a concrete element; (b) the *datum* which is prehended; (c) the *subjective form* which is *how* that subject prehends that datum." (p. 23)

3. For Thirdness, Whitehead adopted the Latin word *nexus* (plural *nexūs*), which represents an instance of connecting or binding together two or more actual entities: "Actual entities involve each other by reason of their prehensions of each other. There are thus real individual facts of the togetherness of actual entities, which are real, individual, and particular, in the same sense in which actual entities and the prehensions are real, individual and particular. Any such particular fact of togetherness among actual entities is called a *nexus*." (p. 20)

An actual entity can exist by itself. A prehension is a directed relation or reaction between two entities. A nexus is a bundle of two or more prehensions; it must therefore include at least three entities. In Kant's terms, a nexus is the *Verbindung* that binds a prehending entity and a prehended entity in a community. In Brentano's analysis of Aristotle's categories, a nexus corresponds to Containment or In-something-ness. The words of Kant, Brentano, Peirce, and Whitehead express different, but related aspects of Thirdness: community, reciprocity, containment, togetherness, and mediation.

Besides the three physical categories, Whitehead maintained "All else is, for our experience, derivative abstraction." He classified the abstractions in the categories of *eternal objects, propositions,* and *subjective forms,* which constitute a triad of abstract Firstness, Secondness, and Thirdness:

1. Whitehead's eternal objects correspond to Plato's forms, but with Aristotle's "correction" that the forms are derivative abstractions rather than the ultimate reality. He maintained that an eternal object is a "pure potential" that can only be described by its manner of "ingression" or instantiation in actual entities. A circle, for example, is an abstraction that can be realized or instantiated in a particular physical object, such as a dinner plate. Whitehead would say that the potentiality of the circle is realized in the dinner plate, thereby contributing a definite form to the baked clay that becomes the plate.

2. For Proposition, both Whitehead and Peirce were strongly influenced by Plato: "The *logos* comes to us by the interweaving (*symplokē*) of the forms with one another" (*Sophist* 259E5). For a simple proposition like cat(Yojo), the form named Cat is predicated of a single entity named Yojo. For a more complex proposition like *Yojo is chasing a mouse,* the syntax of a conceptual graph "interweaves" the forms named Cat, Chase, and Mouse with the relations Agent and Theme:

[Cat: Yojo]←(Agnt)←[Chase]→(Thme)→[Mouse].

The concepts and relations are the warp and woof of the proposition. In the English sentence or the formula in predicate calculus, the weaving is still visible, but the pattern is blurred:

$$(\exists x{:}\mathrm{Cat})(\exists y{:}\mathrm{Chase})(\exists z{:}\mathrm{Mouse})(x{=}\mathrm{Yojo} \wedge \mathrm{agnt}(y,x) \wedge \mathrm{thme}(y,z)).$$

To form the proposition, Whitehead said "The actual entities involved are termed the *logical subject*, and the complex eternal object is the *predicate.*" In this example, the complex pattern is predicated of three entities: Yojo, a mouse, and an act of chasing.

3. As abstract Thirdness, Whitehead's *subjective forms* correspond to the mediating intentions of Peirce and Husserl. He maintained "that there are many species of subjective forms, such as emotions, valuations, purposes, adversions, aversions, consciousness, etc." As a synonym for subjective form, he also used the term *private matter of fact*.

Whitehead's other two categories are principles for generating new categories: his Category 7 of *multiplicities* is made up of "pure disjunctions of diverse entities"; and Category 8 of *contrasts* is a source of distinctions that determine how entities are related in a prehension. Whitehead said "The eighth category includes an indefinite progression of categories, as we proceed from *contrasts* to *contrasts of contrasts* and on indefinitely to higher grades of contrasts."

HEIDEGGER'S CATEGORIES. Husserl's most famous student, Martin Heidegger, shifted the emphasis of phenomenology toward culture and the way it imparts meaning to human practices and artifacts. In his major book *Sein und Zeit* (*Being and Time*), Heidegger distinguished two basic categories: the *Vorhandene* (present-at-hand) and the *Zuhandene* (ready-to-hand). Heidegger's *Vorhandene* entities are independent of human intentions; their characteristics (Firstness) have not been shaped or modified by human needs or desires. The *Zuhandene* entities, which are artifacts designed for some human purpose, are embodiments of Secondness. The culture in which the *Zuhandene* things are used is the Thirdness that explains their Secondness. Like Peirce and Husserl, Heidegger considered the mediating effect of Thirdness to be the primary source of meaning. The *Zuhandene* (Secondness) derive meaning from the culture (Thirdness). The *Vorhandene* (Firstness) do not owe their existence to humans, but human intentionality may project meaning or interpretation upon them. Examples include the emotions expressed in songs and poems about the moon, the stars, the oceans, and the mountains.

Although Heidegger did not explicitly identify Firstness, Secondness, and Thirdness as generative categories, his writings are filled with examples of triads that correspond to Peirce's distinctions. In criticizing the Aristotelian and Scholastic distinction between *essentia* (Firstness) and *existentia* (Secondness), Heidegger

(1975) identified a third mode of being human, *Dasein*, which "knows about itself and knows that it differs from other beings." In addition to the four explicit triads in Kant's categories, Heidegger discovered other examples in Kant's writings:

> Kant enumerates three elements of man's determination: animateness, humanity, and personality. The first determination, animateness, distinguishes man as a living being in general [Firstness]; the second determination, humanity, as a living and at the same time a rational being [Secondness]; the third determination, personality, as a rational being and at the same time a responsible, accountable being [Thirdness]. (1975, p. 131)

Heidegger developed his philosophy without any awareness of Peirce's categories, but in the last few months of his life, he began intently reading a translation of Peirce's works into German (Gray 1977). In his introduction to that translation, the German philosopher Karl-Otto Apel (1975) showed how Peirce's philosophy, although strongly grounded in logic, avoided the split that later developed between the logic-based analytic philosophy and the Continental philosophy of phenomenology and existentialism. European philosophers such as Umberto Eco (1979, 1990) have been using Peirce's work as a basis for reconciling the two traditions.

CATEGORIES OF EMOTIONS.   To make computers more responsive to human needs and attitudes, AI researchers have been developing techniques for recognizing and mimicking human emotions. Systems ranging from Roger Schank's MARGIE (1975) to Lenat and Guha's Cyc (1990), have included emotions in their basic ontologies. In classifying emotions, the psychiatrist Silvano Arieti (1978) developed a three-way partitioning that has strong similarities to Peirce's categories:

1. First-order or *protoemotions* are triggered by the immediate experience of external stimuli or inner bodily status. They include tension, appetite, fear, rage, and satisfaction.

2. Second-order emotions depend on cognitive processes that evoke images associated with first-order emotions: anxiety, anger, wishing, and security. Whereas fear is a response to immediate danger, anxiety is a reaction to remembered, imagined, or expected danger. As a second-order emotion, anxiety may occur at a time and place far removed from the source of the original fear.

3. Third-order emotions involve complex conceptual processes that depend heavily on past experiences and future expectations: love, hate, joy, and sadness. Although they are ultimately derived from first-order experiences, the third-order emotions are so heavily transformed by conceptual processing that the connections may require years of psychoanalysis to trace.

As immediate experiences, the protoemotions are examples of Firstness. As reactions to a cognitive state, the second-order emotions are examples of Secondness. The third-order emotions are the mediating Thirdness; they are richly interconnected systems of images and feelings that motivate language, thought, and action. Love, for example, depends on feelings that are inextricably intertwined with memories, hopes, wishes, and fantasies. Psychiatrists have long been working to unravel the complex interdependencies of emotions, but Arieti cautions, "To discuss adequately what we know about them, which is little in comparison to what remains to be known, would fill many books."

2.3   Top-Level Categories

Aspects of Peirce's three-way distinction or *trichotomy* were discovered by philosophers ranging from Aristotle and the Scholastics to Kant, Hegel, and Whitehead. Even older is the dichotomy between what Heraclitus called *physis* (nature) and *logos* (word, reason, or speech). In Lull's tree of nature and logic (on the cover of this book), the trunk and branches represent nature, and the leaves represent logic. More recently, Quine (1981) illustrated the distinction with the following anecdote:

> Send a man into another room and have him come back and report on its contents. He comes back and agitates the air for a while, and in consequence of this agitation we learn about objects in the other room which are very unlike any agitation of the air. Selected traits of objects in that room are coded in traits of this agitation of the air. The manner of the coding, called language, is complicated and far-fetched, but it works; and clearly it is purely structural, at least in the privative sense of depending on no qualitative resemblances between the objects and the agitation. Also the man's internal state, neural or whatever, in which his knowledge of the objects in that room consists, presumably bears none but structural relations to those objects; structural in the privative sense of there being no qualitative resemblances between the objects and the man's internal state, but only some sort of coding, and, of course, causation. And the same applies to our own knowledge of the objects, as gained from the man's testimony. (p. 176)

As Quine's example illustrates, structural information is embodied in physical matter, but its essence can be transmitted without the matter. Vibrating air, electromagnetic waves, or pulsating neurons may use matter and energy to convey information, but the information itself is independent of the matter or the energy.

Information is measured in *binary digits* or *bits*, which are abstractions from the matter used to encode them. The number of bits depends only on the complexity of the information structure, not on its meaning. In developing *information theory* as a systematic way of counting the bits, Claude Shannon (1948) ignored meaning completely:

> The fundamental problem of communication is that of reproducing at one point either exactly or approximately a message selected at another point. Frequently the messages have *meaning;* that is they refer to or are correlated according to some system with certain physical or conceptual entities. These semantic aspects of communication are irrelevant to the engineering problem.

Although irrelevant to information transmission and storage, the semantic aspects are fundamental to knowledge representation. The central focus of ontology is the classification of the "physical or conceptual entities" that Shannon deliberately ignored.

SYNTHESIS.   The tree in Figure 2.4 is a synthesis of the philosophical insights ranging from Heraclitus to Peirce and Whitehead. The top symbol ⊤ is a neutral representation for the *universal type*. Since everything that exists must be an instance of ⊤, a pronounceable synonym for ⊤ is Entity, which comes from the Latin *ens* (being). Beneath ⊤ is a two-way split between the category Physical for anything consisting of matter or energy and the category Abstract for pure information structures. The third level divides Physical and Abstract in triads according to Peirce's distinction of Firstness, Secondness, and Thirdness. The resulting categories have a strong resemblance to Whitehead's first six categories of existence.

Although the categories in Figure 2.4 have been adopted from Whitehead, they are defined in terms of Peirce's distinction: Prehension is Physical Secondness; Nexus is Physical Thirdness; and Proposition, which Peirce and Whitehead defined equivalently, is Abstract Secondness. The other three are one-word simplifications of Whitehead's terminology: Actuality for Physical Firstness corresponds to actual entity; Form for Abstract Firstness is shorter and more traditional than eternal entity; and Intention for Abstract Thirdness is a concept that Peirce and Husserl used in approximately the same sense as Whitehead's subjective form. The philosophers who inspired Figure 2.4 can no longer comment on how those categories may capture or distort their insights; the ultimate justification for this or any other system of categories must be its applicability to language and reasoning about the world.

CONTRASTS, DISTINCTIONS, AND CATEGORIES.   All perception begins with contrasts: light-dark, up-down, hard-soft, loud-quiet, sweet-sour. Such contrasts, which Whitehead classified in his Category 8, are the source of distinctions for generating the categories of existence: "What are ordinarily termed *relations* are abstractions from contrasts. A relation can be found in many contrasts; and when it is so found, it is said to relate the things contrasted" (1929, p. 228). The contrasts,

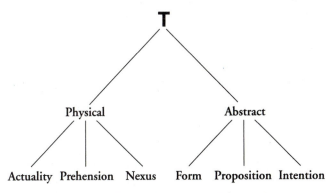

FIGURE 2.4 Top-level categories of an ontology

which relate the categories and determine whether a particular entity belongs to one or another, are more fundamental than the categories themselves.

Contrasts may be expressed in discrete distinctions or continuous gradations, such as a spectrum of color; range of pressure; degree of sweetness; or variation in sound intensity, pitch, duration, and rhythm. The contrast in sound intensity, for example, is the basis for loudness, which can be codified as a dichotomy of loud and quiet; as a trichotomy of loud, medium, and quiet; or as a continuous range of variation. The distinctions and gradations are conceptual interpretations of the perceptual contrasts; they are expressed by the words of language or the predicates of logic. Whitehead also emphasized contrasts of contrasts: the conceptual interpretation of one experience can be contrasted with the interpretation of other experiences to generate higher-level distinctions and more complex conceptualizations.

The distinctions correspond to Leibniz's primitives, which may be combined to generate the categories. The six categories at the bottom of Figure 2.4 are generated by the product of a two-way distinction and a three-way distinction. The combinatorial method always generates highly symmetric structures, but a tree such as Figure 2.4 is not rich enough to display the full symmetry. By the way it's drawn, the tree imposes an ordering: it happens to show the two-way distinction as prior to the three-way distinction. Yet that choice is arbitrary, and either distinction could be placed first. Other structures, such as the graph and the matrix in Figure 2.5, display the combinations without suggesting that either distinction is more fundamental.

The graph on the left of Figure 2.5 is the product of two distinctions. When applied to the top level ⊤, Heraclitus's dichotomy of *physis* and *logos* generates the categories Physical and Abstract. Peirce's trichotomy applied to the top level generates three categories, Independent, Relative, and Mediating:

1. Independent is the category of Whitehead's actual entities and eternal forms as characterized by inherent qualities or Firstness. In logic, independent entities

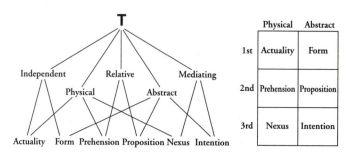

FIGURE 2.5 A graph and a matrix for displaying the categories of Figure 2.4

can be represented by a type label or monadic predicate such as circle(x), potato(x), or elephant(x), which describes some aspect of x without taking into account anything external to x.

2. Relative includes Whitehead's physical prehensions and abstract propositions, both of which can be represented by dyadic predicates. A prehension is a physical relative that relates a prehending entity x to a prehended entity y. A proposition is an abstract relative that relates a form x to an entity y described by x. The proposition that the sun is circular means that the form of a circle can be used to characterize an entity in the sky.

3. Mediating corresponds to Peirce's Thirdness, which includes Whitehead's physical nexūs and subjective forms. As an example, an architectural drawing is an independent entity that consists of pencil marks on paper. It can be described by a monadic predicate whose truth or falsity is determined by the pattern of marks without regard to their meaning. As a relative entity, the pattern of the drawing reflects the structure of some building. It may be expressed by a dyadic relationship between the form of the pencil marks and the physical structure. As a mediating entity, the drawing is a plan for a contractor or builder who translates the pattern of marks to a structure of wood, steel, and concrete. The plan x guides a builder y in the construction of a building z. This irreducible triadic relation cannot be expressed by a conjunction of dyadic relations. (See Exercises 2.6 and 2.7.)

The graph on the left of Figure 2.5 illustrates *multiple inheritance*, where each category on the third level inherits properties from two different categories on the preceding level. The matrix on the right shows another way of representing multiple inheritance: each of the six categories inside the boxes is a combination of the distinctions listed on the top or on the left. The mathematical techniques of graph theory and matrix algebra allow any number of dimensions to be represented. But as the number of distinctions increases, the fine print and criss-crossing lines can make any notation unreadable.

CONTINUANTS AND OCCURRENTS. Whitehead agreed with Heraclitus that all things are in flux, but some things undergo rapid change, while others remain comparatively stable. To accommodate objects in a process-based ontology, he distinguished *enduring objects*, which have a stable identity over some period of time, from the constantly perishing *occasions*, whose successive stages may not resemble one another. An enduring object is called a *continuant*, and a process or event, which does not have enduring characteristics, is called an *occurrent*. The distinction is determined by the way the entity is identified:

- A continuant has stable attributes or characteristics that enable its various appearances at different times to be recognized as the same individual.
- An occurrent is in a state of flux that prevents it from being recognized by a stable set of attributes. Instead, it can only be identified by its location in some region of space-time.

Every appearance of an object is a new event of the same type. As an example, Whitehead (1920) said "You cannot recognize an event; because when it is gone, it is gone. You may observe another event of analogous character, but the actual chunk of the life of nature is inseparable from its unique occurrence. But a character of an event can be recognized. We all know that if we go to the Embankment near Charing Cross we shall observe an event having the character which we recognize as Cleopatra's Needle. Things which we thus recognize I call objects." Cleopatra's Needle is the object (continuant) that explains why each of its appearances (occurrents) have the same shape. A baby's delight in playing the game of peek-a-boo results from the recognition that each appearance of Mommy's face is a sign of her continued existence.

VIEWPOINT. The physical/abstract distinction is independent of the observer's viewpoint, but the continuant/occurrent distinction depends on the choice of time scale. On a scale of minutes, a glacier is a continuant, and an avalanche is an occurrent. But on a scale of centuries, the glacier is a process whose character may be transformed beyond recognition. The changes in a person's facial features are slow enough that friends can recognize an individual as "the same" over the course of a lifetime. Yet each person gains and loses molecules with every bite of food and every breath of air. In about seven years, most of the molecules in the human body have been replaced. A human being, who has a stable identity at a macro level, may be viewed as a constantly changing process at the molecular level. The classification of an entity as a continuant or an occurrent depends on the time scale and level of detail of some observer's point of view.

A performance of a symphony is an occurrent that may last an hour, but a recording of the performance is a continuant that can preserve the information on a magnetic strip that lasts for years. The continuant/occurrent distinction applies to the entities *about which* information is recorded and to the physical media *on which* information is stored. But in Whitehead's terms, the information itself is an eternal object that can be preserved indefinitely, provided that copies are made from time to time. Although information structures do not change, they can represent the form of either a continuant or an occurrent: a static pattern of magnetic spots on a tape may record a dynamic process, such as a movie or a symphony. An abstract type, which is unchanging in itself, can be considered an encoding of information about a continuant or information about an occurrent.

LATTICE OF CATEGORIES. With the binary distinction between continuants and occurrents, the six categories at the bottom of Figure 2.5 are split into twelve categories in Figure 2.6. They are all derived by combinations of the three basic distinctions or dimensions for subdividing the universal type ⊤: Independent, Relative, or Mediating; Physical or Abstract; Continuant or Occurrent. Each of the other categories is a synonym for the combination of categories from which it was derived: Object, for example, could be represented by the acronym IPC for Independent Physical Continuant, and Purpose would be MAO for Mediating Abstract Occurrent. The opposite of the universal type ⊤, which is true of everything, is the *absurd type* ⊥, which is true of nothing. The universal type ⊤ can be considered a synonym for the empty set of no distinctions; ⊥ can be represented by an acronym for the inconsistent combination of all distinctions, IRMPACO.

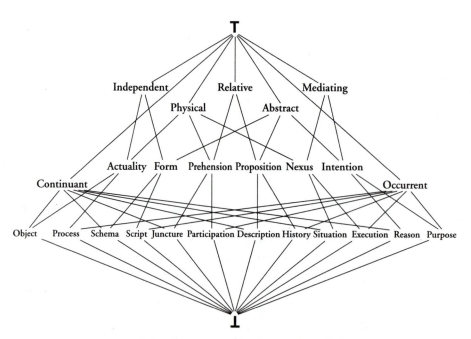

FIGURE 2.6 Lattice generated by the top three distinctions

The symmetric hierarchies generated by Leibniz's method of combination are called *lattices*. When drawn in their full generality, diagrams of lattices can become cluttered with many crossing lines. To simplify the diagram, Figure 2.6 omits ten of the possible combinations, which could be represented by the acronyms PC, PO, AC, AO, IC, IO, RC, RO, MC, and MO. If these categories were added to Figure 2.6, the lattice would contain a total of 37 distinct types, including $\top$ and $\bot$. For common applications, however, the most useful categories are the central twelve, generated by one selection from each of the top three distinctions. Each of the category labels is a technical term that is synonymous with the three-letter acronym that shows its derivation. Informally, short words like Object may be used; but formally, the acronym should be appended in a prefix as IPC-Object or in parentheses as Object (IPC).

- Object (IPC) is an actuality (IP) considered as a continuant (C), which retains its identity over some interval of time. Although no physical entity is ever permanent, an object can be recognized by characteristics that remain stable during its lifetime.
- Process (IPO) is an actuality (IP) considered as an occurrent (O). Depending on the time scale and level of detail, the same actual entity may be viewed as either a stable object or a dynamic process. Even a diamond could be considered a process when viewed over a long time period or at the atomic level of vibrating particles.
- Schema (IAC) is a form (IA) that has the structure of a continuant (C), which does not specify time or timelike relationships. Examples include geometrical forms, the syntactic structures of sentences in some language, and the encodings of pictures in a multimedia system.
- Script (IAO) is a form (IA) that has the structure of an occurrent (O), which represents time or timelike sequences. Examples include computer programs, a recipe for baking a cake, a sheet of music to be played on a piano, or a differential equation that governs the evolution of a physical process. A movie can be described by several different kinds of scripts: the first is a specification of the actions and dialog to be acted out by humans; but the sequence of frames in a reel of film is also a script that determines a process carried out by a projector that generates flickering images on a screen.
- Juncture (RPC) is a prehension (RP) considered as a continuant (C) over some time interval. The prehending entity is an object (IPC) in a stable relationship to some prehended continuant. Examples of junctures include a knot in a string, joints between bones, and connections between parts of a car.
- Participation (RPO) is a prehension (RP) considered as an occurrent (O). The prehending entity is a process (IPO) in a stable relationship to some prehended

continuant. Examples of participation include a dog barking, an apple being eaten, or a sentence being spoken.

- Description (RAC) is a proposition (RA) about a continuant (C), which relates some schema (IAC) as a characterization of the continuant. A schema by itself is an uninstantiated pattern; a description is the application of a schema to describe some continuant, either physical or abstract. In a verbal description, the schema is a sentence that characterizes some aspect of a continuant. A drawing or photograph could also be used as a description when accompanied by a pointer to an object (IPC) the image describes.

- History (RAO) is a proposition (RA) about an occurrent (O), which relates some script (IAO) as a characterization of the occurrent. A computer program, for example, is a script (IAO); a computer executing the program is a process (IPO); and the abstract information (A) encoded in a trace of the instructions executed is a history (RAO). Like any proposition, a history need not be true, and it need not be predicated of the past: a myth is a history of an imaginary past; a prediction is a history of an expected future; and a scenario is a history of some hypothetical occurrent.

- Structure (MPC) is a nexus (MP) considered as a continuant (C) for some reason (MAC) that explains how the junctures of its components are organized for some function. The reason need not be consciously entertained by a human agent: the structure could be a bird's nest, a beaver dam, or a beehive.

- Situation (MPO) is a nexus (MP) considered as an occurrent (O) for some purpose (MAO). The mediating aspect of a situation (MPO) is the purpose (MAO) of some agent that determines why the interaction of entities in the situation is significant. Most verbs express situations, which include an event or state and its participants. Complex situations may have other situations as components: a court trial, for example, may consist of many actions by a judge, jury, lawyers, and witnesses.

- Reason (MAC) is an intention (MA) of some agent concerning some continuant (C). Unlike a description (RAC), a reason (MAC) explains an entity in terms of an intention (MA). For a birthday party, a description might list the presents, but a reason would explain why the presents are relevant to the party.

- Purpose (MAO) is an intention (MA) of some agent that determines the interaction of entities in a situation (MPO). The words and notes of the song "Happy Birthday" form a script (IAO); a proposition about the way people at a party sang the song is history (RAO); and the intention (MA) that explains why they sang the song is purpose (MAO).

Lattices of categories can be derived from the top down, as this one, or they can be derived empirically from an analysis of data. Rudolf Wille and his colleagues (Wille

1992; Ganter & Wille 1996) have been developing lattice techniques for formal concept analysis. They have implemented the techniques in tools for knowledge acquisition, for machine learning from examples, and for classifying large volumes of data, such as the books and documents in a library. Unlike trees, lattices support cross links for showing multiple associations.

To show the twelve central categories from a different perspective, Figure 2.7 arranges them in a matrix instead of a lattice. The three rows are based on Peirce's three-way distinction, and the four columns represent the product of the binary distinction of Physical and Abstract with the binary distinction of Continuant and Occurrent. Each abstract category on the right of Figure 2.7 is said to *characterize* the corresponding physical category on the left: a schema characterizes an object; a script characterizes a process; a description characterizes a juncture; a history characterizes a participation; a reason characterizes a structure; and a purpose characterizes a situation. In conceptual graphs, the concept [Cat: Yojo] asserts that the schema named by the type label Cat characterizes the object named Yojo. Depending on which features are highlighted, the same entity can be characterized in many different ways, such as [Pet: Yojo], [Mammal: Yojo], or [FuzzyBlack-Object: Yojo]. As pure information, all abstract occurrents (scripts, histories, and purposes) are unchanging, but they can be used to characterize changes in physical entities.

The categories of Figure 2.7 provide a framework of twelve boxes for classifying everything that exists, but many more distinctions are needed to subdivide those categories to accommodate the thousands of words of natural languages. Any other distinctions that apply at the top level (category ⊤ or Entity) can be considered as fundamental as those in Figure 2.6. Any distinctions that depend on others as prerequisites can only be applied at lower levels of the lattice. The purpose of the ontology is to provide a framework of distinctions that can be used to discriminate and classify the things that exist and define the words that describe them. But no fixed collection of distinctions or categories is likely to be adequate for describing all things for all time. As Whitehead (1938) said, "We must be systematic, but we should keep our systems open."

	Physical		Abstract	
	Continuant	Occurrent	Continuant	Occurrent
Independent	Object	Process	Schema	Script
Relative	Juncture	Participation	Description	History
Mediating	Structure	Situation	Reason	Purpose

FIGURE 2.7 Matrix of the twelve central categories of Figure 2.6

AXIOMS AND INFERENCES.   Besides classifying things, ontological categories provide hooks to which the definitions and axioms of a knowledge base are attached. By the inference rules of logic, those axioms are inherited from supertypes to subtypes to support inferences about entities at every level of generality. The following axioms are associated with the dichotomy between Physical and Abstract:

- *Location.* If x is physical, then x has a location in space-time. If x is abstract, then x has no physical location, but x might be assigned abstract coordinates in some imaginary space.

- *Mass and energy.* Any physical entity other than empty space must have a positive mass or energy. No abstract entity has mass or energy.

- *Representation.* An abstract entity x may be *encoded* or *represented* in some physical entity y without changing the mass, energy, or location of y.

- *Causality.* Physical entities may causally affect or be affected by other physical entities. Abstract entities cannot have direct causal interactions with other entities, either physical or abstract. They may, however, have indirect causal influences through the mediation of some physical entity x, which *decodes* the representation of some abstract entity y in some physical entity z.

These axioms, which are informally stated in English, could be translated to logic, but such a translation would require an ontology for many other concepts: Space, Time, Mass, Energy, Encoding, Decoding, Representation, Change, Cause, Interaction, and Mediation. They illustrate a fundamental principle of any axiomatic system: the starting primitives cannot be defined in terms of anything more primitive; they can only be specified indirectly by their relationships to other concepts in the system.

The categories at every level of the hierarchy can be characterized by axioms and definitions. But unlike the categories Physical and Abstract, the definitions of the other top-level categories and their subtypes depend on the observer's viewpoint:

- Independent categories are characterized by monadic predicates defined in terms of some entity x by itself (including its inherent parts and properties) and not in terms of anything external to x.

- Relative categories are characterized by dyadic predicates that relate an entity x to some external entity y that can exist independently of x.

- Mediating categories are characterized by triadic or higher predicates that show how an entity x mediates two or more entities ($y,z, \ldots$) and thereby establishes new relationships among them.

- Continuant categories are characterized by a predicate that does not involve time or a timelike succession.

- Occurrent categories are characterized by a predicate that depends on time or a timelike succession.

These categories and their subtypes depend on the way something is represented, classified, or defined. An entity of type Animal may change over time, but it can be classified as a continuant because the defining characteristics of Animal are independent of time. The life of an animal, however, is an occurrent because it is defined as a timelike succession of stages. Different views of the same entity may be described in different words, whose meanings are different concept types with different axioms and definitions.

Each category in the hierarchy inherits all the properties and axioms of every category above it. An instance of Script (IAO), for example, is independent (I); therefore, it can be characterized by a monadic predicate $p(x)$ defined in terms of the parts and properties inherent in x. As an abstraction (A), it can be communicated without transporting the matter in which it is encoded. As an occurrent (O), the characteristic predicate $p(x)$ must involve time or a timelike succession. These properties of the top-level categories apply to subjects in every domain of knowledge. The midlevel categories have more specific, but still broadly applicable properties and axioms. The lowest-level categories inherit all the general knowledge from the top-level and midlevel categories, but they also have much more detailed domain-dependent properties.

The axioms for the top-level categories can be combined with the axioms and definitions for the other categories to derive more specific implications. They can also be combined with detailed facts represented in a database or with physical laws, such as the conservation of mass-energy. As a result, the inference engine of a knowledge-based system could derive implications like the following:

- If x is physical with mass m and x is transported from location l_1 to location l_2, then the total mass at location l_1 is decreased by m, and the total mass at location l_2 is increased by m.
- If x is abstract, an encoding of x in a physical entity y at location l_1 may be copied to an encoding of x in a physical entity z at location l_2 without changing the mass at either location.

Without further qualifications, these implications could only be true in an ideal system where the processes of encoding and decoding are completely reversible. In practical systems, they are only approximately true because physical objects wear out after repeated use. Reasoning about actual systems is always an approximation that depends on the *granularity* of the media, the manufacturing techniques, the measuring instruments, and the users' purposes. Granularity is discussed further in Section 2.7.

2.4 Describing Physical Entities

The same abstract forms may be represented or embodied in many different physical entities. Therefore, physical objects of widely divergent natures could be characterized by the name of the same abstract form. The name of the book *War and Peace*, for example, could refer to an abstract form conceived by Tolstoy or to an embodiment of that form in a physical object made of paper and ink. When computers are used to represent such things, the number of entities, both physical and abstract, is multiplied:

- When *War and Peace* is encoded for computer processing, it becomes a pattern of bits, which is another abstract form that hardly resembles the one that Tolstoy conceived.

- When a computer program formats the bits to recreate a humanly readable copy, the abstract pattern passes through a rapid succession of physical embodiments: reflecting spots on one disk, magnetic spots on another disk, currents flowing in transistors, pulses of light in a laser beam, electrically charged spots on a drum, and dust particles that are attracted to the drum and baked on the paper.

- Despite the profound differences between the physical embodiments, they could all be called by the name of the same abstract form, *War and Peace*. For different purposes, the same physical entity could also be described by different forms: the bound volume could be called *War and Peace* to emphasize its content, or it might be called "a book" to emphasize its physical structure.

William of Ockham admonished philosophers to avoid multiplying entities, but computers multiply them faster than his razor can shave.

      POSSIBLE CONFUSIONS.   For each actual entity, there are many abstract forms that could characterize it from different perspectives. In a computer, each form could be represented in different ways. A curve, for example, might be stored as a pattern of bits or as a mathematical equation. Each representation of a form could have a different name; the names could also have forms; and the forms of the names could have their own representations. A failure to distinguish these entities is a common source of bugs in computer programs. One query system, for example, gave the following answer to a question about U.S. geography:

    Q: *What is the biggest state?*
    A: *Wyoming.*

Alaska is the largest state in area, and California is the largest in population. Wyoming is not the largest by any measure, but it happens to be the last state in alphabetical order. For numbers and character strings, the system would find the largest value by comparing their names with the > operator. For states, it blindly applied the same operator to their names. But unlike numbers, states do not have names that encode their size.

The State of Wyoming, its population, and its land are physical entities; but the name of the state and the measurements of its population and land area are abstract entities. The representations of names and measurements are further abstract entities. Yet programmers sometimes ignore the distinctions and blithely define person as a string or population as a number. In the NIAM methodology for database design (Nijssen & Halpin 1989), the distinctions are carefully preserved: any abstract information structure that can be represented in a computer is called a *lexical object type* (LOT); a physical entity, which cannot be stored in a computer, is called a *nonlexical object type* (NOLOT). That distinction is fundamental to knowledge representation, but the terms LOT and NOLOT show their computer bias by making LOTs primary and calling physical objects by the negative term *nonlexical.* Those terms make the information in the computer seem more real than the world outside.

INTENTIONALITY. As Peirce and Whitehead noted, the way a physical entity is classified depends on the intention or subjective form of some perceiving agent. A proposition, by itself, is a Secondness that characterizes some entity by some abstract form. The mental state of a person who believes or states a proposition is not involved in the proposition. An intention, however, is the mental mediation or Thirdness that directs an agent's attention to some form that characterizes some entity. In his book *Intentionality*, the philosopher John Searle began with a definition: "Intentionality is that property of many mental states and events by which they are directed at or about or of objects and states of affairs in the world."

To illustrate intentionality, Searle presented Figure 2.8, which agents with different intentions might interpret in different ways:

This can be seen as the word "TOOT", as a table with two large balloons underneath, as the numeral 1001 with a line over the top, as a bridge with two pipelines crossing underneath, as the eyes of a man wearing a hat with a string hanging down each side, and so on. In each case, we have a different experience even though the purely physical visual stimuli, the lines on the paper in front of us and the light reflected from them, are constant. But these experiences and the differences between them are dependent on our having mastered a series of linguistically impregnated cultural skills. It is not the failure, for example, of my dog's optical apparatus that prevents him from seeing this figure as the word "TOOT".

Each interpretation of Figure 2.8 could be stated as a different proposition: *There is the word TOOT* or *There is a table with two balloons underneath*. In these statements,

FIGURE 2.8 Searle's example of an ambiguous figure

the word *there* indicates the physical entity, and the phrase following the word *is* specifies some form that is applied to the entity. But the propositions make no reference to any agent, explicit or implicit, who may believe them. A belief is intentional because it involves the agent who relates the form to the entity: *Mary believes that Figure 2.8 shows the word TOOT, but Bill believes that it shows a table with two balloons underneath.* The intentions of Mary and Bill are essential to their beliefs, but not to the propositions that make up the content of those beliefs.

PHENOMENON, ROLE, AND SIGN.   Different intentions lead to different concept types for classifying the same entities. A *structural type* describes an entity by its inherent form or structure, independent of its relationships to external entities. The phrase *a wooden cube*, for example, describes a thing in two ways: the noun *cube* names a geometrical form that describes its shape; the adjective *wooden* describes an embodiment of that form as an object made of wood. Without that adjective, the word *cube* could refer to either an abstract form or a physical object. Formally, a structural type classifies an entity *x* by a monadic predicate that depends only on properties that can be observed in *x* itself. For this example, the phrase *wooden cube* could be translated to a conjunction of two phenomenal predicates, wooden(x) ∧ cube(x).

A *role type* characterizes an entity by some role it plays in relationship to another entity. The type HumanBeing, for example, is a phenomenal type that depends on the internal form of an entity; but the same entity could be characterized by the role types Mother, Employee, or Pedestrian. Role types can apply to things of radically different appearances: entities of the phenomenal types Potato and Steak could serve in the role of Food for some human being; the phenomenal types Horse, Bicycle, and JetPlane describe entities that could play the role of ModeOfTransportation; and HumanBeing and BusinessOrganization describe entities that could play the role of LegalPerson. Formally, role types depend on a dyadic relation: if *x* is classified by a role type, then *x* stands in a dyadic relation to some other entity *y*. Food *x* can be eaten by some animal *y*; a mode of transportation *x* can be used to transport some entity *y*; and a legal person *x* can be a party to some contract *y*. In logic, both entities in a dyadic relationship may be expressed by arguments of a predicate such as foodFor(x,y); an alternate approach, common in natural languages, is to focus on one entity with a concept type such as Food, which leaves the other entity implicit inside the definition of the type.

The biological classifications of plants and animals have traditionally depended on their structure or *morphology*. Newer techniques that use DNA also classify them by structure, but at the molecular level. Classification by role does not depend on an entity's structure: animals of many different forms could be pets, livestock, or vermin; plants could be crops, ornamentals, or weeds. Similar distinctions apply to artifacts and geographical features: nails and buttons could be distinguished by structure or grouped together as fasteners; a river and a mountain might both be tourist attractions, while bodies of water might be considered obstacles or navigable channels.

An entity's appearance independent of context is sufficient to classify it by a phenomenal type, but context is essential for classifying it by role. The type Nail, for example, is a phenomenal type — long and thin with a point at one end. A common use for a nail is to fasten things made of wood; in that context, a nail would be a fastener. But Fastener is a role type that could be applied to things of many different phenomenal types: Nail, Tape, Hook, Button, String, or PaperClip. Although a fastener must have some form, there is no common form for every kind of fastener. In some cases, the form may be predictable from the role. A pet, for example, is usually an animal in a certain role with respect to a human being. Therefore, the role type Pet suggests the phenomenal type Animal. Yet the suggestion is not a strict implication, since a robot, a human, a plant, or even a rock could serve as a pet. Sometimes it may happen that all instances of a certain role type have the same phenomenal type. But new discoveries or inventions might lead to very different forms that could play the same role. Velcro, for example, is a new kind of fastener whose form does not resemble the traditional types like Nail, String, or Button.

Since phenomenal types are monadic and role types are dyadic, Peirce's principle suggests that there should be a third kind of category based on a triadic relation. Indeed, Peirce observed that any physical entity can also serve as a *sign*, which depends on the triadic relation of *representation*: a sign x represents something y to some agent z. If x is Figure 2.8, x may represent soemthing y, such as the word "TOOT" or two balloons under a table, to the reader z. The general study of signs, called *semiotics*, is discussed in Section 6.6.

ADJECTIVES MODIFYING NOUNS.   In elementary logic books, English adjectives and nouns are usually translated to monadic predicates. For many common phrases, that translation produces an acceptable formula in logic:

a happy boy $\Rightarrow (\exists x)(\text{happy}(x) \wedge \text{boy}(x))$.
a shaggy dog $\Rightarrow (\exists y)(\text{shaggy}(y) \wedge \text{dog}(y))$.
a green tree $\Rightarrow (\exists z)(\text{green}(z) \wedge \text{tree}(z))$.

These translations correctly imply that there is some x that is happy and a boy, some y that is shaggy and a dog, and some z that is green and a tree. But when the method is applied to all adjectives and nouns, it runs into serious difficulties. One question-answering program used it to translate the following two sentences to logic:

Sam is a good musician. $\Rightarrow$ good(Sam) $\wedge$ musician(Sam).
Sam is a bad cook. $\Rightarrow$ bad(Sam) $\wedge$ cook(Sam).

Using those translations, the program answered *yes* to the following questions:

Is Sam a bad musician?
Is Sam a good cook?
Is Sam a good bad musician cook?

The problem is caused by the way the adjectives *good* and *bad* modify the nouns. Unlike the adjective *happy*, which applies directly to the person, the adjectives *good* and *bad* apply to some particular role that the person may play. Sam is not being considered good or bad as a human being, but only in the role of musician or cook.

When an adjective is applied to a phenomenal type like Boy, Dog, or Tree, there is only one entity x that it can characterize. But when it is applied to a role type like Musician, Cook, Pet, or Dwelling, it could modify the description of x itself, the role that x plays in relation to some entity y, or the other entity y. Adjectives like *happy, shaggy,* and *green* describe some entity x itself, independent of any role that x may play: a shaggy dog and a shaggy pet are both shaggy in the same way, and the role of pet is independent of the shagginess. Those adjectives may be applied to role types, as in the phrases *happy musician, shaggy pet,* or *green dwelling.* In such combinations, the adjective describes the base entity; the roles of musician, pet, or dwelling are incidental to the modifying adjective. Therefore, the adjective can be represented by a monadic predicate:

a happy musician $\Rightarrow$ $(\exists x)(\text{happy}(x) \wedge \text{musician}(x))$.
a shaggy pet $\Rightarrow$ $(\exists y)(\text{shaggy}(y) \wedge \text{pet}(y))$.
a green dwelling $\Rightarrow$ $(\exists z)(\text{green}(z) \wedge \text{dwelling}(z))$.

The adjectives *good* and *bad*, however, modify the role: a good musician and a good cook are considered good only in relation to music and cooking. Other examples include *nuclear physicist, former senator,* and *alleged thief.* A happy physicist is a happy person, but a nuclear physicist is not a nuclear person; a former senator is not a former person; and an alleged thief is not an alleged person and perhaps not even a thief.

The simplest way to represent an adjective modifying a noun is to invent special predicates like goodMusician(x) or nuclearPhysicist(y). That method gives up the attempt to analyze the meaning further, but it requires a new predicate for every combination of adjective and noun. A more general approach could be based on Richard Montague's technique of treating modifiers as functions that convert one predicate into another. The adjective *good*, for example, would correspond to a function that maps the predicate musician(x) to a predicate that is equivalent to goodMusician(x):

a good musician $\Rightarrow (\exists x)$good(musician)(x).

This formula says that the function *good*, when applied to the predicate *musician*, generates a new predicate good(musician), which is then applied to the entity x. But this approach becomes more complicated with the sentence *Ivan is a poor choice for shortstop, but he's a good choice for catcher*. Choice is a role that implies that Ivan could be chosen for another role, Shortstop or Catcher, for which he might be good or bad. Generalizing the above representation would produce something like

a good choice for catcher $\Rightarrow (\exists x)$good(choice)(catcher)(x).

This formula says that *good* is a function, which when applied to *choice* produces another function, which when applied to *catcher* generates a predicate, which is applied to x.

The representation of adjectives as functions is only a first step. It shows that an adjective modifies a noun, but it does not show how it affects the meaning of the noun. A role type like Musician or Cook describes the role of some human being relative to music or cooking. In Whitehead's terms, it expresses a *prehension*, which consists of three factors: (1) the prehending entity, namely the person or thing the noun refers to; (2) the prehended entity, such as music or cooking; and (3) the subjective form or intention, which determines how the first entity plays the music or cooks the food. An adjective that modifies such a noun could apply to any of the three factors:

1. *Prehending entity.* In the phrases *happy musician, handsome cook,* and *elderly physicist,* the adjective applies directly to the entity referenced by the noun. The relationship of that individual to music, cooking, or physics remains unaffected by the adjective.

2. *Prehended entity.* In the phrases *nuclear physicist* and *pastry chef,* the adjective describes the prehended entity: the branch of physics or the kind of food.

3. *Intention.* In the phrases *good musician, former senator,* and *alleged thief,* the adjective modifies the subjective form or intention that relates the prehending entity to the music, the U.S. Senate, or the act of stealing.

In these examples, the noun implies the role, but sometimes the modifier determines the role. The Loch Ness monster, for example, lives in Loch Ness, but the cookie monster eats cookies. The challenge of finding the correct relation can make natural language understanding difficult for both people and computers.

HAS TEST.   As a test for distinguishing the prehending or prehended entity, apply the pattern "X has Y" to the pair of words that describe them. If the pattern sounds normal or natural, then X is the prehending entity, and Y is the prehended entity. For example, one may say "The car has an engine" or "The car has a color," but not "The engine has a car" or "The color has a car." If the prehended entity is abstract, the *has*-test may sound more natural with the phrase *has knowledge of*: a physicist has knowledge of physics, or a musician has knowledge of music. For some pairs, the *has*-test is one-directional: wholes have parts, but parts do not have the corresponding wholes. For *correlatives*, however, either member of the pair may be the prehending or the prehended entity: a mother has a child, and a child has a mother; a lawyer has a client, and a client has a lawyer; an employer has an employee, and an employee has an employer.

If the same entities are described in different words, the *has* test may find different implicit relationships. If Sam hires his daughter Sue to work in his business, the implicit relationship depends on whether they are described as father-daughter, employer-employee, or partners. The English-based *has*-test can be re-phrased in words related to *have* in other languages. In Aristotle's ontology (Figure 2.3), Having (*echein*) is a basic category for expressing noun-noun relationships. In English translation, his examples are just as appropriate: to "have" virtue, knowledge, height, a cloak, a ring on a finger, a house, land, a wife, or a husband. Such cross-linguistic parallels confirm the validity of Aristotle's use of language as a guide to knowledge representation.

In Figure 2.3, the category Situatedness (*keisthai*) is at the same level as Having. It includes noun-noun relationships for which the *has*-test is not applicable. Earth and sky, for example, are strongly associated, but both patterns, "The earth has the sky" and "The sky has the earth," sound odd or unnatural. The relationship between the earth and the sky is not an instance of Having, but of the other category Situatedness: the earth is situated beneath the sky. The category of Situation in the lattice of Figure 2.6 induces many such relationships among the entities that occur in a situation. The nouns *mother* and *nurture*, for example, are strongly associated, but the *has*-test does not apply to them. The association is induced by the subtype of Situation called Motherhood, which includes mother, child, giving birth, and nurturing.

REPRESENTATIONAL PRIMITIVES.   An uninterpreted logic is *ontologically neutral* in the sense that it is capable of expressing all possible relationships between entities. Some notations, however, may highlight structures that make certain kinds

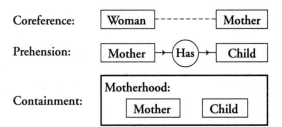

FIGURE 2.9 Three representational primitives

of relationships easier to express than others. Figure 2.9 shows the three primitive structures that are used to assemble conceptual graphs.

Each of the three primitives of Figure 2.9 has a logically equivalent expression in predicate calculus, but the linear notation does not show the structure as clearly:

- *Coreference.* Two concepts that refer to the same entities can be connected by a dotted line, called a *coreference link*, which is usually translated to some form of the verb *be*: the top graph in Figure 2.9 may be read *Some woman is a mother.* In predicate calculus, the coreference link corresponds to equality:

$$(\exists x{:}\text{Woman})(\exists y{:}\text{Mother})x{=}y.$$

- *Prehension.* The most general type of prehension, or "concrete fact of relatedness" in Whitehead's terms, is represented by the relation type Has, which can usually be translated by some form of the verb *have*: the middle graph may be read *Some mother has a child.* In predicate calculus, Has maps to a dyadic predicate has(x,y):

$$(\exists x{:}\text{Mother})(\exists y{:}\text{Child})\text{has}(x,y).$$

- *Containment.* A concept box may contain a nested conceptual graph that describes a nexus or "fact of togetherness." The bottom graph in Figure 2.9 may be read *In some motherhood, there is a mother and a child.* The concept is an abstract container that represents the space-time region of the nexus. In predicate calculus, the container is represented by the description predicate dscr(x,p), which says that some entity x has a description p:

$$(\exists x{:}\text{Motherhood})\text{dscr}(x,$$
$$(\exists y{:}\text{Mother})(\exists z{:}\text{Child})\top).$$

The symbol $\top$ is a place holder for a proposition that is always true. The description predicate is also called *semantic entailment*, represented by the operator $\vDash$. Since dscr(x,p) and the operator $x{\vDash}p$ relate an entity x to a proposition p, they are metalevel operators; in Chapter 5, they are used as a basis for the theory of contexts.

These three primitives can be used to define all other types of conceptual relations. Coreference is equivalent to equality; when combined with negation, it is used to define inequality ≠, which is also called Dffr, for *differ*. In the sample ontology of Appendix B, the Has relation is used to define most of the dyadic relations. The remaining relations, which correspond to Aristotle's category of Situatedness (*keisthai*), are defined in terms of containment. As an example, Figure 2.10 adds more detail to the graph for Motherhood in Figure 2.9.

The two Has relations of Figure 2.10 connect Motherhood to the two principal roles of Mother and Child. The other concepts and relations in the same context show how the mother and child are related to one another:

- The mother, who plays the principal role in the Motherhood nexus, also plays the roles Effector with respect to GiveBirth and Agent with respect to Nurture. The distinction between Agent and Effector depends on whether the action is intentional. In nurturing, the mother must perform the action voluntarily. Giving birth, however, can be done without a voluntary decision; a woman who is anesthetized may give birth while unconscious.

- The child, who has a correlative role with the mother, plays the role of Result with respect to GiveBirth and Recipient with respect to Nurture.

- The concept types GiveBirth and Nurture represent occurrents, which are components of Motherhood. Each of those concepts could also be represented as a nexus that would show further details of how the mother gives birth to or nurtures the child.

- Giving birth and nurturing are two stages of motherhood, related by the relation Successor (Succ) or its inverse Predecessor (Pred).

In Figure 2.10, Has is the only primitive conceptual relation. The five other conceptual relations can be defined as combinations of Has with the corresponding role: Efct is defined as HasEffector; Rslt is HasResult; Agnt is HasAgent; Rcpt is HasRecipient; and Succ is HasSuccessor.

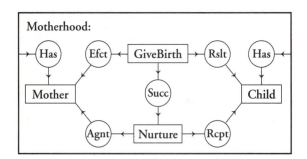

FIGURE 2.10 Showing more detail in the nexus of Motherhood

With correlative concepts like Mother and Child, a nexus for Motherhood includes the child, and a nexus for Childhood includes the mother. The two contexts, however, are not mirror images of one another, since the central focus of a nexus for Childhood is the process of learning and growth. When the graph in Figure 2.10 is translated to predicate calculus, all the detail contained in the context box is added to the proposition nested inside the description predicate:

(∃x:Motherhood)dscr(x,
   (∃y:Mother)(∃z:Child)(∃u:GiveBirth)(∃v:Nurture)
   (has(x,y) ∧ has(x,z) ∧ efct(u,x) ∧ rslt(u,z)
   ∧ succ(u,v) ∧ agnt(v,y) ∧ rcpt(v,z)).

The dscr predicate has two explicit arguments, but it involves three or more entities since its second argument is a proposition (RA).

CLASSIFYING ROLES.   Figure 2.11 shows the hierarchy under Actuality, which classifies independent physical entities (IP) by phenomenon, role, or sign. The category Phenomenon, which includes all phenomenal types, comes closest to Aristotle's category of Substance (*ousia*). The category Role is further subdivided according to Whitehead's distinction between the prehending entity and the prehended entity of a relationship. The category Sign is discussed in Section 6.6 on semiotics.

The distinction between *extrinsic* and *intrinsic* determines the kinds of prehensions. If either entity in a prehension could disappear without affecting the form or existence of the other, the relation between them is extrinsic. If the disappearance of one entity in a prehension changes the appearance or even the existence of the other, the relation between them is intrinsic. That distinction generates three further categories:

- *Composite.* An intrinsic prehending entity, called a *composite*, bears a relationship to each component within itself. Its subtypes are distinguished by the kind of prehension: a whole is made up of its parts; and a substrate (translated from

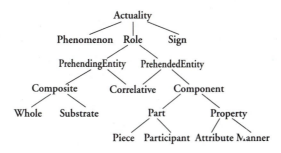

FIGURE 2.11 Classification of actual entities by structure, role, or sign

Aristotle's word *hypokeimenon*) is the underlying material that supports the dependent properties of size, weight, shape, or color.

- *Correlative.* An extrinsic prehending or prehended entity, called a *correlative*, bears a relationship to something outside itself. Examples include mother and child, lawyer and client, or employer and employee. A correlative could be considered the prehending entity of one prehension or the prehended entity of the converse prehension.

- *Component.* An intrinsic prehended entity, called a *component*, bears a relationship to the composite in which it inheres. Its subtypes include parts, whose existence is independent of the whole, and properties, which cannot exist without some substrate.

As a metalevel distinction, Peirce's principle can be applied at different levels of the ontology to generate new triads of categories. The trichotomies in Figure 2.6 and Figure 2.11 are both based on Firstness, Secondness, and Thirdness, but they are applied to different perspectives or aspects of an entity:

- *Essence.* In Figure 2.6, the trichotomy of T as Thing, Reaction, and Mediation is based on the essence or nature of the entities themselves, independent of how they may be described or conceptualized by an agent.

- *Conceptualization.* In Figure 2.11, the trichotomy of Actuality as Structure, Role, and Sign is based on the kind of concept used to describe an entity. By itself, an animal is an instance of Actuality, which could be classified as a horse by its structure, as a pet by its role, or as a sign of its owner's prosperity and favorite hobbies.

The categories are first and foremost a classification of the ways people think and talk about the world. The nature of the world itself directly affects human perception and indirectly the categories they use. But the number of possible ways of viewing the world is far greater than the total number of concepts that anyone has ever conceived.

INDEPENDENCE.   At the fourth level of Figure 2.11, the two categories Composite and Component are subdivided according to Husserl's distinction of *independence* and *dependence*. Fred's car, for example, has parts such as an engine, wheels, doors, and tires, which can be detached and replaced. If separated from the car, they continue to have an independent existence. But the car also has properties that cannot exist independently: size, weight, color, shape, horsepower, fuel consumption, and sex appeal. The weight and shape may be changed by removing or replacing some of the parts, but weight and shape cannot exist without some substrate. This distinction leads to two kinds of intrinsic relations or prehensions: a whole has parts, and a substrate has properties. If Fred's car is considered a whole, its parts such as engine and tires can be removed and continue to exist. The prehension that links Whole to Part is intrinsic, but parts can have an independent existence. The car can also be considered a substrate for properties like color, weight, and sex appeal, but the properties cannot exist independently. The prehension that links Substrate to Property is intrinsic, but properties are not independent.

At the lower right of Figure 2.11, the two categories under Component can be further classified as continuants or occurrents. That subdivision is not completely symmetric because continuants have only spatial parts, but occurrents have both spatial and temporal parts. With those distinctions, the categories under Component are subdivided in five:

- *Piece.* The parts of a continuant are called *pieces.* Examples of pieces include the doors and walls of a house, the states or provinces of a country, or the limbs and organs of an animal.

- *Participant.* The spatially distinguished parts of an occurrent are called *participants.* They include the agent, patient, or recipient of an action, the flammable substance in burning, or the water that falls in rain.

- *Stage.* The temporally distinguished parts of an occurrent are called *stages.* In the life of a human being, for example, the stages would include infancy, childhood, adolescence, and adulthood. Other possibly overlapping stages would include education, motherhood, business career, and retirement.

- *Attribute.* The properties of a continuant, which are usually described by adjectives, are called *attributes.* They include entities like colors, shapes, sizes, and weights.

- *Manner.* The properties of an occurrent, which are usually described by adverbs, are called *manners.* They include entities like the speed of the wind, the style of a dance, or the intensity of a sports competition.

These categories, which are defined by purely semantic distinctions, have a strong correlation with the syntactic categories of natural languages. Continuants are commonly expressed by nouns, and occurrents by verbs. Attributes are expressed by adjectives, and manners by adverbs. Participants are expressed by the *case relations* or *thematic roles* associated with verbs. Stages are often expressed by nouns derived from verbs, such as *retirement,* or by suffixes on role words, such as *infancy* and *motherhood.*

2.5   Defining Abstractions

At the entrance to his Academy, Plato posted the motto "Let no one ignorant of geometry enter here" (*ageōmetrētos mēdeis eisitō*). That slogan expressed his conviction that geometry is the key to understanding all forms. As he said in the *Republic,* "the knowledge at which geometry aims is knowledge of the eternal, and not of anything perishing and transient." Today, mathematicians have defined much richer structures than the geometrical forms of Plato's time: topology, algebra, and set theory; differential equations for representing continuous change; and computer simulations of virtual reality. Mathematical structures, which can be analyzed theoretically and be represented on a computer, have the properties that philosophers from Heraclitus to Quine have postulated for the category of Form: they are abstract, independent of matter and energy, and rich enough to represent or simulate phenomena with sufficient detail to match or exceed the threshold of human perception. Virtual reality, in fact, can be precise enough to trick the human senses into interpreting the simulations as though they were real. In its full generality, mathematics is the theory of all these forms — real, imaginary, and virtual. It includes everything that can be implemented on a computer of any kind: finite or infinite; digital, analog, or neural. Plato summarized that point succinctly: "God eternally geometrizes."

CATEGORIES OF FORMS. Since forms, for both Plato and Whitehead, are eternal, mathematical objects, they do not have a location in either space or time. But they can be used to characterize physical entities that do. The distinction between Continuant and Occurrent divides the category Form in two: Schema includes all the forms and patterns of stable objects; Script includes all the forms of dynamically changing processes. Like read-only procedures in a computer, scripts do not change, but they can determine the flow of processes that are in constant flux. The two categories of Schema and Script can be further subdivided by the distinction between *geometric* and *algebraic*. Figure 2.12 shows the category Form subdivided by those distinctions.

Under SpatialForm are all the schemata that depend on geometrical relations: Plato's forms, the natural shapes of cats, dogs, and people, and the irregular but systematic *fractals*, which are used to simulate trees, grass, ocean waves, and mountain ranges. Under Arrangement are mathematical structures that do not have spatial dimensions: numbers, sets, lists, algebras, grammars, and the data structures

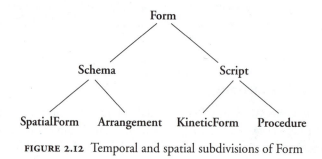

FIGURE 2.12 Temporal and spatial subdivisions of Form

of computer science. The Greek word for arrangement is *taxis*, and the type Arrangement includes the subtypes whose names are derived from *taxis*, including taxonomies and syntax. All the syntactic forms in natural languages, programming languages, and versions of symbolic logic are included under Arrangement. Graphic languages in which distance and position are significant would be under Spatial-Form, but languages like conceptual graphs in which the placement of nodes is not significant would be under Arrangement.

The subtree under Script includes the forms of everything that is in flux. The type KineticForm includes the information in a reel of motion picture film or the patterns and equations for generating motion in virtual reality. The type Procedure includes computer programs, finite-state machines, and Petri nets. It also includes any time- or sequence-dependent specification of actions and events: robot commands, cooking recipes, musical scores, conference schedules, driving directions, and the scripts of actions and dialog in plays and movies. Scripts can also include intermediate cases such as dance choreography or machine controls that may mix spatial information with nonspatial instructions. Although a script is intended to represent a dynamic process, it may have static parts. In a movie film, for example, the sequence of images is a script that determines the motion, but each frame is a schema of a static image.

MONADS.   Everything physical must occupy some region of space and time, but abstract forms can be imagined that are smaller and simpler than anything physically possible. The geometrical *point* and the temporal *instant* are such abstractions: a point is a spatial unit that does not take up any space, and an instant is a temporal unit that takes no time. In abstract algebra, sets, groups, and rings have *elements*, which are not only undefined, but inherently undefinable primitives. When algebra is applied to some subject, the elements may be "identified" with physical things like dogs and people, but the mathematical elements by themselves have no properties other than their relationships to the set and its other elements. For procedures, the elementary units are the *transitions* between states. Like the elements of a set, the transitions of a procedure are abstract entities; they can be associated with real-world processes like baking a cake or with abstract algorithms for computing mathematical functions. Such abstractions — points, elements, instants, and transitions — are fundamental primitives that can be used to define more complex forms.

As a general term for anything that has no parts, Aristotle used the word *monad* (unit). If a monad is "indivisible in every dimension and has position," he called it a *point* (*stigmē*). For each of the subtypes of Form, a corresponding primitive can be defined as a subtype of Monad: a *point* is a monad of spatial form; an *element* is a monad of arrangement in sets, groups, fields, and other algebraic structures; an *instant* is a kinetic monad; and a *transition* is a procedural monad. These labels,

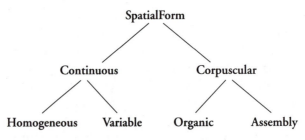

FIGURE 2.13 Hierarchy of spatial forms

however, are merely convenient names for talking about the primitives from which more complex forms are constructed. To say that a number, for example, is a monad of arrangement is no more enlightening than to identify it with a notch on a counting stick. The usefulness of numbers and points results from the axioms of mathematics and their implications for the more complex patterns that are constructed from combinations of primitives. When the points on a map are identified with cities and towns, the theorems of geometry and arithmetic become available for computing distances and directions.

SPATIAL FORMS. Figure 2.13 shows the immediate subtypes under Spatial-Form. The distinction between Continuous and Corpuscular divides SpatialForm according to the presence of internal boundaries that distinguish smooth stuff from lumpy or discrete things. The category Continuous is characterized by indefinite divisibility to the limits of perception by the available sense organs or measuring instruments. It may be as homogeneous as distilled water, or it may vary like the oceans, which differ in temperature and salinity from point to point. The type Corpuscular includes organic structures like trees or animals, which have parts that are not completely separable, even though there are discontinuities. It also includes assemblies like Fred's car, which consists of discrete parts that can be separated and put together to make a car whose form is indistinguishable from the original.

Whether something is considered an unstructured collection or a structured assembly depends on some agent's intention. Fred's car in working order is a highly structured assembly. But if the parts were disassembled and spread out on Fred's lawn, it would be called a collection. Yet if the parts were arranged to spell the name "FRED," they would again form an assembly, although not one that could be used for transportation. Conversely, if Fred's car were towed to the junk yard, the junk dealer might consider it a collection, even though the parts were in the same order they had been in while it was still running.

METHODS OF DEFINITION. Abstract forms can be defined explicitly or implicitly. In an *explicit definition*, a new construct is defined as an abbreviation for some combination of previously defined constructs. An example is the definition of *grandfather*: in any sentence where the word *grandfather* appears, it may be replaced by the phrase *father of a parent*. Another example is the definition of a function *f* by a *λ*-expression:

$$f = (\lambda x)(x^2 + 3x - 7).$$

This definition says that *f* can be used as a synonym for a particular combination of arithmetic operators. It introduces *f* as an abbreviation that could be eliminated by replacing any occurrence of *f* with its definition and assigning the argument of *f* to the variable *x*. Yet explicit definitions have one inherent limitation: they can only combine existing constructs — they cannot introduce fundamentally new ones. When a new theory is being developed, some additional method is needed to introduce the *primitives* in terms of which other things can be defined.

An *implicit definition* does not provide a detachable phrase or expression that can be substituted for the term that is being defined. Instead, it introduces a new term as an undefined primitive whose explicit nature is unknown. The term to be defined is indirectly specified by some constraints or *axioms* that it must satisfy. A *recursive definition*, which defines a function *f* in terms of itself, is always implicit because it is not possible to eliminate *f* by replacing it with the definition. As an example, the factorial function facto(*n*) can be defined recursively by three axioms that refer to facto itself:

- The input argument of facto must be an integer greater than or equal to 0.
- If *n*=0, then facto(0) = 1.
- If *n*>0, then facto(*n*) = *n* × facto(*n*−1).

If a programming language supports recursion, the function facto can be computed by translating each axiom to a statement in a program that calls itself recursively. Sometimes an implicit definition can be replaced by an explicit one. For this example, the recursive definition of facto could be replaced by an explicit loop that could be substituted for facto(*n*). But for a true primitive, there is nothing more primitive that could be substituted for the term to be defined. In dictionaries, every chain of definitions must ultimately stop at undefined primitives, at terms that are specified implicitly, or at terms that are explained by pictures. Sometimes the cycles end with synonyms defined in terms of each other, such as *attribute* and *characteristic*, either of which is a possible primitive.

In his famous textbook *The Elements of Geometry*, Euclid began with primitive terms like *point* and *line*. He gave supposed definitions like "A line is length without breadth"; but since he hadn't defined *length* or *breadth*, it was useless to substitute the phrase *length without breadth* for an occurrence of the word *line*. What gave meaning to the primitive terms were Euclid's five axioms:

1. A straight line can be drawn from any point to any point.
2. A finite straight line can be extended continuously in a straight line.

3. A circle can be described with any center and any distance [from the center].

4. All right angles are equal to one another.

5. If a straight line falling on two straight lines makes the interior angles on the same side less than two right angles, the two straight lines, if extended indefinitely, meet on that side on which the angles are less than the two right angles.

These axioms together with the primitive terms are the implicit basis for getting started. After the primitives have been introduced, other terms, such as *triangle* or *square*, can be introduced by explicit definitions in terms of the primitives. Unlike the primitives, which are always defined by implicit axioms, explicitly defined terms have no additional axioms. When an explicitly defined term is replaced by its definition, there are no leftover assumptions hidden in the axioms.

Euclid's *Elements* set the standard of precision for geometrical reasoning until the nineteenth century, when mathematicians and logicians began to analyze the foundations in greater detail. The German mathematician David Hilbert (1899) reformulated the foundations of geometry with 6 primitive terms and 21 axioms. Although he used traditional words like *point, line,* and *plane,* Hilbert insisted that the informal meanings of the words are irrelevant to the formal axioms. He emphasized the arbitrary nature of the words in one of his most famous aphorisms:

> One must be able to say at all times — instead of points, straight lines, and planes — tables, chairs, and beer mugs.

The only meaning in a mathematical term is the pattern of relationships determined by its axioms. Therefore, terms as different as *plane* and *beer mug* can be used interchangeably if the same axioms are associated with them. Points and lines on a chart might represent the yearly production of beer mugs, the growth of the human population, or the variations in the temperature of the sun.

HIERARCHIES OF THEORIES.   Each of the four categories at the bottom of Figure 2.12 is described by theories taken from a different branch of mathematics. Geometry in all its variations is the theory of SpatialForm; discrete mathematics, as expressed in algebra, logic, set theory, graph theory, and formal grammar, describes the types of Arrangement; calculus and differential equations with their applications to mechanics and fluid dynamics are the theories of KineticForm; and the theories of computer science, such as Turing machines, automata theory, and programming language semantics, are the theories of Procedure.

The axioms and theories associated with any category are inherited through the ontology to form the theories of lower-level subtypes. The theories themselves can also be organized in a hierarchy, which is even more detailed than the hierarchy of ontological categories. Figure 2.14 shows a small excerpt from the infinite hierarchy of possible theories. Each theory is a *generalization* of the ones below it and a

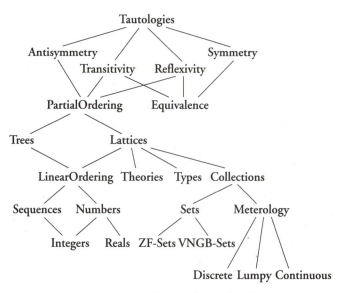

FIGURE 2.14 A generalization hierarchy of theories

specialization of the ones above it. The top theory, which corresponds to the category ⊤ in Figure 2.6, contains all *tautologies* — all the logically true propositions like *p⊃p* that are provable from the empty set. Each theory below Tautologies is derived from the ones above it by adding new axioms; its theorems include all the theorems inherited from above plus all the new ones that can be proved from the new axioms or from their combination with the inherited axioms. Adding more axioms makes a theory larger, in the sense that it contains more propositions. But the larger theory is also more specialized, since it applies to a smaller range of possible models. This principle, which was first observed by Aristotle, is known as the *inverse relationship between intension and extension*: as the meaning or *intension* grows larger in terms of the number of axioms or defining conditions, the extension grows smaller in terms of the number of possible instances. As an example, more conditions are needed to define the type Dog than the type Animal; therefore, there are fewer instances of dogs in the world than there are animals.

Just below Tautologies are four theories named Antisymmetry, Transitivity, Reflexivity, and Symmetry. Each of them includes all tautologies; in addition, each one has a single new axiom. The theory named Equivalence has three axioms, which it inherits from Transitivity, Reflexivity, and Symmetry. The = symbol represents a typical operator that satisfies these axioms:

- *Transitivity.* If *a*=*b* and *b*=*c*, then *a*=*c*.
- *Reflexivity.* For every *a*, *a*=*a*.
- *Symmetry.* If *a*=*b*, then *b*=*a*.

The ≡ operator for logical equivalence also satisfies these axioms.

PartialOrdering, which is the theory of the ≤ operator, inherits the axiom for Antisymmetry instead of Symmetry:

- *Antisymmetry.* If $a \leq b$ and $b \leq a$, then $a = b$.

Two other operators that satisfy PartialOrdering are represented by the ⊂ symbol for subset and the ⊃ symbol for implication. To emphasize the similarity, Peirce adopted a single symbol, ≺, instead of using separate symbols for numbers, sets, and propositions. PartialOrdering has subtheories for Trees and Lattices, which have a common subtheory named LinearOrdering. Among the subtheories of Lattices is the theory named Theories, which contains the axioms that relate all the theories in the hierarchy of theories. The theories of Types and Collections, which are discussed in Section 2.6, are also specializations of the theory of Lattices.

The traditional mathematical theories illustrated in Figure 2.14 are a small part of the infinitely many theories that can be used to describe any subject that can be defined precisely in any language, natural or artificial. When extended to all possible theories, the complete hierarchy is sufficient to formalize all the computer programs that have been written or ever will be written by humans, robots, compilers, and AI systems. Besides the elegant theories that mathematicians prefer to study, the hierarchy contains truly "ugly" theories for the poorly designed and undebugged programs that even their authors would disown. It contains theories for the high-powered formalisms of logicians like Richard Montague and the scruffy programs written by all the hackers of the world.

LATTICE OPERATIONS.   An infinite hierarchy without an index or catalog might contain all the theories that anyone would ever want or need, but no one would be able to find them. To organize the hierarchy of theories, the logician Adolf Lindenbaum showed that Boolean operators applied to the axioms would make it into a lattice:

1. Let the language $\mathcal{L}$ be first-order logic in any suitable notation with any vocabulary $\mathcal{V}$ of types, relations, and constants.

2. If $p_1, \ldots, p_n$ are the axioms of any theory stated in $\mathcal{L}$, insert conjunctions to combine them into a single axiom p:

$$p \equiv p_1 \wedge \ldots \wedge p_n.$$

The axiom p is equivalent to the original list, since the standard rules of inference allow conjunctions to be taken apart or put together. In CGs and other graph notations, there is no difference between a list of formulas and a conjunction of formulas.

3. The theories in the lattice are the *deductive closures* of first-order formulas. For any formula p, closure(p) is the collection of all formulas that are provable from p. If p and q are equivalent ($p \equiv q$), closure(p) is exactly the same theory as closure(q).

With this construction, the Boolean operators applied to the axioms determine the lattice operations on the closures of those axioms:

- *Partial ordering.* The $\supset$ operator, which defines a partial ordering of propositions, can be extended to a partial ordering of theories. If two theories are defined by the axioms p and q, where $p \supset q$, then closure(p) is a specialization of closure(q), represented closure(p)$\supset$closure(q). Conversely, closure(q) is a generalization of closure(p).

- *Supremum.* The *supremum* of two theories is the most specialized generalization. It follows from the disjunction of their axioms: closure($p \lor q$).

- *Infimum.* The *infimum* is the most general specialization of two theories. It follows from the conjunction of their axioms: closure($p \land q$).

- *Top.* The most general theory $\top$ is the theory consisting of all tautologies, which are provable from the empty set. The theory $\top$ is universally true of everything because it says nothing about anything.

- *Bottom.* The bottom of the lattice is the inconsistent theory $\bot$, which results from the deductive closure of any inconsistency, such as closure($p \land \sim p$). The theory $\bot$ includes all possible axioms and is true of nothing.

The lattice operators define a systematic network for inheriting axioms, combining theories, and searching for new ones. In Section 6.5, they are used to classify and relate the techniques of learning, nonmonotonic reasoning, and natural language understanding.

2.6   Sets, Collections, Types, and Categories

The words *set, collection, type,* and *category* have been used by many people in many different ways. In discussing Cyc, Lenat and Guha (1990) explicitly said that they "intermix the usage of *collection, set,* and *category*." Other logicians, philosophers, and knowledge engineers draw finer distinctions:

- *Sets.* In mathematics, a set is a structure with two associated operators: memberOf, represented by the symbol ϵ; and subsetOf, represented by the symbol $\subset$. Those two operators, together with the axioms they obey, give set theory enough structure to serve as the foundation for all of mathematics. But for many applications, sets have too much structure. They are good for talking about discrete things like sets of dogs, integers, and apples, but they are not applicable to the category Continuous in Figure 2.13. One cannot talk about sets of water, air, or maple syrup.

- *Collections.* A collection is a simpler but more general arrangement than a set. Unlike sets, which are based on two operators, a collection has simpler axioms and only one operator, which corresponds to the subset operator ⊂ of set theory. In Figure 2.14, the theory of collections has another specialization called *mereology*, which applies to discrete things like dogs and apples, to continuous stuff like water or maple syrup, and to lumpy stuff like chicken soup with dumplings. In natural languages, *count nouns* like *dog* and *apple* can be represented by sets, but *mass nouns* like *water* or *syrup* require a theory that permits collections without clearly discernible elements.

- *Types.* A type is a specification for a set or collection of entities that exist or may exist in some domain of discourse. In a personnel database, for example, the type Employee may specify conditions for determining the set of employees of some company. The type specification is a monadic predicate whose definition does not change, even though the set of employees may change with every update. Mathematically, every change to a set creates a new set, but the type definition is independent of any change in its instances.

- *Categories.* Before Aristotle, the Greek word *katēgoria* meant an accusation in a law suit. Aristotle generalized the word to mean what may be said or predicated of something. The word *predicate*, in fact, is an English borrowing of the Latin translation of Aristotle's Greek. Since English has inherited both words, *category* and *predicate*, they have acquired slightly different meanings. Today the word *predicate* is closer to Aristotle's meaning of what may be said of something. The word *category* is associated with the process of classifying entities according to some monadic predicate. In that sense, a category may be considered a type used for the purpose of classification.

As Figure 2.14 illustrates, lattice theory applies to all these structures. Therefore, each of them has a corresponding operator for each of the lattice operators. For sets, the partial ordering is determined by the *subset* operator ⊂; the supremum is the *union* ∪; the infimum is the *intersection* ∩; the top is the *universal set* 𝒰; and the bottom is the *empty set* {}. For the other kinds of collections, different authors use different symbols and terminology. In this book, the symbols ∪ for supremum and ∩ for infimum are used for all varieties of types and collections.

SETS AND TYPES.   Concept types are abstract specifications, not sets of things. For every type t, there is a set δt called the *denotation* of t. Figure 2.15 shows δ mapping type labels to sets: Frog is a type in the conceptual system, and δFrog is the set of all frogs in the world. But δ is not a one-to-one mapping from the lattice of types to the lattice of sets. There are many more sets of things in the world than

FIGURE 2.15 Types and denotations

people are aware of, and many types of things that people think about do not exist. Some types, such as Unicorn, map to the empty set; other types, such as Human and FeatherlessBiped, map to the same set; and a randomly selected set of things might not map to any concept type.

In talking about meaning, philosophers have drawn a distinction between the *intension* of a term (its intrinsic meaning or associated concept) and its *extension* or denotation. The types Human and FeatherlessBiped have very different meanings or intensions, but they happen to have the same extension: δHuman = δFeatherlessBiped. Frege used the example of the *evening star* and the *morning star*. Those two terms have different intensions: one means a star that is seen in the morning, and the other means a star that is seen in the evening. Yet both of them have the same denotation or extension, namely the planet Venus.

A semantic basis could be extensional or intensional. An extensional definition of the type Cow, for example, would be a catalog of all the cows in the world. An intensional definition would specify the properties or criteria for recognizing cows without regard to their possible existence. Since the number of cows in the world is large and constantly changing, an extensional definition would be impractical; therefore, the type Cow must be defined by intension. Before Galileo, the types Sun and Moon, each of which had only one instance, could be defined by extension. But new discoveries led astronomers to generalize those concepts, and their extension across the entire universe is now unknown.

In a type hierarchy, the position of a concept type is determined by intension rather than extension. The type Unicorn, for example, has no instances, since there are no existing unicorns. Therefore, its extension is empty. Since the empty set is a subset of all other sets, the extension of Unicorn is a subset of every other set, including the extensions of Cow, Tree, and Asteroid. The description of a unicorn, however, defines it as a mammal with one horn in the middle of its forehead. By intension, the type Unicorn would be placed under Mammal, but not under Cow,

Tree, or Asteroid. For the most general type, the denotation $\delta\top$ is everything that exists. For the absurd type, the denotation $\delta\bot$ is the empty set {}.

In this book, the word *intension*, spelled with an S, is rarely used because it is too easily confused with the word *intention*, with a T. Informally, the word *intension* can be replaced with the more general term *meaning*. Formally, a concept type t represents an intension, and its denotation δt is the extension of the type t.

SET THEORY. In the late nineteenth century, Georg Cantor developed *set theory*, which Frege and Russell adopted as a basis for defining the foundations of mathematics. Before Cantor, the operators of Boolean algebra were used for both propositional logic and a simplified theory of collections:

- *Propositions.* $x+y$ represents the disjunction $x \vee y$, $x \times y$ represents the conjunction $x \wedge y$, and Peirce's operator $x -\!\!< y$ represents implication $x \supset y$.
- *Collections.* $x+y$ represents the union $x \cup y$, $x \times y$ represents the intersection $x \cap y$, and $x -\!\!< y$ represents inclusion or subset $x \subset y$.

Peirce's symbol $-\!\!<$ is actually less confusing than the modern symbols $\supset$ and $\subset$, since $-\!\!<$ points in the same direction for all kinds of partial orderings. The collection of all cats, for example, is included in the collection of all animals, written cats$-\!\!<$animals; and the corresponding implication is written cat$(x)-\!\!<$animal(x).

In developing set theory, Cantor diverged from Boolean algebra by distinguishing an individual entity x from the *singleton set* $\{x\}$ consisting of x by itself. Instead of one operator $-\!\!<$, he defined two operators: $x \in S$ means that x is an element or member of S; and $\{x\} \subset S$ means that $\{x\}$ is a subset of S. Set theory is considered a *refinement:ehp1 of lattice theory because the five lattice operations, when applied to set theory, can all be defined in terms of the more primitive operator* $\in$:

- *Subset.* A$\subset$B means that every element of A is also an element of B: if $x \in$A, then $x \in$B. In particular, every set is a subset of itself: A$\subset$A.
- *Union.* A$\cup$B is the set S that contains all and only the elements in A or B or both: $$A \cup B = S \equiv (\forall x)(x \in S \equiv (x \in A \vee x \in B)).$$
- *Intersection.* A$\cap$B is the set that contains all and only the elements in both A and B: $$A \cap B = S \equiv (\forall x)(x \in S \equiv (x \in A \wedge x \in B)).$$
- *Universal set.* For any collection of sets S_i, the set $\mathcal{U}$ contains all and only the elements that are in each S_i: $$(\forall x)(x \in \mathcal{U} \equiv (\exists S_i)x \in S_i).$$
- *Empty set.* The empty set has no elements: for every x, it is false that $x \in$ {}. The empty set is a subset of every set, including itself: For every set A, {}$\subset$A.

Set theory is more specialized than lattice theory because new operations can be be defined on sets that do not apply to arbitrary lattices. As Figure 2.14 shows, LinearOrdering is a specialization of the theory of lattices, but LinearOrdering and many other kinds of lattices do not have operators that correspond to the following:

- *Proper subset.* A is a proper subset of B if A⊂B and there is at least one element of B that is not in A: A⊂B, and there exists some *b* where *b*∈B, but not *b*∈A.

- *Disjoint sets.* Two sets A and B are said to be *disjoint* if their intersection is empty:
  A∩B = {}.

- *Cardinality.* If S is a finite set, the number of elements in S is an integer N called its *count* or *cardinality*. The cardinality of the empty set {} is defined to be 0.

- *Power set.* For any set S, the set of all subsets of S is called the *power set* of S. If S is a finite set with cardinality N, then the cardinality of the power set of S is 2^N. For this reason, the power set itself is written 2^S.

- *Infinite sets.* No integer is big enough to express the cardinality of an infinite set, and Cantor found that even the old infinity symbol ∞ is too limited. He introduced the Hebrew letter *aleph* with different subscripts to indicate different orders of infinity. The smallest or *countable* infinity, written $\aleph_0$, is defined as the cardinality of the set of all integers. The first *uncountable* infinity $\aleph_1$ is defined as the cardinality of the power set of the integers: $\aleph_1 = 2^{\aleph_0}$. In general, if S is any infinite set, the cardinality of the power set 2^S is the next larger infinity.

For finite sets, all versions are equivalent, but different mathematicians have taken different approaches to the infinite sets. In Figure 2.14, ZF set theory was developed by Zermelo and Fraenkel, and VNGB set theory was developed by von Neumann, Gödel, and Bernays.

CRITICISMS OF SET THEORY. Despite its many applications, set theory has been widely criticized. Some logicians have been critical of the assumptions that lead to uncountable infinities, while some philosophers and linguists have considered sets to be inadequate for representing plurals and mass nouns in ordinary language. David Hilbert called Cantor's hierarchy of infinities a mathematical paradise, but the philosopher Ludwig Wittgenstein called it a swamp of contradictions. Following is a summary of the five kinds of criticisms:

1. *Ontological extravagance.* Starting with a single individual like Tom, set theory leads to an infinite series of sets, all of which have the same content: the singleton set {Tom}, which consists of one element Tom; the set {{Tom}}, which consists of

the set consisting of Tom; and so on with {{{Tom}}}, {{{{Tom}}}}.... In objecting to this luxuriance of sets, the philosopher Nelson Goodman (1956) coined the slogan "No distinction of individuals without distinction of content!"

2. *Discrete elements.* The assumption that every set has a fixed, discrete collection of elements makes set theory awkward or unnatural for representing continuous substances. Drops of rain join to form puddles, which may be splattered into other drops by a passing car. The drops and blobs form and reform without the sharp boundaries that demarcate the elements and subsets of set theory.

3. *Paradoxes.* While using set theory for the foundations of mathematics, Bertrand Russell discovered a set that leads to a contradiction:

$S = \{x \mid \sim x \in x\}.$

This equation defines S as the set of all elements x that are not members of themselves. The contradiction arises from the question of whether S is an element in S. If S is in S, then $S \in S$ implies that S is not in S. But if S is not in S, then $\sim S \in S$ implies that S is in S.

Besides Russell, there is a long parade of mathematicians and logicians who devised versions of set theory to resolve the paradox: Zermelo, Fraenkel, von Neumann, Gödel, Bernays, and Quine. Although easy to state, Russell's paradox is notoriously difficult to avoid. Logicians as distinguished as von Neumann and Quine had contradictions in the solutions they originally published.

4. *Grotesque contortions.* In terms of set theory, many common mathematical concepts become absurdly complicated. Frege, for example, defined the integer 5 as the set of all sets that have exactly five elements. To define a concept that is intuitively obvious to a five-year-old child in terms of infinite sets of sets is repugnant to many mathematicians. Leopold Kronecker, one of Cantor's early critics, declared "God made the integers; all else is the work of man" (*Die ganzen Zahlen hat der liebe Gott gemacht, alles andere ist Menschenwerk*).

5. *Nonconstructive definitions.* For countable sets like the integers, it is possible to generate any element by starting with 0 and counting a finite number of times. Such a process, which is called *constructive*, is the preferred way of defining mathematical concepts, and it is the normal way to program them on a digital computer. The Dutch mathematician L. E. J. Brouwer insisted that all of mathematics should be intuitively constructible by a "languageless activity of the mind having its origin in the perception of a move in time." Brouwer and his colleagues, called the *intuitionists*, would much prefer the child's definition of 5 by counting to a more sophisticated, but nonconstructive definition in set theory.

These criticisms do not detract from the achievements of the many brilliant mathematicians and logicians who have used set theory to define the foundations of mathematics. But they raise doubts about the claim that set theory is the only or even the best choice for the foundations of mathematics. For natural language semantics and the description of continuous substances, set theory has not been as successful, and other options should be considered.

MEREOLOGY.   The Polish logician Stanisław Leśniewski was not satisfied with set theory as the foundation for mathematics. In 1916, he went back to the pre-Cantor Boolean algebra as the basis for a simpler theory that was free of paradoxes. Since he applied it to the study of parts and wholes, he called it *mereology*, from the Greek word *meros* (part). Whitehead (1919, 1920) independently developed a similar theory, which he applied to the description of space-time events. The basic primitive of mereology is *partOf*, which corresponds to the subset operator ⊂ of set theory; but unlike set theory, mereology has no separate membership operator ∈. Mereology addresses the five basic criticisms of set theory:

1. *Simpler ontology.* Without the ∈ operator, mereology cannot create new entities out of old entities since there is no distinction between the individual Tom and the set {Tom}. Leśniewski treated emptiness as nonexistence; therefore, there is no such thing as an empty set {} or elaborate combinations of it such as {{},{{}},{{{}}}}. Most importantly, Cantor's uncountable infinities do not exist because mereology makes no distinction between an entity S and the collection of all its parts. Instead of representing the next larger infinity, the power set 2^S would be S itself.

2. *Continuity.* Mereology can represent collections of discrete elements, called *atoms*, and it can represent an *atomless* continuity that permits indefinite subdivision. It can also represent lumpy mixtures with atoms floating in a continuous soup. Linguists such as Harry Bunt (1985) have used mereology as a more natural representation for the semantics of plurals and mass nouns in natural languages.

3. *No paradoxes.* One of Leśniewski's original goals was to avoid the paradoxes of set theory. In mereology, the collection S that corresponds to Russell's paradoxical set does not exist:

$$S = \{x \mid \sim(x \text{ partOf } x)\}.$$

This equation defines S as the collection of all entities x that are not part of themselves. Since everything is a part of itself, S is {}, which is nothing. There is no contradiction, since S doesn't even exist.

Besides avoiding paradoxes himself, Leśniewski was admired and feared for his ability to find contradictions in the publications of other mathematicians.

He found a contradiction in von Neumann's 1927 version of set theory and later found two more contradictions in von Neumann's revised version of 1931.

4. *More natural definitions.* Unlike set theory, mereology does not provide a mechanism for making anything out of nothing. Therefore, each kind of mathematical structure, such as the integers, must be defined by its own axioms and definitions, which can be as simple or as complicated as the designer wishes. An intuitionist can base the integers on counting, but someone who prefers set theory could add the ϵ operator with its associated axioms.

5. *Constructive definitions.* In developing mereology and its applications to ontology and the foundations of mathematics, Leśniewski adopted the intuitionists' recommendations of following a strictly constructive approach. Although nothing prevents anyone from using mereology in a nonconstructive way, it was designed for constructive procedures.

By itself, mereology does not support Cantor's hierarchy of infinities. But its constructive nature is well suited to computer programming, which cannot be used to implement anything infinite.

AXIOMS FOR MEREOLOGY.   Since mereology was independently invented by different people, it has no standard terminology, notation, or axioms. The collections have been called *collective sets, fusions, individuals, aggregations, aggregates,* and *ensembles.* The basic operator has been called *partOf, in, ingredient,* and *covering.* The symbols that represent these terms are just as varied. In this book, the word *collection* is used as the general term, and the operator that relates a collection to the entities in it is called *partOf.* Two kinds of collections are called *sets* and *aggregates.*

- *Sets.* A set is a collection with two operators, called *subset* ⊂ and *memberOf* ϵ. Any set can be considered a collection by interpreting ⊂ as a synonym for partOf.

- *Aggregates.* An aggregate is a collection with only the partOf operator, which is represented by the symbol ≤. In mereology, there is no distinction between an entity x and an aggregate $\{x\}$ consisting of x. The ϵ operator is not defined for aggregates.

Figure 2.14 shows three specializations of mereology. Discrete mereology corresponds to Boole's version of set theory with no distinction between x and $\{x\}$. The continuous and lumpy versions differ from set theory by allowing arbitrarily divisible stuff.

In set theory, the empty set {} contains nothing, but Leśniewski maintained that the empty aggregate {} *is* nothing. In natural languages, the word *nothing* can be paraphrased by a sentence that begins *It is false that there is something which*, as in the following example:

- *Tom ate nothing.*
- *It is false that there is something which Tom ate.*

Formally, the symbol {} can be defined by a similar paraphrase. Any formula that contains {} can be replaced by an equivalent formula that uses the symbols ~ and ∃ to express nonexistence:

$$P(\{\}) \equiv \sim(\exists x)P(x).$$

This formula may be read *P is true of nothing if and only if there does not exist any x such that P is true of x*. By this equivalence, any statement that contains the symbol {} for nothing can be translated to a statement about nonexistence. For example, two sets *a* and *b* are disjoint if their intersection is the empty set:

$$a \cap b = \{\}.$$

For aggregates, the interpretation of {} as nothing causes this formula to be transformed to the following:

$$\sim(\exists x)\, a \cap b = x.$$

In effect, the symbol {} represents the nonexistent intersection of two disjoint aggregates. (See Exercise 2.7.)

The axioms for the ≤ operator when applied to aggregates are the same as the axioms for ⊂ when applied to sets. They are the three axioms for PartialOrdering illustrated in Figure 2.14. The term *part of* is used for the ≤ operator and *proper part of* for the < operator. Proper parts can be defined in terms of parts:

- *Proper part.* An entity *x* is called a proper part of an entity *y* if *x* is a part of *y* and *y* is not a part of *y*.

$$x < y \equiv (x \leq y \land \sim y \leq x).$$

This definition is not equivalent to the definition of proper subset, which differs from its containing set by at least one element. Since mereology does not have the ∈ operator, another axiom is necessary to ensure the existence of a supplementary part that has no overlap with the proper part:

- *Overlap.* An entity *x* overlaps an entity *y* if they have a common part *z*:

$$\text{overlap}(x,y) \equiv (\exists z)(z \leq x \land z \leq y).$$

- *Supplement.* If an entity *x* has a proper part *y*, then *x* has another proper part *z* that does not overlap *y*:

$$y < x \supset (\exists z)(z < x \land \sim\text{overlap}(z,y)).$$

Another property that is sometimes assumed as an axiom and sometimes proved from other axioms is *extensionality*, which means that two entities with the same parts are the same individual. That property is equivalent to the following proposition:

- *Extensionality.* If every part z of an entity x overlaps an entity y, then x is a part of y:

  $(\forall z)(z \leq x \supset \text{overlap}(z,y)) \supset x \leq y.$

All versions of mereology agree on the axioms of partial ordering for $\leq$, but they may make different assumptions about supplements, overlaps, and extensionality. They may also use different notations and terminology for the operators.

A basic version of mereology allows all possible unions and intersections of entities. It corresponds to set theory without the ϵ operator, with {} interpreted as nonexistence, and with no requirement or prohibition of discrete elements. Leonard and Goodman (1940) defined axioms for this version, which they called the *calculus of individuals*. But Alfred Tarski (1929) had earlier defined more concise but equivalent axioms as a special case of Leśniewski's system. Besides the axioms for part and the definition of proper part, Tarski defined a predicate for *disjoint* and a generalized union (which he called *sum*):

- *Disjoint.* An entity x is said to be disjoint from an entity y if no entity z is part of both x and y.

  disjoint$(x,y) \equiv$
     $\sim(\exists z)(z \leq x \wedge z \leq y).$

- *Generalized union.* An entity x is called a union of all parts of a collection c if every part of c is a part of x and no part of x is disjoint from all parts of c.

  union$(x,c) \equiv$
     $((\forall y)(y \leq c \supset y \leq x) \wedge$
     $\sim(\exists z)(z \leq x \wedge (\forall w)(w \leq c \supset \text{disjoint}(w,z)))).$

Since the definition uses the indefinite article for *a union*, there must be an axiom that ensures there exists exactly one:

- If a collection c is not empty, there exists exactly one entity x which is the union of all parts of c.

  $c \neq \{\} \supset (\exists! x)\text{union}(x,c).$

  NOTE: The quantifier $\exists! x$ states that there exists exactly one x that meets the condition. It is defined in Appendix A.1.

This axiom together with the axioms for the partial ordering of the $\leq$ operator are sufficient to serve as a basis for Tarski's version of mereology and equivalent versions, such as Leonard and Goodman's calculus of individuals. The operators ∪ and ∩ can also be defined:

- *Union.* The union of *a* and *b* includes everything that is a part of *a* or a part of *b*.

  $a \cup b = s \equiv (\forall x)(x \leq s \equiv (x \leq a \lor x \leq b)).$

  This is equivalent to defining *s* as union($s, \{a, b\}$).
- *Intersection.* The intersection of *a* and *b* includes everything that is a part of both *a* and *b*.

  $a \cap b = s \equiv (\forall x)(x \leq s \equiv (x \leq a \land x \leq b)).$

For any aggregate A, the partial ordering ≤ and the two operators ∪ and ∩ define a lattice with the total aggregate A as the top element and the symbol {} as the bottom element.

As Figure 2.14 indicates, different specializations of mereology can describe *discrete* aggregates made up of atoms, *continuous* aggregates with no atoms, or *lumpy* aggregates with a mixture of atoms and continuous stuff. An *atom* is defined as an entity that has no proper parts:

  $\text{atom}(x) \equiv \sim(\exists y)y < x.$

Since everything is part of itself, an atom has no parts other than itself. The axioms for the three kinds of aggregates are defined in terms of atoms:

- *Discrete.* Everything has at least one atom as part.

  $(\forall x)(\exists y)(\text{atom}(y) \land y \leq x).$

  This axiom implies that things can be subdivided up to the point where nothing is left but atoms.
- *Continuous.* Everything has at least one proper part.

  $(\forall x)(\exists y)y < x.$

  This axiom implies that any *x* has a smaller part *y*. But *y* must also have a smaller part *z*, which in turn has a smaller part *w*, and so on indefinitely. It is equivalent to saying that there are no atoms.
- *Lumpy.* Some things are atoms, and some things are continuous.

  $(\exists x)\text{atom}(x) \land$
  $\quad (\exists y)(\forall z)(z \leq y \supset (\exists w)w < z).$

  The first line says that some *x* is an atom, and the second line implies that some *y* is infinitely divisible.

These three axioms are mutually exclusive. Any one of them could be added to the basic axioms for mereology, but any two of them together would cause a contradiction.

Other axioms for mereology may be adopted for specialized applications. Instead of allowing every pair of entities to have exactly one union and intersection, some versions restrict the permissible unions. As an example, a junk dealer and a new-car dealer may both have collections of cars, but they may apply different theories of mereology. If a customer wanted to buy some parts taken from several different cars, the junk dealer would be willing to remove them from the original cars and put them in a new collection for the sale. The junk dealer would therefore subscribe to a mereology with arbitrary intersections and unions. A new-car dealer, however, would be eager to add more accessories to a car, but would be reluctant to take parts out of a brand new car. Therefore, the new-car dealer would enforce the following constraint:

$$(\forall a{:}\text{NewCar})(\forall x,b{:}\text{Entity})$$
$$((x{<}a \land \text{disjoint}(a,b)) \supset {\sim}(\exists y{:}\text{Entity})y{=}x{\cup}b).$$

This formula says that for any new car a and any entities x and b, if x is a proper part of a and a is disjoint from b, then there does not exist an entity y formed as the union of x and b. In other words, don't take parts out of a new car a and put them in something else b.

The combinations of parts and wholes can be constrained in many different ways for different applications. Some of the most interesting and complicated variations are created by the possible changes that may occur over time. Two extended presentations of mereology with applications to ontology are the books *The Structure of Appearance* by Nelson Goodman and *Parts* by Peter Simons. Simons presents a detailed analysis of the variations of mereology, including theories of time-dependent parts and wholes.

COLLECTIVE NOUNS.   The words *collection, set,* and *aggregate* are examples of *collective nouns*, which refer to a plurality of things by a singular noun. Other examples include *bunch, bundle, herd, flock, team, club, group, gang, mob, convoy, crowd, committee, family, clan, audience, population, community, organization, company, corporation, federation,* and *government.* Some of these words, like *set* and *group,* have been adopted by mathematicians who endowed them with formal axioms and operations. Other words like *clan* and *family* are defined by kinship systems that differ from one culture to another. Still others like *team* and *club* have spawned specialized subtypes like baseball teams and bridge clubs, whose members interact according to rigidly defined rules.

Mathematical sets are abstract, but many collective nouns like *herd, crowd,* and *convoy* represent physical entities. Companies and governments can also be considered physical because they can perform actions that have physical effects. The distinction between sets and aggregates can be used to answer Lenat's question of whether sets have mass:

- A mereological aggregate of multiple physical entities is a physical entity. An aggregate of abstract entities is also abstract. But in the usual versions of mereology, an aggregate of a physical entity like the cat Yojo with an abstract entity like the number 7 would be meaningless or undefined.

- In set theory, however, the axioms impose no constraints on the types of the members. A cat and a number could both be members of the set {Yojo,7} because it is a new entity, whose type does not depend on Yojo or 7. A reasonable interpretation is that sets are abstractions, independent of the nature of their members, which may be physical, abstract, or mixed. Therefore, Lenat would be correct in claiming that sets have no mass.

For each kind of collection, the axioms and definitions must specify any constraints on the types of the members or the type of the totality. They must also specify the expected relationships or interactions of the members with each other or with entities that do not belong to the collection. For many common collections, the axioms may be much more complex than abstract set theory. A nuclear family, for example, is restricted to a husband and wife and their children, but the apparent simplicity vanishes when divorce, remarriage, and adoption are considered. An extended family has no clear membership criteria: in-laws of fifth cousins might be included while closer relatives who are not on speaking terms might be excluded. For the U.S. government, the axioms include the Constitution and all the laws, rules, regulations, and treaties created by the legislative and executive branches and their interpretations by the judicial branch.

2.7 Space and Time

The discrete elements and rigid boundaries make set theory awkward for representing continuous space and time. Goodman cited the example of France, which is now divided in a collection of *departments*, but which was formerly divided in a collection of *provinces*. When considered as sets, those two collections cannot be equal because the elements of the two sets are different. In mereology, however, equality of aggregates is determined by their total content, not by the way they happen to be subdivided. The aggregate of all departments is the same entity as the aggregate of all provinces, namely the territory of France. From different viewpoints, the human body can be considered an aggregate of organs, an aggregate of cells, or an aggregate of molecules. Each viewpoint affects the terminology used to talk about the body, but not the body itself.

The representation of space as a set of points introduces other puzzles. At the top of Figure 2.16 is a line segment that is being sliced in two equal halves, which

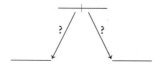

FIGURE 2.16 Where does the midpoint go when a line is divided in two?

are separated at the bottom. A question arises about what happens to the midpoint. If the original line were considered a set of points, it would have just one midpoint. The two halves of the line could not be identical, since only one of them would contain the former midpoint. The other part would contain an uncountably infinite set of points leading up to, but not including the old midpoint. A similar puzzle concerns the bounding line when a rectangle is sliced in half or the bounding plane when a cube is sliced in half: every boundary point must be assigned to one side or the other. This strange property is not only counterintuitive, it contradicts classical Euclidean geometry, which predicts that a line, a rectangle, or a cube can be bisected in two congruent halves.

The paradox of Figure 2.16 did not occur to Aristotle or Euclid, who never said that a line *consisted* of points. They just said that two intersecting lines *determine* a point or that a point *lies on* a line. When Russell and Whitehead collaborated on the *Principia Mathematica*, they used set theory as the foundation for arithmetic. But Whitehead intended to write a fourth volume on geometry, which he planned to base on his own version of mereology, called *extensive abstraction*. Although he never finished that volume, Whitehead wrote two other books (1919, 1920) in which he applied mereology to space-time events. Besides geometry, those two books presented an early version of the ontology that he developed more fully in *Process and Reality.*

SPACE WITHOUT POINTS.   Tarski (1929) used mereology to develop a three-dimensional special case of Whitehead's four-dimensional theory of space-time. Unlike Euclid, who constructed solid geometry as an extension of plane geometry, Tarski adopted spheres as the only primitives and defined a *solid* as any union of one or more spheres. As a model for physics, Tarski's geometry is more realistic, since solid bodies are aggregates of spherelike atoms. At the microscopic level, even the straightest lines and planes have ripples created by the atoms and molecules.

Tarski showed that the concepts of point, line, and plane are not just physically unrealistic, they are theoretically unnecessary to define three-dimensional relationships. His definitions, illustrated in Figure 2.17, are based on mereology with Sphere as the only geometrical primitive:

- *Externally tangent.* The sphere *a* is externally tangent to the sphere *b* if

    1. The sphere *a* is disjoint from the sphere *b*.

2. If any two spheres x and y containing the sphere a as part are disjoint from the sphere b, then either x is a part of y or y is a part of x.

In Euclidean geometry, two tangent objects must have a common boundary point. Since Tarski's geometry has no points, his constraints force the two spheres a and b to be so close together that the containing spheres x and y must also be tangent to b.

- *Internally tangent.* The sphere a is internally tangent to the sphere b if

  1. The sphere a is a proper part of the sphere b.
  2. If x and y are any two spheres that contain the sphere a as part and are part of the sphere b, then either x is a part of y or y is a part of x.

As in the previous definition, the sphere a must be so close to b that x and y must also be tangent to b and to each other.

- *Externally diametrical.* The spheres a and b are externally diametrical to the sphere c if

  1. Each of the spheres a and b is externally tangent to the sphere c.
  2. If any two spheres x and y are disjoint from the sphere c and such that a is part of x and b is part of y, then x is disjoint from y.

To avoid defining the diameter as a line, Tarski imposed constraints that force the two spheres a and b to be on on opposite sides of c.

- *Internally diametrical.* The spheres a and b are internally diametrical to the sphere c if

  1. Each of the spheres a and b is internally tangent to the sphere c.

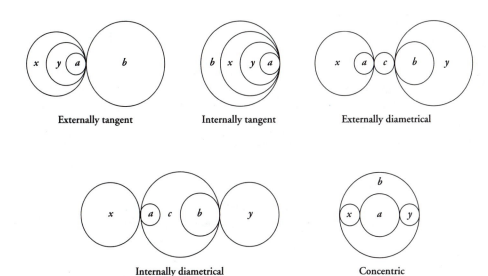

Externally tangent   Internally tangent   Externally diametrical

Internally diametrical   Concentric

FIGURE 2.17 Tarski's constructions for defining relationships between spheres

2. If any two spheres x and y are disjoint from the sphere c and such that a is externally tangent to x and b to y, then x is disjoint from y.

As in the previous definition, the constraint that x and y cannot overlap even if they grow arbitrarily large forces a and b to be diametrically opposite, but inside of c.

- *Concentric.* The sphere a is concentric with the sphere b if any one of the following conditions is satisfied:

    1. The spheres a and b are identical.

    2. The sphere a is a proper part of b; and if any two spheres x and y are externally diametrical to a and internally tangent to b, they are internally diametrical to b.

    3. The sphere b is a proper part of a; and if any two spheres x and y are externally diametrical to b and internally tangent to a, they are internally diametrical to a.

If a and b did not have the same center point, it would be possible to find spheres x and y that met the conditions, but without being internally diametrical to the containing sphere.

Even though Tarski's theory is based on different primitives from Euclid's, they are provably equivalent (see Exercise 2.15). For knowledge sharing, a proof of equivalence between two ontologies is more than an academic exercise. It is necessary to ensure that inference engines that use different axioms and definitions can communicate without generating contradictions.

SETS AT THE METALEVEL.   Instead of starting from scratch with all the axioms needed for a Euclidean style of geometry based on spheres, Tarski chose the simpler task of defining a point as a limit of a set of spheres. Then he just assumed the traditional axioms that are stated in terms of points. That assumption enabled him to adopt the usual terminology of geometry and set theory, but with an important difference: solids consist only of spheres and unions of spheres, not points or sets of points. In effect, the points and sets are fictions. They belong to the *metalanguage* for talking about geometry; they are not part of any actual body. This approach solves the puzzle about the midpoint:

- The parts of a solid are other solids, not points, lines, or planes.
- Similarly, the parts of a two-dimensional surface are other two-dimensional surfaces, which can be constructed from circles (which are the two-dimensional counterparts of spheres).
- The parts of a one-dimensional line are line segments (which are the one-dimensional counterparts of circles or spheres).

- Therefore, the problem about the midpoint vanishes, because a point is just a fictitious limit, not an actual part. When the line segment in Figure 2.16 is divided in two, the two identical halves contain all the actual parts of the original. Since the two segments are separated at the bottom of Figure 2.16, each one has a different, but fictitious limit point, where the original line had only one fictitious midpoint.

The problem vanishes because an ontology for lines need not assume the existence of points. The ontology of points belongs to a different theory, a *metatheory*, which is used for relating Tarski's geometry to Euclid's.

Thinking in Tarski's language is backward from the thinking in point-set geometry: for Tarski, a sphere is an element of a point; in the usual geometry, a point is an element of a sphere. To clarify the distinction, variables in lowercase letters such as x or a can be used for the object level of spheres and solids, and uppercase letters such as X or A can be used for the metalevel of sets and points. Following are Tarski's definitions, written with this convention:

- *Point.* A point A is the set of all spheres that are concentric with a given sphere x.
- *Equidistant.* The points A and B are equidistant from the point C if there exists a sphere x in C such that every sphere y in the points A and B overlaps x, but is not part of x.
- *Interior point.* The point A is an interior point of the solid b if there exists a sphere a that is a member of the point A and a part of the solid b: $a \in A \wedge a \leq b$.

These axioms are metalanguage statements that relate the metalevel vocabulary of set theory to the object-level vocabulary of mereology. In defining the term *equidistant*, for example, Tarski used set theory to talk about a sphere x as a member of C, but he also used mereology for talking about parts. In Euclidean terms, his definition of equidistance implies that the sphere x has a center at point C with points A and B on its surface.

Tarski assumed four axioms, which he stated in a metametalanguage that relates set theory and Euclid's terminology to the object language of spheres and solids. Script letters like $\mathscr{A}$ are used for *metametavariables* that relate Euclid's points to Tarski's spheres:

1. The notions of point and equidistance of two points from a third satisfy all the axioms of ordinary Euclidean geometry of three dimensions.
2. If a is a solid, the set $\mathscr{A}$ of all interior points of a is a nonempty regular open set.
3. If the set $\mathscr{A}$ of points is a nonempty regular open set, there exists a solid a such that $\mathscr{A}$ is the set of all its interior points.

4. If *a* and *b* are solids and all the interior points of *a* are also interior points of *b*, then *a* is a part of *b*.

Since every point is defined as a set of spheres, the set of points $\mathscr{A}$ would be a set of sets of spheres.

In principle, each axiom at the metalevel or the metametalevel could be replaced by one or more axioms at the object level. Axiom 4, for example, could be replaced by the following axiom, which avoids any mention of points:

• If *a* is a solid and *b* is part of *a*, then *b* is also a solid.

Translating the other metalevel axioms to the object level would be more difficult. Axiom 1, in particular, would require a restatement of all the axioms of Euclidean geometry in terms of spheres.

With these definitions and axioms, Tarski was able to prove that the geometry based on spheres has exactly one model, which is isomorphic to ordinary three-dimensional Euclidean geometry. Conversely, the axioms for Euclidean geometry have a model in terms of the geometry based on spheres. Therefore, Tarski's geometry is consistent if and only if traditional Euclidean geometry is consistent. Mathematically, either one can be used for computation. Philosophically, however, Tarski's geometry shows that points can be treated as fictions, not as the basic constituents of space.

TIME WITHOUT INSTANTS.   Consistent with his views about points, Aristotle maintained that instants delimit durations, but they are not parts of durations. More recently, Henri Bergson (1889) developed a philosophy of time based on intervals or durations rather than instants. Whitehead (1919, 1920) adopted a similar approach, but with four-dimensional durations for what he called the *passage of nature*. Tarski's geometry is a three-dimensional special case of Whitehead's four-dimensional theory; time by itself can be represented by a further restriction to one dimension. In all these variations, temporal points or instants are boundaries, not parts of intervals.

In artificial intelligence, a widely used ontology for time is based on the axioms for intervals defined by James Allen (1983, 1984). Later, Allen and Hayes (1985) simplified those axioms by assuming a single primitive meet(i,j), which means that interval i immediately precedes interval j. In terms of mereology and Tarski's geometry, the axioms of Allen and Hayes can be proved as theorems, but some additional assumption is necessary to distinguish past and future. One approach is to assume a special interval called the *distant past*, which includes all time that is long before the period of interest. That assumption is neutral about the question whether the distant past extends backward infinitely far or whether there was a beginning to time. The *meet* relation can be defined in terms of mereology and a special interval named *DistantPast*.

- *Meet.* The interval *i* meets the interval *j* if both *i* and DistantPast are part of some interval *k* that is disjoint from *j*, and if *i* is part of any interval *l* that is disjoint from *j*, then *l* is part of *k*.

meet(*i,j*) ≡
    (∃*k*:Interval)(*i*≤*k* ∧ DistantPast≤*k* ∧ disjoint(*k,j*) ∧
        (∀*l*:Interval)((*i*≤*l* ∧ disjoint(*l,j*)) ⊃ *l*≤*k*)).

The relation meet(*i,j*) for intervals is analogous to Tarski's externally tangent spheres. The added condition about the distant past ensures that *i* precedes *j*. Allen and Hayes defined all other relations between intervals in terms of the meet relation, but some of their definitions are simpler in terms of the mereological relations:

- *Before.* The interval *i* is before the interval *j* if there is some interval *k* such that *i* meets *k* and *k* meets *j*.
- *Equal.* The interval *i* is equal to the interval *j* if *i* is part of *j* and *j* is part of *i*.
- *Overlap.* The interval *i* overlaps the interval *j* if there exist three intervals *a*, *b*, and *c* such that *i*=*a*∪*b*, *j*=*b*∪*c*, *a* meets *b*, and *b* meets *c*.
- *During.* The interval *i* occurs during the interval *j* if there exist two intervals *a* and *b* such that *j*=*a*∪*i*∪*b*, *a* meets *i*, and *i* meets *b*.
- *Starts.* The interval *i* starts the interval *j* if *i* is a proper part of *j* and some interval *k* meets both *i* and *j*.
- *Finishes.* The interval *i* finishes the interval *j* if *i* is a proper part of *j* and both *i* and *j* meet some interval *k*.

Other relations can be defined as inverses or other combinations of these relations; after(*i,j*), for example, is before(*j,i*).

Although Allen and Hayes defined their ontology for time in terms of temporal intervals, they wanted to use the terminology of points in order to talk about beginnings and endings. Therefore, they defined instants or points in time by nests of intervals, just as Tarski defined points as nests of spheres. Another approach is to map the Allen-Hayes intervals to the diameters of spheres in Tarski's geometry:

1. Select an arbitrary line in Tarski's model of Euclidean space and call it Time-Line. Select an arbitrary point *D* on TimeLine, call the part of TimeLine on one side of *D* DistantPast, and call the rest ModernTime.

2. By Tarski's construction, identify every point on TimeLine with a set of concentric spheres. Let *T* be the union of all those sets of spheres. By definition, the center of every sphere in *T* is a point of TimeLine.

3. For every interval i of TimeLine, there is exactly one sphere s in T whose center C is the midpoint of i and whose intersection with TimeLine is a diameter that coincides with i.

4. If the interval i occurs during ModernTime, the two points S and E where the surface of s intersects TimeLine represent the starting and ending points of i. The starting point S can be distinguished from the ending point E because there is some sphere d that includes both S and D as interior points, but E is an exterior point of d.

Because of the mappings between the Allen-Hayes time line, Tarski's geometry, and Euclid's geometry, all the constructions of Euclidean mathematics correspond to equivalent constructions in the other two. The measurements and computations in the Euclidean model, which are usually the simplest, are therefore valid for all three models. Tarski's construction can also be adapted to the non-Euclidean geometries used in relativity theory. Tarski's Axiom 1, which assumes that the constructions of points from spheres satisfy the usual Euclidean axioms, can be replaced by an axiom that assumes any version of four-dimensional geometry used for relativity. In all these variations, the time intervals are considered primary, and the instants are computational fictions, not the actual constituents of time.

ZENO'S PARADOX. The distinction between points and intervals is important for resolving the paradoxes devised by the early Greek philosopher Zeno of Elea. One of the most famous is Zeno's argument that fleet-footed Achilles could never overtake a tortoise in a race if the tortoise had a head start:

- At every instant, both Achilles and the tortoise must have reached some point in the course.
- When Achilles reaches the point from which the tortoise started, the tortoise will have reached a farther point.
- But when Achilles reaches that point, the tortoise will have reached a still farther point.
- Achilles would have to reach an infinite number of intermediate points just to catch up, and he could never overtake the tortoise.

This argument has been debated and analyzed by philosophers and mathematicians since antiquity. Aristotle claimed that the points along the race course were only potential goals, not actual tasks that had to be separately completed. Modern mathematicians analyze it as a sum of an infinite series that converges to a finite limit.

Zeno's argument shows how an inappropriate representation can introduce distractions that confuse or complicate the issue. As Aristotle said, the points along the line are merely potential. By Tarski's construction, they are metalevel fictions used in talking about the line, not actual parts of the line. Bergson (1889) maintained that such problems arise from "confusion of the movement with the space traversed by the mobile entity." His solution was to ignore the points:

> Why does Achilles overtake the tortoise? Because each of Achilles' steps and each of the tortoise's steps are indivisible acts in so far as they are movements, and are different magnitudes in so far as they are space; so that simple addition gives a greater length for the space traversed by Achilles than the sum of the space traversed by the tortoise and its head start.

With Zeno's artificial subdivision, the problem requires the advanced mathematics of infinite series. Bergson, however, represented the problem in terms of the actual movements of Achilles and the tortoise. As a result, he could solve the problem by elementary arithmetic. Both methods generate the same answer: Achilles can indeed overtake the tortoise. But the more natural representation solves the problem with less computation.

TIME'S ARROW.   In Einstein's theory of relativity, three-dimensional space and one-dimensional time are combined in a four-dimensional space-time continuum. That treatment simplifies the equations of physics, but it masks a fundamental asymmetry in time that does not affect space: the difference between past and future. To characterize that difference, Arthur Stanley Eddington (1928) imagined an arrow drawn somewhere in the space-time continuum:

> Let us draw an arrow arbitrarily. If as we follow the arrow we find more and more of the random element in the world, then the arrow is pointing towards the future; if the random element decreases the arrow points towards the past. . . . I shall use the phrase "time's arrow" to express this one-way property of time which has no analogue in space.

The random element is only apparent when there are enough objects in a situation to be statistically significant. If a movie of two billiard balls colliding were played forward or backward, both directions would represent physically possible events. But if any movie showed sixteen billiard balls coalescing into a triangle of fifteen while spitting out the cue ball in the direction of the player, it would be safe to assume that the film was running in reverse. When left to themselves, situations become more randomized with the passage of time, and the effects that are noticeable with a few billiard balls become more pronounced with larger numbers of interacting atoms and molecules.

For physical entities, the measure of randomness is called *entropy*. For abstractions, Shannon (1948) applied the formulas of entropy to measure the amount of *information*. Both entropy and information tend to increase, and their increase is governed by the same mathematical laws. When atoms or billiard balls scatter, the increase in entropy is proportional to the increase in the number of bits required to encode their configuration. Like entropy and information, causality is also intimately connected with time. In his lectures on cause and chance in physics, Max Born (1949) stated three assumptions that dominated the classical view:

- "*Causality* postulates that there are laws by which the occurrence of an entity B of a certain class depends on the occurrence of an entity A of another class, where the word *entity* means any physical object, phenomenon, situation, or event. A is called the cause, B the effect."
- "*Antecedence* postulates that the cause must be prior to, or at least simultaneous with, the effect."
- "*Contiguity* postulates that cause and effect must be in spatial contact or connected by a chain of intermediate things in contact."

Relativity and quantum mechanics have forced physicists to abandon these assumptions as exact statements of what happens at the most fundamental levels, but they remain valid at the level of human experience. After analyzing them in terms of modern physics, Born concluded "chance has become the primary notion, mechanics an expression of its quantitative laws, and the overwhelming evidence of causality with all its attributes in the realm of ordinary experience is satisfactorily explained by the statistical laws of large numbers."

The arrow of time with its implications for entropy, information, and causality is well defined because the universe is still evolving from the big bang, when entropy was extremely low. In a much older universe near thermal equilibrium, the arrow could be undefined or randomly fluctuating. In exceptional circumstances, such as matter and energy falling into a black hole, the arrow of time might even be reversed. A universal ontology should be able to accommodate any novel phenomena discovered by physicists and astronomers. But to describe ordinary events on the earth and the surrounding solar system, the ontology must include a well developed stock of concepts for representing the familiar direction of time and its implications for causality and information flow in everyday life. Those concepts are discussed further in Chapter 4.

CONTINUANTS AND OCCURRENTS. The distinction between continuants and occurrents, which was informally discussed in Section 2.3, can only be formalized in terms of some axiomatization for time. Simons (1987) used time-dependent mereology to state the definitions:

- "A continuant is an object which is in time, but of which it makes no sense to say that it has temporal parts or phases. At any time at which it exists, a continuant is wholly present. Typical continuants come into existence at a certain moment, continue to exist for a period (hence their name) and then cease to exist." A human being, for example, is constantly gaining and losing molecules, but at any time *t* when a person *x* exists, all of *x*'s parts exist at the same time *t*. Even if *x* loses some part, such as a tooth, that tooth (or at least its atoms) would continue to exist at the same time as *x*.

- "Occurrents comprise what are variously called events, processes, happenings, occurrences, and states. They are, like continuants, in time, but unlike continuants they have temporal parts." Examples of occurrents include concerts, sports events, journeys, storms, and earthquakes. A complete specification of an occurrent must include the temporal parts, such as the movements of a symphony or the innings of a baseball game. Although a human being is a continuant, the life of a human being is an occurrent whose stages are spread out over the interval from birth to death.

These definitions apply equally well to physical entities and to the abstractions that encode their structure but without the accompanying matter or energy.

Simons' definitions depend on a coordinate system that separates one-dimensional time from three-dimensional space. They are adequate for ordinary human experience, but they would have to be generalized to four-dimensional space-time for modern theories of physics. That generalization could be based on Eddington's definition of time's arrow in terms of entropy:

- Let $\mathcal{R}$ be any bounded simply connected four-dimensional space-time region. Such a region can always be assumed as the container for an occurrent, whether or not any matter or energy exists in or passes through that region.
- Before a continuant can be found in $\mathcal{R}$, there must exist a continuous path l through $\mathcal{R}$, called a *time line*, which extends from one boundary point t_0 of $\mathcal{R}$ to another boundary point t_1 of $\mathcal{R}$, where the entropy $S(t_0)$ is a minimum and $S(t_1)$ is a maximum. Every point t of the path l must be tangent to the direction of maximum increase in entropy ∇S at the point t.
- If a time line l can be found for the region $\mathcal{R}$, then at each point t of l, define a *snapshot* s as the intersection of $\mathcal{R}$ with a three-dimensional hyperplane perpendicular to l at t.

This construction separates the four-dimensional continuum into a one-dimensional time line and a family of three-dimensional snapshots indexed by the time t. This separation might not be possible at atomic sizes or in the vicinity of a black hole, but when it can be done, it allows the conditions for recognizing a continuant to be defined in purely spatial terms. The criterion that a continuant has only spatial parts can be represented by a *spatial-form predicate* $P(s)$ that depends on the configuration of matter and energy in a snapshot s:

- If there exists a spatial-form predicate $P(s)$ that is true of every snapshot s at time $t_0 \leq t \leq t_1$ in the region $\mathcal{R}$, then a continuant x is said to exist at each time t in the region $\mathcal{R}$.

As an example, the spatial-form predicate P(s) for a sphere would be true if there exists a concentration of matter in s with a boundary that is equidistant from some center point. For the type HumanBeing, a spatial-form predicate would outline the shape of the human body while taking into account possible movements of the limbs.

IDENTITY CONDITIONS.   By itself, a spatial-form predicate can only recognize types. Further *identity conditions* are needed to identify two appearances of the same type as the same individual. A predicate sphere(s), for example, might be sufficient to recognize that a sphere is present at location s, but it could not determine whether two appearances of a sphere at s_1 and s_2 are manifestations of the same sphere or different spheres. Even for the human body, which has many more distinguishing features than a sphere, confusion is possible because of identical twins or changes in age, hair style, or clothing.

The most fundamental identity condition is continuous existence in a region that is just big enough for a single individual of the given type. To state that condition, shrink the region $\mathcal{R}$ to the smallest region $\mathcal{S}$ that is big enough to contain a continuant whose form is recognized by a spatial-form predicate P. Let $\mathcal{S}$ be the subregion of $\mathcal{R}$ that satisfies the following axioms:

- P is true of the intersection of $\mathcal{S}$ with every snapshot s in $\mathcal{R}$:

  $(\forall s{:}\text{Snapshot})(\exists u)((s{<}\mathcal{R} \wedge u{=}\mathcal{S}\cap s) \supset P(u)).$

- There is no proper subregion $\mathcal{T}$ of $\mathcal{S}$ for which P is true of the intersection of $\mathcal{T}$ with every snapshot s in $\mathcal{R}$:

  $\sim(\exists \mathcal{T})(\mathcal{T}{<}\mathcal{S} \wedge (\forall s{:}\text{Snapshot})(\exists u)((s{<}\mathcal{R} \wedge u{=}\mathcal{T}\cap s) \supset P(u))).$

- If $\mathcal{S}$ is continuous from time t_0 to t_1, then $\mathcal{S}$ is assumed to contain a single individual of the type recognized by P.

If there is a spatial discontinuity in $\mathcal{S}$ at some time t, then for ordinary physical objects, the individual recognized by P before t is not the same as the individual recognized by P after t. According to quantum mechanics, however, subatomic particles like electrons can jump from one position to another without being detectable at any intermediate points. Therefore, the continuant/occurrent distinction cannot be assumed at the quantum-mechanical level.

Even for ordinary objects, the definition in terms of spatial continuity requires continuous observation from t_0 to t_1 to avoid the possibility that two similar objects might be interchanged. Without continuous observation, an object's identity can only be guaranteed by indirect means: one sphere, for example, may be locked in a box while a similar one is outside the box. But that guarantee depends on many assumptions: only one person holds the key, that person is trustworthy, and there are no secret side doors in the box. For human beings, eye-witness reports of identity are notoriously unreliable, and identity conditions depend on assumptions about fingerprints, DNA, or memory of obscure personal facts. In general, the recognition of identity depends on inference, and the inference may be mistaken.

GRANULARITY.   Many distinctions about physical objects depend on the observer, the purpose, the application, and the tools available for measuring or manufacturing the objects. The appearance of a substance as continuous, discrete, or lumpy, for example, depends on the ability of an observer to detect fine detail. A sandy beach may look continuous from a distance, but a closer look shows its granular structure. The word *granularity* was introduced in the nineteenth century to describe the limitations of photographs, which cannot record any detail smaller than the grains of silver in the photographic emulsion. That term has since been extended to cover the limitations of any perceptual organs or measuring instruments. For every physical observation, there is always a smallest detectable unit of length, weight, light, sound, pressure, or other measurable quantity. Details smaller than that unit are indistinguishable from one another.

In manufacturing, granularity is a measure of how faithfully the technology can reproduce a physical object of a particular shape. Figure 2.18 shows the ideal shape of a nail and its boundary for a given a *grain* size, the smallest size that a particular machine can measure or reproduce. The boundary is defined as the union of the spheres whose diameter is equal to the grain size and whose centers lie on the surface of the ideal shape. The surface of any actual nail made by that machine would lie somewhere in the boundary determined by the grain size. To define boundaries and discontinuities in terms of ideal shapes with a given granularity, Nicola Guarino, Stefano Borgo, and Claudio Masolo (1997) applied a version of mereology similar to Tarski's geometry of spheres. They showed how such a formalism could be used to define precise semantics for the Express language, which is widely used for engineering specifications.

Besides the granularity caused by the technology for observing and manufacturing physical objects, there is a more fundamental granularity at the atomic level. In

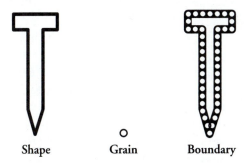

Shape   Grain   Boundary

FIGURE 2.18 Ideal shape of a nail and its boundary for a given granularity.

terms of Peirce's categories, the actual granularity of atoms and quanta is a kind of Firstness, since it depends on the structure of the things themselves. The apparent granularity caused by observational limitations is Secondness, since it depends on an external relationship between an object and an observer. Intentionality creates a deliberate granularity that results from discarding detail that is irrelevant to the purpose at hand. Such granularity is a kind of Thirdness, since it depends on a triadic relationship between an object, an observer, and the observer's reason for ignoring or discarding certain details.

To illustrate the effect of purpose, Jerry Hobbs (1995) discussed different perspectives on a roadway: "When we are planning a trip, we view it as a line. When we are driving on it, we have to worry about our placement to the right or left, so we think of it as a surface. When we hit a pothole, it becomes a volume for us." An engineer who designs roads has radically different views of what is relevant. The engineer must consider the kind of terrain, the slope, the environmental impact, the cost of excavating and moving landfill, the cost of acquiring the land, and the procedures for getting approvals from government authorities. Instead of road maps, the engineer needs maps that show the topography, the natural features, the political subdivisions, and the land ownership. Yet all those views must eventually be reconciled, since the engineer's ultimate purpose is to build roads that are used by the motorists.

Since the three kinds of granularity arise from different sources, each has a different logical status, which must be explicitly noted:

1. *Actual.* Statements about actual granularities can be expressed in conventional first-order logic. The axioms for discrete, continuous, or lumpy aggregates would be assumed as descriptions of the nature of the things themselves.

2. *Epistemic.* Logics of knowledge and belief, called *epistemic logics*, are based on two metalevel predicates that relate an agent a to a proposition p: $know(a,p)$ and $believe(a,p)$. The proposition p, which an agent knows or believes, could be an axiom about the known or believed level of granularity, a measurement for which the granularity results from experimental error, or a conclusion about the granularity deduced from some combination of axioms and measurements.

3. *Intentional.* As Thirdness, intentions require a triadic predicate such as $reason(a,r,x)$, which relates an agent a to an entity x for a reason r. A mining engineer, for example, may treat a slurry of coal in water as continuous when it is being transported through a chute, but lumpy when the coal is being separated from the water. The engineer, who sees that the slurry is epistemically lumpy, may treat it as intentionally continuous, even though at the atomic level both the water and the coal are actually discrete.

In different contexts for different purposes, the same substance may be represented with different axioms, which may even be contradictory. The axioms for a discrete, lumpy, or continuous slurry cannot all be used in the same context for the same object.

Predicates that assert an ideal geometrical shape for an actual entity are almost always approximations. The predicate spherical(x), for example, can never be absolutely true of any physical object, since even the most perfectly machined sphere must be composed of atoms, which would cause tiny ripples on the surface. Epistemically, an object may be classified as a sphere if no imperfections can be detected within the granularity of the available measuring instruments. Intentionally, an agent a may consider an object x as spherical for reason r. A machinist and a chef would have different purposes and hence different criteria for calling a ball bearing or a meatball a sphere. A boulder might be treated as a sphere for computing its approximate speed in rolling down a mountain, but a stonemason might consider it blocklike when building it into a wall. Although the boulder, the meatball, and the ball bearing could never be spherical in actuality, they might be considered epistemically or intentionally spherical by different people for different purposes.

SEARCH FOR PRIMITIVES.   Set theory and mereology are two mathematical theories that supply primitives for defining concepts and relations. They have also been combined with other theories, such as topology to form *point-set topology* and mereology to form *mereotopology*. Another rich source of primitives lies in the vocabularies and syntactic structures that people have found useful for talking about the world. Linguists such as Leonard Talmy (1983, 1996) and Anna Wierzbicka (1996) have been analyzing the vocabularies of diverse languages to find the universal primitives that people use to describe relationships. Other researchers have been applying formal theories to the definition of informal spatial words like *inside* and *through*. In his survey of *qualitative spatial reasoning*, Anthony Cohn (1997) described the wealth of spatial relationships and the variety of theories that people have developed for reasoning about them. Formal theories can define infinitely many structures, and empirical studies of language and the world are necessary to determine which are the most useful, relevant, and expressive.

EXERCISES

1. The Greek philosopher Empedocles developed a theory of four elements, each defined by two properties: Earth is cold and dry, Fire is hot and dry, Air is hot and moist, and Water is cold and moist. Draw a lattice with Matter at the top, ⊥ at the bottom, and the four elements classified according to the two distinctions cold/hot and dry/moist. Then look for other kinds of clas-

sifications that can be arranged in a lattice. In modern physics, for example, many more elements are known, but the subatomic particles can be classified in a lattice according to properties such as *spin, charge, strangeness,* and *charm.*

2. Apply the basic distinctions of Section 2.3 (Independent, Relative, Mediating; Physical, Abstract; Continuant, Occurrent) to analyze the following terms. Based on that analysis, classify the corresponding concept types according to the twelve categories of the matrix in Figure 2.7. For example, the type Elephant would be analyzed as IPC (Independent Physical Continuant), which makes it a subtype of Object.

elephant	number	storm	RR crossing
photograph	water	road map	computation
business	expectation	pregnancy	motherhood
data structure	receipt	tetrahedron	task
imprisonment	traffic	schedule	weather report
dancing	knot	hunger	plan

Some of these terms may have different senses that lead to different classifications; if so, give a brief definition of each sense and its classification. As an aid to the analysis, feel free to use dictionaries or other reference works. A good dictionary is an important tool for the knowledge engineer; the definitions and examples contain background knowledge and reminders that can easily be overlooked.

3. Apply the *has*-test discussed in Section 2.3 to the following pairs of words. If the test is successful, classify the corresponding roles as composites, components, or correlatives in the hierarchy of Figure 2.11. If the *has*-test is not applicable, explain what other kind of relation is likely to hold between the members of the pair.

tail/dog	earth/sky	buyer/seller
airplane/airport	car/driver	car/parking lot
student/teacher	volume/cube	volume/chapter
wife/husband	room/ceiling	tiger/jungle
lumber/saw	cursor/mouse	brother/sister

4. The proverb "Two's company, three's a crowd" illustrates the essential difference between Secondness and Thirdness. If Sally liked Tom at one time and Sally liked Joe at another time, those two dyadic relationships would not create a special relationship between Tom and Joe. But if she likes Tom and Joe at the same time and Tom and Joe both like her, then a triangle is created that induces a rivalry between Tom and Joe. Review various examples of Thirdness, where one entity A mediates between two others B and C, and describe the new relationship

between B and C that is created as a result of A's mediation. A concept A, for example, mediates between a word B and an object C, thereby establishing a *meaning triangle* that enables the word B to refer to the object C.

5. Peirce maintained that Thirdness always involves an irreducible triad that cannot be defined in terms of monadic and dyadic relations. But in conceptual graphs, it is common to represent a triadic relation like give(x,y,z) by a concept type Give linked to its participants by three dyadic relations Agnt (Agent), Thme (Theme), and Rcpt (Recipient):

```
[Give]-
   (Agnt)→[Animate]
   (Thme)→[Entity]
   (Rcpt)→[Animate].
```

Does this representation refute Peirce's claim? If not, why not?

6. Review the discussion of the architectural drawing in Section 2.2. Then consider a triadic predicate buildToPlan(x,y,z) that relates a builder x, a drawing y, and the resulting building z. Suppose that this triadic predicate were defined as a conjunction of three separate dyadic predicates:

$$\text{buildToPlan}(x,y,z) \equiv$$
$$\text{studies}(x,y) \wedge \text{constructs}(x,z) \wedge \text{corresponds}(y,z).$$

Assume that the dyadic predicates *studies, constructs,* and *corresponds* have been adequately defined without an implicit or explicit mention of a missing third argument. For example, the definition of constructs(x,z) might involve the builder x and the methods used to build z, but without any references to the drawing y or its contents. Could any such definition capture the full meaning of the triadic predicate buildToPlan? If not, what is missing?

7. According to Peirce, the defining aspect of Thirdness is "the conception of mediation, whereby a first and a second are brought into relation." That property could be expressed in second-order logic:

$$(\forall x_1, \ldots, x_n : Entity)((\exists y : Mediating)(\exists r : Relation) r(y, x_1, \ldots, x_n)$$
$$\supset (\exists s : Relation) s(x_1, \ldots, x_n)).$$

This formula says that for any entities $x_1, \ldots, x_n$, if some mediating entity y is related to those entities by some relation r, then some relation s, which does not involve the entity y, is also true of those entities. Show how this formula could be specialized to define the buildToPlan predicate.

8. The criteria for classifying entities may be based on Firstness, Secondness, or Thirdness. As an example, consider the following list of items: eraser, pencil,

toothbrush, bar of soap, razor, pocket calculator, apple, sandwich, roll of toilet paper, rubber ducky, book, three-ring binder, towel.

a. By Firstness, the items in that list have little in common. Yet they all share at least one common property. What inherent property of the items was used to sort them in the order listed?

b. By Secondness, the items could be partitioned in two groups according to some external relationships. Make such a grouping.

c. An arbitrary grouping by Secondness could be purely accidental. A grouping by Thirdness, however, must be based on some reason that explains why these groups were selected rather than any others. State the reasons for the grouping in part (b).

Make similar lists of your own that illustrate the principles of classification by Firstness, Secondness, or Thirdness.

9. Mathematicians consider the following "theorem" to be a joke:

THEOREM: All integers are interesting.

PROOF: Let *s* be the set of all integers that are not interesting. Since *s* is a subset of a linearly ordered set that has a smallest element, *s* must either be empty or have a smallest element *u*. But as the smallest uninteresting integer, *u* would be very interesting indeed. Hence the existence of *u* would imply a contradiction. Therefore, the set *s* must be empty, and all integers are interesting.

Use Peirce's categories to explain why this theorem is a joke. Is it possible to give a formal definition of the predicate interesting(n) that would make the theorem more serious? If so, use that definition to prove that most real numbers are not interesting. Are there any useful applications of this or related theorems? Use Peirce's categories to analyze the word *useful*.

10. A description of an event that omitted all interpretation or background knowledge would be almost unintelligible or meaningless. As an example, Devlin and Rosenberg (1996) discussed the following story, which might be told by a visitor from another planet who had learned some English, but knew nothing about human culture:

There are some people. Some of the men are carrying a long wooden box. A man wearing a black robe walks in front of them. The remaining people all walk behind the box.

All the nouns, adjectives, and verbs in this story describe people, objects, and events by the immediate sensory impressions that they create (Firstness) without any consideration of external relationships (Secondness) or context (Thirdness). Compare the following description of the same event:

> A funeral is taking place. The priest, wearing a black robe, is at the head of the procession. The pallbearers carry the coffin. The mourners follow on behind.

The reporter who wrote this description added information that would not be known to an observer who was not familiar with the culture. Using Peirce's categories, explain how that information is conveyed by the following words: *funeral, priest, procession, pallbearer, coffin, mourner, follow*.

11. After working on the previous exercise, find a paragraph in a newspaper or magazine that describes some event, such as a court trial, a wedding, or a baseball game, and rewrite it in the style of a visitor from another planet. In rewriting the paragraph, translate terminology about roles, such as *judge, jury*, or *witness*, to purely descriptive terms that do not depend on the reporter's background knowledge.

12. Review the examples of collective nouns in Section 2.6 and add any others that you may find in a dictionary or thesaurus. Make a list of distinctions that might be useful for classifying them in various ways. For example, *bundle, bunch*, and *aggregate* are often used for collections of nonanimate things, *herd* and *flock* are used for collections of related animals, and many of the other words apply only to collections of people. Various distinctions depend on the purpose of the collection, the permanence of the collection, the criteria that determine membership in the collection, the types of members and the type of the resulting collection, or the structure of relationships among the members. For each kind of collection, describe in English any constraints that would be stated as axioms in a more formal treatment.

13. Leśniewski's interpretation of {} as nonexistence provides a formal way of solving some puzzles that contain the word *nothing*:

> Nothing is better than eternal happiness.
> A ham sandwich is better than nothing.
> Therefore, a ham sandwich is better than eternal happiness.

Translate this puzzle to logic with the {} symbol for the word *nothing*.

a. Assume a dyadic predicate betterThan(x,y) and translate the first premise to a formula using the symbol {}. Use the equivalence in Section 2.6 to eliminate the {} symbol. Then translate the result to an English sentence that avoids using the word *nothing*.

b. Assume that the second premise is an abbreviation for the sentence *For every person x, it is better for x to have a ham sandwich than for x to have nothing.* Using the betterThan predicate to relate propositions, translate that sentence to predicate calculus with the {} symbol. Use the equivalence for eliminating {} to expand the proposition nested inside the argument of the betterThan predicate. Finally, translate the resulting formula back to English.

c. Do the two revised premises imply the conclusion of the syllogism?

14. In conceptual graphs, the word *nothing* can be represented by the concept [Entity: {}]. Use a concept of this form to represent the two premises of the ham-sandwich syllogism in CGs. Assume a dyadic conceptual relation (BetterThan), which can link two concepts of any type. For the second premise, use BetterThan to link two concepts of type Situation that contain nested CGs. To eliminate the {} symbol, suppose that a CG containing a concept of nothing is attached to a subgraph *g*, which contains all the other concepts and relations in the context:

　　[Entity: {}]-*g.*

Then replace that graph with a graph of the following form:

　　¬[[Entity]-*g*].

After eliminating the {} symbol, translate the resulting CGs back to English.

15. Nelson Goodman preferred to use the relation disjoint as the basic primitive of mereology instead of the relation partOf. The following equivalence defines partOf in terms of disjoint:

　　$\text{partOf}(x,y) \equiv (\forall z)(\text{disjoint}(z,y) \supset \text{disjoint}(z,x)).$

In the definitions and axioms of mereology, replace every occurrence of partOf(x,y) or $x \leq y$ with the expression on the right. Then use the rules of inference presented in Appendix A.1 to simplify the results.

16. The variations of mereology differ in the choice of axioms, definitions, and terminology. Some of them lead to logically equivalent constructions, but others are mutually exclusive. Use the rules of inference in Appendix A.1 to prove the following;

a. Write a formula that says there are no atoms and prove that it is equivalent to the axiom that says everything has at least one proper part.

b. Show that the entity *s* derived by a dyadic union $s = a \cup b$ is equal to *s* derived by Tarski's generalized union of the same two parts: union($s,\{a,b\}$).

c. The three axioms for discrete, continuous, or lumpy aggregates are mutually exclusive, and at most one can be added to a theory of mereology. Show that a contradiction of the form $p \wedge \sim p$ can be derived from each of the three pairs of axioms: discrete and continuous; discrete and lumpy; or continuous and lumpy.

17. Tarski stated the definitions illustrated in Figure 2.17 in a stylized version of natural language, not in logical formulas. As an exercise, translate his statements to predicate calculus or conceptual graphs. As a further exercise, prove that Tarski's definitions stated in terms of spheres are equivalent to the usual Euclidean definitions that use points, lines, and planes.

18. Tarski showed how notions such as tangency could be defined for spheres without talking about points or boundaries. In generalizing those notions to arbitrary space-time regions, Whitehead (1929) started with a single primitive connected(x,y), which means that either x and y overlap or they are touching. Then an entity x is defined as a part of y if and only if every entity z that is connected to x is also connected to y:

$x \leq y \equiv (\forall z)(\text{connected}(z,x) \supset \text{connected}(z,y))$.

State the definitions for overlap(x,y) and disjoint(x,y) in terms of connected (x,y). Then show that two externally tangent spheres in Tarski's sense are also externally tangent according to the following definition:

$\text{extTangent}(x,y) \equiv \text{connected}(x,y) \wedge \text{disjoint}(x,y)$.

State the definition of internally tangent in terms of connected(x,y) and show that it is also true of Tarski's internally tangent spheres.

19. A hole is physical because it has a location in space-time, but unlike typical physical entities, a hole is characterized by an absence of matter. By Husserl's distinction, a hole is a dependent entity whose boundaries are defined by an independent physical entity called its *host*. To develop a theory of holes, Roberto Casati and Achille Varzi (1994) started with one undefined primitive, one definition, and one axiom:

- *Primitive.* The dyadic predicate holeIn(x,y) means that x is a hole in or through y.
- *Definition.* hole $= (\lambda x)(\exists y)\text{holeIn}(x,y)$.
- *Axiom.* If x is a hole in y, then y is not a hole:

   $(\forall x,y)(\text{holeIn}(x,y) \supset \sim\text{hole}(y))$.

Translate the following statements to logic, and prove that they follow from the above axiom and definition:

a. If x is a hole in y, then y is not a hole in x.

b No x is a hole in itself.

c. If a hole exists, then something exists that is not a hole.

d. If x is a hole, then x is a hole in something that is not a hole.

Casati and Varzi continued their theory by adding more axioms for the mereology and topology of holes and related features, such as depressions, hollows, tunnels, cavities, and cracks.

20. Show that the relation meet depends only on the interval DistantPast and the relation partOf by eliminating the predicate disjoint from the definition of meet.

21. In Section 2.7, six time relations were defined in stylized English: before, equal, overlap, during, starts, and finishes. Translate the definitions to predicate calculus or conceptual graphs.

22. In Figure 2.12, SpatialForm is shown as a subtype of Schema. In Section 2.7, a spatial form is defined by a predicate $P(s)$, which is true or false about some configuration of matter and energy in a snapshot s. How can these two definitions be reconciled? Give some examples of objects like cars, houses, trees, or dogs, and explain how their spatial forms could be defined by each of these approaches.

23. Review the discussions about the chef and the machinist who have different criteria for meatballs and ball bearings, the motorist and the engineer who view maps and highways from different perspectives, and the mining engineer who treats the same slurry as continuous or lumpy at different times. Find other examples where the same things may be treated at different levels of granularity for different purposes. Is the granularity actual, epistemic, or intentional?

24. The only rooms mentioned in the hotel reservation example (Appendix C) are the ones rented by guests who stay at the hotel. Make a list of other types of rooms in a hotel, including dining rooms, lobbies, ballrooms, meeting rooms, offices, restaurants, exercise rooms, laundry rooms, kitchens, supply rooms, and so on. Organize the list in a type hierarchy with Room at the top. As criteria for subdividing the hierarchy, consider size, purpose, view (scenic, parking lot, light shaft, or windowless), and status (public, reservable, or restricted to hotel employees). Include types of rooms that could be used for different purposes or could be rearranged for meetings and functions of different sizes. The hierarchy should be more complex than a tree: some room types may have more than one immediate supertype; but there should be no cycles — the hierarchy should be an *acyclic graph*.

25. Besides rooms, the hotel reservation example mentioned other kinds of entities, relationships, and events. List those entities and organize them according

to the ontological categories of this chapter. Classify the entities by the techniques suggested for Exercise 2.2 and apply the *has*-test as suggested for Exercise 2.3. Use the hierarchies of categories in Figures 2.6, 2.11, 2.12, and 2.13, as guides for detecting entities that might be missing in your analysis. Include relevant entities that may not have been mentioned explicitly in the problem description.

CHAPTER THREE

Knowledge Representations

Everything in nature, in the inanimate as well as the animate world,
happens according to rules, although we do not always know these rules.
Water falls according to the laws of gravity, and the locomotion of animals
also takes place according to rules. The fish in the water, the bird in the
air move according to rules. All nature actually is nothing but a nexus of
appearances according to rules; and there is nothing at all without rules.
When we believe that we have come across an absence of rules, we can
only say that the rules are unknown to us.

IMMANUEL KANT, *Logic*

3.1 Knowledge Engineering

Knowledge engineering is the application of logic and ontology to the task of building computable models of some domain for some purpose. The features computable, domain, and purpose characterize it as a branch of engineering. Pure mathematics lacks all three: it need not have an application domain; it may define noncomputable or even infinite structures; and it may have no purpose other than the esthetic satisfaction of contemplating elegant abstractions. Empirical sciences have a domain, and they make computable predictions about the domain; but they need not have any purpose other than the pursuit of knowledge. Engineering, however, uses science and mathematics for the purpose of solving practical problems within the constraints of budgets and deadlines. Knowledge engineering can therefore be defined as the branch of engineering that analyzes knowledge about some subject and transforms it to a computable form for some purpose.

INFORMAL SPECIFICATIONS. To illustrate the issues a knowledge engineer must address, consider the problem of translating an informal English specification to an executable program. The following sentence might be part of a larger specification of a traffic simulation system:

> There is a traffic light that automatically turns red or green, but it also has an option for manual control under special circumstances.

The person who wrote this description undoubtedly had a lifetime of experience in driving or walking in a modern city with traffic lights or stop signs at every corner. Yet imagine a Martian who had learned English by monitoring radio broadcasts, but who had never visited the earth. How would the Martian interpret the terms *automatically, option, manual control,* and *special circumstances?* How is the light related to the traffic? Does it move with the traffic? What does it mean for a light to "turn red or green"? Does it rotate? Does it turn, like a maple leaf in autumn, from green to red, and then fall off?

FORMALIZATION. A knowledge engineer who has mastered logic, frames, and rule-based systems is like a Martian when faced with specialized fields such as investment banking, petroleum engineering, or aircraft maintenance. A sentence written by an expert in any of those fields is like the sentence about the traffic light. Every term that might seem "obvious" to the expert is a puzzle that the knowledge engineer must analyze and clarify. A computer is even more like a Martian. When asked whether a computer could automatically write programs from informal specifications, the pioneer in computer science Alan Perlis replied, "It is not possible to translate informal specifications to formal specifications by any formal algorithm." English syntax is not what makes the translation difficult. The difficulty results from the enormous amount of background knowledge that lies behind every word. When the details are added, the sentence about the traffic light could expand to the following specification:

```
The color of the traffic light X may be either red
or green. X has an automatic control switch, which
may be either on or off.
If the automatic control switch is on,
  then X behaves according to the following two rules:
    When the color of X becomes green,
      it remains green for g seconds;
      then it changes to red.
    When the color of X becomes red,
      it remains red for r seconds;
      then it changes to green.
```

This revised version is an *interpretation* of the original text that makes some further assumptions. The new variables g and r, for example, depend on the assumption that the light stays green or red for a fixed duration whenever it changes color. Some such assumptions are necessary to make the specification detailed enough to be computable, but they are based on outside information, which must come from the knowledge engineer's background knowledge, from various reference sources, or from a discussion with an expert. Besides making assumptions and adding detail, the knowledge engineer must translate the detailed specification to a computable form.

PRINCIPLES OF KNOWLEDGE REPRESENTATION.   Three experts in knowledge representation, Randall Davis, Howard Schrobe, and Peter Szolovits (1993), wrote a critical review and analysis of the state of the art. They summarized their conclusions in five basic principles about knowledge representations and their role in artificial intelligence:

1. *A knowledge representation is a surrogate.* Physical objects, events, and relationships, which cannot be stored directly in a computer, are represented by symbols that serve as *surrogates* for the external things. The symbols and the links between them form a model of the external system. By manipulating the internal surrogates, a computer program can simulate the external system or reason about it.

2. *A knowledge representation is a set of ontological commitments.* Ontology is the study of existence. For a database or knowledge base, ontology determines the categories of things that exist or may exist in an application domain. Those categories represent the *ontological commitments* of the designer or knowledge engineer.

3. *A knowledge representation is a fragmentary theory of intelligent reasoning.* To support reasoning about the things in a domain, a knowledge representation must also describe their behavior and interactions. The description constitutes a *theory* of the application domain. The theory may be stated in explicit axioms, or it might be compiled into executable programs.

4. *A knowledge representation is a medium for efficient computation.* Besides representing knowledge, an AI system must encode knowledge in a form that can be processed efficiently on the available computing equipment. As Leibniz realized, some of the most interesting problems can be represented easily enough, but solving them may require an enormous amount of time and effort to compute. New developments in computer hardware and programming theory have had a major influence on the design and use of knowledge representation languages.

5. *A knowledge representation is a medium of human expression.* A good knowledge representation language should facilitate communication between the *knowledge engineers* who understand AI and the *domain experts* who understand the application. Although the knowledge engineers may write the definitions and rules, the domain experts should be able to read them and verify whether they represent a realistic theory of the domain.

These five principles can be used as a framework for discussing the issues of knowledge representation and illustrating them in terms of the traffic light example.

SURROGATE. A computational model is a surrogate for some real or hypothetical system — in this case, the traffic light. Each of the significant entities, such as the current time or the color of the light, is assigned a variable that serves as an internal surrogate for the external entity. Then the values of those variables can be transformed, either procedurally or declaratively, to simulate the behavior of the system. The procedural approach uses programs or rules that operate on the variables of the model $\mathcal{M}$:

1. Represent each possible event by an operation that changes $\mathcal{M}$ in an appropriate way.
2. Design a control structure that triggers each operation at the moment when its starting conditions become true.
3. Run the programs to see how the model $\mathcal{M}$ evolves in time.

Programs can be executed directly by a computer. Rules must be interpreted by some other program called an *inference engine*. For better performance, an optimizing compiler could be used to translate the rules to programs that run directly on the underlying computer.

The declarative approach is based on constraints or *axioms* that define the *preconditions, postconditions,* and transformations for each event that may occur in the model. Instead of executing programs to simulate the events, it uses theorem-proving techniques to derive their consequences. For any simulation that can be computed procedurally, the declarative approach can derive the same result by deduction:

1. Describe the starting state S by a collection of formulas.
2. Add the description of S to the axioms for the model $\mathcal{M}$.
3. To determine the state of $\mathcal{M}$ at any later time t, start with the axioms of $\mathcal{M}$ and the description of S, and prove a theorem that describes the state of $\mathcal{M}$ at time t.

In effect, the theorem prover serves as an interpreter that "executes" the axioms. The challenge, however, is to make it efficient. That is an engineering task of solving a problem within the constraints of budgets and deadlines.

ONTOLOGICAL COMMITMENTS. By Quine's criterion, the ontological commitments are determined by the types of variables in the knowledge representation.

For the traffic light example, the variables stand for the significant entities, such as the light itself, the current time, the current color, the last time when the color changed, the duration the light is red or green, and the switch for automatic control. Those commitments may be represented by variables in predicate calculus, by concepts in a graph, or by slots in data structures called *frames, schemas,* or *templates.* Following is a template for trafficLight, written in a rule-based language called CLIPS:

```
(deftemplate trafficLight
    (slot name            (type SYMBOL))
    (slot currentColor    (allowed-values red green))
    (slot redTime         (type FLOAT))
    (slot greenTime       (type FLOAT))
    (slot whenChanged     (type FLOAT))
    (slot autoSwitch      (allowed-values on off))  )
```

This template has six *slots,* each with a *facet* that restricts the values that may be stored in the slots. The template and its slots represent the primary ontological commitments. The facets add further commitments to the existence of entities of type Float and Symbol. Those entities do not belong to the object domain of traffic lights, but to the metalanguage domain used to talk about the symbols that represent traffic lights.

After the template has been defined, it can be *instantiated* by an *assert* statement, which inserts values in the slots. The autoSwitch slot would have the initial value *on,* but it could be turned off for manual control.

```
(assert (trafficLight
    (name           Blinky)
    (currentColor   green)
    (redTime        60)
    (greenTime      60)
    (whenChanged    0)
    (autoSwitch     on)  ))
```

The template corresponds to a structure or record definition in a programming language. Each assertion for that template allocates and initializes the storage for a new instance. In logic, the slots correspond to dyadic predicates or relations such as redTime(x,y), where the first variable x represents the traffic light and the second variable y represents the current value in the slot.

MEDIUM FOR EFFICIENT COMPUTATION. Both the procedural and the declarative approaches can be transformed to a computable form. If the utmost in efficiency is necessary for some problem, then a low-level programming language that maps directly to hardware may be the fastest. The following program simulates the traffic light by a loop that alternately sets the color to red or green:

```
loop while autoSwitch;
    set currentColor to red;
    wait redTime;
    set currentColor to green;
    wait greenTime;
    end loop;
```

This program could be used either to simulate a traffic light or to drive a microprocessor that controls an actual traffic light. As a knowledge representation, however, it lacks one essential feature: there is no way to get information out of it. The traffic light doesn't explain why it changes color, it doesn't keep a record of its color changes, and it doesn't answer questions about the average time it was red or green or was being operated under manual control.

If statistics about the traffic light are unimportant or irrelevant, then a programming loop may be the best way to simulate it. But if the traffic light itself is significant, then more instructions would be needed to keep records about the light and its changes. Those are *metalevel* instructions that support reasoning about the traffic light, but they could easily become much more voluminous and time-consuming than the original loop. To handle the detail, various *simulation languages* have been developed that operate on two levels in parallel: at the object level, they compute the effects of each action performed by the objects in the simulated system; at the metalevel, they monitor the objects and record information about them. The first modern *object-oriented language*, Simula-67, was originally designed for simulation. O-O languages are still popular for simulation, since the metalevel instructions can be *encapsulated* inside procedures associated with each object.

The declarative way to simulate the traffic light is to translate the English description to formulas in logic and to prove theorems about its states. Following are two axioms that represent the conditions for the light to turn green or red:

$(\forall x{:}\text{TrafficLight})(\forall t{:}\text{Time})(\forall r{:}\text{Duration})$
$\quad((\text{turnsRed}(x,t) \wedge \text{redTime}(x,r) \wedge \text{autoSwitch}(\text{on}))$
$\qquad \supset \text{turnsGreen}(x,t+r)).$
$(\forall x{:}\text{TrafficLight})(\forall t{:}\text{Time})(\forall g{:}\text{Duration})$
$\quad((\text{turnsGreen}(x,t) \wedge \text{greenTime}(x,g) \wedge \text{autoSwitch}(\text{on}))$
$\qquad \supset \text{turnsRed}(x,t+g)).$

The first axiom says that for any traffic light x, time t, and duration r, if x turns red at time t, the red time of x is r, and the autoswitch is turned on, then x turns green at time $t + r$. The second axiom is the same, but with green and red interchanged.

Many different kinds of theorem provers have been developed for variations of logic and related declarative languages. Prolog was the first and is still the most popular *logic-programming language*. Following are the translations of the two axioms to Prolog rules:

```
turns_green(X,T2) ← traffic_light(X) & turns_red(X,T)
    & red_time(X,R) & auto_switch(on) & sum_times(T,R,T2).
turns_red(X,T2) ← traffic_light(X) & turns_green(X,T)
    & green_time(X,G) & auto_switch(on) & sum_times(T,G,T2).
```

These two rules are logically equivalent to the axioms, but with the syntactic changes necessary for Prolog: each variable begins with a capital letter; the quantifiers are omitted, since all Prolog variables are assumed to be universally quantified; and the implication operator ⊃ is turned backward for the Prolog implication, which is represented by ←, <-, or :- in different dialects. The predicate sum_times would also have to be defined to make the proper conversions when seconds are added to hours and minutes.

Before these rules can be used computationally, the starting conditions for the traffic light would have to be asserted separately. The following four Prolog assertions correspond to the CLIPS assertion for the instance named Blinky (with the name written in lowercase to distinguish it from the Prolog variables).

```
traffic_light(blinky). red_time(blinky, 60).
green_time(blinky, 60). turns_green(blinky, 0:00).
```

These propositions assert that Blinky is a traffic light, it has a red time of 60 seconds, it has a green time of 60 seconds, and it turns green at time 0:00. From the two rules and the four assertions, a Prolog inference engine can deduce conclusions of the following form:

```
turns_red(blinky,0:01). turns_green(blinky,0:02).
turns_red(blinky,0:03). turns_green(blinky,0:04).
```

These conclusions would be generated in response to Prolog goals for the questions *When does Blinky turn red?* or *List all times when Blinky turns red or turns green.* Unlike the procedural loop, which continuously updates the variables to simulate the light, the Prolog rules make predictions about the light in answer to specific questions.

There are two major families of rule-based expert systems: the *backward-chaining* systems are supported by inference engines, which, like Prolog, are based on logical deduction; the *forward-chaining* systems are also based on logic, but they have procedural aspects that resemble the programming loop. Following is a forward-chaining rule written in stylized English supplemented with variables:

```
if there is a trafficLight x,
  the currentColor of x is red,
  the redTime of x is r,
  the whenChanged of x is t,
  the autoSwitch is on,
  the currentTime is now,
  now ≥ t + r,
then modify currentColor of x to green,
  modify whenChanged of x to now.
```

This rule can be translated line by line to CLIPS, in which variables are marked by the ? symbol:

```
(defrule turnsGreen
  ?x <- (trafficLight
    (currentColor red)
    (redTime ?r)
    (whenChanged ?t)
    (autoSwitch on) )
  (currentTime ?now)
  (test (>= ?now (+ ?t ?r)))
=>
  (modify ?x
    (currentColor green)
    (whenChanged ?now) ))
```

The logic-based rules, which are true for all time ($\forall t$:Time), make predictions about when the light will turn red or green. The forward-chaining rule, however, is stated in terms of a constantly changing time called *now*. It lies dormant until the time $t + r$ becomes *now*; then, like the procedural loop, it modifies data in working memory. In effect, the if-part of the rule is as declarative as logic, and the then-part is as procedural as the loop. An inference engine must keep track of the changing patterns in working memory and activate each rule when all its conditions become true.

FRAGMENTARY THEORY OF REASONING. The procedural loop, the logical formula, and the forward-chaining rule illustrate three different strategies for reasoning about a traffic light: the instructions in the loop carry out a step-by-step simulation of the states of the light; the logical formulas support a theorem prover that can make a prediction about the light at any time t; and the forward-chaining rules, which lie dormant until their conditions become true, spring into action to update the current state description. Any of these three reasoning strategies could also be used by humans who may be thinking about a traffic light. Each one has advantages and disadvantages, which may make it the preferred strategy for certain purposes.

The procedural approach is best suited to representing processes that have a natural sequence of operations. Each operation maps to a block of machine instructions, and the structure of the program mirrors the structure of the problem. But procedures are not as suitable for representing relationships where there is no natural time sequence. For such problems, the sequential nature of the procedure is an arbitrary imposition that may obscure or distort the structure of the problem. Even when time is significant, a pure procedural approach may still be unsuitable: a system with parallel operations and unforeseeable "surprises" can be difficult or impossible to map to a strictly sequential procedure.

Logic is best suited to describing patterns of relationships with criss-crossing dependencies that have no natural linearization. A graph logic is good for displaying such dependencies, but a linear notation such as predicate calculus can also express them in an equivalent form. To represent time sequences, logic must be supplemented with an appropriate ontology for time. Versions of *temporal logic* make time a privileged entity and explicitly represent the context-dependent time *now*. Parallel processes can also be represented in logic, but they require a context mechanism with message-passing operators for communicating between processes. Such mechanisms require further ontological assumptions about contexts, messages, and the axioms for relating them. They are described further in Chapters 4 and 5.

MEDIUM FOR HUMAN EXPRESSION.   Since knowledge engineers must work with experts in other fields, they must be able to communicate with them in languages and notations that avoid the jargon of AI and computer science. Conceptual graphs and other diagrams have been used successfully as a communication medium between knowledge engineers and domain experts (Slagle et al. 1990). Figure 3.1 shows a conceptual graph equivalent to the logical formula or Prolog rule.

As Figure 3.1 illustrates, a conceptual graph may be more readable than linear rules, but the graphs are not self-explanatory. A domain expert who had never seen CGs before would need some explanation about the distinction between ovals and boxes, the directions of the arrows, and the conventions for coreference labels like *x and ?x. As an alternate notation, the conceptual graph could be translated to stylized English:

> If a traffic light x turns red at time t,
>> has a red time of a duration r,
>>> and has autoswitch in the state on,
>
> then x turns green at a time, which is the sum of t and r.

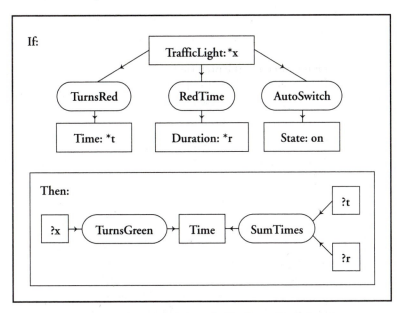

FIGURE 3.1 A conceptual graph for the traffic-light rule

This stylized English version requires less explanation, and it could be used as an alternate or a supplement to a formalized knowledge representation language. But specialized diagrams have become traditional in most fields: flow diagrams with tanks, pipes, and boilers in chemical engineering; circuit diagrams with transistors and resistors in electrical engineering; pieces on a board in chess; or notes and staves in music. Experts in any of those fields would prefer their familiar diagrams to any other notation, including natural language.

Translating an informal diagram to a formal notation of any kind is as difficult as translating informal English specifications to executable programs. But the converse can be much easier: a formal representation in conceptual graphs or any other system of logic can be translated automatically either to stylized natural language or to traditional kinds of diagrams. Walling Cyre and his students have developed a *scripting language* for translating conceptual graphs to circuit diagrams, block diagrams, and visual depictions (Cyre et al. 1994). With such tools, a logical specification written by the knowledge engineer could be translated automatically to visual diagrams for the domain expert, to executable code for the computer, or to natural language for documentation, explanations, and help facilities.

SIMULATION AND THEOREM PROVING. The procedural loop, the Prolog rules, and the forward-chaining rules represent three different ways of simulating the behavior of the traffic light. Yet simulation has certain limitations: it can only predict what would happen in a specific case; it can never prove a general theorem. Logic has greater flexibility; it can be used to design a simulator, but it can also be used to prove theorems:

- Blinky turns green at every even-numbered minute.
- Blinky turns red at every odd-numbered minute.
- Blinky turns green 30 times per hour.
- Blinky will spend 50 percent of its time red.
- A traffic light with red time r and green time g will be red for $r/(r+g)$ of the time.
- A traffic light with red time r and green time g will turn green an average of $3600/(r+g)$ times per hour.

If the simulator were run for a long time, the results would suggest the patterns predicted by these theorems. Yet any patterns observed in the data might be caused by chance or by an unusual selection of starting conditions. Since the simulation was started at time 0, the theorem prover and the simulator would both show that Blinky turns green at every even-numbered minute. But only the theorem prover can explain how the results follow from the starting conditions.

Theorem proving can derive general principles with absolute certainty. But if a system is complex and changeable, the number of exceptions may make the rules so complex that finding a proof could be difficult or impossible. Even when a proof can be found, a simulation would be useful to check for possible errors in the starting assumptions or to give a survey of typical results. Ideally, simulation and theorem proving can supplement one another: patterns that are suggested by simulation can be verified by theorem proving.

The question of whether knowledge should be encoded declaratively in some form of logic or procedurally in a programming language is one of the oldest and still most hotly contested issues in AI and computer science in general. A declarative specification is usually the most concise and easiest to verify, but a low-level procedure is usually the most efficient. For programs that are only executed once, the human time is far more valuable than the computer time. If execution time is critical, optimizing compilers may be able to generate efficient code from declarative specifications. But for special purposes, suitable compilers might not be available, and some human programmer would have to translate the specifications to optimized code.

PERSISTENCE.   Both the simulator and the theorem prover determine what happens at the discrete time points when the light changes color. But further information is needed to determine what happens in the intervals between color changes. The English statement that the light "remains green" or "remains red" is not captured in the formal axioms. To determine the light's color in the intervening intervals, the axioms for the traffic light must be supplemented with two additional axioms of *persistence*:

$$(\forall x{:}\text{TrafficLight})(\forall t{:}\text{Time})(\forall t_1{:}\text{Time})(\forall r{:}\text{Duration})$$
$$((\text{turnsRed}(x,t_1) \land \text{redTime}(x,r)$$
$$\land\ (t{=}t_1 \lor (\text{before}(t_1,t) \land \text{before}(t,t_1{+}r)))\ )$$
$$\supset \text{color}(x,\text{red},t)\ ).$$

This axiom says that if the traffic light x turns red at time t_1 and its red time is r, then at any time t in the interval $(t_1,t_1{+}r)$ its color is red. The next axiom states the equivalent conditions for green:

$$(\forall x{:}\text{TrafficLight})(\forall t{:}\text{Time})(\forall t_1{:}\text{Time})(\forall g{:}\text{Duration})$$
$$((\text{turnsGreen}(x,t_1) \land \text{greenTime}(x,g)$$
$$\land\ (t{=}t_1 \lor (\text{before}(t_1,t) \land \text{before}(t,t_1{+}g)))\ )$$
$$\supset \text{color}(x,\text{green},t)\ ).$$

Axioms of persistence are a cumbersome way of saying something that should be obvious. Unfortunately, computers cannot recognize the obvious unless they are explicitly told how. These cumbersome axioms are a special-case solution to the more general *frame problem*, which is discussed in Section 4.7. The general approach to that problem is based on Leibniz's principle of *sufficient reason*: Nothing at all can happen without some reason (*Nihil omnino fit sine aliqua ratione*). Leibniz's principle is a metalevel axiom that is used to generate one or more lower-level axioms for each particular example. In this case, it implies that the light's color should remain unchanged unless some reason for change can be found.

3.2 Representing Structure in Frames

Besides representing knowledge, a language must be able to analyze knowledge in low-level primitives and organize it in high-level structures. In natural language, the basic unit is the word, and the basic structure is the sentence. But higher-level structures like paragraphs, sections, chapters, and volumes are needed to classify and organize the knowledge. In symbolic logic, the basic units are predicates, which are connected by operators like $\land$, $\lor$, and $\supset$ to create formulas. In conceptual graphs, the basic units are concepts and relations, which are linked to one another in graphs. Besides linking, a knowledge representation language must have methods of grouping or nesting that can organize knowledge and package it in larger structures.

SCHEMATA. Aristotle used the term *schema* for his patterns of valid syllogisms. That word, with its plural *schemata* (accent on the first syllable), has been adopted by philosophers and psychologists for the patterns that organize elements of knowledge into larger structures. Immanuel Kant (1787) maintained that a schema has an associated rule that can accommodate all possible aspects of a concept:

> Indeed, our pure sensory concepts are not based on images of objects, but on schemata. For the concept of a triangle in general, no image could ever be adequate. It would never attain the generality of the concept, which applies to all triangles, whether right — angled, obtuse-angled, or acute-angled; it would always be limited to a part of this domain. The schema of the triangle can exist nowhere but in thought, where it signifies a rule of synthesis for constructing pure spatial figures in the imagination. Still less is an object of experience or its image ever adequate to an empirical concept, which is immediately connected to the schema of imagination as a rule for determining our intuition according to a certain general concept. The concept Dog signifies a rule according to which my imagination can construct the figure of a four-footed animal in general, without being restricted to any particular image supplied by experience or to any possible image I may draw *in concreto*. (A:141, B:180)

In his theory of memory, the psychologist Frederic Bartlett (1932) also adopted the term *schema*, for which he gave the following definition:

> . . . an active organization of past reactions, or of past experiences, which must always be supposed to be operating in any well-adapted organic response. That is, whenever there is any order or regularity of behavior, a particular response is possible only because it is related to other similar responses which have been serially organized, yet which operate, not simply as individual members coming one after another, but as a unitary mass. (p. 201)

Kant and Bartlett had important insights that guided their researches, but their definitions were too vague to be implemented in a computer system. The psychologist Otto Selz, who was deeply influenced by Kant, represented schemata as networks of concepts in his theory of *schematic anticipation* (1913, 1922). In Selz's theory, a schema with incomplete information serves as a goal that directs the thinking processes to search for specific values to complete it. Selz's schemata for directing thought have a strong resemblance to the backward chaining rules in AI.

FRAMES. The similarities of AI patterns to the schemata of Kant, Selz, and Bartlett is not accidental. At Carnegie-Mellon University, Allen Newell and Herbert Simon cited Selz's influence on their work on problem solving (1972). In his famous paper on frames, Marvin Minsky (1975) cited Bartlett as a source of inspiration, but he defined frames in more implementable terms:

> A *frame* is a data structure for representing a stereotyped situation, like being in a certain kind of living room or going to a child's birthday party. Attached

to each frame are several kinds of information. Some of this information is about how to use the frame. Some is about what one can expect to happen next. Some is about what to do if these expectations are not confirmed.

We can think of a frame as a network of nodes and relations. The "top levels" of a frame are fixed, and represent things that are always true about the supposed situation. The lower levels have many *terminals* — "slots" that must be filled by specific instances of data. Each terminal can specify conditions its assignments must meet. (The assignments themselves are usually smaller "sub-frames.") Simple conditions are specified by markers that might require a terminal assignment to be a person, an object of sufficient value, or a pointer to a sub-frame of a certain type. More complex conditions can specify relations among the things assigned to several terminals.

When Minsky published his paper on frames, it had an electrifying effect on everybody working in AI, but the effects were different on people with different viewpoints. Some people immediately set out to implement frame systems according to Minsky's guidelines; two of the earliest were the Frame Representation Language (FRL) by Goldstein and Roberts (1977) and the Knowledge Representation Language (KRL) by Bobrow and Winograd (1977). Other people claimed that their "networks" or "records" or "chunks" already served the same purpose as frames. Still others, such as Patrick Hayes (1979), maintained that everything in frames could be represented equally well in logic. Those reactions are justified to a certain extent, but the importance of Minsky's paper was his emphasis on the need for structure in organizing a knowledge base.

Since Minsky's paper first appeared, more than 50 versions of frame systems have been implemented. For knowledge sharing, Peter Karp and Thomas Gruber (1996) have designed the Generic Frame Protocol, which supports the basic operations for accessing and maintaining a knowledge base of frames. GFP has no preferred notation, because it is intended to be syntactically neutral, and sample frames in this book are written in a LISP-like notation that maps to GFP. Following is a frame that defines the type TrafficLight:

```
(defineType          TrafficLight
    (supertype       Object)
    (currentColor    (type Color) (oneOf (red green)))
    (redTime         (type Duration))
    (greenTime       (type Duration))
    (whenChanged     (type PointInTime))
    (autoSwitch      (type State) (oneOf (on off))) )
```

This frame definition bears a strong resemblance to the CLIPS template definition. The most obvious difference is the second line, which declares Object to be the supertype of TrafficLight. Another difference is that the type restrictions allow a wider range of types, such as Color, Duration, PointInTime, and State. Some types may be primitive, but frame definitions can create new ones. The types Duration and PointInTime, for example, might be stored as floating-point numbers, but they would have different interpretations: a duration could be added to a point in time, but two points in time could not be added to one another. The CLIPS assertion for Blinky corresponds to an *instance definition*:

```
(defineInstance    Blinky
  (type            TrafficLight)
  (currentColor    green)
  (redTime         (60 second))
  (greenTime       (60 second))
  (whenChanged     (0:00 hour))
  (autoSwitch      on) )
```

With user-defined types, frames can represent measures by a pair that has a numeric value and a unit, such as second or hour.

Besides creating types and instances, frame definitions specify supertypes to form a hierarchy with inheritance. As an example, the following frame declares the type Truck with supertype Vehicle and with slots for unloaded weight, maximum gross weight, cargo capacity, and number of wheels:

```
(defineType          Truck
  (supertype         Vehicle)
  (unloadedWt        (type WtMeasure))
  (maxGrossWt        (type WtMeasure))
  (cargoCapacity     (type VolMeasure))
  (numberOfWheels    (type Integer))  )
```

For the facets in this frame, the type Integer would be a built-in type, but WtMeasure and VolMeasure could be defined by frames that specify a slot for the numeric value and a slot for the unit of measure, such as tons, pounds, or cubic meters. A type TrailerTruck could be defined as a subtype of Truck:

```
(defineType          TrailerTruck
  (supertype         Truck)
  (hasPart           (type Trailer))
  (numberOfWheels 18)  )
```

This frame introduces the hasPart slot and restricts the value of the number-OfWheels slot to 18. As a result, the type TrailerTruck would *inherit* the information for Truck by a process of merging the slots for the Truck frame with the slots for the TrailerTruck frame. The TrailerTruck frame would effectively have the following definition:

```
(defineType        TrailerTruck
  (supertype       Truck)
  (unloadedWt      (type WtMeasure))
  (maxGrossWt      (type WtMeasure))
  (cargoCapacity   (type VolMeasure))
  (hasPart         (type Trailer))
  (numberOfWheels  18) )
```

In the process of inheritance, the supertype slot is treated differently from the other slots. Instead of being inherited, it points to the frame from which the other slots are inherited. The slots for weight and cargoCapacity, which are not mentioned in the TrailerTruck frame, are copied from the Truck frame. Since the number-OfWheels slot occurs in both frames, the facets are merged. In this example, the type facet for TrailerTruck would be checked to ensure that the value 18 is an integer. In case of conflicts between the two specifications, the facets for the subtype override the facets inherited from the supertype.

MAPPING FRAMES TO LOGIC.   As Patrick Hayes has long insisted, the purely declarative information in a frame can be translated to any notation for first-order logic. The instance definitions use the existential conjunctive (EC) subset: only the existential quantifier ∃ and the conjunction ∧ are required. In CGs, each slot maps to a dyadic relation with a concept to hold the type specification and the current value:

```
[TrafficLight: Blinky]-
  (currentColor)→[Color: green]
  (redTime)→[Duration: <60,second>]
  (greenTime)→[Duration: <60,second>]
  (whenChanged)→[PointInTime: <0:00,hour>]
  (autoSwitch)→[State: on].
```

Except for punctuation, this graph looks very frame-like. In the linear notation for CGs, a hyphen following a concept indicates that its attached relations are continued on subsequent lines. In predicate calculus, the dyadic relations become dyadic predicates:

$(\exists x{:}\text{TrafficLight})(x{=}\text{Blinky} \land$
  $\text{currentColor}(x,\text{green}) \land$
  $\text{redTime}(x,{<}60,\text{second}{>}) \land$
  $\text{greenTime}(x,{<}60,\text{second}{>}) \land$
  $\text{whenChanged}(x,{<}0{:}00,\text{hour}{>}) \land$
  $\text{autoswitch}(x,\text{on})\ ).$

The process of instantiating the frame has the effect of merging the slots in the instance frame with the slots in the type frame. In conceptual graphs and predicate calculus, that merger is based on a rule of inference called *unification*.

The type frames map to lambda expressions or CG type definitions. Following are the Truck and TrailerTruck frames translated to CG type definitions:

```
type Truck(*x) is
  [Vehicle: ?x]-
    (UnloadedWt)→[WtMeasure]
    (MaxGrossWt)→[WtMeasure]
    (CargoCapacity)→[VolMeasure]
    (NumberOfWheels)→[Integer].
```

This graph defines a truck as a vehicle whose unloaded weight is a weight measure, whose maximum gross weight is a weight measure, whose cargo capacity is a volume measure, and whose number of wheels is an integer. A trailer truck is then defined as a type of truck:

```
type TrailerTruck(*x) is
  [Truck: ?x]-
    (HasPart)→[Trailer]
    (NumberOfWheels)→[Integer: 18].
```

In predicate calculus, the CG type definitions map to monadic lambda expressions that are equivalent line by line to the CG and frame definitions:

Truck =
  $(\lambda x{:}\text{Vehicle})($
    $(\exists y_1{:}\text{WtMeasure})\text{unloadedWt}(x,y_1) \land$
    $(\exists y_2{:}\text{WtMeasure})\text{maxGrossWt}(x,y_2) \land$
    $(\exists y_3{:}\text{VolMeasure})\text{cargoCapacity}(x,y_3) \land$
    $(\exists y_4{:}\text{Integer})\text{numberOfWheels}(x,y_4).$
TrailerTruck =
  $(\lambda x{:}\text{Truck})($
    $(\exists y_1{:}\text{Trailer})\text{hasPart}(x,y_1) \land$
    $(\exists y_2{:}\text{Integer})(\text{numberOfWheels}(x,y_2) \land y_2{=}18)).$

Besides the EC subset for the instances, the type definitions use the λ symbol, which has the effect of stating that the type frame is implicitly true of every instance of the given type. Other combinations of quantifiers are not permitted in frames.

Since the concepts and relations in these graphs have been translated directly from the frames, some relations have names like HasPart instead of the usual CG relation Part. Long names like CargoCapacity or NumberOfWheels may be used in conceptual graphs and predicate calculus, but they can also be defined in terms of more primitive concepts and relations. The concept type WtMeasure could be defined as an amount that is characteristic (Chrc) of some weight:

type WtMeasure(*x) **is**
   [Amount: ?x]←(Chrc)←[Weight].

Following is a definition of the dyadic relation MaxGrossWt in terms of the concept type MaxGrossWeight:

relation MaxGrossWt(*x,*y) **is**
   [Vehicle: ?x]→(Chrc)→[MaxGrossWeight]-
   (Chrc)→[Amount: ?y].

This definition says that the MaxGrossWt relation links a vehicle x to its characteristic maximum gross weight, which has a characteristic amount y. Another definition is necessary to relate the concept type MaxGrossWeight to the simpler types:

type MaxGrossWeight(*x) **is**
   [Vehicle: *y]→(Chrc)→[Weight: ?x]-
     (Chrc)→[Amount]→(GE)→[Amount]←(Sum)-
       ←[Amount]←(Chrc)←[UnloadedWeight]←(Chrc)←[?y]
       ←[Amount]←(Chrc)←[Weight]←(Chrc)←[Cargo]←(In)←[?y].

This definition says that maximum gross weight x is a weight x that is characteristic of a vehicle y, where x has an amount that is greater than or equal to (GE) an amount, which is the sum (using the triadic relation Sum) of the amount of the unloaded weight of y plus the amount of the weight of the cargo in y. These definitions can be translated to predicate calculus, but the arithmetic computations are beyond the expressive power of frames. Some frame systems support them by *procedural attachments* that invoke procedures in an external language.

    A knowledge base in frame systems has two parts: a hierarchy of type definitions and a collection of instances. The instance frames, which use only existential-conjunctive logic, are equivalent in expressive power to a relational or object-oriented database. Hector Levesque (1986) called the EC subset *vivid logic* because it is capable of expressing all concrete facts. It cannot, however, express negations, implications, or generalizations. As an example of the limitations of EC logic, consider the statement *There is no hippopotamus in this room.* That statement cannot be expressed in EC logic because it requires a negation. Yet an adult hippopotamus is a four-ton beast. If one were present, it would certainly be noticed. Those last two sentences, however, go beyond EC logic because they express a generalization and an implication. By itself, EC logic can be used to catalog the presence of every item in a room, but it cannot state or imply the absence of anything, not even a hippopotamus.

FRAMES AND SYLLOGISMS.   A frame is a package of propositions about some type or some instance of a type. Logically, a frame that defines n slots for a type t is a conjunction of n universal affirmative (type A) propositions that are true for every instance of the type t. The truck frame, for example, asserts four type A propositions:

Every truck

- is a vehicle.
- has an unloaded weight, whose value is a weight measure.
- has a maximum gross weight, whose value is a weight measure.
- has a cargo capacity, whose value is a volume measure.
- has a number of wheels, whose value is an integer.

A frame that defines n slots for an instance x is a conjunction of n particular affirmative (type I) propositions that are true of x. The instance frame for X39071D asserts two type I propositions:

X39071D

- is a truck.
- has a cargo capacity of 25 cubic meters.
- has 6 wheels.

Note that the English reading *is a* may represent either the supertype slot or the instanceOf slot. That ambiguity can be confusing because the two kinds of slots support different kinds of operations: the supertype slot represents a universally quantified proposition (type A); and the instanceOf slot represents an existentially quantified proposition (type I). The implications of the two quantifiers are very different.

The two principal rules of inference in frame systems are based on the syllogisms Barbara and Darii. Barbara supports inheritance from supertypes to subtypes:

    A: Every truck has a cargo capacity.
    A: Every trailer truck is a truck.
    A: Therefore, every trailer truck has a cargo capacity.

The syllogism Darii supports inheritance from type frames to instance frames:

    A: Every truck has a cargo capacity.
    I: X39071D is a truck.
    I: Therefore, X39071D has a cargo capacity.

In both forms of inheritance, the major premise of the syllogism is a type A proposition that comes from a type frame. The minor premise of Barbara is a type A proposition that says everything of type s is also of type t; the conclusion is a type

A proposition about type *s*. The minor premise of Darii is a type I proposition that says some instance *x* is of type *t*; the conclusion is a type I proposition about *x*.

MULTIPLE INHERITANCE. Syllogisms and frame systems support *multiple inheritance*, which allows a type to have multiple supertypes or an instance to have multiple types. To represent the sentence *Some Peterbilt is a TrailerTruck*, the following definition specifies an instance named ZF437TT, which has two types, Peterbilt and TrailerTruck:

```
(defineInstance   ZF437TT
  (type           Peterbilt)
  (type           TrailerTruck) )
```

The new instance ZF437TT inherits all the attributes of both types Peterbilt and TrailerTruck. Following is a frame that defines the type Peterbilt as a truck that is manufactured by the company Peterbilt, Inc.

```
(defineType        Peterbilt
  (supertype       Truck)
  (manufacturedBy  PeterbiltInc) )
```

Inheritance is performed by copying the slots from three type frames: Peterbilt, TrailerTruck, and their common supertype Truck. ZF437TT would effectively have the following definition:

```
(defineInstance   ZF437TT
  (type           Peterbilt)
  (type           TrailerTruck)
  (manufacturedBy PeterbiltInc)
  (unloadedWt     (type WtMeasure))
  (maxGrossWt     (type WtMeasure))
  (cargoCapacity  (type VolMeasure))
  (hasPart        (type Trailer))
  (numberOfWheels 18) )
```

Five new slots have been added to this frame by repeated syllogisms of types Barbara and Darii. As these examples illustrate, each frame groups related information about a type or an instance in a convenient package; inheritance allows automatic inference of multiple propositions; and the inferences can be implemented efficiently by the list handling or pointer handling operators of programming languages.

KL-ONE. Although parenthesized notations have been popular in AI, Minsky originally described a frame as "a network of nodes and relations." Ronald Brachman (1979) designed a network notation for his Knowledge Language One (KL-ONE),

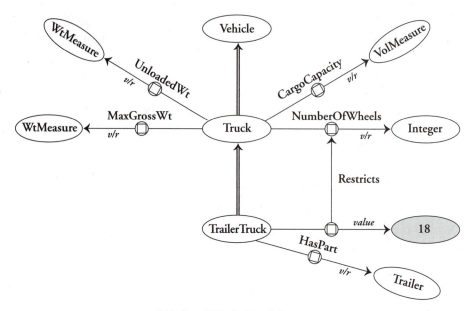

FIGURE 3.2 Truck and TrailerTruck frames in KL-ONE

which is the ancestor of many frame systems. Woods and Schmolze (1992) reported that about 20 systems have been implemented in the KL-ONE tradition. Figure 3.2 shows the information in the Truck and TrailerTruck frames represented in a KL-ONE network. The network has nine ovals for concept nodes and nine arrows, which represent different kinds of links. The white ovals represent *generic concepts* for the types, as distinguished from the shaded oval, which is an *individual concept* for the instance 18. The oval marked with an asterisk * indicates that Integer is a built-in or primitive type. The concepts Truck and TrailerTruck are defined in Figure 3.2, but Vehicle, Trailer, WtMeasure, and VolMeasure would have to be defined by other KL-ONE diagrams.

What distinguishes KL-ONE from earlier frame systems is not so much its network notation as its clearly defined semantics. Some of the early AI systems had an ad hoc structure that was severely criticized in two famous papers, "What's in a Link" by William Woods and "Artificial Intelligence Meets Natural Stupidity" by Drew McDermott. In responding to those critiques, Brachman drew a clear distinction between the different kinds of links in a semantic network. The double-line arrows represent subtype-supertype links from TrailerTruck to Truck and from Truck to Vehicle. The arrows with a circle in the middle represent *roles*, which correspond to the slots other than supertype in the previous frames. The Truck node has four roles labeled UnloadedWt, MaxGrossWt, CargoCapacity, and NumberOfWheels. The TrailerTruck node has two roles, one labeled HasPart and one that restricts the NumberOfWheels role of Truck to the value 18. The notation *v/r* at the target end of the role arrows indicates *value restrictions* or type constraints on the permissible values for those roles.

During the Middle Ages, the critiques by Woods and McDermott would have been unecessary. Logic, as presented by Aristotle and Peter of Spain, was the first of the *seven liberal arts* taught to every university graduate. In fact, the similarity between the KL-ONE network in Figure 3.2 and Peter's version of the Tree of Porphyry in Figure 1.1 is striking: the double-line arrows represent the relationship from species to genus or from one genus to the next higher genus; the roles represent the differentiae that distinguish each category from its genus. The individual concepts in KL-ONE represent the instances at the bottom of the Tree of Porphyry; the generic concepts correspond to the species and genus nodes higher in the tree. Even the process of inheritance is the same: for each defined category, the differentiae are derived by merging all the roles or slots along the path from the defined node up to the top.

CLASSIFICATION.   Besides drawing careful distinctions between the kinds of concepts and links, Brachman et al. (1991) emphasized the importance of automatic classification in *generalization* or *subsumption* hierarchies:

> The most notable feature of Classic's family of languages is the "self-organization" of the concepts defined: Because concepts have clear definitions, it is possible to have the *system* organize them into the subsumption hierarchy, rather than have the user specify their exact place. This is important because standard logic and production systems, for example, do not address the knowledge engineering issue of organizing large collections of knowledge.

Both classification and inheritance are logical operations that can be performed by the standard rules of inference. Systems like KL-ONE and Classic, however, implement them with specialized techniques for high performance. This is a trade-off of expressive power for efficiency: classification and inheritance do not provide the full deductive capability of first-order logic; nor do they provide the full computational power of a programming system; but they do support an important subset of knowledge engineering services efficiently and automatically.

To increase the computational power, frame systems can be made into *hybrids*, in which the frame language is combined with either a programming language or a more expressive version of logic. Brachman, Fikes, and Levesque (1983) designed KRYPTON as a hybrid that combined KL-ONE for reasoning about *terminology* (T-box) with a version of first-order logic for reasoning about *assertions* (A-box). The T-box does automatic classification and high-speed inheritance, and the A-box supplements the T-box with a more expressive system of logic. The hybrid combines the advantages of both: automatic classification in the T-box; greater expressive power in the A-box; and the efficiency of T-box inheritance as a supplement to A-box deduction.

REASONING IN FRAME SYSTEMS. For a knowledge-based configurator, Wright et al. (1993) used a version of Classic implemented in C. They remarked that the language "lacks true disjunction and has no way to express negation. Nevertheless, we have not encountered major problems when we encoded the product knowledge for our AT&T Network Systems products." The knowledge in Classic, as in many related frame systems, is organized in three parts:

1. *T-Box.* A terminological hierarchy of concept definitions, all of which have a form that can be represented by lambda expressions, as in the examples above.

2. *A-Box.* An assertional database of descriptors for individual objects; each descriptor is a conjunction of one or more instantiations of concept definitions that describe the object. Since the database is grouped around objects rather than relations, Brachman et al. (1991) call it an *object-centered* database.

3. *Rule base.* A collection of rules consisting of a left-side L and a right-side R. In each rule, L is a single concept definition, and R is either another concept or a function $r(x)$ whose result is a concept.

The Classic rules therefore correspond to statements of type A in syllogisms:

```
A: Every L is an R.
```

In predicate calculus, each rule can be translated to a statement in one of the following two forms:

$(\forall x{:}L)R(x).$
$(\forall x{:}L)assert(r(x),x).$

The first rule says that every x of type L is also an R. The second rule has the same condition, but it applies a function r, whose result $r(x)$ is a concept that is asserted about x. As an example, $r(x)$ might compute the age of x from the current date and x's date of birth.

The Classic rules are executed whenever an object x is classified as some concept that matches the left side of a rule. If x is classified as an instance of L, then all rules that have L or any supertype of L as their left side are executed. For each one, the right side R or the result of the function call that generates R is instantiated and added to the descriptor of x. Each rule execution corresponds to one inference according to the syllogism Darii:

A: Every L is R.
I: x is L.
I: Therefore, x is R.

Besides Darii for adding new information to the A-Box, Classic uses syllogisms of type Barbara for inheriting information about the concept definitions in the T-Box. Since a trailer truck is defined as a kind of truck, the definition of trailer truck inherits all the properties defined for truck.

Since Classic does not represent negations, it cannot directly express statements of type E or O. However, Classic does allow two concepts, such as Truck and Corvette, to be declared *disjoint*. That declaration is logically equivalent to a statement of type E:

No Corvette is a truck.

Statements of this type can be used as the major premise in the syllogisms Celarent and Ferio. In doing consistency checks, Classic uses inferences of type Celarent to insure that the definitions in the T-box are consistent. When an assertion about an individual is made, it uses inferences of type Ferio to insure that the A-box is consistent. Although these inferences cannot support all of FOL, they can be executed efficiently. For full generality, Classic, like most frame systems, depends on subroutine calls to a host language such as LISP or C.

DEFINITIONAL LOGICS.   Frame systems in the KL-ONE family have merged with restricted versions of typed or sorted logics to form a family of knowledge-representation languages called *definitional logics* or *terminological logics* (Bläsius et al. 1989). The systems in that family are characterized by three common features:

1. Emphasis on the logical operators that are most useful for defining and classifying concept types in a *subsumption* or type-subtype hierarchy.

2. Restrictions that limit the use of operators and inference rules that might make the classification problem computationally inefficient or even undecidable.

3. A formal semantic foundation based on Tarski-style model theory.

Logically, the common core of all these systems is the existential-conjunctive subset of logic with new types defined by monadic lambda-expressions or their equivalent. Classification and consistency checks within that subset can be computed efficiently — in *polynomial time* compared to the *exponential time* that is sometimes required for full first-order logic.

The source of inefficiency, however, is not the expressive power of the logic, but the nature of the problems to be solved. In the original implementation of the LOOM system, Robert MacGregor (1991) restricted its expressive power to the common core of the definitional logics. At the request of the users, MacGregor (1994) designed an extended system called PowerLoom, which supports full first-order logic. In the worst case, those extensions could cause an exponential increase in computing time. In practice, the worst cases are rare; the average increase in computer time for typical applications has been about a factor of 2 in the LISP implementation of PowerLoom. A C++ implementation runs much faster; its speed enables it to outperform LOOM on every problem that LOOM can solve. Furthermore, PowerLoom can solve problems that could not be stated in LOOM.

3.3   Rules and Data

During the 1970s, universities took the lead in designing *rule-based expert systems*, while Ted Codd at IBM developed the theory of *relational databases*. Expert systems and database systems differ more in quantity than in quality: expert systems use repeated executions of rules on relatively small amounts of data, while database systems execute short chains of rules on large amounts of data. The differences, however, are decreasing as database systems perform increasingly complex operations and expert systems are used in larger applications. Today, the SQL language for relational databases has evolved to support the same logical functions as the expert systems of the 1970s and 1980s.

The convergence of the two kinds of systems results from their common logical foundations: they both store data in the existential-conjunctive (EC) subset of logic, and they use the same rules of inference to answer questions, perform updates, and check constraints. The two primary rules are called *modus ponens* (mode of putting) and *modus tollens* (mode of taking away):

- *Modus ponens.* From the formulas p and $(p \supset q)$, infer the consequent q.
- *Modus tollens.* From the formulas $\sim q$ and $(p \supset q)$, infer the denial of the antecedent $\sim p$.

Although each rule of inference is simple by itself, the power comes from the combinations of rules and their repeated executions in lengthy chains and branches. Repeated execution of modus ponens is called *forward chaining*, and repeated modus tollens is called *backward chaining*. As an example, consider the following chain of implications:

$$p \supset q. \ q \supset r. \ r \supset s.$$

Forward chaining proceeds in the direction of the implications: given an assertion p, the first rule leads to the new assertion q; then q plus the second rule produces r; finally r plus the third rule produces s. Backward chaining goes in the reverse direction: given a negation $\sim s$, the last rule produces $\sim r$; then $\sim r$ plus the middle rule produces $\sim q$; and $\sim q$ plus the first rule produces $\sim p$. In applications, forward chaining is commonly used to make insertions and modifications to a database or working memory, and backward chaining is used to answer questions. See Exercises 3.6 to 3.9 for a small expert system that can be implemented in forward-chaining rules to update a database or in backward-chaining rules to answer a question.

The first system that combined forward and backward chaining with a relational database was Planner, designed by Carl Hewitt (1971) at MIT. At Stanford, Ted Shortliffe (1976) designed MYCIN as a backward-chaining system for diagnosing bacterial infections. Its successor EMYCIN became the prototype for a family of commercial expert systems. At Carnegie-Mellon University, early work by Allen Newell and Herbert Simon on the General Problem Solver (1963) evolved into a series of forward-chaining systems. The version called OPS5 (Official Production System #5) became the prototype for another family of commercial expert systems; the CLIPS language, which is used in some examples in this book, is a widely used descendant of OPS5. Robert Kowalski in England, Maarten van Emden in the Netherlands, and Alain Colmerauer in France collaborated to develop logic into a backward-chaining language called Prolog. Ideas from all of these approaches influenced programmers, who combined them with frames, semantic networks, and databases in a sometimes bewildering variety of ways.

MICROPLANNER, PROLOG, AND SQL.   Microplanner, a language derived from Planner, pioneered techniques that have been used in both expert systems and relational databases. As an example, Figure 3.3 shows a database for representing blocks and pyramids that Terry Winograd (1972) implemented in Microplanner. On the right side of Figure 3.3 are two database relations, named Objects and Supports. The Objects relation identifies each object in the stack, its shape, and its color. The supports relation shows which objects are supporters and supportees. Winograd used Microplanner as both a database query language and a problem-solving language for updating and transforming the database. He then wrote a parser that translated English questions to backward-chaining queries and English commands to forward-chaining tasks. The resulting system, called SHRDLU, combined question answering and problem solving with a natural language interface.

To answer the question *Which block supports a pyramid?* SHRDLU generated a sequence of three *goal statements* in Microplanner:

```
(goal (objects ?x1 block ?))
(goal (objects ?x2 pyramid ?))
(goal (supports ?x1 ?x2))
```

The first goal searches the objects relation for an object x1 of shape block, the second searches for an object x2 of shape pyramid, and the third searches the supports relation to determine whether x1 supports x2. The prefix ? marks variables; by itself, the symbol ? is called an *unnamed variable, wild card,* or *don't-care symbol,* which matches any value.

To answer a query, Microplanner, Prolog, and SQL use a technique called *backtracking.* For the sequence of three goals, they try to satisfy each goal by finding appropriate values for the variables x1 and x2. If some goal cannot be satisfied, they

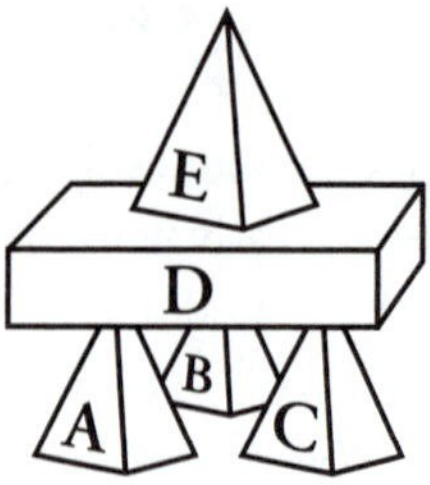

OBJECTS			SUPPORTS	
ID	SHAPE	COLOR	SUPPORTER	SUPPORTEE
A	pyramid	red	A	D
B	pyramid	green	B	D
C	pyramid	yellow	C	D
D	block	blue	D	E
E	pyramid	orange		

FIGURE 3.3 A stack of blocks represented by database relations

backtrack to a previous goal and try a different option. All three systems would perform an equivalent series of operations:

1. Search the objects relation to find some block x1;
   if there are no more blocks, then stop and report failure.

2. Search the objects relation to find some pyramid x2;
   if no more pyramids, backtrack to step 1 to find another block x1.

3. Check whether x1 supports x2;
   if so, stop and return x1 as the answer;
   if not, backtrack to step 2 to find another pyramid x2.

For the database shown in Figure 3.3, they would find the block D at step 1 and the pyramid A at step 2. Since D does not support A, they would backtrack to step 2 to try pyramid B, then C, and finally E. Since D supports E, they would stop with D as the answer for the variable x1.

The equivalent queries in Prolog or SQL have a different syntax, but the same semantics. In Prolog, variables must begin with an uppercase letter, the keyword *goal* is omitted, and the relation name is written outside the parentheses. But Prolog expresses the same three subgoals, which are executed in the same order:

```
objects(X1,block,*) & objects(X2,pyramid,*) & supports(X1,X2).
```

The first subgoal searches the objects relation for a block X1, the second searches objects for a pyramid X2, and the third checks whether X1 supports X2. The asterisk * is the don't-care symbol, which matches anything. In SQL, the syntax is more verbose, but the underlying operations are the same as in Prolog and Microplanner:

```
select supporter
  from supports, objects x1, objects x2
    where x1.shape = 'block'
    and x2.shape = 'pyramid'
    and supporter = x1.id
    and supportee = x2.id
```

This SQL query selects the supporter from the database relations named supports. The objects relation is listed twice on line 2, since the system must find two distinct objects x1 and x2. The where clause expresses the same conditions as the Prolog and Microplanner goals: the shape value for x1 is 'block'; the shape value for x2 is 'pyramid'; the supporter is equal to the id (identifier) of x1; and the supportee is equal to the id of x2.

For a small database like Figure 3.3, backtracking would take very little time, but it could become significant for a large database. To improve performance, most implementations of commercial database systems perform various kinds of optimizations: indexes and hash coding to reduce the amount of search, reordering of subgoals to reduce the amount of backtracking, and compilers to translate interpreted languages to directly executable code. For this example, consider the effect of interchanging the second and third goals:

```
(goal (objects ?x1 block ?))
(goal (supports ?x1 ?x2))
(goal (objects ?x2 pyramid ?))
```

As before, the first search would find the block D as the value for x1. Then the second search would find that D supports E, which would become the value for the variable x2. Finally, the third search would check that E is a pyramid. With this ordering of goals, the correct answer would be found without any backtracking. By reordering the sequence of execution, an optimizer can reduce the number of futile searches while preserving the significant ones.

The optimal ordering of goals depends on the structure of the database and the relative numbers of each kind of object. Since the database in Figure 3.3 has four pyramids but only one block, the best ordering is to search for blocks before pyramids. But if there were fewer pyramids, it would be better to search for a pyramid first. In general, the order of searching is highly data dependent, and database optimizers determine the search order at the time the query is processed. In Prolog and Microplanner, however, there is no automatic reordering of goals, and the programmer must choose the order in advance. It is possible, however, to write a preprocessor that optimizes a query before translating it to Prolog. The Chat-80 query system (Warren & Pereira 1982), which translated English questions to Prolog, performed the same kinds of optimizations used in SQL databases. As this discussion illustrates, logic determines the structure of the query; a good compiler can manage the bookkeeping details to optimize performance. (See Exercise 3.13 for techniques of optimizing performance by reordering the goals.)

PLURALS AND SETS. Moving from singular to plural in English can be done by adding *s* to the nouns and dropping *s* from the verbs. In logic, however, set notation tends to become more cumbersome. As an example, SHRDLU translates the English question *Which blocks are supported by 3 pyramids?* to the following Microplanner code:

```
(find all ?x1
  (goal (objects ?x1 block ?))
  (find 3 ?x2
    (goal (objects ?x2 pyramid ?))
    (goal (supports ?x2 ?x1)) ))
```

The find operator in Microplanner executes a goal repetitively to find as many answers as required: on the first line, all; and on the third line, 3. In English, this code may be paraphrased *Find all x1 where each x1 is a block and it is possible to find three x2 where each x2 is a pyramid and x2 supports x1.*

Prolog requires an equivalent of the find operator to perform repeated searches and accumulate the results. Some versions of Prolog provide a setof predicate that can perform such searches (Walker et al. 1990). It takes three arguments: setof(V,G,L), where V is a variable that keeps track of each object to be found, G is some Prolog goal to be executed repeatedly, and L is a list that accumulates all the values of V that satisfy the goal G. The following Prolog goal uses two nested setof predicates, which correspond to the two nested find operators in Microplanner:

```
setof(X1,
  objects(X1,block,*) &
  setof(X2, objects(X2,pyramid,*) & supports(X2,X1), L2) &
  length(L2,3)),
  L1).
```

In this example, the outer setof predicate starts on line 1 with the variable X1 representing the blocks to be found; lines 2, 3, and 4 represent the goal to be satisfied by appropriate values of X1; and line 5 specifies the list L1, which will accumulate all X1's that satisfy the goal. In English, this Prolog goal may be read *Accumulate a set of all X1 to the list L1, where each X1 is a block and the set of all X2 that are pyramids that support X1 are accumulated to the list L2, which must have a length of 3.*

Since databases are designed to handle large sets, the SQL language has built-in operators to manipulate them. The select verb corresponds to the find operator in Microplanner and the setof predicate in Prolog. SQL also has a special group-by clause that replaces the nested find:

```
select supportee
  from supports, objects x1, objects x2
    where supportee = x1.id
      and x1.shape = 'block'
      and supporter = x2.id
      and x2.shape = 'pyramid'
        group by supportee having count(supporter) = 3
```

In English, this query may be paraphrased *Select all supportees from the supports and objects relations where each supportee is equal to the id of x1 and the shape of x1 is block and each supporter is equal to the id of x2 and the shape of x2 is pyramid and group the answers by supportees, selecting only those supportees that have a count of three supporters.*

As these examples illustrate, all three languages perform equivalent operations to derive the answer; but each of them uses a different syntax. None of them are as simple as the original English question. To simplify the translation from English to logic, conceptual graphs have a notation with a close correspondence to the features of natural languages. The first question *Which block supports a pyramid?* maps to the following CG:

```
[Block: ?]←(Inst)←[Support]→(Thme)→[Pyramid].
```

The question mark in the first concept corresponds to the select verb in SQL. It asks which block is the instrument (Inst) of support, where the theme (Thme) is a pyramid. The relations Inst and Thme are linguistic relations, which are summarized in Appendix B.

The second question *Which blocks are supported by 3 pyramids?* uses plural nouns and passive voice. In conceptual graphs, plurals are marked by the generic plural symbol {*}. The transformation from active to passive causes the relations Inst and Thme to be interchanged:

```
[Block: {*}?]←(Thme)←[Support]→(Inst)→[Pyramid: Col{*}@3].
```

The question mark corresponds to the word *which*; the symbol {*} corresponds to the *s* ending on the nouns; and the prefix Col before the second {*} is an abbreviation of *collectively*, which corresponds to the group-by clause in SQL. The graph may be read *Which blocks are supported by 3 pyramids collectively?* By representing logic in a form that is close to natural language, conceptual graphs can serve as an intermediate language for mapping to lower-level languages like SQL.

RULES AND VIEWS. Rule-based languages like Prolog and CLIPS were specifically designed to perform long chains of implications, but SQL, an acronym for Structured Query Language, had little or no support for implication. Over the years, implications have been added to SQL, but with terminology that obscures their logical foundation: SQL implications used in backward chaining are called *views*, and those used in forward chaining are called *triggers*. To illustrate the correspondence, the following Prolog rule defines the predicate sup_color, which relates supporters to the colors of the objects they support:

```
sup_color(S,C) ← supports(S,X) & objects(X,*,C).
```

The arrow in a Prolog rule points to the left because the inference engine starts with the conclusion and works backward to the antecedent. This rule says that sup_color is true of S and C if S supports some X and X is an object with color C. Following is the corresponding SQL view:

```
create view sup_color
  as select supporter, color
    from supports, objects
      where supportee = id;
```

This statement defines sup_color as a new relation whose values are taken from the supporter of the supports relation and from the color of the objects relation where the supportee in supports is equal to the id in objects. In both SQL and Prolog, relations like sup_color, which are defined by rules, may be used in the same way as relations that are defined by a table of facts.

Although Prolog can represent all SQL views, many features of Prolog such as recursion were not available in SQL. As an example, the following Prolog rule uses recursion to define the predicate ind_supports (indirectly supports):

```
ind_supports(S,X) ← supports(S,X)
                  | supports(S,Y) & ind_supports(Y,X).
```

This rule may be read *S indirectly supports X if either S supports X or S supports some Y and Y indirectly supports X.* After ind_supports has been defined, the setof predicate can be used to find all the direct or indirect supporters of some object, such as the pyramid E:

```
setof(S, ind_supports(S,'E'), L).
```

When this query is executed, the Prolog system accumulates all the supporters of E and puts them in the list L. In this case, L contains the other four objects, [A,B,C,D].

The lack of recursion in SQL has been a handicap for many common applications: listing parts and subparts in a bill of materials; searching the management hierarchy of a business; or finding dependencies in a schedule of tasks and subtasks. In such applications, the only way to solve those problems has been to invoke multiple SQL queries from a *host language* like COBOL or C. Finally, some implementations of SQL have begun to support recursion, which is scheduled to become standard in a future version called SQL3. Following is a recursive query that finds all objects that directly or indirectly support the pyramid E:

```
with ind_supports (supporter, supportee)
  as ((select *
      from supports)
    union all
    (select s.supporter, x.supportee
      from supports s, ind_supports x
```

```
      where s.supportee=x.supporter))
select supporter
   from ind_supports
   where supportee='E'
```

In this example, the with clause defines a recursive table named ind_supports, and the select statement at the end retrieves all objects that support E. The difference between Prolog and SQL results from the select statements, which retrieve an entire set at once. Then the SQL definition uses the union operator to combine the sets. In Prolog, however, the operators normally process one item at a time; to collect all the answers to a query, the setof predicate must be used.

LOGICAL FOUNDATIONS.   SQL, Prolog, and Microplanner use the same strategy for handling quantifiers: the variables in a query are governed by existential quantifiers, and the variables in a rule are governed by universal quantifiers. This convergence on a common strategy is no accident. It follows from the logical form of the database and the algorithms for searching it. Every database used by those languages — as well as every commercial database, whether relational, hierarchical, or object-oriented — implements the existential-conjunctive subset of logic. The two database relations in Figure 3.3, for example, can be mapped to that form with only the $\exists$ quantifier and the $\land$ operator. Every row of the objects relation maps to a proposition of the following form:

$$(\exists x{:}\text{Object})(\text{id}(x,\text{A}) \land \text{shape}(x,\text{pyramid}) \land \text{color}(x,\text{red})).$$

This formula says *There exists an x of type object whose id is A and whose shape is pyramid and whose color is red.* Every row of the supports relation maps to a proposition of the form,

$$(\exists x{:}\text{Support})(\text{supportee}(x,\text{A}) \land \text{supporter}(x,\text{D})).$$

This formula says *There exists an x of type support whose supportee is A and whose supporter is D.* This small subset of logic is sufficient to represent all the things that exist in the universe, their properties, and their relationships to every other thing. It forms the common logical core of every software system that stores and retrieves data of any kind.

EC logic can represent everything stored in a database, but it cannot represent negations, disjunctions, implications, or universal quantifiers. Therefore, it cannot represent queries of the following forms:

- *Which pyramids are not supported by a block?*
- *Is any block red or yellow?*
- *Does every block support a pyramid?*
- *Which block supports every orange pyramid?*

The three languages discussed so far can indeed represent these queries. They do so by a metalevel technique called *negation as failure*: if they fail to find an answer in the database, they assume falsehood. When negation is used in all possible combinations with ∃ and ∧, the logic can then represent the universal quantifier and all Boolean operators. The universal quantifier ∀, for example, is defined by the following equivalence:

$$(\forall x)P(x) \text{ is equivalent to } \sim(\exists x)\sim P(x).$$

Suppose that $P(x)$ means "x is a person." The formula for "Every x is a person" would then be equivalent to the formula for the sentence "It is false that there exists an x that is not a person."

Since database languages represent ∀ by combining negation with ∃, they usually require double negations to express queries with universal quantifiers. As an example, the query *Which block supports every orange pyramid?* would be represented by the following Prolog goal:

```
objects(X1,block,*) & ê(objects(X2,pyramid,orange) & êsupports(X1,X2)).
```

In English, this goal may be read *Find a block X1 where it is false that there exists an X2 where X2 is an orange pyramid and X1 does not support X2*. The same combination of double negations is also used to represent universal quantifiers in Microplanner and SQL. Following is the SQL query on the left with the corresponding parts of the Prolog goal on the right:

SQL QUERY	PROLOG GOAL
`select id.x1`	
`from    objects x1`	`objects(X1,`
`where  x1.shape = 'block'`	`block,*)`
`  and not exists`	`& ê`
`    (select *`	`(`
`    from objects x2`	`objects(X2,`
`    where x2.shape = 'pyramid'`	`pyramid,`
`      and x2.color = 'orange'`	`orange)`
`      and not exists`	`& ê`
`        (select *`	
`        from    supports`	`supports(`
`        where   supporter = x1.id`	`X1,`
`          and   supportee = x2.id))`	`X2) ).`

This convoluted way of writing queries that represent the word *every* follows from the common semantics of languages as seemingly different as Prolog and SQL.

FORWARD CHAINING. In Prolog and SQL, backward chaining is used to answer a question without causing any side effects. A forward-chaining rule, however, performs some action, which normally has a side effect of changing something in working memory. Such rules have two parts: a *pattern* that is matched to something in the database or working memory, and an *action* to be performed if the pattern match succeeds:

```
pattern => action.
```

This kind of rule is called a *production rule*. When it is executed, the inference engine searches working memory for some combination of data that matches the pattern. If the match succeeds, the action on the right is executed to assert, retract, or modify facts or to call external programs that perform some computation. Unlike the left arrow in a backward-chaining language like Prolog, the arrow in a forward-chaining rule typically points to the right.

An important use of forward-chaining rules is to check and correct possible violations of *integrity constraints* on database relations. In SHRDLU, for example, an object of shape box is defined to *contain* any object it supports. Therefore, SHRDLU checks every new assertion for the supports relation to determine whether the supporter is a box. If so, it asserts that the box contains the supportee. Following is the equivalent rule in CLIPS:

```
(defrule checkForBoxSupporter
  (supports ?x ?y)
    (objects ?x box ?)
=>
  (assert (contains ?x ?y)) )
```

The pattern part of this rule is invoked for every assertion that some x supports some y. Then if x is an object of shape box, the action part asserts that x contains y. To make the contains relation transitive, the following rule checks whether the supporter x is contained in some z. If so, it also asserts that z contains y.

```
(defrule makeContainsTransitive
  (supports ?x ?y)
  (contains ?z ?x)
=>
  (assert (contains ?z ?y)) )
```

Together, these two rules maintain the consistency of the contains, supports, and objects relations with respect to the constraint that boxes contain anything they support, either directly or indirectly. The rule that makes the contains relation transitive may be invoked recursively if there happens to be a nest of boxes in which the outer boxes contain the inner boxes as well as their contents.

Forward chaining rules may also be used to retract an assertion after updating the database with the implications of the assertion. The following rule updates the supports relation after an assertion that some object x is put on another object y:

```
(defrule updateEffectsOfPutOn
  ?newPutOn <- (putOn ?x ?y)
=>
  (if ?oldSupport <- (supports ?z ?x)
    then (retract ?oldSupport) )
  (assert (supports ?y ?x))
  (retract ?newPutOn) )
```

This rule asserts that if x is put on y, the new supporter of x is y. If x had been supported by some z, the rule would retract the information about the old support. It also retracts the putOn assertion itself, whose effects have been taken into account by changes to the database. To avoid deleting the new assertion, the rule must not assert the new supporter before retracting the old one. In pure logic, ordering cannot affect the results, but the action part of a forward-chaining rule introduces procedural dependencies.

The rule for putOn illustrates the *cascading updates* that often occur in databases and knowledge bases. A single assertion about putOn causes one assertion and one retraction for the supports relation. Then the two rules for contains would be triggered by the supports assertion to check whether the supporter was a box or was contained in a box. In the most common case where x is not being moved into or out of a box, the pattern parts of those rules would not match, and no further updates would occur. If x happened to be put into a box, those rules would update the contains relation. But if x were being removed from a box, the putOn rule would violate the constraints on the contains relation. See Exercise 3.15 and the answers at the back of the book for further discussion of the putOn rule and the revisions that are necessary to preserve the constraints on the contains relation.

SQL TRIGGERS. To support forward-chaining rules in SQL, some versions implement *triggers*, which will become standard in SQL3 (Chamberlin 1996). Each trigger is invoked by an insertion, deletion, or update to a database relation. The two CLIPS rules for preserving the constraints on the contains relation can be rewritten as SQL triggers, but the rules must be repackaged: one rule is triggered by insertions to the contains relation, and two others are triggered by insertions to the supports relation. The following trigger checks whether the new containee is also a supporter. Like the CLIPS rules, it may make recursive insertions into the contains relation.

```
create trigger check_container
  after insert on contains
  referencing new as x
  for each row
    insert into contains
      select x.container supportee
      from supports
      where x.containee = supporter
```

This trigger inserts another row (x.container, supportee) into the contains relation for each row in which the new containee is also a supporter.

The next two triggers check for insertions to the supports relation: one checks whether the new supporter is a box, and the other checks whether the new supporter is contained in some box. Both triggers could be invoked if a box is being inserted into a box or onto some object that is already in a box. The following trigger checks whether shape of the new supporter is a box. If so, it inserts the row (x.supporter, x.supportee) into the contains relation. The effect is to copy the new rows of the supports relation whose supporter is a box into the contains relation.

```
create trigger check_box_supporter
  after insert on supports
  referencing new as x
  for each row
  when ('box'=(select shape from objects
    where id=x.supporter) )
  insert into contains
    values(x.supporter, x.supportee)
```

The next trigger checks whether the new supporter is contained in a box. If so, it inserts all rows of the form (container, x.supportee) into the contains relation to show that everything supported by x.supporter also has the same container.

```
create trigger check_supporter_in_box
  after insert on supports
  referencing new as x
  for each row
  when (x.supporter in
    (select containee from contains) )
  insert into contains
    select container x.supportee
    from contains
    where containee = x.supporter
```

Both of these triggers may cause recursive insertions into contains. The complexity of these examples results from the complex ways that boxes and other objects can be stacked and nested. In a procedural language, the programs would be even more complex.

IMPLEMENTING LOGIC IN PRACTICAL SYSTEMS.   In the 1970s, the research on expert systems and relational databases showed that logic-based systems could be fast enough to compete with traditional computer programs. During the 1980s, the research was implemented in practical systems. The rule-based expert systems solved problems that had been abandoned as too complex to be programmed in conventional languages. In several debates on database languages, Ted Codd, Chris Date, and other relational advocates showed that SQL was simpler and more concise than an older language developed by the CODASYL DBTG (Data Base Task Group). In reply, one of the CODASYL defenders made the infamous claim that "programmers enjoy a challenge." Yet SQL was not widely accepted until relational databases could compete with the older systems in performance.

Microplanner was ahead of its time in implementing forward chaining and backward chaining over a relational database. But even on the small databases in SHRDLU, it acquired a reputation for inefficiency. Gerald Sussman and Drew McDermott (1972) developed a rival system called Conniver, which they described in the report "Why Conniving is Better than Planning." The design goal for Conniver was to improve performance by giving programmers more control over the search strategy. Unfortunately, it led them to use clever tricks rather than clean logical design.

After Microplanner, most rule-based systems were specialized for one way of applying rules: backward chaining for Prolog and languages in the MYCIN tradition; and forward chaining for languages like OPS5 and CLIPS. Prolog has a simpler structure than Microplanner, which supports more efficient compilers and interpreters. Prolog also uses a powerful pattern-matching technique called *unification*, which supports a logic-based method for manipulating data structures. To improve the speed of pattern matching, CLIPS and other languages derived from OPS5 maintain a *rete network*, which maintains pointers to partial matches and helps avoid redundant searches. When CLIPS rules are entered, the compiler constructs a network of pointers from data elements to the rules that might be affected by updates to the data.

Performance is the main reason for the structural differences between the CLIPS rules and the SQL triggers. In CLIPS, the makeContainsTransitive rule, for example, is invoked by an update to either the supports or the contains relations. The rete network enables either update to invoke the same rule. Since SQL databases do not use a rete network, the SQL programmer must explicitly state the conditions for invoking the triggers. For the check_container trigger, the condition is "after insert on contains"; for the other two triggers, the condition is "after insert on supports."

As these examples illustrate, logic serves as the common foundation for database and expert systems. Good compilers can simplify the interfaces by deriving the information necessary to optimize performance directly from the logic. Without an optimizer, Microplanner was inefficient even on the toy databases in SHRDLU. With optimization, SQL database systems routinely manage terabytes of data while responding to requests from thousands of users around the world.

3.4 Object-Oriented Systems

The *object-oriented programming systems* (OOPS) combine a declarative style for specifying objects with a procedural style for defining the actions by and upon those objects. Object-oriented declarations, which specify the same kind of information as frames, are organized in a type or class hierarchy that supports the same kind of inheritance. Instead of separating the declarations that define an object from the procedures that operate on them, the O-O systems integrate the declarations and the operations for each type of object in a single package. In effect, an O-O language has three components: a programming language, a frame system, and a structure that *encapsulates* the procedures with the frames. Various kinds of languages have been extended to object-oriented languages: C to C++; Prolog to Object Prolog; COBOL to Object COBOL; SQL to OQL; and CLIPS to COOL.

O-O DECLARATIONS.   To illustrate the similarities and differences, the frame examples can be translated to Java, one of the most popular object-oriented languages. Following is a Java declaration for a *class* that corresponds to the Truck frame:

```
public class Truck extends Vehicle {
    // Define an instance variable for each slot in the frame.
    private WtMeasure unloadedWt, maxGrossWt;
    private VolMeasure cargoCapacity;
    private Wheel[] wheels;

    // The methods return the current values of the private variables.
    public WtMeasure unloadedWt() {return unloadedWt;};
    public WtMeasure maxGrossWt() {return maxGrossWt;};
    public VolMeasure cargoCapacity() {return cargoCapacity;};
    public int numberOfWheels() {return wheels.length;};
}
```

The top line declares Truck as an *extension* or subtype of Vehicle. The Truck class inherits declarations from the Vehicle class in the same way frames inherit from supertypes. The *instance variables*, which correspond to the slots in frames, are declared *private* to restrict access by other objects. To read or modify them, other objects must invoke one of the procedures or *methods* defined in the Truck class or one of its subclasses. The TrailerTruck class extends Truck with another variable for the trailer and a method called a *constructor*, which initializes some of the variables:

```
public class TrailerTruck extends Truck {
  // Inherits from Truck and adds the following:
  private protected Trailer trailer;

  // Constructor to initialize each new TrailerTruck.
  public TrailerTruck() {
    trailer = new Trailer;
    wheels = new Wheel[18];
    for (int i=0; i<18; i++)
      wheels[i] = new Wheel;
    }
  }
```

The constructor creates a new object of type Trailer, which it assigns to the variable named trailer. To initialize the variable wheels, it creates an array to hold 18 wheels and creates a new instance of Wheel for each element of the array. Some other Java program could create a new TrailerTruck with an assignment statement like the following:

```
tt = new TrailerTruck;
```

When this statement is executed, the TrailerTruck constructor is invoked, and a pointer to the new TrailerTruck is assigned to the variable tt. The Wheel and Trailer classes might have their own constructors, which in turn could create other objects.

MAPPING FRAMES AND RULES TO OBJECTS.   The supertype slot in a frame corresponds to the extends qualifier in a Java class definition. The other slots correspond to instance variables. The inheritance of slots in frames corresponds to the inheritance of variables and methods. Yet neither the frames nor the purely declarative definitions in Java provide a complete programming system. Each of them must be supplemented with procedural code in order to do something useful. Frames and O-O systems differ in the way they allow procedures to access the slots or instance variables:

- To a host language like LISP or C, frames look like a network of globally accessible records. The programs can read the slots, modify them, and follow chains of pointers from one frame to another. Although a frame system may have a recommended set of operators for doing "safe" operations on the frames, a programmer who uses the host language can ignore the recommendations and manipulate the frames as if they were ordinary data structures.

- In an O-O system, the objects can be *encapsulated.* Only programs or methods in the declaration of the object class or one of its subclasses can access private variables directly. To access information from an object, external programs must invoke one of the class methods, which have complete control over the local data.

The C++ language, for example, combines the procedural language C with a frame system for declarations and inheritance. What distinguishes C++ from a hybrid of C with a separate frame system is the packaging that supports encapsulation and the strict type checking that enforces it.

Compilers can automate the translations from logic to the declarative parts of object definitions. Frames in PowerLoom have been compiled to C++ declarations, and type definitions in Cyc have been compiled to Java (Peterson et al. 1998). Generating procedural code from logic specifications is more difficult, but many special cases can be automated:

- *Backward chaining.* Deterministic Horn-clause rules, which require no backtracking, can be translated to if-then statements and recursive subroutine calls. This technique, called *recursive descent,* is widely used to translate grammar rules to executable code. Terry Winograd used it to parse a subset of English for his SHRDLU system.

- *Forward chaining.* To support an SQL-style of triggers, the Java library defines two classes, called *Observer* and *Observable.* Each object of type Observable maintains a list of pointers to objects of type Observer, which may be affected by changes in the observable data. Whenever a change occurs, the observable sends an update message to each of its observers. A method in the observer can then perform the equivalent of the action part of a CLIPS rule or an SQL trigger.

See Chapter 4 for the representation of general procedures in a declarative style.

ENCAPSULATION.   By encapsulating objects, O-O languages provide a way of distinguishing the external behavior of objects from their internal structure. The first O-O language was Simula-67 (Dahl & Nygaard 1968), which was designed for simulating a system of interacting objects. In an O-O simulation, the Truck class might have methods that determine how trucks move and interact with traffic signals, warehouses, and dispatchers. The way an individual truck behaves is determined by its internal structure and processes, not by an external program. In effect, each object instance is an autonomous agent whose behavior is determined by its class methods and the inputs it receives from other objects.

Encapsulation helps to localize information about each object, but relationships between objects introduce further complexities. As an example, consider the three classes Truck, Person, and Driver. The Truck and Person classes are distinct, but Driver would be a subclass of Person. Somehow, trucks and drivers should be associated, but the association is not a permanent one:

- At different times, each driver might drive different trucks, and each truck might be driven by different drivers.

- If the information about the current driver is placed in the Truck class, the question *Which truck is Sam driving?* would require a search through all the trucks in the database.

- If the information about the truck is placed in the Driver class, the question *Who is driving truck #587?* would require a search of every driver.

- If duplicate information is placed in both the Truck and the Driver classes, then the possibility of *update anomalies* arises. Each time a truck is reassigned, three objects must be changed: the Truck object, the old Driver, and the new Driver. Errors could arise if different programs happened to access data from those objects while they were being modified.

- A common technique in frame and O-O systems is to create a special class or type called Trip, which would specify the truck, driver, dates, cargo, starting point, and destination for a single trip. A new instance of Trip would be created for each assignment of a truck and driver, and no instance would ever be reused. The instance object for the driver Sam and the instance for truck #587 would each contain a pointer to their common instance of Trip.

Objects like Trip can simplify the update problem, but further conventions are needed for distributed systems. Different branch offices in different cities might have local databases for keeping track of trucks, drivers, and trips. When the trucks and drivers are moving from city to city, a safe and secure locking and updating strategy is essential. Such issues have been studied in great detail for database systems.

Since frames lack the O-O encapsulations, frame systems permit coding techniques that might compromise the integrity of the objects. Yet encapsulation is not always an advantage. The proliferation of methods whose only purpose is to return the current value of a variable such as weight or cargo capacity increases the overhead. Although the time to invoke one method is negligible, the overhead may become significant in operations on large sets and databases. A query about the average weight of all trucks could take more time in an O-O system than in a system that scans a linked list of frames. To improve performance, some languages like

C++ and Java allow "friendly" programs to access their local variables. Such compromises are useful, but potentially dangerous.

LOGIC-BASED O-O SYSTEMS. Frame systems and O-O systems that depend on procedures cannot state a general proposition directly. Instead, they encode the proposition in some procedure that determines how it is used. Consider the information that every trailer truck has eighteen wheels. That information could be used for many different purposes: to answer the question *How many wheels does a trailer truck have?*; to initialize the number of wheels, as in the Java definition for Trailer-truck; or to print an error message when a trailer truck with a different number of wheels is found. In logic, a single assertion could be used for all those purposes, but in a procedural system, the information must be encoded in a different program for each purpose. Besides the programming effort for writing multiple encodings, inconsistencies can arise when different parts of the code are updated and modified by different programmers at different times.

To represent the encapsulated objects of object-oriented systems, logic must support *contexts* whose structure reflects the nest of encapsulations. In conceptual graphs, contexts are represented by concept boxes that contain nested graphs that describe the referent of the concept. In predicate calculus, the nesting can be represented by the *description predicate* dscr(x,p), which relates an object x to a proposition p that describes x. Chapter 5 discusses the semantics of contexts, the description predicate, and the rules of inference for importing and exporting information from the contexts. To illustrate the encapsulation, Figure 3.4 shows a graph for a birthday party that occurred at the point in time (PTim) of 26 May 1996.

The concept box with the label BirthdayParty says that there exists a birthday party, but it doesn't specify any details. The PTim relation indicates that it occurred on the date 26 May 1996. Figure 3.4 may be translated to the following formula in predicate calculus:

($\exists x$:BirthdayParty)(date(26May1996) $\land$ ptim(x,26May1996)).

This formula says that there exists a birthday party x, 26 May 1996 is a date, and the point in time of x was 26 May 1996. To see the details of what happened during the party, it is necessary to open the box and look inside. With a graphic display and a mouse for pointing, a person could click on the box, and the system would expand it to the context in Figure 3.5. In that graph, the large outer box is the same

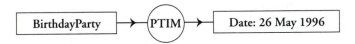

FIGURE 3.4 A birthday party on 26 May 1996

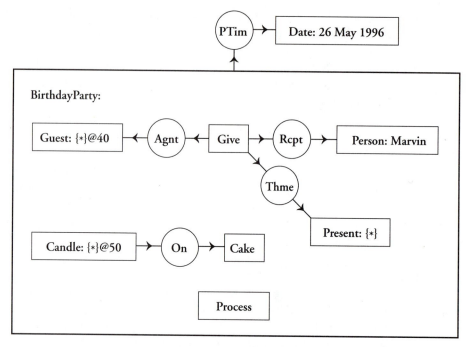

FIGURE 3.5 Expanded view of the birthday party context

concept of type BirthdayParty that was shown in Figure 3.4, but now the expanded box contains nested conceptual graphs that describe the party.

Inside the large box in Figure 3.5, the first graph says that 40 guests are giving presents to a person named Marvin, and the second one says that 50 candles are on a cake. The relations Agnt, Ptnt, and Rcpt are linguistic case relations that indicate the agent (guests who are giving), the patient (presents that are being given), and the recipient (the birthday boy, Marvin). The notation {*} indicates a set of things, and the qualifiers "@40" and "@50" indicate the count of elements in the sets.

The nested graphs in Figure 3.5 describe the birthday party. In predicate calculus, the corresponding formula uses the description predicate $dscr(b,p)$, which relates the birthday party b to a nested proposition that describes it:

$(\exists b$:BirthdayParty$)($date$(26$May$1996) \wedge$ ptim$(b,26$May$1996) \wedge$
    dscr$(b,$
        $(\exists x$:Set$)(\exists z_1$:Give$)(\exists z_2$:Set$)(\exists y$:Set$)(\exists z_3$:Cake$)(\exists p$:Process$)$
            $($person$($Marvin$) \wedge$ rcpt$(z_1,$Marvin$) \wedge$
            count$(x,40) \wedge (\forall m_1 \epsilon x)($guest$(m_1) \wedge$ agnt$(z_1,m_1)) \wedge$
            count$(y,50) \wedge (\forall m_2 \epsilon y)($candle$(m_2) \wedge$ on$(m_2,z_3)) \wedge$
            $(\forall m_3 \epsilon z_2)($present$(m_3) \wedge$ thme$(z_1,m_3))$ $))).$

This formula says that there is a birthday party b on the date 26 May 1996; b is described by the proposition that there exist a set x, an instance of giving z_1, a set z_2, a set y, a cake z_3, and a process p; the person Marvin is the recipient of the giving z_1; the set x has 40 members, and for all m_1 in x, m_1 is a guest and m_1 is an agent of z_1; the set y has 50 members, and for all m_2 in y, m_2 is a candle and m_2 is on the cake z_3; and for all m_3 in the set z_2, m_3 is a present and m_3 is a theme of the giving z_1. The logical effect of the context box or the description predicate is to *quote* the nested proposition, which may hold under different conditions from the containing context.

ZOOMING IN AND ZOOMING OUT.   At the bottom of the box in Figure 3.5 is another concept [Process]. By clicking on that box, a person could expand it to a context that shows the steps in the process. In Figure 3.6, the process box contains three other nested contexts: a state with duration 15 seconds, followed by an event that occurs at the point in time 20:23:19 Greenwich Mean Time, followed by a state with duration 5 seconds. The relation Dur represents duration, PTim represents point in time, and Succ represents successor. Dur links a context to a time interval during which the graphs that describe the context are true; PTim links a context to a time point, which may be considered a very short interval whose starting and ending times are not distinguishable.

At the top of Figure 3.6, two new variables *x and *y appear on the concepts of the 40 guests and the 50 candles. Those variables mark defining nodes that are referenced by variables of the form ?x for the guests and ?y for the candles in graphs nested inside the process context. In the pure graph notation, variables are not needed, since coreference links are shown by dotted lines. But when the graphs contain a lot of detail, variables can help reduce the clutter. An interactive display could provide an option of showing coreference links either as variables or as dotted lines.

In Figure 3.6, the graphs nested inside the concepts of type State and Event are too small to be read. By clicking on the box for the first state, a person could zoom in to see the details in Figure 3.7. The expanded state shows the candles ?y burning while the guests ?x sing the song "Happy Birthday." Then the event box could be expanded to show Marvin blowing out the candles, and the next state would show the candles smoking for 5 seconds. Context boxes can encapsulate details at any level. At a lower level, the concept [Sing] might be expanded to show one guest singing in the key of G while another is singing in G flat. In this way, the encapsulated description of any object could be contained in a single context box, which could be expanded to show the details or contracted to hide them.

TRANSLATIONS TO NATURAL LANGUAGE.   Although conceptual graphs are quite readable, they are a formal language that would normally be used by program-

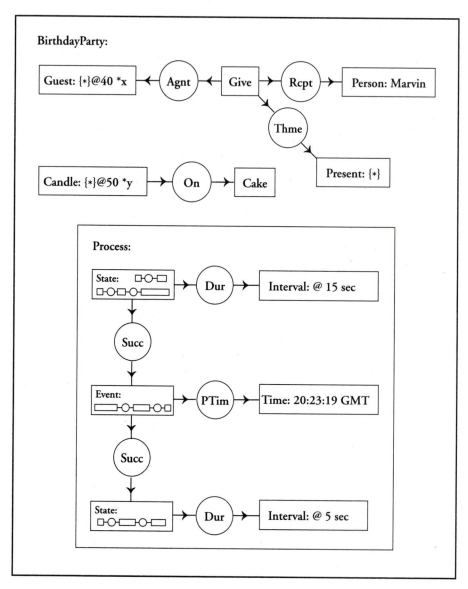

FIGURE 3.6 Expanded view of the birthday party to show details of the process

mers, systems analysts, and other professionals. End users would usually prefer natural languages. But even programmers use natural language for comments, documentation, and help facilities. Since conceptual graphs were originally designed as a semantic representation for natural language, they can help form a bridge between computer languages and the natural languages that everyone reads,

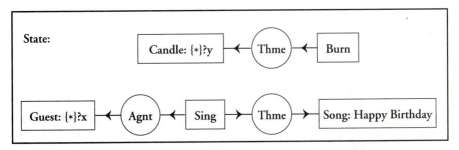

FIGURE 3.7 Expanded view of the first state of the process in Figure 3.6

writes, and speaks. A stylized English description could be generated by translating each context of Figure 3.6 to a sentence or paragraph:

> There is a birthday party b on 26 May 1996.
>
> In b, 40 guests x are giving presents to the person Marvin. 50 candles y are on a cake.
>
> There is a process p.
>
> In the process p, there is a state s_1 with a duration of 15 seconds. The state s_1 is followed by an event e at the time 20:23:15 GMT. The event e is followed by a state s_2 with a duration of 5 seconds.
>
> In the state s_1, the candles y are burning. The guests x are singing the song "Happy Birthday."
>
> In the event e, the person Marvin blows out the candles y.
>
> In the state s_2, the candles y are generating smoke.

Translating a natural language to a formal language is difficult because of the ambiguities in ordinary language, but translating a statement in an unambiguous formal language to a natural language sentence is much simpler. The hardest part of language generation is the task of deciding what to say and how to organize it in sentences and paragraphs. For stylized English, that process can be simplified by mapping the context structure of conceptual graphs to the English paragraphs. Such stylized language may not be elegant, but it is useful for comments and explanations.

OBJECTS AND THEORIES. There is a close correspondence between the hierarchy of theories in the ontology of Figure 2.14 and the hierarchy of types or classes in O-O systems. The two kinds of hierarchies can be compared point by point:

- Each object-oriented class corresponds to some type in the ontology.
- For each object class, the preconditions and postconditions for its methods or procedures are the axioms of the theory associated with the corresponding type in the ontology.

- Every instantiation of an object class is described by propositions (or their abbreviations in frame-like slots) that are consistent with the axioms.
- Multiple inheritance in O-O systems corresponds to multiple inheritance in the hierarchy of theories. If object class C inherits from classes A and B, then the theory for C is formed by merging the axioms for A and B.

The preconditions, postconditions, and class definitions can all be specified in first-order logic.

The biggest difference between procedural and logic-based O-O languages lies in the implicit order of execution in the procedural code. For subjects that have a natural time sequence, that implicit order can often simplify the representation. For subjects that have no natural sequence, the order of execution is irrelevant or potentially misleading. Graphics user interfaces (GUIs), for example, are especially difficult to program in procedural languages because the order of execution is not determined by the linear flow of the program instructions, but by the user's selections on a computer display. To accommodate the nonsequential dependencies, GUIs are usually driven by an *event-based* mechanism that invokes short procedures in an order determined by the user. Chapter 4 presents an event-based formalism called *Petri nets*, their application to concurrent processes, and their translation to logic.

3.5   Natural Language Semantics

Natural languages are the ultimate knowledge representation languages. They are used by everyone from infants learning their first words to scientists discussing the most advanced theories of the universe. Aristotle began his study of knowledge representation with an analysis of the semantic categories and relationships expressed in natural language. Those same categories correspond to the types or classes that are encoded in the latest AI languages and object-oriented systems. Natural language semantics is related to knowledge representation as physics is related to mathematics: one is a source of empirical data, and the other is a source of rich formalisms and computable operations. They stimulate and complement each other.

After thousands of years of evolution in intimate contact with every aspect of human experience, natural languages have attained a greater flexibility and expressive power than any artificial language. Mathematics is more concise because its vocabulary is so small that each concept can be represented by a single character; the equation "$2+2=4$" uses the same number of symbols as the English "Two plus two equals four." Besides the limited vocabulary, the limited syntax of mathematics and programming languages also helps to avoid ambiguity and vagueness. There is no such thing as a vague computer program. Like the magic incantations in Goethe's "Sorcerer's Apprentice" (*Zauberlehrling*), a program always does something very precise, although what it does may have no relationship to what was intended. Despite their potential ambiguity and vagueness, natural languages serve as the ultimate foundation for defining the formal languages. The textbooks that define and explain them are all written in natural languages. Even when an artificial language is defined in an artificial metalanguage, the original metalanguage used to start the cycle of definitions is always a natural language.

BACKGROUND KNOWLEDGE. The expressive power of natural languages, which is their greatest strength, is also one of the greatest obstacles to efficient, computable operations. Since the early 1950s, highly talented linguists, logicians, and computer scientists have been working on the problem of language under-standing by computer. Yet no program today can read and understand a newspaper at the level of an average high-school student. The crux of the problem is not in syntax, because modern grammars and parsers are powerful enough to analyze almost any sentence in a newspaper in a fraction of a second. The major difficulty is to represent the vast amount of background knowledge necessary to understand those sentences. To illustrate the issues, consider the problem of designing a system that could produce a satisfactory response to the following request, entered either by voice or by keyboard:

> *Show me the scene from* Casablanca *where Humphrey Bogart says "Play it again, Sam."*

There are two distinct parts to this problem. The first part requires the system to analyze the sentence outside the quotation as language about a movie. The second part requires the system to find a scene in the movie that contains the quoted sentence (which does not actually occur in the form quoted). Both parts of the sentence contain problems, but of very different kinds:

1. Understanding the part outside the quotation marks requires a parser that is able to analyze every word and its syntactic and semantic role in the sentence. It also requires a semantic interpreter that can find and use a considerable amount of domain knowledge about movies: e.g., Casablanca is a movie rather than a city; Humphrey Bogart is an actor who portrays a character in the movie; a movie consists of a time-indexed sequence of scenes; and scenes contain dialog made up of sentences spoken by characters portrayed by actors.

2. Finding the quoted sentence raises a new set of problems. Searching the sound track for a spoken sentence is a difficult and time-consuming task. If the script of the movie is searched instead, the scenes must be cross-indexed to the lines of the script. The sentence as quoted never occurs in the script, but there is a passage where the character Bogart portrays tells the character named Sam to "play it."

Putting enough domain knowledge into the system to handle problems of the first kind is not easy, but for small domains, it can be done. Yet current systems require highly skilled knowledge engineers who are familiar with both the application domain and the linguistic patterns used in talking about the domain. For each domain, someone would have to add different knowledge and vocabulary. The following examples illustrate typical applications:

- Understanding a question about a Tang Dynasty horse and giving a museum visitor directions to the appropriate floor, wing, room, and exhibit case,
- Finding a person in a large organization by function rather than by name; e.g., "Find me a programmer at Chase Manhattan Bank who is familiar with computer graphics,"
- Selecting one of 500 television channels that might have a program that matches the range of interests of two or more people in a family.

In current natural language systems, the background knowledge for understanding these questions must be hand-coded by a linguist or a trained specialist who has mastered the specialized formats and commands of the computational system. The challenge is to design a system that could acquire sufficient background knowledge from a museum guide, an administrator in a company personnel department, or an assistant producer at a TV station — especially if the guide, administrator, or producer had no prior linguistic or computer training.

The second part of the problem involves *information retrieval,* which could be done by a search engine that matches words in the request to words in the database. One search engine, which is devoted to finding quotations from famous movies, failed to find the quotation when given the request "play it again," but it succeeded when given just the two words "play it." Another search engine, which invokes several others to find as much material as possible on the World Wide Web, is appropriately named "Dogpile." For this example, the pile includes the exact quotation and even an excerpt of the soundtrack with Humphrey Bogart speaking it. To find that selection, however, the user must either wade through thousands of irrelevant texts or make intelligent guesses of keywords to narrow down the selection. A more challenging task is to find the name of the song Sam plays. A person who already knows the exact name, "As Time Goes By," can find the lyrics by giving the name to the search engine, but it is much harder to find the song without giving its name. Keyword search is highly effective when the person asking the question already knows some of the words that occur in the answer. Finding conceptual patterns expressed in different words or in a different language is much more difficult.

For a museum search, the keywords *Tang* and *horse* would quickly locate the correct exhibit. The words *China* and *horse* might find the answer, but with some extraneous references to pottery and draft animals. To find a programmer who knows about graphics would be easy if the bank had a department with the word *graphics* in the title. Otherwise, a graphics expert might be working in a publication department or an international loan department. For selecting TV channels, the result is more likely to be influenced by the advertisers who are promoting their wares than by the people who are looking for entertainment. The problem of getting the best answer to any question depends less on the input language than on the way the knowledge in the system is organized, represented, and used.

LANGUAGE ANALYSIS.   To illustrate the difference between what is easy and what is difficult, it is helpful to consider an example from an implemented system. The following sentence from an Italian newspaper was successfully processed by a system called DANTE, which was implemented by Velardi et al. (1988).

L'associazione degli industriali a approvato un nuovo piano di investimenti nel mezzogiorno.
(The association of the industrialists approved a new project of investments in the south.)

DANTE took input sentences from news services and analyzed their word forms (*morphology*), their grammar (*syntax*), and their meaning (*semantics*). Figure 3.8 shows the stages of processing a sentence and translating it to conceptual graphs.

Each of the three stages in sentence processing depends on a repository of linguistic knowledge: dictionaries of word forms for the morphology, grammar rules for the syntax, and conceptual patterns for the semantics. Following is a brief summary of what happens in each stage:

1. *Morphology.* The first stage looks up all the words in a dictionary, determines their root forms plus inflections, expands contractions, and finds the parts of speech. The word *degli* (of the) is a contraction of the preposition *di* (of) and the masculine plural article *gli* (the). The word *approvato* (approved) is the past participle of the verb *approvare* (to approve).

2. *Syntax.* The second stage uses grammar rules to compute a *parse tree*, which represents the syntax as a combination of phrases and subphrases. On the right of Figure 3.8 is a tree for the first noun phrase (NP). That phrase has three parts: an article, *la*; a noun, *associazione* (association); and a prepositional phrase (PP). The prepositional phrase has two parts: a preposition, *di* (of); and another noun phrase, *gli industriali* (the industrialists).

3. *Semantics.* Finally, a *semantic interpreter* scans the parse tree and translates it to a conceptual graph that represents the meaning. The graph at the bottom of Figure 3.8 contains two concepts linked by a conceptual relation. The concept [Association: #] represents the phrase *the association*; the concept [Industrialist: {*}#] represents *the industrialists*; and the relation (Part) represents "to have as part." Altogether, the conceptual graph means "the association has as parts the industrialists."

**L'associazione degli industriali ha approvato
un nuovo piano di investimenti nel mezzogiorno.**

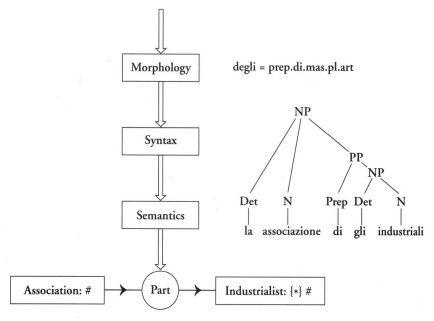

FIGURE 3.8 Stages in analyzing a natural language sentence

For the entire sentence, DANTE generated the conceptual graph shown in Figure 3.9.

CONCEPTS AND RELATIONS.   The seven circles in Figure 3.9 represent conceptual relations. They are derived from word inflections like the tense markers on verbs, the word order for distinguishing subject from object, and prepositions like *di* (of) or *nel* (in the). Following is a brief description of each of them:

- Agent (Agnt) links a concept of an action to a concept of an animate being (person, animal, or robot) that performs it: *approve has the association as agent.*
- Theme (Thme) links a concept of an event or state to a concept of the principal entity that is involved: *approve has project as theme.*
- Past (Past) marks the past tense: *approve occurred in the past.*
- Part (Part) links a concept of an entity to some other concept that represents a part of the entity: *the association has the industrialists as parts.*
- Attribute (Attr) links one concept to another one that represents some attribute of the first: *a project has the attribute new.*

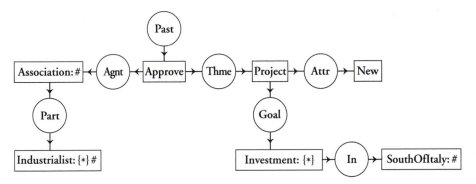

FIGURE 3.9 Conceptual graph that represents the input sentence

- Goal (Goal) links a concept to another one that represents its goal: *a project has the investments as goal.*
- In (In) links a concept whose referent is contained in the referent of the concept it is linked to: *the investments are in the south of Italy.*

These low-level relations, which are derived from linguistic categories, are the basic building blocks for defining more complex relations in databases and expert systems.

RESOLVING AMBIGUITIES. Ambiguous words and phrases are a common source of complexity in natural languages. For the sample sentence, DANTE found the following ambiguities:

- The morphological analyzer found that the word *industriali* was three ways ambiguous: it could be a plural noun meaning "industrialists"; it could be a plural adjective meaning "industrial"; or it could be the imperative form of the verb *industriare* (to be busy) with an attached or enclitic pronoun *li* (it). This ambiguity in the morphology was resolved in the syntactic stage because only the noun was permissible in the given context.
- The word *piano* is even more ambiguous. The morphological stage found the following options for parts of speech and possible meanings:

  As a noun, it could mean project, plan, plane (surface), story (of a building), or pianoforte.
  As an adjective, it could mean plain, smooth, or clear.
  As an adverb, it could mean gently, slowly, or quietly.

In the given context, the syntax ruled out the possibility of adjective or adverb, but it could not determine the correct meaning of the noun. To resolve that ambiguity, the DANTE developers decided that the type label Project was general enough to represent both *project* and *plan.* They decided that the other meanings were less likely in the domain of financial news and adopted the brute-force solution of deleting them from the dictionary.

- The Italian word *mezzogiorno*, like the French *midi*, literally means midday or noon. But since the sun at noon is in the south, *midi* has come to mean the south of France, and *mezzogiorno* means the south of Italy. In this case, the ambiguity was resolved by checking the choice of preposition: *a mezzogiorno* would mean at noon, but *nel mezzogiorno* means in the south.

- In dictionaries, the preposition *di*, like its English counterpart *of*, has dozens of word senses. But the large number of word senses does not indicate a lot of meaning. Instead, it indicates that the word has very little meaning in itself and that most of its meaning is derived from context. In the phrase *the association of the industrialists*, it represents the Part relation; but in *plan of investments*, it represents the Goal relation. To select the correct relation, DANTE checks the semantic patterns associated with the words linked by the preposition.

As these examples illustrate, current systems can adequately deal with the linguistic problems of syntax and morphology. The semantic problems, however, require a large dictionary of word meanings, a broad range of background knowledge, and an inference engine that can use the knowledge effectively. Several projects around the world are developing methods to encode and use such knowledge. The Cyc system designed by Doug Lenat and R. V. Guha (1990) has the world's largest and most detailed knowledge base, and the Cyc developers are collaborating with linguists and lexicographers to link that knowledge with machine-readable dictionaries.

QUESTION ANSWERING.   After building up a knowledge base of conceptual graphs, DANTE could answer questions or select documents that contain relevant information. Figure 3.10 shows the processing steps in question answering.

The input question *Che cosa si approva?* (What thing is approved?) is analyzed by the same processes used for the original text. The result is a *query graph* that represents the meaning of the question. It is a conceptual graph that contains one or more concepts with a question mark in the referent field, as in [Thing: ?]. The question mark, which is derived from the question word *che* (what), serves as a trigger that initiates a search through the knowledge base. As an answer, the search engine finds a conceptual graph that specializes the concept [Thing: ?] to the concept [Project] for the purpose of [Investment: {*}]. Finally, the generation stage translates the answer graph to the sentence *Si approva un progetto di investimenti* (A project of investments is approved). If the user wanted more detail, DANTE could also retrieve the original text from which the answer was derived.

INFERENCE.   A knowledge representation at the conceptual level can support inferences that are not possible at the level of character strings. For the question

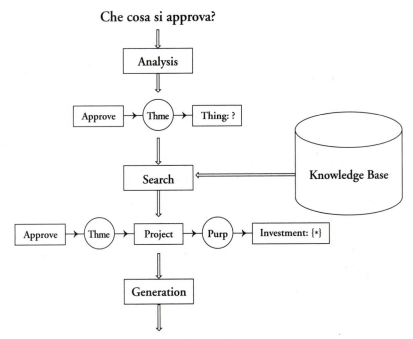

Che cosa si approva?

Si approva un progetto di investimenti.

FIGURE 3.10 Stages in answering a question

What do the industrialists belong to?, DANTE could answer *an association that approved a project of investments.* That inference depends on the variety of linguistic expressions for the Part relation: *the association of the industrialists; the industrialists in the association;* or *the industrialists belong to the association.* But many questions require a deeper knowledge of the subject. As an example, DANTE analyzed the following sentence correctly:

> *Il consiglio di amministrazione ha raggiunto un accordo sulla nomina di Raul Gardini a presidente del gruppo Montedison al posto di Mario Schimberni.*
> (The board of directors has reached an agreement on the appointment of Raul Gardini as president of the Montedison group in the post of Mario Schimberni.)

From that input, DANTE could answer the question *Who was appointed president of the Montedison group?* But the next two questions are much harder to answer:

- *Who was president of the Montedison group before the appointment?*
- *Who was president of the Montedison group after the appointment?*

To answer these questions, a system must have specialized knowledge: the board of directors of a company has the power to appoint the president; making such decisions requires an agreement by the board; after an appointment, the person who was appointed assumes the post to which he or she was appointed; since there is only one president at a time, the previous president must stop being president when a new one is appointed. With its purely linguistic knowledge, DANTE could not answer such questions; but with its more detailed background knowledge, the Cyc system could.

3.6 Levels of Representation

To be useful, a computer program must represent information about things in the world, but the computerized information passes through many levels of representations of representations of representations. As an example, Figure 3.11 shows an image that represents a person named Harry, the letters "Harry" used to represent the sound of his name, and four ways of encoding the letters. The symbol 0x486172727900 is the C language representation of the hexadecimal representation of the ASCII encoding of the character string; and X'C8819999A8' is the PL/I representation of the corresponding EBCDIC encoding. On the right side of Figure 3.11 are two strings of 1s and 0s that represent the bits stored on disk or transistors.

The number of levels shown in Figure 3.11 is a small fraction of the variety of representations that actually occur. Neither the person Harry nor the actual bits in the computer can be printed on paper. The image on the left is a rough caricature that may resemble the person, but it is not the real physical person. The strings of 1's and 0's on the right are not the actual magnetic spots on a disk or the currents flowing in transistors. To print the character string 'Harry' in the chosen font and size, each 8-bit sequence in the ASCII encoding was mapped to a Postscript specification of the curves that represent the shapes of the letters. Then another computer inside the printer converted the Postscript commands to a pattern of dots, which were used to modulate a laser beam, which modified charged spots on a plate, which attracted black dust particles, which were finally baked on paper in the shape of letters. The procedure is more outlandish than anything Rube Goldberg ever conceived, but somehow it works.

KNOWLEDGE LEVELS.   In moving from left to right in Figure 3.11, the focus shifts from physical objects to names to computer-oriented details. In analyzing

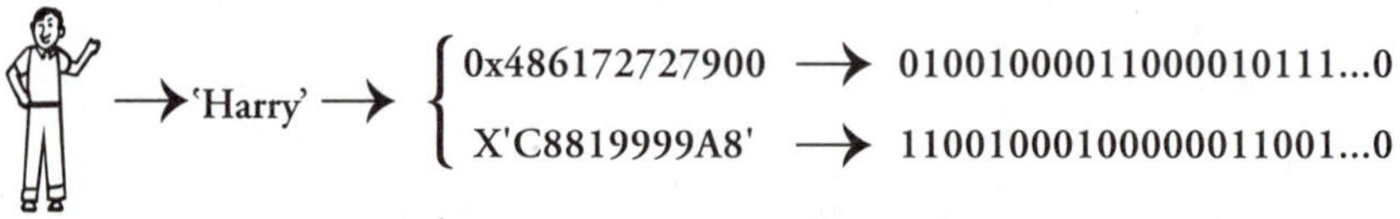

FIGURE 3.11 A physical object and some computer representations

that shift, John McCarthy and Patrick Hayes (1969) drew a sharp distinction between the declarative, logic-like representations, which they called the *epistemological level*, and the more procedural encodings, which they called the *heuristic level*. The epistemological level is solely devoted to knowledge about objects and processes in the application domain, while the heuristic level introduces data structures for representing the objects and programs for simulating the processes. Ron Brachman (1979) renamed the heuristic level the *implementational level* and split the epistemological level into four separate levels:

1. *Implementational.* The level of data structures such as atoms, pointers, lists, and other programming notions.

2. *Logical.* Symbolic logic with its propositions, predicates, variables, quantifiers, and Boolean operators.

3. *Epistemological.* A level for defining concept types with subtypes, inheritance, and structuring relations.

4. *Conceptual.* The level of semantic relations, linguistic roles, objects, and actions.

5. *Linguistic.* The level of arbitrary concepts, words, and expressions of natural languages.

Lenat and Guha (1990) adopted the McCarthy-Hayes terminology for the Cyc system, but they made essentially the same distinctions that Brachman made. The heuristic level in Cyc corresponds to Brachman's implementational level, and the Cyc epistemological level has sublevels that match Brachman's other four: the Cyc constraint language corresponds to level 2; the Cyc definitions correspond to level 3; and the Cyc ontology corresponds to levels 4 and 5.

COMPETENCE LEVELS. A *robot* is an AI system that receives signals from the environment and acts on the environment in a way that helps it to achieve some preestablished goals. In what he called the *subsumption architecture* for mobile robots, Rodney Brooks (1986) distinguished eight *levels of competence*, each with increasingly more sophisticated goals and means for achieving them:

1. *Avoiding.* Avoid contact with other objects, either moving or stationary.

2. *Wandering.* Wander around aimlessly without hitting things.

3. *Exploring.* Look for places in the world that seem reachable and head for them.

4. *Mapping.* Build a map of the environment and record the routes from one place to another.

5. *Noticing.* Recognize changes in the environment that require updates to the mental maps.

6. *Reasoning.* Identify objects, reason about them, and perform actions on them.

7. *Planning.* Formulate and execute plans that involve changing the environment in some desirable way.

8. *Anticipating.* Reason about the behavior of other objects, anticipate their actions, and modify plans accordingly.

Each of these levels depends on and *subsumes* the competence achieved by the earlier levels. Each level responds to signs, signals, or stimuli from the input sensors and generates output for the motor mechanisms. Yet the robot as a whole does not depend on a strict control hierarchy. The first few levels by themselves could support an insectlike intelligence that responds directly to immediate inputs without doing abstract reasoning or planning. The higher levels could inhibit the lower levels and take control for more sophisticated or intelligent behavior, but the lower levels would still be capable of automatic, reflexlike reactions to danger signals.

The behavior of the lower levels depends primarily on immediate inputs. The higher levels depend more heavily on internal representations, such as maps of the environment, memories of previous inputs, stored patterns for recognizing familiar objects, and established habits for repeatable behaviors. Every level responds to signs from the external environment and from other internal levels, but there is an increase in complexity from the automatic responses at the lower levels to the knowledge-based reasoning at the higher levels.

DESIGN LEVELS.   For his *Information System Architecture* (ISA), John Zachman (1987) distinguished five separate levels, with the distinctions between levels based on design issues. Zachman's top three levels correspond to the epistemological level, and his bottom two levels correspond to the heuristic or implementational level. His first level, called the *scope,* and his second level, called the *enterprise model,* describe aspects of the world independent of how they might be represented in a computer. At the third level, called the *system model,* the descriptions are still implementation-independent, but the selection of details is made by a systems analyst who works on the border between the computer and the outside world. At the bottom two levels, Zachman distinguished the *technology model* from the *components.* At the technology level, an application programmer relates data structures designed for efficient computation to data structures that represent physical objects at the top levels. At the component level, a system programmer deals with implementation details whose connections to the outside world are no longer apparent.

Zachman organized his five levels in a matrix with six columns to show thirty different perspectives on the knowledge representation. To illustrate the ISA framework, Sowa and Zachman (1992) drew Figure 3.12, which shows the kind of information that goes in each cell. These are English descriptions of some of the

	What?	How?	Where?	Who?	When?	Why?
	Entity/Rel	*Function/Arg*	*Location/Link*	*Agent/Work*	*Time/Cycle*	*Ends/Means*
Scope *Planner*	Oz,OCRA, cars, fees, licenses, car histories.	Register, transfer, collect, enforce.	Emerald City, Munchkin Land Kansas, Hollywood.	Director, managers, clerks, car owners.	Time of sale, transfer, registration, destruction.	Regulate sales, raise money, trace cars.
Enterprise Model *Owner*	Each car is of a particular model.	Ownership is transferred by registration of the transfer.	Registrations are recorded at offices of OCRA.	An OCRA clerk must record each registraiton.	When a car is constructed, transferred, or destroyed.	Keep accurate records and collect fees.
System Model *Designer*	Functional dependency from car to model.	Car history updated by transfer module.	Each office must have a connection to OCRA HQ.	A clerk must enter information at a terminal.	DB updates occur at irregular intervals.	Old batch system does not respond fast enough.
Technology Model *Builder*	Car relation has a column for model identifier.	Transfer done by COBOL prog XFR397A.	B.O. records are backed up at OCRA headquarters.	Clerk completes form REG972 to initiate registration.	Each module is invoked by a menu selection.	Efficient, reliable service within budget.
Component *Sub-Contractor*	MODELID PIC X(15).	SELECT SNO FROM HIST WHERE...	Install TCP/IP link to OZNET.	Install cordons to guide queue for clerks.	Use popup windows selected by mouse.	Meet specifications for each mocule.
Working System	Data	Function	Network	Organization	Schedule	Strategy

FIGURE 3.12 Design levels in the Zachman ISA framework

data, functions, network, organization, schedules, and strategies of the Oz Car Registration Authority (OCRA), which was adapted from an ISO report on *conceptual schemas* (van Griethuysen 1987). Each of the five rows in Figure 3.12 describes the entire OCRA system at one level of detail. Each is a complete, self-contained description from the viewpoint of a certain type of person: a planner who is proposing the general idea; the owner or manager who would use the system from day to day; a designer who works out the underlying details; a builder who is in charge of constructing the system; or a subcontractor who assembles individual components:

1. *Scope.* The first row corresponds to an executive summary, which describes in gross terms the purpose of the system, its scope, its cost, and what it would do. The entities in this row are discussed without mentioning any implementation details.

2. *Enterprise model.* The next row describes the system from an operational point of view, as it would appear to the people who work with it in the daily routines of business. The entities at the enterprise level are the people, resources, products, and tasks of the business.

3. *System model.* The third row describes the information system as designed by a systems analyst who must determine the data elements and functions that represent business entities and processes. The information entities are data structures that represent physical entities in the row above and procedures that simulate the behavior of those entities.

4. *Technology model.* The fourth row deals with the technology used to implement the information elements in the third row. It is the representation used by the programmers who must map the system analyst's view to the programming languages, I/O devices, and related components of the computer system.

5. *Components.* The last row represents the detailed specifications that are given to programmers who code individual modules without concern for the global context or purpose. They are the people who design abstract algorithms that are independent of the application domain. Sorting routines, for example, could be used equally well to sort employee names, stock market quotes, or chemical formulas.

In designing the ISA framework, Zachman emphasized its applicability to physical objects in the top row, to low-level programming details in the bottom row, and to mixed interfaces in the intermediate rows. The first object-oriented language, Simula 67, was designed to simulate the kinds of objects that populate the top rows of the ISA framework, but current O-O textbooks tend to concentrate on the technology at the bottom rows. The major contribution of the ISA framework is its global view of all the rows and columns and their interrelationships. It helps to remind programmers that the information objects they manipulate inside the computer refer to physical objects on the outside.

The six columns of the ISA framework correspond to the six question words in English: *what, how, where, who, when,* and *why.* Each column contains one perspective at each row: what entities are in the system, how do they behave, where are they, who works with the system, when do events occur, and why do the events take place? Immediately below each question word is a pair of words that indicate the basic concept type that answers the question word and the kind of relation associated with that concept. At the bottom of each column is a single word that summarizes the collective contribution of the things in that column to the working system:

1. *Entity/Relationship.* The answer to the question *What?* is a list of the entity types at each level. Each of the entities has one or more relationships that link it to other entities. The representation of all the entities and their relationships to other entities constitutes the total *data* of the working system.

2. *Function/Argument.* The answer to *How?* is a list of functions performed by the system. Each function takes one or more entity types as arguments. The totality

of all the individual functions and arguments constitutes the overall system *function.*

3. *Location/Link.* The answer to *Where?* is a list of the significant locations, which may be physical rooms, buildings, and cities or logical sites inside a computer system. Each location has one or more links that connect it to other locations. The connection of all the locations and links constitutes the *network.*

4. *Agent/Work.* The answer to *Who?* is a list of the agents that play some role in the system. The agents include humans, such as employees and customers, and computerized agents that operate automatically. Each agent has associated activities, tasks, or work that he/she/it performs. The totality of all the agents and their work constitutes the *organization.*

5. *Time/Cycle.* The answer to *When?* is a list of times when significant events take place. Each point in time occurs on some cycle, which may be periodic, such as a billing cycle, or irregular, such as demand-driven events initiated by various agents. The totality of times and cycles determines the *schedule.*

6. *Ends/Means.* The answer to *Why?* is a list of the ends or purposes for each entity, function, location, agent, or time. Each end has an associated means by which it may be accomplished. The totality of all ends and means constitutes the *strategy.*

Although Figure 3.12 uses English in all thirty cells, different languages, linear or graphic, are often used for different rows and columns. The scope may be described by a list of words, but it could be supplemented with charts, tables, and maps. Many people recommend formal languages for *enterprise modeling* (Petrie 1992), but natural languages supplemented with charts and tables are commonly used. For the system model, tools and languages have been designed for *computer-aided software engineering* (CASE), but informal notations supplemented with natural language comments are also used. At the technology level, the dominant languages are programming languages like COBOL or Java, database languages like SQL, or various application packages that define problem-oriented languages and interfaces. At the component level, the languages tend to be machine-oriented languages like COBOL, FORTRAN, or C, which are supported by efficient compilers. Altogether, the Zachman ISA framework represents a checklist of 30 viewpoints to consider in the analysis, design, and implementation of an information system.

MEANING TRIANGLE. The ISA levels illustrate some of the relationships between symbols, objects, and meaning. Figure 3.13 organizes those relationships in a *meaning triangle.* On the lower left is an image of a person named Harry. On the right is a printed symbol that represents his name. The cloud on the top is an iconic

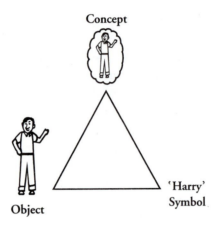

FIGURE 3.13 The meaning triangle

suggestion of the unprintable mental concept or neural excitation induced by light beams bouncing off Harry's body. Ogden and Richards (1923) popularized the term *meaning triangle*, but Aristotle was the first to make the distinction:

> Spoken words are symbols of experiences [*pathēmata*] in the psyche; written words are symbols of the spoken. As writing, so is speech not the same for all peoples. But the experiences themselves, of which these words are primarily signs, are the same for everyone, and so are the objects of which those experiences are likenesses. (*On Interpretation* 16a4)

Both Frege and Peirce adopted the three-way distinction from Aristotle and used it as the semantic foundation for their systems of logic. Frege's terms for the three vertices of the meaning triangle were *Zeichen* (sign) for the symbol, *Sinn* (sense) for the concept, and *Bedeutung* (reference) for the object. As an example, Frege cited the terms *morning star* and *evening star*. Both terms refer to the planet Venus, but their senses are very different: one means a star seen in the morning, and the other means a star seen in the evening. Following is Peirce's definition:

> A sign, or *representamen*, is something which stands to somebody for something in some respect or capacity. It addresses somebody, that is, creates in the mind of that person an equivalent sign, or perhaps a more developed sign. That sign which it creates I call the *interpretant* of the first sign. The sign stands for something, its *object*. It stands for that object, not in all respects, but in reference to a sort of idea, which I have sometimes called the *ground* of the representamen. (CP 2.228)

The terms *morning star* and *evening star* are distinct signs that create different interpretants in the mind of the listener. Both interpretants stand for the same object, the planet Venus, but in respect to a different ground, namely, whether the planet is seen in the morning or in the evening.

Aristotle observed that symbols could symbolize other symbols, as "written words are symbols of the spoken." Frege said that his logic could be used as a language to talk about the logic itself. But Peirce went further than either of them in recognizing that multiple meaning triangles could be linked together to generate an arbitrary number of levels. Figure 3.14 shows three linked triangles that represent the relationships between Zachman's levels in Figure 3.12.

The triangle on the left relates Harry as a physical object at the enterprise level to his name, which is an information object at the system level. The middle triangle relates 'Harry' to the symbol 0x486172727900, which represents the character string as a programmer might see it at the technology level. The triangle on the right relates the string to its bit representation at the component level. At the top of each triangle is a cloud that suggests the concepts in the minds of a manager who is thinking about Harry, a systems analyst who is thinking about the name, and a programmer who is thinking about the string. Since thought clouds are not physically observable or printable, each one has a box above it that represents the concept as a node in a conceptual graph. The concept of the person Harry is linked by the characteristic (Chrc) relation to a concept of the nam, which is linked by the representation (Repr) relation to a concept of the string 0x486172727900.

METALEVELS. Besides linking the triangles side by side as in Figure 3.14, Peirce also considered the concept or interpretant at the top of each triangle as another sign that could form another triangle. The concept would be represented by a *metalevel symbol*, whose interpretant would be a metalevel concept. As an

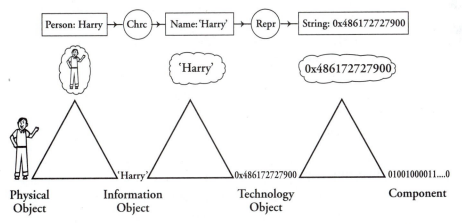

FIGURE 3.14 Linked meaning triangles representing Zachman's ISA levels

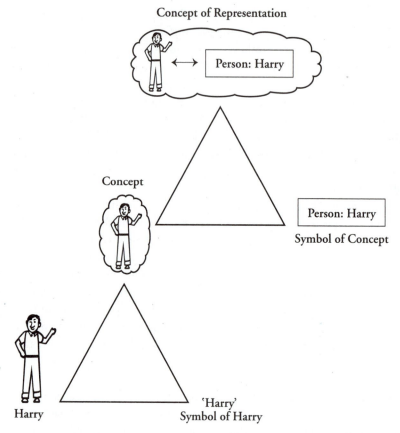

FIGURE 3.15 The concept of the representation of the concept of Harry

example, Figure 3.15 has a metalevel triangle stacked on top of the triangle from Figure 3.13. The bottom triangle relates the person Harry to the symbol 'Harry' and the concept of Harry. The top triangle relates the mental concept of Harry to the printable symbol [Person: Harry] and the concept of representation in the mind of a knowledge engineer.

As these examples show, meaning triangles may be linked side by side or stacked to generate arbitrarily many levels. Figure 3.14 could be extended with further triangles on the right to show how a computer engineer would relate the bits to transistors or how a printer designer would relate them to dots on paper. Figure 3.15 could be extended with more triangles on top for representing the metalevels used in talking about words, language, or even theories of representation. Natural languages are a rich source of metalanguage about language: the word *red*, for example, refers directly to physical patches of a certain color; the word *color* is a metaterm that refers to the way a red patch may be distinguished from a patch of blue or yellow; the word *characteristic* is a metametaterm that refers to the mode of distinguishing by color, shape, size, or texture; and the word *mode* is a metametametaterm about the act of distinguishing. Despite the breadth and depth of levels, Peirce's system of symbols is ultimately grounded in physical objects and processes. At the bottom left corners of Figures 3.13, 3.14, and 3.15, for example, is the real physical person Harry. Some symbols may refer to mental, fictional, or hypothetical objects, but the foundation of the system as a whole rests on solid ground.

MENTAL PROCESSES.   The clouds in Figures 3.13, 3.14, and 3.15 suggest the mental processes that support thought. The philosophers Ludwig Wittgenstein (1953) and Gilbert Ryle (1949) deliberately avoided talk about mental processes because knowing the meaning of a word does not depend on understanding the nature of those processes. Since Wittgenstein never talked about mental processes, some people have confused his position with a behavioristic denial of such processes. But Wittgenstein himself was careful to avoid that confusion. He criticized idle speculation about "the yet uncomprehended process in the yet unexplored medium," but he added, "And now it looks as if we had denied mental processes. And naturally we don't want to deny them." What Wittgenstein denied was that an understanding of mental processes is necessary to understand the normal use of language. Children learn the meaning of a word by seeing how adults use it. Philologists determine the meaning of a Latin word by analyzing Latin texts, even though the brains that composed those texts have long since crumbled into dust. Conceptual analysis, either formal or informal, is the basic method of determining meanings, and it requires no peering into the inner workings of brains or machines.

Wittgenstein declined to speculate about mental processes, partly because they were unobservable, but primarily because the nature of meaning does not depend on the nature of the mental processes. But some of his followers, such as Norman Malcolm (1977), went much further than the master in dismissing AI, theoretical linguistics, and cognitive psychology as a "mythology of inner guidance systems" (p. 169). Malcolm is correct in saying that a study of the human brain cannot explain the meaning of a word. He is also justified in doing conceptual analysis of language without considering "inner guidance systems." But he is wrong in dismissing such systems as unimportant, uninteresting, or even nonexistent. The meaning triangle does not depend on whether concepts are represented in a spiritual soul, a bloody brain, or silicon chips. But some kind of representation is necessary to complete the triangle.

Aristotle, Frege, and Peirce would agree that physical objects and the signs that represent them are publicly observable, but that the senses, interpretants, or experiences in the psyche are not directly observable. None of them used introspection to study the mental contents or neurosurgery to study the neural excitations.

Instead, they developed formal systems of logic for representing and reasoning about the logically necessary but physically unobservable concepts. They did not consider logic to be a *descriptive science* about the way people think or reason, but a *normative science* for evaluating the results of the reasoning. No matter how the reasoning happens to be carried out, the results must be tested against the norms of sound reasoning as determined by logic.

EXERCISES

1. The earliest traffic lights had only two colors, red and green. Later, yellow was introduced as a warning that a green light was about to become red. Then some cities began to use combinations such as red and yellow or green and yellow as signals for pedestrians. Finally, WALK and DON'T WALK lights were introduced, with blinking DON'T WALK lights as a warning that the light was about to change. Simulating all those lights would require different extensions to the procedural loop, the logical axioms, or the forward-chaining rules. In Section 3.1, the traffic light used as an example had only two colors, red and green. Revise the specifications to include another color, yellow:

   a. First, revise the informal description to mention that a green light turns yellow before it turns red.

   b. Then revise the more detailed English specifications to state the conditions more precisely.

   c. Then revise the rules, programs, formulas, and CGs in Section 3.1 to incorporate the new color and the conditions for dealing with it.

   Try to make the implementations as systematic as possible so that they could readily be extended to handle WALK and DON'T WALK lights.

2. Herbert Simon (1989) emphasized the importance of diagrams as an aid to formulating the representations necessary for solving a problem. As an example, he gave the following English statement:

   A weight W1 is supported by a string A that runs over a pulley B; the other end of the string is attached to a second weight W2. The pulley B is supported by another string C, which runs over a second pulley D, then under a third pulley E, and finally is attached at its end to the ceiling. The second pulley D is also attached by a string to the ceiling. The third pulley E, supported by string C, supports another string F, which is attached to the weight W2. Thus W2 is supported by both strings A and F. The system is in equilibrium, and W1 weighs one pound. What is the weight of W2?

Study this statement and do the following exercises:

a. Draw a diagram that shows the pulleys, strings, weights, and their relationships as described in the problem statement.

b. Solve the problem by analyzing the diagram and determining the forces that support the weight W2.

c. Analyze the methods you used to solve the problem and state them as general principles that could be used to solve similar problems.

d. Develop systematic guidelines for translating a problem statement about weights and pulleys into some knowledge representation language that could be used to find the solution.

e. Apply those guidelines to this problem statement and show that the resulting representation is capable of getting the same answer that you derived by analyzing the diagram.

3. The World-Wide Parcel Delivery Service (WWPDS) ships parcels via local trucks, long-distance trucks, and planes. Define the frames or object classes for a system that would enable WWPDS to keep track of parcels, trucks, planes, truck drivers, and air crew at every stage of their travels. The frame for Trip should have subframes for LocalTrip by local truck, IntermediateTrip by long-distance truck, and LongTrip by plane. Each trip has a single truck or plane and a single driver or air crew. Local trips start and return to the same WWPDS distribution center, making a number of customer stops to pick up and deliver parcels. Intermediate trips start and end at a WWPDS distribution center, with 0 or more stops at airports or other WWPDS distribution centers. Long trips start and end at an airport with 0 or more stops at other airports. If necessary, make reasonable assumptions about the way WWPDS plans their trips and assigns parcels, personnel, and equipment to the trips.

4. Study the CG type definition of MaxGrossWeight. Then translate the English sentence *The unloaded weight of a vehicle is the difference between the weight of the vehicle minus the weight of any cargo in it* to a CG definition of the concept type UnloadedWeight. To represent the difference, assume a triadic relation Diff whose third argument is equal to the first minus the second. Translate the CG definitions of MaxGrossWeight and UnloadedWeight to lambda expressions in predicate calculus.

5. In Section 3.2, the claim was made that EC logic, as used in frames and relational databases, could not express the absence of a hippopotamus. Yet those systems are routinely used to express the absence of something just by

failing to mention it. Why doesn't that approach refute the claim that EC logic cannot state or imply that something is absent?

6. The following sentences about the weather explain a phenomenon called the *lake effect*. They represent the kind of knowledge that may be encoded in expert system rules.

> If a lake is warmer than the air above it, the air is saturated. If air is saturated, it rises. If air rises, it becomes cooler. If moisture precipitates in air that is above freezing, it is raining. If moisture precipitates in air that is below freezing, it is snowing. If saturated air becomes cooler, moisture precipitates. If wind is blowing from the west and location x is east of y, then the attributes of the air at x are the same as at y.

Define an ontology for describing the air at location x that is sufficient to represent the knowledge in these sentences. Then translate each sentence to an implication in predicate calculus that uses that ontology. For example, the first sentence might be translated to the formula,

$$(\forall x{:}\text{Location})(\text{lakeWarmerThanAir}(x) \supset \text{air}(x,\text{saturated})).$$

Literally, this formula may be read *For every location x, if a lake warmer than the air is at x, then the air at x is saturated*. Note that the air predicate relates a location to an attribute of the air at that location. In this example, the attribute *saturated* is a constant, but the second argument of the air predicate could be a variable. The ontology may include such constants as well as predicates.

7. Following are some statements about geography and the weather. Translate them to predicate calculus using the same ontology you defined for the previous exercise.

> Buffalo is east of Lake Erie. Lake Erie is warmer than the air above it. The air over Lake Erie is below freezing. Wind from the west is blowing over Lake Erie.

From these statements and the rules for the previous exercise, perform the following deductions with pencil and paper:

a. Use forward chaining to prove that it is snowing in Buffalo.

b. What other conclusions can be deduced from the above sentences by forward chaining?

c. Represent the question *Is it snowing in Buffalo?* by the formula that corresponds to the negation *It is not snowing in Buffalo*. Then use backward chaining to derive a contradiction, i.e., a formula of the form ~p where p is one of the formulas derived from the above sentences.

d. Many expert systems generate explanations by translating a sequence of inference steps to natural language sentences. For this example, list each rule and fact used in the backward-chaining deduction; then reverse that list, and translate each formula to an English sentence. The result should be a paragraph that explains why it is snowing in Buffalo.

8. The lake-effect rules can be used to explain the weather patterns at various places around the Great Lakes, which lie on the border between the United States and Canada. Explore the following extensions to those rules and facts:

a. Deduce the implications of the following facts, which explain how Watertown, New York, got its name:

> Watertown is east of Lake Ontario. Lake Ontario is warmer than the air above it. The air over Lake Ontario is above freezing. Wind from the west is blowing over Lake Ontario.

b. The wind across the Great Lakes, which typically blows from the west, may sometimes come from other directions. Add another rule to predict the weather in Cleveland, Ohio, which is south of Lake Erie.

c. Instead of adding more rules, add eight facts of the form opposite(n,s), opposite(ne,sw), and opposite(e,w). Then generalize the lake-effect rules to accommodate wind from any of the eight directions.

d. Translate the modified rules to English sentences.

9. In pure logic, the same rules can be used in forward or backward chaining without modification, but most expert-system tools are designed for one method or the other. Readers who know some such tool may use it to implement the lake-effect rules:

a. For languages in the OPS5 family like CLIPS, a direct translation of the lake-effect rules would be executed by forward chaining. Backward chaining can be simulated by defining special working memory elements to represent goals. Giarratano and Riley (1994) show how to simulate a backward-chaining inference engine in CLIPS; that simulation would be adequate for small problems like the lake-effect rules, but it would be inefficient for larger problems.

b. For languages like Prolog and expert systems in the MYCIN family, a direct translation of the rules would be executed by backward chaining. Most languages in the MYCIN family cannot simulate forward chaining, but Prolog is rich enough to implement interpreters for forward chaining. Many textbooks on Prolog, such as Walker et al. (1990), show how to implement various kinds of interpreters.

c. Microplanner and some of the more sophisticated expert-system shells support both forward and backward chaining, but they usually require each rule to be tailored for a specific inference method. Some hybrid systems support multiple inference methods by providing multiple languages, such as OPS5 and Prolog.

d. In SQL, views support backward chaining, and triggers support forward chaining. Although the lake-effect rules could be represented as views or triggers, the SQL language and its implementations are not designed to facilitate such applications. Readers who know SQL might try implementing the lake-effect rules to see how they would perform.

Winograd's book on SHRDLU (1972) is obsolete for techniques of natural language processing, but it is still useful as a source of examples of forward and backward chaining. The SHRDLU implementation shows how English explanations can be generated by translating the steps of a proof to English sentences. Buchanan and Shortliffe (1984) discuss the importance of such translations for explaining the results of an expert system.

10. After solving the previous exercises about the weather, state some English sentences that represent the knowledge that might be encoded in an expert system for some other subject. Sample topics might be taken from photography, cooking, choosing college courses, finding a job, or debugging a computer program. Define a suitable ontology for representing the sentences, translate them to predicate calculus, and do the same kinds of forward and backward-chaining deductions as in the previous exercises.

11. Review the translation of music to logic in Sections 1.2 and 1.4. Then translate the music examples to a rule and frame representation:

a. Define a frame for the type Note, with slots for tone, duration, and next. Then specify the melody in Figure 1.5 by an instance frame for each note. For each note, the next slot should either be nil or contain the identifier of the following note. Don't bother to write all 32 instances; just show the frames for the first few notes and the last note.

b. Use stylized English to write a forward-chaining rule that checks the sequence of frames and prints a warning message if it finds a tritone between any note and the next. Assume an inference engine that will check the conditions in the if-part of a rule and automatically invoke the rule when its conditions become true. The then-part may contain one or more actions, such as an assignment statement, a print statement, or a subroutine call.

c. Extend the frames to represent the two-voice harmony in Figure 1.8. Instead of representing the duration as a slot in each note, define a frame for the type Interval with slots for start time, ending time, and duration. Then add a slot to the Note frame that specifies the identifier of the instance of the interval in which it is sounded.

d. Add a slot named simul to the frame definition to indicate a list of notes that are sounded simultaneously. Then write a forward-chaining rule that checks the frames and fills in the simul slots. Assume that the if-part of a rule can contain conditions such as "The time in the start slot of the interval named in the interval slot of the note x is equal to the time in the start slot of the interval named in the interval slot of the note y." If you decide to use more concise abbreviations, define them.

e. Finally, write a forward-chaining rule that checks the frames to find any dissonant intervals that may be sounded simultaneously. If the next notes do not resolve the dissonance to a harmonious interval, print a warning message. Assume that the harmonious intervals are *unisons* (two identical notes sung in different voices), *thirds* (two notes separated by one other, such as G and B), *fourths* (G and C), *fifths* (G and D), *sixths* (G and E), and *octaves* (G and the next higher G). Assume that dissonant intervals include *seconds* (such as G and A), *tritones* (C and F#), *sevenths* (G and F#), and *ninths* (a G and the A in the next higher octave).

If you are familiar with a frame or rule-based language that is suitable for this exercise, you may use its notation instead of stylized English. Otherwise, use the syntax for frames shown in Section 3.2, and write the rules in a stylized English similar to the examples in Section 3.1. The if-part of a rule should check conditions without changing any values; the then-part of a rule may perform some action such as calling a subroutine or changing values in the slots.

12. After writing the frames and rules for the previous exercise, write the corresponding representations in another language, either one discussed in this chapter or some other language you may happen to know.

13. The techniques for optimizing the search in SQL, Prolog, and Microplanner are essentially the same. Some optimizations are independent of the data, but others depend on the number of instances stored in a relation. Consider the three goals that SHRDLU generated to answer the question *Which block supports a pyramid?*

```
(goal (objects ?x1 block ?))
(goal (objects ?x2 pyramid ?))
(goal (supports ?x1 ?x2))
```

A translation of the English sentence to Prolog or SQL would generate three equivalent goals, which would cause the same number of database accesses. Study the effects of optimization in the following cases:

a. Assume that each goal statement causes one database access whenever execution reaches the statement directly or by backtracking. For this sequence of goals and the database in Figure 3.3, count the number of DB accesses that must be made to find the answer. Then count the number of accesses that would be made if the second and third goals were interchanged.

b. Draw another diagram in which there are more blocks than pyramids, and enter the data in the objects and supports relations to represent that diagram. Then count the number of DB accesses that would be made for the original sequence of goals and for the revised sequence with the second and third goals interchanged. Would any other ordering of the goals reduce the number of accesses with this new database? If so, count the number of accesses with your new sequence of goals for both the original database in Figure 3.3 and the new database.

c. Different kinds of DB accesses take different amounts of time. The fastest ones test a single row of the table for each access; each subsequent execution of the same goal would step to the next row without requiring any search. Other DB accesses must search for a row with a particular value in a particular column, such as the identifier B or the color red. If a column with N entries has an *index*, a search for a particular value in the column could be done by a binary search that tests $\log_2 N$ rows for each DB access. The most complicated DB accesses perform a data-dependent test that requires a sequential search; they must test an average of $N/2$ rows for each DB access, and an index would not speed up the search. For the three goals in this exercise, which would test one row at each access, which would test $\log_2 N$ rows, and which would test $N/2$ rows? How would a reordering of the goals affect the number of tests?

d. Most SQL database systems support indexes that enable binary searches, but the database designer must specify whether an index should be created for a particular column of a table. If the DB designer does not specify an index, no binary searches can be done. Repeat the analysis for parts a, b, and c of this exercise, but instead of simply counting DB accesses, find the total number of rows that must be tested, assuming either a sequential search or a binary search. State the answers in terms of the number of rows N in the tables, and estimate the improvement that an index could make for table sizes $N=8$, $N=64$, and $N=32768$.

14. The SHRDLU system translated the sentence *Find the biggest block that supports a pyramid* to Microplanner code of the following form:

```
((goal (objects ?x1 block ?
   (goal (objects ?x2 pyramid ?)
   (goal (supports ?x1 ?x2)
   (not
     (and
        (goal (objects ?x3 block ?)
        (goal (objects ?x4 pyramid ?)
        (goal (supports ?x3 ?x4))
        (goal (moresize ?x3 ?x1)) )))
```

This code was inefficient, even for rather small databases. Study this code and the discussion of Microplanner in Section 3.3, and solve the following problems:

a. Translate the Microplanner code to a version of stylized English that uses the same variable names and sequence of searching. Assume that the objects relation has another column for the volumes of the objects and that more-size is defined by comparing the volumes.

b. Translate the code to some programming language you happen to be familiar with. The translation to Prolog or SQL would be the most direct, but the code could also be translated to a rule-based language like CLIPS or to a procedural language like C.

c. Assume that the underlying Microplanner implementation does a sequential search to look up a value in its database of relations. If there are N blocks in the database and each block supports an average of k other blocks, how would the execution time of the Microplanner code or its direct translation to a procedural language vary as a function of k and N?

d. Assume that the database relations are indexed by object identifiers so that a value could be found by a binary search. For the same Microplanner or English code, how would the expected search time vary in terms of k and N?

e. Assume that the system you are using has a sorting procedure whose execution time is proportional to $N\log N$. Rewrite the stylized English to take advantage of the sorting procedure. How would the expected search time vary assuming binary search or sequential search?

15. The CLIPS rule named updateEffectsOfPutOn modifies the supports relation to represent the effect of an assertion of the form (putOn ?x ?y). But it does not modify the contains relation if ?x happens to be removed from a box.

How should that CLIPS rule be revised to accommodate the following possibilities?

a. The original SHRDLU system was designed to simulate a robot named Shakey, which could only pick up one object at a time. For that case, assume that ?x does not contain or support any other objects.

b. Assume that a more stable robot might be able to move an object and anything it supports in a single putOn operation. That object might be a box, or it might be a block that supports a box.

If x is a box nested inside another box, the single act of removing x and its contents would cause multiple violations of the constraints. Make sure that your revised rules correct any violations that may occur. Readers who are familiar with Java should try using the Observer and Observable classes to implement the equivalent of the CLIPS rules or the SQL triggers in the examples of Section 3.3.

16. Analyze the encoding of the music examples in logic, frames, rules, and other languages, and compare the various languages according to the five principles of knowledge representation that were discussed in Section 3.1. Besides the music examples, review other examples, either in this book or in other sources you may know. Draw a table with five columns for the five principles and with one row for each of the n languages you have analyzed. In the $5n$ boxes of the table, rate each language on a scale of 0 (worst) to 10 (best) according to how well it satisfies the corresponding principle. Is a single number in each box adequate for evaluating the various knowledge representation languages? If not, discuss aspects of the languages that cannot be adequately measured by a single number.

17. Study the sample sentences discussed in Section 3.6. Find some sentences in a newspaper that have about the same degree of complexity. Analyze the ambiguities, both in syntax and in word senses. Look up each word in a dictionary to check for any unusual meanings that might confuse a computer program. For each ambiguity, determine the background knowledge a computer would need to determine the correct syntax and word sense.

18. A major theme of this chapter is the common logical foundation for various frame-based, rule-based, and object-oriented systems. Many other notations, such as HTML and XML, have been developed as special cases of the Standard Generalized Markup Language (SGML). The foundation for SGML is the existential-conjunctive (EC) subset of logic supplemented with an ontology for character strings. The *tags* defined in SGML specify an ontology for documents and their parts, such as paragraphs, sections, chapters, indexes,

tables, and graphical inserts. Select any special-purpose declarative notation that has been developed for any application domain. Then analyze the subset of logic it expresses and the underlying ontology represented in it. Show how that notation could be translated to predicate calculus or conceptual graphs.

19. Analyze the hotel reservation example in Appendix C according to the Zachman ISA Framework, as described in Section 3.5. The first stage of the analysis addresses the ISA Level 1 or Scope. For each question word *What, How, Where, Who, When,* and *Why,* make a list of the relevant terms in the problem statement that answer the question. For the question What, list the terms that represent entities, such as hotel, room rate, or cancellation number. For How, list the functions, such as make reservation, put on wait list, or check out. For Where, list locations, such as national park, hotel, or room. For Who, list the kinds of people, such as guest or reservation clerk. For When, list the events, such as time of check in, time of change in room rates, or time of expiration of a wait list. For Why, list the purpose or motivation, such as time stamp for auditing, accommodating guests' preferences for room type, making rooms available for new guests, or collecting payments.

20. Begin implementing parts of the hotel reservation system in some language that illustrates principles that were discussed in this chapter: a rule-based language like Prolog or CLIPS; the database language SQL; or an object-oriented language like Java. Review your answers to other exercises based on the hotel reservation example and determine whether your earlier analysis can be used as an aid to the implementation. If you modify or depart from your previous analysis, explain why.

This exercise could be done as a class project, with different students using different languages or tools to implement the same parts of the system. Then compare the implementations to evaluate the suitability of each language for various aspects of knowledge representation.

CHAPTER FOUR

Processes

*I have heard from a learned man that the motions of the sun, moon,
and stars constitute time, and I did not agree. For why shouldn't the
motions of all bodies in general be time? Indeed, if the lights of heaven
should cease, and a potter's wheel run round, would there be no time by
which we might measure those revolutions? Could we say either that it
moved with equal pauses, or if it sometimes moved slower, sometimes
faster, that some revolutions were longer, others shorter? Or even while
we were saying this, wouldn't we also be speaking in time?*

ST. AUGUSTINE, *Confessions*

4.1 Times, Events, and Situations

Charles Sanders Peirce was the first modern logician to treat processes and events
as entities distinct from the things that participate in the processes. Another
pioneer in logic, Alfred North Whitehead (1929), went further in making processes the primary entities in his ontology. Yet elementary logic books relegate
processes to a secondary status in comparison with the more stable things called
objects. A typical logic book would map a sentence like *Brutus stabbed Caesar* to
the formula

stabbed(Brutus,Caesar).

This translation ignores the detail implicit in the English sentence. It would require
different predicates for present, past, and future tenses; it does not allow further
relations to be linked to the verb, such as an adverb *violently* or a prepositional
phrase *with a shiny knife*; and it cannot support cross references from other sentences, such as *The stabbing was violent.*

During the 1960s, the need to treat events as first-class entities was independently rediscovered in linguistics, philosophy, and artificial intelligence. One
of the most persistent advocates of *event semantics* has been the philosopher Donald Davidson (1967), who waged a long campaign to get philosophers to admit

quantified variables for representing events. In linguistics, Terence Parsons (1990) used *event variables* to represent the sentence *Brutus stabbed Caesar*:

($\exists I$:Interval)(before(I,now) $\land$
    ($\exists t$:Time)($t \in I$ $\land$
        ($\exists e$:Stabbing)(agent(e,Brutus) $\land$ patient(e,Caesar) $\land$ culminates(e,t)))).

The first line of the formula says that there exists an interval I, where I is before now. The second line says that there exists a time t, which is contained in I. The third line says that there exists a stabbing event e, the agent of e is Brutus, the patient of e is Caesar, and e culminates at time t. With the proliferation of predicates and variables, Parson's representation is more complex than the simple *stabbed* relation, but it captures more of the meaning in the English sentence.

SITUATIONS AND EVENTS.   With his *correlational nets*, Silvio Ceccato (1961) was one of the first computational linguists to map nouns, verbs, and adjectives to nodes with equivalent status. Other versions of semantic networks (Quillian 1966; Schank & Tesler 1969) also represented the basic content words of language with equivalent concept nodes. Since conceptual graphs combine Peirce's logic with the semantic networks of AI, they represent attributes and events with the same kinds of concept nodes used for concrete things. Figure 4.1 shows a conceptual graph for the sentence *Brutus stabbed Caesar violently with a shiny knife*. The conceptual relations Agnt for *agent*, Ptnt for *patient*, and Inst for *instrument* correspond to the *thematic roles* used by linguists. The relation Attr for *attribute* links the knife to the instance of shininess. The relation Manr for *manner* applies to processes usually expressed by verbs in the same way that Attr applies to objects expressed by nouns. Surrounding the graph for the entire sentence is a concept of type Situation, which is linked to the relation Past, which indicates the past tense of the verb.

The graph in Figure 4.1 incorporates some abbreviations that simplify the notation. The Past relation, which is not a primitive, is defined by the following *lambda expression*:

```
Past = [Time: #now]←(Succ)←[Time]←( PTim)←[Situation: λ].
```

This definition says that there is a time #now, which is the successor (Succ) of some *reference time*, which is the point in time (PTim) of a situation, which is marked as the formal parameter by the Greek letter λ. The current time #now is neither a constant nor a variable; it is an *indexical* that must be resolved to the time specification of some containing context. Other examples of indexicals include #I and #you for the speaker and listener; #this and #that for objects indicated by location or pointing; and the general indexical marker # for the definite article *the*.

When a concept of type Situation contains a conceptual graph in its referent field, the graph itself is not the referent, but a symbol that describes the referent.

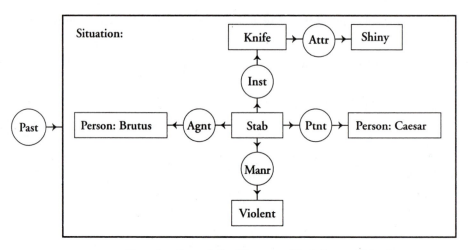

FIGURE 4.1 Conceptual graph for "Brutus stabbed Caesar violently
with a shiny knife."

Figure 4.1 asserts that there once existed a situation described by the proposition that
Brutus stabbed Caesar violently with a shiny knife. When the abbreviations for
situations and tenses are expanded, Figure 4.1 may be written in the following form:

```
[Time: #now]←(Succ)←[Time]←(PTim)←[Situation]-
  (Dscr)→[Proposition:
    [Stab]-
      (Agnt)→[Person: Brutus]
      (Ptnt)→[Person: Caesar]
      (Inst)→[Knife]→(Attr)→[Shiny]
      (Manr)→[Violent]  ].
```

The hyphens following the concepts [Situation] and [Stab] indicate that the relations
attached to them are listed on subsequent lines. The Dscr relation indicates that the
situation is described by the proposition stated by the nested conceptual graph.

Before a conceptual graph can be translated to predicate calculus, the indexicals
must be resolved to constants or variables. For this example, assume that the
sentence was uttered in a context whose point in time was 15 March 1996. Then
#now could be replaced by the constant 15Mar1996, and the graph could be
translated to the following formula:

$(\exists t{:}time)(\exists s{:}situation)(time(15Mar1996) \wedge succ(t,15Mar1996) \wedge ptim(s,t) \wedge$
$\quad dscr(s, (\exists x{:}knife)(\exists y{:}stab)(\exists z{:}violent)(\exists w{:}shiny)(person(Brutus) \wedge$
$\quad\quad person(Caesar) \wedge agnt(y,Brutus) \wedge ptnt(y,Caesar) \wedge$
$\quad\quad inst(y,x) \wedge manr(y,z) \wedge attr(x,w))))$.

This formula may be read *There exist a time t and a situation s, where t has 15Mar1996 as successor, the point in time of s is t, and s is described by the proposition that there exist a knife x, a stabbing y, an instance of violence z, an instance of shininess w, where Brutus is a person, Caesar is a person, y has agent Brutus, y has patient Caesar, y has instrument x, y has manner z, and x has attribute w.*

The graph in Figure 4.1 implicitly contains every detail of the formula, but it has a more direct mapping to English. Each of the six concept nodes inside the situation box expresses one of the six content words in the sentence. Each of the six circles corresponds to some syntactic feature: (Past) to the *-ed* ending on the verb; (Inst) to the preposition *with*; (Attr) to the word order of adjective modifying a noun; (Manr) to the *-ly* ending on the adverb; and (Agnt) and (Ptnt) to the subject and object, which are shown by word order in languages like English and Chinese or by case markers in Latin and Japanese.

MULTIPLE OCCURRENCES. The Past relation in Figure 4.1, which is attached to a concept of type Situation, shows that everything described inside the box occurred at some time in the past. That relation could also be attached directly to the verb, where it would indicate that the event expressed by the verb occurred in the past without explicitly saying anything about the time of the other entities. As an example, the sentence *Yojo chased a mouse* could be translated to a CG with the Past relation attached to the concept [Chase]:

```
(Past)→[Chase]-
      (Agnt)→[Cat: Yojo]
      (Thme)→[Mouse].
```

This graph indicates that the chasing occurred in the past, but it says nothing about the mouse, which ceased to exist shortly after the event. To show that that all three entities occurred together in the same situation, the Past relation can be attached to a concept of type Situation, which encloses the concepts of the act and its participants:

```
(Past)→[Situation:
   [Cat: Yojo]←(Agnt)←[Chase]→(Thme)→[Mouse] ].
```

Both graphs are permissible representations of the English sentence, but the second explicitly indicates the scope of the tense marker.

When a sentence in the past tense is translated to a CG, the simplest representation is to attach the tense relation to the concept expressed by the verb. Then a later inference step could widen the scope of the tense to include the entire situation. Sometimes, however, that inference step is not permissible. As an example, consider the sentence *Yojo chased two mice*, as represented by the following conceptual graph:

```
(Past)→[Chase]-
      (Agnt)→[Cat: Yojo]
      (Thme)→[Mouse: {*}@2].
```

The symbol {*} represents a *generic plural*, the qualifier @2 indicates two distinct entities, and the type label of the concept indicates that the entities are mice. This graph happens to be true, but the graph with the past tense attached to an enclosing situation would be false, because there was never a situation when Yojo was chasing two mice at the same time.

The paradox of sentences that are true in the past tense, but were never true in the present was discovered by Diodorus Cronus in the fourth century B.C.. The CG in Figure 4.2, which illustrates his paradox, may be read *Alma had three husbands, Gustav, Walter, and Franz*. That sentence, which is true in the past tense, was never true in any present because Alma Maria Schindler Mahler Gropius Werfel married her husbands sequentially rather than collectively. The prefix Dist on the set {Gustav, Walter, Franz} indicates a distributive (one at a time) relationship between the elements of the set and the proposition asserted by rest of the conceptual graph.

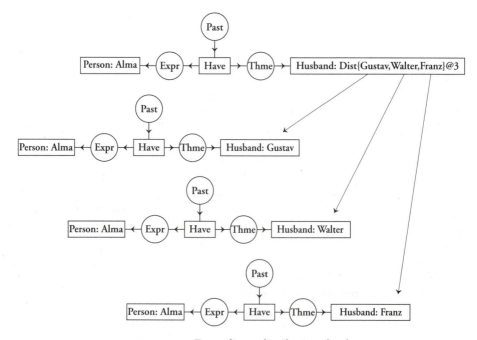

FIGURE 4.2 Expanding a distributive plural

The arrows in Figure 4.2 show how a distributive plural referent is expanded to three separate conceptual graphs, one for each of the three individuals in the set. The definition of the Past relation includes an implicit existential quantifier for some reference time that precedes the current time #now. For the unexpanded graph at the top of Figure 4.2, the Past relation could not be moved to an enclosing situation because it contains only one implicit reference time. But for the expanded graphs, the three separate Past relations would each include a separate existential quantifier in their definitions. Therefore, they could be moved to three separate enclosing situations, each of which would have its own reference time.

If Alma had married her husbands collectively, the plural referent would have the prefix Col, as in the concept [Husband: Col{Gustav, Walter, Franz}@3]. If this concept were expanded, only the relations directly attached to it would be copied. The resulting graph would have three copies of the Theme relation (Thme):

```
(Past)→[Have]-
        (Expr)→[Person: Alma]
        (Thme)→[Husband: Gustav]
        (Thme)→[Husband: Walter]
        (Thme)→[Husband: Franz].
```

For this graph, the Past relation could be moved to an enclosing situation. In general, the collective marker Col allows the Past relation to be moved, since it implies that there is only a single event involved in multiple relationships. The distributive marker Dist, however, blocks the move, since the expanded graphs might not be true at the same time. A plural without any prefix, like [Mouse: {*}@2], does not distinguish between the collective and distributive interpretations. Therefore, a tense marker on such a graph cannot be moved without further evidence of the existence of all participants in the same situation. In effect, the marker {*} specifies only the minimal information that the original noun phrase was plural; the other information must come from other words in the sentence, such as *together* or *simultaneously*. Sometimes, general background knowledge or the discourse context may be needed to resolve the scope.

ADVERBIAL MODIFIERS. The question of whether an adverb modifies the verb or the entire situation raises the same kinds of issues as tense markers. Robert Moore (1995) cited the following examples:

John sang strangely.
Strangely, John sang.

Moore observed that in the first sentence, the manner of singing is considered strange. Perhaps John sang "Happy Birthday" off key or with unusual variations in the melody. In logic, the concept [Strange] or the corresponding predicate could be linked directly to [Sing] by the manner relation (Manr):

```
(Past)→[Situation:
   [Person: John]←(Agnt)←[Sing]→(Manr)→[Strange] ].
```

This graph says that there existed a situation in the past in which John was the agent of singing in a strange manner. For this sentence, the Past relation could also have been attached directly to the concept [Sing], and the surrounding concept box for the situation could have been omitted.

In the second sentence, the fact that John sang is considered strange, even though his manner of singing might have been quite pleasant. Perhaps he stood up during a funeral service and began singing "Happy Birthday" to the deceased. Therefore, the Manr relation is attached to the concept of type Situation:

```
(Past)→[Situation:
   [Person: John]←(Agnt)←[Sing] ]→(Manr)→[Strange].
```

In this graph, the manner of the situation is marked as strange, and the manner of singing is not indicated.

In English, the *-ly* ending distinguishes the adverb *strangely* from the adjective *strange*. That syntactic distinction may signal a difference in the conceptual relation:

- *Manner.* Adverbs, which usually modify verbs, commonly express the manner of performance or happening of some occurrent.
- *Attribute.* Adjectives, which usually modify nouns, commonly express an attribute of some continuant.

This correlation, however, does not hold when an occurrent is expressed by a noun or a gerund. For the sentence *John's singing was strange,* the semantics of the concept overrides the syntax of the word: the gerund *singing* is modified by the adjective *strange,* but the concept [Sing] would be linked to the concept [Strange] by the Manr relation. Many languages, such as German and Chinese, do not have a syntactic marker for distinguishing adjectives from adverbs. In those languages, semantics alone determines the choice of relation.

ACTIONS AS ROLES. The same criteria used to classify objects by phenomenal types or role types can also be used to classify actions. Some verbs directly describe an action's form or structure, but others describe an action by its role. Consider the sentence *Mary hid the ball by placing it in a box.* Hiding and placing are two different ways of describing exactly the same action. An external observer could see Mary "placing" the ball by the form of her action, but could not tell that she was "hiding" it without knowing her intentions. As another example, consider the next two sentences:

The mayor spent a long time outlining his proposals. He spoke for nearly three hours.

The three verbs, *spending, outlining,* and *speaking,* describe the same activity. Speaking determines the form, which an external observer can recognize even without being able to understand the language. Outlining, however, does not refer to the activity (Firstness), but to the results (Secondness). Spending time ignores the nature of the activity and refers only to its duration, which is a different aspect of the result. In conceptual graphs, the three verbs would be represented by three separate concepts with coreference links drawn between them. The concept [Speak] would represent the form; the two concepts [Outline] and [SpendTime] refer to the same activity, but with emphasis on different effects.

With different verbs, the same action could be described by its form (Firstness), by its effects (Secondness), or by the agent's intentions (Thirdness). As an example, a person may walk (Firstness) into a forest and disappear from view (Secondness). If the person's intention (Thirdness) was to disappear, then the act of walking would be an act of hiding. The next three sentences describe another act in each of those ways:

1. Brutus *stabbed* Caesar.

2. Brutus *killed* Caesar.

3. Brutus *murdered* Caesar.

By Firstness, an act of stabbing can be recognized by objective criteria at the instant it happens. No other events or mental attitudes need to be considered to identify an act as stabbing. But an act of stabbing cannot be identified as killing unless a second event of dying occurs. Caesar had time to ask "Et tu, Brute?" before the stabbing could be interpreted as a killing. Murder is Thirdness that depends on the motives of the agent. Determining whether an act of stabbing that resulted in killing should be considered a murder may depend on subtle clues whose interpretation could require a judge, a jury, and a lengthy trial.

4.2 Classification of Processes

Processes can be described by their starting and stopping points and by the kinds of changes that take place in between. Figure 4.3 shows the category Process subdivided by the distinction of continuous change versus discrete change. In a continuous process, which is the normal kind of physical process, incremental changes take place continuously. In a discrete process, which is typical of computer programs or idealized approximations to physical processes, changes occur in discrete steps called

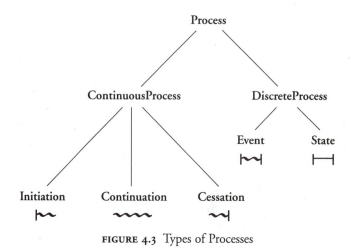

FIGURE 4.3 Types of Processes

events, which are interleaved with periods of inactivity called *states.* A continuous process with an explicit starting point is called an *initiation;* one with an ending point is a *cessation;* and one whose endpoints are not being considered is a *continuation.*

Beneath each of the five categories at the leaves of Figure 4.3 is an icon that illustrates the kind of change: a vertical bar indicates an endpoint, a wavy horizontal line indicates change, and a straight horizontal line indicates no change. A discrete process is a sequence of states and events that may be symbolized by a chain of straight and wavy lines separated by vertical bars. A continuous process may be symbolized by a continuous wavy line with occasional vertical bars. Those bars do not indicate a break in the physical process, but a discontinuity in the way the process is classified or described. The weather, for example, varies by continuous gradations, but different time periods may be classified as hot or cold, cloudy or sunny.

The categories in Figure 4.3 could be differentiated further by considering an agent's *intentions.* A cessation that satisfies the agent's goals is a *success;* one that does not satisfy the goals is a *failure.* Suppose, for example, that Farmer Brown plowed the east field on Monday, stopped on Monday evening, and then plowed the west field on Tuesday. If Brown had promised to finish the work in two days, the activity could be considered a single event with a successful completion on Tuesday and a temporary pause on Monday evening. If each field was considered separately, the same activity could be classified as two events with a successful completion at the end of each day. But if Brown had promised to finish the work in one day, the cessation on Monday evening might be considered a failure.

In language, the features of *tense* and *aspect* relate the event described by a verb to the type of process and to the *reference times* of one or more observers. The *simple tenses* — past, present, and future — relate the time of an event to the time of the speech. The *compound tenses,* such as past perfect or future perfect, involve an additional reference time in some real or hypothetical past or future. Aspect describes the initiation, continuation, or completion of some action with respect to the reference times. As in the example of Farmer Brown, whether an action is continuing or completed may depend on some agent's intentions. The definitions of many verbs depend on the intentions of their agents, and the same physical process described by different verbs can be classified in very different ways. Different classifications, in turn, have different implications: depending on the verb that is applied, Brown may be praised for a success or blamed for a failure.

FLUENTS.   Isaac Newton used the word *fluent* for a time-dependent physical quantity, such as position, pressure, or temperature. Leibniz developed the more general notion of a *function*, whose values could depend on an argument of any type, including time. Newton's fluents can be considered special cases of Leibniz's functions. They can also be considered indexicals whose referents depend on the current context. As examples, Exercises 1.18 and 1.19 illustrated two ways of representing time dependencies:

- *Implicit.* With temporal logic, the operator □ for *always* means *for every temporal context*, and ◊ for *sometimes* means *for some context*. Then everything within the scope of □ or ◊, including predicates like part(x,y), is a fluent governed by an implicit quantifier for time.
- *Explicit.* With the quantifiers ($\forall t$:Time) and ($\exists t$:Time), everything that can change must have an explicit argument for time, as in the triadic predicate part(x,y,t). In effect, the variable t serves as the index of a separate context for every instant of time.

Fluents and indexicals can be considered abbreviations that allow one argument of a function or relation to be left implicit. When they are translated to predicate calculus, the extra variable t is either hidden in the definition of an operator like □ or shown explicitly with a quantifier like ($\forall t$:Time). In conceptual graphs, the PTim relation links a context to an explicit concept for the point in time, and relations like the tense marker Past hide the time concept inside the definition.

In AI, the term *fluent* has been generalized beyond Newton's physical quantities and beyond time-dependent functions to any kind of state or situation-dependent property. Even the property of being president can be considered a fluent, as in the following example:

> The president of the United States is elected every four years.
> Bill Clinton is the president of the United States.
> Therefore, Bill Clinton is elected every four years.

The fallacy in this syllogism results from an undistributed middle term: the definite article indicates that the phrase *the president* is a context-dependent indexical. In the major premise, it is within the scope of the quantifier *every four years*, which introduces a new context for each election. The minor premise, however, is only true within the context of Bill Clinton's time in office. Many other role types, such as Employee, Client, or DesignatedDriver, can be also treated as fluents.

BASIC DISTINCTIONS. In his book *Features and Fluents*, Erik Sandewall presented a comprehensive analysis of fluents, their representation in logic, and the techniques for reasoning about them. For knowledge representation, the interactions of fluents with time, change, sequencing, and context are major concerns. Sandewall presented a list of distinctions for classifying processes according to the complexity of their interactions with fluents:

- *Discrete or continuous.* In physics, *continuous* processes are represented by *differential equations*. On digital computers, time is divided into *discrete* time points, called *integer time* when they are numbered 0, 1, 2. . . . Continuous processes can be approximated by decreasing the time step and thereby increasing the number of points that must be represented, stored, and computed. Differential equations represent the limiting case when the time step approaches zero and the number of points approaches infinity.

- *Linear or branching.* A *linear* order of time points and their associated events creates a deterministic process that is easy to represent and compute. Conditional alternatives, however, create *branching time*, with a nondeterministic increase in the future possibilities that must be represented and analyzed.

- *Independent or ramified.* If the fluents are *independent*, a change to one has no effect on the others; in a *ramified* process, a change to one can cause changes in the others. Sandewall drew a three-way distinction: *local independence*, where all the fluents are independent; *local ramification*, where an event that changes one fluent only changes other fluents that are directly involved in the current event; and *structural ramification*, where the effects of changing one fluent may propagate to other events and cause indirect changes to remotely related fluents.

- *Immediate or delayed.* If the changes caused by an event occur *immediately*, they can be represented or simulated during the same time step as the event. A *delayed* effect, however, does not cause an observable change until some subsequent states or events.

- *Sequential or concurrent.* In a *sequential* process, only one event occurs at any instant. In a *concurrent* process, multiple independent events occur in parallel.

- *Predictable or surprising.* A *predictable* process follows a script that specifies all the possible causes and effects of each event. A *surprising* or *exogenous* event causes a change that is not anticipated by the script.

- *Normal or equinormal.* Some processes have a highly probable or *normal* flow of events that can be assumed as the default. In an *equinormal* process, multiple courses of events are equally likely, and no single outcome can be considered the default.

- *Flat or hierarchical.* In a *flat* process, each event is described by a short list of the changes it can cause. In a *hierarchical* process, any event may be composed of subevents. A third option is a *recursively hierarchical* process, in which some events are composed of subevents of the same type.

- *Timeless or time-bound.* The simplest processes to analyze involve a fixed number of *timeless* objects that are neither created nor destroyed during the process. *Time-bound* objects, which may be created or destroyed during the interval of interest, lead to processes with an ever-changing inventory of objects.

- *Forgetful or memory-bound.* In a *forgetful* process, the future course of events depends only on the current state, not on the history of how the current state came about. A *memory-bound* process retains some information from earlier states, which may affect future outcomes.

The product of these distinctions generates an ontology with $2^8 \times 3^2$ or 2304 categories of processes. The first option in each distinction leads to a process as predictable as a clock; the later options lead to richer but more complex processes. Unfortunately for computational purposes, most naturally occurring processes involve some or all of the later options.

Sandewall's list does not exhaust all the possible distinctions for classifying processes and fluents. A system designer, for example, might distinguish a process *local* to a single system from a process *distributed* across a network. Sandewall did not consider that distinction .because the location of a process is independent of the methods for reasoning about it. For different purposes, new categories can be generated by adding more distinctions to the list or by deleting some that are not relevant.

4.3 Procedures, Processes, and Histories

Discrete processes can be simulated by digital computers, but continuous processes are more naturally simulated by analog computers. Yet if the time step is small enough, the granularity of a digital simulation might not be noticeable. Movies and television, for example, represent continuous motion by a sequence of discrete frames. *State-transition diagrams*, which represent states by circles and events by arrows that connect the circles, are a common representation for discrete processes. *Finite-state machines* are the simplest and most widely used version of state-transition diagrams. *Petri nets*, designed by Carl Adam Petri (1962), are a generalization of state-transition diagrams for representing concurrent processes. For object-oriented design, Petri nets have been adopted as the basis for *activity diagrams* in the Unified Modeling Language (UML).

For programming the original von Neumann machine, Herman Goldstine and John von Neumann (1947) designed *flow charts*, which are complementary to finite-state machines. In a flow chart, boxes represent computational events, and diamonds represent decisions where the flow of control can take an alternate path. In a finite-state machine, circles represent states, and arcs mark the transitions from one state to the next. Figure 4.4 shows how a flow chart and a finite-state machine can be merged to form a Petri net, which is more general than either of them. The circles of the Petri net, which are called *places*, correspond to the states of the finite-state machine; the bars, called *transitions*, correspond to the events of the flow chart.

The same kinds of notations used to specify computer procedures can also be used to specify, describe, or approximate discrete processes of any kind. Petri nets are especially convenient for representing *cause* and *effect*: each transition represents a possible event, the input states of a transition represent the causes, and the output states represent the effects. By executing the Petri net interpretively, a computer can simulate the processes and causal dependencies.

MAPPING TO LOGIC. In the diagrams of Figure 4.4, the states are labeled p, q, r, s, and t; the events are labeled a, b, d, e, and f; the diamond labeled c in the flow chart represents a condition, which corresponds to the arc of the finite-state machine from state r to s if c is true and to the arc from state r to t if c is false. The state p is the *precondition* of the event a, and the state q is the *postcondition* of a and the precondition of the next event b. If the condition c is true in state r, the successor event is d; if c is false, the successor event is f. Any of the three diagrams in Figure 4.4 could be mapped to logic in either the predicate calculus or the conceptual graph notation. But a representation for Petri nets would be general enough to subsume the other two.

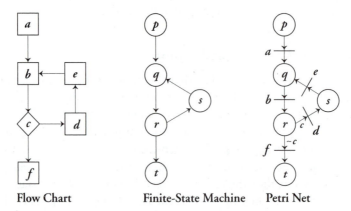

Flow Chart   Finite-State Machine   Petri Net

FIGURE 4.4 Three graphic notations for specifying procedures

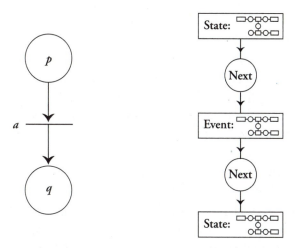

FIGURE 4.5 Translating a Petri net to a conceptual graph

Figure 4.5 shows the first transition of the Petri net and its translation to a conceptual graph. The input place p is described by a concept of type State, which contains a nested conceptual graph that describes p. The Next relation links that state to a concept of type Event, which contains another nested conceptual graph that describes the event a. Another Next relation links the event a to the state q, which contains a nested graph that describes q. In a general Petri net, a transition may have multiple input or output places. In the corresponding conceptual graph, the event concepts would have multiple predecessor or successor states linked to the events by relations of type Next.

A conceptual graph that describes a Petri net can be translated directly to predicate calculus. For each state or event x that is described by nested conceptual graph g, the description predicate $dscr(x,\varphi(g))$ would link x to the formula $\varphi(g)$, which is derived from the nested CG. The graph in Figure 4.5 would map to the following formula:

$(\exists p{:}\text{State})(\exists a{:}\text{Event})(\exists q{:}\text{State})$
$(dscr(p,\varphi(p\text{-graph})) \wedge next(p,a) \wedge dscr(a,\varphi(a\text{-graph}))$
$\wedge\ next(a,q) \wedge dscr(q,\varphi(q\text{-graph}))).$

In this formula, the nested conceptual graphs that describe p, a, and q are abbreviated p-graph, a-graph, and q-graph. The operator φ applied to these graphs produces the corresponding formulas in predicate calculus. The dscr predicates represent the CG convention that a nested graph describes the referent of a concept.

The conceptual graph in Figure 4.5 represents a history of the execution of some process. Unlike a procedure, which may be executed many times, the CG states and events have implicit existential quantifiers to indicate that they existed at one particular time. To distinguish processes, procedures, and histories, some further distinctions must be observed:

- A *process* is an evolving sequence of states and events, in which one of the states or events is marked *current* at a context-dependent time called #now.
- A *procedure* is a pattern or *script* that determines the types of states and events that may occur in an entire family of processes. Each process in the family is called an *activation* of the procedure.
- A *history* is a record of the sequence of states and events that existed in the evolution of some process. Each state and event of a history may be marked with a *time stamp* that records its point in time or duration.

In a Petri net, the places (empty circles) represent types of states. An instance of a state is represented by a dot or *token* inside the circle. Without tokens, a Petri net is a procedure that specifies a sequence of types of states and events. A token passing through the places represents a process, and a record of the passage is a history.

In logic, the distinction between procedures, processes, and histories is determined by the quantifiers on the variables of a formula or the referents of a conceptual graph. Figure 4.6 shows three CGs derived from the Petri net. The one on the left is a procedure, in which the first state is marked with a universal quantifier ∀. It implies that every state of that type is followed by an event of the type described in the next concept box, which is followed by another state of the type described in the third concept box. The graph in the middle shows a process. It has the same sequential structure as the procedure, but its first state has an attached relation (PTim), which indicates that a state of the specified type exists at the point in time #now. The graph on the right is a history in which the first and third boxes have attached relations (Dur) to indicate their duration; the event in

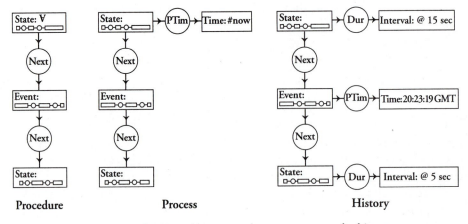

Procedure   Process   History

FIGURE 4.6 Representing a procedure, a process, and a history

the middle has an attached PTim relation to indicate its point in time. For representing procedures, the conceptual graphs or the corresponding formulas contain one or more universal quantifiers; for processes, they include one or more indexicals, such as #now; and for histories, they contain only constants and existential quantifiers.

BRANCHES AND LOOPS.   The CGs in Figures 4.5 and 4.6 represent linear processes with no loops or branches. But in Figure 4.4, the two alternatives at state *r* create a branch, and the arc from *e* to *q* creates a loop. For branches and loops, the simple translation of Figure 4.5 cannot be used:

- *Branches.* When the flow of control takes a branch, the states and events on the path not taken never occur, and the concepts that represent them should not have existential quantifiers.
- *Loops.* When the flow of control loops back to a place that was previously visited, a new instance of that type of state occurs. In CGs, a separate concept box is needed to distinguish the new instance from the previous instance.

These issues, which occur in every mapping from a procedural language to a logic-based language, were first formalized by C. A. R. Hoare (1969). His axioms, based on preconditions and postconditions, describe the changes that occur as a computer executes a procedure by following the branches and loops and executing commands along the way.

If a branch does not create a loop, it can be represented with the operator ∨ in predicate calculus or an If-Then-Else block in CGs. Following is the CG representation of the branch in Figure 4.4 from state *r* to event *d* or event *f.* Labels such as *r*-graph or *c*-graph represent the nested conceptual graphs that describe the corresponding states, events, and conditions of the Petri net.

```
[State: *r r-graph]
[If: [State: ?r c-graph]
   [Then: [?r]→(Next)→[Event: d-graph] ]
   [Else: [?r]→(Next)→[Event: f-graph] ] ].
```

The first line represents a state labeled *r, which is described by the nested *r* graph. The If-context contains a concept asserting that the *c* graph is also true of the state ?r. If that assertion is true, the next event is described by the *d* graph; otherwise, the next event is described by the *f* graph.

The concepts that represent the *d* or *f* events are nested inside the Then or Else contexts. Without the nesting, the implicit existential quantifiers in the concepts would incorrectly suggest that instances of both event types *d* and *f* would exist. With the nesting, the events would only exist within one or the other of the mutually exclusive Then or Else contexts. Since predicate calculus does not have an if-then-else operator, the translation from the CG uses an equivalent construction with the ∨ operator:

$$(\exists r{:}\text{State})(\text{dscr}(r,\varphi(r\text{-graph})) \wedge$$
$$(\text{dscr}(r,\varphi(c\text{-graph})) \wedge$$
$$(\exists d{:}\text{Event})(\text{next}(r,d) \wedge \text{dscr}(d,\varphi(d\text{-graph}))))$$
$$\vee (\text{dscr}(r,\sim\varphi(c\text{-graph})) \wedge$$
$$(\exists f{:}\text{Event})(\text{next}(r,f) \wedge \text{dscr}(f,\varphi(f\text{-graph}))))).$$

The first line says that there exists a state r, which is described by the translation of the r-graph to predicate calculus. The next two lines present the first option: the translation of the c-graph is true of r and the next event d after r is described by the d graph. The last two lines present the second option: the translation of the c-graph is not true of r and the next event f after r is described by the f-graph. When the if-then-else construction is mapped to an ∨ operator, the condition c must be tested in both options, once with and once without a negation.

In logic, recursively defined types and relations are used to represent the equivalent of a loop. Following is the CG definition of a recursive event type named Loop1:

```
[Type: Loop1]→(Def)→[LambdaExpression:
  [Event: λ
    [Event: d-graph]→(Next)→[State: s-graph]-
      (Next)→[Event: e-graph]→(Next)→[State: q-graph]-
      (Next)→[Event: b-graph]→(Next)→[State: r-graph *r]
    [If: [State: ?r c-graph]
      [Then: [?r]→(Next)→[Loop1] ]] ]].
```

This definition says that the type Loop1 is defined by a lambda expression whose formal parameter is an event described by a nested conceptual graph. In the nested CG, there is a sequence of events and states described by the graphs d, s, q, b, and r. The last state in that sequence is marked by the coreference label *r. Finally, the If-Then implication says that if the condition stated by the c graph is true of the state marked ?r, then the state ?r is followed by another occurrence of the composite event type Loop1.

Recursion is commonly used to represent loops in logic, formal grammars, and logic-programming languages. A recursive formula can be derived by translating the CG definition:

$$\text{Loop1} = (\lambda l{:}\text{Event})\text{dscr}(l,$$
$$(\exists d{:}\text{Event})(\exists s{:}\text{State})(\exists e{:}\text{Event})$$
$$(\exists q{:}\text{State})(\exists b{:}\text{Event})(\exists r{:}\text{State})$$
$$(\text{dscr}(d,\varphi(d\text{-graph})) \wedge \text{next}(d,s) \wedge$$
$$\text{dscr}(s,\varphi(s\text{-graph})) \wedge \text{next}(s,e) \wedge$$

$$\text{dscr}(e, \varphi(e\text{-graph})) \land \text{next}(e, q) \land$$
$$\text{dscr}(q, \varphi(q\text{-graph})) \land \text{next}(q, b) \land$$
$$\text{dscr}(b, \varphi(b\text{-graph})) \land \text{next}(b, r) \land$$
$$(\text{dscr}(r, \varphi(c\text{-graph})) \supset$$
$$(\exists l_1{:}\text{Loop1})\text{next}(r, l_1)\ ))).$$

Since the event of type Loop1 is only used for the recursive call, there is no need to add the label Loop1 to the permanent type hierarchy. Instead, a macro named While, which is defined in Appendix A.5, can be used to simplify the representation of loops. With that macro, the Petri net in Figure 4.4 could be written as the following CG:

```
[State: p-graph]→(Next)→[Event: a-graph]→(Next)→[State: q-graph]-
   (Next)→[Event: b-graph]→(Next)→[State: r-graph]-
   (Next)→[While: c-graph
     [Loop:
       [Event: d-graph]→(Next)→[State: s-graph]→(Next)→[Event: e-graph]-
         (Next)→[State: q-graph]→(Next)→[Event: b-graph]-
         (Next)→[State: r-graph] ]]-
   (Next)→[Event: f-graph]→(Next)→[State: t-graph].
```

The first two lines are a translation of the Petri net states and events from p through r. The third line introduces the While loop, which continues as long as the condition described by the c graph is true. The nested loop contains the sequence from d through r, and the last line finishes with the event f and state t. Although the usual predicate calculus notation does not support macro definitions, it would be possible to extend the notation with a construction similar to the While loop.

PROCEDURAL OR DECLARATIVE. Conventional programming languages are usually called *procedural,* and logic is the epitome of nonprocedural or *declarative* languages. Yet the examples show that logic can represent the same kinds of procedures as a programming language. The primary difference is that logic requires explicit relations or predicates to express the sequence, while procedural languages depend on the implicit sequence of the program listing. Ideally, programmers should use whatever notation they find easiest to read and write, and compilers should translate that notation to different code for different purposes: a logic-based language for program analysis, or machine-oriented code for high-speed execution.

4.4 Concurrent Processes

Although flow charts and finite-state machines can represent branches and loops, they limited to sequential processes. The major strength of Petri nets is their ability to represent parallel or concurrent processes. Every other mechanism or

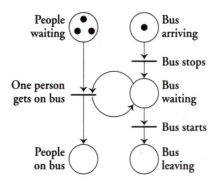

FIGURE 4.7 Petri net for a bus stop

formalism for representing discrete concurrent processes can be treated as a variation or special case of a Petri net. The *tokens* that flow through a Petri net are generalizations of the *markers* that Ross Quillian (1966) and Scott Fahlman (1979) implemented in their versions of semantic networks. To illustrate the flow of tokens, Figure 4.7 shows a Petri net for a bus stop where three tokens represent people waiting and one token represents an arriving bus.

At the upper left of Figure 4.7, each of the three dots is a token that represents one person waiting at the bus stop. The token at the upper right represents an arriving bus. The transition labeled *Bus stops* represents an event that *fires* by removing the token from the arriving place and putting a token in the waiting place. When the bus is waiting, the transition labeled *One person gets on bus* is *enabled;* it fires by first removing one token from the place for *People waiting* and one token from the place for *Bus waiting* and then putting one token in the place for *People on bus* and putting a token back in the place for *Bus waiting*. As long as the bus is waiting and there are more people waiting, that transition can keep firing. It stops firing when either there are no more people waiting or the *Bus starts* transition fires by removing the token for the waiting bus and putting a token in the place for *Bus leaving*. Figure 4.7 simulates a bus driver who stops whether or not anyone is waiting and leaves even when more people are still trying to get on. A Petri net for a more thoughtful bus driver would require more states and events for checking whether anyone is waiting.

When the nodes and tokens of a Petri net are identified with particular features of a process, they can represent all the categories of discrete processes in the ontology of Section 4.2. In *colored* or *typed* Petri nets, the colors represent the type of state for each place, the type of event for each transition, and the type of objects or data associated with the tokens that flow through the net. When a colored Petri net is translated to logic, the colors map to type labels on the concepts of CGs or the variables of typed predicate calculus. Each transition in a colored Petri net is defined either by another Petri net or by a subroutine written in a programming language. Nested definitions can support hierarchical and recursively hierarchical processes. For memory-bound processes, data associated with the tokens can represent information about earlier states.

FLOW OF TOKENS. Figure 4.8 shows a concurrent Petri net and a conceptual graph that describes the execution of the Petri net from time $t=0$ to $t=8$. In the conceptual graph on the right of Figure 4.8, concepts of the form [A-State] or [B-Event] are used as abbreviations for concepts with nested CGs, such as [State: *a*-graph] or [Event: *b*-graph]. For the time measures, a concept of the form [@5sec] is an abbreviation for [Interval: @5sec], which is an abbreviation for the graph

```
[Interval]→(Chrc)→[Amount: <5,sec>].
```

The expanded graph may be read *an interval that has a characteristic amount of 5 seconds.*

The diagram in the upper left of Figure 4.8 is an example of a Petri net at a particular time $t=0$. The token in place *a* represents a state of type *a*, which occurs at time $t=0$. The flow of tokens through a Petri net is governed by three rules:

- *Enabled.* Whenever a transition has one or more tokens in each of its input places, it is said to be *enabled.*
- *Active.* An enabled transition may become *active* by removing one token from each input place.
- *Finished.* An active transition finishes by adding one token to each output place. The event from activation to finish is called a *firing* of the transition.

The token in place *a* enables transition *b*. When *b* becomes active, it removes the token from place *a*. When *b* finishes, it adds one token to each of its three output places *c*, *d*, and *e*. At the bottom left of Figure 4.8 is the Petri net at time $t=8$, just after the firing of transition *b*.

On the right of Figure 4.8 is a conceptual graph that describes the states that occurred just before and just after the firing of transition *b*. It says that a state of type A (represented by a dot in place *a*) lasted for a duration (Dur) of 5 seconds, which started (Strt) at the time 0:00:00. The Next relation shows that the A-State was followed by a B-Event, which had a duration of 3 seconds. The event finished at the time $t=8$, which is the sum of the time 0:00:00 plus the two durations of 5 seconds for the state and 3 seconds for the event. The successors of the event were states of types C, D, and E, which had durations of 11, 4, and 13 seconds, respectively.

In terms of the categories of Chapter 2, a Petri net without any tokens represents a script (A1O) that determines the behavior (P2O) of a family of processes (P1O). A token in a place represents a proposition (A2) that some condition (P2C) is true at the current time #now. Figure 4.3, which is an extension of the lattice in Figure 2.6,

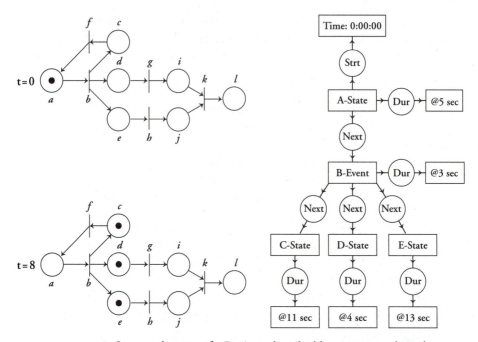

FIGURE 4.8 States and events of a Petri net described by a conceptual graph

shows states and events as types of occurrents (O), which represent the changes (events) and the absence of change (states) that occur in discrete processes. The conceptual graph on the right of Figure 4.8 represents a history (A2O) that describes the sequence of states before and after an event of type B.

In a colored Petri net, each token carries some associated data, which may be generated by one transition, stored temporarily in a place, and later used by another transition. The color of a token represents the type of entity represented by the data, which may be abstract or physical. For example, a *PERT chart* (Project Analysis and Review Technique) is a special case of a Petri net used in project management. Each transition represents one task to be performed as part of an overall project. The input arcs of each task show how it depends on the results of previous tasks, and the output arcs show other tasks that depend on it. The tokens that flow through the net can represent the people who perform the tasks, the resources used in the tasks, or the money paid for the completion of a task. Since no task may depend on itself, a PERT chart cannot have cycles: it must be an *acyclic* Petri net.

TIMING DIAGRAM.   Conceptual graphs and predicate calculus are general-purpose notations that may become cluttered with detail for specific kinds of problems. A special-purpose notation, such as the *timing diagram* in Figure 4.9, is a more succinct way of showing the history of states and events that occur as the Petri net in

Figure 4.8 is executed. The calibrated arrow at the bottom represents the flow of time. The diagram above the time arrow shows sequences of events (wavy lines) and states (straight lines) separated by vertical bars at various points in time.

At the left of Figure 4.9, a state of type A begins at time $t=0$ and ends at $t=5$. Then an event of type B occurs that corresponds to the firing of transition b in Figure 4.8. After 3 seconds, states of type C, D, and E begin. Each of those states is followed by an event of the type determined by the Petri net. The token in place c, for example, enables transition f, which is fired in an event of type F. At time $t=22$, that event is completed, and another token appears in place a to show another state of type A. Meanwhile, other states and events are following parallel paths, as in a multithreaded operating system.

The Petri net, the conceptual graph, and the timing diagram are different ways of representing aspects of discrete processes. The Petri net highlights the procedure, which determines a family of processes, but it does not show the details of the times and durations of any particular process. The timing diagram explicitly shows the flow of time and the parallel threads of processes made up of discrete states and events. The multiple paths in the timing diagram show the states where resources are waiting to be used and the *critical path* that has no wait states: every resource along a critical path is used as soon as it becomes available.

As complete representations for logic, conceptual graphs and predicate calculus are general enough to represent everything that can be represented in a Petri net, a timing diagram, or any other notation for discrete processes. That generality, however, comes at the expense of a more detailed notation that can become less readable: the conceptual graph has many more nodes and arcs, and the predicate calculus has many more predicates and variables. The general and special notations complement one another: Petri nets and timing diagrams show fewer relationships, but they highlight them more clearly.

MEASURING TIME.   As St. Augustine observed, the motions of the heavenly bodies do not constitute time, but they can be used to measure its passage. Any

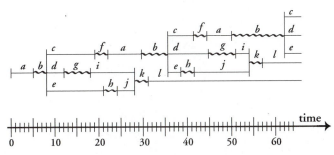

FIGURE 4.9 A timing diagram for representing a history of states and events

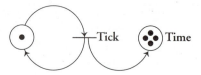

FIGURE 4.10 A Petri net for a clock at time $t=4$

other objects whose motions are sufficiently regular could also be used as a standard for measuring time. Galileo used his own heartbeats to time falling bodies. Clocks have been based on dripping water, sifting sand, swinging pendulums, and the vibrations of springs, tuning forks, crystals, and atoms. Figure 4.10 shows a Petri net for a clock that could be based on any such process. The transition named Tick is enabled by the token at the left. When the transition fires, it immediately replaces that token and adds another token to the place labeled Time. The four tokens that have accumulated in that place indicate that four ticks of the clock have elapsed. The time unit for one tick might be a month for a clock based on the moon, a second for water drops, or a nanosecond for a vibrating crystal.

The clock in Figure 4.10 measures time by the number of tokens that have accumulated in the Time place, but the tokens might accumulate so fast that some additional mechanism may be needed to count them. Inside a mechanical clock, most of the gears are used to translate the high-speed ticks of a pendulum or vibrating spring to the much slower movement of the hour and minute hands. A digital clock would use a *counter* to translate a sequence of pulses to a number that counts how many pulses occurred. Figure 4.11 shows a Petri net that could be used to count tokens. It has four places: the input place accepts new tokens from some process, such as the clock; the even place indicates a count of 0; the odd place indicates a count of 1; and the carry place accumulates tokens that overflow beyond the limit of 1.

By itself, a one-bit counter is not very useful, but multiple copies of the counter can be linked together to count as high as desired. The carry place of each counter would be merged with the input place for the next higher bit; with n one-bit counters, the combined counter could measure times up to 2^n. The Petri net could

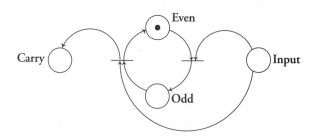

FIGURE 4.11 A Petri net for a one-bit counter

be extended with more transitions for drawing a notch on a line at every tick, a slightly longer notch at every 5 ticks, and the current total at every 10 ticks. As a result, the Petri net could print a calibrated arrow, such as the one at the bottom of Figure 4.9. The combined clock, counter, and printer could be used as a standard for timing other Petri nets, such as Figure 4.8. All methods of measuring time are based on the same principle: select some process whose ticks are assumed to be regular, and use the count of ticks to measure the progress of other processes. In effect, qualitative observations are more fundamental than quantitative measurements: every measuring instrument ever invented is based on counting instances of some repetitive event type that is recognized by qualitative similarities.

SYNCHRONIZING PROCESSES.   The transitions of a Petri net are independent of one another and may fire asynchronously. That property makes them a better model for independent activities than a strictly sequential computer program. But if two processes have to cooperate, Petri nets can also be used to represent the control primitives, synchronizing mechanisms, network protocols, and deadlock management techniques.

As an example of interacting processes, Figure 4.12 shows a Petri net for two processes that produce messages and one process that consumes them. The six-place producer loop contains two tokens, each of which represents a process that is in some stage of producing messages. The five-place consumer loop contains only one token, which represents a process that is consuming messages. Two additional places, named Buffer Full and Buffer Empty, are used to synchronize the processes and ensure that sufficient buffers are available to hold the messages.

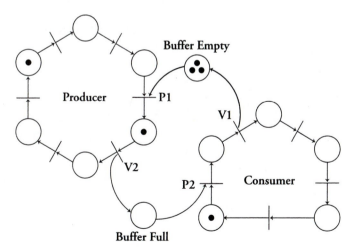

FIGURE 4.12 A Petri net with producers and consumers
interacting via semaphores

The two tokens on the producer loop move independently of one another; one token might overtake and pass the other. The single token on the consumer loop is even more independent. But to prevent messages from being lost, the two places labeled Buffer Empty and Buffer Full enforce synchronization between producers and consumers:

- *Buffer empty.* The three tokens in this place indicate three instances of empty buffers ready to be filled with messages. When a token on the producer loop reaches the transition labeled P1, it cannot pass unless there is at least one token in the buffer-empty place. If there is, the P1 transition removes one token from each of its input places and puts a token in its output place. More tokens accumulate in the buffer-empty place whenever the consumer passes through transition V2 and returns an empty buffer.

- *Buffer full.* The absence of a token in this place indicates that there are no buffers filled with messages. Therefore, the token on the consumer loop must wait at transition P2 until a producer token passes through transition V2 and puts a buffer containing a message in the buffer-full place. When a token appears in the buffer-full place, the consumer can pass through P2 and read the message; then it can pass through V2 to return the empty buffer.

These two places and the transitions that add or remove tokens implement a synchronizing mechanism called a *semaphore*, which was introduced by the Dutch computer scientist Edsger Dijkstra.

In operating systems, a semaphore is represented by a variable that maintains a count of available resources of some type. The two permissible operators on semaphores, called P and V, must be performed as uninterruptable actions:

- *Free.* The V operation frees some resource, such as a buffer, to make it available to other processes. It adds 1 to the semaphore s to show that another resource is available.

  $s := s + 1.$

  The letter V comes from the Dutch word *vrij* (free).

- *Pass.* The P operation makes a request for some resource and waits until it becomes available. If one or more resources are available, it subtracts 1 from s and lets the process pass through:

  If $s = 0$ then wait.
  If $s > 0$ then $s := s - 1$; pass.

- The letter P comes from the Dutch word *passeer* (pass).

For the Petri net in Figure 4.12, the variables for the Buffer-Empty and Buffer-Full semaphores would represent the number of tokens in the corresponding places.

THEOREMS ABOUT PETRI NETS.   The places and transitions of a Petri net form a static pattern of types; the tokens flowing through the net form a dynamic pattern of instances. From the pattern of types, it is possible to prove theorems that predict the permissible changes in the instances:

- If a transition has n input places and m output places, then every time it fires, there is a net gain of $(m-n)$ tokens on the Petri net.

This theorem follows immediately from the rule for firing transitions. An enabled transition fires by removing one token from each input place and adding one token to each output place. For the Petri net in Figure 4.8, transition b (which is called a *fork*) causes a net gain of $(3-1)$ or 2 tokens whenever it fires. Transition k (which is called a *join*) causes a gain of $(1-2)$ or a loss of 1 token whenever it fires. None of the other transitions cause any gain or loss, since they all have the same number of inputs and outputs.

Each token in a Petri net corresponds to a separate *thread* or *task* in a multitasking system. The timing diagram in Figure 4.9 shows that one thread starts at time $t=0$ with the single token in state a. After transition b, there are three threads, which become two after transition k. At time $t=64$, there are five threads, caused by two more firings of transition b and one of transition k. Two of the threads at the end of Figure 4.9 correspond to tokens in state l, which is not an input to any transition. Those threads will remain dormant indefinitely. In an operating system, such dormant tasks cause *memory leaks*; they keep accumulating until they fill all available computer storage without performing any useful service. That problem, which is often caused by programs that do not maintain a balance between task opening and closing, can be avoided by the following theorem:

- If for every transition, the number of inputs equals the number of outputs, then the number of tokens on the Petri net remains constant.

A special case is a conventional flow chart or finite-state machine, which is translated to a Petri net such as Figure 4.4 with exactly one input and one output for every transition.

Another way to avoid useless threads is to ensure that every path that leads to an n-way fork eventually brings the threads together with an n-way join. Figure 4.12 illustrates that solution. Although the number of tokens on the net may increase or decrease over time, there is an upper bound and a lower bound on the possible total at any moment. The following theorem can be used to determine those bounds:

- On any cycle, if every place has one input arc and one output arc that is part of the cycle, then the number of tokens on the cycle remains constant (even though the number of tokens on the net as a whole may be changing).

Note that this theorem depends only on the number of inputs and outputs to each place of the cycle, not to each transition. Figure 4.12 has three cycles that meet that condition. The first two are the producer loop, which has two tokens, and the consumer loop, which has one token. But there is also the buffer cycle in the middle, which has one place that overlaps the producer cycle and one place that overlaps the consumer cycle. In Figure 4.12, the buffer cycle has four tokens, one of which is shared with the producer cycle. The upper bound is $2+1+4$ or seven tokens, which would occur when there are no tokens in the shared places. The lower bound of four tokens would occur when both tokens on the producer cycle are in one shared place and the single token of the consumer cycle is in the other shared place. Figure 4.12 shows an intermediate state with six tokens.

4.5   Computation

As purely declarative notations, logic and mathematics have no inherent directionality. A computation, however, always has a purpose. It must thread its way through a tangle of relationships to find the answer to some question. As an example, Newton's famous equation relates the force F on a body to its mass m and acceleration a:

$$F = ma.$$

By the way it's written, this equation suggests that force is the unknown result to be computed from the given mass and acceleration. Yet the equation could just as well be used to compute the mass from F and a or the acceleration from F and m.

Similar observations apply to logical implications, which can be used in forward-chaining or backward-chaining applications. The following implication was discussed in Section 1.4 as a rule for the harmonious resolution of a dissonant chord:

$(\forall x,y{:}\text{Note})((\text{simul}(x,y) \land \text{tone}(x,\text{Ti}) \land \text{tone}(y,\text{Fa})) \supset$
$\qquad (\exists z,w{:}\text{Note})(\text{next}(x,z) \land \text{tone}(z,\text{Do}) \land \text{next}(y,w) \land \text{tone}(w,\text{Mi}))\ ).$

According to the way this formula is written, the expected reading would proceed from left to right: *For every note x and y, if x and y are simultaneous, the tone of x is Ti, and the tone of y is Fa, then there exist notes z and w, where the next note after x is z, whose tone is Do, and the next note after y is w, whose tone is Mi.* The if-then implication seems to suggest that a composer writing music should follow the rule in the way it is written: after writing a dissonant chord, follow it with a harmonious resolution. In practice, the composer might plan ahead to the final chord and then apply the rules backward to derive a series of chords with an intermediate dissonance before the final harmony.

The relationships stated in logic and mathematics are like a road map: they affect every possible route, but they don't determine any particular direction a driver should take. The directionality of a computation, like the route the driver chooses, depends primarily on the starting point and the desired goal. A road map is a statement of constraints the driver must observe to find a route with the best balance of speed, economy, convenience, and scenery. The constraints stated in a road map or a logical formula determine the options; the driver's goals determine the direction.

DATAFLOW DIAGRAMS. Functions are relations that behave like one-way streets in guiding a computation. In graphic form, they correspond to *dataflow diagrams*, which have a preferred directionality. By definition, a *function* is a relation that has one argument called the *output*, which has a single value for each combination of values of the other arguments, called the *inputs*. In conceptual graphs, the output concept of a function is attached to its last arc, whose arrow points away from the circle. If f is a function from type T1 to type T2, the constraint of a single output for each input can be stated by an axiom in a conceptual graph or predicate calculus:

$[T1: \forall] \rightarrow (f) \rightarrow [T2: @1].$
$(\forall x{:}T1)(\exists! y{:}T2)f(x,y).$

Both the graph and the formula say that for every input of type T1, f has exactly one output ($\exists! y$) of type T2. Since the distinction between functions and other relations is important for many applications, it is useful to have a special notation that marks a relation as a function. In Figure 4.13, the diamond nodes indicate that the relations Sum, Pred, and CS2N are functional.

The variables ?a, ?b, and ?c are inputs that refer to concept nodes on other graphs. The output variable *x marks a defining node that could be referenced elsewhere by ?x. The functions Sum and Prod each take two numbers as input and generate one number as output. The function CS2N converts a character string input to a number as output. Figure 4.13 could be mapped to the following expression in predicate calculus supplemented with an infix notation for the mathematical operators:

$x = (a + b) * \text{cs2n}(c).$

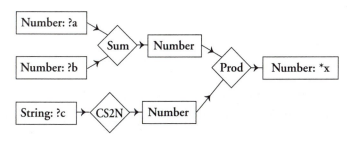

FIGURE 4.13 A dataflow diagram with functional relations

This equation looks like an assignment statement, and it could be translated to one in a conventional programming language. But the converse does not hold: not every assignment statement can be translated to a dataflow diagram. The following assignment statement, for example, could never be interpreted as a true equation for any value of x:

$$x = x + 1.$$

Such assignments, which change the value of a variable, cannot be represented in a dataflow diagram. The programming languages that correspond to dataflow diagrams are called *functional*. Variables in those languages are not truly variable, since their values can never be modified after their first assignment. For that reason, they are also called *single assignment languages*.

Without loops and branches, dataflow diagrams cannot support a complete programming system. When supplemented with a conditional operator and the ability to call diagrams recursively, however, they form the basis for a language that can specify any computable function. Only three control mechanisms are needed for a complete *functional programming language:* recursive function definition, function application, and a conditional operator. As an example, Figure 4.14 shows a conceptual graph for defining the function facto, which computes the factorial x of a nonnegative integer n.

The relation Sub1 subtracts 1 from its input; it corresponds to the function sub1 in LISP or the decrement operator in C. The conditional relation Cond corresponds to an if-then-else expression or the ternary ?: operator in C. In Figure 4.14, the first argument of Cond is the truth value of $2 > n$; if true, the output of Cond is the second argument 1; otherwise, the output of Cond is the third argument, which results from

relation Facto(*n,*x) is functional

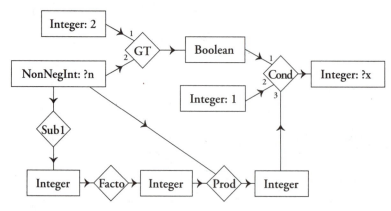

FIGURE 4.14 Using a conceptual graph to define a recursive function

the recursive call. The keyword *functional* is a metalanguage abbreviation for the axiom that there exists exactly one output x for every input n. The next three lines show how the conceptual graph would be translated to a lambda expression in predicate calculus, a function in C, and a function in LISP:

- *Predicate calculus.* facto = $(\lambda n{:}\text{Integer})\text{cond}(2{>}n, 1, n{*}\text{facto}(n{-}1))$.
- *C.* int facto(int n) { return ((2>n) ? 1 : n*facto(— n)); }
- *LISP.* (defun facto (n) (if (> 2 n) 1 (* n (facto (sub1 n)))))

These translations illustrate the equivalence between a specification in logic and a purely functional specification in a programming language. For convenience, efficiency, and the ability to control multiple processes, languages like C and LISP support many other features, but the functional mechanisms alone are sufficient to simulate a Turing machine. For parallel machines, functional languages can often achieve higher efficiency than conventional languages because all the dependencies are specified before compile time; no surprises can occur that would interrupt the parallel processes.

COMPUTING WITH PETRI NETS.   When a dataflow diagram such as Figure 4.13 is translated to a Petri net, concepts map to places, and relations map to transitions. But recursive diagrams, such as Figure 4.14, would cause the Petri net to grow and shrink dynamically. Each recursive call to Facto would cause the label Facto to be replaced by a copy of its defining graph. That new copy, which is invoked to compute another value, is erased after it returns the result. For efficiency, an optimizing compiler would avoid copying the entire graph; instead, it could use a *pushdown stack* to store only the changeable data.

    If concurrent processes have interacting side effects, dataflow diagrams can be supplemented with general Petri nets. Kurt Jensen (1992) took advantage of that distinction in his system for compiling colored Petri nets to executable code. He used the functional language ML (Stansifer 1992) to specify the basic computation within a transition and developed graphic tools to simulate the interactions between transitions. This distinction enables the different kinds of computations to be specified, tested, and debugged in a modular fashion. After the testing and debugging, the complete Petri nets are compiled to C for efficiency and portability.

    Petri nets are especially useful for *event-driven* programs that respond to unpredictable surprises from outside the computer system. Some large applications were implemented with Jensen's tools: a radar simulation system, electronic money transfer between banks, and communication protocols for a digital telephone network. Since the activity diagrams in UML are based on Petri nets, such tools can be used to simulate UML models and compile them to executable code.

MESSAGE PASSING.   Surprises in event-driven systems are commonly represented by passing *messages* from one process to another. The kinds of systems can be distinguished by the way the sending process communicates with the receiving process:

- *Synchronous or asynchronous.* In synchronous communication, the process that sends the message waits for an answering message before continuing. In asynchronous communication, the process that sends the message continues without waiting for a response.

- *Addressed or associative.* In addressed communications, the sending process invokes a particular process by its address, name, or other identifier. In associative or *pattern-directed* communication, the process that sends the message does not know the identity of the process that accepts and responds to the message. Instead, the sending process puts the message in a pool, called a *blackboard* or *bulletin board* (BB), and the responding process selects a message from BB that matches a pattern it is prepared to handle. In the Java language, BB is called the *InfoBus.*

Combinations of these two distinctions lead to four kinds of communication by message passing:

1. Synchronous addressed communication corresponds to a function or subroutine call, in which the calling program is suspended until the called program returns a result.

2. Asynchronous addressed communication supports parallel processing for input/output devices and mutithreaded operating systems.

3. Synchronous associative communication is based on an *agenda* for ordering or prioritizing tasks in forward-chaining languages such as CLIPS.

4. Asynchronous associative communication resembles the New York Stock Exchange, with a pandemonium of brokers making trades for buyers and sellers who never know each other's identity. It is used in distributed processing, triggers in database systems, and data sharing among independent Java programs that communicate via the InfoBus.

Logically, addressed communications correspond to backward-chaining inferences, and associative communications correspond to forward-chaining inferences. The question of whether a process waits or continues is an implementation issue that does not affect the logical relationships, but it does affect efficiency. Synchronous communication is easier to control, but asynchronous communication can keep more processes active at the same time.

Associative communication, whether synchronous or asynchronous, requires a common place, such as the bulletin board BB, where the processes deposit their messages and look for new messages that match their patterns. Since CLIPS is a synchronous language, the only active process is the *inference engine*. The CLIPS BB is the working memory that stores all the facts; the inference engine carries out all the pattern matching, sequencing, and rule execution. For asynchronous associative communication, the common place can become as busy as the floor of a stock exchange. Despite the apparent chaos, useful work can be accomplished as long as the processes follow well-defined rules for the formats of messages and the ways of sending and receiving them.

LINDA. The language *Linda*, designed by David Gelernter (1985), has a simple but powerful set of rules for asynchronous associative communication. In Linda, messages are passed via BB as *n-tuples* or lists of *n* data items. There are three kinds of tuples:

- *Data.* A data tuple represents a fact that is being asserted, a value that has been computed, or a response to some earlier message. It looks like an instance frame, an assertion in CLIPS, or a row of a relational database.
- *Patterns.* A pattern tuple, like a condition in CLIPS, has a variable marked with ? in zero or more of the slots in the tuple. When a process requests a data tuple from BB, it provides a pattern tuple. If the pattern matches some data tuple currently in BB, the variables in the pattern tuple are replaced with values from the corresponding slots in the data tuple.
- *Executables.* An executable or *live* tuple differs from a data tuple by containing an expression in one or more slots. For each expression, a new process is started asynchronously to evaluate the expression before the result is placed in BB.

In effect, the Linda bulletin board resembles a relational database, in which a *BB manager* responds to requests from multiple concurrent processes. The sample database in Figure 3.3 could be stored in BB as a collection of data tuples:

```
(objects A pyramid red)     (supports A D)
(objects B pyramid green)   (supports B D)
       . . .                     . . .
```

To ask a question like *What is the name and shape of a green object?*, some process would send a request to BB with the pattern tuple (objects ?name ?shape green). The BB manager would match this pattern to a data tuple and replace the variable ?name with "B" and the variable ?shape with "pyramid". If no matching data tuple is found, the two Linda operators InP and ReadP send a negative response, but the In and Read operators keep the requesting process waiting until a matching tuple is placed in BB.

Processes communicate by six possible operations that put tuples in BB or take

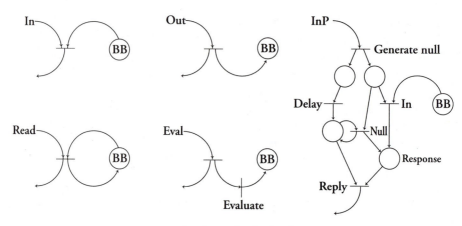

FIGURE 4.15 Petri nets for the Linda operators

matching tuples out of BB. Figure 4.15 shows the Petri nets that represent the following Linda operators:

1. *In.* The In operator sends a pattern tuple to BB, which is matched to some data tuple in BB. If a matching tuple is found, it is sent to the calling process. If no match, the calling process must wait until some other process sends a matching data tuple to BB. The Petri net for the In operator is in the upper left of Figure 4.15.

2. *Read.* The Read operator is like In, but with one extra feature: when a matching tuple is found in BB, a copy is sent to the calling process, and the original is returned to BB. Its Petri net is like the net for In, but with an arc to return the tuple to BB.

3. *Out.* The Out operator sends a data tuple to BB and lets the sending process continue. Its Petri net is in the upper middle of Figure 4.15.

4. *Eval.* The Eval operator evaluates the expressions of an executable tuple and sends the resulting tuple to BB. Its Petri net resembles the net for Out, but with a transition labeled Evaluate before the result goes to BB. For each expression in the executable tuple, Eval starts a separate process. Depending on the complexity of those expressions, the new processes could call Eval recursively to start more processes.

5. *InP.* The InP operator is like In, but if no matching tuple is found in BB, it sends a *null tuple* to the requesting process instead of making it wait. The Petri net for InP, which is shown on the right side of Figure 4.15, has four additional transitions and places. The first transition generates a null tuple for its left output and passes the original pattern tuple to the right output. The transition

labeled In is the same as the In operator. The one labeled Delay pauses to give In a chance to search for a match; then it passes the null tuple to its output place. If In finds a match, the matching tuple is sent to the place labeled Response; otherwise, the transition labeled Null passes the null tuple to the Response place and deletes the original pattern tuple, which is still waiting. Finally, the transition labeled Reply passes whatever tuple is in the Response place to the original process and deletes the leftover null tuple.

6. *ReadP.* The ReadP operator is like InP, but if a match is found, it sends a copy of the matching data tuple to Response and sends the original data tuple back to BB. Its Petri net, which is not shown in Figure 4.15, is like the net for InP, but with one extra arc to return the tuple to BB.

From the calling program, the six Linda operators appear to be ordinary subroutine calls. They can be called from languages like FORTRAN and C, which do not have any built-in features for multitasking. With the addition of Linda calls, such languages have been used to implement highly parallel distributed systems (Carriero & Gelernter 1990). In a Petri net, the Linda operators can be called as subnets; to the calling net, they look like simple transitions whose internal details are not visible. For examples, see the exercises at the end of this chapter.

A Linda-like system could be designed for any form of knowledge representation, including frames, Prolog terms, or conceptual graphs. Logically, BB is a repository of facts and goals that can be accessed in parallel by multiple inference engines. Computationally, many systems implement Linda-like operations in various ways. An SQL database, for example, can be viewed as a bulletin board with indexed tables of tuples that are accessed concurrently by multiple distributed processes. Sandewall's category of surprises could be represented in SQL or any other Linda-like system by processes that deposit "surprising" messages in the database or BB. Processes that are sensitive to surprises could use SQL queries or the Linda ReadP operation to check for messages that might affect their outcome.

4.6 Constraint Satisfaction

A computation follows a method to achieve a goal that satisfies certain constraints. In procedural languages, the programmer states the method in detail and leaves the goal unstated, except perhaps in the comments and documentation. In nonprocedural languages, the programmer states the goal and lets the computer system select an appropriate method. In either kind of language, the constraints must always be specified. The SQL database language is a typical nonprocedural language: the programmer specifies a goal in the select clause of a query and the logical constraints in the where clause; then the database system determines an appropriate method for satisfying the constraints.

By itself, a *constraint* is a proposition stated in some logic-based language. What makes a constraint different from an ordinary statement is the ulterior purpose behind it: some agent has declared that the constraint *must* be true. Computationally, some goal triggers a search for a combination of values that make the constraint true. The method of searching depends on both the goal and the constraints. In SQL, for example, very different search methods would be generated by different select options with the same where clause.

GENERATE AND TEST.   For his system of rotating disks, Ramon Lull discovered a general method for solving constraint-satisfaction problems: *generate and test.* Figure 4.16 shows the two-step flow chart: the box at the top contains a generator that assigns values to all variables each time it is invoked; the diamond applies all the tests to see whether the latest assignment solves the problem. In Lull's system, the generate box corresponds to a systematic method of rotating the circles to generate possible combinations, and the test corresponds to Lull's tables and diagrams for checking the resulting combinations. In a modern programming language, the generate box could be implemented by a nest of loops, a backtracking method, or some other method of systematically stepping through all possibilities. Whenever a new combination of values is generated, all tests are applied. If any of them fail, the algorithm goes back to generate a new combination.

The generate-and-test algorithm has one important property: it is general enough to solve all constraint satisfaction problems. For realistic problems, how-

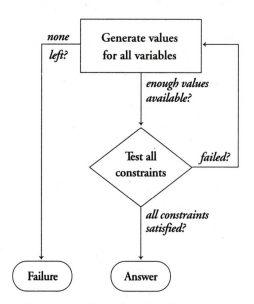

FIGURE 4.16 Generate-and-test algorithm for constraint satisfaction

ever, it is impossibly slow, since its execution time increases exponentially with the number of variables. Its saving grace is that many of the most useful programs can be converted to highly optimized ones just by changing the order of generating values and testing constraints. The general method of reordering, which is used in relational database systems and many AI systems for planning and problem solving, is called *constraint propagation*.

CRYPTARITHMETIC PROBLEM. To illustrate the effects of constraint propagation, consider the puzzle SEND+MORE=MONEY, which is an example of a *cryptarithmetic problem*. The goal is to replace the letters with digits that make the equation true; each letter represents a single digit, no digit is repeated, and the initial digits S and M must not be zero. In their studies of human problem solving, Allen Newell and Herbert Simon (1972) studied how people solve such puzzles in the hope of finding heuristics for making AI programs more natural. Yet a conscious imitation of human techniques is unnecessary. An optimal solution that is remarkably similar to the best human approaches can be derived directly from an analysis of the logical constraints. An optimizing compiler could use such an analysis to determine an efficient sequence of execution.

The constraints are derived from the equation SEND+MORE=MONEY and the rules of arithmetic. Besides the eight variables S, E, N, D, M, O, R, Y, there must be four variables to represent possible carries: let $C1$ represent a carry from the units position; $C2$, a carry from the tens position; $C3$, a carry from the hundreds position; and $C4$, a carry from the thousands position. Then the puzzle determines five constraint equations:

$$D + E = Y + 10 \times C1.$$
$$N + R + C1 = E + 10 \times C2.$$
$$E + O + C2 = N + 10 \times C3.$$
$$S + M + C3 = O + 10 \times C4.$$
$$C4 = M.$$

The carries $C1$, $C2$, $C3$, and $C4$ are restricted to be 0 or 1 with possible repetitions; the other variables are restricted to 0 through 9 with no repetitions; and the leading digits must not be zero: $S>0$ and $M>0$.

The structure of the generate-and-test algorithm and the method of optimization would be essentially the same in any programming language. The unoptimized code, which corresponds to the flow chart in Figure 4.16, would be translated to two separate blocks of code for the generate box and the testing diamond. The generate box would use some method of iterating, such as looping, recursion, or backtracking. At each iteration, it would generate the next combination of values for all variables. Then the code for the testing diamonds would check whether all the constraints are satisfied. If not, it would loop or backtrack to the generate box

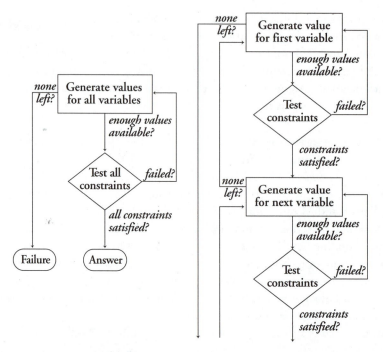

FIGURE 4.17   Optimizing the generate-and-test algorithm
by constraint propagation

to find another combination. When it finally finds a satisfactory combination, the program exits with the answer.

In the back of this book, the answer to Exercise 4.17 gives a solution in Prolog, which is more concise than most other languages. For problems of this kind, a few lines in Prolog would expand to a page of code in LISP or many pages in C. The unoptimized version of the Prolog program eventually finds the correct combination: M=1, S=9, O=0, E=5, N=6, R=8, D=7, and Y=2. The total CPU time is about 13 seconds on an IBM 3090 computer. Although 13 seconds is not a long time for a complex problem, this problem could be solved in just a few milliseconds with a different ordering of the generating and testing.

OPTIMIZATION.   By constraint propagation, the unoptimized program can be improved by interleaving the operations of generating values and testing constraints. The optimized version corresponds to the flowchart on the right side of Figure 4.17. Following are two metalevel principles that determine which constraints to move:

- When values have been generated for all variables in a constraint, test that constraint before new values are generated for other variables.

- If all remaining constraints depend on variables that have not yet been assigned a value, generate values for the constraint that has the smallest *choice space*.

To define the size of a choice space for a constraint, let $x_1, x_2, \ldots, x_n$ be the variables that have not yet been assigned values. Then let *choice*(x_i) be the number of possible values x_i can assume. The size of the choice space is defined as the product *choice*(x_1)×...×*choice*(x_n).

To illustrate these principles, apply them systematically to optimize the SEND+MORE = MONEY problem. The first constraint to test is the one with the smallest choice space: C4=M. Since M is determined by the value of C4, its choice space is limited to the two possible values of C4. The further constraint M>0 eliminates the value 0 and completely determines the values M=1 and C4=1. The beginning of the optimized program therefore has no choices:

- Assign M=1 and C4=1.
- The available values that can be assigned to other variables are [0,2,3,4, 5,6,7,8,9].

After the values of C4 and M are determined, the next most restricted constraint is S+M+C3=O+10×C4. In this equation, three variables, S, O, and C3, are without values; a choice for any two determines the third. Since C3 is limited to 0 or 1 and S is restricted by the further constraint that S>0, the choice space is 2×8 or 16. All the other equations have a choice space of 112 or more. The procedure should then choose a nonzero value for S, choose a value for C3, compute the value of O from the choices for S and C3, and check whether the computed value for O is one of the possible values left in the list R8. The next part of the optimized program would be

- Choose 0 or 1 for C3, and choose a nonzero value for S from the availability list.
- Compute O := S + M + C3 − 10×C4.
- If O is not in the available list, backtrack to make another choice.

The next most restricted constraint is E+O+C2=N+10×C3, in which the variables E, N, and C2 need values. There are two choices for C2, and seven for E or N. Since E and N have the same choice space, either one can be chosen first to determine a value for the other; the choice space is 2×7 or 14.

- Choose 0 or 1 for C2, and choose E from the availability list.
- Compute N := E + O + C2 − 10×C3.
- If N is not in the available list, backtrack.

Now the most restricted constraint is $N+R+C1=E+10 \times C2$. Only R and C1 require values, and picking 0 or 1 for C1 determines R:

- Choose 0 or 1 for C1.
- Compute $R := 10 \times C2 + E - N - C1$.
- If R is not in the available list, backtrack.

Finally, the last constraint to be tested is $D+E=Y+10 \times C1$, in which only D and Y need values. Picking a value for either one determines the other. The end of the program is

- Choose a value for D from the availability list.
- Compute $Y := D + E - 10 \times C1$.
- If Y is not in the available list, backtrack.

This optimized reordering of the generating and testing can be translated to any programming language. The improvement in performance is dramatic: the Prolog version takes only four milliseconds — more than 3200 times faster than the unoptimized version. See Exercises 4.15 and 4.16 and the answers at the back of the book for further discussion of this problem.

OBSERVATIONS ON THE METHOD. The optimized program is still a form of generate and test, but a more distributed form, represented by the flowchart on the right side of Figure 4.17. Instead of having a single block that generates all combinations followed by another block that tests all constraints, the optimized version repeatedly generates a few combinations and immediately tests them. Reordering the sequence of generating and testing improves performance in three ways:

1. Dependencies in the constraints allow certain values to be computed deterministically from the values already generated for other variables. In this example, the choice spaces for M, O, N, R, and Y were narrowed down to 1.

2. Some constraints, such as $M>0$ and $S>0$, do not determine a unique value, but they help reduce the size of the choice spaces.

3. Other constraints serve as filters that break up the monolithic generate block into a sequence of smaller generate blocks separated by constraint testing, as in the flowchart on the right of Figure 4.17.

With weak constraints that have a large choice space, the filtering effect is of little value. The worst case arises when every constraint requires values for all variables before it can be tested; then reordering is not possible. For many practical problems, however, each constraint depends on a small subset of the variables. The generate block on the left side of Figure 4.17 can then be partitioned into a separate block for each subset of variables. The ideal case occurs when the constraints that separate the blocks filter out all but one combination. Such filtering breaks the problem into separable subproblems that completely eliminate backtracking. Then the total number of combinations that have to be tested is the sum of the choice spaces in each subblock rather than their product. In practice, the reordering reduces but does not eliminate the backtracking. In this example, even a partial reduction is good enough to improve performance by a factor of 3200.

METALEVEL HEURISTICS. Generate and test is an exhaustive search for the best possible solution. Constraint propagation is a metalevel technique that reorganizes the search to improve performance, but it still finds the best solution if one exists. *Heuristics* are also metalevel techniques for guiding the search, manipulating constraints, or evaluating different solutions at the object level. Unlike generate and test or constraint propagation, most heuristics cannot guarantee that a solution they find is the best possible. There are many such techniques, including *genetic algorithms*, which simulate an evolutionary search for gradually improved methods. Peirce emphasized three ways of using logic: *deduction, induction,* and *abduction.* His third method, abduction, uses heuristics to guess a solution, followed by deduction to verify its correctness. As a universal language for representing declarative information, logic is equally suitable for deductive algorithms that determine the best solution and metalevel heuristics that search for acceptable solutions.

4.7 Change

Reasoning about change and its causes and effects is one of the most important but difficult problems for AI. Formally, a change occurs when certain facts that are true in a situation s_1 are no longer true in a later situation s_2. The problem lies in identifying which facts remain true, which change, how they change, when they change, and why. Although the focus of this book is on representation rather than reasoning, the choice of representation can have a major effect on the way the reasoning is carried out and on its ultimate success or failure.

SITUATION CALCULUS. In an early memo, John McCarthy (1963) introduced a representation called the *situation calculus*, which has become one of the most popular logic-based methods for reasoning about change. His basic idea was to represent cause by a metalevel operator, which treats propositions as fluents that are true in certain situations:

$$\text{cause}(\pi)(s).$$

McCarthy said that this formula is "intended to mean that the situation s will lead in the future to a situation that satisfies the fluent π. Thus cause(π) is itself a propositional fluent." As an example, he wrote

$$(\forall s\text{:Situation})(\forall p\text{:Person})$$
$$[(\text{raining} \wedge \text{outside}(p)) \supset \text{cause}(\text{wet}(p))](s).$$

McCarthy's brackets enclose a propositional fluent, which is applied to the situation s to derive a proposition. The complete formula may be read *For every situation s and person p, if it is raining and p is outside, then p will become wet in a situation caused by s.*

Over the years, everybody who has used the situation calculus has adapted it to his or her preferred notation. To convert McCarthy's formula to a conceptual graph, move the brackets to enclose the proposition about the situation:

$$[\text{Situation: } \forall^* s$$
$$(\forall p\text{:Person})((\text{raining} \wedge \text{outside}(p)) \supset \text{cause}(s,\text{wet}(p)))\,].$$

The result is a hybrid notation: the brackets represent a concept of type Situation with a universal quantifier; the nested formula states a proposition that describes the situation; and the metalevel cause predicate has an extra argument s to relate the situation to its effects. This hybrid could be translated to a pure CG form by replacing the nested formula with an equivalent conceptual graph. In the CG form, the concept box corresponds to an implicit description predicate dscr(s,p). Following is a translation back to predicate calculus notation:

$$(\forall s\text{:Situation})\text{dscr}(s,$$
$$(\forall p\text{:Person})((\text{raining} \wedge \text{outside}(p)) \supset \text{cause}(s,\text{wet}(p)))).$$

This formula says that every situation s is described by the proposition that every person who is outside when it is raining gets wet. In this formula, the link between the situation s and the nested proposition is shown explicitly by the metalevel description predicate. That predicate enables McCarthy's fluents to be replaced by ordinary predicates and propositions.

For problem solving with the situation calculus, Cordell Green (1969) used a theorem prover based on a rule of inference called *resolution*. But since his theorem prover was a first-order system without metalevels, Green translated McCarthy's notation to a form without fluents or metalevel operators. In Green's notation, every predicate has an explicit argument for the situation:

$$(\forall s\text{:Situation})(\forall p\text{:Person})$$
$$((\text{raining}(s) \wedge \text{outside}(p,s)) \supset \text{getWet}(p,s)).$$

This formula may be read *For every situation s and person p, if it is raining in s and p is outside in s, then p gets wet in s.* Unfortunately, Green's first-order notation also requires axioms to say what does not happen:

($\forall s$:Situation)($\forall p$:Person)
    ((raining(s) $\land$ inside(p,s)) $\supset$ ~getWet(p,s)).

This formula says that every person who stays inside in a situation in which it is raining does not get wet.

The need to say what does not happen has been one of the major drawbacks of the situation calculus. In Section 3.1, axioms of persistence were needed to say that after a traffic light turns red or green, it remains that color until something causes it to change. For many applications, the number of axioms that say what does not happen tend to overwhelm the axioms about the changes that actually do happen. McCarthy and Hayes (1969) called such a proliferation of negative axioms the *frame problem.* That name tends to be confusing since the frame problem primarily affects the situation calculus, and it usually does not occur with frame representations.

SOLVING THE FRAME PROBLEM.   Leibniz's principle of sufficient reason is the key to solving the frame problem: *Nothing at all happens without some reason.* That principle is a metalevel statement that cannot be used in purely first-order theorem provers. Nevertheless, it has been implemented in many systems, both logic-based and procedural. The first explicit solution to the frame problem was by Richard Fikes and Nils Nilsson (1971) with their system called STRIPS (Stanford Research Institute Problem Solver):

> While Green's formulation represented a significant step in the development of problem solvers, it suffered some serious disadvantages connected with the "frame problem" that prevented it from solving nontrivial problems. In STRIPS, we surmount these difficulties by separating entirely the processes of theorem proving from those of searching through a space of world models. This separation allows us to employ separate strategies for these two activities and thereby improve the overall performance of the system. Theorem-proving methods are used only *within* a given world model to answer questions about it concerning which operators are applicable and whether or not goals have been satisfied.

The world models of STRIPS correspond to McCarthy's situations. Each model is a collection of statements in the existential-conjunctive (EC) subset of logic. The metalevel for reasoning about the models is implemented in LISP procedures that search the network of models, generate the changed models by adding or deleting propositions, and test whether the newly generated models have reached the desired goals. The search strategy is based on *means-ends analysis*, a technique pioneered by Newell, Shaw, and Simon (1959) with the General Problem Solver (GPS).

In the STRIPS formalism, every possible action by a robot has three associated propositions or lists of propositions. The act of pushing, for example, has the following description:

- *Signature.* push(Object:k, Location:m, Location:n).
- *Precondition.* atRobot(m) $\land$ at(k,m).
- *Delete list.* atRobot(m), at(k,m).
- *Add list.* atRobot(n), at(k,n).

The signature states the types of entities to which the act applies: the robot pushes an object k from location m to location n. The delete and add lists are limited to statements in EC logic, but the precondition is an arbitrary first-order statement that must be true to enable the action. To simulate the act of pushing, STRIPS uses a resolution theorem prover called QA3 (Question-Answering System #3) to verify that the precondition is true in the current model. Then it generates the changed model by making a copy of all the statements in the current model, deleting the ones on the delete list, and adding those on the add list. As a result, the propositions in the changed model say that the robot and the object k, which were originally at location m, are now at location n.

STRIPS avoids the frame problem by using a two-level or *stratified* reasoning method. By copying the current world model as the first step in generating the next one, STRIPS obeys Leibniz's metalevel principle of leaving everything unchanged that is not affected by the current action. Without the metalevel, additional axioms are needed for every action and every changeable thing that is not affected by that action. The resulting explosion of first-order axioms is typical of systems that do not have a metalevel. Exercise 1.37, for example, shows how the single metalevel statement of Exercise 1.36 expands to 499,500 first-order statements. With an appropriate use of metalanguage, the proliferation of axioms caused by the frame problem disappears.

Variations of the STRIPS technique have been implemented in many systems of *model-based reasoning*. Like STRIPS, many of them implement the metalevel in a procedural language; Robert Kowalski (1979) showed how logic could do STRIPS-like metareasoning declaratively; others do the metalevel reasoning by techniques of *belief revision* or *theory revision*, which are described in Section 6.5. The reason frame systems do not suffer from the frame problem is that they must always use a two-level implementation, since the subset of logic expressed by frames is too limited to represent everything. Therefore, they combine the EC subset of logic for representing world models with a procedural language for metalevel manipulation of the models.

Similar techniques are used for temporal reasoning in database systems: the current state of the database is a world model, which requires only EC logic; the precondition for an action is tested with an SQL query; and the deletions and additions are performed by database updates.

YALE SHOOTING PROBLEM.   Steve Hanks and Drew McDermott (1987) posed a problem that has raised controversies about the role of logic in reasoning about time. Named after their university, the Yale shooting problem concerns a person who is alive in a situation s_0. In their version of the situation calculus, they replaced McCarthy's metalevel cause operator with a function named result:

- Situation s_1 is the result of a gun being loaded in s_0:

  s_1 = result(load,s_0).

- Situation s_2 is the result of waiting for some interval of time after s_1:

  s_2 = result(wait,s_1) = result(wait, result(load,s_0).

- Situation s_3 is the result of the victim being shot by the gun:

  s_3 = result(shoot,s_2)
      = result(shoot, result(wait, result(load,s_0))).

Figure 4.18 shows a finite-state machine whose states represent the situations and whose arcs represent the actions that transform one situation to the next. The problem is to determine whether the victim is alive or dead in situation s_3.

Hanks and McDermott found that the axioms of persistence in situation calculus cannot definitely predict the fate of the victim. With their representation, the state of a person being alive would normally persist, but the state of a gun being loaded would also persist. The situation calculus cannot determine whether the gun switches state from loaded to unloaded or the victim switches state from alive to dead. The length of time spent waiting between situation s_1 and s_2, for example, is not specified. If the waiting time had been a minute, the gun would be likely to remain loaded. But if the time had been a year, it's more likely that someone would have unloaded it. The person or persons who carried the gun, loaded it, pulled the trigger, or perhaps unloaded it are not mentioned, and their motives are unknown. The type of weapon, the distance between the assassin and the victim, the victim's movements, and the assassin's shooting skills are unknown. Without further information, no system of logic by itself can determine exactly what would happen.

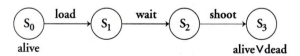

FIGURE 4.18 A finite-state machine for the Yale shooting problem

As someone who has long worked on logic-based approaches to AI, McDermott had hoped that logic alone would be able to give a unique answer to the Yale shooting problem and other similar, but more practical problems. He reluctantly concluded that the versions of *nonmonotonic logic* used for reasoning about time cannot by themselves solve such problems:

> The whole point behind the development of nonmonotonic formal systems for reasoning about time has been to augment our logical machinery so that it reflects in a natural way the "inertia of the world." All of this effort is wasted if one is trying merely to express constraints on the physics of the world: we can solve the problem once and for all by saying "once a fact becomes true it stays true until the occurrence of some event causes it to become false.". . . Many researchers, however, would not be satisfied with using logic only as a notation for expressing ontological theories.

McDermott's method of solving the problem "once and for all" is a paraphrase of Leibniz's principle of sufficient reason. But as Leibniz observed, every entity in the universe has some influence on every other entity. Only an omniscient being such as God could account for the potentially infinite number of events that might cause a change. To determine which of those events are significant, finite reasoners — human or computer — must use background knowledge about physics to select the most likely causes and effects.

DISTRIBUTED SITUATIONS.   As Figure 4.18 illustrates, the usual situation calculus is equivalent in structure to a finite-state machine, which can only represent a single-threaded sequence of situations and events. When multiple agents interact, however, they create distributed processes that are more naturally represented by Petri nets. Figure 4.19, for example, shows two representations for a robot r pushing an object k from m to n: on the left, a finite-state machine that corresponds to the situation calculus; and on the right, a Petri net. A token in a circle indicates that the corresponding condition is true at the indexical time *now*.

For the situation calculus, the finite-state machine shows the preconditions and

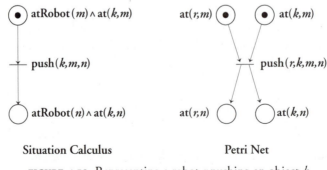

Situation Calculus   Petri Net

FIGURE 4.19 Representing a robot r pushing an object k

postconditions for a robot pushing an object, as Fikes and Nilsson stated them in STRIPS. Since finite-state machines correspond to Petri nets with just one token on the entire net, any version of the situation calculus that can be modeled by an FSM can only represent a single active agent, such as a robot working alone. The Petri net on the right, however, shows a distributed representation with separate input and output states for the robot r and the object k. With multiple circles and tokens, a Petri net can represent any number of active or passive entities, whose states can be updated independently.

For the Yale shooting problem, Figure 4.20 takes advantage of the greater expressive power of Petri nets to show causal links between states and events that involve different participants. Following are the mappings from Petri nets to a distributed version of the situation calculus:

- *Places.* Every place on the Petri net represents a type of condition that can be expressed by a proposition stated in predicate calculus or conceptual graphs. The seven places in Figure 4.20 represent seven types of conditions that might be true at some time in the past, present, or future.

- *Tokens.* A token in a place means that the corresponding condition is true at the indexical time *now*, which is the point in time of the current situation. Instead of representing situations by single nodes, as in finite-state machines, a Petri net represents the current situation by a conjunction of the conditions for all the places that currently contain tokens. In Figure 4.20, the initial situation is described by a conjunction of two propositions: the assassin has a gun, and the victim is alive.

- *Events.* Every transition represents a type of event, whose precondition is the conjunction of the conditions for its input places and whose postcondition is the conjunction of the conditions for its output places. In the example, the Misfire event has no output conditions. When it occurs, its only effect is to erase a token from the place labeled Firing-pin-struck, thereby disabling the event Gun-fires.

- *Arcs.* The arcs that link places and transitions have the effect of the add and delete lists in STRIPS. For any transition, the input arcs correspond to the delete list because each of them erases a token from its input place, thereby causing the corresponding proposition to become false. The ouput arcs correspond to the add list because each of them adds a token to its output place, thereby asserting the corresponding proposition.

- *Persistent places.* A place that is linked to a transition by both an input and an output arc is *persistent* because its condition remains true when that transition fires. In the example, the place labeled Assassin-has-gun persists after the assassin loads the gun or pulls the trigger. For all the other places in Figure 4.20, their preconditions become false after their tokens are used as input to some transition.

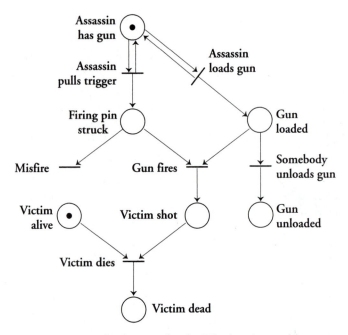

FIGURE 4.20 A Petri net for the Yale shooting problem

Figure 4.20 elaborates the Yale shooting problem with further detail. This elaboration is by no means unique, since any problem can be analyzed and extended with any amount of detail.

Questions about future situations can be answered either by executing the Petri net interpretively or by proving theorems about which states are reachable. To determine what happens to the victim, trace the flow of tokens through Figure 4.20:

1. If the assassin loads the gun and pulls the trigger before anyone unloads it, the gun can fire, shooting the victim, who ends up dead.

2. If somebody unloads the gun before the assassin pulls the trigger, the gun misfires, and the victim remains alive.

3. Even if the gun is loaded when the assassin pulls the trigger, there is a slight chance of a misfire because of some other malfunction. In that case, the victim also remains alive.

With these possibilities, the most that can be concluded is a disjunction:

Misfire ∨ Victim-dead.

A conclusion of this form is inevitable unless further information eliminates the possibility that the gun misfires or somebody unloads it.

CAUSAL NETWORKS. Network notations that resemble Petri nets have been used in many AI systems for representing cause and effect. Chuck Rieger (1976) developed a version of *causal networks*, which he used for analyzing problem descriptions in English and translating them to a network that could support metalevel reasoning. Benjamin Kuipers (1984, 1994), who was strongly influenced by Rieger's approach, developed methods of *qualitative reasoning*, which serve as a bridge between the symbolic methods of AI and the differential equations used in physics and engineering. Judea Pearl (1988, 1996), who has developed techniques for applying statistics and probability to AI, introduced *belief networks*, which are causal networks whose links are labeled with probabilities.

To resolve the indeterminism that occurs at disjunctive nodes, Pearl would compute or estimate the probabilities of each of the options. When one option is much more likely than the other, he would derive a qualitative solution by assigning a small value ε to the unlikely option and the complementary value $(1-\varepsilon)$ to the more likely option. For the network shown in Figure 4.20, there are three disjunctive nodes, each of which has one likely path and one unlikely path.

1. The first disjunction occurs at the top, where the order of loading the gun or pulling the trigger is not specified. Unless the assassin were grossly incompetent, the probability of pulling the trigger before loading the gun would be a small value ε_1, and the option of loading first would be $(1-\varepsilon_1)$.

2. After the gun is loaded, the probability that someone might happen to unload it shortly thereafter is another small number ε_2.

3. If the gun is unloaded, the probability of a misfire is 100 percent, since the transition labeled Gun-fires would not be enabled. But if the gun is loaded, the likelihood of a misfire is a small value ε_3.

If the network correctly captures the relevant causal dependencies, the probabilities at different disjunctive nodes would be independent. Therefore, the probability of any possible outcome would be the product of all the options along the path from start to finish. The primary path, which takes each of the more likely options, would have a probability that corresponds to informal intuitions:

$$(1-\varepsilon_1)(1-\varepsilon_2)(1-\varepsilon_3).$$

If each of the ε options has a probability of 10 percent or less, the probability that the victim dies would be at least 72.9 percent. For a variety of problems in temporal reasoning, Peter Grünwald (1997) compared the solutions obtained with Pearl's belief networks to other proposed methods. For each of them, he showed that Pearl's approach was equivalent to, more general than, or intuitively more convincing than the others.

As this example illustrates, Petri nets are causal networks that can be executed interpretively, be compiled to efficient procedures, or serve as the basis for metalevel analysis. The theorems that were proved at the end of Section 4.4 illustrate one way to perform such analysis. Another way is to map the Petri nets to *linear logic*, in which the proof procedures mimic the firing of Petri net transitions by moving truth markers from the inputs to the outputs of an implication. Although some versions of linear logic are not decidable, Anne Troelstra (1992) showed that Petri nets are equivalent to a version of linear logic whose outcomes are decidable. That result implies that causality problems expressible in Petri nets can be solved either by direct execution or by metalevel analysis about how they could be executed.

EXERCISES

1. As Diodorus Cronus observed, sentences like *Alma married three husbands* can be true in the past tense even though there was never a time when the present tense of those sentences was true. Find similar examples, state the conditions under which they could be true or false, and represent them in conceptual graphs.

2. Study the representation of the song "Frère Jacques" in Sections 1.2 and 1.4. Then draw a Petri net that would represent the singing of the song:

   a. Draw a Petri net with 34 places, which represent a starting state, a stopping state, and the 32 notes of the melody. Inside the circle for each note, write its tone and duration. There should also be 33 transitions: one to start the first note, one after the last note, and 31 to represent the next relations between notes.

   b. After you have drawn the Petri net for one voice singing the melody, modify the net to allow multiple voices to sing it as a round, with each new voice entering at the third measure of the melody. It is possible to make this revision without adding any new places or transitions; one additional output arc to one of the transitions would be sufficient. Would this modified Petri net ever stop?

   c. Make another modification to the Petri net to allow any number n of voices to sing, where $n \geq 1$. Design it so that the first voice will begin when n tokens have been placed in the start state, voice $i+1$ will begin when voice i reaches measure 3, and all singing will stop when the n-th voice has finished. Hint: This modification requires just one new place.

   d. Study the mapping from the conceptual graph to the Petri net, and generalize it to an algorithm for mapping any CG that represents a melody to the corresponding Petri net. Then show how the Petri net could be translated to a language like Java or Basic that could play the melody. How would you represent multiple voices singing in parallel in the programming language you chose?

This exercise illustrates the transfer of information from one representation to another: musical score ⇒ conceptual graph ⇒ Petri net ⇒ computer program ⇒ program execution ⇒ sound. It is possible to write programs to perform such translations automatically.

3. A PERT chart for project management is acyclic, but a Petri net for a continuous process such as an assembly line would have cycles to represent repetitive processes. Draw a Petri net for a bakery that has one or more chefs who bake cakes, one or more people who decorate the cakes with icing and personalized messages, and one or more sales clerks who take orders and send the finished cakes to their destinations.

4. In conventional programming languages, memory-bound processes can be represented by procedures that have the side effect of changing their internal data. To avoid such side effects, Jensen used the functional language ML to implement the transitions of colored Petri nets. Yet memory-bound processes can still be represented in such nets by saving the changed data in the tokens rather than the places or transitions. How could that technique be used to represent memory associated with a single task or thread in a multitasking system? How could it be used to represent memory that is always associated with a specific transition, independent of which task or thread invokes that transition? Show that these techniques can represent memory-bound processes without changing internal data in the places or transitions.

5. Draw a new Petri net by merging the output place of the net for the clock in Figure 4.10 with the input place of the one-bit counter in Figure 4.11.

   a. Apply the theorems about Petri nets in Section 4.4 to show that for every two ticks of the clock there is a net gain of one token on the combined Petri net. In which place does that token appear?

   b. Add three more copies of the one-bit counter to the new net to create a 4-bit counter that measures times from $t=0$ to $t=15$.

   c. Apply the theorems to show that for every 16 ticks of the clock there is a net gain of one token on this net.

   d. If the clock ticked every nanosecond, how much time would elapse before a 32-bit counter would generate an overflow token?

NOTE: A 4-bit register, which does not seem very large, is still the typical size of the data path for the microprocessors used in many appliances such as clocks, calculators, cameras, and washing machines. After repeated doubling in size, the first 4-bit microprocessor, the Intel 4004, evolved into the Pentium (Faggin et al. 1996).

6. Using the techniques of Section 4.3, translate the Petri net for the clock in Figure 4.10 and the Petri net for the one-bit counter in Figure 4.11 to conceptual graphs. Then translate the CGs to predicate calculus.

7. Design a Petri net for a general purpose counter (GPC) that could be used as a component in a larger Petri net. GPC should have the following properties:

   a. GPC can represent integers from 0 to $2^N - 1$ for some fixed positive integer N.

   b. GPC has four places labeled Reset, Increment, Decrement, and Request-Count, each of which may receive tokens from transitions outside of GPC. No other place in GPC may receive tokens from outside.

   c. GPC has three places labeled CurrentCount, Overflow, and Underflow, from which transitions outside of GPC may remove tokens. No transitions outside of GPC may remove tokens from any other place in GPC.

   d. The initial state of GPC has no tokens in any place that is accessible from the outside. It may have tokens in certain internal places, such as the place labeled Even in Figure 4.11.

   e. Whenever a token appears in Reset, GPC restores the distribution of tokens in its initial state.

   f. Whenever a token appears in Increment, GPC removes that token and changes some places internal to GPC. If GPC is currently at the top of its range, GPC puts a token in Overflow and resets the initial distribution of tokens in all internal places of GPC, but it leaves any tokens in externally accessible places unchanged.

   g. Whenever a token appears in Decrement, GPC removes that token and changes some places internal to GPC. If GPC is currently at the bottom of its range, GPC puts a token in Underflow and causes all tokens to disappear from all places internal to GPC.

   h. Whenever a token appears in RequestCount, GPC removes that token and puts a token in CurrentCount that has an associated integer n in the range of 0 to $2^N - 1$. That integer represents the number of tokens removed from Increment minus the number removed from Decrement since the most recent occurrence of any one of the following events: the initial state, a token removed from Reset, a token put in Overflow, or a token put in Underflow.

   HINT: The Linda operators of Figure 4.15 could be used as subnets to implement the reset operation in GPC. When a token appears in the Reset place,

GPC would invoke the Out subnet to send the data tuple (reset all) to BB. For every other place in GPC, there would be a token waiting for a transition that invokes the Read subnet with the pattern tuple (reset all).

8. Translate the dataflow CG in Figure 4.13 and the recursive CG in Figure 4.14 to Petri nets. Then translate the Petri nets to programs in some procedural language. Run the programs and check the results.

9. Study the Petri nets in Figure 4.15 for defining the Linda operations. Which Linda operations increase or decrease the number of tokens in the blackboard (BB)? Analyze the flow of tokens through the net for the operation InP in the case that a matching tuple was found in BB and in the case that no match was found. Verify the following properties:

   a. If the four places in the net are empty (no tokens) at the beginning of the execution of InP, then the four places will also be empty at the completion of InP whether or not a matching tuple is found.

   b. If no matching tuple is found, the number of tokens in BB remains unchanged.

   c. If a matching tuple is found, the number of tokens in BB decreases by one.

   d. There is no danger that the Petri net for InP might remove a tuple from BB, but a null tuple would be returned instead of the one from BB.

10. Design a Petri net named BB Manager to implement all six Linda operations. It should have the following properties:

    a. BB Manager should have one output place and six input places labeled In, Read, Out, Eval, InP, and ReadP.

    b. Each token received in an input place should be associated with a tuple and the identifier (ID) of the sender. Each token generated for the output place should be associated with the expected response for the corresponding Linda operation and the ID of the original sender.

    c. Whenever BB Manager removes a token from an input place labeled In, Read, InP, or ReadP, it should take one of the following two actions before removing another token from the same input place:

       • If the tuple associated with the input token matches some tuple in BB, BB Manager completes the operation by generating the expected output for the output place.

       • If the tuple associated with the input token does not match some tuple in BB, BB Manager returns the token with its original tuple and ID to its original input place.

d. Let t_1 and t_2 be two times, $t_1 < t_2$, when BB Manager is not in the process of performing any Linda operations.

- At time t_1, let B be the total number of tokens in BB, and let N be the total number of tokens in all places other than the input places, the output places, and BB.

- During the interval between t_1 and t_2, let C be the number of completed requests, where

$$C = C_{In} + C_{Read} + C_{Eval} + C_{Out} + C_{InP} + C_{ReadP}.$$

- Show that at time t_2 the total number of tokens in all places other than the input, output, and BB remains N, and the number of tokens in BB is

$$B + C_{Out} + C_{Eval} - C_{In} - C_{InP} - C_{Read} - C_{ReadP}.$$

e. In Figure 4.15, the Delay transition waits for a time independent of the number of tokens in BB. Revise the Petri net for BB Manager to count the number of tokens in BB and to add another input to Delay from the current count so that the waiting time might be extended if there are many tokens in BB. If you have not yet implemented a general purpose counter according to the specifications in Exercise 4.6, you may assume that someone has designed one for you.

f. Performance can usually be improved by minimizing the number of transitions executed for each operation and maximizing the number of threads executed in parallel. In designing the Petri net for BB Manager, try to optimize performance without violating conditions a, b, c, and d.

This exercise shows how Petri nets can be used for designing software and verifying its correctness in a way that is independent of any particular machine or implementation language.

11. In Section 4.4, the firing rules for Petri nets were defined in English, and several theorems about Petri nets were derived from those rules by informal arguments. Define an ontology of types and relations for making statements about Petri nets in some version of logic. Using that ontology, translate the definitions and theorems to logical graphs or formulas. Then use the rules of inference for that version of logic to prove that the theorems follow from the definitions.

12. Some Petri nets can be decomposed into a collection of finite-state machines that interact by passing messages. As an example, show that the producer-consumer net in Figure 4.12 could be decomposed into finite-state machines that interact by means of a bulletin board managed by Linda operators:

a. Make copies of the three cycles of Figure 4.12 to form seven separate Petri nets, each with a single token: two producer loops, one consumer loop, and four buffer loops.

b. Each of the separated nets should have a copy of one P transition and one V transition that came from the original net. Erase the extra arcs of the P and V transitions that were connected to the other loops.

c. Show that the separated nets are now equivalent to finite-state machines.

d. To represent the original interactions, two transitions on each of the separated nets can be replaced by calls to Linda operators. Which transitions are they? Which Linda operators are used for each of them? What is the format of the tuples that are sent to and from BB?

Discuss possible applications in which a collection of finite-state machines might be more convenient than a unified Petri net. When might a unified Petri net be preferable?

13. Instead of decomposing Figure 4.12 into seven finite-state machines, as in Exercise 4.12, show that it could be decomposed into three finite-state machines by the following method:

a. Design three finite-state machines, two for the producers and one for the consumer.

b. Synchronize the producer machines with the consumer machine by passing messages via Linda operators.

c. Each message should consist of a pair of the form (*state, buffer-pointer*), where *state* is one of {empty, full} and *buffer-pointer* is a variable for pattern tuples or the address of a buffer for a data tuple.

Specify which transitions invoke Linda operators and which operators are invoked. What are the advantages and disadvantages of the decomposition of Figure 4.12 to three or seven machines? Discuss kinds of applications for which one method or the other might be preferable.

14. The Petri net in Figure 4.8 cannot be decomposed into separate finite-state machines by the methods described in the previous exercises. What features of Figure 4.8 prevent that method from being used? Show that Figure 4.8 could be decomposed into finite-state machines by means of other Linda operators.

15. Can all Petri nets be represented by finite-state machines that interact via Linda operators? Which features of Petri nets are the most difficult to simulate by combinations of Linda operators?

16. Draw two Petri nets for the SEND+MORE=MONEY problem. The first net should correspond to the unoptimized flowchart in Figure 4.16. The second net should correspond to the optimized flowchart in Figure 4.17. In the places of the Petri nets, write the conditions that are true in the corresponding states. Draw the transitions as boxes and write brief descriptions of the corresponding events inside the boxes.

17. Solve the SEND+MORE=MONEY problem in any suitable programming language. Prolog would be the easiest language to use, but the generate-and-test algorithms described in Section 4.6 could also be implemented in procedural languages, such as Java or C. Write both an optimized and an unoptimized version, corresponding to the two flowcharts in Figure 4.17. Compare the execution times of the two versions on the computer you are using.

18. The where clause of the SQL language is general enough to represent the constraints of the SEND+MORE=MONEY problem, but most implementations of SQL are not optimized to solve such problems. Readers who are familiar with SQL might try using it to solve that problem. First create a table called Numbers with a column called Digit, which would contain the digits 0 through 9. Then write an SQL query with a where clause that states the constraints on S.Digit, E.Digit, N.Digit, and so on. Use the features of SQL to state a query with a single where clause that corresponds to the unoptimized flowchart of Figure 4.16. Then rewrite the query with separate select statements nested inside the where clause to represent the optimized flowchart. With an ideal optimizing compiler, both queries should take the same amount of time; try running the queries to check the difference in performance.

19. Classic AI systems such as Microplanner, described in Section 3.3, and STRIPS, described in Section 4.7, pioneered techniques that have now become commonplace. The problems they addressed are still significant for modern database and knowledge-base systems.

   a. The STRIPS world models, which are conjunctions of relations whose arguments are all constants, are equivalent to the data stored in a relational database. Some of the relations in a world model might depend on others; the NextTo relation, for example, could be computed from the values of the At relation. In performing the adds and deletes for an action, STRIPS would encounter the kinds of problems typical of database updates. Describe some of those problems and possible ways of handling them.

   b. Readers who are familiar with computational complexity should note that STRIPS uses a resolution theorem prover to verify that the precondition of an action, which might be an arbitrary first-order statement, is true in the current world model. Does that mean STRIPS is expected to solve NP-complete problems?

20. To represent more detailed causal links in the Yale shooting problem, try adding more states and transitions to the finite-state machine in Figure 4.18 and the Petri net in Figure 4.20. Is it possible to draw an extended finite-state machine that represents some version or approximation to the states and events represented in Figure 4.20? What kinds of interactions can be represented in Petri nets, but not in finite-state machines? Give examples.

21. Review the techniques of Exercises 4.12 to 4.15 for decomposing Petri nets into finite-state machines that interact via the Linda operators. Use that approach to decompose the Petri net of Figure 4.20 into four separate finite-state machines: one for the assassin, one for the victim, one for the gun, and one for the unknown person or persons who might unload the gun. Show which Linda operators are used to communicate between the finite-state machines, the points where each machine invokes a Linda operator, and the formats of the messages that are sent or received.

22. Judea Pearl's method of computing the probabilities determined by a causal network depends on which nodes correspond to conjunctions (∧ operators) and which correspond to disjunctions (∨ operators). Formulate a general principle that can be used to determine at a glance which nodes are conjunctive or disjunctive. Although Petri nets do not have an explicit method for representing negations, it is possible to implement the technique of negation as failure, as described in Section 3.3. Show how. Find an example of a Petri net in this chapter that uses negation as failure.

23. To represent negation explicitly, some extended versions of Petri nets have *inhibit arcs*, whose input is a place and whose output is a transition. When a token is in the input place of an inhibit arc, the output transition is prevented from firing. If there is no token in the input place of any inhibit arc, the output transition can fire in the normal way by removing a token from each of the ordinary input places and putting a token in each of the output places. How could inhibit arcs be used in Figures 4.15 and 4.20?

24. Petri nets represent discrete processes, but most physical processes are continuous. As an example, the following passage from the medieval Arabic philosopher Avicenna (Ibn Sina) discusses causal links between two continuous processes:

> The mind is not at all repelled by the statement "When Zayd moved his hand, the key moved" or "Zayd moved his hand, then the key moved." The mind is repelled, however, by the statement "When the key moved, Zayd moved his hand," even though it is [rightly] said "When the key moved, *we*

knew that Zayd moved his hand." The mind, despite the temporal coexistence of the two movements, assigns a (causal) priority for one, a posteriority for the other. For it is not the existence of the second movement that causes the existence of the first; it is the existence of the first movement that causes the second. (Translated by Nicholas Rescher 1967)

Since Petri nets are designed for the kinds of discrete operations that are representable in digital computers, they cannot faithfully represent all the details of continuous interactions. One approach is to ignore the details and represent an entire action by a single transition: one transition would represent Zayd moving his hand, and another would represent the key moving. Another approach is to approximate a continuous process by a series of discrete steps: each partial movement by Zayd's hand would cause a partial movement of the key. Draw Petri nets for each of these two representations; in both of them, show that the movement of the key is causally dependent on the movement of Zayd's hand.

25. Review Section 4.2 with Sandewall's list of distinctions for classifying processes with interacting fluents. Show how each type of process could be represented in a Petri net. Give some examples of Petri nets with multiple options, and show how it would be possible to generate all 2,304 combinations.

26. Exercise 4.3 about the bakery did not mention exceptional cases, which might require workers to interrupt certain tasks to perform other tasks with a higher priority. A sales clerk, for example, might be interrupted by a telephone call while addressing a package. A chef might spill something while mixing cake batter. Revise the Petri net for the bakery to accommodate such interruptions. To avoid recursive interrupts, assume that the bakery has a telephone-answering machine, whose operation should also be represented in the Petri net. To simplify the representation of interrupts, post interrupt messages to a bulletin board with the Linda operators; then specify when the Petri nets for interruptible tasks check the bulletin board. If convenient, the Linda operators could also be used to communicate between the workers to state when a cake is finished or to specify the type of cake or the decorations.

27. Isaac Newton (1687) assumed that space and time are "absolute" entities that exist independent of any physical objects or processes:

- "Absolute, true, and mathematical time, of itself, and from its own nature, flows equably without regard to anything external, and by another name is called duration."
- "Absolute space, in its own nature, without regard to anything external, remains always similar and immovable."

Whitehead (1929) observed that Newton's view has been highly successful for developing mathematical physics, but that it conflicts with common sense and with the more recent developments in relativity and quantum mechanics:

> For the purposes of science, it was an extraordinarily clarifying statement, that is to say, for all the purposes of science within the next two hundred years, and for most of its purposes since that period. But as a fundamental statement, it lies completely open to skeptical attack; and also, as Newton himself admits, diverges from common sense — "the vulgar conceive those quantities under no other notions but from the relation they bear to sensible objects."

In response, Whitehead described his own philosophy as "an attempt to return to the conceptions of the vulgar." He considered "actual entities" as the fundamental reality and defined space and time as abstractions from actual entities and their relationships.

Is the discussion of the clock in Figure 4.10 more compatible with Newton's view or with Whitehead's? What implications would either view have on the classification of space and time in the twelve categories of Figure 2.7? How would measurements, dates, and geographical coordinates be classified? What about other kinds of physical measurements such as temperature? Can the physical notions be generalized to measurements in other fields such as a stock market index or intelligence quotient (IQ)? Where would those entities be classified in the categories of Figure 2.7? The issues raised in this exercise could be answered in a paragraph, an essay, or a dissertation.

28. Show how the representations for time and causality in Petri nets could be related to the physical concepts discussed in Section 2.7. How could Born's postulates for cause, antecedence, and contiguity be stated in terms of Petri nets? What would correspond to a region, a time line, or a snapshot? What kinds of regions would correspond to continuants and occurrents? How would you define a spatial form predicate $P(s)$ that applies to a snapshot s?

29. After working on the previous exercise, check the answers at the back of the book. Then write some suggestions or guidelines that might help a knowledge engineer analyze physical processes and map them to Petri-net simulations.

30. List the kinds of events discussed in the hotel reservation example in Appendix C. Draw a Petri net that shows the states and events that may take place from the time a guest makes a reservation to the time of check-out. Inside the circles of the Petri net, write a short description of the conditions that must be true in each state. Enlarge the transition bars to boxes, and write a short

description of what happens in the corresponding events. Include various exceptional cases, such as a guest walking in without a reservation.

Some places in the net might have multiple tokens, each one representing a clerk who is waiting for some guest to request a service. Design the Petri net to ensure that no clerk is doing more than one task at a time, but a clerk who finishes a task should be available to perform other services for other guests.

Some of the interactions in the Petri net might be more conveniently expressed by messages sent via the Linda operators. If you choose to use messages, show which transitions invoke Linda operators and the formats of the tuples they send or receive. For time-dependent conditions, you may assume that a Petri net for an alarm clock uses the Linda Out operator to send a message to BB. It is not necessary to show the internal details of the alarm clock net.

CHAPTER FIVE

Purposes, Contexts, and Agents

*Can we realize for an instant what a cross-section of all existence at a
definite point of time would be? While I talk and the flies buzz, a sea gull
catches a fish at the mouth of the Amazon, a tree falls in the Adirondack
wilderness, a man sneezes in Germany, a horse dies in Tartary, and twins are
born in France. What does that mean? Does the contemporaneity of these
events with one another, and with a million others as disjointed, form a
rational bond between them, and unite them into anything that means for us
a world? Yet just such a collateral contemporaneity, and nothing else, is the
real order of the world. It is an order with which we have nothing to do but
to get away from it as fast as possible. As I said, we break it: we break it into
histories, and we break it into arts, and we break it into sciences; and then
we begin to feel at home. We make ten thousand separate serial orders of it,
and on any one of these we react as though the others did not exist.*
WILLIAM JAMES, *The Will to Believe and Other Essays*

5.1 Purpose

In Peirce's terms, purpose is the Thirdness that relates some mind or mindlike entity
(first), which directs the course of a process (second) toward some goal (third). That
mindlike entity need not be human or even animal; both Peirce and Whitehead
believed in a continuity of mental aspects from the atomic level to the human level,
and perhaps beyond. For knowledge representation, purpose determines the selection of subject matter, the categories for representing it, and the *intentional granularity* or level of detail that is considered relevant.

    FINAL CAUSES.   For purpose, Aristotle used the word *telos*, which is the goal
or *final cause* of an action. In Figure 5.1, the positions in the games of go and
go-moku show how purpose can have a causal effect. Both games are played with
the same equipment and with the same kind of moves: two players take turns
placing black and white stones on the intersections of a 19×19 grid. At a purely
syntactic level, the moves in the two games appear to be the same:

1. The game starts with an empty board.
2. The player with the black stones places one stone on any empty intersection.

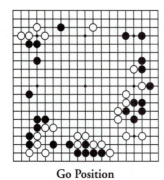 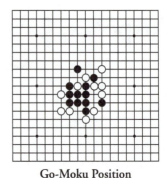

Go Position   Go-Moku Position

FIGURE 5.1 The effect of purpose on the course of a game

3. The player with the white stones places one stone on any empty intersection.

4. Repeat from step #2 until the players agree that either one side has won or there is no advantage in making any further moves.

5. Finally, compute the score to determine which player wins.

The difference between the games results from the way the score is computed at step #5. The method of scoring at the end affects every move from the very beginning.

The two board positions in Figure 5.1 are typical of intermediate stages in the two games: a go position usually has stones scattered around the edges, but a go-moku position has stones clustered in the middle. Those patterns result from the final scoring rules:

- *Go.* The purpose of go is to surround territory: the players get one point for every empty intersection surrounded by their stones, and none for the space that the stones actually occupy.

- *Go-moku.* The purpose of go-moku is to get five adjacent stones of the same color in a straight chain, vertically, horizontally, or diagonally.

The scoring rules for go encourage the players to begin placing stones in loosely related positions near the corners and edges, where it is easier to surround a block of space. The first move in go is usually close to one of the four corners. The go-moku rules encourage the players to place stones close together, where they can form a chain or block an opponent's attempt to form a chain. Unlike go, the best opening move in go-moku is to occupy the center. Although the same moves are legal in the two games, the scoring procedure at the end determines the purpose of the stones and affects the choice of moves from the beginning.

Purpose depends on a goal-seeking agent, but the agent need not be conscious: a computer program that searches for favorable moves can play games that resemble experienced human play. Those programs are not mindlike at the human level, but Peirce (1906) would have classified them somewhere between crystals and bees, which he considered capable of a mediating Thirdness. The crystalline lattices and the storage of honey for the winter are the final causes that explain the individual actions of the swarms of molecules and bees. For such entities, the goal-directed Thirdness is not derived from a conscious choice; instead, it is compiled into their computer programs, molecular structure, or genetic code.

COMPLEMENTARITY.   A continuant is an object that retains its identity over an extended period of time; an occurrent is an ever-changing process whose stages evolve from, but are not identical to one another. That distinction may seem clear in the abstract, but in practice, no physical object can remain unchanged over any extended interval. The changeable nature of all things was a major theme of Heraclitus: "One cannot step twice into the same river, nor can one grasp any mortal substance in a stable condition, but it scatters and again gathers; it forms and dissolves, and approaches and departs." In one sense, the Hudson River is the "same" river that Henry Hudson explored in 1609, but in another sense, it is in a constant state of flux.

Whether a river is considered a continuant that retains its identity over centuries or an occurrent that differs from one moment to the next depends more on the viewer than on the thing itself. As Whitehead (1938) observed:

> In logical reasoning, which proceeds by use of the variable, there are always two tacit presuppositions — one is that the definite symbols of composition can retain the same meaning as the reasoning elaborates novel compositions. The other presupposition is that this self-identity of each variable can be preserved when the variable is replaced by some definite instance. . . . The baby in the cradle and the grown man in middle age are in some senses identical and in other senses diverse. Is the train of argument in its conclusions substantiated by the identity or vitiated by the diversity? (p. 146)

For some purposes, the baby x can be considered the same person as the adult x. But a baby and an adult play very different roles in society, and the identity $x=x$ cannot be assumed for x at different times. The interpretation of an entity as a continuant or an occurrent depends on the concept used to characterize it.

The various ways of classifying things lead to complementary ontologies. At a conceptual level, they resemble the quantum mechanical issue of whether an electron is a wave or a particle. For some purposes, either view could be considered correct: either the wave theory or the particle theory could be used to describe the behavior of an electron. For some experiments, one view may be easier to apply or calculate than the other. When they both apply, they predict the same observable results. But a mixture of the two theories cannot be used without producing contradictions. The physicist Niels Bohr (1934, 1958) called this practice of alternately using two incompatible descriptions of the same system the *principle of complementarity*. A similar principle holds for any aspect of the world that may be described by potentially contradictory theories. For legal purposes, a human being may be considered a person whose identity remains constant for a lifetime. But for other purposes, the same "person" may be classified at different times as a baby, a teenager, or an adult. Each view highlights a different aspect of what it means to be a human being. Each one may be appropriate in some context; but if both views are applied to the same individual in the same context, contradictions can arise.

Although human beings may be described as processes, the type Person classifies a human being as a continuant whose identity remains the same throughout a lifetime. In the following graph, the dotted line is a *coreference link*, which shows that a person named Tom in 1976 is the same individual as a person named Tom in 1997:

```
[Year: 1976]←(PTim)←[Person: Tom]- - -[Person: Tom]→(PTim)→[Year: 1997].
```

But consider the following graph:

```
[Baby: Tom]- - -[Adult: Tom].
```

This graph says that there exists some individual named Tom who is both a baby and an adult. That graph is just as contradictory as the corresponding sentence in English or formula in predicate calculus:

baby(Tom) $\wedge$ adult(Tom).

By the rules of classical logic, additional qualifiers can make a statement contradictory, but they can never remove a contradiction. With more PTim relations, the graph or the corresponding formula would still be contradictory:

```
[Year: 1976]←(PTim)←[Baby: Tom]- - -[Adult: Tom]→(PTim)→[Year: 1997].
```

Baby and Adult are incompatible concepts that characterize different stages of a process — a human life. When viewed as a process, Tom cannot be in both stages in the same context. But the concept type Person describes Tom as a continuant whose identity remains constant independent of any physical change. If Tom and the Hudson River are viewed as continuants, then "the same person" can step into "the same river" many times during the course of a lifetime. But if they are both viewed as processes, then neither the human being nor the river can be "the same" at two different encounters.

CONTEXTS. Complementary ways of describing the same object can be mixed, but only when the contexts are explicitly distinguished. Figure 5.2 shows the person Tom coreferent with a baby in a situation in 1976 and coreferent with

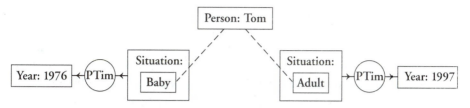

FIGURE 5.2 Incompatible concepts for describing Tom at different times

an adult in 1997. That graph may be read as the sentence *Tom was a baby in 1976 and an adult in 1997.* The type Person classifies Tom as a continuant that has a long-term duration. The concepts Baby and Adult are also continuants, but they describe Tom at shorter intervals of his lifetime. The concepts [Baby] and [Adult] may both be coreferent with [Person: Tom] in different situations, but there is no situation in which they could be coreferent with each other. Figure 5.2 can be translated to the following formula in predicate calculus:

$(\exists x{:}\text{Person})(\text{name}(x,\text{Tom}) \wedge$
$\quad (\exists y{:}\text{Situation})(\text{year}(1976) \wedge \text{ptim}(y,1976) \wedge$
$\quad\quad \text{dscr}(y, \text{baby}(x))) \wedge$
$\quad (\exists z{:}\text{Situation})(\text{year}(1997) \wedge \text{ptim}(z,1997) \wedge$
$\quad\quad \text{dscr}(z, \text{adult}(x)))).$

This formula may be read *There exists a person x named Tom, and there existed a situation y in the year 1976, which is described by x being a baby, and there existed a situation z in the year 1997, which is described by x being an adult.* The two situations described by the propositions nested inside the *dscr* predicates effectively create *opaque contexts.* The descriptions inside those contexts can refer to the individual *x,* which is quantified outside; but neither of the nested contexts can refer to or contradict any information in the other.

Complementarity is not a property of the world itself, but of the conceptual systems used to classify and talk about the world. A dualistic view of an electron as either a wave or a particle is only an approximation. Its real nature is best described in purely quantum mechanical laws, which may be difficult for people to visualize; but that is a limitation of human imagination, not a characteristic of the electron itself. A similar caveat applies to complementary views of a person as a baby, a child, a teenager, a young adult, a mature individual, or a senior citizen. Those terms classify the continuous process of growth as a series of discrete jumps. Discontinuities between stages can lead to disputes and misunderstandings: A two-year-old girl protested "Mom, I'm not a baby any more!" Apparently, the mother still classified her according to the type Baby, but the girl wanted to jump to the next stage and assume the axioms appropriate to the type Child.

IDENTITY.   Even a concept as fundamental as identity depends on purpose. Mathematicians usually assume that everything is identical to itself: $(\forall x)x{=}x$. But Heraclitus stated the equally fundamental principle that everything is in a state of flux. Plato and Aristotle reconciled these two principles by noting that the abstract mathematical forms are the only things for which identity is true without qualifications. For the Greeks, the *logos* is unchanging, but the *physis* is in flux.

In terms of the categories of Chapter 2, identity holds without qualifications only for the abstract branch of the lattice. For the physical branch, the *identity conditions* depend on which features are considered significant. One of the oldest paradoxes of identity is the *ship of Theseus*, all of whose parts were supposedly replaced, one by one, over the years until not a single piece of the original remained. Could one say that it was still the same ship? Would it be more accurate to say that the old ship was repaired or that it was replaced by a new ship? This philosophical puzzle still creates serious problems for inventory control systems. The U.S. Army, for example, keeps track of rifles, but it does not keep track of every individual part. A soldier whose rifle has a broken or worn-out part can request a new part with a minimum of paperwork. But a policy of unrestricted replacement would allow someone to steal a complete rifle by requesting parts one at a time. To prevent that possibility, the army established a policy that the identity of a rifle is determined by its stock, which is the only part that cannot be replaced. If it is broken, a soldier must request an entirely new rifle.

The army's solution to the problem of identity is the usual way of making a naturally occurring concept precise — by an artificial convention that may be accepted by consensus or legislated by some authority. In a database or knowledge base, identity is determined by unique serial numbers or *surrogates*. But the surrogates do not automatically solve the problem of identity. They are just a mechanism for recording whatever convention has been adopted.

VERBS AS NEXUS.   In Peirce's terms, a verb is a syntactic unit for representing the mediating Thirdness that relates the participants. The concept type Chase, for example, involves three entities: an animate chaser, a mobile entity that is being chased, and the act of chasing itself. The type Give involves four entities: a giver, a gift, a recipient, and the act of giving. In Whitehead's terms, the process expressed by the verb serves as a *nexus* or "particular fact of togetherness." The nexus binds the participants together in a bundle of interlocking relationships or *prehensions*. In a conceptual graph, the nexus may be represented by a context box, which is linked to the concepts that represent the participants by conceptual relations that express the prehensions.

To illustrate various ways of representing verbs, Figure 5.3 shows three conceptual graphs for the sentence *A cat is chasing a mouse*. The top graph represents the act of chasing by a conceptual relation that directly links the cat to the mouse. The

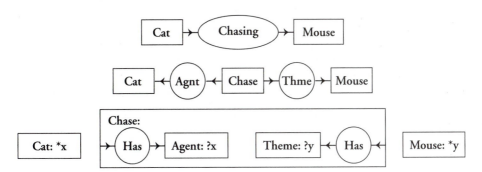

FIGURE 5.3 Three ways of saying that a cat is chasing a mouse

middle one uses the concept [Chase] to represent the act as a separate entity, which is linked to the cat and the mouse by the agent (Agnt) and theme (Thme) relations. The bottom graph uses a context box to represent the concept [Chase] as a nexus with two Has relations, which link the act of chasing to the agent x and the theme y.

The graph with the Chasing relation links the cat to the mouse without showing the act of chasing as a separate entity. It maps to the kind of formula used in elementary logic books:

$$(\exists x{:}\text{cat})(\exists y{:}\text{mouse})\text{chasing}(x,y).$$

The middle graph with the agent and theme relations has a more direct mapping to and from the thematic relations in natural languages. It maps to the following formula:

$$(\exists x{:}\text{cat})(\exists y{:}\text{mouse})(\exists z{:}\text{chase})(\text{agnt}(z,x) \wedge \text{thme}(z,y)).$$

The bottom graph, in which Has is the only relation type, shows Chase as a nexus with prehensions that bind the agent and theme. The Has relation is the primitive that links one of Whitehead's *prehending entities* to its *prehended entity*. In this example, the context box labeled Chase expresses the nexus, and the two Has relations represent the prehensions that link the nexus to the agent x and the theme y. In the linear notation, that graph may be written

```
[Cat: *x] [Mouse: *y]
[Chase: *z [?z]→(Has)→[Agent: ?x] [?z]→(Has)→[Theme: ?y]].
```

In the translation to predicate calculus, there are three existentially quantified variables: x for the cat, y for the mouse, and z for the chase. The description predicate *dscr* is used to relate the nexus z to the proposition stated by the nested conceptual graph. In predicate calculus, the graph maps to the following formula:

$$(\exists x{:}\text{cat})(\exists y{:}\text{mouse})(\exists z{:}\text{chase})$$
$$\text{dscr}(z, \text{has}(z,x) \wedge \text{agent}(x) \wedge \text{has}(z,y) \wedge \text{theme}(y)).$$

This formula may be read *There exists a cat x, a mouse y, and an instance of chasing z; the chase z is described by the proposition that z has x as agent and y as theme.*

Whenever the information expressed by the nested graph is true under the same conditions as the information in the outer context, the Has relations can pivot around the context wall, and the inner graphs or subgraphs can be moved to the outside. When the Has relations are moved outside, the bottom graph of Figure 5.3 becomes

```
[Cat]- - -[Agent]←(Has)←[Chase]→(Has)→[Theme]- - -[Mouse].
```

Following is the corresponding formula:

$$(\exists x{:}\text{cat})(\exists y{:}\text{mouse})(\exists z{:}\text{chase})$$
$$(\text{has}(z,x) \wedge \text{agent}(x) \wedge \text{has}(z,y) \wedge \text{theme}(y)).$$

The context box or the description relation serves as a "firewall" that separates the encapsulated information from the information in the outer context. The effect of exporting the nested information is to erase the firewall between the two contexts.

Every conceptual relation that expresses a thematic role can be defined in terms of Has and the corresponding concept type for that role. As an example, the following equation defines the Agnt relation by a dyadic lambda expression that includes the concept [Agent].

```
Agnt = [Act: λ1]→(Has)→[Agent]- - -[Animate: λ2].
```

This definition says that the Agnt relation links an act $\lambda 1$ to an animate being $\lambda 2$, where the act has an agent, which is coreferent with that animate being. In principle, all conceptual relations can be defined in terms of concepts linked by the primitive dyadic relation Has and coreference links.

DEFINING VERB SENSES.   Figure 5.4 shows the type Chase defined by a graph that shows how the agent and theme are related. It may be read *The agent of the chase is an animate being, which is rapidly following a mobile entity, which is the theme of the chase; the animate being's purpose in following is to catch the mobile entity.* As an instance of Peirce's category Thirdness, purpose is represented by a triadic relation that links the agent who has the intention, an act performed by that agent, and an intended situation, which is the reason why the agent performed the act. The context box around the intended situation separates it from the act of following, since the catching takes place in a separate situation after the following. If the chase is unsuccessful, the catching might not occur at all.

The graph nested inside the context describes the bundle of prehensions that constitute the nexus expressed by the verb. In Figure 5.4, the verb *chase* expresses the concept type Chase. The graph inside the context of [Chase] describe the nexus. The two Has relations link the context box to the concepts [Agent] and [Theme],

type Chase(*x) is

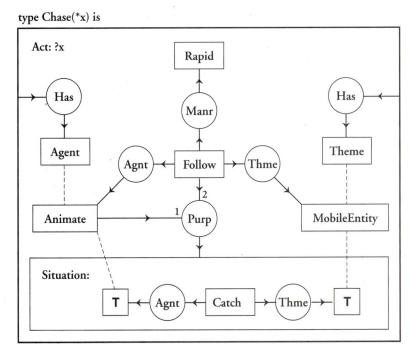

FIGURE 5.4 A definition of the concept type Chase

which represent the roles of the two principal participants. Those concepts are coreferent with the concepts [Animate] and [MobileEntity], which represent the types of entities that can play the roles of agent and theme. The rest of the graph states the conditions for an action to be considered a chase: the animate being is rapidly following the mobile entity for the purpose of catching it.

Since conceptual graphs are a system of logic, the associated rules of inference can transform the definition or combine it with other definitions and axioms to derive the consequences. The effect of the purpose relation (Purp) could be specified by several axioms:

- *Time sequence.* If an agent x performs an act y whose purpose is a situation z, the start of y occurs before the start of z.
- *Contingency.* If an agent x performs an act y whose purpose is a situation z described by a proposition p, then it is possible that z might not occur or that p might not be true of z.
- *Success or failure.* If an agent x performs an act y whose purpose is a situation z described by a proposition p, then x is said to be *successful* if z occurs and p is true of z; otherwise, x is said to have *failed*.

type ChaseAway(*x) is

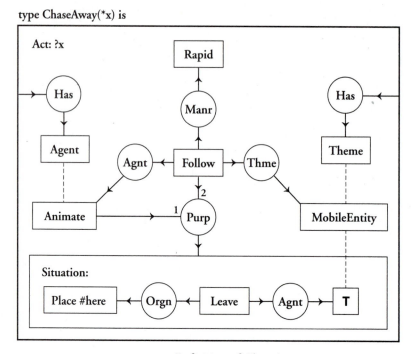

FIGURE 5.5 Definition of ChaseAway

When applied to the definition of Chase, these axioms predict that a successful act of chasing would enable the agent to catch the theme, but there is a possibility that the act might fail.

Different senses of a word map to concept types with different definitions. Figure 5.5 shows a definition of the type ChaseAway, which is a sense of the verb *chase* in which the agent does not intend to catch the theme. Instead, the agent's purpose is to cause the theme to leave the place where the agent happens to be. Inside the situation box, the origin of leaving is represented by a place marked with the indexical #here. Like the indexical #now, it must be resolved to some concept specified in a containing context.

Since predicate calculus does not have a syntax for contexts, it cannot support a mechanism for representing and resolving indexicals. It would, however, be possible to extend predicate calculus with a notation for marking contexts. Then that notation could also be used to represent indexicals.

5.2 Syntax of Contexts

The word *context* has been used with a variety of conflicting meanings in linguistics, philosophy, and artificial intelligence. Some of the confusion results from an ambiguity in the English word. Dictionaries list two major senses of the word *context*:

- The basic meaning is a section of linguistic text or discourse that surrounds some word or phrase of interest.
- The derived meaning is a nonlinguistic situation, environment, domain, setting, background, or milieu that includes some entity, subject, or topic of interest.

The word *context* may refer to the text, to the information contained in the text, to the thing that the information is about, or to the possible uses of the text, the information, or the thing itself. The ambiguity about contexts results from which of these aspects happens to be the central focus. These informal senses of the word suggest criteria for distinguishing the formal functions:

- *Syntax.* The syntactic function of context is to group, delimit, quote, or package a section of text.
- *Semantics.* The quoted text may describe or refer to some real or hypothetical situation. That nonlinguistic referent is the derived meaning of the word *context.*
- *Pragmatics.* The word *interest*, which occurs in both senses of the English definition, suggests some reason or purpose for distinguishing the section of linguistic text or nonlinguistic situation. That purpose is the pragmatics or the reason why the text is being quoted.

In LISP, a context is represented by the quote operator, which blocks an expression from being executed as a program. In logic, a quote blocks the standard rules of inference and allows the definition of new rules for interpreting the text. In general, a context delimits text that is interpreted by some special rules for some particular purpose. Purpose is the central issue that must be distinguished in any formal theory of context.

PEIRCE'S CONTEXTS.   In 1883, C. S. Peirce invented the algebraic notation for predicate calculus. A dozen years later, he developed a graphical notation that more clearly distinguished contexts. Figure 5.6 shows his graph notation for delimiting the context of the proposition under discussion. In explaining that graph, Peirce (1898) said, "When we wish to assert something about a proposition without asserting the proposition itself, we will enclose it in a lightly drawn oval." The line attached to the oval links it to a relation that makes a *metalevel* assertion about the nested proposition. The primary function of Peirce's contexts is to separate the two levels: the propositions outside the context make metastatements about the propositions inside.

The oval supports the basic syntactic function of grouping related information

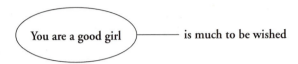

FIGURE 5.6 One of Peirce's graphs for talking about a proposition

in a package. But besides notation, Peirce developed a theory of the semantics and pragmatics of contexts and the rules of inference for importing and exporting information into and out of the contexts. For first-order logic, the only metalevel relation is *negation*. By combining negation with the existential-conjunctive subset of logic, Peirce developed *existential graphs* (EGs), which are based on three primitives:

1. *Existential quantifier:* A bar or linked structure of bars, called a *line of identity*, represents ∃.

2. *Conjunction:* The *juxtaposition* of two graphs in the same context represents ∧.

3. *Negation:* An *oval enclosure* with no lines attached to it represents ~ or the denial of the enclosed proposition.

When combined in all possible ways, these three primitives can represent full first-order logic. When used to state propositions about nested contexts, they form a metalanguage that can be used to define modal and higher-order logic.

To illustrate the use of negative contexts for representing FOL, Figure 5.7 shows an existential graph and a conceptual graph for the sentence *If a farmer owns a donkey, then he beats it*. The EG on the left has two ovals with no attached lines; by default, they represent negations. It also has two lines of identity, represented as linked bars: one line, which connects *farmer* to the left side of *owns* and *beats*, represents an existentially quantified variable (∃x); the other line, which connects *donkey* to the right side of *owns* and *beats*, represents another variable (∃y).

In CGs, a context is defined as a concept whose referent field contains nested

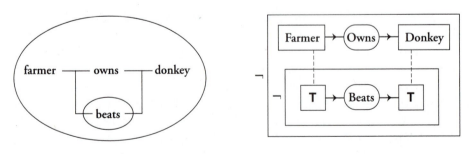

Existential Graph   Conceptual Graph

FIGURE 5.7 EG and CG for "If a farmer owns a donkey, then he beats it."

conceptual graphs. Since every context is also a concept, it can have a type label, coreference links, and attached conceptual relations. Syntactically, Peirce's ovals are squared off to form boxes, and the negation is explicitly marked by a ¬ symbol in front of the box. The primary difference between EGs and CGs is in the treatment of lines of identity. In EGs, the lines serve two different purposes: they represent existential quantifiers, and they show how the arguments are connected to the relations. In CGs, those two functions are split: the concepts [Farmer] and [Donkey] represent typed quantifiers (∃x:Farmer) and (∃y:Donkey), and arcs marked with arrows show the connections of relations to their arguments. In the inner context, the two concepts represented as [⊤] are connected by coreference links to concepts in the outer context.

When the EG of Figure 5.7 is translated to predicate calculus, *farmer* and *donkey* map to monadic predicates; *owns* and *beats* map to dyadic predicates. The implicit conjunctions are represented with the ∧ symbol. The result is an untyped formula:

$$\sim(\exists x)(\exists y)(\text{farmer}(x) \wedge \text{donkey}(y) \wedge$$
$$\text{owns}(x,y) \wedge \sim\text{beats}(x,y)).$$

The CG maps to the equivalent typed formula:

$$\sim(\exists x\text{:Farmer})(\exists y\text{:Donkey})(\text{owns}(x,y) \wedge \sim\text{beats}(x,y)).$$

A nest of two ovals, as in Figure 5.7, is what Peirce called a *scroll*. It represents implication, since ~(p ∧~q) is equivalent to $p{\supset}q$. Using the ⊃ symbol, the two formulas may be rewritten

$$(\forall x)(\forall y)((\text{farmer}(x) \wedge \text{donkey}(y) \wedge$$
$$\text{owns}(x,y)) \supset \text{beats}(x,y)).$$
$$(\forall x\text{:Farmer})(\forall y\text{:Donkey})(\text{owns}(x,y) \supset \text{beats}(x,y)).$$

The algebraic formulas with the ⊃ symbol illustrate a peculiar feature of predicate calculus: in order to keep the variables x and y within the scope of the quantifiers, the existential quantifiers in the phrases *a farmer* and *a donkey* must be moved to the front of the formula and translated to universal quantifiers. This puzzling feature of logic has posed a problem for linguists and logicians since the Middle Ages. The *donkey sentence* represented in Figure 5.7 is one of a series of sentences the Scholastics used to illustrate the problems of mapping language to logic.

Besides attaching a relation to an oval, Peirce used colors or *tinctures* to distinguish contexts other than negation. Figure 5.8 shows one of his examples, but with shading instead of color. The graph contains four ovals: the outer two form a scroll for *if-then*; the inner two represent possibility (shading) and impossibility (shading inside a negation). The outer oval may be read *If there exist a person, a horse, and water*, the next oval may be read *then it is possible for the person to lead the horse to the water and not possible for the person to make the horse drink the water.*

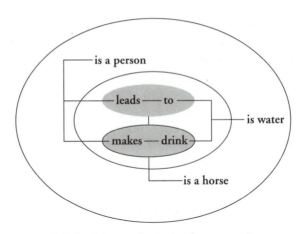

FIGURE 5.8 EG for "You can lead a horse to water, but you can't make him drink."

The notation -leads-to- represents a triadic predicate leadsTo(x,y,z), and -makes-drink- represents makesDrink(x,y,z). In the algebraic notation with $\Diamond$ for possibility, Figure 5.8 maps to the following formula:

$\sim(\exists x)(\exists y)(\exists z)(\text{person}(x) \wedge \text{horse}(y) \wedge \text{water}(z) \wedge$
$\sim(\Diamond\text{leadsTo}(x,y,z) \wedge \sim\Diamond\text{makesDrink}(x,y,z))\,)$.

With the symbol $\supset$ for implication, this formula becomes

$(\forall x)(\forall y)(\forall z)((\text{person}(x) \wedge \text{horse}(y) \wedge \text{water}(z)) \supset$
$(\Diamond\text{leadsTo}(x,y,z) \wedge \sim\Diamond\text{makesDrink}(x,y,z))\,)$.

This version may be read *For all x, y, and z, if x is a person, y is a horse, and z is water, then it is possible for x to lead y to z, and not possible for x to make y drink z.* Although logically explicit, this reading is not as succinct as the original proverb, *You can lead a horse to water, but you can't make him drink.*

DISCOURSE REPRESENTATION THEORY. The logician Hans Kamp once spent a summer translating English sentences from a scientific article to predicate calculus. During the course of his work, he was troubled by the same kinds of irregularities that puzzled the Scholastics. In order to simplify the mapping from language to logic, Kamp (1981a,b) developed *discourse representation structures* (DRSs) with an explicit notation for contexts. In terms of those structures, Kamp defined the rules of *discourse representation theory* for mapping quantifiers, determiners, and pronouns from language to logic (Kamp & Reyle 1993).

Although Kamp had not been aware of Peirce's existential graphs, his DRSs were structurally equivalent to Peirce's EGs. The diagram on the left of Figure 5.9

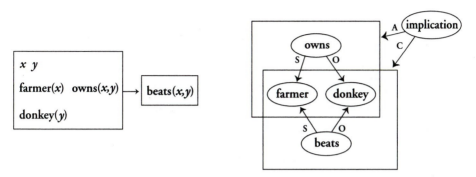

FIGURE 5.9 DRS and PSN for "If a farmer owns a donkey, then he beats it."

is a DRS for the donkey sentence, *If there exist a farmer x and a donkey y and x owns y, then x beats y.* The two boxes connected by an arrow represent an implication where the antecedent includes the consequent within its scope.

The DRS and EG notations look quite different, but they are exactly isomorphic: they have the same primitives, the same scoping rules for variables or lines of identity, and the same translation to predicate calculus. Therefore, the DRS in Figure 5.9 maps to the same formula as the EG in Figure 5.7:

$$\sim(\exists x)(\exists y)(\text{farmer}(x) \wedge \text{donkey}(y) \wedge$$
$$\text{owns}(x,y) \wedge \sim\text{beats}(x,y)).$$

Not all context notations have the same structure. On the right of Figure 5.7 is another notation that uses boxes: the *partitioned semantic network* (PSN) designed by Gary Hendrix (1979). Instead of nested contexts, Hendrix adopted overlapping contexts. Like EGs, CGs, and DRSs, the PSN notation supports complete first-order logic, but the PSN overlapping contexts do not have the same scope as the EG, CG, and DRS forms.

Peirce's motivation for the EG contexts was to simplify the logical structure and rules of inference. Kamp's motivation for the DRS contexts was to simplify the mapping from language to logic. Remarkably, they converged on context representations that are isomorphic. Therefore, Peirce's rules of inference and Kamp's discourse rules apply equally well to contexts in the EG, CG, or DRS notations. For notations with a different structure, such as PSN or predicate calculus, those rules cannot be applied without major modifications.

RESOLVING INDEXICALS. Besides inventing a logical notation for contexts, Peirce coined the term *indexical* for context-dependent references, such as pronouns and words like *here, there,* and *now.* In CGs, the symbol # represents the general indexical, which is usually expressed in English by the definite article *the.* More specific indexicals are marked by a qualifier after the # symbol, as in #here, #now, #he,

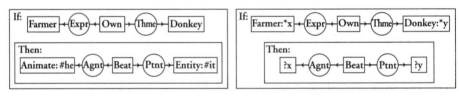

CG with indexicals   CG with indexicals resolved

FIGURE 5.10 Two conceptual graphs for "If a farmer owns a donkey, then he beats it."

#she, or #it. Figure 5.10 shows two conceptual graphs for the sentence *If a farmer owns a donkey, then he beats it.* The CG on the left represents the original pronouns with indexicals, and the one on the right replaces the indexicals with the coreference labels ?x and ?y.

In the concept [Animate: #he], the label Animate indicates the semantic type, and the indexical #he indicates that the referent must be found by a search for some type of Animate entity for which the masculine gender is applicable. In the concept [Entity: #it], the label Entity is synonymous with ⊤, which may represent anything, and the indexical #it indicates that the referent has neuter gender. The search for referents starts in the inner context and proceeds outward to find concepts of an appropriate type and gender. The CG on the right of Figure 5.10 shows the result of resolving the indexicals: the concept for *he* has been replaced by [?x] to show a coreference to the farmer, and the concept for *it* has been replaced by [?y] to show a coreference to the donkey.

Predicate calculus does not have a notation for indexicals, and its syntax does not show the context structure explicitly. Therefore, the CG on the left of Figure 5.10 cannot be translated directly to predicate calculus. After the indexicals have been resolved, the CG on the right can be translated to the following formula:

$$(\forall x{:}\text{Farmer})(\forall y{:}\text{Donkey})(\forall z{:}\text{Own})$$
$$((\text{expr}(z,x) \wedge \text{thme}(z,y)) \supset$$
$$(\exists w{:}\text{Beat})(\text{agnt}(w,x) \wedge \text{ptnt}(w,y))).$$

Note that this formula and the graph it was derived from are more complex than the CG in Figure 5.7. In order to compare the EG and the CG directly, that diagram represented the verbs by relations Owns and Beats, which do not explicitly show the linguistic roles. In Figure 5.10, the concept Own represents a state with an experiencer (Expr) and a theme (Thme). The concept Beat, however, represents an action with an agent (Agnt) and a patient (Ptnt). In general, the patient of an action is more deeply affected or transformed than a theme. See Appendix B.4 for a summary of these linguistic relations.

TRANSFORMATION RULES. In analyzing the donkey sentences, the Scholastics defined transformations or conversion rules from one logical form to another. As an example, a sentence with the word *every* can be converted to an equivalent sentence with an implication. The sentence *Every farmer who owns a donkey beats it* is equivalent to the one represented in Figures 5.7, 5.9, and 5.10. In CGs, the word *every* maps to a universal quantifier in the referent of some concept:

```
[ [Farmer: λ]←(Expr)←[Own]→(Thme)→[Donkey]: ∀]-
  (Agnt)←[Beat]→[Entity: #it].
```

In this graph, the quantifier ∀ does not range over the type Farmer, but over the subtype defined by the nested lambda expression: just those farmers who own a donkey. The symbol ∀ represents a *defined quantifier*, which causes the surrounding CG to be expanded to the following form:

```
¬[ [Farmer: λ]←(Expr)←[Own]→(Thme)→[Donkey]: *x]
  ¬[ [⊤: ?x]←(Agnt)←[Beat]→[Entity: #it] ].
```

The ∀ symbol in a CG triggers a *transformation rule*, as described in Appendix A.2. That rule or some procedure that simulates it transforms the original CG to the more primitive form.

Other transformation rules are used to expand the defined types and relations, such as the impossibility relation (¬Psbl), which is defined as the negation of possibility (Psbl):

relation ¬Psbl(*p) **is**
```
  ¬[Proposition: (Psbl)→[Possible: ?p]].
```

This rule says that a proposition p is not possible if it is false that p is possible. Such transformation rules can be used to map CGs derived from different sentences to a common logical form.

The transformation of a universal quantifier to an implication has been known since medieval times. But the complete catalog of all the rules for resolving indexicals is still an active area of research in linguistics and logic. For the sentence *You can lead a horse to water, but you can't make him drink,* many more transformations must be performed to generate the equivalent of Peirce's EG in Figure 5.8. The first step is be the generation of a logical form with indexicals, such as the CG in Figure 5.11, which may be read literally *It is possible* (Psbl) *for you to lead a horse to water, but it is not possible* (¬Psbl) *for you to cause him to drink the liquid.*

A parser and semantic interpreter that did a purely local or *context-free* analysis of the English sentence could generate the four concepts marked as indexicals by # symbols in Figure 5.11:

- The two occurrences of *you* would map to the two concepts of the form [Person: #you].

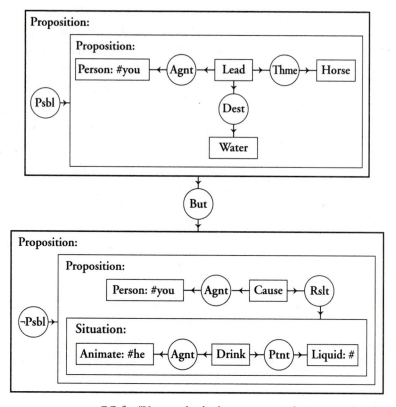

FIGURE 5.11 CG for "You can lead a horse to water, but you can't make him drink."

- The pronoun *him* represents a masculine animate indexical in the objective case, whose concept is [Animate: #he].

- The missing object of the verb *drink* is presupposed by the concept type Drink, which requires a patient of type Liquid. The implicit concept [Liquid: #] is marked as an indexical, so that the exact referent can be determined from the context.

The indexicals would have to be resolved by a context-dependent search, proceeding outward from the context in which each indexical is nested.

CONVERSATIONAL IMPLICATURES. Sometimes no suitable referent for an indexical can be found. In such a case, the person who hears or reads the sentence must make further assumptions about implicit referents. The philosopher Paul Grice (1975) observed that such assumptions, called *conversational implicatures*, are often necessary to make sense out of the sentences in ordinary language. They are justified by the charitable assumption that the speaker or writer is trying to make a meaningful statement but, for the sake of brevity, may leave some background information unspoken. To resolve the indexicals in Figure 5.11, the listener would have to make the following kinds of assumptions to fill in the missing information:

1. The two concepts of the form [Person: #you] would normally be resolved to the listener or reader of the sentence. Since no one is explicitly mentioned in any containing context, some such person must be assumed. That assumption corresponds to drawing an if-then nest of contexts with a hypothetical reader *x* coreferent with *you*:

   ```
   [If: [Person: *x]- - -[Person: #you]
     [Then: . . .]].
   ```

   This graph may be read *If there is a person x who is the the listener you, then . . .*, where the three dots are a place holder for the graph in Figure 5.11. After that graph is inserted in place of the dots, every occurrence of #you would be replaced by ?x. The resulting graph could be read *If there exists a person x, then x can lead a horse to water, but x can't make him drink the liquid.*

2. The concept [Animate: #he] might be resolved to either a human or a beast. Since the reader is referred to as *you*, the most likely referent is the horse. But in both CGs and DRSs, coreference links can only be drawn between concepts under one of the following conditions:

   • The antecedent concept [Horse] and the indexical [Animate: #he] both occur in the same context.

   • The antecedent occurs in a context that includes the context of the indexical.

   In Figure 5.11, neither of these conditions holds. To make the second condition true, the antecedent [Horse] can be *exported* or *lifted* to some containing context, such as the context of the hypothetical reader *x*. This assumption has the effect of treating the horse as hypothetical as the person *x*. After a coreference label is assigned to the concept [Horse: *y], the indexical #he could be replaced by ?y.

3. The liquid, which had to be assumed to make sense of the verb *drink*, might be coreferent with the water. But in order to draw a coreference link, another assumption must be made to lift the antecedent concept [Water: *z] to the same hypothetical context as the reader and the horse. Then the concept [Liquid: #] would become [Liquid: ?z].

The result would be the following CG with all indexicals resolved:

```
[If: [Person: *x] [Horse: *y] [Water: *z]
   [Then:
      [Proposition:
         (Psbl)→[Proposition: [Person: ?x]←[Lead]-
            (Thme)→[Horse: ?y]
            (Dest)→[Water: ?z] ]]→(But)-
      [Proposition:
         (¬Psbl)→[Proposition: [Person: ?x]←(Agnt)←[Cause]-
            (Rslt)→[Situation:
               [Animate: ?y]←(Agnt)←[Drink]→(Ptnt)→[Liquid: ?z]] ]]]].
```

This CG may be read *If there exist a person x, a horse y, and water z, then the person x can lead the horse y to water z, but the person x can't make the animate being y drink the liquid z.* This graph is more detailed than the EG in Figure 5.8 because it explicitly shows the conjunction *but* and the linguistic roles Agnt, Thme, Ptnt, Dest, and Rslt. Before the indexicals are resolved, the type labels are needed to match the indexicals to their antecedents. Afterward, the *bound concepts* [Person: ?x], [Horse: ?y], [Animate: ?y], [Water: ?z], and [Liquid: ?z] could be simplified to just [?x], [?y], or [?z].

As this example illustrates, indexicals occur in the intermediate stage of translating language to logic, and their correct resolution may require nontrivial assumptions. Many programs in AI and computational linguistics follow rules of discourse representation to resolve indexicals. The problem of making the correct assumptions about conversational implicatures is more difficult. The kinds of assumptions needed to understand ordinary conversation are similar to the assumptions that are made in nonmonotonic reasoning (see Section 6.4). Both of them depend partly on context-independent rules of logic and partly on context-dependent background knowledge.

5.3   Semantics of Contexts

As William James (1897) observed, an arbitrary region of space-time has no intrinsic meaning. The best way to deal with the bewildering confusion of events in some region of space and time is to "break it. . . . We make ten thousand separate serial orders of it, and on any one of these we react as though the others did not exist." A context is a package of information about one of those separated chunks of the world. Semantics determines how those packages relate to those chunks.

SITUATIONS AND PROPOSITIONS.   Logicians such as Saul Kripke (1963a,b) and Richard Montague (1974) developed theories of semantics based on models of possible worlds. Each model represents an unbounded region of space-time with all the heterogeneous complexity of William James's example. To avoid such large, open-ended models, Jon Barwise and John Perry (1983) developed *situation seman-tics* as a theory that relates the meaning of sentences to smaller, more manageable chunks called *situations*. Each situation is a configuration of some aspect of the world in a bounded region of space and time. It may include people and things with their actions and speech; it may be real or imaginary; and its time may be past, present, or future.

Situation semantics is a theory about the flow of information: from situations in the world, to speakers who perceive and talk about those situations, to listeners who interpret the speech by thinking about and acting upon the situations.

- Speaker's information flow: Situation ⇒ Perception ⇒ Statement.
- Listener's information flow: Statement ⇒ Interpretation ⇒ Action ⇒ Modified situation.

This flow relates the abstract symbols of language to the physical situations people live in and talk about. Without the physical situations at both ends, the symbols would be *ungrounded*. Symbols acquire meaning by the process of *symbol grounding*, which as Peirce insisted depends on triadic relationships: the speaker expresses a *concept* of an *object* by a *symbol*, which the listener interprets by an equivalent concept "or perhaps a more developed one."

Figure 5.12 shows a concept of type Situation, which is linked by two image relations (Imag) to two different kinds of images of that situation: a picture and the associated sound. The description relation (Dscr) links the situation to a proposition that describes some aspect of it. It is equivalent to the *entailment operator, x⊨p*, which means that p is a true proposition about x. The proposition is linked by three statement relations (Stmt) to statements of the proposition in three different languages: an English sentence, a conceptual graph, and a formula in the Knowledge Representation Language (KIF). As the diagram illustrates, the sound image and the picture image capture information that is not stated in the propositional forms, but even they are only partial representations.

The sound and the picture, which are displayed graphically in Figure 5.12, would be stored in some conventional representation, such as a GIF or JPEG file. The CG could be mapped to the following formula in predicate calculus:

$$(\exists s{:}\text{Situation})(\exists p{:}\text{Proposition})(\exists g{:}\text{CG})$$
$$(\exists x{:}\text{Sound})(\exists y{:}\text{Picture})(\exists z{:}\text{English})(\exists w{:}\text{K IF})$$
$$(\text{dscr}(s,p) \wedge \text{imag}(s,x) \wedge \text{imag}(s,y)$$
$$\wedge \text{stored}(x,\text{clankety.wav}) \wedge \text{stored}(y,\text{plumber.gif})$$
$$\wedge \text{stmt}(p,z) \wedge \text{stmt}(p,g) \wedge \text{stmt}(p,w)$$
$$\wedge \text{literal}(z,\text{"A plumber is carrying a pipe."})$$
$$\wedge \text{literal}(g,\text{"[Plumber]}{\leftarrow}\text{(Agnt)}{\leftarrow}\text{[Carry]}{\rightarrow}\text{(Thme)}{\rightarrow}\text{[Pipe]"})$$
$$\wedge \text{literal}(w,\text{"(exists ((?x plumber) (?y carry) (?z pipe))}$$
$$\text{(and (agnt ?y ?x) (thme ?y ?z)))"})).$$

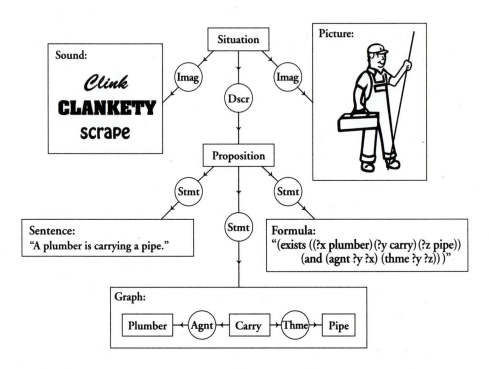

FIGURE 5.12 A CG representing a situation of a plumber carrying a pipe

The stored relation links images to the names of files in which they are stored, and the literal relation links linguistic entities to the character strings used to express them. A multimedia system can display them in any form that is convenient for the users.

McCARTHY'S CONTEXTS.   John McCarthy is one of the founding fathers of AI, whose collected work (McCarthy 1990) has frequently inspired and sometimes revolutionized the application of logic to knowledge representation. In his "Notes on Formalizing Context," McCarthy (1993) introduced the predicate ist($\mathcal{C}$,p), which may be read "the proposition p is true in context $\mathcal{C}$." For clarity, it will be spelled out in the form isTrueIn(p,$\mathcal{C}$). As illustrations, McCarthy gave the following examples:

> isTrueIn("Holmes is a detective", contextOf("Sherlock Holmes stories")).
> isTrueIn("Holmes is a Supreme Court Justice", contextOf("U.S. legal
> history")).

In these examples, the context *disambiguates* the referent of the name *Holmes* either to the fictional character Sherlock Holmes or to Oliver Wendell Holmes, Jr., the first appointee to the Supreme Court by President Theodore Roosevelt. In effect, names behave like indexicals whose referents are determined by the context.

One of McCarthy's reasons for developing a theory of context was his uneasiness with the proliferation of new logics for every kind of modal, temporal, epistemic, and nonmonotonic reasoning. The ever-growing number of modes presented in AI journals and conferences is a throwback to the Scholastic logicians who went beyond Aristotle's two modes *necessary* and *possible* to *permissible, obligatory, doubtful, clear, generally known, heretical, said by the ancients,* or *written in Holy Scriptures.* The medieval logicians spent so much time talking about modes that they were nicknamed the *modistae.* The modern logicians have axiomatized their modes and developed semantic models to support them, but each theory includes only one or two of the many modes. McCarthy (1977) observed:

> For AI purposes, we would need all the above modal operators in the same system. This would make the semantic discussion of the resulting modal logic extremely complex.

Instead of an open-ended number of modes, McCarthy hoped to develop a simple but universal mechanism that would replace all the modal logics with first-order logic supplemented with metalanguage about contexts. His student R. V. Guha (1991) implemented contexts in the Cyc system and showed that a first-order object language supplemented with a first-order metalanguage could support versions of modal, temporal, default, and higher-order reasoning.

McCarthy and his students have shown that the predicate isTrueIn can be a powerful tool for building knowledge bases, but the predicate isTrueIn mixes the syntactic notion of containment (is-in) with the semantic notion of truth (is-true-of). One way to resolve the semantic status is to assume a mapping from McCarthy's contexts to Barwise and Perry's situations:

$$(\forall \mathcal{C}{:}\text{Context})(\exists s{:}\text{Situation})(\forall p{:}\text{Proposition})(\text{isTrueIn}(p,\mathcal{C}) \equiv \text{dscr}(s,p)).$$

This formula says that for every context $\mathcal{C}$ in McCarthy's sense, there exists a situation s in Barwise and Perry's sense; furthermore, for every proposition p, p is true in the context $\mathcal{C}$ if and only if the situation s is described by p. For Figure 5.12, the context $\mathcal{C}$ would include the proposition that a plumber is carrying a pipe, but it would also include all the propositions that are entailed by the sound and picture images: the plumber is carrying a toolbox, he works for Acme Plumbing Co., he is dragging the pipe with a clankety noise, he is wearing a cap with the letter A on it, and so forth. The predicate isTrueIn$(p,\mathcal{C})$ means that p is one of those propositions.

MEANINGFUL SITUATIONS.   Barwise and Perry (1983) identified a situation with a bounded region of space-time. But in James' terms, an arbitrary region of space and time contains "disjointed events" with no "rational bond between them." A meaningful situation is far from arbitrary, as the following examples illustrate:

- A college lecture could be considered a situation bounded by a fifty-minute time period in a spatial region enclosed by the walls of a classroom. But if the time were moved forward by thirty minutes, the region would include the ending of one lecture and the beginning of another. That time shift would create an unnatural "situation."

- If the space were shifted left by half the width of a classroom, it would include part of one class listening to one teacher, part of another class listening to a different teacher speaking on a different topic, and a wall between the two lectures. That shift would create an even more unnatural situation than the time shift.

- Another transformation might fix the coordinate system relative to the sun instead of the earth. Then the region that included the class at the beginning of the lecture would stay behind as the earth moved. Within a few minutes, it would be in deep space, containing nothing but an occasional hydrogen atom.

Even more complex situations would be needed for the referents of the Sherlock Holmes stories or the U.S. legal history. The first is fictional, and the second is intertwined with all the major events that happened in the United States from 1776 to the present. The space-time region for a fictional situation does not exist, and the space-time region for the U.S. legal history cannot be separated from the region of its political, economic, or cultural history.

In discussing the development of situation theory, Keith Devlin (1991) observed that the definitions were stretched to the point where situations "include, but are not equal to any of simply connected regions of space-time, highly disconnected space-time regions, contexts of utterance (whatever that turns out to mean in precise terms), collections of background conditions for a constraint, and so on." After further discussion, Devlin admitted that they cannot be defined: "Situations are just that: situations. They are abstract objects introduced so that we can handle issues of context, background, and so on."

For Devlin, situations are undefinable objects whose purpose is to simplify the problems of reasoning about contexts. For McCarthy, contexts are undefinable objects whose purpose is to simplify the problems of reasoning about situations. Peirce and James, the two founders of *pragmatism*, focused on what is common in these two circular definitions: the notion of purpose. Space-time coordinates are not sufficient to distinguish a meaningful situation from a disjointed collection of events. Some agent for some purpose must pick and choose what is relevant.

MEANING-PRESERVING TRANSLATIONS.   Informally, different statements in different languages can mean "the same thing." Formally, that "thing," called a *proposition*, represents abstract, language-independent, semantic content. As an abstraction, a proposition has no physical embodiment that can be written or spoken. Only its statements in particular languages can be expressed as strings of symbols.

According to Peirce (1905), "The meaning of a proposition is itself a proposition. Indeed, it is no other than the very proposition of which it is the meaning: it is a translation of it." Mathematically, Peirce's informal statement may be formalized by defining a proposition as an *equivalence class* of sentences that can be translated from one to another while preserving meaning. Some further criteria are necessary to specify what kinds of translations are considered to "preserve meaning." Formally, a *meaning-preserving translation f* from a language $\mathcal{L}_1$ to a language $\mathcal{L}_2$ may be defined as a function that satisfies the following constraints:

- *Invertible.* The translation function f must have an inverse function g that maps sentences from $\mathcal{L}_2$ back to $\mathcal{L}_1$. For any sentence s in $\mathcal{L}_1$, $f(s)$ is a sentence in $\mathcal{L}_2$, and $g(f(s))$ is a sentence in $\mathcal{L}_1$. All three sentences, s, $f(s)$, and $g(f(s))$ are said to *express* the proposition p.

- *Proof preserving.* When a sentence s in $\mathcal{L}_1$ is translated to $f(s)$ in $\mathcal{L}_2$ and back again to $g(f(s))$ in $\mathcal{L}_1$, the result might not be identical to s. But according to the rules of inference of language $\mathcal{L}_1$, each one must be provable from the other: $s \vdash g(f(s))$, and $g(f(s)) \vdash s$. Similarly, $f(s)$ and $f(g(f(s)))$ must be provable from each other by the rules of inference of language $\mathcal{L}_2$.

- *Vocabulary preserving.* When s is translated from $\mathcal{L}_1$ to $\mathcal{L}_2$ and back to $g(f(s))$, the logical symbols like $\forall$ and the syntactic markers like commas and parentheses might be replaced by some equivalent. However, the same *content words* or symbols that represent categories, relations, and individuals in the ontology must appear in both sentences s and $g(f(s))$. This criterion could be relaxed to allow terms to be replaced by synonyms or definitions, but arbitrary content words or predicates must not be added or deleted by the translations.

- *Structure preserving.* When s and $g(f(s))$ are mapped to *Peirce Normal Form* (with negation $\sim$, conjunction $\wedge$, and the existential quantifier $\exists$ as the only logical operators), they must contain exactly the same number of negations and existential quantifiers, nested in semantically equivalent patterns.

These four criteria ensure that the sentences s and $g(f(s))$ are highly similar, if not identical. If s is the sentence *Every farmer who owns a donkey beats it*, then the sentence $g(f(s))$ might be *If a farmer x owns a donkey y, then x beats y*. Those sentences use different logical and syntactical symbols, but they are provably equivalent, they have the same content words, and they have the same structure when expressed with only $\wedge$, $\sim$, and $\exists$.

Attempts to apply formal definitions to natural languages are fraught with pitfalls, exceptions, and controversies. To avoid such problems, the definition of meaning-preserving translation may be restricted to formal languages, like CGs and KIF. The sample sentence in Figure 5.12 could be defined as part of a formal language called *stylized English*, which happens to contain many sentences that look like English. Yet even for formal languages, the four criteria require further explanation and justification:

- *Invertible.* The functions f and g are not exact inverses, since $g(f(s))$ might not be identical to s. To ensure that f is defined for all sentences in $\mathcal{L}_1$, the language $\mathcal{L}_2$ must be at least as expressive as $\mathcal{L}_1$. If $\mathcal{L}_2$ is more expressive than $\mathcal{L}_1$, then the inverse g might be undefined for some sentences in $\mathcal{L}_2$. In that case, the language $\mathcal{L}_2$ would express a superset of the propositions of $\mathcal{L}_1$.

- *Proof preserving.* Preserving provability is necessary for meaning preservation, but it is not sufficient. It is a weak condition that allows all tautologies to be considered equivalent, even though the proof of equivalence might take an exponential amount of time. Informally, the test to determine whether two sentences "mean the same" should be "obvious." Formally, it should be computable by an efficient algorithm — one whose time is linearly or polynomially proportional to the length of the sentence.

- *Vocabulary preserving.* Two sentences that mean the same should talk about the same things. The sentence *Every cat is a cat* is provably equivalent to *Every dog is a dog*, even though one is about cats and the other is about dogs. Even worse, both of them are provably equivalent to a sentence about nonexistent things, such as *Every unicorn is a unicorn*. An admissible translation could make some changes to the syntactic or logical symbols, as in the sentence *If something is a cat, then it is a cat*. It might replace the word *cat* with *domestic feline*, but it should not replace the word *cat* with *dog* or *unicorn*.

- *Structure preserving.* Of all the logical operators, conjunction $\land$ is the simplest and least controversial, while negation $\sim$ introduces serious logical and philosophical problems. Intuitionists, for example, deny that $\sim\sim p$ is identical to p. For *relevance logic*, Anderson and Belnap (1975) disallowed the *disjunctive syllogism*, which is based on $\lor$ and $\sim$, because it can introduce extraneous information into a proof. Computationally, $\sim\sim p$ and p have different effects on the binding of values to variables in Prolog, SQL, and many expert systems. The constraints on quantifiers and negations help ensure that formulas in the same equivalence class have the same properties of decidability and computational complexity.

These conditions impose strong constraints on translations that are said to preserve meaning. They ensure that the content words or predicates remain identical or synonymous, they preserve the logical structure, and they prevent irrelevant content from being inserted.

EXAMPLES OF MEANING-PRESERVING TRANSLATIONS. To illustrate the issues, consider meaning-preserving translations between two different notations for first-order logic. Let $\mathscr{L}_1$ be predicate calculus with Peano's symbols $\wedge$, $\vee$, $\sim$, $\supset$, $\exists$, and $\forall$, and let $\mathscr{L}_2$ be predicate calculus with Peirce's symbols $+$, $\times$, $-$, $\prec$, Σ, and $\varPi$. Then for any formulas or subformulas p and q in $\mathscr{L}_1$, let f produce the following translations in $\mathscr{L}_2$:

- *Conjunction.* $p \wedge q \Rightarrow p \times q$.
- *Disjunction.* $p \vee q \Rightarrow -(-p \times -q)$.
- *Negation.* $\sim p \Rightarrow -p$.
- *Implication.* $p \supset q \Rightarrow -(p \times -q)$.
- *Existential quantifier.* $(\exists x)p \Rightarrow \Sigma_x p$.
- *Universal quantifier.* $(\forall x)p \Rightarrow -\Sigma_x -p$.

The sentences generated by f use only the operators $\times$, $-$, and Σ, but the inverse g is defined for all operators in $\mathscr{L}_2$:

- *Conjunction.* $p \times q \Rightarrow p \wedge q$.
- *Disjunction.* $p + q \Rightarrow p \vee q$.
- *Negation.* $-p \Rightarrow \sim p$.
- *Implication.* $p \prec q \Rightarrow p \supset q$.
- *Existential quantifier.* $\Sigma_x p \Rightarrow (\exists x)p$.
- *Universal quantifier.* $\mathrm{Pi}_x p \Rightarrow (\forall x)p$.

The functions f and g meet the criteria for meaning-preserving translations: they are invertible, proof preserving, vocabulary preserving, and structure preserving. Furthermore, the proof of equivalence can be done in linear time by showing that two sentences s and t in $\mathscr{L}_1$ map to the same form with the symbols $\wedge$, $\sim$, and $\exists$.

The functions f and g in the previous example show that it is possible to find functions that meet the four criteria. They don't map any sentences to the same equivalence class unless they can be said to "preserve meaning" in a very strict sense, but they leave many closely related sentences in different classes: permutations such as $p \wedge q$ and $q \wedge p$; duplications such as p, $p \wedge p$, and $p \wedge p \wedge p$; and formulas with renamed variables such as $(\exists x)P(x)$ and $(\exists y)P(y)$. To include more such sentences in the same equivalence classes, a series of functions $f_1, f_2, \ldots$, can be defined, all of which have the same inverse g:

1. *Sorting.* The function f_1 makes the same symbol replacements as f, but it also sorts conjunctions in alphabetical order. As a result, $p \wedge q$ and $q \wedge p$ in $\mathscr{L}_1$ would both be mapped to $p \times q$ in $\mathscr{L}_2$, which would be mapped by g back to $p \wedge q$. Therefore, f_1 groups permutations in the same equivalence class. Since a list of

N terms can be sorted in time proportional to $N \log N$, the function f_1 takes just slightly longer than linear time.

2. *Renaming variables.* The function f_2 is like f_1, but it also renames the variables to a standard sequence, such as $x_1, x_2, \ldots$. For very long sentences with dozens of variables of the same type, the complexity of f_2 could increase exponentially. A typed logic can help reduce the number of options, since the new variable names could be assigned in the same alphabetical order as their type labels. For the kinds of sentences used in human communications, most variables have different types, and the computation time for f_2 would be nearly linear.

3. *Deleting duplicates.* After f_1 and f_2 sort conjunctions and rename variables, the function f_3 would eliminate duplicates by deleting any conjunct that is identical to the previous one. The deletions could be performed in linear time.

For the kinds of sentences that people speak and understand, the total computation time of all three functions would be nearly linear. Although it is possible to construct sentences whose computation time would increase exponentially, those sentences would be hopelessly unintelligible to humans. What is unnatural for humans would be inefficient for computers.

This series of functions shows how large numbers of closely related sentences can be reduced to a single *canonical form.* If two sentences express the same proposition, their canonical forms, which can usually be calculated efficiently, would be the same. The function f_2 has the effect of reducing sentences to *Peirce Normal Form* (PNF) — the result of translating a sentence from predicate calculus to an existential graph and back again. As an example, consider the following sentence, which Leibniz called the *Praeclarum Theorema* (splendid theorem):

$$((p \supset r) \wedge (q \supset s)) \supset ((p \wedge q) \supset (r \wedge s)).$$

This formula may be read *If p implies r and q implies s, then p and q imply r and s.* When translated to $\mathcal{L}_2$ by f_3 and back to $\mathcal{L}_1$ by g, it has the following Peirce Normal Form:

$$\sim((\sim(p \wedge \sim r) \wedge \sim(q \wedge \sim s)) \wedge \sim(\sim(p \wedge q) \wedge \sim(r \wedge s))).$$

This form is not as readable as the original, but it serves as the canonical representative of an equivalence class that contains 864 different, but highly similar sentences. The function f_3, which deletes duplicates, can reduce an infinite number of sentences to the same form. Such transformations can factor out the differences caused by the choice of symbols or syntax.

To account for synonyms and definitions, another function f_4 could be used to replace terms by their defining lambda expressions. If recursions are allowed, the replacements and expansions would be equivalent in computing power to a Turing machine; they could take exponential amounts of time or even be undecidable.

Therefore, f_4 should only expand definitions without recursions, direct or indirect. Since the definitions may introduce permutations, duplications, and renamed variables, f_4 should expand the definitions before performing the reductions computed by f_3. Without recursion, the expansions would take at most polynomial time.

MEANING IN NATURAL LANGUAGES. When functions like the f_i series are extended to natural languages, they become deeply involved with the problems of syntax, semantics, and pragmatics. In his early work on *transformational grammar*, Noam Chomsky (1957) hoped to define transformations as meaning-preserving functions. But the transformations that moved phrases and subphrases had the effect of changing the scope of quantifiers and the binding of pronouns to their antecedents:

- *Every cat chased some mouse.*
  ⇒ *Some mouse was chased by every cat.*
- *We do your laundry by hand; we don't tear it by machine.*
  ⇒ *We don't tear your laundry by machine; we do it by hand.*

To account for the implications of such transformations, Chomsky (1982) developed his theory of *government and binding*, which replaced all transformations by a single operator called *move-α* and a set of constraints on where the phrase α could be moved. In his most recent *minimalist* theory, Chomsky (1995) eliminated movement altogether and formulated the principles of grammar as a set of logical constraints. With that theory, both language generation and interpretation become constraint-satisfaction problems of the kind discussed in Section 4.6. The common thread running through these theories is Chomsky's search for a syntax-based characterization of the meaning-preserving translations.

AI-based computational linguistics has also involved a search for meaning-preserving translations, but with more emphasis on semantics and pragmatics than on syntax. Roger Schank (1975), for example, developed his *conceptual dependency theory* as a canonical representation of meaning with an ontology of eleven primitive action types. Although Schank was strongly opposed to formalization of any kind, his method of reducing a sentence to canonical form could be viewed as a version of function f_4. In his later work (Schank & Abelson 1977; Schank 1982), he went beyond the sentence to higher-level structures called *scripts, memory organization packets* (MOPs), and *thematic organization packets* (TOPs). These structures, which have been implemented in framelike and graphlike versions of EC logic, address meaning at the level of paragraphs and stories. Stuart Shapiro and his colleagues have implemented versions of *propositional semantic networks*, which support similar structures in a form that maps more directly to logic (Shapiro 1979; Maida & Shapiro 1982; Shapiro & Rapaport 1992). Shapiro's propositional nodes serve the same purpose as Peirce's ovals and McCarthy's contexts.

Besides the structural forms of syntax and logic, the meaning-preserving translations for natural languages must account for the subtle interactions of many thousands of words. The next two sentences, for example, were adapted from a news report on finance:

- *The latest economic indicators eased concerns that inflation is increasing.*
- *The latest economic indicators heightened concerns that inflation is increasing.*

The first sentence implies that inflation is not increasing, but the second one implies that it is. The negation, which is critical for understanding the sentences, does not appear explicitly. Instead, it comes from an implicit negation in the meaning of the noun *concern*: if some agent x has a concern about y, then x hopes that some bad event does not happen to y. The concern is eased when the bad event less likely to occur, and the concern is heightened when the bad event is more likely to occur. In the normal use of language, people understand such sentences and their implications. For a computer to understand them, it would require detailed definitions of the words, background knowledge that rising inflation is bad for the economy, and the reasoning ability to combine such information. Doug Lenat and his group in the Cyc project have been working since 1984 on the task of encoding and reasoning with the millions of rules and facts needed for such understanding.

TINCTURED EXISTENTIAL GRAPHS.   Peirce (1906) introduced colors to distinguish contexts of different types. Conveniently, the *heraldic tinctures*, which were used to paint coats of arms in the middle ages, were grouped in three classes: *metal, color,* and *fur.* Peirce adopted them for his three-way distinction of *actual, modal,* and *intentional* contexts:

1. An actual context is a true description of some aspect of the world. Peirce used the metallic tincture *argent* (white background) for "the actual or true in a general or ordinary sense," and three other metals (*or, fer,* and *plomb*) for "the actual or true in some special sense." Figure 5.13 shows that an actual context can be designated by a monadic relation such as True, which does not refer explicitly or implicitly to any other context.

2. A modal context is a description of some possibility relative to what is actual. Figure 5.13 shows a dyadic relation (Possible) between the actual and modal contexts. The monadic Psbl relation leaves the actual context implicit. Peirce used four heraldic colors to distinguish modalities: *azure* for logical possibility (dark blue) and subjective possibility (light blue); *gules* (red) for objective possibility; *vert* (green) for "what is in the interrogative mood"; and *purpure* (purple) for "freedom or ability."

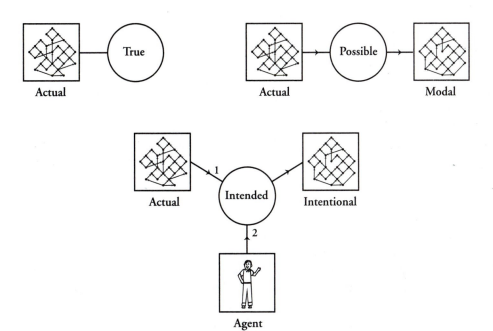

FIGURE 5.13 Actual, modal, and intentional contexts

3. An intentional context describes what some agent intends relative to what is actual. Figure 5.13 uses a triadic relation to show the agent and the actual context explicitly, but one or both of them may be left implicit. Peirce used four heraldic furs for intentionality: *sable* (gray) for "the metaphysically, or rationally, or secondarily necessitated"; *ermine* (yellow) for "purpose or intention"; *vair* (brown) for "the commanded"; and *potent* (orange) for "the compelled." Bertrand Russell called these modes *propositional attitudes* because they represent some agent's attitude toward a proposition.

Throughout his analyses, Peirce distinguished the logical operators, such as ∧, ~, and ∃, from the tinctures, which, he said, do not represent "differences of the *predicates*, or *significations* of the graphs, but of the predetermined objects to which the graphs are intended to refer." In effect, the tinctures belong to the metalanguage that describe how logic applies to the *universe of discourse*.

> The nature of the universe or universes of discourse (for several may be referred to in a single assertion) in the rather unusual cases in which such precision is required, is denoted either by using modifications of the heraldic tinctures, marked in something like the usual manner in pale ink upon the surface, or by scribing the graphs in colored inks.

In Peirce's contexts, the oval enclosures distinguish the syntax, the universe of discourse determines the semantics, and the nature of the universe of discourse determines the pragmatics.

CLASSIFYING CONTEXTS.   The first step toward a theory of context is a classification of the types of contexts and their relationships to one another. Any of the tinctured contexts may be nested inside or outside the ovals representing negation. When combined with negation in all possible ways, each tincture can represent a family of related modalities:

1. The first metallic tincture, argent, corresponds to the white background Peirce used for his original existential graphs. When combined with existence and conjunction, negations on a white background support classical first-order logic about what is actually true or false "in an ordinary sense." Negations on the other metallic backgrounds support FOL for what is "actual in some special sense." A statement about the physical world, for example, would be actual in an ordinary sense. But Peirce also considered mathematical abstractions, such as Cantor's hierarchy of infinite sets, to be actual, but not in the same sense as ordinary physical entities.

2. In the algebraic notation, $\Diamond p$ means that p is possible. Then necessity $\Box p$ is defined as $\sim\Diamond\sim p$. Impossibility is represented as $\sim\Diamond p$ or equivalently $\Box\sim p$. Instead of the single symbol $\Diamond$, Peirce's five colors represent different versions of possibility; for each of them, there is a corresponding interpretation of necessity, impossibility, and contingency:

    - *Logical possibility.* A dark blue context, Peirce's equivalent of $\Diamond p$, would mean that p is consistent or not provably false. His version of $\Box p$, represented as dark blue between two negations, would therefore mean that p is provable. Impossible $\sim\Diamond p$ would mean inconsistent or provably false.
    - *Subjective possibility.* In light blue, $\Diamond p$ would mean that p is believable or not known to be false. $\Box p$ would mean that p is known or not believably false. This interpretation of $\Diamond$ and $\Box$ is called *epistemic logic.*
    - *Objective possibility.* In red, $\Diamond p$ would mean that p is physically possible. As an example, Peirce noted that it was physically possible for him to raise his arm, even when he was not at the moment doing so. $\Box p$ would mean physical necessity according to the laws of nature.
    - *Interrogative mood.* In green, $\Diamond p$ would mean that p is questioned, and $\Box p$ would mean that p is not questionably false. This interpretation of $\Diamond p$ corresponds to a proposition p in a Prolog goal or the where-clause of an SQL query.

- *Freedom.* In purple, $\Diamond p$ would mean that p is free or permissible; $\Box p$ would mean that p is obligatory or not permissibly false; $\sim\Diamond p$ would mean that p is not permissible or illegal; and $\Diamond\sim p$ would mean that p is permissibly false or optional. This interpretation of $\Diamond$ and $\Box$ is called *deontic logic.*

3. The heraldic furs represent various kinds of intentions, but Peirce did not explore the detailed interactions of the furs with negations or with each other. Don Roberts (1973) suggested some combinations, such as negation with the tinctures gules and potent to represent *The quality of mercy is not strained.*

Although Peirce's three-way classification of contexts is useful, he did not work out their implications in detail. He wrote that the complete classification of "all the conceptions of logic" was "a labor for generations of analysts, not for one."

In the current generation, theories like situation semantics address the problems of classifying and reasoning about intentional contexts, but the number of intentional combinations is very large. Many intentional verbs come in pairs like *hope* and *fear, know* and *believe,* or *seek* and *avoid.* When combined with negations, these verbs generate more complex patterns than the relationships between the two basic modes $\Diamond$ and $\Box$. As an example, the predicate hope(a,p) could mean that the agent a hopes that the proposition p will become true. Then the predicate fear(a,p) would mean that a hopes that p will not become true:

$$\text{fear}(a,p) \equiv \text{hope}(a,\sim p).$$

An agent a is *indifferent* to p if a neither hopes nor fears that p:

$$\text{indifferent}(a,p) \equiv \sim\text{hope}(a,p) \land \sim\text{fear}(a,p).$$

An agent a is *ambivalent* about p if a both hopes that p and fears that p:

$$\text{ambivalent}(a,p) \equiv \text{hope}(a,p) \land \text{fear}(a,p).$$

Given the definition of fear in terms of hope, ambivalence would mean that a hopes that p will come true and that p will not come true:

$$\text{ambivalent}(a,p) \equiv \text{hope}(a,p) \land \text{hope}(a,\sim p).$$

If conjunction is assumed to commute with hope, this formula would imply that a hopes for a contradiction $p \land \sim p$. Such states occur in science-fiction movies when someone like Captain Kirk presents a computer with an unresolvable dilemma.

5.4 First-Order Reasoning in Contexts

Syntactically, contexts are enclosures for propositions. Semantically, some agent asserts, believes, or assumes that the propositions they enclose describe some situation. Pragmatically, the contexts separate an agent's statements about a situation from metalevel statements about the agent's intentions or attitudes toward those statements. This section develops techniques for first-order logic, in which negation is the metalevel operator that denies the statements in a context. The next section extends the techniques to modal and intentional operators, which make a broader range of metastatements about contexts.

Soundness and Completeness. Semantic tests, stated in terms of the *entailment operator* ⊨, provide criteria for evaluating the rules of inference, which define the *provability operator* ⊢. Two desirable properties are *soundness*, which means that everything provable is true, and *completeness*, which means that everything true is provable. Rules of inference are *sound* if provability (⊢) preserves truth as determined by semantic entailment (⊨):

- *Soundness.* $(\forall s:\text{Situation})(\forall p,q:\text{Proposition})(s \models p \supset (p \vdash q \supset s \models q))$.

This formula says that for every situation s and propositions p and q, if s entails p, then if q is provable from p, s also entails q. Completeness is the converse of soundness:

- *Completeness.* $(\forall s:\text{Situation})(\forall p,q:\text{Proposition})((s \models p \supset s \models q) \supset p \vdash q)$.

For every situation s and propositions p and q, if s entails p implies that s entails q, then q is provable from p.

The three operators ⊃, ⊢, and ⊨ represent different ways of formalizing *if-then*: ⊃ is a Boolean operator that appears in ordinary formulas of logic; ⊢ and ⊨ are *metalevel operators* that appear in statements about logic. Semantic entailment is more fundamental than provability because it derives the truth of formulas from facts about the world. Provability depends on the rules of inference of a particular version of logic, and those rules must be justified in terms of entailment.

For classical first-order logic, the distinction between ⊢ and ⊨ can be ignored because soundness and completeness guarantee that they are equivalent. For other versions of logic, however, they must be carefully distinguished. Kurt Gödel (1931) proved the *incompleteness* of higher-order logic by finding propositions entailed by ⊨ that are not provable by ⊢. Nonmonotonic logic, which is discussed in Chapter 6, is not even sound. Instead of preserving truth, the nonmonotonic rules of inference preserve only the weaker property of consistency: all true statements must be consistent, but not all consistent statements are true.

Import-Export Rules. Besides proposing contexts, McCarthy emphasized the need for *lifting rules* that import and export information in and out of contexts. To be sound, those rules must preserve truth. Therefore, if a context 𝒞 describes some situation s, a proposition p can only be moved into 𝒞 if s entails p. The rules of inference for moving p consist of those transformations that preserve the semantic constraint that $s \models p$. That constraint, however, mixes a physical situation s with an abstract proposition p. To be computable, the rules must relate the abstract entities p and $\mathscr{C}$ by means of purely symbolic relationships such as provability.

The import-export rules, which relate abstract contexts and propositions, must be justified by relationships between physical situations and the entities they contain. Their semantics depends on the things that are described by the three kinds of contexts:

- *Actual.* Contexts that describe actual situations in the physical world or the abstract world of mathematics can be described in first-order logic. Therefore, a proposition p can be moved to a context $\mathscr{C}$ if the first-order rules of inference permit.

- *Modal.* The semantics of possibility and necessity is formulated in terms of infinite families of possible worlds, which are questionable ontologically and intractable computationally. To be computable, semantic theories based on possible worlds must be related to operations on contexts that describe finite situations in those worlds.

- *Intentional.* The semantics of intentions must relate possible worlds to the agents who think about and act upon those worlds. It has all the complexity of modality with the added complexity of reasoning about agents who may be reasoning about other agents who are changing the worlds while everyone is trying to reason about them.

A primary goal of context theory, for both Peirce and McCarthy, was to preserve a first-order style of reasoning. As Peirce observed, the tinctures that mark the kinds of context represent "the nature of the universe or universes of discourse"; they do not represent "differences of the predicates or significations of the graphs."

PEIRCE'S RULES OF INFERENCE.   With his algebraic notation, Peirce followed Boole in doing inference by algebraic manipulation of formulas. But when he developed existential graphs, he discovered five inference rules that state the conditions for importing and exporting statements in and out of contexts. Although Peirce originally stated the rules for existential graphs, they can be adapted to any notation, including conceptual graphs, predicate calculus, and discourse representation structures.

Peirce's rules are based on the principle that generalization in a positive context or specialization in a negative context preserves truth. As an example, suppose that a brown dog is eating a bone in the kitchen. Then the following generalizations must also be true:

- A dog is in the kitchen.
- A brown animal is eating.
- An animal is eating something in a room.

Each of these generalizations is derived from the original by erasing some phrase or by replacing a term like *dog* with a more general term like *animal*. In a negative context, any sentence can be specialized. If there is no cat in the kitchen, then there is no cat of any kind doing anything in the kitchen:

- No black cat is under the table in the kitchen.
- No striped cat is eating a fish in the kitchen.
- No orange cat with white paws is sleeping in the kitchen.

As these examples illustrate, a true statement that has no negations can be generalized to another true statement by relaxing any condition. Conversely, a true statement containing a negation can be converted to another true statement by adding more conditions to the part inside the negation. This principle holds for any number of nested negations: truth is preserved by generalization in a positive context (no negations or any even number of negations) or by specialization in a negative context (any odd number of negations).

For existential graphs, Peirce observed that a simple graph with no negations can be generalized by erasing any subgraph, and it can be specialized by adding some graph or graphs to it. The most general of all graphs is the *blank* or empty graph in which everything has been erased. The blank graph, which can never be false, is Peirce's only axiom: any graph that can be derived from the blank is a theorem. For graphs with negations, Peirce stated five rules of inference:

1. *Erasure.* In a positive context, any graph or subgraph may be erased.
2. *Insertion.* In a negative context, any graph or subgraph may be inserted.
3. *Iteration.* If a graph or subgraph p occurs in a context $\mathscr{C}$, another copy of p may be written in the same context $\mathscr{C}$ or in any context nested in $\mathscr{C}$.
4. *Deiteration.* Any graph that could have been derived by iteration may be erased: any graph or subgraph p may be erased if a copy of p occurs in the same context or any containing context.
5. *Double negation.* Two negations with nothing between them may be erased or inserted around any graph or collection of graphs in any context. In particular, a double negation may be drawn around the blank or empty collection.

The rules of erasure and insertion have no inverses; if q is derived from p by one of those rules, then p cannot be derived from q. The rule of deiteration is the inverse of iteration, and double negation is its own inverse; if q is derived from p by those rules, then p can be derived from q by the inverse rules. These five rules define a sound and complete inference procedure for propositional logic. The same rules support full first-order logic with equality when they are used to erase or insert a line of identity.

PROOF IN EXISTENTIAL GRAPHS. To show how Peirce's rules are applied to existential graphs, consider the proof of Leibniz's *Praeclarum Theorema*:

$$((p \supset r) \wedge (q \supset s)) \supset ((p \wedge q) \supset (r \wedge s)).$$

Figure 5.14 shows that the EG proof takes seven steps starting from an empty sheet; each step is numbered with the rule that is applied. The EG at the end of the proof has four pairs of ovals, each pair corresponding to one of the $\supset$ symbols in the algebraic form. It would be possible to simplify the final graph by erasing a double negation, but then the exact correspondence with the algebraic notation would be lost.

Peirce's rules are the simplest and most general rules of inference ever discovered. In the *Principia Mathematica*, which was published 13 years later, the equivalent of Figure 5.14 required a total of 43 steps starting from five nonobvious axioms. One of those axioms was redundant, but the proof of its redundancy was not discovered by the authors or by any of their readers for 16 years. The axioms and rules of the *Principia* can be proved as theorems in terms of Peirce's rules. In fact, all other rules of inference for classical first-order logic can be derived as special cases of Peirce's rules: *natural deduction* by Gerhard Gentzen (1935), *tableaux* by Evert Beth (1955), and *resolution* by Alan Robinson (1965a).

PROOF IN ALGEBRAIC NOTATION. Although Peirce's rules apply to any notation for logic, some adjustment is needed to accommodate differences in syntax:

- *Blanks.* In graph logic, the blank is represented by an empty sheet of paper or by a context with nothing in it. In algebraic notation, the blank must be represented by a place holder, such as the letter T for *truth*.
- *Conjunctions.* In graph logic, there is no need for ∧ symbols between conjuncts. In algebraic notation, an ∧ symbol must be added when a new conjunct is inserted, and the extra ∧ symbol must be erased when a conjunct is erased.

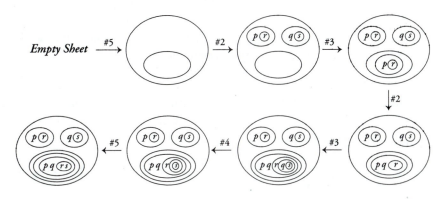

FIGURE 5.14 Proof of the Praeclarum Theorema

In EGs, the nested contexts explicitly show the negations, but in algebraic notation, implicit negations are buried inside the definition of every operator other than $\wedge$ and $\exists$. For each operator, a special rule is needed to determine how the operator affects the *negation depth* of its operands:

- *Negation.* A negation $\sim$ increases the negation depth by one. For any expression of the form $\sim p$, the negation depth of the operand p is one greater than the negation depth of the containing context.

- *Conjunction.* A conjunction $\wedge$ has no effect on the number of negations. For an expression $p \wedge q$, the negation depth of both p and q is the same as the negation depth of the containing context.

- *Disjunction.* Since $p \vee q$ is defined as $\sim((\sim p) \wedge (\sim Iq))$, a disjunction $\vee$ increases the negation depth of both p and q by two.

- *Implication.* Since $p \supset q$ is defined as $\sim(p \wedge \sim q)$, an implication $\supset$ increases the negation depth of p by one and the negation depth of q by two.

- *Existential.* The existential quantifier $\exists$ has no effect on the number of negations. For an expression $(\exists x)p$, the negation depth of p is the same as the negation depth of the containing context.

- *Universal.* Since the universal quantifier $(\forall x)p$ is defined as $\sim(\exists x)\sim p$, it increases the negation depth of p by two.

Existence and conjunction have no effect on the depth of nesting. Logically, philosophically, and computationally, they are the two simplest operators. Negation adds one to reverse the sign of a context: positive to negative or negative to positive. Implication reverses only the sign of its antecedent. Disjunction and the universal quantifier, which increase the depth by two, do not change the sign, but they do introduce more computational complexity than $\exists$ and $\wedge$.

For each step in the proof of Figure 5.14, the same rule can be applied to the algebraic formula, although the linear notation makes the transformations more complex:

1. By rule #5, start by drawing two negative contexts around the blank or T: $\sim(T \wedge \sim T)$. Writing this formula as an implication,

   $T \supset T.$

2. By rule #2, the first T may be replaced with any specialization. In particular, it may be replaced with the entire left side of the formula to be proved:

   $((p \supset r) \wedge (q \supset s)) \supset T.$

3. By rule #3, copy $(p \supset r)$ into the same context with T and erase the now unneeded place holder T:

   $((p \supset r) \wedge (q \supset s)) \supset (p \supset r).$

4. By rule #2, insert q into the antecedent of $(p{\supset}r)$ in the conclusion:

$((p \supset r) \wedge (q \supset s)) \supset ((p \wedge q) \supset r).$

5. By rule #3, copy $(q{\supset}s)$ into the same context as r at the end of the formula:

$((p \supset r) \wedge (q \supset s)) \supset ((p \wedge q) \supset (r \wedge (q \supset s))).$

6. By rule #4, erase the last copy of q and replace it with the blank or T:

$((p \supset r) \wedge (q \supset s)) \supset ((p \wedge q) \supset (r \wedge (T \supset s))).$

7. Finally, $(T{\supset}s)$ is equivalent to the double negation $\sim(\sim(s))$; therefore, by rule #5,

$((p \supset r) \wedge (q \supset s)) \supset ((p \wedge q) \supset (r \wedge s)).$

This example shows why no one but Peirce ever discovered these rules: the linear form obscures the nested structure of contexts, but the EG form makes the nesting obvious. The graphs enabled Peirce to see patterns in the rules of inference that no one else discovered in their full generality. Once those patterns are recognized in graph form, they can be adapted to any other notation. The adaptations require a definition of the way each operator affects positive and negative contexts and the method of generalizing or specializing a statement in any context.

Cut-and-Paste Theorem. For theorem proving, Peirce's rules are equivalent to the other systems of classical FOL. For reasoning in contexts, however, they have a remarkable property that is not shared with any other system of first-order rules: they can be applied inside deeply nested contexts. Whereas the traditional rules like *modus ponens* can only be applied to a formula that is outside of any nest, Peirce's rules depend on the sign of the context, not its depth. Therefore, they can be applied in exactly the same way in an outer context at depth 0 or in a context nested inside 2 or 22 negations. Any proof that can be carried out on a blank sheet of assertion can be "cut out" and "pasted" into any positive context nested at any depth. The formal statement of this property is called the *cut-and-paste theorem*:

- *Theorem:* If a statement q can be derived from a statement p by Peirce's rules of inference in the outermost context (nesting level 0), and if a copy of p occurs in any positively nested context $\mathscr{C}$, then the proof of q from p can be replicated by equivalent steps inside the context $\mathscr{C}$.

- *Proof:* Let the proof of q from p at level 0 be some sequence of statements $s_1, \ldots, s_n$, where the first step $p = s_1$ and the last step $q = s_n$. Since Peirce's rules depend only on the sign of a context, not its depth, every inference from s_i to s_{i+1} that is permissible at the blank sheet of assertion must also be permissible in #. Therefore, a copy of the sequence of graphs from $p = s_1$ to $q = s_n$ can be replicated inside $\mathscr{C}$.

This theorem shows how Peirce's rules can support complex operations at any level of a nest of contexts. They allow all the steps of a proof to be carried out inside any positive context.

Strictly speaking, the cut-and-paste theorem is not an ordinary theorem of logic, but a *metatheorem* about logic. It is a general statement about the kinds of theorems that can be derived. Other useful metatheorems can be derived from the cut-and-paste theorem as *corollaries* — theorems with short proofs. As an example, the rule of *modus ponens*, which is normally applied outside of any context, can be derived from Peirce's rules. By the cut-and-paste theorem, it can therefore be used in nested contexts.

GENERALIZED MODUS PONENS. The first step in generalizing any rule of inference, including *modus ponens*, is to show that it follows from Peirce's rules:

- Given two statements p and $p{\supset}q$, rewrite the implication in the form $\sim(p{\wedge}\sim q)$.
- By the rule of deiteration, the nested copy of p can be replaced by the blank or T to form $\sim(T{\wedge}\sim q)$.
- By the rule for deleting T and the $\wedge$ symbol, this statement is equivalent to $\sim\sim q$.
- By double negation, the two $\sim$ symbols may be erased to form q.
- Finally, p can also be erased.

By the cut-and-paste theorem, *modus ponens* can therefore be used in nested contexts. The rule can be generalized further, as illustrated in Figure 5.15.

Each oval in Figure 5.15 represents a negative context. Inside the contexts, there may be arbitrarily many statements represented in any notation for logic. Three statements are shown explicitly: p, $q{\supset}r$, and r. In this example, p is assumed

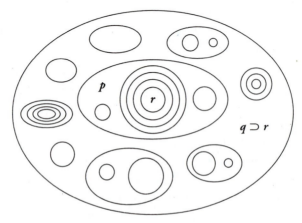

FIGURE 5.15 Applying generalized *modus ponens* inside a nest of contexts

to be a specialization of q (i.e., $p \vdash q$), and r is derived from p and $q \supset r$ by the rule of *generalized modus ponens* (GMP). Following is a theorem that states GMP:

- *Generalized modus ponens.* Let $\mathscr{C}$ be any positive context nested inside two contexts $\mathscr{C}_1$ and $\mathscr{C}_2$. The contexts $\mathscr{C}_1$ and $\mathscr{C}_2$ may be either positive or negative, and either or both could be the same as $\mathscr{C}$ itself. If a statement p occurs in $\mathscr{C}_1$ and a statement $q \supset r$ occurs in $\mathscr{C}_2$ where p is a specialization of q, then by GMP, the statement r may be inserted in the context $\mathscr{C}$.

- *Proof.* By iteration, the statement p and the statement $q \supset r$ may be copied into the context $\mathscr{C}$. Since $\mathscr{C}$ is positive, the rule of erasure allows the copy of p to be replaced by any generalization, such as q. Since $\mathscr{C}$ now contains q and $q \supset r$, *modus ponens* can be used to derive r. Any intermediate results can also be erased since $\mathscr{C}$ is positive.

To emphasize the contexts, Figure 5.15 uses a hybrid notation that mixes algebraic formulas like $q \supset r$ with nested ovals that represent $\sim(. . .)$. Two rules can be used to check the nesting of any context in a nest of ovals:

- *Negation depth.* To determine the negation depth of any context $\mathscr{C}$, draw a line l from inside $\mathscr{C}$ to the outside of the largest oval. The line l should always go from an inner context to an enclosing one, and never from an outer to an inner one; if necessary, l may be curved to avoid going in and out of extra ovals. Then the negation depth of $\mathscr{C}$ is equal to the number of ovals crossed by l.

- *Enclosures.* To determine whether a context $\mathscr{C}$ is nested inside a context $\mathscr{D}$, check whether every line drawn from $\mathscr{C}$ to the outside must pass through $\mathscr{D}$.

By the first rule, the negation depth of the context of r in Figure 5.15 is 6, the depth of p is 2, and the depth of $q \supset r$ is 1. By the second rule, the context of r is nested inside the context of p and the context of $q \supset r$. Therefore, the conditions for applying GMP to derive r are satisfied.

Although the conditions are easiest to check in a notation with explicit contexts, the rule of GMP can be applied directly to statements in any notation for first-order logic. Following is an algebraic formula that satisfies the conditions:

$$(s \wedge \sim(t \vee u) \wedge \sim(v \wedge (q \supset r) \wedge \sim(t \vee (k \wedge p \wedge (l \vee (m \wedge n)))))).$$

In this formula, the context that includes $(m \wedge n)$ happens to be positive, and it is nested inside contexts that contain p and $q \supset r$. Therefore, the following formula can be derived by GMP:

$$(s \wedge \sim(t \vee u) \wedge \sim(v \wedge (q \supset r) \wedge \sim(t \vee (k \wedge p \wedge (l \vee (m \wedge n \wedge r)))))).$$

All the common rules of inference, including resolution and natural deduction, can be derived as special cases of Peirce's rules. The same techniques used to prove GMP can be used to derive generalized forms of those rules. Therefore, a knowledge-based system could use those rules to prove theorems inside any positive context nested at any depth. The question-answering methods of SQL, the Horn-clause rules in Prolog, and the Aristotelian syllogisms for frames support proof procedures that can be carried out inside any positively nested contexts.

EXPORTING INFORMATION FROM A CONTEXT.   For first-order logic, Peirce's rules of inference determine how information may be moved across context boundaries. The rules of iteration and deiteration insert and erase information in an inner context that is duplicated in an outer context. But there are no direct rules for exporting information from an inner context to an outer one or from any context to a neighboring one. The rule of double negation, however, does allow information to be exported by the drastic measure of erasing two context walls; it causes everything in the doubly nested context to merge with the containing context. To export partial information while preserving the nest of contexts, double negation can be combined with the other rules to derive a more general version of GMP called *hypergeneralized modus ponens* (HMP):

- *Hypergeneralized modus ponens.* Let $\mathcal{D}$ be a positive context that contains an implication $\mathcal{C}$ of the following form:

  $(p_1 \wedge \ldots \wedge p_n) \supset (q_1 \wedge \ldots \wedge q_m).$

  If a specialization of every p_i occurs in $\mathcal{D}$ or some context that contains $\mathcal{D}$, then a copy of any q_j may be written in $\mathcal{D}$ or any context nested in $\mathcal{D}$.

- *Proof.* To preserve $\mathcal{C}$ unchanged, make another copy of it in $\mathcal{D}$ by the rule of iteration, and do all further operations on the copy. Call that copy $\mathcal{C}_2$, and write it with explicit contexts:

  $\neg[\, p_1, \ldots, p_n \neg[\, q_1, \ldots, q_m \,]\,] \ .$

  Since a specialization of each p_i occurs in some context that contains $\mathcal{C}_2$, erase each p_i in $\mathcal{C}_2$ to produce

  $\neg[\, \neg[\, q_1, \ldots, q_m \,]\,] \ .$

  Then erase the double negation to export all the qs to $\mathcal{D}$. Since $\mathcal{D}$ is positive, any unwanted information can be erased, leaving just q_j in $\mathcal{D}$. Now q_j may be copied to any context nested in $\mathcal{D}$ by the rule of iteration. If q_j is no longer wanted in $\mathcal{D}$, it can also be erased.

HMP is a generalized version of the rule of *hyperresolution,* which was defined by Alan Robinson (1965b). Unlike hyperresolution, HMP can be performed inside contexts nested at any positive depth. Furthermore, HMP does not require the formulas to be converted to *clause form,* which was another notation invented by

Gentzen. Peirce's rules provide a unifying framework for deriving Gentzen's rules of natural deduction and Robinson's rules of resolution.

Sometimes the rule of HMP may be blocked because one or more of the conditions p_i cannot be erased. In that case, it is still permissible to export a deeply nested statement as the conclusion of an implication. Those ps that cannot be erased become conditions in the antecedent of the implication. The following rule of *qualified export* (QE) allows a suitably qualified proposition to be exported, even if it happens to be nested inside many levels of negations with many other propositions occurring at each level:

- *Qualified export.* Let q be a statement in a positive context $\mathscr{C}$, which is nested at any depth inside another positive context $\mathscr{D}$; let $p_1, \ldots, p_n$ be a list of all statements contained in negative contexts that are contained in $\mathscr{D}$ and that contain $\mathscr{C}$. Then an implication of the following form may be written in $\mathscr{D}$:

  $(p_1 \wedge \ldots \wedge p_n) \supset q.$

  This statement is called a *qualified export* of q, for which each p_i is called a *qualification* of q.

- *Proof.* Copy the entire nest of contexts in $\mathscr{D}$ that contain $\mathscr{C}$, and call it $\mathscr{C}_2$. Then in every positive context of $\mathscr{C}_2$, erase every statement other than q. As a result, $\mathscr{C}_2$ has the following form, possibly with extra double negations of the form $\neg[\neg[\ldots]]$ separating some adjacent items in the list of ps:

  $\neg[\, p_1, \ldots, p_n \neg[\, q\,]].$

  Erase the extra double negations, and write the result in the form of an implication.

For examples of QE, see Exercise 5.17 and the answers at the back of the book. Other variations of qualified export can be formulated to account for differences in time, modality, and intentionality.

5.5 Modal Reasoning in Contexts

Leibniz introduced *possible worlds* as the foundation for modal semantics: a proposition p is necessarily true in the real world if it is true in every possible world, and p is possible in the real world if there is some accessible world in which it happens to be true. In the algebraic notation for logic, Peirce followed Leibniz by representing necessity with a universal quantifier that ranges over all "states of affairs." In the graphic notation for logic, he used a pad of paper instead of a single "sheet of assertion." Graphs that are necessarily true are copied on every sheet; those that are possibly true are drawn on some, but not all sheets. The top sheet contains assertions about the real world, and the other sheets describe related possible worlds.

KRIPKE'S WORLDS.   In developing axioms for modal logic, Clarence Irving Lewis (1918) was strongly influenced by Peirce, but he did not develop a model theory that related the axioms to the possible worlds or states of affairs. Saul Kripke (1963a,b) developed such a theory with *model structures* having three components:

- *Possible worlds.* A set K of entities called *possible worlds,* of which one *privileged world* w_0 represents the real world.
- *Accessibility relation.* A relation $R(u,v)$ defined over K, which says that world v is *accessible* from world u.
- *Evaluation function.* A function $\Phi(p,w)$, which maps a proposition p and a possible world w to one of the two truth values {T,F}. The world w semantically entails p if $\Phi(p,w)$ has the value T, and w entails $\sim p$ if $\Phi(p,w)$ has the value F:

  $w \vDash p \equiv \Phi(p,w) = T.$
  $w \vDash \sim p \equiv \Phi(p,w) = F.$

For the real world w_0, the evaluation function Φ determines whether p is contingently true or false. To determine whether p is necessary or possible, Kripke defined $\Diamond p$ and $\Box p$ by considering the truth of p in the worlds that are accessible from w_0:

- *Possibility.* p is possible in the real world w_0 if p is true of some world w accessible from w_0:

  $\Diamond p \equiv (\exists w : \text{World})(R(w_0, w) \land \Phi(p,w) = T).$

- *Necessity.* p is necessary in w_0 if p is true of every world w accessible from w_0:

  $\Box p \equiv (\forall w : \text{World})(R(w_0, w) \supset \Phi(p,w) = T).$

These definitions are a formal statement of Leibniz's intuition. Kripke's major contribution was to show how Lewis's axioms determine constraints on R:

- *System T.* Two basic axioms of System T are $\Box p \supset p$ (Necessity implies truth) and $p \supset \Diamond p$ (Truth implies possibility). They require every world to be accessible from itself; hence, R must be reflexive:

  $\text{reflexive}(R) \equiv (\forall w : \text{World})R(w,w).$

- *System S4.* System T with Lewis's axiom S4, $\Box p \supset \Box \Box p$, requires R to be transitive:

  $\text{transitive}(R) \equiv (\forall u,v,w : \text{World})((R(u,v) \land R(v,w)) \supset R(u,w)).$

- *System S5.* System S4 with axiom S5, $\Diamond p \supset \Box \Diamond p$, requires R to be symmetric:

  $\text{symmetric}(R) \equiv (\forall u,v : \text{World})(R(u,v) \supset R(v,u)).$

For System S5, the properties of reflexivity, transitivity, and symmetry make R an *equivalence relation.* Those properties cause the collection of all possible worlds to be partitioned in disjoint equivalence classes. Within each class, all the worlds are accessible from one another, but no world in one class is accessible from any world in another class.

The world of Sherlock Holmes stories, for example, is similar enough to the real world w_0 that it could be in the same equivalence class. The proposition that Sherlock Holmes assisted Scotland Yard is possible in w_0 because there is some accessible world w in which it is true:

$$(\exists w: \text{World})(R(w_0, w) \land \Phi(\text{"Sherlock Holmes assisted Scotland Yard"}, w) = T).$$

A cartoon world with talking mice and ducks, however, is too remote to be accessible from the real world. Therefore, it is not possible for ducks to talk in w_0. Business contracts further partition the cartoon worlds into disjoint classes: the world of Disney characters is not accessible from the world of Looney Tune characters. Therefore, Donald Duck can talk to Mickey Mouse, but he can't talk to Bugs Bunny or Daffy Duck.

CRITICISMS OF POSSIBLE WORLDS.   Possible worlds provide a metaphor for interpreting modality, but their ontological status is dubious. Truth is supposed to be a relationship between a statement and the real world, not an infinite family of fictitious worlds. In his novel *Candide*, Voltaire satirized Leibniz's notion of possible worlds. In that same tradition, Quine (1948) ridiculed the imaginary inhabitants of possible worlds:

> Take, for instance, the possible fat man in that doorway; and, again, the possible bald man in that doorway. Are they the same possible man, or two possible men? How do we decide? How many possible men are there in that doorway? Are there more possible thin ones than fat ones? How many of them are alike? Or would their being alike make them one?

After Kripke developed his model structures for possible worlds, Quine (1972) noted that models prove that the axioms are consistent, but they don't explain what the modalities mean:

> The notion of possible world did indeed contribute to the semantics of modal logic, and it behooves us to recognize the nature of its contribution: it led to Kripke's precocious and significant theory of models of modal logic. Models afford consistency proofs; also they have heuristic value; but they do not constitute explication. Models, however clear they be in themselves, may leave us at a loss for the primary, intended interpretation.

By relating the modal axioms to model structures, Kripke showed the interrelationships between the axioms and the possible worlds. But the meaning of those axioms remains hidden in the accessibility relation R and the evaluation function

Φ. The functional notation $\Phi(w,p)=T$ gives the impression that Φ computes a truth value. But this impression is an illusion: the set of worlds K is an undefined set given *a priori*; the relation R and function Φ are merely assumed, not computed. Nonconstructive assumptions cannot be used to compute anything; nor can they explain how Quine's possible fat men and thin men might be "accessible" from the real world with an empty doorway.

HINTIKKA'S MODEL SETS.   Instead of assuming possible worlds, Jaakko Hintikka (1961, 1963) independently developed an equivalent semantics for modal logic based on collections of propositions, which he called *model sets*. He also assumed an *alternativity relation* between model sets, which serves the same purpose as Kripke's accessibility relation between worlds. As collections of propositions, Hintikka's model sets describe Kripke's possible worlds in the same way that McCarthy's contexts describe Barwise and Perry's situations. The predicate isTrueIn can be used to relate a Hintikka model set $\mathcal{M}$ to a Kripke world w:

$$(\forall \mathcal{M}:\text{ModelSet})(\exists w:\text{World})(\forall p:\text{Proposition})$$
$$(\text{isTrueIn}(p,\mathcal{M}) \equiv w \vDash p).$$

This formula says that for any model set $\mathcal{M}$, there exists a possible world w for which a proposition p is true in $\mathcal{M}$ if and only if w semantically entails p.

The primary difference between model sets and contexts is size: Hintikka defined model sets as *maximally consistent* sets of propositions that could describe everything in the real world or any possible world. But total information about the entire world is far too much to be comprehended and manipulated in any meaningful way. A context is an excerpt from a model set in the same sense that a situation is an excerpt from a possible world. Its basis can be chosen as a finite set of propositions that describe some situation, even though the deductive closure of that set may be infinite.

Figure 5.16 shows mappings from a Kripke possible world w to a description of w as a Hintikka model set $\mathcal{M}$ or a finite excerpt from w as a Barwise and Perry situation s. Then $\mathcal{M}$ and s may be mapped to a McCarthy context $\mathcal{C}$. This is an example of a *commutative diagram*, which shows a family of mappings that lead to the same result by multiple routes. From a possible world w, the mapping to the right extracts an excerpt as a situation s, which may be described by the propositions in a context $\mathcal{C}$. From the same world w, the downward mapping leads to a description of w as a model set $\mathcal{M}$, from which an equivalent excerpt would produce the same context $\mathcal{C}$.

The combined mappings in Figure 5.16 replace the mysterious possible worlds with finite, computable contexts. Hintikka's model sets support operations on well-defined symbols instead of imaginary worlds, but they may still be infinite. Situations are finite, but like worlds they consist of physical or fictitious objects that

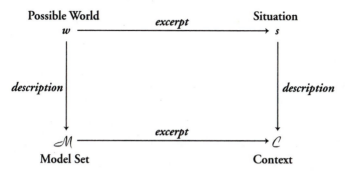

FIGURE 5.16 Ways of mapping possible worlds to contexts

are not computable. The contexts in the lower right of Figure 5.16 are the only things that can be represented and manipulated in a digital computer. Any theory of semantics that is stated in terms of possible worlds, model sets, or situations must ultimately be mapped to a theory of contexts in order to be computable.

DUNN'S LAWS AND FACTS. If the accessibility relation R is assumed as a primitive, modality cannot be explained in terms of anything more fundamental. To make accessibility a derived relation, Michael Dunn (1973) introduced pairs $<\mathcal{M},\mathcal{L}>$, where $\mathcal{M}$ is a Hintikka-style model set called the *facts* of a possible world and $\mathcal{L}$ is a subset of $\mathcal{M}$ called the *laws* of that world. Finally, Dunn showed how the accessibility relation from one pair to another is defined by constraints on which propositions are chosen as laws. As a result, the accessibility relation is no longer primitive, and the modal semantics does not depend on imaginary worlds. The ultimate source of modality is some agent, called the *lawgiver*, who chooses the laws.

Philosophers since Aristotle have recognized that modality is related to laws; Dunn's innovation lay in making the relationships explicit. Let $<\mathcal{M}_1,\mathcal{L}_1>$ be a pair of facts and laws that describe a possible world w_1, and let the pair $<\mathcal{M}_2,\mathcal{L}_2>$ describe a world w_2. Dunn defined accessibility from the world w_1 to the world w_2 by the constraint that the laws $\mathcal{L}_1$ are a subset of the facts in $\mathcal{M}_2$:

$$R(w_1,w_2) \equiv \mathcal{L}_1 \subset \mathcal{M}_2.$$

According to this definition, the laws of the first world w_1 remain true in the second world w_2, but they may be demoted from the status of laws to just ordinary facts. Dunn then restated the definitions of possibility and necessity in terms of laws and facts. In Kripke's version, possibility $\Diamond p$ means that p is true of some world w accessible from the real world w_0:

$$\Diamond p \equiv (\exists w \text{World})(R(w_0,w) \land w \vDash p).$$

By substituting the laws and facts for the possible worlds, Dunn derived an equivalent definition:

$\Diamond p \equiv (\exists \mathcal{M}:\text{ModelSet})(\text{laws}(\mathcal{M}) \subset \mathcal{M}_0 \wedge p \in \mathcal{M}).$

Now possibility $\Diamond p$ means that there exists a model set $\mathcal{M}$ whose laws are a subset of the facts of the real world $\mathcal{M}_0$ and p is a fact in $\mathcal{M}$. By the same substitutions, the definition of necessity becomes

$\Box p \equiv (\forall \mathcal{M}:\text{ModelSet})(\text{laws}(\mathcal{M}) \subset \mathcal{M}_0 \supset p \in \mathcal{M}).$

Necessity $\Box p$ means that in every model set $\mathcal{M}$ whose laws are a subset of the facts of the real world $\mathcal{M}_0$, p is also a fact in $\mathcal{M}$.

Dunn performed the same substitutions in Kripke's constraints on the accessibility relation. The result is a restatement of the constraints in terms of the laws and facts:

- *System T.* The constraints $\Box p \supset p$ and $p \supset \Diamond p$ require every world to be accessible from itself. That property follows from Dunn's definition because the laws $\mathcal{L}$ of any world are a subset of the facts $\mathcal{M}$.

- *System S4.* System T with Lewis's axiom S4, $\Box p \supset \Box \Box p$, requires that R must also be transitive. It imposes the tighter constraint that the laws of the first world must be a subset of the laws of the second world: $\mathcal{L}_1 \subset \mathcal{L}_2$.

- *System S5.* System S4 with axiom S5, $\Diamond p \supset \Box \Diamond p$, requires that R must also be symmetric. It constrains both worlds to have exactly the same laws: $\mathcal{L}_1 = \mathcal{L}_2$.

In Dunn's theory, the term *possible world* is an informal metaphor that does not appear in the formalism: the semantics of $\Box p$ and $\Diamond p$ depends only on the choice of laws and facts. In the pairs $<\mathcal{M},\mathcal{L}>$, all formulas are purely first order, and the symbols $\Box$ and $\Diamond$ never appear in any of them.

COMPLETING THE PUSHOUT.   In the commutative diagram of Figure 5.16, the downward arrow on the left corresponds to Dunn's mapping of possible worlds to model sets, and the rightward arrow at the top corresponds to Barwise and Perry's mapping of possible worlds to situations. The branch of mathematics called *category theory* has methods of completing such diagrams by deriving the other mappings. Given the two arrows at the left and the top, the technique called a *pushout* defines the two arrows on the bottom and the right:

- *Left.* The downward arrow on the left side of the diagram maps each possible world w to a model set $\mathcal{M}$ of facts that describe w. Since every proposition p in $\mathcal{M}$ must be true of w, the evaluation function $\Phi(p,w)$ maps to membership: $p \in \mathcal{M}$. The laws $\mathcal{L}$ of w can be chosen as any subset of necessary propositions in w whose deductive closure is the intersection of all $\mathcal{M}$ for worlds accessible from w.

- *Top.* The rightward arrow at the top maps w to a finite region s selected from w called a situation. The excerpt is chosen by some agent who decides how much of the world is relevant and what level of granularity is appropriate for its description.

- *Bottom.* The rightward arrow on the bottom is determined by the choice of s at the top. Every proposition p in $\mathcal{M}$ that is true of s ($s \models p$) is copied to the context $\mathcal{C}$. The laws of $\mathcal{C}$ are those laws in $\mathcal{M}$ that happened to be copied: $\mathcal{C} \cap \mathcal{L}$.

- *Right.* The downward arrow at the right maps the situation s to a context $\mathcal{C}$ that describes s. It produces the same result as the mapping on the bottom because it must satisfy the same constraints: every proposition p in $\mathcal{M}$ that is true of s must be in $\mathcal{C}$; the laws of $\mathcal{C}$ are the laws in $\mathcal{M}$ that are included in $\mathcal{C} \cap \mathcal{L}$.

Since the domains of each of the four mappings in Figure 5.16 are noncomputable structures, the mappings themselves are not computable. Their purpose is not to support computation, but to determine how theories about noncomputable possible worlds and situations can be adapted to computable contexts. After the theories have been transferred to contexts, the possible worlds and situations are unnecessary for further reasoning and computation.

SITUATIONS AS PULLBACKS.   The inverse of a pushout, called a *pullback*, is an operation of category theory that "pulls" some structure or family of structures backward along an arrow of a commutative diagram. For the diagram in Figure 5.16, the model set $\mathcal{M}$ and the context $\mathcal{C}$ are symbolic structures that have been studied in logic for many years. The situation s, as Devlin observed, is not as clearly defined. One way to define a situation is to assume the notion of context as more basic and to say that a situation s is whatever is described by a context $\mathcal{C}$. In terms of the diagram of Figure 5.16, the pullback would start with the two mappings from w to $\mathcal{M}$ and from $\mathcal{M}$ to $\mathcal{C}$. Then the situation s in the upper right and the two arrows $w{\rightarrow}s$ and $s{\rightarrow}\mathcal{C}$ would be derived by a pullback from the starting arrows $w{\rightarrow}\mathcal{M}$ and $\mathcal{M}{\rightarrow}\mathcal{C}$.

The definition of situations in terms of contexts may be congenial to logicians for whom abstract propositions are familiar notions. For people who prefer to think about physical objects, the notion of a situation as a chunk of the real world may seem more familiar. The commutative diagram provides a way of reconciling the two views: starting with a situation, the pushout determines the propositions in the context; starting with a context, the pullback defines the situation. The two complementary views are useful for different purposes: for a mapmaker, the context is derived as a description of some part of the world; for an architect, the concrete situation is derived by some builder who follows an abstract description.

LEGISLATING MODALITIES.   As the multiple axioms for modal logic indicate, there is no single version that applies to all problems. The complexities increase when different interpretations of modality are mixed, as in Peirce's five versions of possibility, which could be represented by colors or by subscripts, such as $\Diamond_1, \Diamond_2, \ldots, \Diamond_5$. Each of those modalities is derived from a different set of laws that may interact with the other laws:

- The combination $\Box_2\Diamond_1 p$, for example, would mean that it is subjectively necessary that p is logically possible.
- According to the definition of $\Box_2$, someone must know that $\Diamond_1 p$.
- Since what is known must be true, the following statement would be a theorem for that combination of modalities:

$$\Box_2\Diamond_1 p \supset \Diamond_1 p.$$

Similar analysis would be required to derive the axioms and theorems for all possible combinations of the five kinds of possibility with the five kinds of necessity. Since subjective possibility depends on some agent, the number of possible combinations escalates when multiple agents interact.

With the metalevel predicate isTrueIn, McCarthy sought to reduce the proliferation of modalities to a process of metalevel reasoning about the propositions that are true in a context. For an agent to declare which true propositions happen to be laws, a triadic metalevel predicate is needed: legislate($a,p,\mathscr{C}$) would say that some agent a *legislates* that p is a law in $\mathscr{C}$. Peirce's five kinds of possibility depend on who has the authority to legislate:

- *Logical possibility.* The only statements that are logically necessary are tautologies: those statements that are provable from the empty set. No special lawgiver is needed for the empty set; alternatively, every agent may be assumed to legislate the empty set:

$$\{\} = \{p\text{:Proposition} \mid (\forall a\text{:Agent})(\forall \mathscr{C}\text{:Context})\text{legislate}(a,p,\mathscr{C})\}.$$

The empty set is the set of all propositions p where every agent a legislates p as a law of every context $\mathscr{C}$.

- *Subjective possibility.* A proposition p is subjectively possible for an agent a if a does not know p to be false. The subjective laws for any agent a are all the propositions that a knows:

$$\text{SubjectiveLaws}(a) = \{p\text{:Proposition} \mid \text{know}(a,p)\}.$$

To relate knowledge to legislation, the following formula may be adopted as an axiom:

$$(\forall a\text{:Agent})(\forall p\text{:Proposition})(\forall \mathscr{C}\text{:Context})$$
$$(\text{know}(a,\text{isTrueIn}(p,\mathscr{C})) \equiv \text{legislate}(a,p,\mathscr{C})).$$

This formula says that a knows that p is true in $\mathscr{C}$ if and only if a legislates p as a law of $\mathscr{C}$.

- *Objective possibility.* The laws of nature define what is physically possible. The symbol *God* may be used as a place holder for the lawgiver:

LawsOfNature $=$ {p:Proposition | $(\forall x$:Entity)legislate(God,p,x)}.

If God is assumed to be omniscient, this set is the same as everything God knows or SubjectiveLaws(God). What is subjective for God is objective for everyone else.

- *Interrogative mood.* A proposition is not questioned if it is part of the common knowledge of the parties to a conversation. For two agents a and b, common knowledge can be defined as the intersection of their subjective knowledge or laws:

CommonKnowledge(a,b) $=$ SubjectiveLaws(a) $\cap$ SubjectiveLaws(b).

- *Freedom.* Whatever is free or permissible in a context $\mathscr{C}$ must be consistent with the laws, rules, regulations, ordinances, or policies of any lawgiver who has the authority to legislate what is obligatory in $\mathscr{C}$:

Obligatory($\mathscr{C}$) $=$
   {p:Proposition | $(\exists a$:Agent)(authority(a,$\mathscr{C}$) $\wedge$ legislate(a,p,$\mathscr{C}$)}.

This interpretation, which defines deontic logic, makes it a weak version of modal logic since consistency is weaker than truth. The usual modal axioms $\Box p \supset p$ and $p \supset \Diamond p$ do not hold for deontic logic, since people can violate the laws.

Reasoning at the metalevel of laws and facts is common practice in courts. In the United States, the Constitution is the supreme law of the land; any law or regulation of the U.S. government or any state, county, or city in the U.S. must be consistent with the U.S. Constitution. But the tautologies and laws of nature are established by an even higher authority. No one can be forced to obey a law that is logically or physically impossible.

EXPORTING MODAL INFORMATION. A prerequisite for exporting nested information is that the inner and outer contexts have the same modal, temporal, and intentional status. If the status is different, the exported information must be enclosed in a *modal qualification* that states the conditions under which the information is true. There are two basic metalevel statements about a context that can be used to justify import and export rules:

- *Description.* If a context $\mathscr{C}$ describes an entity x, then any proposition p that also describes x can be imported into $\mathscr{C}$. Furthermore, any proposition p that is true in $\mathscr{C}$ can be exported from $\mathscr{C}$ in the form dscr(x,p):

$(\forall \mathscr{C}$:Context$)(\forall x$:Entity$)(\forall p$:Proposition$)$
   (dscr(x,$\mathscr{C}$) $\supset$ (dscr(x,p) $\equiv$ isTrueIn(p,$\mathscr{C}$)).

This formula says that if a context $\mathcal{C}$ describes an entity x, a proposition p describes x if and only if p is true in $\mathcal{C}$.

- *Communication.* A *trusted source,* such as an oracle or a dependable sensing device, may assert propositions in the outermost context, which could then be imported into other contexts. In effect, the outermost context can serve as a bulletin board for posting messages to any nested contexts.

These operations can move information in a first-order nest of contexts, but they depend on metalevel conditions that go beyond pure FOL.

Other rules can also be formulated for moving information about parts of objects at various points in time, but further qualification is necessary. The following rule, for example, might be derived from the rule of description:

- *Identity.* If two contexts describe exactly the same entity x, then any proposition p in either one may be exported to the other.

This rule would follow from the rule of description, since p could be exported from one context in the form dscr(x,p) and imported into the other. However, the exported form may have to be qualified to avoid incompatibilities, such as the example of Tom the baby and Tom the adult in Figure 5.2. At one time, Tom might have dark hair, then gray hair, and finally no hair. From the contexts in Figure 5.2, the next two propositions could be exported in qualified form:

ptim(dscr(Tom,baby(Tom)),1976).
ptim(dscr(Tom,adult(Tom)),1997).

A description at one point in time cannot be imported into a context for a different time unless some other information implies that the property can be expected to hold. Age changes in a highly predictable way; hair color is less predictable; but name and sex tend to remain unchanged unless some notable event occurs.

STRATIFIED METALEVELS. The STRIPS system, which was discussed in Section 4.7, solved the frame problem by using a *stratified* reasoning method with a separate object language and metalanguage. Metalevel reasoning is powerful, but it can sometimes create paradoxes with examples like "This sentence is false." Tarski (1935) developed the theory of stratified metalevels to avoid such paradoxes: every metalevel can refer to anything in any level beneath itself, but no level can refer to its own symbols or truth values.

1. Let the object language $\mathcal{L}_0$ refer to entities in some *universe of discourse* $\mathcal{D}$, but $\mathcal{L}_0$ cannot refer to its own symbols or the truth values of its own statements.

2. The metalanguage $\mathcal{L}_1$ can refer to the original $\mathcal{D}$, to the symbols of $\mathcal{L}_0$, to the truth values of statements in $\mathcal{L}_0$, and to the relationships between the language

$\mathscr{L}_0$ and $\mathscr{D}$. The language $\mathscr{L}_1$ is still first order, but its universe of discourse has been enlarged from $\mathscr{D}$ to $\mathscr{L}_0 \cup \mathscr{D}$.

3. The metametalanguage $\mathscr{L}_2$ is also first order, but its universe of discourse is $\mathscr{L}_1 \cup \mathscr{L}_0 \cup \mathscr{D}$.

4. In general, the nth metalanguage includes all the languages beneath itself, their domains of discourse, and the truth values of statements in those languages. But no language can refer to its own symbols or to the truth values of its statements.

Every metalanguage can be used to formalize the semantics of any level beneath itself, but no level can refer to its own semantics.

For many applications, the metalogic applied to contexts and propositions has the same structure as the logic for reasoning about physical objects like blocks, pyramids, and boxes. That clean separation of levels arises when the details of the object level statements in $\mathscr{L}_0$ do not interact with the details of the metalanguage $\mathscr{L}_1$. Consider the next two formulas:

- *If block x is on block y and y is in box z, then x is also in z.*

  $(\forall x,y{:}\text{Block})(\forall z{:}\text{Box})((\text{on}(x,y) \land \text{in}(y,z)) \supset \text{in}(x,z))$.

- *If proposition p implies proposition q and p is true in context $\mathscr{C}$, then q is also true in $\mathscr{C}$.*

  $(\forall p,q{:}\text{Proposition})(\forall \mathscr{C}{:}\text{Context})(((p \supset q) \land \text{isTrueIn}(p,\mathscr{C})) \supset \text{isTrueIn}(q,\mathscr{C}))$.

According to the ontology of Chapter 2, the entities in the first statement are physical, and the entities in the second are abstract. For the rules of inference, however, the ontology is irrelevant, since the rules depend only on the syntax, not the subject matter. Therefore, the same kind of logic can be used to reason about blocks in boxes as to reason about propositions in contexts.

At the metalevel, propositions can be moved and sorted in contexts in the same way that blocks or pyramids are moved and sorted in boxes. In STRIPS, that method was used at the metalevel to add, delete, or copy propositions in the current context in order to derive the next context. After the sorting has been done, first-order rules of inference are applied to the propositions inside the contexts:

- All metalevel statements about the truth, likelihood, or evidence for the propositions in a context $\mathscr{C}$ are contained in contexts outside of $\mathscr{C}$.

- Rules of inference that are sensitive to the internal structure of a proposition p may not be used in the same context in which p is qualified by modal or intentional operators like $\Diamond p$ or $\text{hope}(a,p)$.

- Dunn's technique of replacing modal and intentional operators by metastatements about laws and facts can be used to transform a context $\mathscr{C}$ to a collection of first-order statements about some entity x: dscr($\mathscr{C}$,x). As before, the ontological nature of x as abstract or physical is irrelevant to the formal transformations.

- If $\mathscr{C}$ describes x, any proposition p entailed by x is true in $\mathscr{C}$:

$(\forall\mathscr{C}{:}Context)(\forall x{:}Entity)(\forall p{:}Proposition)$
$((dscr(x,\mathscr{C}) \wedge x\vDash p) \supset isTrueIn(p,\mathscr{C}))$.

- When all propositions in $\mathscr{C}$ are in first-order form, entailment $\vDash$ is equivalent to provability $\vdash$. Therefore, Peirce's first-order rules and the variations derived from them can be used within the context.

In short, metalevel reasoning is first-order reasoning about the way statements are sorted in contexts. After the sorting has been done, the propositions in a context can be handled by the usual FOL rules. At every level of the Tarski hierarchy of metalanguages, the reasoning process is governed by first-order rules. But first-order reasoning in language $\mathscr{L}_n$ has the effect of higher-order or modal reasoning for every language below n. At every level n, the model theory that justifies the reasoning in $\mathscr{L}_n$ is a conventional first-order Tarskian theory, since the nature of the objects in the domain &scriptd$_n$ is irrelevant to the rules that apply to $\mathscr{L}_n$.

Agents who use stratified languages to communicate do not feel restricted in what they can say: if they want to talk about the language they are currently using, they just move to the next higher metalanguage to discuss it. Natural languages, in fact, are commonly used as metametalanguages: every metalevel uses the same syntax and vocabulary, but the speakers use it to refer to statements that can be considered a level beneath the one they are currently using. If a paradoxical statement such as "This sentence is false" happens to arise, the speakers resolve the paradox by clarifying the strata with a retraction such as "The statement I just made [i.e. at level $n-1$] was false."

EXAMPLE.   To illustrate the interplay of the metalevel transformations and the object-level inferences, consider the following statement, which includes direct quotation, indirect quotation, indexical pronouns, and metalanguage about belief:

> *Joe said, "I don't believe in astrology, but they say that it works even if you don't believe in it."*

This statement could be translated word for word to a conceptual graph in which the indexicals are represented by the symbols #I, #they, #it, and #you. Then the resolution of the indexicals could be performed by metalevel transformations of the graph. Those transformations could also be written in stylized English:

1. First mark the indexicals with the # symbol, and use square brackets to mark the multiple levels of nested contexts:

```
Joe said
  [#I don't believe [in astrology]
  but #they say
    [[[#it works]
    even if #you don't believe [in #it] ]].
```

2. The indexical #I can be resolved to the speaker Joe, but the other indexicals depend on implicit background knowledge. The phrase "they say," like the French "on dit" or the German "man sagt," refers to the commonly accepted wisdom of Joe's community; it could be translated "every person believes." The two occurrences of #it refer to astrology, but the three nested contexts about astrology have different forms; for simplicity, they could all be rewritten "astrology works." When no explicit person is being addressed, the indexical #you can be interpreted as a reference to any or every person who may be listening. For this example, it could be assumed to be coreferent with "every person" in the community. With these substitutions, the statement becomes

```
Joe said
  [Joe doesn't believe [astrology works]
  but every person x believes
    [[astrology works]
    even if x doesn't believe [astrology works] ]].
```

3. If Joe's statement was sincere, Joe believes what he said. The word *but* could be replaced with the word *and*, which preserves the propositional content, but omits the contrastive emphasis. A statement of the form "p even if q" means that p is true independent of the truth value of q. It is equivalent to $((q \supset p) \wedge ((\sim q) \supset p))$, which implies p by itself. The statement can therefore be rewritten

```
Joe believes
  [Joe doesn't believe [astrology works]
  and every person x believes [astrology works] ].
```

4. Inside the context of Joe's beliefs, the detailed syntax of the nested context [astrology works] can be ignored. Therefore, a first-order rule of inference can be applied to substitute the constant "Joe" for the quantifier "every person x":

```
Joe believes
  [Joe doesn't believe [astrology works]
  and Joe believes [astrology works] ].
```

5. At this stage, the context of Joe's beliefs can be translated to propositional logic by using the symbol p for the sentence "Joe believes [astrology works]":

```
Joe believes [p ∧ ~p].
```

This transformation exposes the contradiction in the context of Joe's beliefs.

For computer analysis of language, the most difficult task is to determine the conversational implicatures and the background knowledge needed for resolving indexicals. After the implicit assumptions have been made explicit, the translation to logic and further deductions in logic are straightforward.

In the process of reasoning about Joe's beliefs, the context [astrology works] is treated as an encapsulated object whose internal structure is ignored. When the levels interact, however, further axioms are necessary to relate them. Like the iterated modalities $\Diamond\Diamond p$ and $\Diamond\Box p$, iterated beliefs occur in statements like *Joe believes that Joe doesn't believe that astrology works*. One reasonable axiom is that if an agent *a* believes that *a* believes *p*, then *a* believes *p*:

$$(\forall a{:}\text{Agent})(\forall p{:}\text{Proposition})(\text{believe}(a,\text{believe}(a,p)) \supset \text{believe}(a,p)).$$

This axiom enables two levels of nested contexts to be collapsed into one. The converse, however, is less likely: many people act as if they believe propositions that they are not willing to admit. Joe, for example, might read the astrology column in the daily newspaper and follow its advice. His actions could be considered evidence that he believes in astrology. Yet when asked, Joe might continue to insist that he doesn't believe in astrology.

MODEL THEORY IN CONTEXTS.   Tarski's model theory, with its stratified metalevels, maps directly to the framework of contexts. A first-order logic $\mathcal{L}_0$ can be used to describe some situation in the world, and the levels above $\mathcal{L}_0$ can be used to represent the model theory and proof theory for $\mathcal{L}_0$:

1. Let the language $\mathcal{L}_0$ be ordinary first-order logic in any suitable notation, and let the domain $\mathcal{D}_0$ be some collection of physical objects, such as the SHRDLU blocks world.

2. Let the context $\mathcal{C}_0$ be the deductive closure of some statements written in $\mathcal{L}_0$ that happen to be true of the objects in $\mathcal{D}_0$. By construction, $\mathcal{C}_0$ must be consistent.

3. Let the language $\mathcal{L}_1$ be an extension of $\mathcal{L}_0$ and its domain to include the blocks of $\mathcal{D}_0$, all the syntactic features of $\mathcal{L}_0$, and the predicate isTrueIn$(p,\mathcal{C}_0)$ for any formula p in $\mathcal{L}_0$.

4. Let the context $\mathcal{C}_1$ be a statement of Tarski's model theory for $\mathcal{L}_0$ formulated in language $\mathcal{L}_1$ with the predicate isTrueIn$(p,\mathcal{C}_0)$ replacing the predicate isTrue(p). If Tarski's model theory is consistent, then context $\mathcal{C}_1$ must also be consistent.

5. To continue this technique, any established logical theory could be stated in contexts that include $\mathcal{C}_0$ and $\mathcal{C}_1$. A context $\mathcal{C}_2$, for example, could state the

first-order rules of inference for language $\mathcal{L}_0$ and prove that those rules preserve truth as defined by the model theory in $\mathcal{C}_1$.

6.   The framework also allows statements in a context $\mathcal{C}_n$ to use the triadic *legislate* predicate to formalize theories about the agents in lower contexts and their knowledge and intentions. At level n, such theories would be stated in first-order logic, but they would have the effect of a modal or higher-order logic in contexts below n.

This construction shows that the framework of nested contexts by itself does not introduce any inherent inconsistencies. People who use that framework, however, might say something inconsistent in one of the contexts, but such inconsistencies would be the fault of the people who use the framework, not of the framework itself. In fact, the framework serves as a "firewall" that prevents inconsistencies that are local to one context from spreading globally. The inconsistency in Joe's statement about astrology, for example, would not affect his statements about other subjects.

5.6   Encapsulating Objects in Contexts

The example of the birthday party in Section 3.4 shows how contexts can encapsulate the logical descriptions of the static structures and the dynamic processes associated with an object. The rules of inference of logic allow those descriptions to be inherited from supertypes to subtypes. Logic is also capable of representing the other features of object-oriented languages:

- Distinction between the definition of an object class and the instances of each object,
- Distinction between the definition of a method and the process that results from the activation of the method,
- Time sequence of steps in the execution of a method,
- Messages passed to an object that trigger the execution of its methods.

These features do not require changes in the logic itself, but they require some definitions and conventions about the way logic is used to represent them.

Without explicit contexts, the statements that describe different objects or kinds of objects cannot be distinguished. Figure 5.17, for example, shows a conceptual graph that describes typical cars: *Every car is of some model, and it has as parts an engine, four wheels, and a body.* The CG statement can be translated directly to predicate calculus:

$$(\forall c{:}\text{Car})(\exists m{:}\text{Model})(\exists e{:}\text{Engine})\ (\exists b{:}\text{Body})(\exists w{:}\text{Set})$$
$$(\text{kind}(c,m) \wedge \text{part}(c,e) \wedge \text{part}(c,b) \wedge \text{count}(w,4) \wedge (\forall x{\in}w)(\text{wheel}(x) \wedge \text{part}(c,x))).$$

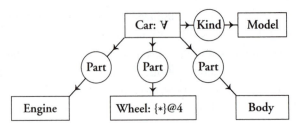

FIGURE 5.17 A conceptual graph that describes cars

The conceptual graph or the corresponding formula could be placed anywhere on a sheet of paper or in computer storage. The axioms that describe how cars behave would be stored in the same area, along with many other axioms that describe other kinds of objects. To separate the information about cars from the information about other things, Figure 5.18 shows the graph from Figure 5.17 encapsulated inside a context that defines the object class Car.

The class definition in Figure 5.18 has a universal quantifier ∀ to show that it applies to every car *c. Inside the definition context, the nested graph shows that each car ?c is a kind of model *m, and it has as parts an engine *e, a set of 4 wheels *w, and a body *b. This graph is equivalent to the unencapsulated graph in Figure 5.17. Below that graph are six other concepts that describe procedures, called *methods*, associated with cars: StartEngine, Accelerate, StopEngine, TurnLeft, Brake, and TurnRight. Each of these concepts is itself a nested context, which contains graphs that describe what happens when the method is invoked.

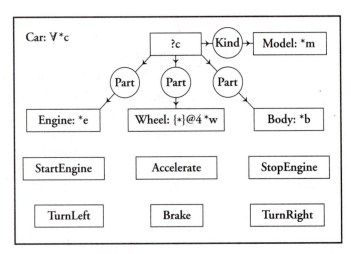

FIGURE 5.18 Encapsulated definition of the Car class

OBJECT INSTANCE. When a new instance of a class is created, a unique identifier, called a *surrogate*, is generated to identify it. A surrogate corresponds to the *object identifier* (OID) in the O-O languages. Like OIDs, surrogates are *local symbols* that are not meaningful outside the system. For externally visible references, an instance may also have a name or serial number that could appear after the type label in the concept box. Those are *public symbols* that can be printed, copied, and shared with external systems. Figure 5.19 shows a car with serial number PCXX999 at the point in time 9:51:02 Greenwich Mean Time.

A class definition is a timeless statement that is always true of all its instances. But each instance is created at a specific time and passes through a series of states during its lifetime. In Figure 5.19, the relation PTim for point in time shows that the car exists at 9:51:02 GMT. Unless that time is overridden by another PTim relation, it also applies to everything in the nested contexts. The concepts in the class definition have existential quantifiers to indicate that some engine or body must exist for each car, but they don't specify their names or other identifiers. In a context for a specific instance, however, many of the concepts are *individual*

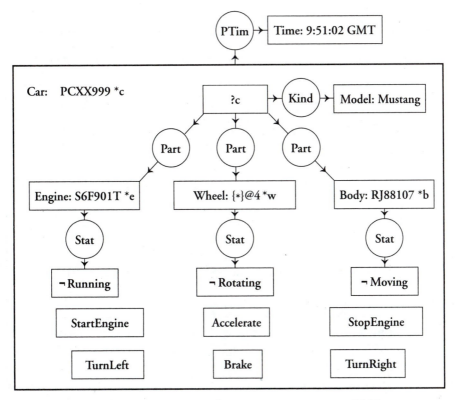

FIGURE 5.19 An instance of car PCXX999 at 9:51:02 GMT

concepts, identified by their names, serial numbers, or surrogates. The model *m of the car has the name Mustang; the car's engine *e has a serial number S6F901T; its four wheels *w are not named; and its body *b has a serial number RJ88107. The engine is in the state not running, the wheels are in the state not rotating, and the body is in the state not moving.

OBJECT METHODS. In Chapter 4, Petri nets were used to illustrate the difference between procedures and processes. That same distinction applies to the nested contexts for the methods associated with O-O classes and instances. In the class definition of Figure 5.18, the six boxes for the methods contain procedure definitions that apply to every car; the boxes in the object instance of Figure 5.19 contain active processes for the particular car PCXX999. Class definitions contain procedures, and object instances contain processes.

By the technique of zooming discussed in Section 3.4, the StartEngine context in Figure 5.18 can be expanded to show the detail in Figure 5.20. When the StartEngine method for the instance in Figure 5.19 is activated, it begins in the state described by Figure 5.20. But as the process continues, the conceptual graphs

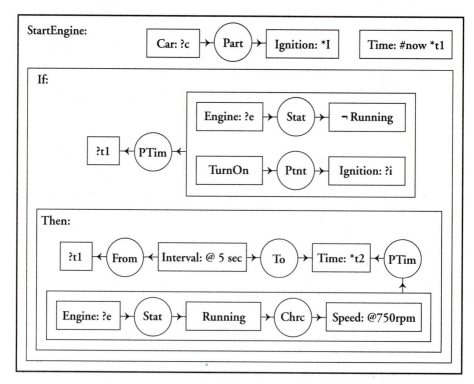

FIGURE 5.20 Expanded view of the StartEngine context in Figure 5.18

from the procedure are combined with other graphs from the car context and new information from a message to start the engine. The rules of inference determine the step-by-step transformation of the graphs that describe the state of the car at each instant.

Inside the context of Figure 5.20, some graphs represent local data for each instance, and other graphs specify the time sequence of events in the process. The graph at the top shows that the car ?c, which is defined in the containing context, has as part an ignition system *i. The concept [Time: #now *t1] specifies *t1 as coreferent with the current time #now. Below that is an if-then block that determines what happens when the process is activated. The if-context specifies the preconditions at time ?t1: the engine ?e is not running, and the ignition ?i is turned on. When those conditions become true, the then-context specifies the postconditions: at a time *t2, which follows ?t1 by an interval of 5 seconds, the engine ?e is in a state (Stat) of running with a characteristic (Chrc) speed of 750 rpm.

PASSING MESSAGES.   Since the definition of the StartEngine procedure in Figure 5.20 must be true for all times, it cannot contain a reference to the specific time of any particular instance. Instead, it contains the indexical referent #now, which must be resolved to a time specification of some instance. When the procedure is activated in the environment of car PCXX999, the indexical #now and the associated label *t1 would be resolved to the current time 9:51:02 GMT, which is specified in Figure 5.19.

To activate the procedure, a *message* such as Figure 5.21 must be asserted in the context of car PCXX999. It contains two indexical referents, each indicated by a # symbol: the first # symbol refers to the StartEngine context, and the second # symbol refers to the ignition. The reason for the indexicals is that from the outside of the car, only its serial number PCXX999 is known. The originator of the message (either a human or a program) may know that there exists a procedure for starting the engine and that it is triggered by turning on the ignition, but the specific object identifiers are not known outside the context of the car. In CGs, the # symbol serves

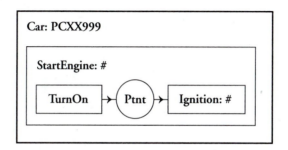

FIGURE 5.21 A message to start the engine

the same purpose as the indexical *this*, which refers to the current object instance in O-O languages like Java and C++.

EXECUTING A PROCEDURE.   Operations on graphical structures are easier to show than to describe. The steps for initiating and running a procedure could best be seen from an on-line demonstration or a video recording. But within the limitations of the printed page, the following steps describe what would be seen. Each step is justified by a rule of inference described in Section 5.4. The complete sequence of steps constitutes a proof that the message in Figure 5.21 would cause the engine to begin running at 750 rpm. A compiler could translate this sequence of inferences directly to an executable procedure.

1. Export the following graph from the context of the message in Figure 5.21:

    `[StartEngine: # [TurnOn]→(Ptnt)→[Ignition: #]].`

2. Import this graph into the context of car PCXX999 in Figure 5.19.

3. Resolve the # symbol on the concept [StartEngine: #] to the [StartEngine] box in Figure 5.19.

4. Initialize the description of the StartEngine box in Figure 5.19 by copying the definition from Figure 5.20. This copy is justified by the universal quantifier ∀ on the class definition (Figure 5.18), which implies that the definition, including any expanded contexts in it, must be true of every instance of the class.

5. Replace the #now indexical in the StartEngine box with the current time 9:51:02 GMT.

6. Export the following graph from the StartEngine box in the message (Figure 5.21):

    `[TurnOn]→(Ptnt)→[Ignition: #].`

7. Import this graph into the StartEngine box.

8. Resolve the # symbol on [Ignition: #] by replacing it with the label ?i to indicate a coreference link to the concept [Ignition: *i].

9. Join the two concepts of type Ignition that are now in the context of the StartEngine box.

At this point, if a viewer pressed the pause button on a theorem prover, the StartEngine box would look like Figure 5.22. That graph shows a stage in the evolution of the StartEngine process after the message was sent to the car PCXX999 and the new information was linked with the previous state description. The next step is to trigger the if-then block to determine what changes would occur to the car.

The process in Figure 5.22 would continue according to the rules of inference

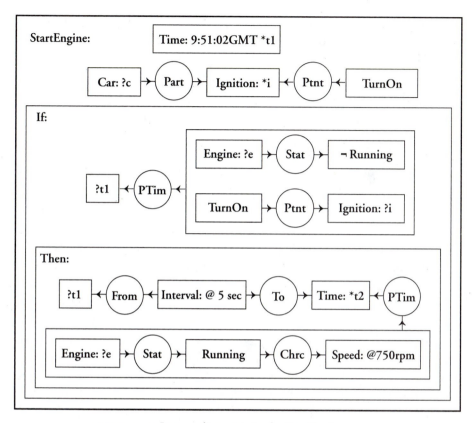

FIGURE 5.22 Intermediate state in the StartEngine process

for an if-then block. The if-context specifies the conditions, and the then-context specifies the resulting changes. By the rules described in Section 5.4, an if-then block would be executed by applying the rule of deiteration to erase the graphs in the if-context. Then the resulting double negation would be erased, and the final state would be described by the graph that emerges from the then-context. Following are the steps in the process continuing from Figure 5.22.

1. Since the defining node *t1 has the value 9:51:02, that value may be copied to the two references marked by ?t1 in the if-context and the then-context.

2. As a result of Step #1, the time specification in the if-context has become identical to the specification on the containing context for the car PCXX999 in Figure 5.19. By the rule of time deiteration, the following subgraph may be erased:

```
[Time:  9:51:02  GMT]←(PTim)←[. . .]
```

3. Deiteration may be applied when the nested graph is a subgraph or generalization of a graph in a containing context. Therefore, the following graph may be erased from the if-context, since it is a subgraph of a graph in the containing context in Figure 5.19:

```
[Engine: ?e]→(Stat)→[¬Running].
```

4. Then the following graph is the only one left in the if-context:

```
[TurnOn]→(Ptnt)→[Ignition: ?i].
```

By deiteration, this graph may also be erased since it is a subgraph of a graph in a containing context in Figure 5.22.

5. Now there is nothing left between the inner and outer negations of the if-then block, and both negative contexts may be erased.

6. The graph in the then-context, which has now been removed from the if-then nest, specifies that an interval of five seconds has lapsed from ?t1 to *t2, which must therefore be 9:51:07 GMT.

As a result of these steps, the graph in Figure 5.22 is transformed to Figure 5.23, which represents the final state of the StartEngine process. Yet the information that the engine ?e is running at a speed of 750 rpm will be true only after the point in time 9:51:07 GMT. Since the time for car PCXX999 in Figure 5.19 is still marked as 9:51:02, the rule of time deiteration cannot yet be applied. Therefore, the information about the running engine must remain inside the nested context.

RESULTING STATE. After five seconds have elapsed, the time specification for car PCXX999 becomes identical to the time specification of the nested context. Then the rule of deiteration can be applied to erase the nested time specification,

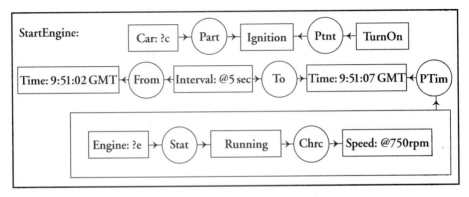

FIGURE 5.23 Final state of the StartEngine process

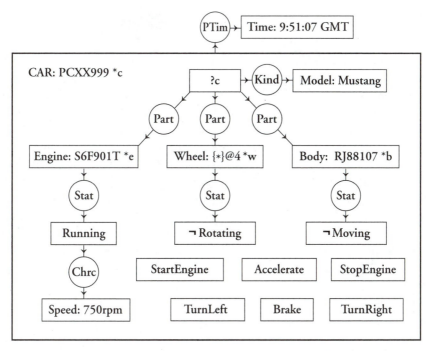

FIGURE 5.24 State of car PCXX999 at 9:51:07 GMT

and the information about the running engine can be exported from the nested context to the context of car PCXX999. There it can be combined with the other graphs in Figure 5.19 to derive Figure 5.24, which shows the engine running at a speed of 750 rpm. By Leibniz's principle of sufficient reason, those parts of the description that have not been affected by any inference rule remain unchanged.

USING MULTIPLE NOTATIONS. This example shows how the inference rules for conceptual graphs can execute a procedure. But as Chapter 4 showed, other notations, such as finite-state machines or Petri nets, can often represent procedures more concisely. Those notations, however, can be defined in terms of conceptual graphs, and the rules for processing them can be defined in terms of Peirce's rules of inference. Therefore, those notations may be nested inside CG contexts. For the car example, Gerard Ellis (1995) used CGs to represent a finite-state machine and the detailed specifications inside each state. The resulting CGs were more concise than the steps from Figure 5.19 to 5.24. But nested CG contexts can also accommodate other notations, such as Petri nets, predicate calculus, or stylized natural language. Even a domain-dependent notation such as a musical score can be represented and manipulated inside the boxes of a conceptual graph. The only prerequisite is a formal definition of the notation and the rules of inference in terms of CGs.

5.7   Agents

The word *agent* has become popular for describing software systems that automatically perform useful tasks, such as searching the Internet, sorting e-mail notes, or generating help messages. Another common term is *softbot*, which suggests a similarity to robots, but without an embodiment in hardware. Literally, an agent is something that acts, but more detail is needed to distinguish a software agent from an ordinary computer program. Carl Hewitt, who has been doing research on agents since his early work on Planner (1971), remarked that a major embarrassment of the field is that no one can agree on a definition of *agent*. The psychologists David Moffat and Nico Frijda (1995) observed: "The word *agent* is a technical term without a generally agreed usage. It can refer to something as trivial as a persistent computer program, like the Unix *at* daemon; or to an independent system with enough knowledge and interactive capabilities to ensure its effectiveness in a wide range of somewhat unforeseen circumstances. The biological model for this latter kind of agent would be an animal of some kind, somewhere on the scale from insect to human."

There is no shortage of definitions, theories, or implementations of agents, just a shortage of agreement. In a survey of the research, Michael Wooldridge and Nicholas Jennings (1995) listed four attributes that are common to most versions of agents:

- *Autonomous.* Agents are self-regulating or *autonomous*, from the Greek *auto* (self) and *nomos* (law). They guide their actions according to their own internal laws or directives.

- *Social.* Agents communicate with other agents, including humans, by some *agent communication language* (ACL).

- *Reactive.* Agents perceive aspects of the environment and react appropriately.

- *Proactive.* Agents can take the initiative in performing goal-directed actions.

Other properties claimed for various agents include mobility, veracity, benevolence, rationality, intentionality, desire, obligation, commitment, deliberation, flexibility, selectivity, and robustness. Many of those terms have never been clearly defined for humans, and some people question whether they could be meaningfully applied to computer systems.

PSYCHOLOGY OF AGENTS.   Linguistically, an agent is an animate being that can perform some action, and an action is an event that is initiated or carried out by some animate being. The circularity in those definitions might be broken by determining what characteristics of an animate being are necessary for it to play the role of an agent. Then those features could be generalized to a definition of *agent* that would apply to people, animals, robots, and certain kinds of software.

The word *animate* comes from the Latin *anima*, which means breath or soul;

the Scholastics used *anima* as a translation of the Greek *psychē,* which also means breath or soul. The basis for the modern terminology is Aristotle's treatise *Peri Psychēs,* which is called *De Anima* in Latin or *On the Soul* in English. Aristotle defined the psyche as the *logos* or principle that determines what it is for something to be a living entity. Instead of a single principle of the psyche that covered all living things, Aristotle found six related functions, which he arranged in a hierarchy: nutrition, perception, desire, locomotion, imagery, and thought:

> We must inquire for each kind of living thing, what is its psyche; what is that of a plant, and what is that of a human or a beast. The reason why the functions are arranged in this order must also be considered. For without nutrition, there does not exist perception, but in plants, nutrition is found without perception. Again, without the sense of touch none of the other senses exists, but touch exists without the others, for many animals have neither vision nor hearing nor sense of smell. And of those that can perceive, some have locomotion, while others have not. Finally and most rarely, they have reason and thought. Those mortal creatures that have reason have all the rest, but not all those that have each of the others have reason; some do not even have imagery, but others live by this alone. The rational intellect requires a separate principle (*logos*). An appropriate definition of each of these functions would be the most appropriate for the psyche as well. [414b32]

Aristotle's hierarchy of functions was based on his extensive study of the plants and animals known in his day. With his criteria, he was the first to recognize that sponges were primitive animals rather than plants. The subdivisions in the tree of Porphyry (Figure 1.1) are based on his distinctions of animate/inanimate, sensitive/insensitive, and rational/irrational. Aristotle's hierarchy also resembles the competence levels that Rodney Brooks (1986) defined for mobile robots (see Section 3.6). In fact, Aristotle's levels may help to clarify and refine the competence levels: nutrition, which Brooks omitted, is necessary for a robot to recharge its batteries; and desire or something like it is necessary to determine goals for the robot at every level, from the most primitive nutrition to the most sophisticated planning.

ARTIFICIAL PSYCHES. What distinguishes a software agent from an ordinary program is a unifying principle that gives it a certain autonomy. Following Aristotle, that principle may be called its *psyche,* and its definition can be based on an appropriate definition of each of its functions. The six functions of the psyche, which Aristotle applied to living things from plants and insects to humans, can serve as metaphors for the functions of artificial agents:

- *Nutrition.* For a robot or embodied agent, nutrition is the act of recharging its batteries or energy stores from time to time. For a software agent, nutrition is the procurement of computer time and storage space from a host system. A computer virus is a parasite that steals the time and space; a more benign agent lives in a symbiotic relationship with its host, providing useful services in exchange for room and board.

- *Perception.* For a robot, perception depends on input sensors and the ability to interpret the inputs. A television camera, for example, may provide a stream of data; to see, however, the robot must convert the data to a representation of objects in the environment. For a software agent, perception requires access to input devices of the host and the ability to interpret data from those devices.

- *Desire.* Aristotle's general word for desire is *orexis*, which causes an agent to reach for what is desired — one that doesn't reach is *anorexic*. He distinguished three aspects of desire: appetite (*epithymia*), passion (*thymos*), and will (*boulēsis*). He classified appetite and passion as feelings shared with beasts and will as the result of rational thought. In their psychology of agents, Moffat and Frijda (1995) made a similar distinction between preference and will. For a software agent, the built-in equivalent of appetite or passion gives it a preference for certain kinds of states. Its will is determined by a logically derived plan for reaching a preferred state.

- *Locomotion.* For mobile robots, locomotion is a basic function that may be further divided into subfunctions, such as Brooks's competence levels. Software agents, which operate in some host system, may use the input/output devices of the host to explore the environment, including anything reachable via computer networks.

- *Imagery.* Aristotle's term *phantasia*, according to the Liddell and Scott dictionary, means the appearance, presentation, or representation of images "whether immediate or in memory, whether true or illusory." The processing of imagery by computer is an active research topic in artificial intelligence. Like Aristotle, many researchers believe that important aspects of animal-level intelligence can be achieved by manipulating imagelike data structures rather than propositions (Glasgow et al. 1995).

- *Thought.* Aristotle reserved the highest level of the psyche for rational thought. His term for *rational animal* was *zōon logon echon* (animal having logos). For software agents, rational thought corresponds to the deductive and planning capacity that transforms the motivating forces of appetite and passion into will. A rational agent must be able to perceive relevant aspects of a situation, evaluate their desirability, and determine plans for transforming the current situation into a more desirable one.

The notion of *psyche* with its hierarchy of functions provides a framework for classifying agentive behavior. The psyche of an agent is its functional organization, and its level of sophistication depends on how much of the Aristotelian range of function it is able to support.

Consciousness.   One function of the psyche that is noticeably absent from Aristotle's list is *consciousness*. In the introduction to his translation of Aristotle's *De Anima*, D. W. Hamlyn (1968) criticized that absence:

> Aristotle's dealings with the traditional mind-body problem are perfunctory. He assumes in general that his concern is with functions which are those of both body and soul. Indeed this must be so, given his account of the soul as the form of the body. But there is an almost total neglect of any problem arising from psycho-physical dualism and the facts of consciousness. Such problems do not seem to arise for him. The reason appears to be that concepts like that of consciousness do not figure in his conceptual schema at all; they play no part in his analysis of perception, thought, etc. (Nor do they play any significant role in Greek thought in general.)

Recent work in AI and cognitive psychology has moved away from a sharp mind-body dualism. The new developments have reawakened an interest in Aristotle's continuity of mindlike phenomena. In their commentary, the philosophers Martha Nussbaum and Hilary Putnam (1992) concluded, "Aristotle's thought really is, properly understood, the fulfillment of Wittgenstein's desire to have a "natural history of man." It is also, in a different way, the fulfillment of Aquinas' desire to find that our truly natural being is the being that we live every day, and that God has not screened our real nature behind some arbitrary barrier."

One reason why the Greeks did not distinguish consciousness as a separate function of the psyche is that their vocabulary, despite its overall richness, did not have a corresponding term. In English, the single word *consciousness* is applied to several different functions:

- *Wakefulness.* The most characteristic feature of consciousness is the state of being awake instead of being asleep. This function depends on physiological processes that are shared by the higher vertebrates, especially mammals.
- *Attention.* Another aspect of consciousness is the ability to focus attention on certain sensory inputs while ignoring others. Selective attention is characteristic of animal perception, even at the level of worms, insects, and Brooks's robots.
- *Mental imagery.* Consciousness also includes the subjective experience of images of the external world, which differ from the imagery of dreams by an accompanying feeling of reality. Perhaps the basis for that difference is not the conscious brain, but the sleeping brain, which shuts down the motor mechanisms in order to prevent dreamers from injuring themselves.
- *Metalevel reasoning.* A fourth aspect of consciousness involves metalevel reasoning about the imagery, about its reality, and about the self who reasons about reasoning. This function, which includes *self-awareness* as a special case, depends more on a logical distinction between language and metalanguage than on the underlying psychology or physiology.

Although Aristotle did not have a single word for consciousness, he did discuss aspects of all these functions. Far from being a hindrance, the lack of a blanket term for consciousness may have saved the Greeks from confusing the different functions.

REACTIVE AGENTS.   The simplest examples of agents include thermostats and alarm clocks, which *react* to stimuli but have no ability to form plans. In his examples, Aristotle said that if an eye were an independent being, its psyche would be the ability to see; if an axe were a living thing, its psyche would be the ability to cut. By the same principle, the psyche of a thermostat would be its ability to maintain the temperature within a narrow range; for an alarm clock, it would be the ability to sound an alarm when a preset time is reached. A thermostat takes nutrition from an electrical source, its perception is based on a thermometer for detecting the temperature of the environment, its desire is derived from a built-in "yearning" or *epithymia* to keep the temperature as close as possible to a preset ideal, and its ability to act is limited to turning the furnace on or off. An alarm clock has a psyche that is about as complex as a thermostat's, but instead of sensing the environment, it checks its own internal clock.

In general, the behavior of a *reactive agent* is defined by a script that determines its next action from its current state, the inputs from its sensors, and a limited amount of memory of past states. The mobile robots that deliver mail and supplies in hospitals and factories are more sophisticated than alarm clocks, but their complexity results from a longer script with more built-in options. Their script determines their "desire" to follow an internal map of the environment and deliver packages to the specified addresses. Programming notations such as Petri nets are commonly used to write such scripts. Figure 5.25 shows a Petri net for simulating the behavior of reactive agents playing the game of Hide and Seek. It was adapted from an example in the *PlayNet* notation designed by Norman Badler, Barry Reich, and Bonnie Weber (1997).

The four tokens at the top left represent four agents who are playing the role of *hiders*, and the token at the top right represents a single *seeker*. The game starts when the seeker enters the transition labeled Start. From there, a token for the seeker goes to the Count transition, while another token to the Gate place enables the hiders to leave the starting place and hide. After counting, the seeker calls out a warning: "Ready or not, here I come." The Warn transition removes the token from the Gate place and blocks any remaining hiders who haven't found a hiding place.

After the warning, the seeker enters a seeking state while the hiders watch. If the seeker isn't looking in their direction, the hiders may enter the Run-home transition. The transition labeled Seen begins a confrontation between the seeker and one of hiders. When it fires, a single token representing the pair of both agents enters the Chase place. The chase ends when either the Evade transition or the Tag transition fires. After Evade, the hider goes to the Safe place, and the seeker goes

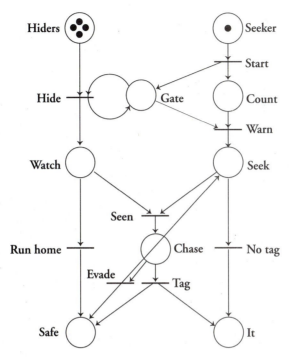

FIGURE 5.25 Petri net for the game of Hide and Seek

back to Seek. After Tag, the seeker goes to the Safe place to play the role of hider in the next game, and the hider goes to the It place to become the next seeker. If none of the hiders are tagged, the seeker goes to the It place and remains the seeker for another game.

Figure 5.25 shows a global view of the states and actions of all five agents. Instead of using a single net for all agents, Badler, Reich, and Weber designed their PlayNets as separate finite-state machines for each agent with the interactions controlled by messages from one net to another. The corresponding PlayNets can be derived by decomposing the global Petri net into separate finite-state machines that pass messages via the Linda operators (as described in Section 4.5 and Exercise 4.12). Figure 5.26 shows a decomposition of Figure 5.25 into separate nets for each player in the game. The seeker would follow the net on the right, and each hider would use a copy of the net on the left. To emphasize the similarities with Figure 5.25, the Petri net notation is also used in Figure 5.26, but these nets are equivalent to finite-state machines, since each net has only one token and every transition has exactly one input and one output.

In Figure 5.25, four transitions depend on inputs from both a hider and a seeker: Hide, Seen, Evade, and Tag. For each of those transitions, there is a pair of

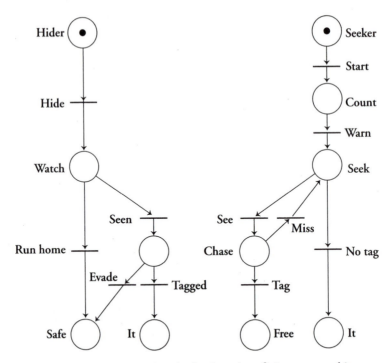

FIGURE 5.26 Decomposing the Petri net into finite-state machines

transitions in Figure 5.26. One member of each pair sends a message, and the other member of the pair must wait until the message is received:

- *Start→Hide.* The Start transition calls the Linda operator Out to send the tuple (hide) to the bulletin board. For each copy of the hider net, the Read operator is called with the pattern (hide). When the BB manager finds a matching tuple, the token at the top can enter the Hide transition. At the Warn transition, the seeker net uses the In operator to remove the (hide) tuple from BB and block any remaining hiders.

- *See→Seen.* When a hider is seen, the seeker enters the See transition, which calls the Out operator to send a tuple of the form (see *name*). In the Watch place, each hider periodically checks BB by calling the InP operator with the pattern (see *name*), where *name* is the hider's own name. If the hider finds that tuple, it enters the Seen transition; otherwise, it may enter the Run-home transition.

- *Evade→Miss.* If a hider that is being chased successfully avoids being tagged, it enters the Evade transition, which calls Out to send the tuple (*name* evaded) to BB. In the Chase place, the seeker periodically calls the InP operator with the pattern (*name* evaded). If it finds that tuple, it enters the Miss transition.

- *Tag→ Tagged.* If the seeker successfully tags the hider during a chase, it sends the tuple (tag *name*). During the chase, the hider periodically calls InP with the pattern (tag *name*). If it finds that tuple, it enters the Tagged transition.

For the interaction between the Start and Hide transitions, the BB place serves the same purpose as the Gate place in Figure 5.25. The other three pairs of transitions were derived by splitting single transitions in the original net. For all four pairs, the receiving net must call a Linda operator to check BB while the token is still in the place immediately before the corresponding transition.

Note the choice of verbs that name the transitions. The names of the sending transitions are active forms of transitive verbs: Start, See, Evade, and Tag. Linguistically, the agents of those transitions are the agents (Agnt) of the concepts represented by the verbs. Two of the receiving transitions are named by passive verb forms (Seen and Tagged) whose agents are affected by the action. The other two are named by intransitive verbs (Hide and Miss) whose agents are involved in intransitive actions that are caused by the sending transitions. This choice of names for the transitions illustrates the close correspondence between linguistic and computational notions of agency. Not all Petri nets have transitions with such a close mapping to natural language verbs, but when such mappings exist, they should not be ignored. They can help guide a knowledge engineer who is analyzing a problem specification or a linguist who is designing a system for talking to or about automated agents.

BELIEFS, DESIRES, AND INTENTIONS.   More sophisticated than reactive agents are *rational agents*, which can plan their own course of action. The philosopher Michael Bratman (1987) distinguished three factors that determine such plans: *beliefs, desires,* and *intentions*. Bratman insisted that all three are essential, and that none of them is reducible to the other two. Peirce would have agreed: the appetitive aspect of desire is a kind of Firstness; belief is a kind of Secondness that relates a proposition to a situation; and intention is a kind of Thirdness that relates an agent, a situation, and the agent's plan for action in the situation. In Aristotle's terms, the plan is determined by a *boulēsis*, which a rational agent, motivated by appetites and passions, derives from its beliefs about the situation.

To formalize Bratman's approach, Philip Cohen and Hector Levesque (1990) extended Kripke's model structures to accommodate beliefs, desires, and intentions (BDI). Instead of the triples of Kripke's models, Cohen and Levesque introduced *octuples* for BDI models:

$$<\Theta, P, E, Agnt, T, B, G, \Phi>.$$

Θ is a set of entities called *things;* P is a set of entities called *people;* E is a set of *event types;* Agnt is a function defined over events, which specifies some entity in P as the *agent* of the event; T is a set of possible worlds or *courses of events,* each of which is a function from a sequence Z of time points to event types in E; $B(w_1, p, t, w_2)$ is a *belief accessibility relation*, which relates a course of events w_1, a person p, and a time point t to some course of events w_2 that is accessible from w_1 according to p's beliefs; $G(w_1, p, t, w_2)$ is a *goal accessibility relation*, which relates a course of events w_1, a person p, and a time point t to some course of events w_2 that is accessible from w_1 according to p's goals; and the BDI Φ is an evaluation function similar to Kripke's Φ.

Although the development of agents for practical applications is a rapidly growing field, much of the elegant theory has had little influence on the practical design of robots and software agents. Quine's criticisms of Kripke's models apply with equal force to the BDI models: they are useful for proving consistency, they show that Bratman's informal discussions can be formalized, but they are not explanations. As with Kripke models, all eight components of the BDI models are undefined sets that are assumed *a priori*, without being computed or observed. In response to such criticisms, Levesque, Reiter, and their colleagues (1996) set out to demonstrate the usefulness of their theory by applying it to robot control. They implemented a Prolog-like language called GOLOG, which maps the abstract symbols to sensors that receive inputs from the external world and to effectors that perform actions upon the world. Other logicians, such as Anand Rao and Michael Georgeff (1993) and Kurt Konolige (1997), have also turned to robotics in order to give their abstract theories some physical embodiment. Meanwhile, computational linguists have been implementing speech systems to map the same abstract symbols to and from natural languages. Besides demonstrating the abstract theories, such tools can improve the interfaces between people and their cars, robots, and other machines.

COMBINING RATIONAL AND REACTIVE TECHNIQUES.   In practical applications, reactive agents that follow fixed scripts are the most commonly used. Some of the scripts are written in conventional programming languages. Other scripts are generated by a human who guides a robot arm through a sequence of actions. Marcel Schoppers (1987) developed a technique for automatically generating *universal plans*, which consist of precompiled reactions to a large number of circumstances a robot might encounter. The precompiled reactions enable the robot to respond instantly in unpredictable environments when long-range deductive planning would be impractical. Matthew Ginsberg (1989a,b) complained that compiling and storing universal plans would take too much time and space to be practical, but Schoppers (1989) replied that they would be effective in many common applications.

Robert Kowalski (1995) showed that logic can be used as a metalanguage to reconcile the controversies over reactive or rational agents. In effect, the first stage of compiling a universal plan is the metalevel, and the plan itself is a collection of object-level rules that are applied when their preconditions arise. Logic could be used for both stages: compiling the rules and applying them. The metalevel could be computed in advance, as in universal planning, or it could computed "just in time" to generate object-level rules immediately before they are used. Schoppers suggested that rules compiled just in time could also be saved in a cache for later reuse. When faced with a novel situation, a robot might take some time to "stop and think"; but if a similar situation occurred later, the cached rules could be used immediately.

Metalevel reasoning can also be used to analyze, model, or implement the competence levels for Rodney Brooks's robots. The lower levels may be controlled by precompiled reactive rules. Each higher level is a metalevel, which can monitor the levels beneath it, interrupt them, override them, or even reprogram them. The highest levels can support rational planning for generating new rules or metalanguage for asking and telling other agents about likely plans and rules. Meanwhile, the lowest levels would behave like conditioned reflexes in responding to stimuli, unless overruled by one of the higher levels. The stratified metalevels discussed in Section 5.5 provide a framework that can integrate stimulus-response reactions at the lower levels with conscious planning and reflection at the higher levels.

EXERCISES

1. The go position in Figure 5.1 was reached at move 53 of a famous game between the master Karigane (Black) and the champion Honinbo Shusai (White). After 287 moves, White won with four more points of territory than Black. The go-moku game, however, is nearly finished. From the brief summary of go-moku in the discussion, it is possible to determine which player has the next move in Figure 5.1. Which player has a winning strategy? What is it?

2. Translate the next two sentences to conceptual graphs:

   a. *Two chickens are in a coop.*

   b. *One chicken pecked the other chicken.*

   For sentence a, represent the plural referent by {*}@2. For b, represent the past tense by the relation Past attached to the concept for the verb, the word *one* by an indexical #one in the referent of a concept, and the phrase *the other* by an indexical #other.

3. If sentences a and b in the previous exercise were contiguous sentences in the same paragraph, they might be assumed to represent information about the same situation. Resolve the indexicals in the following steps:

   a. Assume that both chickens are in the same coop collectively. Therefore, the referent of the chicken concept could be represented by Col{*}@2. Study the example of Alma's husbands in Section 4.1, and use the same method for expanding the concept to a separate concept for each chicken.

b. To resolve the indexical #one, draw a coreference link to one of the chicken concepts and then erase the indexical #one.

c. To resolve #other, draw a coreference link to a concept of a chicken other than the one selected in part b and then erase #other.

d. Finally, translate the resulting CG to predicate calculus.

4. After resolving the indexicals in the previous exercise, review the donkey and horse examples in Section 5.2. Then translate the following sentence to a conceptual graph: *Every chicken coop has a chicken that is pecked by every other chicken in the coop.* Represent the first *every* by $\forall$ in a concept whose type is a lambda expression, represent *every other* by the combination $\forall$#other, and represent the last *the* by #.

5. For the CG derived in the previous exercise, expand the two $\forall$ quantifiers to the if-then form. To expand $\forall$#other, treat the combination in the same way as the single $\forall$ quantifier; but in the final step, erase only $\forall$, leaving #other in the referent field. Finally, resolve all the indexicals to coreference labels and translate the result to predicate calculus.

6. Give more examples of sentences with indexicals that have about the same level of complexity as the sentences about the donkeys and the chickens. Select sentences from various domains. The sentence about chickens in a coop, for example, could be mapped to one about workers in an office: *Every department has a secretary who is given assignments by every other member of the department.* Represent the sentences in conceptual graphs with indexicals, resolve the indexicals to coreference links or coreference labels, and translate the result to predicate calculus.

7. Hans Reichenbach (1947) defined a concise notation for linguistic tenses in terms of three time points: the *speech time* S, the *event time* E, and a *reference time* R. For the default present tense, which is represented by a CG context with no tense marker, all three time points coincide: $S=E=R$. For the past tense relation (Past), which was defined in Section 4.1, E and R coincide and precede S: $E=R<S$. For the past perfect tense (PPrf), the specification $E<R<S$ maps to the following CG definition:

```
PPrf = [Time: #now *s]←(Succ)←[Time: *r]-
       (Succ)←[Time: *e]←(PTim)←[Situation: λ].
```

Use the definitions of the Past and PPrf relations to translate the following sentence to a conceptual graph: *The mouse ate the cheese after the cat had left.*

a. Translate the two clauses *the mouse ate the cheese* and *the cat had left* to two contexts of type Situation, each of which has a nested CG and an attached relation of type Past or PPrf.

b. Define a dyadic conceptual relation (Aftr), which links a situation at some point in time that is a successor of the point in time of another situation. Then use the Aftr relation to link the situations for the two clauses of the sentence.

c. Expand the CG by replacing the relations Past, PPrf, and Aftr with their definitions.

d. State reasonable assumptions about conversational implicatures that can be used to relate the various concepts of type Time in the resulting CG. Use those assumptions to simplify the CG by joining coreferent concepts that appear in the same context.

Next, define a dyadic conceptual relation (Bfor) as the inverse of (Aftr), define the future perfect relation (FPrf) according to the specification $S<E<R$, and use these two relations to represent the sentence *The mouse will have eaten the cheese before the cat returns*. Finally, expand the defined relations, and simplify the resulting CG.

8. The meaning-preserving function f_2, which was defined in Section 5.3, causes the following two formulas to be placed in the same equivalence class:

$$((p \supset r) \wedge (q \supset s)) \supset ((p \wedge q) \supset (r \wedge s)).$$
$$\sim((\sim(p \wedge \sim r) \wedge \sim(q \wedge \sim s)) \wedge \sim(\sim(p \wedge q) \wedge \sim(r \wedge s))).$$

Give some other examples of the 864 formulas in the equivalence class determined by f_2. Show how the number 864 was derived.

9. Find some examples of sentences that use the modal words *can* or *must* to express possibility or necessity. For each sentence, state the axiom, law, rule, principle, or convention that determines what is possible or necessary. The governing rule is often highly context dependent: if someone says "You can't park here," the reason may be physical (the space is too small), legal (the town ordinance prohibits it), or personal ("I saw it first."). If the same sentence may be used in several widely different contexts, give a brief explanation of each.

10. There is a common superstition about hope and fear: if you hope something will happen and you mention it, then it won't become true; but if you fear something will happen and you mention it, then it will become true. State that superstition in predicate calculus, using the predicates hope(a,p) and fear(a,p) from Section 5.3 and two new predicates, mention(a,p) and becomeTrue(p).

11. The protoIndoEuropean word *arktos* (bear) survived in Greek and in a related form *ursus* in Latin, but it has been replaced by words derived from *brown* in the Germanic languages and by words like *m'edv'ed'* (honey-knower) in Russian and other Slavic languages. What superstition related to the one about hope and fear might explain that fact? State it in predicate calculus.

12. Different interpretations of the superstition about hope and fear might be translated to different formulas in predicate calculus. Find an interpretation that would imply a contradiction if a person who was ambivalent about a proposition p happened to mention p. Assuming that $\sim$becomeTrue(p) is not equivalent to becomeTrue$(\sim p)$, revise that formula to avoid the contradiction. Give a proof that the first version would lead to a contradiction and that the second would not. Then write an English explanation of the contradiction and its resolution that would be intelligible to someone who had no knowledge of symbolic logic. Ask one of your nonmathematical friends to read and comment on your explanation.

13. Study the examples of situations defined by fictional stories, historical periods, and actual space-time coordinates. Give some pairs of a "meaningful" situation and a related one that is as disjointed as the examples by William James. For each pair, state some property that distinguishes the meaningful situation from its disjointed relative. Identify some agent, human or otherwise, for whom that property is significant.

14. Rudolf Carnap (1947) defined a proposition as an equivalence class of sentences that can be proved to be logically equivalent to one another. Richard Montague (1974) defined a proposition p as a function from possible worlds to truth values: for each world w, $p(w) = T$ if p makes a true statement about w; and $p(w) = F$ if p is false about w. Compare these two definitions to each other and to the definition in Section 5.3 in terms of meaning-preserving functions. Which definitions generate the same equivalence classes? Which definitions have the most or fewest equivalence classes? Which definitions are the most or least efficient to compute? Give some examples that illustrate the differences.

15. Quine (1960) formulated a controversial hypothesis about the "indeterminacy of translation" that has not been definitively confirmed or rejected by empirical studies of actual languages:

> The thesis is this: manuals for translating one language into another can be set up in divergent ways, all compatible with the totality of speech dispositions, yet incompatible with one another. In countless places, they will diverge in giving, as their respective translations of a sentence of the

one language, sentences of the other language which stand to each other in no plausible sort of equivalence however loose.

To illustrate his thesis, Quine gave several examples:

a. A manual might translate English *rabbit* to *gavagai* in language $\mathcal{L}$. Yet the native speakers of $\mathcal{L}$ might intend *gavagai* to mean "undetached rabbit parts" and no evidence could ever be found to distinguish their intended meaning from the English meaning of *rabbit*.

b. The sentence *Neutrinos have no mass* has no unique translation into a language that lacks the concepts of modern physics (including the English language of Shakespeare's time). At best, the sentence would have to be expressed by a lengthy paraphrase, and different manuals might give different and incompatible paraphrases.

Is Quine's thesis compatible with the definition of propositions in terms of meaning-preserving functions? If not, show the incompatibility. Otherwise, restate Quine's thesis in terms of propositions defined by meaning-preserving functions. What kind of evidence from exotic languages might count for or against Quine's thesis or your restatement of it?

16. Section 2.2 illustrated the problems of translating Aristotle's Greek terms to English; one of the most difficult words to translate is *logos*. The word *psychē*, which was discussed in Section 5.7, has no suitable English translation, since the common word *soul* distorts Aristotle's meaning. Do these examples support Quine's thesis of the indeterminacy of translation? Why or why not?

17. Study the proof of the Praeclarum Theorema in Figure 5.14 and the corresponding proof in algebraic notation. Verify that each formula in the algebraic proof is equivalent to the corresponding EG in Figure 5.14. Then choose some other notation for logic, such as conceptual graphs, discourse representation structures, or KIF. Restate Peirce's rules of inference for the notation you have chosen, and show that they support a proof with the same steps as the proof in Figure 5.14.

18. For the following pairs of formulas, check whether generalized *modus ponens* can be used to derive the second formula from the first. If GMP does not apply, explain why not, and determine whether the second formula follows from the first by some other rule discussed in Section 5.4.

a. Following are two steps at the end of an alternate proof of the Praeclarum Theorema:

$((p \supset r) \land (q \supset s)) \supset ((p \land q) \supset T)$.
$((p \supset r) \land (q \supset s)) \supset ((p \land q) \supset (r \land s))$.

b. For the next two formulas, assume that p is a specialization of q (i.e., $p \vdash q$).

$(s \wedge \sim(t \vee u) \wedge \sim(v \wedge (q \supset r) \wedge (t \vee (k \wedge p \wedge (l \vee (m \wedge n))))))$.
$(s \wedge \sim(t \vee u) \wedge \sim(v \wedge (q \supset r) \wedge (t \vee (k \wedge p \wedge (l \vee (m \wedge n \wedge r))))))$.

c. Assume $p \vdash q$:

$(p \wedge (q \supset r)) \supset m$.
$(p \wedge (q \supset r)) \supset (m \wedge r)$.

d. Assume $p \vdash q$:

$(p \vee (q \supset r)) \supset m$.
$(p \vee (q \supset r)) \supset (m \wedge r)$.

Whether one context is nested inside another is determined by their representation in Peirce Normal Form. In case of doubt, expand one or more of the operators to definitions in terms of $\wedge$ and $\sim$.

19. Following are some formulas that occur in a positive context $\mathcal{D}$:

$(p \wedge q) \supset (r \wedge (s \supset t))$.
$(u \wedge r) \equiv ((p \wedge \sim w) \equiv (\sim v \wedge s))$.
$q \wedge u \wedge \sim v$.

Show how the following formulas may be derived in $\mathcal{D}$ by one or more inference rules, including at least one application of the rule of qualified export.

a. $p \supset r$.

b. $(p \wedge s) \supset t$.

c. $(r \wedge s) \supset p$.

Estimate the amount of computation needed to verify these formulas by truth tables.

20. In the discussion of metalevels in Section 5.5, the statement "This sentence is false" was cited as an example of a paradox that could be resolved by a nonparadoxical statement such as "The statement I just made was false." What features make the first sentence paradoxical and the second acceptable? Is it a coincidence that both of those sentences contain indexical terms such as *this* and *I*? Tenses also have an indexical effect; is it coincidental that the first is in the present tense and the second is in the past tense? If natural languages use the same vocabulary at every metalevel, how can words like *true* and *false* be used in nonparadoxical ways to refer to truth values at multiple levels?

21. In Section 5.5, the laws that determine Peirce's five kinds of modality were defined in terms of a triadic predicate legislate$(a, p, \mathscr{C})$, where a is an animate agent. That approach leads to the assumption of God as the lawgiver for the laws of nature. Some philosophies avoid the assumption of a personal God by introducing an impersonal logos or Tao. With such a metaphysics, the laws that determine the modal operators $\Box$ and $\Diamond$ could be given by a monadic function $logos(x)$, where x is some appropriately chosen entity. For each of the five kinds of modality, how would x be chosen? For each of those entities, what kind of laws are determined by $logos(x)$?

22. Study the example of the StartEngine process (Section 5.6), which was represented in conceptual graphs. List the sequence of operations that are carried out in that process and represent them in a Petri net, according to the correspondences between Petri nets and logic that are presented in Chapter 4.

23. Compare Aristotle's functions of the psyche, as discussed in Section 5.7, with Rodney Brooks's competence levels for mobile robots, as discussed in Section 3.6. How can an analysis of nutrition and desire help to refine the competence levels? How can Peirce's categories help to analyze, refine, and classify the levels? Can such analysis resolve or at least clarify the controversies about artificial intelligence and the question of whether anything computer systems can do might be comparable with human or animal intelligence?

24. After a process specified by a Petri net has finished, some tokens may be left in one or more places. Sometimes those tokens are intended to remain in those places, but often, they represent bugs or unusual conditions that had not been accommodated by the design. In Figure 5.25, the presence of a token in the Gate place allows the hiders to hide. But when that token is removed by the Warn transition, tokens that may be left in the Hide place cannot leave. Add more detail to the rules of the game to specify what should happen to the remaining hiders. One possibility is that a hider who has not found a hiding place automatically becomes "It" for the next game. Another possibility is that the seeker immediately starts to chase hiders who have not been able to hide. A third possibility is that a hider who has not yet found a hiding place can request more time. Show how the Petri net can be revised for each of these rule changes.

25. In Figure 5.26, a hider who reads a tuple of the form (see *name*), where *name* matches the hider's own name, goes to the transition labeled Seen. No explicit conditions determine when a hider might enter the Run-Home transition. Without modifying Figure 5.26, show how a revised choice of Linda operators could be used to control the actions in more detail: a hider might run home while the seeker was chasing some other hider; a seeker who missed the current hider would try to stop other hiders from running home; and a seeker who failed to tag anyone might give up the search by sending a message that everyone could run home free. Specify the places or transitions where the

messages would be sent or received, and show the formats of the pattern and data tuples.

26. Write axioms for the game of Hide and Seek based on the Petri nets of Figures 5.25 and 5.26. For each transition, write an axiom for the preconditions and the postconditions. Your axioms should be consistent with the mapping from Petri nets to logic in Chapter 4, but the predicates may have names that correspond more directly to the terms that describe the game. For each axiom, write a sentence in stylized English that uses the same variable names but would be readable by someone who is not familiar with symbolic logic. The list of all the sentences in stylized English should form a readable description of the complete set of rules for Hide and Seek while remaining as close as possible to the axioms. If you feel that more detail should be added to the stylized English in order to make it more complete or readable, add the same detail to the axioms so that the stylized English sentences remain faithful translations of the statements in logic.

27. After writing the axioms of Hide and Seek for the previous exercise, use those axioms as the specifications for writing a program that simulates several agents playing the game of Hide and Seek. A logic-based language like Prolog or a rule-based language like CLIPS should support a more direct translation of the axioms than a procedural language, but you may use any language you prefer. The graphics and multithreading features would make Java a good language to use for displaying the actions of each agent during the course of the game. In whatever language you choose, include the stylized English versions of your axioms as comments in the program. Try to keep the structure of your programs as close as possible to the original Petri nets and axioms. If the nature of the programming language causes you to modify or deviate from the original axioms, include comments in the program to explain the deviations.

This exercise could be done as a class project, with different students or groups of students using different languages. The various groups could make interim presentations of their progress to the class. After the first stage of the project, all the groups should agree on a common set of axioms. The groups should be encouraged to borrow ideas from each other in order to improve their programs while keeping them faithful to the original axioms. Compare the different languages on various criteria, such as ease of programming, ease of maintenance and modification, and ease of implementing various features of the game.

28. The following legal case was reported at a meeting of the American Association for Forensic Science by AAFS President Don Harper Mills:

On 23 March 1994, Ronald Opus, who had been acting despondent, wrote a suicide note and jumped from the roof of a ten-story building. Before jumping, Opus could not see that a safety net had been set at the eighth-floor level to protect some window washers. But as he fell past the ninth floor, he was hit by a shotgun blast from an open window. The medical examiner found that the net would have prevented the suicide and that Opus had died of a shotgun wound to the head. Therefore, Opus's death appeared to be a homicide rather than a suicide.

If an agent x intends to kill y, but kills z in the attempt, x is guilty of the murder of z. In this case, the person who fired the shotgun was an elderly man who lived with his wife on the ninth floor. The man admitted that he had threatened his wife with the shotgun, but he never intended to kill her, since the gun had been kept unloaded. But this time, the gun happened to be loaded, the shot missed his wife, and Opus was killed. Both the man and his wife claimed that Opus's death was an accident.

During the investigation, additional facts emerged: the old lady had cut off her son's financial support; and a witness claimed to have seen the son loading the shotgun. Apparently the son had expected to get revenge by causing his father to kill his mother during one of their frequent arguments. Therefore, the son's intentions made him responsible for the death of Ronald Opus. The medical examiner, however, discovered a crucial fact that led him to conclude the death was a suicide.

Translate this report to logic, and deduce the crucial fact.

29. In the previous exercise, the medical examiner's conclusion depends on the definition of *suicide*. Show that that conclusion follows from the definition of suicide as self-murder. Give another definition that would imply that Ronald Opus is guilty of self-murder, but not of suicide. Which definition seems closer to the informal intuitions?

30. Legal reasoning involves three kinds of tasks: representation of the laws themselves; representation of the background knowledge about the subject to which the laws are applied; and the logical inferences that lead to a conclusion. Of the three, the most difficult is usually the analysis and representation of the open-ended amount of background knowledge. For the exercise about Ronald Opus (5.28), make a list (in English) of all the background knowledge a computer would need to understand the case, such as information about falling bodies, safety nets, and the multiple word senses of *floor* and *story*.

Knowledge Soup

Human knowledge is a process of approximation. In the focus of experience, there is comparative clarity. But the discrimination of this clarity leads into the penumbral background. There are always questions left over. The problem is to discriminate exactly what we know vaguely.

ALFRED NORTH WHITEHEAD, *Essays in Science and Philosophy*

I've often said that every poem solves something for me in life. I go so far as to say that every poem is a momentary stay against the confusion of the world. . . . We rise out of disorder into order. And the poems I make are little bits of order.

ROBERT FROST, *A Lover's Quarrel with the World*

Get rid, thoughtful Reader, of the Okhamistic prejudice of political partisanship that in thought, in being, and in development the indefinite is due to a degeneration from a primal state of perfect definiteness. The truth is rather on the side of the Scholastic realists that the unsettled is the primal state, and that definiteness and determinateness, the two poles of settledness, are, in the large, approximations, developmentally, epistemologically, and metaphysically.

CHARLES SANDERS PEIRCE, *Collected Papers* 6.348

6.1 Vagueness, Uncertainty, Randomness, and Ignorance

Some of the knowledge in people's heads may be represented in propositions, more of it in imagelike forms, and the rest of it in habits, vague intuitions, and "gut feelings" that are never verbalized or visualized. Whatever its form, the knowledge is far too complex and disorganized to be called a knowledge base. Its fluid, heterogeneous, ever changing, and often inconsistent nature could be better characterized as *knowledge soup*. The soup may contain many small chunks, corresponding to the typical frames, rules, and facts in AI systems; it may also contain large chunks that correspond to entire theories. The chunks should be internally consistent, but they may be inconsistent with one another. The inconsistencies arise from various sources:

- Generalizations that omit "obvious" assumptions: Birds fly. But what about penguins? a day-old chick? a bird with a broken wing? a stuffed bird? a sleeping bird?

- Abnormal conditions: If you have a car, you can drive from New York to Boston. But what if the battery is dead? Your license has expired? There is a major snowstorm?

- Incomplete definitions: An oil well is a hole drilled in the ground that produces oil. But what about a dry hole? a hole that has been capped? a hole that formerly produced oil? Are three holes linked to a single pipe one oil well or three?

- Conflicting defaults: Quakers are usually pacifists, and Republicans are not. But what about Richard Nixon, who was both a Quaker and a Republican? Would he or wouldn't he be a pacifist?

- Unanticipated applications: The parts of the human body are described in anatomy books. But is hair a part of the body? hair implants? a wig? a wig made from a person's own hair? a hair in a braid that has broken off from its root? fingernails? plastic fingernail extenders? a skin graft? artificial skin used for emergency patches? a bandage? a bone implant? an artificial implant in a bone? a heart transplant? an artificial heart? an artificial leg? teeth? fillings in the teeth? a porcelain crown? false teeth? braces? a corneal transplant? contact lenses? eyeglasses? a tattoo? make-up? clothes?

Since these inconsistencies are most apparent in ordinary speech, many people assume that they are merely linguistic problems that would not occur in a purified language like logic. Yet that assumption is wrong. All of those problems are caused by the complexity of the world itself. A logical predicate like bodyPart(x) would solve nothing; the intermediate cases of hair and fingernails would raise the same questions of truth and falsity as the English noun phrase *body part*.

The knowledge soup has a loose organization characterized by the "disorder" and the "leftover questions" discussed by the mathematician, logician, and philosopher Alfred North Whitehead and the poet Robert Frost. Whitehead said that the problem is to "discriminate exactly what we know vaguely," and Frost said that the task is to make "little bits of order" that organize, interpret, and give meaning to the disorder. For both of them, language is a tool for discriminating and creating structure out of the primordial knowledge soup. That structure is essential for precise reasoning, and any reasoning system — human or artificial — must either find structure in the soup or create structure that can provide, in Peirce's terms, "a solid foundation for great and weighty thought."

MULTIPLE USES OF THE SAME WORDS. Much of the vagueness and ambiguity results from the use and reuse of the same words in different domains and applications. Figure 6.1 illustrates nine different kinds of things to which the word *chair* might be applied. On the right are five questions about different characteristics of chairs. The only common characteristics are a backrest and a platform wide enough to sit on. Those are the *necessary conditions* for something to be a chair, but they are not sufficient to exclude all nonchairs. The toilet shown at the bottom of Figure 6.1 has those features, but it is not usually called a chair. An even more extreme example is a stairway, whose steps would be wide enough to sit on and whose risers could be used as a backrest. Yet a stairway is much less chairlike than a toilet. As Wittgenstein said, the common concepts of ordinary life can only be characterized by a loose set of family resemblances, not by a definitive set of necessary and sufficient conditions.

Another word with multiple meanings is *wall,* which may be defined as a vertical surface used as a *boundary* of a room or as a *separator* between rooms. The genus or supertype is VerticalSurface, which is a necessary condition for something to be a wall. But the alternatives in the definition indicate two distinct subtypes: Wall₁ is a vertical boundary, and Wall₂ is a vertical separator. For some applications, the two subtypes are compatible, since the same structure could be used as both a boundary and a separator at the same time. But for other applications, the two meanings may be in conflict. An interior decorator may think of the two sides of a wall as distinct surfaces, each of which is the boundary Wall₁ of a distinct room. In that sense, each surface is part of a different room, whose color and texture must match the furnishings of its room. A construction contractor, however, may think of a wall as a separator Wall₂, which divides a space into two rooms without being part of either one. Conflicts may arise if the tenants of adjoining apartments want to make incompatible modifications of "their" walls.

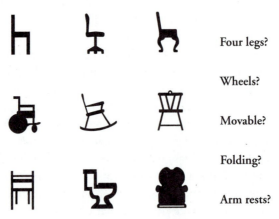

Four legs?

Wheels?

Movable?

Folding?

Arm rests?

FIGURE 6.1 What criteria distinguish chairs from nonchairs?

Whenever disputes arise, philosophers since Socrates have resolved them by drawing distinctions. Perhaps the wall is a composite structure with Sheetrock on each surface and a wooden frame in the middle. Therefore, the wooden frame could be treated as a separator Wall₂ outside of either room, but each surface could be considered as a boundary Wall₁, which would be part of the room it faces. Yet that distinction depends on the method of construction. If the wall consists of a single layer of bricks, there would be no clear way of distinguishing the boundaries from the separator. Problems like these do not arise from the nature of language, but from the nature of the world: there are more methods of constructing walls than there are distinct words for them in the English language. Such difficulties, which can be illustrated with simple things like chairs and walls, become even more acute with complex things like automobiles. At the beginning of the twentieth century, the word *automobile* was the equivalent of the term *horseless carriage*. Those automobiles looked like carriages, most of their parts were interchangeable with carriages, and they even had attachments for hitching a horse in case of a breakdown. But today the computerized metal cabins that are still called automobiles have little similarity to the original horseless carriages. Changes in the world cause changes in the meanings of words.

For database and knowledge-base design, ever-changing applications require multiple, often conflicting definitions of the same terms. Consider expert systems designed to assist automobile drivers, airplane pilots, ship captains, and locomotive engineers. Those applications share many common terms, such as *time, speed, distance, fuel consumption, equipment condition,* and *passenger safety.* Yet the details of the applications are so radically different that the definitions of those terms have little in common. A major difference is the number of degrees of freedom in the motion:

- Rigid tracks confine a train's motion to one dimension.
- At a gross level, a car's motion is also one dimensional, but at a detailed level, the driver must maneuver in two dimensions to keep the car in lane and avoid other cars and obstacles.
- A ship's motion is also two dimensional, but its greater inertia causes a change in course to take minutes instead of the split-second maneuvers that are possible with a car.
- An airplane moves in three dimensions, but changes in attitude introduce three more degrees of freedom.

Besides differences in motion, there are different kinds of signals to consider and different ways of planning a course and following it. As a result, a driver, a pilot, a captain, and an engineer have totally different ways of thinking and reacting. A person who is both a driver and a pilot would have two independent modes of thought with little or nothing in common. Expert systems designed for each of these tasks would have few, if any, common concepts and rules.

VAGUENESS IN SCIENTIFIC LANGUAGE.   Frege and Russell hoped that the vagueness of ordinary language would not infect the purified technical language of science. Yet even in computer science, where ambiguities can be disastrous, the most central and important terms have slightly different meanings in different applications. Consider the term *assignment statement* in different programming languages. The following statements are supposed to add A to B and assign the result to X:

```
APL:        X ← A + B
C:          X = A + B;
FORTRAN:    X = A + B
Pascal:     X := A + B;
PL/I:       X = A + B;
```

On the surface, these statements seem to perform equivalent operations, but with minor differences in notation. If A, B, and X are numbers of the same type, the results would be the same in each of the languages. But major differences arise when the data types are different. The C language does not do automatic type conversions. FORTRAN and PL/I do type conversions to or from integer and floating-point, but Pascal only does automatic conversion from integer to floating and would generate an error message if A+B happened to be a floating-point number and X were an integer. APL also does automatic conversions in evaluating A+B; but in doing the assignment, it could change the type of X instead of converting the result of A+B to X's previous type. PL/I does many other kinds of automatic conversions and would even convert character strings to and from numbers. APL and PL/I both allow A, B, and X to be arrays as well as simple scalars; but PL/I places more restrictions on the dimensions of the arrays, while APL has fewer restrictions. Because of these differences, terms like *addition* or *assignment statement* can be given a precise definition only for a single programming language. In some cases, the language standards are so loose that the definition may change with every compiler or even every modification of a compiler. With technical terms, as with common terms, changes in the world cause changes in meaning.

Seemingly insignificant differences, mentioned only in footnotes in the language manuals, are the bane of system programmers who have to develop software that runs on more than one operating system or even a new version of the same operating system. The following joke characterizes the notorious difficulty of keeping definitions consistent from one version to the next:

Q: *How was God able to create the world in just six days?*
A: *He had no installed user base.*

The millions of installed copies of a computer system impose stringent constraints on the definitions of every function and datatype. When designing a new system, it is usually easier to start from scratch, as God did, and ignore the old definitions. As a result, every word that is used to describe both the old system and the new one acquires another layer of ambiguity.

PARADOX OF THE HEAP. Continuity gives rise to a gradually shifting vagueness that is related to, but not quite the same as the vagueness that varies by discrete jumps when the same word is applied to different domains. One of the oldest problems of continuity is the paradox of the *heap*: One grain of sand does not form a heap; neither do two grains, five grains, or ten grains. In general, if *n* grains of sand do not form a heap, then neither do *n*+1 grains. By the axiom of mathematical induction, it should not be possible to form a heap by adding one grain of sand at a time. This paradox arises in many different variations: One farmer found that he could easily lift a newly born calf. Each day, the calf grew slightly heavier, but if the farmer could lift the calf one day, he should still be able to lift it the next day. By lifting the calf every day, the farmer thought that he would eventually become strong enough to lift a fully grown cow. Such paradoxes, which are caused by the vague boundaries of words like *heap* and *heavy*, arise in every domain where discrete words are applied to a continuous spectrum or range of gradations: color, weight, length, happiness, warmth, humidity, noise, pain, sweetness, and wealth.

LIQUIDS. Fluids like gases and liquids have no fixed shape, and they can be subdivided far beyond the limits of human perception. In developing an ontology for liquids, Patrick Hayes (1985) analyzed the problems of representing, referring to, and talking about liquids in their various forms. He classified the informal ways of talking about liquids according to three distinctions, two of which are further subdivided:

1. Bulk or divided.
2. Still or moving.
   - If moving, either slow or fast.
3. Supported or unsupported.
   - If supported, either by a two-dimensional surface or by a three-dimensional shape.

These features can be combined to generate 2×3×3 or 18 subcategories. Following is a list of the possible combinations and a typical example of each:

1. Bulk, still, supported on a surface: *a wet surface or film of liquid.*
2. Bulk, still, supported by a shape: *a body of liquid in a container.*

3. Bulk, still, unsupported: *a blob of liquid floating weightless in a spacecraft.*

4. Bulk, moving slow, on a surface: *a sheet of rain flowing along a sloping roof.*

5. Bulk, moving fast, on a surface: *waves lapping on a shore or a stream hitting a surface.*

6. Bulk, moving slow, supported by a shape: *liquid flowing in a channel, as a river or an aqueduct.*

7. Bulk, moving fast, supported by a shape: *liquid pumped along a pipeline.*

8. Bulk, moving slow, unsupported: *a falling column, as a waterfall or a stream poured from a jug.*

9. Bulk, moving fast, unsupported: *a waterspout, fountain, or jet from a fire hose.*

10. Divided, still, on a surface: *dew on grass or condensation on a window.*

11. Divided, moving slow, on a surface: *condensed droplets flowing down a cold glass.*

12. Divided, moving fast, on a surface: *raindrops driven along the windshield of a moving car.*

13. Divided, still, supported by a shape: *mist filling a valley.*

14. Divided, moving slow, supported by a shape: *mist flowing down a valley.*

15. Divided, moving fast, supported by a shape: *mist blown along a tube.*

16. Divided, still, unsupported: *mist or cloud.*

17. Divided, moving slow, unsupported: *rain or shower.*

18. Divided, moving fast, unsupported: *spray, splash, or driving rain.*

This list shows how the selection of words in a language forces continuous phenomena into a limited number of describable states. In the world itself, there are continuous gradations of droplet size and speed of flow. Three-dimensional shapes allow an unlimited range of variations: networks of pipes and conduits, bottles of various shapes and sizes, natural boundaries like river and ocean bottoms, or fanciful shapes like a milk pitcher in the form of a cow. No finite set of categories can cover all the possibilities.

MULTIPLE PERSPECTIVES. Some apparent inconsistencies result from different perspectives or views of the same phenomena. Figure 6.2 shows three different views of the same object. When viewed end on, it looks like a circle; when viewed from the side, it looks like a square; and when viewed from an angle, it can be seen as a cylinder. A superficial comparison of only the right and left views might suggest an inconsistency, since no figure drawn on a plane can be both round and square at the same time. But when the object is considered three dimensional, the inconsistency vanishes, since its projections into different planes can be very different.

The apparent inconsistencies that arise with geometrical figures become even

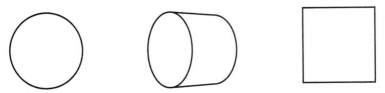

FIGURE 6.2 Three views of an object that is both round and square

more complex and pervasive with abstract ideas and modes of thought in different cultures. The anthropologist Clifford Geertz (1983) observed that cultural differences may be created as much by vocational specialization as by geographical distance:

> The problem of how a Copernican understands a Ptolemaian, a fifth republic Frenchman an *ancien régime* one, or a poet a painter is seen to be on all fours with the problem of how a Christian understands a Muslim, a European an Asian, an anthropologist an aborigine, or vice versa. We are all natives now, and everybody else not immediately one of us is an exotic. What looked once to be a matter of finding out whether savages could distinguish fact from fancy now looks to be a matter of finding out how others, across the sea or down the corridor, organize their significative world. (p. 151)

In knowledge engineering as in anthropology, the most fundamental assumptions are usually left unsaid. When asked about them, the expert tends to say, "Oh, but that's obvious! Of course! You mean you didn't know that!?!" The knowledge engineer or the anthropologist may have to spend days, weeks, or even years asking probing questions to dig out the underlying assumptions. Some experts may be highly articulate, but others may have a limited ability to express the distinctions verbally. Following is an excerpt from a dialog between a knowledge engineer and an expert repairman:

> Knowledge engineer: *I'm not sure what you want the system to do — determine whether a malfunction has occurred, determine what caused it, or determine what action to take in order to correct it.*
> Repairman: *What's the difference?*

The expert was highly skilled in fixing the device, but he had never analyzed his actions verbally or even thought of them as separate stages. But the knowledge engineer must do that analysis in order to design an expert system that performs a similar function. If the analysis is incomplete or inaccurate, the resulting system may contain arbitrary restrictions, inconsistent data, or limitations that make future extensions impossible.

INTENTIONAL GRANULARITY. Every branch of science and engineering uses models that enhance certain features and ignore others. For calculating the orbit of a satellite, relativity and quantum mechanics are ignored; the influences of the earth, moon, and sun are significant, but the other planets and asteroids may be ignored. In thermodynamics, individual molecules are ignored, and temperature, pressure, entropy, and other quantities depend on averages of sextillions of molecules. In fluid mechanics, the equations are so difficult to evaluate that every application requires major simplifications. For most subsonic flows, even air is treated as an incompressible fluid.

Science is a loose collection of subfields, each focused on a narrow range of phenomena. But the high degree of specialization causes details outside the primary focus of attention to be ignored, simplified, or approximated. In every subfield, problem solving requires abstractions that select relevant knowledge and approximate irregular features by simpler structures. Reasoning only becomes precise, formal, and deductive after the intractable details have been thrown away: a boulder tumbling down a mountainside may be modeled as a sphere rolling down a cone. But sometimes the seemingly irrelevant details may suddenly become significant. In the early days of aerodynamics, one mathematician "proved" that it was impossible for anything to travel faster than the speed of sound. Unfortunately, the proof depended on someone else's simplified equations for velocities that were much less than the speed of sound.

6.2 Limitations of Logic

In developing formal logic, Aristotle took Greek mathematics as his model. Like his predecessors Socrates and Plato, Aristotle was impressed with the rigor and precision of geometrical proofs. His goal was to formalize and generalize those proof procedures and apply them to philosophy, science, and all other branches of knowledge. Yet not all subjects are equally amenable to formalization. Greek mathematics achieved its greatest successes in astronomy, where Ptolemy's calculations remained the standard of precision for centuries. But other subjects, such as medicine and law, depend more on deep experience than on brilliant mathematical calculations. Significantly, two of the most penetrating criticisms of logic were written by the physician Sextus Empiricus in the second century A.D. and by the legal scholar Ibn Taymiyya in the fourteenth century.

Sextus Empiricus, as his nickname suggests, was an empiricist. By profession, he was a physician; philosophically, he was an adherent of the school known as the Skeptics. Sextus maintained that all knowledge must come from experience; his epithet *Empiricus* comes from the Greek *empeirikos* (experienced), which is derived from *en* (in) and *peiran* (try or attempt). In propounding his views, he wrote several polemics entitled *Against the Philosophers, Against the Physicians,* and *Against the Logicians.* As an example, he cited the following syllogism:

Every human is an animal.
Socrates is human.
Therefore, Socrates is an animal.

Sextus questioned the source of evidence for the major premise *Every human is an animal.* A universal proposition that purports to cover every instance of some category must be derived by induction from particulars. If the induction is incomplete, then the universal proposition is not certain, and there might be some human who is not an animal. But if the induction is complete, then the particular instance Socrates must have been examimed already, and the syllogism is redundant or circular. Every one of Aristotle's valid forms of syllogisms contains at least one universal affirmative or universal negative premise. Therefore, the same criticisms apply to all of them: the conclusion must be either uncertain or circular.

The Aristotelians answered Sextus by claiming that universal propositions could be true by definition: since the type Human is defined as rational animal, the essence of human includes animal; therefore, no instance of human that was not an animal could exist. This line of defense was attacked by the Islamic jurist and legal scholar Taqi al-Din Ibn Taymiyya. Like Sextus, Ibn Taymiyya agreed that the form of a syllogism is valid, but he did not accept Aristotle's distinction between essence and accident (Hallaq 1993). According to Aristotle, the essence of human includes both rational and animal. Other attributes, such as laughing or being a featherless biped, might be unique to humans, but they are *accidental* attributes that could be different without changing the essence. Ibn Taymiyya, however, maintained that the distinction between essence and accident was arbitrary. Human might just as well be defined as laughing animal, with rational as an accidental attribute.

As an example of the difference between essence and accident, Hallaq mentioned the English word *date,* which names a fruit whose accidental attributes could be ripe or unripe. But in Arabic, there are three words for *date* at different stages of maturity: *busr* for unripe dates; *rutab* for somewhat ripe dates; and *tamr* for fully mature dates. In English, the single word *date* suggests the essence of a fruit whose accidental attributes happen to change with time; but in Arabic, the three different words suggest three distinct essences. Ibn Taymiyya would say that such verbal distinctions express mental categories, not actual reality: dates grow the same and taste the same no matter what they're called. An Aristotelian, however, would reply that those mental categories reflect real differences in the chemical composition of dates at different stages of ripeness. Such arguments, which have continued for centuries, still have the power to provoke debates about the choice of categories in a database or a knowledge base.

CASE-BASED REASONING.   Denouncing logic would be pointless if no other method of reasoning were possible. But Ibn Taymiyya had an alternative: the legal practice of reasoning by cases and analogy. In Islamic law, a new case is *assimilated* to one or more previous cases that serve as precedents. The mechanism of assimilation is analogy, but the analogy must be guided by a cause that is common to the new case as well as the earlier cases. If the same cause is present in all the cases, then the earlier judgment can be transferred to the new case. As an example, it is written in the Koran that grape wine is prohibited, but nothing is said about date wine. The judgment for date wine would be derived in four steps:

1. Given case: Grape wine is prohibited.

2. New case: Is date wine prohibited?

3. Cause: Grape wine is prohibited because it is intoxicating; date wine is also intoxicating.

4. Judgment: Date wine is also prohibited.

In practice, the reasoning may be more complex. Several previous cases may have a common cause but different judgments. Then the analysis must determine whether there were mitigating circumstances that affected the operation of the cause. But the principles remain the same: analogy guided by rules of evidence and relevance determines the common cause, the effect of the mitigating circumstances, and the judgment.

Besides arguing in favor of analogy, Ibn Taymiyya also replied to the logicians who claimed that syllogistic reasoning was certain, but analogy was merely probable. He was willing to grant that logical deduction was certain when applied to purely mental constructions in mathematics. But in any reasoning about the real world, universal propositions can only be derived by induction, and induction must be guided by the same principles of evidence and relevance used in analogy. Figure 6.3 illustrates Ibn Taymiyya's argument: Deduction proceeds from a *theory* containing universal propositions. But those propositions must have earlier been derived by induction using the methods of analogy. The only difference is that induction produces a theory as intermediate result, which is then used in a subsequent process of deduction. By using analogy directly, legal reasoning dispenses with the intermediate theory and goes straight from cases to conclusion. If the theory and the analogy are based on the same evidence, they must lead to the same conclusions.

Both Sextus Empiricus and Ibn Taymiyya admitted that logical reasoning was valid, but they doubted the source of evidence for universal propositions about the real world. What they overlooked was the pragmatic value of having a good theory: a small group of scientists can derive a theory by induction, and anyone else can apply it without redoing the exhaustive analysis of cases. But until the seventeenth century, there were no comprehensive theories that could explain physical phenomena. Even in astronomy, Ptolemy derived his cycles and epicycles by trial and error

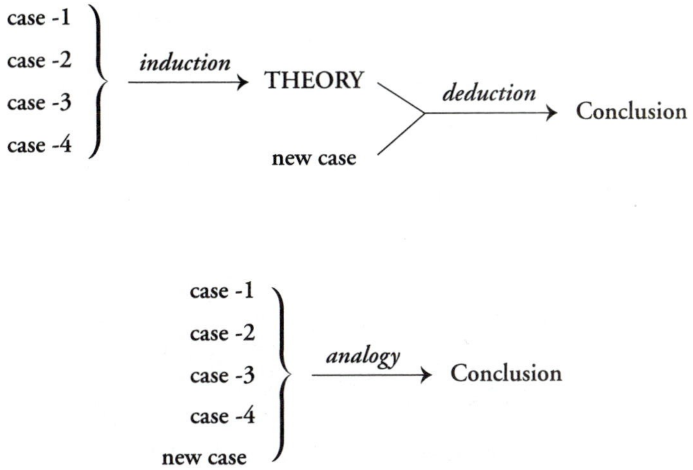

case -1
case -2 ⎫ *induction* THEORY *deduction* Conclusion
case -3 ⎬ ─────────▶ ─────────▶
case -4 ⎭
        new case

case -1
case -2 ⎫
case -3 ⎬ *analogy* Conclusion
case -4 ⎭ ─────────▶
new case

FIGURE 6.3 Induction and deduction compared to reasoning by analogy

without a unifying theory to explain them. In 1687, Isaac Newton published the first theory of physics that had universally quantified propositions with real explanatory power. His three laws of motion explained everything from the orbits of the planets to the fall of an apple, the tick of a pendulum, and the trajectory of a cannonball. Yet three hundred years later, very few areas of human knowledge come close to Newtonian mechanics in mathematical precision. Automotive engineers use sophisticated computers to design cars, but the people who drive them learn their skills by trial and error. Lawyers use computers to search for cases, but they still reason by analogy, using methods much like Ibn Taymiyya's. Furthermore, lawyers must be able to explain their reasoning to twelve jurors who have no special training in logic or the subject matter of the case.

EXCEPTIONS. Although Sextus and Ibn Taymiyya could not know of the great advances in modern science and logic, their criticisms are still valid today. Similar points were raised by the mathematician, logician, and philosopher Alfred North Whitehead, who with Bertrand Russell coauthored the *Principia Mathematica*, one of the most comprehensive treatises on logic ever written. Whitehead fully appreciated the power of logic and the value of a good theory, but in *Modes of Thought* he noted the difficulties of making logic fit the world:

- "It should be noticed that logical proof starts from premises, and that premises are based upon evidence. Thus evidence is presupposed by logic; at least, it is presupposed by the assumption that logic has any importance." (p. 67)
- "The premises are conceived in the simplicity of their individual isolation. But there can be no logical test for the possibility that deductive procedure, leading to the elaboration of compositions, may introduce into relevance considerations

from which the primitive notions of the topic have been abstracted. . . . Thus deductive logic has not the coercive supremacy which is conventionally conceded to it. When applied to concrete instances, it is a tentative procedure, finally to be judged by the self-evidence of its issues." (p. 144)

- "The topic of every science is an abstraction from the full concrete happenings of nature. But every abstraction neglects the influx of the factors omitted into the factors retained." (p. 196)

The erroneous "proof" that nothing can travel through air faster than the speed of sound shows how ignoring the tacit presuppositions can invalidate a deduction. The general equations for fluid mechanics are so complicated that exact solutions are impossible to derive, except in highly simplified special cases. One common simplification is to assume that all speeds are much less than the speed of sound. But the equations based on that assumption cannot be used for speeds that approach or exceed the speed of sound.

A common source of errors in applying logic to physical phenomena is the all-inclusive nature of the universal quantifier $\forall$, which admits no exceptions. With its more limited nature, the existential quantifier $\exists$ is less problematical: any sensory stimulation whatever is sufficient evidence that something exists. The difficulty, however, lies in determining exactly what exists. When a word, concept, or predicate is applied to natural phenomena, there are always intermediate or vague cases for which the applicability of the term is uncertain. Some of the vagueness results from a mismatch of the continuous world with the discrete set of words in language or predicates in logic:

- Languages (both natural and artificial) are made up of discrete symbols organized in well-defined syntactic structures.
- The world is made up of an endless variety of things, forms, substances, gradations, changes, and continuous flows with imperceptible transitions from one to another.

As a result of this mismatch, no symbolic notation (logic, frames, production rules, semantic networks, or even natural language) can capture the full richness of the world.

The continuous gradations and open-ended range of exceptions make it impossible to give complete, precise definitions for any concepts that are learned through experience. Kant (1800) observed that artificial concepts invented by some person for some arbitrary purpose are the only ones that can be defined completely:

Since the synthesis of empirical concepts is not arbitrary but based on experience, and as such can never be complete (for in experience ever new characteristics of the concept can be discovered), empirical concepts cannot be defined.

> Thus only arbitrarily made concepts can be defined synthetically. Such definitions... could also be called *declarations*, since in them one declares one's thoughts or renders account of what one understands by a word. This is the case with *mathematicians*.

Kant explicitly stated a theme that has been repeated with variations by philosophers from Heraclitus to the present. Two of the more recent statements are the principles of *family resemblance* by Ludwig Wittgenstein (1953) and *open texture* by Friedrich Waismann (1952):

- *Family resemblance.* Empirical concepts cannot be defined by a fixed set of necessary and sufficient conditions. Instead, they can only be defined by giving a series of examples and saying "These things and everything that resembles them are instances of the concept."

- *Open texture.* For any proposed definition of empirical concepts, new instances will arise that "obviously" belong to the category but are excluded by the definition.

These principles imply that all classifications are approximations. For any collection of concepts, new examples will inevitably arise that don't quite fit any of the existing categories. But deductive reasoning requires precise definitions, clearly stated axioms, and formal rules of inference.

PROTOTYPES AND DEFINITIONS. Aristotle introduced the method of formal definition in terms of genus and differentiae, and he also began the systematic description and classification of animal and plant species. But as biology developed, the classification of species came to be based on *prototypes* rather than formal definitions. William Whewell (1858) gave a classic description of biological practice:

> Natural groups are given by Type, not by Definition. And this consideration accounts for that indefiniteness and indecision which we frequently find in the descriptions of such groups, and which must appear so strange and inconsistent to anyone who does not suppose these descriptions to assume any deeper ground of connection than an arbitrary choice of the botanist. Thus in the family of the rose-tree, we are told that the *ovules* are *very rarely* erect, the *stigmata usually* simple. Of what use, it might be asked, can such loose accounts be? To which the answer is, that they are not inserted in order to distinguish the species, but in order to describe the family, and the total relations of the ovules and the stigmata of the family are better known by this general statement. . . .
>
> The type-species of every genus, the type-genus of every family, is then one which possesses all the characters and properties of the genus in a marked and

prominent manner. The type of the Rose family has alternate stipulate leaves, wants the albumen, has the ovules not erect, has the stigmata simple, and besides these features, which distinguish it from the exceptions or varieties of its class, it has the features which make it prominent in its class. It is one of those which possess clearly several leading attributes; and thus, though we cannot say of any one genus that it *must* be the type of the family, or of any one species that it *must* be the type of the genus, we are still not wholly to seek; the type must be connected by many affinities with most of the others of its group; it must be near the center of the crowd, and not one of the stragglers.

In responding to Whewell, the philosopher John Stuart Mill (1865) argued that the practice of defining a category by prototype does not exclude the possibility of finding a formal definition in terms of necessary and sufficient conditions:

> The truth is, on the contrary, that every genus or family is framed with distinct reference to certain characters, and is composed, first and principally, of species which agree in possessing all those characters. To these are added, as a sort of appendix, such other species, generally in small number, as possess *nearly* all the properties selected; wanting some of them one property, some another, and which, while they agree with the rest *almost* as much as these agree with one another, do not resemble in an equal degree any other group. Our conception of the class continues to be grounded on the characters; and the class might be defined, those things which *either* possess that set of characters, *or* resemble the things that do so, more than they resemble anything else.
>
> And this resemblance itself is not, like resemblance between simple sensations, an ultimate fact, unsusceptible of analysis. Even the inferior degree of resemblance is created by the possession of common characters. Whatever resembles the genus Rose more than it resembles any other genus, does so because it possesses a greater number of the characters of that genus, than of the characters of any other genus. Nor can there be the smallest difficulty in representing, by an enumeration of characters, the nature and degree of resemblance which is strictly sufficient to include any object in the class. There are always some properties common to all things which are included. Others there often are, to which some things, which are nevertheless included, are exceptions. But the objects which are exceptions to one character are not exceptions to another: the resemblance which fails in some particulars must be made up for in others. The class, therefore, is constituted by the possession of *all* the characters which are universal, and *most* of those which admit of exceptions.

The arguments by Whewell and Mill are compatible for closed classes whose members have long been known and thoroughly analyzed. They disagree, however, on open-ended classes for which many members have never been discovered or analyzed. Whewell's argument would have been stronger if he had not chosen such a common example as the Rosaceae. Critical examples arise with prehistoric animals such as dinosaurs and early hominids, for which the fossil record is fragmentary and many species are known only by a single jaw bone or just a tooth. That is the lesson of Waismann's principle of open texture: it is not possible to state the necessary and sufficient conditions for class membership when many or even most of the members have never been discovered.

The nineteenth-century debate between Whewell and Mill was continued by Wittgenstein with his discussion of family resemblance. More recently, it was revived in AI debates over the use of logic or prototypes for definitions. In general, formal definitions are possible in any subject where the person who states a definition has the authority to make it true by *legislation*. Government legislatures are the prototype for legislating, but anyone who has the power to make rules also has the power to legislate definitions: schools, businesses, clubs, parents, computer programmers, participants in a discussion, engineers who invent a new device, and authors who write a book or article on a new subject. In empirical subjects, formal definitions are possible, but only when all the evidence has been gathered. When the evidence is incomplete, definitions by prototype are not only useful, but necessary. Since all children and most adults are constantly learning about things that were previously unknown (at least to them), the human brain is designed to learn better and faster through prototypes than through formal definitions. Even mathematicians and logicians need examples to sharpen their insights into the meaning of a new definition. Prototypes and other examples are difficult to use in deductive reasoning, but they are the raw material for inductive reasoning.

PROPOSITIONS AND CONTINUOUS MODELS. The limitations of logic cast doubt on the *knowledge representation hypothesis*, as stated by Brian Cantwell Smith (1982):

> Any mechanically embodied intelligent process will be comprised of structural ingredients that (a) we as external observers naturally take to represent a propositional account of the knowledge that the overall process exhibits, and (b) independent of such external semantical attribution, play a formal but causal and essential role in engendering the behavior that manifests that knowledge.

The view of knowledge as a collection of propositions characterizes the discrete, symbolic systems of AI, but it is incompatible with Kant's undefinable concepts, Wittgenstein's family resemblances, Waismann's open textures, and any other view that considers continuity to be an essential and irreducible aspect of the world. After many years of working on problems of knowledge representation, Smith (1996) tempered his earlier views by trying to balance the need for clear conceptual categories in language and thought with the vague, indistinct gradations that occur in nature:

> Think of the truism that someone possessed only of "book knowledge" of a given subject matter, especially one far from common sense and experience, is liable to reach spectacularly dumb conclusions. Or that a constant diet of perception and action is needed to keep inference from gradually drifting astray.

Instead of his earlier propositional account, Smith maintained that "high-level conceptual inference will turn out, essentially and inextricably, to rest on a constant underlying connective tissue of non-conceptual content, between and among and through all the explicit conceptualized steps."

Smith's later hybrid of propositional and analog reasoning is compatible with the *modeling hypothesis* formulated by Kenneth Craik (1952):

> If the organism carries a *small-scale model* of external reality and of its own possible actions within its head, it is able to carry out various alternatives, conclude which is the best of them, react to future situations before they arise, utilize the knowledge of past events in dealing with the present and the future, and in every way react in a fuller, safer, and more competent manner to the emergencies which face it.

For the AI community, Marvin Minsky (1965) summarized Craik's hypothesis in a catchy slogan: "The brain is a machine for making models." If the models are built from discrete elements in discrete relationships, then all the features could be completely captured in propositions. But the models can also accommodate continuous simulations, numeric computations, and nonnumeric images. Such simulations have evolved into the branch of computer science called *virtual reality*. Although digital simulations always have an actual granularity, the computations can be refined to a level beyond the epistemic granularity of human perception or the intentional granularity of any particular human purpose.

6.3   Fuzzy Logic

One approach to the limitations of logic is to increase the number of truth values beyond the classical 1 for true and 0 for false. A three-valued logic has a third truth value for *unknown* or *undefined*. A four-valued logic may add another value to represent an overdefined or inconsistent state. The ultimate generalization of *many valued* or *multivalued* logic was developed by the Polish logician Jan Łukasiewicz (1930), who assumed a continuous range of truth values from 0.0 to 1.0. But unlike classical first-order logic, for which independent developers converged on semantically equivalent definitions, the various theories of multivalued logic have diverged with a variety of interpretations. Furthermore, the various interpretations resemble, overlap, compete with, or are confused with the continuous range of numbers derived by other methods:

- *Fuzzy logic.* In order to represent vagueness or uncertainty, Lotfi Zadeh (1975) developed *fuzzy logic*, with a continuous range of *possibilities* from 0 for impossible to 1.0 for certain. For his expert systems, Ted Shortliffe (1976) tagged each rule and assertion with a *certainty factor* that ranges from +1.0 for true to −1.0 for false. Some people claim that possibilities and certainty factors are different, while others treat them as two names for the same concept. Since Zadeh's notion of possibility is very different from the ◊ operator in modal logic, the term *certainty factor* may be adopted as a less confusing alternative.

- *Statistics.* Traditional statistics and probability theory are based on explicit, objective counting of frequencies. The resulting probabilities have a continuous range of values with some similarities to the continuous range of fuzzy possibilities or certainty factors. When statistical evidence is sufficient, computed frequencies are usually more reliable than certainty factors derived from somebody's best guess. The Bayseian theory of *subjective probabilities*, however, depends on human judgment in much the same way as fuzzy logic. For his version of certainty factors, Shortliffe adapted ideas from both Bayesian theory and fuzzy logic. Other experts, such as Judea Pearl (1988), maintained that "Fuzzy logic is orthogonal to probability theory — it focuses on the ambiguities in describing events, rather than the uncertainty about the occurrences or nonoccurrences of events." Meanwhile, Enrique Ruspini (1996) developed one of the best interpretations of fuzzy logic by explicitly relating it to probability theory.

- *Neural networks.* Arrays or networks of active elements, popularly called *neural networks*, have been used to compute continuous ranges of numbers that resemble the values computed by statistics and fuzzy logic. They have been most successful for pattern recognition and for learning systems that adjust their outputs in response to inputs. Mathematically, they compute functions that are related to the statistical techniques, and theoretical studies treat them as a method of implementing statistical procedures.

- *Virtual reality.* For reasoning about continuous quantities, numerical computation is often simpler and more efficient than logical deduction. With recent advances in computer hardware, numerical simulation of physical situations can be carried out efficiently and in great detail. When attached to appropriate sensors and I/O devices, such simulations have led to the new field of virtual reality. But the same simulations can also be used to make predictions and test alternatives that would be difficult or impossible to represent in logical symbols and propositions. In effect, virtual reality gives the computer a kind of "mental imagery" that can be used as an alternative or a supplement to logic. Images are often more convenient than symbolic systems for reasoning about space, time, and other continuously varying aspects of the world.

These techniques have been successfully used in applications for which classical logic has not been applicable. Yet the continuous numbers represent many different things: truth values, possibilities, certainty factors, objective probabilities, subjective probabilities, approximations, measures of relevance, measures of utility, or just some undefined "weighting factors." Their successful application to practical problems is encouraging, but some guidelines are necessary to determine which techniques are appropriate for each kind of problem.

FUZZY PREDICATES AND OPERATORS.   In 1965, Zadeh introduced *fuzzy set theory* with a continuous range of membership values for the operator ϵ. Later he combined fuzzy set theory with Łukasiewicz's many-valued logic for a version of *fuzzy logic*. For the nine chairlike things in Figure 6.1, a membership value of 1.0 might be assigned to the chairs with four fixed legs; 0.9 to the desk chair, the rocking chair, the folding chair, and the upholstered arm chair; 0.8 to the wheelchair; and 0.7 to the toilet. To indicate its slight similarity to chairs, a stairway might have the value 0.3. Zadeh also assigned numeric values to *hedging terms* like *almost, more or less, likely,* or *very likely.* The statement that Quakers are likely to be pacifists might have a certainty factor 0.8.

By representing intuitive judgments, fuzzy logic can sometimes handle situations with insufficient data for the usual statistical tests. The words *young* and *old,* for example, are applied to people at various stages of life, but there are no statistical tables that relate a person's age to the probability of being called young or old. Instead of objective statistics, fuzzy logic uses an intuitive or subjective assignment of certainty. Figure 6.4 shows someone's best guess about the certainty factors for the predicates young(x) and old(x) as functions of age.

The two graphs for *young* and *old* cross at age 36, which has the neutral or

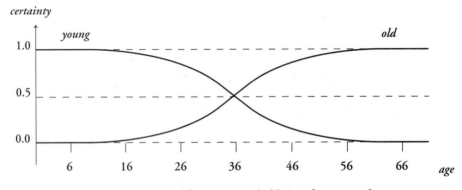

FIGURE 6.4 Certainty of young(x) and old(x) as functions of age x

unknown certainty of 0.5. To represent the qualifier *very*, Zadeh proposed to square the values of the base distributions:

$$\text{veryYoung}(x) = (\text{young}(x))^2.$$
$$\text{veryOld}(x) = (\text{old}(x))^2.$$

Figure 6.5 shows the graphs for the two functions veryYoung(x) and veryOld(x), which were derived by squaring the functions shown in Figure 6.4. At age 36, both of these predicates would have the value 0.25. Around that age, a person might be classified simultaneously as not very young and not very old.

COMPUTING CERTAINTY FACTORS.   For rule-driven expert systems, the range -1 to $+1$ for certainty factors is convenient because the symmetry simplifies the computation. As an example, consider the problem of Nixon, the Republican Quaker. First assume the following certainty factors about Nixon:

certainty("Nixon is a Republican", 0.9).
certainty("Nixon is a Quaker", 0.7).

The first line says that Nixon is a Republican with a high certainty (0.9). The second line says that his Quaker affiliation is somewhat less certain (0.7). The next two rules determine the pacifist inclinations of Republicans and Quakers:

rule("If x is a Republican, then x is a pacifist", -0.8).
rule("If x is a Quaker, then x is a pacifist", 0.8).

The first line assigns a negative certainty -0.8 to the rule that if x is a Republican, then x is a pacifist. The second line assigns the positive certainty $+0.8$ to the rule that a Quaker is a pacifist.

The next step is to combine the certainty of the premises with the certainty of the rules to compute the certainty of the conclusions. Shortliffe's basic rule is to multiply the certainties. According to the first rule, the certainty that Nixon is a

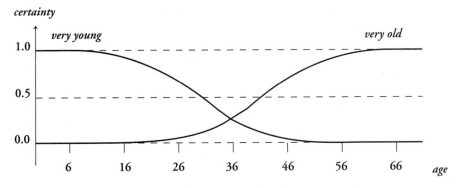

FIGURE 6.5 Certainty of veryYoung(x) and veryOld(x) as functions of age x

pacifist would be the product of 0.9 (Nixon is a Republican) with -0.8 (the certainty of the rule). Therefore, Nixon is a pacifist with the negative certainty -0.72. According to the second rule, he is a pacifist with a positive certainty 0.56. His nonpacifist inclinations would therefore outweigh his pacifism.

As in the Nixon example, different proofs may lead to conflicting or reinforcing conclusions. For the MYCIN family, Shortliffe proposed the following rule for combining the contributions of two different proofs that have the certainty factors c_1 and c_2:

$$\text{CombinedCF}(c_1, c_2) = \begin{cases} c_1 + c_2 - c_1 c_2, & \text{if } c_1, c_2 \geq 0 \\ \dfrac{c_1 + c_2}{1 - \min(\text{abs}(c_1), \text{abs}(c_2))}, & \text{if } c_1, c_2 \text{ are of opposite signs.} \\ c_1 + c_2 + c_1 c_2, & \text{if } c_1, c_2 \leq 0 \end{cases}$$

If the two certainty factors c_1 and c_2 have the same sign, the conclusions reinforce one another. For the Nixon example, the different signs cause a conflict. With the middle option, the values $c_1 = -0.72$ and $c_2 = +0.56$ result in the combined certainty factor -0.36. The negative value suggests that Nixon is somewhat unlikely to be a pacifist.

CONTEXT DEPENDENCE. An all-purpose certainty factor, as in Figures 6.4 and 6.5, is likely to be wrong or misleading in any specific context. At age 16, a college student would be considered young, but a high-school student would be considered average. Age 26 would be considered young for a professor, typical for a graduate student, old for an undergraduate, and very old for a high-school student. Age 35 is the minimum for the U.S. president, and even at age 46, Bill Clinton was considered young. An astute observer remarked, "Ever since I was in first grade, I've believed that old is fifteen years past my own age." Since the pronoun *I* is an indexical, any word like *young* or *old* that is defined in terms of it would also be an indexical, and its current value would be context dependent. In general, all fuzzy terms are highly context dependent. A machine shop and a butcher shop would have very different standards for terms like *accurate*.

The practice of treating *very* as an operator for squaring the distribution function is also questionable. An ordinary resistor, for example, might have a 20% tolerance: its resistance in ohms could vary ±20% around the stated value. A resistor with a 10% tolerance might be called accurate, and one with a 5% tolerance might be called very accurate. According to Zadeh's rule, the distribution function for very accurate resistors could be derived by squaring the distribution for accurate resistors. But suppose a manufacturer makes all three kinds of resistors on the same assembly line, but uses the following procedure for grading them:

1. Measure the resistance of each resistor that comes off the line.
2. If it's outside the 20% tolerance, discard it.

3. If it's between 10% and 20%, call it standard.
4. If it's between 5% and 10%, call it accurate.
5. If it's better than 5%, call it very accurate.

With this manufacturing process, a batch of accurate resistors is guaranteed to contain none that are very accurate. Like the descriptive terms *young* and *accurate*, hedging terms like *very* are also context dependent.

As problems become more complex with more interacting variables, the context dependencies become even more critical. In surveying the methods of calculating uncertainty in medical diagnostics, Chandrasekaran (1994) observed that the usual techniques do not properly account for context dependencies:

> Bayesian approaches, fuzzy set theory, Dempster-Shafer theory, and uncertainty factor calculus were all available to us. All these calculi shared one important property or assumption about human expertise — that there was a situation and goal-independent way of combining uncertainties.

Expert physicians, however, used reasoning techniques that

> differed from context to context and problem-solving goal to problem-solving goal. We had to resist the mathematical attractions of an abstract calculus. Instead, we developed a formalism in which we could incorporate the uncertainty-combining behavior of experts, who were compiling a complex of background knowledge in such context-specific rules.

In the absence of information about context, fuzzy logic and related statistical methods may be useful as a first approximation. But human experts use domain-dependent models that support different reasoning techniques for each type of application.

FUZZY CONTROL SYSTEMS. The most successful applications of fuzzy techniques have been in control systems for such things as camera focus, elevator scheduling, subway brakes, washing machines, and sake fermenting (Hirota 1993). In those applications, fuzzy systems do not behave like theorem provers, but more like analog computers for simulating continuous phenomena. Figure 6.6 shows how the temperature of a house can vary with a furnace controlled by an ordinary thermostat.

At the starting time in Figure 6.6, the room temperature is at the desired temperature T, and the furnace is off. The value ε represents the permitted deviance from T before the furnace changes state: when the room temperature falls below $T-\varepsilon$, the furnace goes on; when the room temperature rises above $T+\varepsilon$, the furnace goes off. As Figure 6.6 shows, the furnace is either turned on 100 percent or turned off completely. Meanwhile, the room temperature tends to oscillate beyond the desired limits of $T-\varepsilon$ and $T+\varepsilon$.

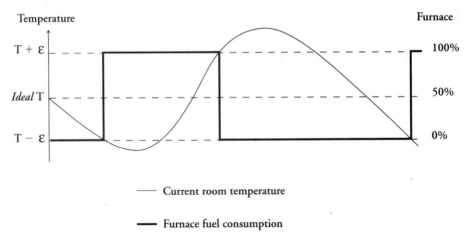

FIGURE 6.6 Room temperature controlled by a thermostat with discrete settings

Figure 6.7 shows the more gradual change in temperature and fuel consumption that is possible with a fuzzy thermostat. Instead of the discrete on-off states of the conventional thermostat, the fuzzy thermostat begins to feed some fuel to the furnace as soon as the temperature begins to fall below T. When the temperature starts to rise, the thermostat reduces fuel even before the ideal setting T has been reached. As a result, the room temperature stays closer to the ideal, and the furnace operates more efficiently at a moderate setting instead of oscillating between the extremes.

ANALOG CONTROL SYSTEMS. The graph in Figure 6.7 is typical of analog systems, which have been used to control industrial processes for years. A sophisti-

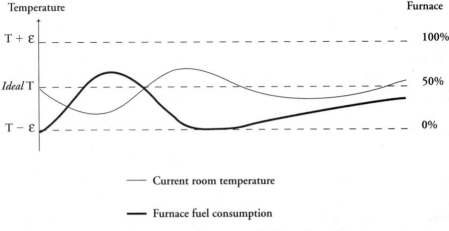

FIGURE 6.7 Room temperature controlled by a fuzzy thermostat

cated analog control system might compute fuel consumption as a function of several variables:

$$\text{fuel} = f\left(T_O, T_i, \frac{dT_i}{dt} \right).$$

The three principal inputs to f are the outside temperature T_o, the inside temperature T_i, and the rate of change of the inside temperature with respect to time dT_i / dt. The function f requires more input data than the simple thermostat shown in Figure 6.6: one sensor must monitor the outside temperature while another monitors the inside temperature. Furthermore, the control system must maintain a clock, check the inside temperature at frequent intervals, and compute its rate of change. Those sensors would be much more expensive than a household thermostat, which has a single on-off switch connected to a spring that expands or contracts with temperature. Yet the sensors would still be cheap compared to an analog control system, which could only be justified for a major industrial application.

For a home furnace or for a thermostat in every room of a large building, the cost of the sensors and the computer must be kept small. Today the cost of a digital computer chip is insignificant compared to the cost of the fuel that can be saved with a well-regulated furnace. A sophisticated program on a cheap computer chip may be able to save a great deal in fuel consumption while improving room comfort. Fuzzy computing techniques on a digital computer can often serve as an economical replacement for the more expensive analog control systems.

CRITICISM OF FUZZY LOGIC. The philosopher Susan Haack (1978, 1996) was one of the early critics of fuzzy logic, and she has continued to sharpen her arguments against the claims that natural language justifies or even requires "degrees of truth." Her most serious criticism is not that fuzzy logic is vague, but that it is too precise: instead of modeling the way people talk and think about vagueness, fuzzy logic forces an unwarranted quantification of vagueness. Such quantification might be useful if it could help solve some of the problems of knowledge soup discussed in Section 6.1. But fuzzy logic and numeric certainty factors offer little or no help:

- Incomplete generalizations: Fuzzy logic might assign a certainty factor like 0.8 to the proposition "Birds fly." But that value is a poor compromise between the actual values of 1.0 for normal healthy adult sparrows and 0.0 for penguins. In any particular case, the correct inference depends on context-dependent conditions, such as a broken wing or location in Antarctica, not on certainty factors or likelihoods.

- Abnormal conditions: Assigning certainty factors to the various situations that might arise in driving from New York to Boston may be useful in contingency planning, but it doesn't help in reasoning about a specific situation once it occurs.

- Incomplete definitions: A geological survey or an accounting system requires clear-cut definitions of things like oil wells. The definition must specify whether a single pipe connected to three holes is counted as one oil well or three.

- Conflicting defaults: Fuzzy logic might be useful for deciding the likelihood that Nixon is a pacifist, but only if the certainty factors on the premises had been well chosen. Large amounts of data provide the only solid basis for choosing certainty factors; but with a sufficient amount of data, conventional statistics is more dependable than fuzzy logic.

- Unanticipated applications: The certainty that a predicate applies to an individual cannot be determined without considering the context. A person might be tall for a high school student but short for a basketball player. Someone might consider a sock part of the foot when taking measurements for ski boots, but not when treating a broken ankle.

Despite the criticisms, the proponents of fuzzy techniques point to a growing list of successful applications. The journal *IEEE Expert* devoted an entire issue (August 1994) to criticisms by Charles Elkan and responses by 22 researchers in the field, including Lotfi Zadeh. Some were sympathetic to Elkan's comments and some were hostile, but the only consensus about fuzzy values was that they are not conventional truth values. Elkan and his commentators did agree that fuzzy control systems have been useful, but better guidelines are needed to determine when they are appropriate and which features lead to success or failure in a particular application.

QUANTIFYING CONTINUITY AND VAGUENESS. Fuzzy systems address two issues that create difficulties for classical logic: continuity and vagueness. Peirce observed that each of them violates a law of two-valued logic:

- *Excluded middle.* In classical logic, there is no middle value between true and false or 1 and 0. Yet any continuous function with a value 1 at some point and a value 0 at another point must assume intermediate values somewhere in between. If warm(x) is a continuous predicate with a value true when $x = 30°C$ and false when $x = 10°C$, there must be some region around 20°C where its truth value is unknown, indeterminate, meaningless, or undefined.

- *Noncontradiction.* Peirce remarked that it is "easy to be certain. One has only to be sufficiently vague" (CP 4.237). By covering a broad range of possibilities, a vague statement can be both true and false or neither true nor false. The vague statement *It's warm in here* is more likely to be true than the more precise statement *The temperature is 29 degrees Celsius*. The statement *It's comfortable in here* may be true and false for different people; even for one person, the temperature may be pleasant, but the chairs may be hard.

By making vague statements precise, science increases their likelihood of being proven false by experimental tests. Clocks, thermometers, and scales replace vague words like *early, warm,* and *heavy* with numbers that designate a narrow, objectively measurable range. Those numbers do not change the nature of language or logic, but they enable people to use it precisely when precision is important.

Fuzzy values resemble the quantities measured by clocks and thermometers more than they resemble truth values. There are no standard units for measuring camera focus, laundry dirt, or subway brakes, and fuzzy methods provide a way of deriving numbers for quantifying those subjects. But for each application, the methods of deriving the fuzzy values depend critically on the subject matter and the user's purpose. That dependency indicates that fuzzy methods are very different from the domain-independent methods of logic. Instead, they resemble techniques of measurement and approximation, which relate a statement in some language to some domain. As Whitehead observed, "The topic of every science is an abstraction from the full concrete happenings of nature." Fuzzy techniques, like other methods of approximation, can help to quantify the mismatch between abstractions and reality.

6.4 Nonmonotonic Logic

Classical logic is *monotonic*: adding axioms to a theory monotonically increases the number of theorems that can be proved. If a theory implies a car can be driven from New York to Boston, new information about a dead battery or snow conditions can never block the proof. If a contradiction arises, the old proofs are not blocked; instead, everything becomes provable. The versions of *nonmonotonic logic* allow new information to increase or decrease the number of conclusions that can be derived. Information that Tweety is a penguin blocks the conclusion that Tweety can fly. Information about snow conditions can make a driver rethink the options for getting to Boston. Nonmonotonic reasoning is also called *defeasible* because an earlier proof might no longer be feasible when new information becomes available.

VARIATION BY DISCRETE STEPS. Unlike fuzzy logic, nonmonotonic logic depends on discrete changes in context rather than a continuous range of certainties. For a certain kind of wall, fuzzy logic might generate the answer 0.83 for the question of whether the wall is a part of the room, but an apartment dweller who wants to remodel needs a yes or no answer. For a particular wall, a crisp answer can be deduced by discrete reasoning from a guideline such as "If a wall consists of multiple layers, an apartment owner may replace or remodel a non-load-bearing surface layer." For the assignment statements in programming languages, each case can be defined separately without fuzzy edges between cases. For the cars, trains, ships, and airplanes, each system would have distinct concepts and rules, not a continuous range of rules. Intermediate cases may exist: a streetcar has some similarities to a train, but it also runs on city streets like an automobile. An expert system for streetcars might therefore share some of the rules for trains and cars. But the rules do not vary continuously: a discrete subset of the rules for trains and cars would be adopted for streetcars.

Instead of the continuous range of membership of fuzzy set theory, Fritz Lehmann and Anthony Cohn (1994) used *egg-yolk diagrams* for grouping things in a series of discrete levels of membership. Figure 6.8 shows a diagram for the chairlike objects from Figure 6.1. In the yolk are three examples that have all the typical features of chairs: a seat, a backrest, and four fixed legs. The egg white contains things that differ from typical chairs in one way or another: they move, they fold up, they have wheels, or they don't have discrete legs. The toilet is a borderline case, and the footstool and staircase are outside, but close to the chair group. Egg-yolk diagrams show discrete levels of variation rather than continuous variation. Without a specific purpose, the question of whether a wheelchair or a rocking chair is more chairlike is meaningless. The way they vary from the central group may be significant in some contexts and irrelevant in others.

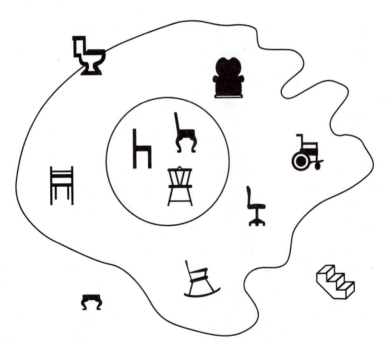

FIGURE 6.8 The egg-yolk theory of word meaning

For the Cyc system, Lenat and Guha (1990) originally tagged the rules and facts with certainty factors. But uncertainties in the choice of certainty factors caused too many spurious inferences. A fuzzy value of 0.8 for the wheelchair and 0.9 for the rocking chair might lead to a good conclusion in one context, but an erroneous conclusion in another. They replaced the certainty factors with context-dependent defaults and obtained better results with five discrete options: *unconditionally true, true by default, unknown, false by default,* and *unconditionally false.* Whether a default is accepted or rejected depends on the context, not on a context-independent number.

DEFAULTS IN FRAMES. The oldest, simplest, and most popular way of dealing with defaults and exceptions is to tag slots in a frame with *default values.* The value 18, for example, might be the default for the number of wheels of trailer trucks, but it could be overridden for a particular subtype. Such default values are called *ad hoc* because they address a local feature without checking global constraints. Programs that had only been tested with 18-wheelers might suddenly fail because the code was inconsistent with values other than 18.

The ease of attaching a default value to a slot in a frame makes default reasoning look deceptively simple. The toy examples in books and manuals often reinforce that impression. Following are two frames taken from a book on expert systems:

```
(defineType      Bird
   (supertype      Vertebrate)
   (covering       (default feathers))
   (reproducesBy   (default lays-eggs))
   (flies          (default true) )
(defineType      Penguin
   (supertype      Bird)
   (flies          default false) )
```

The first frame says that the default value of the flies slot for the Bird frame is true. The second frame says that the type Penguin is a subtype of Bird; therefore, it would normally inherit all the slots and values from Bird. However, the default value for flies is overridden by the value false for Penguin. The first frame would therefore imply that birds normally fly, and the second frame would make an exception for penguins.

This example, which was designed to illustrate defaults, also illustrates the popular technique of "coding first and thinking later." The frames have three slot names: *covering* is a participle whose associated value is a plural noun; *reproducesBy* is a verb-preposition pair whose value is a gerund-noun pair; and *flies* is a verb whose value is true or false. The meaning of those slots and values is not defined by any systematic relationship to logic, language, or the real world. It is defined only by the procedures that manipulate the character strings in the slots, and they are allowed to do anything at all. Superprogrammers, who can keep all relationships in mind at all times, may be able to use ad-hoc defaults effectively. But maintenance and modification over long periods of time can introduce inconsistencies in the best of code, and some computer-aided method of detecting and avoiding them is desirable.

DEFAULT LOGIC. The first systems of nonmonotonic logic evolved from attempts to formalize and systematize the ad-hoc defaults used in frames. Jon Doyle and Drew McDermott (1980) and Ray Reiter (1980) developed *default logic* as a method of preserving global consistency while supporting local defaults. Reiter started with a typical rule that says $a(x)$ implies $\gamma(x)$:

$$(\forall x)(a(x) \supset \gamma(x)).$$

Then he added a special predicate $\beta(x)$, which may be called the *normality condition*. The resulting *default rules* are implications that check for normality before the conclusion is asserted. In Reiter's notation, they are written

$$\frac{a(x) : \beta(x)}{\gamma(x)}.$$

This rule says that if some predicate a is true of x and it is consistent to believe the normality condition β of x, then conclude γ of x. The following rule says that birds can fly if it is consistent to believe they can:

$$\frac{\mathrm{bird}(x) : \mathrm{canFly}(x)}{\mathrm{canFly}(x)}$$

In this case, $a(x)$ is bird(x); $\beta(x)$ and $\gamma(x)$ are both canFly(x). The difference between this rule and the ad-hoc default is the consistency check before the default is asserted.

For many defaults, the normality condition β is the same as the conclusion γ, but general default rules can accommodate an arbitrary expression for β. For the example of driving a car to Boston, $a(x)$ might be the statement "x is a car"; $\beta(x)$ might be "x has all parts in working order"; and $\gamma(x)$ might be the conclusion "x can be driven from New York to Boston." If all the normality conditions in β are consistent with current beliefs, the default rule would imply that the car could be driven to Boston. But if the driver later discovered that the battery was dead, the new belief would block the earlier conclusion. By allowing new information to block a conclusion, default rules provide a nonmonotonic effect.

ABNORMALITY. Instead of representing defaults in terms of the normality predicate, John McCarthy (1980) introduced the *abnormality* predicate abnormal(x) as the negation of $\beta(x)$. Then Reiter's default rule can be restated

$$(\forall x)(a(x) \land \text{consistent}(\sim\!\text{abnormal}(x))) \supset \gamma(x).$$

Since ~abnormal(x) is consistent if and only if abnormal(x) is not provable, the default rule can also be written

$$(\forall x)(a(x) \land \sim\!\text{provable}(\text{abnormal}(x))) \supset \gamma(x).$$

The principle of *negation as failure*, which was discussed in Chapter 3, defines negation as a failure to prove. For systems based on that principle, which include most database and expert systems, the expression ~provable(abnormal(x)) can be simplified to ~abnormal(x):

$$(\forall x)(a(x) \land \sim\!\text{abnormal}(x)) \supset \gamma(x).$$

These transformations show how any system based on negation as failure can be used to implement default logic. As an example, the default rule that birds can fly is expressed by the following Prolog rule, which says that x can fly if x is a bird and x is not abnormal:

```
canFly(X) ← bird(X) & ¬abnormal(X).
```

Then abnormality for birds can be defined by a list of common exceptions:

```
abnormal(X) ← bird(X) &
  (penguin(X) | ostrich(X) | kiwi(X) | chick(X)).
```

This rule says that x is abnormal if x is a bird and x is a penguin, an ostrich, a kiwi, or a chick. Then suppose that someone asserts that Tweety is a bird:

```
bird(tweety).
```

At this point, abnormal(tweety) cannot be proved. Therefore, the first rule would imply canFly(tweety). But if someone later said that Tweety was a penguin, the following assertion would cause abnormal(tweety) to be provable, and canFly (tweety) would no longer be provable:

```
penguin(tweety).
```

This example illustrates the fundamental characteristic of nonmonotonic reasoning: new information blocks an earlier conclusion.

In SQL, an abnormality table could be defined as a *view*. Suppose that a table named *animal* has columns for the identifier (id), type, species, and growth stage of individuals that are known in the database. Then the following definition would create a view named *oddbirds*, which would extract a column of identifiers for all the birds that are abnormal in one way or another.

```
create view oddbirds
  as select id
      from animal
        where type = 'bird'
        and species = 'penguin' or 'ostrich' or 'kiwi'
  union
    select id
      from animal
        where type = 'bird'
        and growth_stage not equal 'adult'
```

This view supports the same kinds of inferences as McCarthy's abnormality predicate. Tweety the penguin would not appear in the list of odd birds until his species is known. A newly hatched ostrich would be selected twice, but the union operator in SQL would delete the duplicate. Like Molière's gentleman, who was amazed to learn that he had been speaking prose all his life, most SQL programmers have been using nonmonotonic logic without knowing it.

OPEN AND CLOSED WORLDS.   The technique of negation as failure has a nonmonotonic effect because most databases are incomplete: they contain some but not all the significant facts about their domain of discourse. As Leibniz observed, only an omniscient being such as God could have complete knowledge of the world. With their limited powers of observation and reasoning, mere mortals (whether animals or robots) are limited to knowledge about finite situations. Even for those situations, they could never obtain complete knowledge about all possible details. For mathematical theories, however, Leibniz maintained that mortal beings could obtain complete knowledge, since they could choose to limit the domain to a finite set of axioms that they would declare true by definition. Reiter (1978) used the criterion of completeness to distinguish two categories of databases:

- *Closed worlds.* A database that either stores or deduces every true proposition about its domain is called a *closed world.* In a closed world, negation as failure is equivalent to ordinary negation, since any proposition that is not stored or provable is guaranteed to be false. When all relevant facts are known, there is no need for defaults, and all reasoning is monotonic.

- *Open worlds.* A database in which some facts about the domain are unknown or unprovable is called an *open world.* In an open world, some propositions are known to be true, and some are known to be false, but there is a large middle area of propositions whose truth value is unknown. That middle area is the province of nonmonotonic reasoning, which uses defaults, probabilities, and heuristics to make "educated guesses" about the missing information.

Any database constructed from measurements or observations of situations in the real world is almost certainly incomplete. Like Leibniz's mathematical theories, closed-world databases are artificial constructions, such as virtual reality or databases whose contents are constrained by the rules of a business organization. An airline reservation system, for example, has a closed database because the absence of a reservation implies that the reservation does not exist. A passenger's protest does not have a nonmonotonic effect of causing a reservation to exist.

Reiter's two categories of databases can be extended with a third category, called *semi-open*, in which some subdomains are closed by definition, but other subdomains contain observed or measured information that is typically incomplete. A personnel database, for example, may be semi-open: the domain of employees can be closed by definition, since anyone not listed would not be an employee; but other subdomains, such as the employees' address or list of children, might contain missing or incomplete information. In SQL, the keyword *mandatory* is used to declare domains that are required to be closed.

KNOWLEDGE AND BELIEF. In a closed world, knowledge and belief are identical: every proposition known to be true is believed, and all the others are unbelievable because they are known to be false. In an open world, beliefs and defaults are tentative excursions into the province of what is unknown. Robert Moore (1985) developed a version of nonmonotonic logic based on beliefs rather than defaults. He called his theory *autoepistemic* logic, from the Greek *auto* (self) and *epistēmē* (knowledge). To maintain a consistent set of beliefs, the inference rules for autoepistemic logic must perform the same kinds of consistency checks as default logic. Any belief that is inconsistent with current knowledge must be discarded. The nonmonotonic effect is the result of discarding inconsistent beliefs in the light of new knowledge.

Theories of beliefs and defaults are derived from different intuitions, but their axioms lead to the same kinds of logical and computational systems: knowledge takes precedence over belief in the same way that facts take precedence over defaults. In effect, a default is a believable proposition that has a high probability of being true. Formally, default logic and autoepistemic logic are isomorphic: every axiom and inference rule that applies to either one can be translated to an equivalent axiom or rule for the other. Teodor Przymusinski (1991) proved that both of them are also equivalent to logics based on negation as failure. The proof of equivalence means that any rule-driven system based on negation as failure, which includes Prolog, SQL, and most expert systems, can be used as a tool for implementing default logic or autoepistemic logic.

CONFLICTING DEFAULTS. The goal of nonmonotonic logic is to maintain consistency between facts and defaults. But the defaults may be inconsistent with one another. Consider the next two default rules:

$$\frac{\text{Quaker}(x): \text{pacifist}(x)}{\text{pacifist}(x)}, \quad \frac{\text{Republican}(x): {\sim}\text{pacifist}(x)}{{\sim}\text{pacifist}(x)}$$

The first rule says that if x is a Quaker and it is consistent to believe that x is a pacifist, then conclude that x is a pacifist. The second says that if x is a Republican and it is consistent to believe that x is not a pacifist, then conclude that x is not a pacifist. The diagram on the left of Figure 6.9 shows Richard Nixon as both a Republican and a Quaker. If the Quaker rule happened to be executed first, the conclusion would be pacifist(Nixon), and the Republican rule would be blocked. But if the Republican rule happened to be first, the conclusion would be ~pacifist(Nixon), and the Quaker rule would be blocked. Such a system would maintain consistency, but the choice between the two options is purely arbitrary.

The diagram on the right of Figure 6.9 shows a kind of conflict that often occurs between the default attributes of a type and a supertype. Elephants are normally gray, but royal elephants are white. A conflict arises because Clyde, a royal elephant, is also an elephant. The usual solution to this conflict is to assume that defaults for the more specific types override or take *priority* over defaults inherited from supertypes. In terms of the egg-yolk representation, a royal elephant is in the egg white for Elephant. Since Clyde is also a royal elephant, he is likely to deviate from the egg-yolk elephants in the same way as his immediate supertype RoyalElephant.

The priority assumption that works for Clyde does not resolve the conflict for

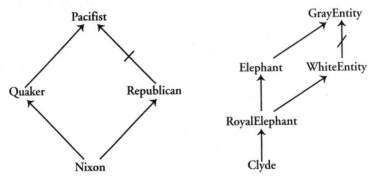

FIGURE 6.9 Two examples of conflicting defaults

Nixon because Quaker and Republican are both at the same level. Some rule-based languages, such as Prolog, execute rules in the order in which they are listed. A programmer can take advantage of that order by listing the more likely option Republican before the less likely option Quaker. If the first option leads to a contradiction, the Prolog inference engine backtracks to try one of the later options. Some languages that do not have ordered rules, such as CLIPS, allow a numeric priority level to be assigned to different options.

Rule order in Prolog and numeric priority in CLIPS support a linear ordering of defaults. But a fixed linear order has two weaknesses: first, it depends on some programmer's best guess about the importance or likelihood of the various options; second, most conflicts arise because of nonlinear dependencies, such as the diamond patterns in Figure 6.9. To represent those dependencies, some graph or network-based approaches have been developed:

- *Inheritance with defaults.* Scott Fahlman (1979) designed a network language (NETL) for inheritance with defaults. It was based on a mechanism of propagating markers, which trigger computations in the same way as tokens in a Petri net. NETL was a complex system that mixed many different mechanisms, and Fahlman did not analyze all their logical implications in detail. Rich Thomason and David Touretzky (1991) did a formal analysis of such mechanisms that confirmed many of Fahlman's informal intuitions, but clarified and corrected others.

- *Truth-maintenance systems.* Jon Doyle (1979) designed a truth-maintenance system (TMS) as a network of propositions linked by implications. Each node represents a proposition that is *in* or *out*, depending on its consistency with a given set of axioms and the other nodes that are currently marked *in*. The techniques have been extended to *nonmonotonic* (NMTMS), *justification-based* (JTMS), *logic-based* (LTMS), and *assumption-based* (ATMS) truth-maintenance systems. In effect, a TMS is a bookkeeping system for metalevel reasoning about logical dependencies among propositions. For nonmonotonic logic, it can improve efficiency by replacing global consistency checks with local tests in a limited region of the network.

PRIORITIZED DEFAULTS. Benjamin Grosof (1997) used metalanguage to specify the priorities of different defaults. To illustrate the technique, he adapted an example from Etherington and Reiter (1983) about the shell-bearing properties of molluscs. The first two axioms, which have no exceptions, say that every nautilus is a cephalopod, and every cephalopod is a mollusc:

- $(\forall x)(\text{nautilus}(x) \supset \text{cephalopod}(x))$.
- $(\forall x)(\text{cephalopod}(x) \supset \text{mollusc}(x))$.

By default, every mollusc is shell bearing; a cephalopod, however, is usually not shell bearing; but a nautilus is shell bearing. Grosof represented those defaults by named axioms:

- Mol: $(\forall x)(\text{mollusc}(x) \supset \text{shellBearer}(x))$.
- Cep: $(\forall x)(\text{cephalopod}(x) \supset \sim\text{shellBearer}(x))$.
- Nau: $(\forall x)(\text{nautilus}(x) \supset \text{shellBearer}(x))$.

If any instance x happened to trigger the Cep axiom together with the Mol or Nau axioms, a contradiction would arise. To resolve that conflict, the next two metalevel statements assert that the Nau axiom takes priority or *overrides* the Cep axiom, and the Cep axiom overrides the Mol axiom:

- overrides(Nau,Cep).
- overrides(Cep,Mol).

Whenever the condition parts of two or more named axioms happen to be true for the same instance, the theorem prover checks which axioms have priority. Then it ignores the axioms that are overridden. When all axioms are represented in a Horn-clause form (Prolog style), Grosof proved that a partial ordering of defaults determines a unique, noncontradictory solution for every instance. Given that Molly is a mollusc, Sophie is a cephalopod, and Natalie is a Nautilus, these axioms would predict that Molly and Natalie are shell bearing, but Sophie is not. Exercise 6.11 is another of Grosof's examples that shows how prioritized defaults can be used by a software agent for sorting email.

COMPUTATIONAL COMPLEXITY.   One weakness of default logic is intractability. In classical logic, the rule of modus ponens requires a pattern match that can be done in linear time. Yet even if each rule takes linear time, a complete proof could take exponential time, because a very large number of rules may be executed. In default logic, however, each rule by itself requires a consistency check that could be as complex as an entire proof in conventional logic. A proof with defaults could require an exponential number of rules, each of which might take exponential time.

In contrast with the complexity of default logic, frame systems are usually quite efficient. Inheritance allows an inference to be performed just by following a chain of pointers and copying some data. A default simply cancels one value and replaces it with another. Yet that efficiency is purchased at the expense of reduced expressive power: many kinds of inferences cannot be handled by inheritance alone. If framelike inheritance were the only inference rule, default logic could also do consistency checks as efficiently as a frame system. There is no magic: frame notation cannot solve an unsolvable problem; it merely limits the expressive power so that the difficult questions cannot be asked.

Of the logically respectable versions of nonmonotonic logic, the most efficient are implemented in database and expert system languages like Prolog, CLIPS, and SQL. When the variables in those languages are restricted to the scalar values of a relational database, they form an even more restricted language called *Datalog*, in which proofs can be done in polynomial time. Although buggy programs can be written in any language, those systems have sound foundations that can be used to support logically secure implementations (Apt, Blair, & Walker 1988; Van Gelder 1988).

6.5 Theories, Models, and the World

The problems of knowledge soup result from the difficulty of matching abstract theories to the physical world. The techniques of fuzziness, probability, defaults, revisions, and relevance are different ways of measuring, evaluating, or accommodating the inevitable mismatch. Each technique is a metalevel approach to the task of finding or constructing a theory and determining how well it approximates reality. To bridge the gap between theories and the world, Figure 6.10 shows models as Janus-like structures, with an engineering side facing the world and an abstract side facing the theories.

On the left is a picture of the physical world, which contains more detail and complexity than any humanly conceivable model or theory can represent. In the middle is a mathematical model that represents a domain of individuals $\mathcal{D}$ and a set of relations $\mathcal{R}$ over $\mathcal{D}$. If the world had a unique decomposition into discrete objects and relations, the world itself would be a universal model, of which all accurate models would be subsets. But as the examples in this book have shown, the selection of a domain and its decomposition into objects depends on the

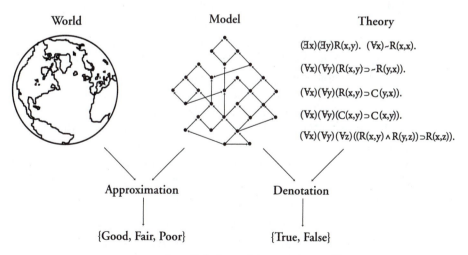

FIGURE 6.10 Relating a theory to the world

intentions of some agent and the limitations of the agent's measuring instruments. Even the best models are approximations to a limited aspect of the world for a specific purpose. Engineers express that point in a pithy slogan: *All models are wrong, but some are useful.*

On the right of Figure 6.10 are the axioms of a theory that describes the world in terms of the individuals and relations in the model. Alfred Tarski (1935) introduced *model theory* as a way of defining the *denotation* operator δ, which determines the truth value of a sentence in terms of a model. If s is any sentence that uses only the names of individuals and relations in the model, δs is either true or false. For finite models that can be stored in a computer, Tarski's relational structures resemble the tables of a relational database or the ground-level facts asserted in Prolog. To make the resemblance into an exact equivalence, the *closed-world assumption* must be added: every relationship not found in the tables is assumed to be false. With that assumption, the denotation operator δ can be computed by an SQL query or a Prolog goal. If a model is stored in a database, a theory can be verified by translating each axiom to an SQL query and checking whether it is true or false.

FACTS, FICTIONS, AND HYPOTHESES. In a model of an actual situation, all the entities in the domain $\mathscr{D}$ exist in the world. But to represent the semantics of natural languages, logic must also accommodate plans for the future, historical entities that no longer exist, hypotheses whose truth value is unknown, and stories in which some or all the characters and events are fictitious. The Sherlock Holmes stories, for example, mix fictional characters with actual places and institutions in London. Histories that purport to be factual may contain dubious material that would not be admitted in a court of law, and even a court must be able to talk about entities whose existence is in dispute. Models for scientific theories, history books, and fictional stories must be able to represent mixtures of contemporary, historical, hypothetical, and fictional entities. In a library, books about one topic may be classified as fact, and books about another as fiction. Yet those are metalevel classifications. At the object level, the language of a novel is indistinguishable from the language of a history book. Today, the standard way to verify information about anybody — living, dead, or fictional — is to search the Internet.

The problems of fictitious and hypothetical entities troubled Plato, Aristotle, and all the philosophers who have thought about logic ever since. Karel Lambert (1967) coined the term *free logic* for logics that allow variables to refer to entities whose existence is dubious. In a collection of papers on free logic (Lambert 1991), the fourteen authors defined more than fourteen versions:

- The basic language of all versions looks like classical first-order logic. Some versions add special vocabulary such as a quantifier (E!x) or a predicate exists(x) to indicate that x actually exists somewhere in the world.

- The major difference between free logic and classical FOL is in the model theory. Instead of a single domain $\mathcal{D}$ of individuals, the domain is split in two disjoint sets: an *inner domain* $\mathcal{D}_i$ of ordinary entities that exist in the real world and an *outer domain* $\mathcal{D}_o$ of problematical entities that may not exist.

- The various model theories differ in the truth values assigned to simple sentences that mention entities in $\mathcal{D}_o$. The sentence *Ancient Greeks worshipped Zeus* would be true in *positive free logic*, false in *negative free logic*, and indeterminate in *neutral free logic*.

The characteristic feature of all versions is freedom from assumptions about the existence of referents for both the general terms (entity and relation types) and the singular terms (names and definite descriptions).

The definition of free logic is broad enough to accommodate the models illustrated in Figure 6.10. Such models support a version of positive free logic whose language is identical to classical first-order logic:

- The domain $\mathcal{D}$ of the model is an arbitrary set whose elements are called *surrogates*. A conventional model is a special case in which the surrogates are actual entites in the world. In a computer, the surrogates may be *object identifiers* (OIDs) or *universal resource locators* (URLs) that are easier to store on a disk than physical trees, cows, and people.

- The rules of inference and the denotation operator δ are the same as in classical FOL.

- The logic is free because there is no requirement that the surrogates correspond to entities in the world. The inner domain $\mathcal{D}_i$ consists of the elements of $\mathcal{D}$ for which there exists a one-to-one mapping to some set of entities in the world. The remaining surrogates constitute the outer domain $\mathcal{D}_o$.

- The framework of contexts presented in Chapter 5 may be used to express metalevel statements about the logic, the models, and the correspondence between the surrogates and the world. A context A could contain a theory $\mathcal{T}$, a context B could contain a model $\mathcal{M}$, and both A and B could be nested in a context C that contained metalevel statements relating $\mathcal{T}$ to $\mathcal{M}$.

The framework of contexts and metalevels allows more flexibility than just a two-way split in the domain. Different concept types in the ontology may have different identity conditions that determine how the entity that corresponds to a particular surrogate is recognized. Objects and events, for example, could be represented by similar kinds of surrogates in the model, but the criteria for recognizing their real-world counterparts would be very different. The fuzzy rules and default options discussed in Sections 6.3 and 6.4 could also be treated as metalevel criteria about the adequacy of a model with respect to the world, not as modifications to the logic or the denotation operator. Computationally, the surrogates and models could be stored in a relational database, and all the programs based on classical FOL, including theorem provers, query processors, and expert system shells, could be used to manipulate them.

FINDING THE BEST THEORY. Although the world is bigger than any human can comprehend or any computer can compute, the set of all possible theories and models is even bigger. The entire universe contains a finite number of atoms, but the lattice of theories discussed in Section 2.5 is infinite, and the number of possible models of those theories is uncountably infinite. The ultimate task of science is to search that vast infinity in the hope of finding a theory that gives the best answers to all possible questions. Yet that search may be in vain. Perhaps no single theory is best for all questions; even if one theory happened to be the best, there is no assurance that it would ever be found; and even if somebody found it, there might be no way to prove that it is the best.

Engineers have a more modest goal. Instead of searching for the best possible theory for all problems, they are satisfied with a theory that is good enough for the specific problem at hand. When they are assigned a new problem, they look for a new theory that can solve it to an acceptable approximation within the constraints of available tools, budgets, and deadlines. Although no one has ever found a theory that can solve all problems, people everywhere have been successful in finding more or less adequate theories that can deal with the routine problems of daily life. As science progresses, the engineering techniques advance with it, but the engineers do not have to wait for a perfect theory before they can do their work.

NAVIGATING THE LATTICE OF THEORIES. The infinite lattice of theories resembles "The Library of Babel" envisioned by the poet, storyteller, and librarian Jorge Luis Borges (1941). His library consists of an infinite array of hexagonal rooms with shelves of books containing everything that is known or knowable. Unfortunately, the true books are scattered among infinitely many readable but false books, which themselves are an insignificant fraction of the unreadable books of random gibberish. In the story by Borges, the library has no catalog, no discernable organization, and no method for distinguishing the true, the false, and the gibberish. In a prescient anticipation of the World Wide Web, Borges described people who spend their lives aimlessly searching through the rooms with the hope of finding some hidden secrets. But no matter how much truth lies buried in such a collection, it is useless without a method of organizing, evaluating, indexing, and finding the books and the theories contained in them.

From each theory, the partial ordering of the lattice defines paths to more general theories above and more specialized theories below. Figure 6.11 shows four basic ways of moving along the paths from one theory to another: *contraction, expansion, revision,* and *analogy.*

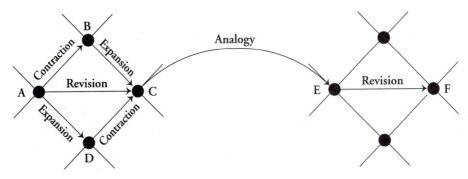

FIGURE 6.11 Navigating the lattice of theories

To illustrate the moves through the lattice, suppose that theory A is Newton's theory of gravitation applied to the earth revolving around the sun and that F is Niels Bohr's theory about an electron revolving around the nucleus of a hydrogen atom. The path from A to F is a step-by-step transformation of the old theory to the new one. The revision step from A to C replaces the gravitational attraction between the earth and the sun with the electrical attraction between the electron and the proton. That step can be carried out in two intermediate steps:

- *Contraction.* Any theory can be contracted or reduced to a smaller, simpler theory by deleting one or more axioms. In the move from A to B, axioms for the gravitational force would be deleted. Contraction has the nonmonotonic effect of blocking proofs that depend on the deleted axioms.

- *Expansion.* Any theory can be expanded by adding one or more axioms to it. In the move from B to C, axioms for the electrical force would be added. The net result of both moves is a substitution of electrical axioms for gravitational axioms.

Unlike contraction and expansion, which move to nearby theories in the lattice, analogy jumps to a remote theory, such as C to E, by systematically renaming the types, relations, and individuals that appear in the axioms: the earth is renamed the electron; the sun is renamed the nucleus; and the solar system is renamed the atom. Finally, the revision step from E to F uses a contraction step to discard details about the earth and sun that have become irrelevant, followed by an expansion step to add new axioms for quantum mechanics.

By repeated contraction, expansion, and analogy, any theory or collection of beliefs can be converted into any other. Multiple contractions would reduce a theory to the *empty* or *universal theory* ⊤ at the top of the lattice that contains only the tautologies that are true of everything. Multiple expansions would lead to the *inconsistent* or *absurd theory* ⊥ at the bottom of the lattice, which contains all axioms and is true of nothing. Each step through the lattice of theories is simple in itself, but the infinity of possible steps makes it difficult for both people and computers to find the best theory for a particular problem. Newton became famous for finding the axioms that explain the solar system, and Bohr won the Nobel Prize for revising them to explain the atom.

THEORY REVISION.   The techniques of nonmonotonic logic depend on meta-level reasoning about defaults, consistency, abnormality, priorities, or the failure to prove. Instead of using nonmonotonic logic, the philosophers Isaac Levi (1980) and Peter Gärdenfors (1988) have maintained that it is conceptually simpler to keep first-order logic and use explicit metalevel reasoning about the axioms of a theory. The process of *theory revision* or *belief revision* is a metalevel technique for modifying axioms to construct a new theory that forms a better match to a given collection of facts. It can be considered a method of navigating the infinite lattice of first-order theories.

If the axioms of a theory are *independent*, expansion or contraction can be done by adding or deleting one axiom at a time. But dependencies among the axioms make the operations more difficult. As an example, consider a theory that happens to include axioms of the following form:

$p. \quad q. \quad p{\supset}q.$

Deleting q by itself would have no effect, since the other two propositions imply q: their deductive closure would bring q back into the fold. To delete q completely, one of the other propositions must also be deleted, but there is no obvious way of deciding which one. Expansion is more risky because the addition of a single proposition that happens to contradict one of the others causes the entire theory to degenerate into the absurd theory $\perp$. To avoid falling into the pit of $\perp$, Levi recommended that revising a theory $\mathcal{T}$ by a new proposition p proceed in two steps: first contract $\mathcal{T}$ by removing $\sim p$ and anything that implies $\sim p$ before expanding with p. Such methods have been codified in the *AGM axioms* for theory revision, named for their authors, Carlos Alchourrón, Peter Gärdenfors, and David Makinson (1985). The AGM axioms are metalevel guidelines equivalent in power to the nonmonotonic logics discussed in Section 6.4.

THEORIES AS EXPLANATIONS.   The lattice of theories with the AGM axioms is better organized than the uncataloged library of Babel. But it shows only the possible pathways; it does not explain why anyone should prefer one path to another. In terms of Peirce's categories, the view of a theory as a deductive closure is determined by its syntactic form or Firstness. Given axioms $\mathcal{A}$, the deductive closure $\mathcal{T}$ is defined as the set of all propositions that are derivable from the axioms by the provability operator $\vdash$:

$$\mathcal{T} = \{p \mid \mathcal{A} \vdash p\}.$$

This is a definition of $\mathcal{T}$ by Firstness, since it has no dependencies on anything outside of $\mathcal{T}$. If $\mathcal{T}$ is expressed in first-order logic, for which the inference rules are sound and complete, it coincides with the set of all propositions that are semantically entailed by every entity that is described by the axioms $\mathcal{A}$:

$$\mathcal{T} = \{p \mid (\forall x{:}\text{Entity})(\text{dscr}(x,\mathcal{A}) \supset x \vDash p)\}.$$

This is a definition of $\mathcal{T}$ by Secondness, since the entailment operator $\vDash$ relates the propositions in $\mathcal{T}$ to entities that are external to $\mathcal{T}$. The Secondness of a theory is its applicability to the description of entities outside of itself. But by itself, a description is not sufficient for an explanation.

In the empirical sciences, a theory is more than a collection of propositions. To be meaningful, it must have applications (Secondness) and explanatory power (Thirdness). Explanation is Thirdness because it relates a theory (first) to some entity (second) in a way that enables some agent (third) to make predictions about properties of the entity that are not explicitly described.

1. If the applications are ignored, a theory is nothing more than the deductive closure (Firstness) of a set of axioms. The formulas of the theory are abstract patterns that characterize some form; the word *formula*, in fact, is a Latin word meaning "little form."

2. If the formulas of a theory are treated as summaries of observed data (Secondness), but without any consideration of their predictive or explanatory power (Thirdness), then the theory could be considered an instance of type Proposition.

3. In the empirical sciences, a theory must have an application (Secondness), and the deductive steps of a proof must serve as an explanation (Thirdness) of the cause-and-effect relationships in the application domain. As Thirdness, an explanation always involves an intention that relates an observer, a theory, and a domain.

The same forms may be applied to different domains. The differential equation for an oscillator, for example, may be applied to a radio circuit, a sound wave, or the springs in a car's suspension; each application would be a different proposition. For an application (Secondness) to provide an explanation (Thirdness), some agent must have an intention to use the formulas as an explanation.

ABDUCTION.   Peirce coined the term *abduction* for the process of generating hypotheses, whose consequences are later developed by deduction. The term has been adopted by AI researchers for an initial stage of hypothesis formation to be followed by a later stage of deduction from the hypotheses. Abduction may be considered a process of selecting chunks of knowledge from the soup, evaluating their relevance to the problem at hand, and assembling them into a consistent theory. It may be performed at various levels of complexity:

- *Reuse.* Do an associative search for a predefined theory that can be reused for the current problem.
- *Revise.* Find a theory that approximately matches the problem at hand and use belief revision techniques to tailor it for the current situation.
- *Combine.* Search for scattered fragments of knowledge and perform repeated steps of belief revision to combine them into a complete theory.

Abduction and deduction may be used iteratively. Peirce noted that after a hypothesis is formed by abduction, its consequences must be tested by deduction. If the implications do not match reality, the hypothesis must be revised in another stage of abduction. Figure 6.12 illustrates the use of abduction for extracting a theory or parts of a theory from the knowledge soup, belief revision for modifying the theory, and deduction for answering questions.

As an example, consider a bridge player who is planning a line of play. The knowledge soup for bridge includes tactics like finesses and endplays, probability estimates for various card distributions, and techniques for analyzing a given bridge hand to find an optimal line of play. In double-dummy bridge (where all 52 cards are arranged face up) there is no uncertainty, and success depends only on precise deduction. But in a normal game, each player sees half the cards dealt, and the distribution of the remaining cards must be guessed from probabilities and hints from the bidding and play. In planning the play, a bridge player combines abduction and deduction:

- *Abduction.* Imagine the possible distributions of the unseen cards and estimate their likelihood. Each possibility constitutes one theory about the current deal.
- *Deduction.* Determine optimal strategies for each distribution and search for a compromise that wins the maximum number of tricks with the favorable distributions while limiting the losses with the unfavorable ones.

Depending on the novelty of the situation, either of these phases could be simple or complex. In abduction, a bridge player might quickly recall a similar hand from prior experience or spend considerable time imagining a novel distribution and doing a lengthy analysis to compute the odds. In deduction, the player might already have a predefined pattern for a routine finesse or need to make detailed inferences to work out a complex endplay. The two phases may be iterated: if deduction does not determine a winning strategy, another phase of abduction may be used to find a different distribution that could lead to a better strategy. For routine bridge hands, a bridge player might complete both phases in a few seconds, but a complex hand might require several minutes of thinking before the first card is played. During the play, new information is obtained at each trick; it may

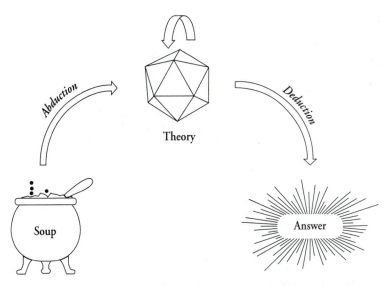

FIGURE 6.12 Crystallizing theories out of knowledge soup

confirm one of the hypotheses, or it may be a "surprise" that forces the player to return to the abduction stage and generate a new hypothesis.

The example of the bridge player shows how abduction could use statistics with a continuous range of probabilities for dealing with uncertainty, while deduction uses a two-valued logic. The two phases of reasoning may be stated more generally:

- *Abduction.* Use associative search to find chunks in the knowledge soup that match the current situation and use statistical measures to determine their relative importance. If no chunk matches exactly, find several chunks that match partially and combine or modify them to form a theory that applies.

- *Deduction.* Apply the theory to find a solution to the current problem. If new information conflicts with the theory, go back to the abduction phase to modify it or to find a better one.

Some problems may require more emphasis on one phase or the other. In poker, uncertainty predominates, and deduction is minimal. In chess, uncertainty vanishes, and deduction predominates. Yet even in chess, the limit on thinking time requires a cut-off of deduction and the use of heuristic measures for evaluating positions. Most situations in life require a combination of both kinds of thinking.

As another example of abduction and deduction, consider whether Nixon is a pacifist. The two phases in the reasoning process would proceed as follows:

- *Abduction.* Considering what is known about Nixon, search for related items about Republicans and Quakers. In this case, evidence of political activity and absence of strong religious activity suggest that his Republican principles outweigh his Quaker principles. Therefore, a first approximation to a theory of Richard Nixon would start with everything typical of Republicans; knowledge about Quakers would be added only if there were no conflict with the knowledge about Republicans.

- *Deduction.* In the theory of Nixon constructed by abduction, the Republican views about pacifism would remain, and the Quaker views would be lost. Therefore, the conclusion would be that Nixon is not a pacifist.

For this example, most of the work is done in the abduction phase, which depends on metalevel information about the relevance of the competing theories. See Exercises 6.14 and 6.15 for a comparison of this technique to the method of prioritized defaults discussed in Section 6.4.

For the problem about driving to Boston, the initial theory would include only the most salient propositions:

If you have a car, you can drive 55 mph on a highway.

New York is about 200 miles from Boston.

If the driving time between two locations is four hours or less

it is reasonable to consider driving between them.

For most drivers, this is a familiar theory that would be retrieved in the abduction phase. But when the engine fails to start, the mismatch between the theory and reality forces the driver to revise the theory. The first condition, "if you have a car," must be qualified: "if you have a car and it is in working order." Another abduction step would be needed for find a theory about how to fix a nonworking car. There is no limit to the number of abduction steps that may be needed: while the driver is trying to find someone with jumper cables to get the engine started, it may start to snow.

COMBINING KNOWLEDGE SOURCES.   Marvin Minsky (1987) has been skeptical of the notion of a unified, monolithic reasoner based on pure logic. Instead, he has a vision of mind as a society of interacting agents, each specialized for one aspect of knowledge or intelligence. The appearance of unity would result from averaging over a large number of independent agents. To implement his view, Minsky suggested that AI systems should be designed as societies of interacting agents, each of which might find a niche where it could contribute its knowledge or talents to the overall flow of thought. Precise, logical reasoning might be done by some of the agents, but others might pursue independent trains of "thought" that sometimes lead to conflicts and sometimes to harmonious resolution.

The most direct source of knowledge about the world is observation. An indirect approach, commonly used in engineering, is to construct a model of some

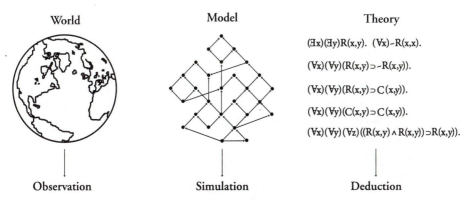

World	Model	Theory
		$(\exists x)(\exists y)R(x,y).$ $(\forall x)\sim R(x,x).$
		$(\forall x)(\forall y)(R(x,y)\supset \sim R(x,y)).$
		$(\forall x)(\forall y)(R(x,y)\supset C(x,y)).$
		$(\forall x)(\forall y)(C(x,y)\supset C(x,y)).$
		$(\forall x)(\forall y)(\forall z)((R(x,y)\wedge R(x,y))\supset R(x,y)).$
Observation	Simulation	Deduction

FIGURE 6.13 Three sources of knowledge about the world

existing or proposed system and observe the simulated behavior in circumstances that would be expensive, dangerous, or unethical to recreate in the real world. Deduction from a theory is even more indirect: the axioms of the theory are abstractions from patterns of relationships in the model, which itself is an abstraction from the world. Figure 6.13 shows the world, a model, and a theory together with methods for extracting knowledge from them.

The three knowledge sources in Figure 6.13 are complementary rather than competing. To answer a question, the choice of method depends on the available data, the computing resources, the required precision, and the amount of time and money that can be devoted to the study. As an example, consider a question about tomorrow's weather:

1. *Observation.* Weather satellites gather enormous amounts of data about the weather across the world. By watching the movement of air masses, a forecaster can see where tomorrow's air, with its temperature and moisture, is coming from.

2. *Simulation.* With supercomputers, meteorologists can model the earth's atmosphere at various altitudes and study the transfer of heat and moisture to and from the ground, the oceans, and the sky. After a simulation, they can read the data for any particular time and place.

3. *Deduction.* Before the days of satellites and supercomputers, forecasters predicted the weather by applying general rules to a relatively small amount of data. Since the prevailing winds come from the west, tomorrow's weather in New York can often be derived from a few rules applied to yesterday's measurements in Chicago and Pittsburgh. The lake effect rules in Exercises 3.6 through 3.9 illustrate the use of deduction for predicting rain or snow in Buffalo and Cleveland.

In practice, all three of these knowledge sources are used in combination. Computer simulations are constantly updated and recalibrated with the latest observations; and global models are supplemented with rules to deal with local features, such as cities, lakes, and mountains. Like a carpenter or a plumber, a reasoning system must have a truckload of tools to handle different aspects of the same problem.

In the progression from left to right of Figure 6.13, some detail is lost at each level of abstraction, but each loss is compensated by an increase in generality. With minor adjustments, an engineering model can be adapted to many different situations, and a scientific theory can be applied by engineers working in different domains. The equations of fluid mechanics, for example, apply to the earth's atmosphere, to the ocean currents, and even to the flow of magma deep beneath the earth's crust. Because of their generality, abstract theories suggest new models and supply the categories for interpreting new data. Only raw feelings are truly direct; every recorded observation is an interpretation of sensory input in terms of the categories of some preconceived theory. Knowledge acquisition involves a constant cycling from data to models to theories and back to a reinterpretation of the old data in terms of the new theories. Beneath it all, there is a real world, which people learn to approximate through repeated cycles of abstraction and reinterpretation.

6.6   Semiotics

The knowledge soup consists of collections of *signs* — images, symbols, words, and concepts with associated feelings. An important step toward managing the complexity of the knowledge soup is to analyze and classify the kinds of signs it contains. The study of signs, called *semiotics*, was independently developed by C. S. Peirce and the linguist Ferdinand de Saussure. The term comes from the Greek *sēma* (sign); Peirce originally called it *semeiotic*, and Saussure called it *semiology*, but *semiotics* is the most common term today. Saussure (1916) defined it as a general subject that includes all of linguistics as a special case:

> Language is a system of signs that express ideas, and is therefore comparable to a system of writing, the alphabet of deaf-mutes, symbolic rites, polite formulas, military signals, etc. But it is the most important of all these systems.
>
> A science that studies the life of signs within society is conceivable; it would be part of social psychology and consequently of general psychology; I shall call it semiology. . . . Semiology would show what constitutes signs, what laws govern them. Since the science does not yet exist, no one can say what it would be; but it has a right to existence, a place staked out in advance. Linguistics is only part of the general science of semiology; the laws discovered by semiology will be applicable to linguistics, and the latter will circumscribe a well-defined area within the mass of anthropological facts.

Just as Saussure the linguist classified linguistics as a branch of semiotics, Peirce the logician classified logic as a branch of semiotics. In applying his trichotomy of Firstness, Secondness, and Thirdness, Peirce (1897) divided semiotics into three branches:

1. *Syntax.* "The first is called by Duns Scotus *grammatica speculativa.* We may term it *pure grammar.* It has for its task to ascertain what must be true of the representamina used by every scientific intelligence in order that they may embody any *meaning.*"

2. *Semantics.* "The second is logic proper. It is the science of what is quasi-necessarily true of the representamina of any scientific intelligence in order that they may hold good of any *object*, that is, may be true. Or say, logic proper is the formal science of the conditions of the truth of representations."

3. *Pragmatics.* "The third. . . I call *pure rhetoric.* Its task is to ascertain the laws by which in every scientific intelligence one sign gives birth to another, and especially one thought brings forth another." (CP 2.229)

The words *syntax, semantics,* and *pragmatics* were introduced by Charles Morris (1938) in his presentation of Peirce's three branches of semiotics. As Peirce developed it, semiotics is an observational science, which formulates general laws that govern the nature and use of signs by "any scientific intelligence," which he defined as "an intelligence capable of learning by experience." By that term, Peirce included animal intelligence and even mindlike processes in inanimate matter.

ARBITRARY NATURE OF SYMBOLS. Saussure used the terms *signifier* and *signified* for Peirce's distinction between *sign* and *interpretant.* Instead of Peirce's triadic relationship of sign, interpretant, and object, Saussure (1916) emphasized the role of signs in distinguishing what is considered to be an object:

A language does not simply assign arbitrary names to a set of independently existing concepts. It sets up an arbitrary relationship between signifiers of its own choosing on the one hand, and signifieds of its own choosing on the other. Not only does each language produce a different set of signifiers, articulating and dividing the continuum of sound in a distinctive way, but each language produces a different set of signifieds; it has a distinctive and thus "arbitrary" way of organizing the world into concepts or categories.

In emphasizing the arbitrary nature of signs, Saussure denied that the world naturally divides into distinct objects that are waiting to be labeled. Instead, the categories of language draw attention to certain aspects of the world that are considered as objects. Different languages, cultures, and individuals make different selections from the continuum of possibilities that may be treated as significant.

CLASSES OF SIGNS.   In developing his theory of signs, Peirce (1867) started with the trichotomy of icon, index, and symbol. That is the *relational trichotomy*, which is determined by the way the sign is related to its object. Later, Peirce (1897) recognized that the relational trichotomy is based on Secondness — the relationship between a sign and its object. He therefore looked for two other trichotomies based on the Firstness or Thirdness of the sign. The signs in the first or *material trichotomy* signify by the nature of the sign itself; those in the third or *formal trichotomy* signify by some formal rule that associates sign and object. The matrix in Figure 6.14 shows Peirce's three trichotomies of signs, with the name and a brief description of each kind of sign.

Different aspects of the same situation may be analyzed according to the different kinds of signs in Figure 6.14. As an example, consider a situation with a ringing telephone and the associated signs. The following examples illustrate the material trichotomy:

1. *Qualisign* (material quality): A ringing sound as a pure sensory experience, independent of its source in a telephone, doorbell, or alarm clock.

2. *Sinsign* (material indexicality): A ringing sound coming from the direction of a telephone.

3. *Legisign* (material mediation): The convention that a ringing telephone means that someone is trying to call.

The relational trichotomy is determined by the relationship between sign and object:

1. *Icon* (relational quality): An image that resembles a telephone: ☎.

2. *Index* (relational indexicality): A finger pointing toward a telephone: ☞ ☎.

3. *Symbol* (relational mediation): A ringing sound used on a radio program to suggest a telephone call.

The formal trichotomy is determined by the conventions of some language, either natural or artificial:

1. *Rheme* (formal quality): A word such as *telephone*, which represents the possible existence of a telephone.

2. *Dicent Sign* (formal indexicality): A sentence formed of rhemes used to assert actual existence: "You have a phone call from your mother."

3. *Argument* (formal mediation): A sequence of dicent signs, such as a syllogism, used to express a lawlike relationship: "It may be an emergency. Therefore, you should answer the phone."

Since a "scientific intelligence," as Peirce said, is capable of learning from experience, the interpretation of the same physical signs may change over time. The icon ☎, for

	1. Quality	2. Indexicality	3. Mediation
1. Material	**Qualisign** *A quality which is a sign.*	**Sinsign** *An actual existent thing or event which is a sign.*	**Legisign** *A law which is a sign.*
2. Relational	**Icon** *Refers by virtue of some similarity to object.*	**Index** *Refers by virtue of being affected by object.*	**Symbol** *Refers by virtue of some law or association.*
3. Formal	**Rheme** *A sign of qualitative possibilty.*	**Dicent Sign** *A sign of actual existence.*	**Argument** *A sign of law.*

FIGURE 6.14 Peirce's three trichotomies of signs

example, resembles an old-fashioned telephone. When it is used to refer to a modern telephone, it has become a symbol rather than a pure icon: habitually used icons tend to evolve into symbols.

SEMIOTIC ANALYSIS. Classification is a necessary first step in any science, but the benefits of science come from the theories that relate the categories and the applications that use them to explain the phenomena. As an application of the semiotic categories, consider the following story, which is summarized from a newspaper clipping:

> One family noticed that their telephone would no longer ring. But if they happened to pick up the phone when their dog was barking, they would often find a caller waiting for them. After some investigation, they discovered that the dog's leash was short-circuited to the telephone wires, and the dog was getting an electrical shock whenever someone tried to call. They repaired the phone lines, and things returned to normal for both the dog and the humans.

A barking sound, by itself, is a *qualisign*. Its occurrence served as a *sinsign* that drew the attention of the humans to the dog. When they saw no obvious signs of anything unusual about the dog, they ignored the barking. Over time, however, the habitual association between the barking and the telephone suggested some new law that made barking a *legisign* for a telephone caller. Then the humans began to wonder how that new law was related to known laws about dogs and telephones. They compared the old legisign that relates a ringing telephone to a phone call to the new legisign that relates a barking dog to a phone call. As existing objects, the dog and the telephone were both sinsigns. Those objects were attached to cables, which in turn were sinsigns of electrical conduits. After following the chain of sinsigns, the humans discovered a point of contact, which was an index of a relation between the sinsigns. By applying the laws of electricity (which are themselves signs), they were able to infer another law — an explanation of the causal links from telephone call to electric shock to barking dog.

But the dog also has "scientific intelligence," which is capable of using signs and learning from experience. From its point of view, the electrical shock was a painful sinsign, and pain may be a legisign of some threatening agency. By habit (or instinct, which is a genetically programmed habit), the dog used barking as a legisign to inform the members of its pack (the human family) that something was wrong. Over time, the dog learned a new legisign that barking had a causal effect in stopping the shock.

This semiotic analysis depends on the assumption that people and dogs are capable of recognizing signs and learning from experience. It also assumes some mental capacity that can support triadic relationships of sign, object, and interpretant. It does not, however, assume anything about the nature of that mental capacity or its implementation in neural networks or a language of thought. Peirce noted that mental images are merely the result of neural processes; they are not the mechanisms themselves, about which "there is no reason for supposing a power of introspection; and, consequently, the only way of investigating a psychological question is by inference from external facts" (CP 5.249).

APPLICATIONS OF SEMIOTICS.   Because of its broad scope, semiotics has been applied to subjects ranging from psychoanalysis to literary criticism (Eco 1979, 1990). For AI, semiotics can help resolve philosophical puzzles that have generated heated controversies about the nature of intelligence and its simulation by machine. Following are some ongoing controversies that could be clarified by a semiotic analysis:

1. *Chinese room.* The philosopher John Searle (1980) proposed a thought experiment that stimulated a decade of debate. He imagined a "Chinese room," which received questions written in Chinese characters and generated appropriate answers in Chinese. Inside the room was a man who knew no Chinese, but who followed a book of rules for manipulating the characters in order to transform the input questions to the output answers. Assuming that the Chinese speakers who submitted questions were satisfied with the answers, Searle

asked whether one could therefore assume that the system could be said to "understand" Chinese.

Searle maintained that neither the room as a whole nor any part of it such as the man plus the rulebook could truly be said to understand Chinese. He therefore concluded that a computerlike process of following rules could not achieve humanlike understanding. The ensuing debates went off on many tangents, including the issue of whether connectionist or neural simulations could more readily achieve understanding than rule following.

In terms of Peirce's categories, a native Chinese speaker, the Chinese room, the man inside the room, a digital computer that follows rules, and a neural network are all semiotic systems that are capable of relating signs and signs of signs. The differences between them are not the result of a mysterious process of "understanding," but of differences in the way the signs, objects, and interpretants are related. As semiotic systems, the primary difference between the Chinese room and a native Chinese speaker is that the room lacks sensory inputs and motor outputs for relating symbols to external objects. Therefore, its semiotics is limited to metalanguage that relates one kind of symbols to another. The question of whether the symbols are being manipulated by a human being, a digital computer, or a neural network is irrelevant. A robot with sensory inputs and motor outputs would be a more complete semiotic system than a windowless Chinese room with a human being inside.

2. *Symbolic and imagelike reasoning.* The role of symbols and images in reasoning has been discussed by philosophers and psychologists for centuries. With the advent of computers that can process either images or symbols, the debate has sharpened into arguments over the relative advantages or disadvantages of reasoning by symbol manipulation or by transforming analog *depictions*. In a special issue of the journal *Computational Intelligence*, Janice Glasgow (1993) presented a position paper, "The Imagery Debate," which was followed by two dozen responses by experts in AI and psychology. The discussants in that debate presented examples, made cogent remarks, and took various positions on the issue of whether imagery and symbols are competing or complementary.

From a semiotic point of view, images and symbols are more than complementary; they are necessary components of a complete system of reasoning. Peirce regarded images or icons as primary, and symbols as derived from them by habitual association:

> The only way of directly communicating an idea is by means of an icon; and every indirect method of communicating an idea must depend for its establishment upon the use of an icon. Hence, every assertion must contain an icon or set of icons, or else must contain signs whose meaning is only explicable by icons. . . .

> Symbols grow. They come into being by development out of other signs, particularly from icons, or from mixed signs partaking of the nature of icons and symbols. We think only in signs. These mental signs are of a mixed nature; the symbol parts of them are called concepts.

Wittgenstein (1922) drew a similar distinction between what can be said and what can be shown. Everything that can be said is symbolic; some symbols can be explained by combinations of other symbols; but the ultimate explanations can only be shown by icons.

3. *Subsymbolic processes.* In a book comparing the symbolic and connectionist paradigms, John Dinsmore (1992) observed that the mapping from external objects to internal symbols depends on "mysterious processes" that are not themselves symbolic:

> It follows that there can never be a complete, strictly symbolic theory of cognition. Work in connectionism. . . suggests that dropping down to a lower, *subsymbolic*, level allows mysterious processes to be analyzed more successfully in terms of a nonsymbolic vocabulary.

Peirce would agree with this observation. He maintained that symbols are the end product of a complex process of perception, interpretation, and habituation, which begins with sensory impressions or qualisigns. When the resulting symbols are communicated in a language, either natural or artificial, their intended physical referents can only be determined through the aid of one or more indexes. Of the nine categories of signs in Figure 6.14, the five ranging from qualisigns to indexes could be called subsymbolic, and the three from rhemes to arguments could be called *supersymbolic*.

Peirce's categories provide a vocabulary for describing neural networks as semiotic systems that span the gulf between sensory inputs and symbolic outputs. In the network of Figure 6.15, the uninterpreted signals on the left are *qualisigns* that propagate through the nodes and arcs to generate signals that represent symbols on the right. The learning algorithms used with neural networks create a pattern of *weights* on the arcs that amplify or inhibit the signals. In the *hidden layers* of the network, some signals represent *sinsigns* that indicate the existence of external features or combinations of features, and the patterns of weights that are created by the learning algorithms determine the conditioned reflexes or *legisigns* that map qualisigns to symbols. Peirce would be the first to admit that further analysis and experiments are necessary, but his framework provides a "nonsymbolic vocabulary" for discussing and interpreting them.

4. *Phenomenology.* The philosopher Hubert Dreyfus (1992) has long criticized the goals and methods of AI. He based his philosophy on *phenomenology*, especially in the version developed by Martin Heidegger. His most famous

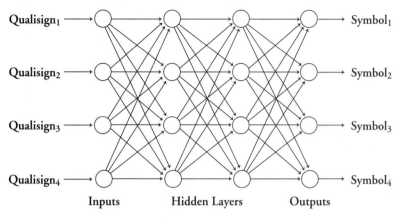

FIGURE 6.15 A neural network for mapping qualisigns to symbols

convert is Terry Winograd, who developed the SHRDLU system discussed in Section 3.3. In the book about SHRDLU, Winograd (1972) claimed that it could "understand natural language." After becoming disillusioned by its limitations, Winograd took the opposite position of denying that AI systems could ever attain true understanding. In a later book (Winograd & Flores 1986), he presented Heidegger's view that it is meaningless to talk about objects and their properties without considering their purpose:

> Another aspect of Heidegger's thought that is difficult for many people to assimilate to their previous understanding is his insistence that objects and properties are not inherent in the world, but arise only in an event of *breaking down* in which they become *present-at-hand* (*vorhandene*). One simple example he gives is that of a hammer being used by someone engaged in driving a nail. To the person doing the hammering, the hammer as such does not exist. It is a part of the background of *readiness-to-hand* (*Zuhandenheit*) that is taken for granted without explicit recognition or identification of an object. It is part of the hammerer's world, but it is not present any more than are the tendons of the hammerer's arm.

In Peirce's terms, the agent's intention in hammering is the Thirdness that gives meaning to the hammer as Secondness in its relationship to the nails and wood. The hammer's Firstness — its "hammerness" or *vorhandene* aspect — becomes significant for human purposes only when the Secondness breaks down, as when the hammer "slips from grasp or mars the wood." Peirce would have been sympathetic to Winograd's recognition of Thirdness, but he always insisted on a proper balance of all three categories: the importance of Thirdness (pragmatics) in no way diminishes the importance of Secondness (semantics) or Firstness (syntax).

This brief discussion cannot do justice to the volumes of commentary that have been written on these topics, but it shows how the semiotic categories draw attention to key issues. By themselves, the categories cannot solve all the problems of knowledge soup, but they are a prerequisite for analyzing, classifying, and stating them precisely. By providing a rich, highly nuanced vocabulary, Peirce's semiotics can help to clarify and resolve some of the endless debates about artificial intelligence. In fact, Peirce himself might have suggested *computational semiotics* as a less contentious name for AI.

EXERCISES

1. Review the examples discussed in Section 6.1 and find more examples at about the same level of detail from various subjects you are familiar with. Select examples from both technical subjects and everyday life. For each example, determine the source of the vagueness or inconsistency and explain why it would create difficulties for a reasoning system.

2. The party game called Horse, Bird, and Muffin shows how categories that are never defined by necessary and sufficient conditions can still be used as effective standards for classification. In the game, the players try to classify people (either celebrities in the news or their friends and associates) by estimating each one's proportions of horselike, birdlike, or muffinlike qualities. As an example, President Clinton might be classified as having a large amount of muffin, but with a considerable amount of horse. His wife, Hillary Rodham Clinton, however, might be classified as mostly horse with some bird. As a class exercise, spend about 15 minutes (preferably at the end of a class period) describing well-known local personalities by their proportion of horse, bird, and muffin.

3. Study the paradox of the heap mentioned in Section 6.1 and the related example of the farmer who thought he could become strong enough to lift a cow. Consider the other modes of continuous variability mentioned in that section: color, weight, length, happiness, warmth, humidity, noise, pain, sweetness, and wealth. Select one of these modes of variability and formulate a paradox similar to the examples of the heap or the farmer.

4. Fuzzy writing more often results from fuzzy thinking than from an inherent fuzziness in language itself. Disciplined literary genres, such as Japanese haiku, help to avoid fuzziness by forcing the author to observe, analyze, and think precisely before starting to write. Each haiku is a poem of exactly seventeen syllables that expresses strong emotion while using only concrete words. For the following exercises, practice writing short descriptions of no more than three sentences (about fifty words), in which every word has a crisp meaning.

Avoid words like *beautiful* or *charming*; instead, use concrete words that would lead the reader to feel that the subject is beautiful or charming. Also avoid intensifiers or hedging words like *very* or *somewhat*.

a. Describe several houses on a street with enough precision that a reader can use the written description to distinguish them. Do not adopt the style of real-estate ads, which are explicit about the number of rooms and bathrooms, but describe the appearance by emotional terms like *attractive* or *exciting*.

b. Write captions for pictures of art works, such as sculptures and paintings, that might be presented on a website. The captions should not give an explicit description, since the readers can look at the pictures. Instead, direct the readers' attention to significant aspects of the artist's technique. For example, if a painting shows a woman looking happy or sad, point out what aspects of her expression, gestures, posture, clothing, surroundings, or lighting convey that impression.

c. Write short descriptions or captions for several objects of the same type, such as butterflies, automobiles, or tropical fish. Assume that they would be used either to identify the objects (as in part a) or to point out significant features (as in part b).

The time for the observation and analysis to write three succinct sentences may take longer than the time to write two rambling pages. Disciplined prose is just as hard to write in natural language as in any programming language or knowledge representation language.

5. Ignoring tacit presuppositions can sometimes be a matter of life or death. More than 100 people were killed in the collapse of two walkways that were suspended over the lobby of a major hotel. The diagram on the left of Figure 6.16 shows the original design, which supported the walkways by suspension rods nearly 14 meters long. Since rods of that length are difficult to work with, the contractor who built the walkways decided to use shorter rods, as in the diagram on the right of Figure 6.16. In calculating the stress points, the engineer made certain assumptions that were invalidated by the contractor's design change. Which connecting points were the first to fail? Why?

6. In the book *To Engineer Is Human*, Henry Petroski discussed many design failures, including the one mentioned in Exercise 6.5. Find similar examples, either in Petroski's book or in other sources. Show how minor changes in assumptions or seemingly insignificant details can make a catastrophic difference in the results. Engineers summarize that principle in Murphy's Law: "If something can go wrong, it will."

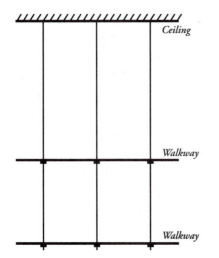
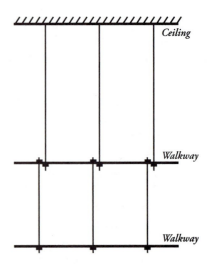

As the engineer designed it   **As the contractor built it**

FIGURE 6.16 Two suspended walkways that collapsed after a major
structural failure

7. Some of the examples in this chapter, such as the paradox of the heap, illustrate
the vagueness caused by continuous variation, where barely noticeable differences have little effect individually, but may become significant by repeated
accumulation. Other examples, such as the structural failure of the walkway
supports in Exercise 6.5, illustrate discontinuities: a seemingly minor alteration
may have have a catastrophic effect. Review the examples of knowledge soup
discussed in this chapter. Classify them as continuous, discontinuous, or other.
Can you find any distinctions for making further subclassifications, especially of
the category "other"?

8. Generalize the definition of abnormality in Section 6.4 to include animals
other than birds: mammals that lay eggs; amphibians that live in trees; a
"growth stage" of dead or stuffed; or the pandas and kinkajous, which belong
to the class Carnivora, but do not eat meat. To accommodate expansions and
revisions, new entries, especially at the species level, should be accommodated
by changing the data rather than the rules. Implement the definitions in
Prolog, SQL, CLIPS, or some other rule-based language.

9. Far from being competitors, logic and statistics are commonly used together
to compute probabilities. If a proposition p is true in m states out of a possible
n states and each state is equally likely, then the probability of p is m/n. Apply
that principle to the following statements to compute the probabilities that

the Giants will play the Buccaneers, Lions, Redskins, or Vikings in the first round of the National Football League playoffs:

- If the Buccaneers, Lions, and Vikings all win their last game of the regular season, the Giants will play the Vikings.
- If the Redskins and Vikings lose, the Giants will play the Vikings.
- If the Lions lose and either the Redskins or the Vikings win, but not both, the Giants will play the Lions.
- If the Redskins win and either the Lions or Vikings win, but not both, the Giants will play the Redskins.
- If the Buccaneers lose and the Lions and Vikings win, the Giants will play the Buccaneers.

None of the Giants' possible opponents are playing one another; therefore, the outcomes of all the games are independent. If the probability of each win or loss is 50%, compute the probabilities that the Giants will play each of the four possible opponents. Compute the probabilities if the Buccaneers, Lions, Redskins, and Vikings have winning probabilities b, l, r, and v respectively.

10. Review the definitions of open, closed, and semi-open databases in Section 6.4. Give examples of application domains whose databases would typically be open, closed, or semi-open. What features of the applications would lead to each kind of database? For your examples of a closed database or subdomain, state the axioms, constraints, or assumptions that require the domain to be closed. Could defaults or statistical techniques help to fill the knowledge gaps in your examples of open or semi-open databases? Which gaps could or could not be filled by defaults?

11. Sorting email according to its importance is a typical metalevel operation that can be specified with prioritized defaults. Suppose that Karen has defined the following rules for a software agent that sorts her email:

- Mail from a retail store is usually unimportant.
- But mail from a store from which Karen is awaiting a delivery is important.
- However, mail from Karen's favorite store, fave.com, is always important.

Translate these three rules to axioms in logic, and use Grosof's technique (described in Section 6.4) for naming the axioms and asserting priorities. Then add the following information about particular instances: baby.com, fave.com, and paris.com are retailers, and Karen is awaiting a delivery from paris.com. Trace the inference steps that Karen's agent would take in classifying message #54 from baby.com, #81 from paris.com, and #117 from fave.com.

12. The technique of applying prioritized defaults described in Section 6.4 can be interpreted as a walk through the infinite lattice of theories described in Section 6.5. Whenever a default theory is applied to a particular aspect of the world, only a consistent subset of axioms is selected. That selection represents an ordinary first-order theory somewhere in the lattice. When the axioms are applied to a different aspect of the world, a different subset of first-order rules is selected. That new selection is a revision of the theory selected for the first application. Apply this approach to select the theory that determines that Molly the mollusc has a shell. Show how that theory can be revised to determine the theories applied to Sophie the cephalopod and Natalie the Nautilus. For Exercise 6.11, do a similar analysis to determine the theories that Karen's email agent selects for messages #54, #81, and #117. This exercise illustrates the principle that a default theory can be interpreted as an abbreviated representation for a family of first-order theories together with metalevel criteria for determining which theory is most appropriate for any particular application.

13. Exercise 3.9 showed how a proof could be explained by translating each step to stylized natural language. Using that technique, write a paragraph that starts with an assertion that Sophie is a cephalopod or that message #117 is from fave.com and explains the implications in terms that could be understood by someone who has never studied formal logic. In your paragraph, explain both the default steps and the classical inference steps.

14. Show how the problem about Nixon the Republican Quaker can be solved by theory revision and by nonmonotonic logic with prioritized defaults. For both methods, use the following two axioms:

   Qua: $(\forall x)(\text{quaker}(x) \supset \text{pacifist}(x))$.
   Rep: $(\forall x)(\text{republican}(x) \supset \sim\text{pacifist}(x))$.

   For nonmonotonic logic, treat these as two named axioms, and state which one overrides the other. For theory revision, treat them as two separate one-axiom theories that float in the knowledge soup, and state the metalevel conditions for selecting one theory or the other.

15. Although a partial ordering of defaults is more flexible than a linear order, no fixed ordering can handle all possible circumstances. After solving Exercise 6.14, add another Republican Quaker named Bob, who is very religious and not politically active. Show how the methods of theory revision and prioritized defaults could be adapted to generate plausible conclusions about Nixon and Bob. Add more people with various combinations of political and religious convictions and show what conclusions theory revision and prioritized defaults would generate.

16. In Section 6.3, the problem of Nixon the Republican Quaker was solved by adjusting certainty factors. Show that the same techniques can be used to generate a plausible conclusion about Bob. Can they also be used to reason about shell-bearing molluscs? Compare the techniques of fuzzy logic, prioritized defaults, and theory revision and evaluate their applicability to different kinds of problems. Which is the most general? Which is the most *ad hoc*? Which is the most efficient? Which gives the best answers to the most questions? Which has the best theoretical justification? Would you trust your life to a car or airplane that was controlled by any of these theories?

17. Some aspects of musical notation are iconic, such as the mapping of high-low pitch to the up-down position of notes on the staff. Other aspects are symbolic, such as the notations for sharps, flats, and the duration of notes. Some aspects are indexical, such as the Italian phrase *Da capo al segno* (from the beginning to the sign). Apply Peirce's classifications in Figure 6.14 to the various features. Examine several musical scores and do a semiotic analysis to classify the kinds of signs and the information they convey.

18. Explain how the three knowledge sources described in Section 6.5 — observation, simulation, and deduction — form a Peircean triad. Review the levels and metalevels of representation in Section 3.6 and Peirce's classification of signs in Section 6.6. Then do a semiotic analysis of the relationships implicit in Figures 6.10 and 6.13. Depending on the depth and detail of the analysis, this exercise could be answered in a paragraph, a term paper, a dissertation, or an encyclopedia.

19. The two trichotomies that form the basis for the table of nine kinds of signs in Figure 6.14 have some similarities to the trichotomy of Independent, Relative, and Mediating in Figure 2.6 and the trichotomy of Structure, Role, and Sign in Figure 2.11. Compare those applications of Peirce's principle, and examine other applications in Sections 2.6, 5.4, and 6.5. What similarities do you find? Is it possible to generalize those trichotomies to incorporate the nine kinds of signs into a more general version of the lattice in Figure 2.6? What new categories are added to the more generalized lattice? Give examples of concept types that are subtypes of those new categories.

20. Many of the hotel policies stated in Appendix C have multiple options with defaults. Select some of those options and show how they could be represented with the kinds of default rules discussed in Section 6.4. Do any of those defaults conflict with one another? If so, name the default rules and state which ones override others. If not, add some features to the problem statement that would introduce possible conflicts and define prioritized defaults to represent them.

CHAPTER SEVEN

Knowledge Sharing
and Acquisition

> *The only way to rectify our reasonings is to make them as tangible as those*
> *of the Mathematicians, so that we can find our error at a glance, and*
> *when there are disputes among persons, we can simply say: Let us*
> *calculate, without further ado, in order to see who is right.*
> GOTTFRIED WILHELM LEIBNIZ, *"The Art of Discovery"*

> *The purpose of computing is insight, not numbers.*
> RICHARD HAMMING, *Numerical Methods for Scientists and Engineers*

> *Our life is frittered away by detail. . . Simplify, simplify.*
> HENRY DAVID THOREAU, *Walden*

7.1 Sharing Ontologies

To the problems of knowledge representation, knowledge sharing adds the further difficulty of relating different choices of representation by different people for different purposes. Each of the three aspects of knowledge representation — logic, ontology, and computation — poses a different kind of problem:

- *Logic.* Different implementations support different subsets and variations of logic. Transferring information from a smaller, less expressive subset to a larger one can usually be done automatically. Transfers in the opposite direction, however, are only possible for information that can be expressed in the common subset of the two versions.

- *Ontology.* Different systems may use different names for the same kinds of entities; even worse, they may use the same names for different kinds. Sometimes two entities with different definitions are intended to be the same, but the task of proving that they are indeed the same may be difficult, if not impossible.

- *Computation.* Even when the names and definitions are identical, computational or implementational side effects may cause the same knowledge to behave differently in different systems. In some implementations, the order of entering rules and data may have an effect on the possible inferences and the

results of computations. Sometimes the side effects may cause a simple inference on one system to get hung up in an endless loop on another system.

These three aspects of knowledge sharing are interdependent. For applications in
library science, humans usually process the knowledge. Therefore, the major attention has been directed toward standardizing the terminology used to classify and
find the information. With its emphasis on computer processing, artificial intelligence requires deep, precise axiomatizations suitable for extended computation and
deduction. But as these fields develop, the requirements are beginning to overlap.
More of the librarian's task is being automated, and the AI techniques are being
applied to large bodies of information that have to be sorted, searched, and
classified before extended deductions are possible.

To address such issues, standards bodies, professional societies, and industry
associations have developed standards to facilitate sharing. Yet the standards themselves are part of the problem. Every field of science, engineering, business, and the
arts has its own specialized standards, terminology, and conventions, but the various
fields cannot be isolated. Medical instruments, for example, must be compatible
with the widely divergent standards developed in the medical, pharmaceutical,
chemical, electrical, and mechanical engineering fields. The standards for hospital
operating rooms must take into account heating, lighting, and air conditioning.
Medical computer systems must be compatible with all of the above plus the
standards for billing, inventory, accounting, payroll, patient records, scheduling,
email, networks, databases, and government regulations. The first requirement is to
develop standards for relating standards.

The three quotations at the beginning of this chapter present desirable, but
sometimes conflicting goals for the techniques of knowledge sharing and acquisition. In his search for mathematical precision, Leibniz led the way to symbolic logic
and calculating machines for knowledge representation. Computer science pioneer
Richard Hamming contributed many innovations to the development of computer
systems, but he was always sensitive to the broader human implications. Yet their
contributions, which simplified some aspects of life, have introduced more of the
details that Thoreau hoped to escape. Even in his cabin on Walden Pond, Thoreau
found some details too daunting — he made periodic visits home, bringing a bag
of laundry for his mother to deal with. The tools for knowledge acquisition should
enhance precision, insight, and simplicity while providing an automatic washer-
dryer to take care of the dirty laundry.

PROBLEMS OF ALIGNING ONTOLOGIES.   Related concepts in the ontologies
underlying different languages and knowledge bases can seldom be put in an exact
one-to-one alignment. Concepts in one ontology may be subtypes, supertypes, or
siblings of the related concepts in another ontology. Figure 7.1 shows the concept

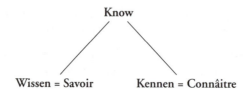

FIGURE 7.1 Subtypes of Know expressed in French and German

type Know, which represents the most general sense of the English word *know,* and two of its subtypes. On the left are the German concept type Wissen and the French concept type Savoir, which correspond to the English sense of knowing-that. On the right are the German Kennen and the French Connâitre, which correspond to the English sense of knowing-some-entity.

Figure 7.2 shows a more complex pattern for the senses of the English words *river* and *stream* and the French words *fleuve* and *rivière.* In English, size is the feature that distinguishes *river* from *stream;* in French, a *fleuve* is a river that flows into the sea, and a *rivière* is either a river or a stream that flows into another river. In translating French into English, the word *fleuve* maps to the French concept type Fleuve, which is a subtype of the English type River. Therefore, *river* is the closest one-word approximation to *fleuve;* if more detail is necessary, it could also be translated by the phrase *river that runs into the sea.* In the reverse direction, *river* maps to River, which has two subtypes: one is Fleuve, which maps to *fleuve;* the other is the English-French hybrid BigRivière, whose closest approximation in French is the single word *rivière* or the phrase *grande rivière.*

Even when words are roughly equivalent in their literal meanings, they may be quite different in *salience.* In the type hierarchy, Dog is closer to Vertebrate than to Animal. But since Animal has a higher salience, people are much more likely to refer to a dog as an animal than as a vertebrate. To illustrate the way salience affects word choice, Figure 7.3 shows part of the hierarchy that includes the English Vehicle and the Chinese Che. The English types Car, Taxi, Bus, Truck=Lorry, and Bicycle are subtypes of Vehicle. The Chinese types do not exactly match the English: Che is a supertype of Vehicle that includes Train (HuoChe), which is not usually considered a vehicle in English. The type QiChe (Energy-Che) has no English equivalent, and it includes Car, which has no Chinese equivalent.

In English, the specific words *car, bus,* and *taxi* are commonly used in speech,

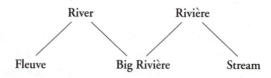

FIGURE 7.2 Hierarchy for River, Stream, and their French equivalents

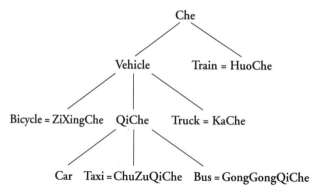

FIGURE 7.3 Hierarchy for English Vehicle and Chinese Che

and the generic *vehicle* would normally be used only in a technical context, such as traffic laws. In Chinese, however, the word *chē* is the most common term for any kind of a vehicle. When the specific type is clear from the context, a Chinese speaker would simply say *Please call me a chē, I'm waiting for the 5 o'clock chē*, or *I parked my chē around the corner*. The fact that *chē* is both a standalone word and a component of all its subtypes enhances its salience; the fact that *chuzuqiche* and *gonggongqiche* are four-syllable words decreases their salience. Therefore, it would sound unnatural to use the word *chuzuqiche*, literally the exact equivalent of *taxi*, to translate the sentence *Please call me a taxi*. In translations from Chinese, the type Che would have to be specialized to a subtype to avoid sentences like *I parked my mobile entity around the corner*. George Lakoff (1987) presents many more examples of the effect of salience in natural languages.

Misalignments between ontologies arise from a variety of cultural, geographic, linguistic, technical, and even random differences. Geography probably contributes to the French distinction, since the major rivers in France flow into the Atlantic or the Mediterranean. In the United States, however, there are major rivers, such as the Ohio and the Missouri, which flow into the Mississippi. The Chinese preference for one-syllable words that can either stand alone or form part of a compound leads to the high salience for *chē*. The English tendency to drop syllables leads to highly salient short words like *bus* and *taxi* from *omnibus* and *taxicab*, which itself is a contraction of *taximeter cabriolet*.

Figure 7.4 shows a "bowtie" inconsistency that sometimes arises in the process of aligning two ontologies. On the left is a mathematical ontology in which Circle is represented as a subtype of Ellipse, since a circle can be considered a special case of an ellipse in which both axes are equal. On the right is a representation that is sometimes used in object-oriented programming languages: Ellipse is considered a subclass of Circle, since it has more complex methods. If both ontologies were merged, the resulting hierarchy would have an inconsistency. To resolve the inconsistency, some

FIGURE 7.4 A bowtie inconsistency between two ontologies

definitions must be changed, or some of the types must be relabeled. In most graphics systems, the mathematical definitions are preferred because they support more general transformations.

ONTOLOGIES AND AXIOMS.   The most widely used ontology for natural language processing is WordNet, developed by George Miller (1995) and his colleagues (Fellbaum 1998). WordNet contains thousands of English words classified by concept types called *synsets* (synonym sets). The synsets are organized in a hierarchy of types and subtypes with a few other associated relations, but with no axioms or formal definitions. An even larger ontology is EDR (Electronic Dictionary Research), which includes 400,000 concept types with the Japanese and English terms that express them (Yokoi 1995). The Cyc system (Lenat 1995) has the most detailed definitions and axioms for its concepts. To facilitate knowledge sharing, these groups have been collaborating with ANSI and ISO committees to develop standards for *aligning* ontologies and their associated axioms. Since WordNet is freely available on the World Wide Web, it is being used as a starting point, but adjustments and revisions are inevitable as inconsistencies between the ontologies are resolved.

Different applications require different amounts of detail in the ontologies and different levels of logic in the representation. Following are the requirements for some typical applications:

- *Information retrieval* (IR). Many search engines on the World Wide Web use arbitrary character strings as the keywords for indexing documents. They are useful for many purposes, but they often find thousands of irrelevant documents (low precision) while missing some of the most significant ones (low recall). Both recall and precision can be improved with ontologies that organize concepts in a generalization hierarchy and show the common relations linked to them. Ontologies like WordNet and EDR, which have thousands of words but very few axioms, are commonly used for IR.

- *Machine translation* (MT). For more than thirty years, MT systems have been used to generate quick drafts of a text in a new language. Ontologies at the level of WordNet and EDR have been used for resolving ambiguities, but most commercial MT systems do not translate the source documents to a logical form that can use detailed axioms at the level of Cyc.

- *Database question answering* (QA). Unlike IR and MT systems, which depend on users to understand the documents, a QA system must analyze the question in sufficient detail to know what it is asking for. Some early QA systems, which were largely based on keywords, were useful for finding data (as an IR system), but their answers were often highly misleading (see the examples in Section 7.2). A robust and reliable QA system must be sensitive to as many logical features of the input as a problem-solving system. The axioms and background knowledge of Cyc would be valuable for analyzing the input questions and doing the inferences necessary to answer them.

- *Problem solving.* Chess-playing programs illustrate the highly-specialized problem solvers that are designed for a specific task or a narrow range of tasks. Commercially practical examples occur in most of the major engineering, financial, scientific, and business applications. Such applications typically have small ontologies with a few dozen or a few hundred concept types. But those ontologies have associated axioms that are far more detailed and specialized than any of the large ontologies, including Cyc. Narrow ontologies, which are tailored for a single application, create serious difficulties for knowledge sharing and reuse. The engineers who design automobiles and the drivers who use them have completely different ways of thinking and talking about them. The workers in auto repair shops face the challenge of becoming multilingual in the ontologies of different manufacturers and drivers.

- *Automatic programming.* In the early days of computers, the term *automatic programming* was applied to compilers that translated high-level languages to machine language. Since then, the term has come to mean the much more difficult task of translating informal specifications written in natural language to formal, executable programs. That task, which is discussed in Section 3.1, was seriously pursued in AI research projects during the 1960s and 1970s. The conclusion of that research was that the problem is far more difficult than anyone had imagined. It would require a total integration of every aspect of language understanding, every reasoning technique ever developed, and broad coverage dictionaries and encyclopedias axiomatized to a depth and precision that has so far been achieved only on very small problems. This is an example of an *AI complete* problem, which cannot be solved until all the outstanding research issues in AI have been settled.

The result of aligning WordNet, EDR, and Cyc with other ontologies would be valuable for most of these tasks. But the problems of knowledge soup discussed in Chapter 6 must always be kept in mind. The standards for relating and aligning ontologies must be systematic, but they must also be open to unforeseen and unforeseeable extensions, modifications, and revisions.

NATURAL LANGUAGE AND PROBLEM SOLVING.   For natural language processing, an ontology must be able to accommodate anything that anyone might say. Its concepts must cover the full range of word senses in the language. For problem solving, the axioms are the major concern, and colorful details expressed in the source language are often irrelevant. As a typical AI problem, consider the *MC puzzle* about missionaries and cannibals who want to cross a river:

> Three missionaries wearing flowing robes and three cannibals wearing loincloths are walking together from one village to another. Along the way, they come to a river where they find a boat that is big enough to hold two people at a time. They want to get everyone across the river, but the missionaries are afraid of being eaten if at any time the cannibals on either bank of the river outnumber the missionaries. How can they manage to get all six people safely across?

The task of translating this English paragraph to any notation for logic and analyzing the conditions of the puzzle is more difficult than the task of solving the puzzle itself. To illustrate the complexity, Figure 7.5 shows a conceptual graph for the first sentence. Literally, it may be read *A set of people consisting of the union of a set x of three missionaries who are wearing flowing robes and a set y of three cannibals who are wearing loincloths are walking together from a village to a village that is different from the first one.*

This sentence illustrates several kinds of problems that arise in translations from language to logic. The word *together* in the original sentence indicates a

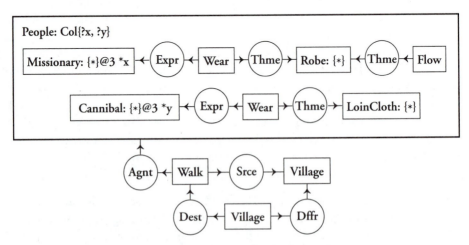

FIGURE 7.5 Conceptual graph for the first MC sentence

collective set Col{?x,?y}, which consists of the union of sets *x* and *y*. But that sentence also contains four other plural nouns: *missionaries, cannibals, robes,* and *loincloths.* No special words or syntactic markers indicate how the corresponding collections are related to one another and to the instances of wearing. In Figure 7.5, the *generic plural* marker {*} leaves open the issue of how many robes or loincloths the people are wearing and how they may be sharing them. If the language analyzer had sufficient background knowledge, it might guess that each of the three mission-aries was likely to wear a separate robe:

```
[Missionary: Dist{*}@3 *x]←(Expr)←[Wear]-
    (Thme)→[Robe]←(Thme)←[Flow].
```

The distributive prefix Dist indicates that each of the three missionaries is wearing a distinct robe. A similar analysis would be needed for the cannibals and their loincloths. See Section 4.1 for other examples of distributive and collective sets.

At the bottom of Figure 7.5, the phrase *one village* was mapped to the concept [Village], which indicates that there exists a village. The word *another* is an indexi-cal, which indicates the existence of a village that is different from the other village. Indexicals like these, which were discussed in Section 5.2, can be resolved by domain-independent rules. Some of the other indexicals, however, require more background knowledge: *the way, they,* and *the cannibals on either bank.* The phrase *the missionaries,* which occurs twice in the paragraph, is an indexical with different referents at each occurrence. The first occurrence refers to all three missionaries, but the second occurrence refers to just those missionaries who are on the same bank as the cannibals. A mistake in resolving the referents might lead to the loss of some missionaries.

Logical features that are critical for problem solving are less important for many applications of natural language processing. For IR, the search engines on the World Wide Web can retrieve dozens of student papers and analyses of the MC puzzle when given just the phrase "missionaries and cannibals." They even find solutions to the problem written in Lisp, Prolog, Java, and other languages. Finding a previously written program is often just as useful as automatically generating a new one. For MT, the logical details of the plurals and indexicals are almost irrelevant: even a crude translation of the English statement to another language would convey enough of the content and purpose that a reader of the target language could understand the relationships. The burden of supplying the back-ground knowledge and deriving the logical constraints is placed on the human reader rather than the machine.

REPRESENTATIONS FOR PROBLEM SOLVING.   After the MC paragraph has been translated to some knowledge representation language, it is still much too complex for most problem-solving programs. Many details, such as the flowing robes and loincloths, are irrelevant. Other details, such as the fear of being eaten and the desire to cross the river, are necessary as motivation, but they do not appear in the final representation. In analyzing the MC puzzle, Saul Amarel (1968) derived a series of six representations, each with progressively less detail. His simplest and most efficient representation for each state is a triple $<m,c,b>$, which represents the number of missionaries m, cannibals c, and boats b on the starting side of the river. The initial state is $<3,3,1>$, and the goal state is $<0,0,0>$. The conditions of the puzzle are translated to axioms, which state the constraints on the form of permissible triples:

- For any state $<m,c,b>$, $0 \leq m \leq 3$, $0 \leq c \leq 3$, $0 \leq b \leq 1$, ($m=0$ or $m \geq c$), and $((3-m)=0$ or $(3-m) \geq (3-c))$.
- For any state $<m_1,c_1,1>$, the next state is $<m_2,c_2,0>$, where $1 \leq (m_1+c_1) - (m_2+c_2) \leq 2$.
- For any state $<m_1,c_1,0>$, the next state is $<m_2,c_2,1>$, where $1 \leq (m_2+c_2) - (m_1+c_1) \leq 2$.

After the English statement has been translated to logical formulas, the problem could be solved by constraint-satisfaction methods, as described in Section 4.6. Doing the translation, however, is the difficult part. Writing a general program that could translate a wide range of problems from English to logic is still an AI complete research problem.

ELABORATION TOLERANCE. With minor changes, Amarel's triples could be used for different numbers of missionaries, cannibals, and boats. But such a highly specialized representation cannot accommodate major changes in the structure of the problem. John McCarthy (1997) coined the term *elaboration tolerance* for the ability of a representation to accommodate changes in structure. As examples, he discussed several kinds of elaborations of the MC puzzle:

- *Political correctness.* The missionaries are in no danger, since the cannibals only eat enemies they capture in war. But if the missionaries outnumber the cannibals, they might convert them and reduce ethnic diversity. Find a solution to the puzzle that avoids the conversion of cannibals.
- *An oar on each bank.* In the initial state, there is one oar on each side of the river. The boat can carry one person with one oar, but two oars are needed for it to carry two persons.
- *Bridge.* Instead of a boat, there is a bridge that can accommodate two persons at a time.
- *Bad boat.* Suppose the boat had a leak. One solution might require a repair stage before the boat could be used. Another solution might require one person to bail and row.

- *Restrictions on rowers.* Case 1: the missionaries can't row. Case 2: only one missionary and one cannibal can row.
- *Restrictions on sizes.* Case 1: the biggest cannibal eats the smallest missionary if they are alone together. Case 2: the biggest cannibal fills the boat. Case 3: the biggest missionary fills the boat.
- *Island.* There is an island in the middle of the river where extra cannibals can be parked until the missionaries get across.
- *Time dependencies.* Cannibals are initially not hungry, but rowing makes them hungry. If the strongest of the missionaries rows fast enough, the cannibals won't get hungry enough to eat the missionaries.
- *Conversion.* A cannibal left alone with three missionaries is converted to a missionary. A missionary who goes too long without food becomes a cannibal.
- *Pregnancy.* One of the missionaries or cannibals happens to be pregnant and has a baby during the crossing. Babies can't row, but they don't take up much space in the boat. They also raise issues of whether the property of being a missionary or a cannibal is inherited or acquired and whether it is manifested at birth or takes some time to develop.

These elaborations, although stated in terms of a toy problem, are typical of the kinds of revisions and extensions that occur in any program as new features and functions are added. A drawback to reusing programs written by other people is the difficulty of adapting them to such changing requirements, especially if they are poorly documented. (As examples, see some of the MC programs found on the World Wide Web.) Specialized representations, which may be highly efficient for one version, are usually the hardest to modify or extend. A general representation in logic is usually the easiest to extend: the revisions can be made by adding and deleting axioms, as in the theory revision systems discussed in Section 6.5. See Exercises 7.1 to 7.6 for further discussion of these issues.

7.2   Conceptual Schema

Every program encodes knowledge about some application or domain of applications, but the conventions for encoding the knowledge depend on some programmer's ingenuity. Figure 7.6 illustrates current practice: application programs are connected to the database and the user interface by thin lines supported by subroutine calls. Each of the circles processes the same logical information about the same application domain. But for each of them, the information must be encoded in different formats, in different languages, and with features that are optimized for one circle but are possibly redundant or incompatible with the features needed for any other circle. As a result, current systems are plagued with special-purpose encodings that are difficult to design, implement, debug, maintain, use, and reuse.

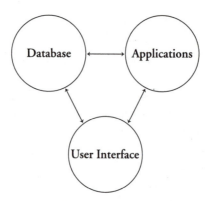

FIGURE 7.6 Calling interfaces in current systems

The need for standardized ways of encoding knowledge has been recognized since the 1970s. The American National Standards Institute (ANSI) proposed that all pertinent knowledge about an application domain should be collected in a single *conceptual schema* (Tsichritzis & Klug 1978). Figure 7.7 illustrates an integrated system with a unified conceptual schema at the center. Each circle is specialized for its own purposes, but they all draw on the common application knowledge represented in the conceptual schema. The user interface calls the database for query and editing facilities, and it calls the application programs to perform actions and provide services. Then the database supports the application programs with facilities for data sharing and persistent storage. The conceptual schema binds all three circles together by providing the common definitions of the application entities and the relationships between them.

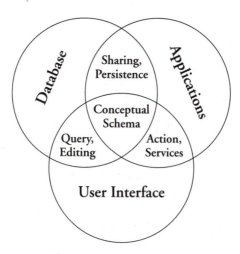

FIGURE 7.7 Conceptual schema as the heart of an integrated system

INTEGRATED SYSTEMS.   For more than twenty years, the conceptual schema has been the key to integrated application design, development, and use. Unfortunately, there were no full implementations. Yet partial implementations of some aspects of the conceptual schema have formed the foundation of several important developments: the *fourth generation languages* (4GLs); the *object-oriented programming systems* (OOPS); and the tools for *computer-aided software engineering* (CASE). Each of these approaches enhances productivity by using and reusing common data declarations for multiple aspects of system design and development. Each of them has been called a solution to all the world's problems; and each of them has been successful in solving some of the world's problems. But none of them has achieved the ultimate goal of integrating everything around a unified schema. One programmer characterized the lack of integration in a poignant complaint:

> Any one of those tools by itself is a tremendous aid to productivity.
> But any two of them together will kill you.

Each tool reshapes the world in its own image with its own data structures and programming techniques. It may be highly efficient within its sphere of influence, but it frustrates peaceful coexistence with other systems based on a different world view. The most serious challenge for all such systems is to accommodate the billions of dollars of existing software — the so-called *legacy systems*. Even if all the programs in the world were magically converted to some new standard, they would not work unless they could process the volumes of old data in the old formats.

The enhanced productivity of the 4GLs, the O-O languages, and the CASE tools is derived from a common strength: improved methods of representing application knowledge in a form that can be used and reused by multiple system components. Their limitations result from a common weakness: the inability to share that knowledge with systems that use a different representation. The potential for conflict is inevitable: sharing requires a common representation, but independently developed systems almost invariably use different representations. In order to support knowledge sharing among heterogeneous systems, the conceptual schema must be general enough to accommodate anything that can be represented in any current system, any legacy system inherited from the past, and any new system that may be developed in the future.

UNIVERSAL LANGUAGES.   To express anything that can be represented in any past, present, or future system requires a *universal language* — one that can represent anything and everything that can be said. Fortunately, universal languages do exist. There are two kinds:

1. *Natural languages.* Everything in the realm of human experience that can be expressed at all can be expressed in a natural language, such as English, French,

Japanese, or Swahili. Natural languages are general enough to explain and comment on any artificial language, mathematical notation, or programming language ever conceived or conceivable. They are even general enough to serve as a *metalanguage* that can explain themselves or other natural and artificial languages.

2. *Logic.* Everything that can be stated clearly and precisely in any natural language can be expressed in logic. There may be aspects of love, poetry, and jokes that are too elusive to state clearly. But anything that can be implemented on a digital computer in any programming language can be specified in logic. Logic can also be used as a metalanguage for defining other formal languages, including itself.

Although anything that can be stated clearly and precisely can be expressed in logic, attaining that level of precision may not be easy. Chapter 6 discussed the limitations of logic in dealing with the complexities of the knowledge soup. Yet logic is all there is: every programming language, specification language, and requirements definition language can be defined in logic; and nothing less can meet the requirements for a complete definition system.

NEED FOR LOGIC.   In the early work on conceptual schemas, Thomas Steele (1975) advocated logic as "the only acceptable choice" for representing database definitions, constraints, and queries. Yet Steele's advice was not heeded, partly because of the unreadability of predicate calculus. But without a solid foundation in logic, a database system cannot be trusted for critical applications. One question-answering system, which was widely used during the 1980s, was advertised as capable of "understanding English," but it did not understand logic. As an example, it included a personnel database for a sample company. Using that database, it correctly answered the following question:

Who are all of the exempt female managers?

The advertising claimed that the system could handle "incorrect grammar." That was true, only because it completely ignored grammar. When the words in the above question were scrambled in the following ways, it would still produce the same answer:

Managers female exempt the of all are who?
Who the be of females all manager on exempts of of?

It discarded all function words such as *a, the, are,* and *of* as "noise words." The only words it saved from this query are *exempt, female,* and *manager.* Regular users learned to type just the basic keywords:

manager female exempt?

Despite its rudimentary treatment of meaning, it was useful for many simple queries. Its major drawback, however, was that it couldn't handle complex queries. Even worse, users had no easy way to tell when a query would be handled correctly or incorrectly. Following are some actual responses:

Q: *How many managers are exempt?*
A: 36

Q: *How many managers are nonexempt?*
A: 5

Q: *How many managers are not exempt?*
A: 5

So far, all of these answers are correct.

Q: *How many exempt managers are not exempt?*
A: *Your request contains a logical inconsistency.*

This is a good response that tells the user that the query was not stated correctly. But note the following response:

Q: *How many exempt managers are nonexempt?*
A: 41

Instead of saying that the request was inconsistent, it answered 41, which is the total number of all managers in its database.

Questions that might seem simple to the user often turned out to be surprisingly difficult for the system. Following is another strange response:

Q: *Are all managers men?*
A: *yes*

On the surface, this response might not seem strange. It could indicate a typical male chauvinist company. But consider the next response:

Q: *Are all managers women?*
A: *yes*

These two responses suggest the following question:

Q: *How many men are also women?*
A: 441

The answer 441 happens to be the total number of employees in the company. Either everybody in the company is a hermaphrodite, or the logic used by the query system is highly unusual.

The manuals did not explain the rules of logic assumed by the system, since logic was considered "too technical" for the average user. By trial and error, however, an experienced user could discover the following implicit rules:

1. If two terms refer to different database fields, connect them with a logical *and*.
2. If two terms refer to the same database field, connect them with a logical *or*.
3. Assume that *not* negates the next database term, and ignore intervening "noise words."
4. Map all quantifying terms to the existential quantifier $\exists$.

These rules are good enough to answer many questions correctly. By rule 3, the system was able to detect the inconsistency in the question *How many exempt managers are not exempt?* But instead of analyzing the word *nonexempt* as a synonym for *not exempt*, it treated it as just another term that might occur in the same database field as *exempt*. By rule 2, it interpreted the question *How many exempt managers are nonexempt?* as though it meant *How many managers are either exempt or nonexempt?* The answer to that question is *all of them* or 41.

Some of the most egregious errors were the result of rule 4, which treats all quantifiers as existential. Because of that rule, the system could not distinguish *any, every, all,* or *some.* Therefore, it treated the questions *Are all managers men?* and *Are all managers women?* as though they were stated *Are any managers men?* and *Are any managers women?* Finally, by throwing away what it considered "noise words," the system treated the question *How many men are also women?* as if it had been stated *How many men and women are there?* The answer to that question is the total, 441.

Many people found the system useful because it was much easier to learn than SQL or any other formal query language. Although it made occasional errors, most of its answers were correct. Furthermore, the system always generated an *echo*: an English paraphrase that showed exactly how it interpreted the input question. But since most of its answers were correct, the users didn't always read the echo. Ironically, the more successful the system became in answering routine questions, the more likely that users would ignore the echo, and the more dangerous its mistakes could become. For a medical database, imagine what might happen if the system treated the following two questions as synonymous:

> *Did every patient who received drug X survive?*
> *Did any patient who received drug X survive?*

The system would answer yes to both of these questions even if 90 percent of the patients died after taking drug X. Some people bought the database system because it was easy to use and it generated attractive reports with colored bar charts and pie charts. But a patient who might be given drug X would undoubtedly prefer a system that paid more attention to logic than to pretty pictures.

ENTITY-RELATIONSHIP DIAGRAMS. Every reliable database language does have a logical foundation. SQL, for example, supports all of first-order logic, although with a notation that is more difficult to read and write than predicate calculus. Even professional programmers rarely write a correct SQL query on their first try, especially when it involves database joins. Many database design languages also support subsets of logic. They include graphic notations such as entity-relationship (E-R) diagrams (Chen 1976) and NIAM (Nijssen & Halpin 1989; Wintraecken 1990). Those notations have proved to be valuable for many purposes. Yet none of them are as general and flexible as logic, and none of them can be used by themselves for a complete system design and specification.

To illustrate some of the issues, Figure 7.8 shows an entity-relationship diagram for part of a university database. The four boxes represent the entity types Department, Course, Section, and Student. The four diamonds represent relations between those types: Offers is a 1-to-n relation between departments and courses; Has is a 1-to-n relation between courses and sections; Enrolls is an n-to-m relation between students and sections; and Major is an n-to-1 relation between students and departments.

E-R diagrams represent some of the information needed for a conceptual schema: a list of the entity types, the permissible relations between them, and some of the constraints on those relations. But they are too limited to express everything needed for data and program specification. Following are the kinds of information that cannot be expressed in E-R diagrams:

- *Instances.* E-R diagrams only represent types and cannot say anything about particular instances of those types. It is not possible, for example, to use E-R as a language for a database update, such as *Student Tom Jones, who is majoring in biology, is enrolled in Section M1B of Course Calculus I.*

- *Integrity constraints.* They can only express constraints on one relation at a time. The following constraint cannot be expressed because it involves two relations, Enrolls and Has: *No student may be enrolled in two or more sections of the same course.*

- *Programs.* They cannot express procedures, time dependencies, dataflows, state transitions, or mathematical formulas.

- *Object-oriented systems.* Although some versions of E-R have been extended to show type or class hierarchies, they cannot represent object encapsulations, message passing, or the operations an object performs in response to a message.

These weaknesses do not imply that E-R diagrams are bad for what they can do. But they do imply that E-R diagrams are incomplete as a design and specification language. Richer languages are needed to supplement them.

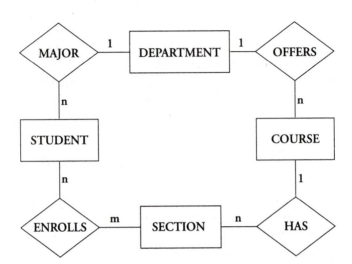

FIGURE 7.8 Entity-relationship diagram for a university database

CONCEPTUAL GRAPHS AND KIF.   To provide a more expressive basis for the conceptual schema, the NCITS T2 committee has developed ANSI standards for two logic-based languages: the Knowledge Interchange Format (KIF) as an inter-change format between heterogeneous systems and conceptual graphs (CGs) as a presentation format with better readability for human users. Although the KIF and CG notations look different, their semantics are identical. The two standards have been developed in parallel to ensure that anything written in one can be translated automatically to the other. Therefore, any information transmitted via KIF could be presented in CGs, and vice-versa. As an example, Figure 7.9 shows a conceptual graph for an assertion that could not be stated in an E-R diagram: *Student Tom Jones majors in the Biology Department, he enrolls in Section M1B, and Course Calculus I has Section M1B.*

Each concept box has two parts: the *type label* on the left of the colon corresponds to the entity types in the E-R diagram; the *referent* on the right designates an instance of the type, such as Tom Jones or M1B. To translate Figure 7.9 to KIF, a concept like

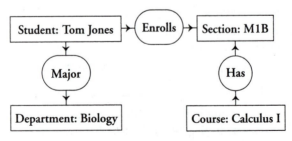

FIGURE 7.9 An assertion stated as a conceptual graph

[Student: Tom Jones] becomes the parenthesized pair (student Tom_Jones). Each relation with *n* arguments becomes a list of *n* elements, starting with the name of the relation. The relationship between Tom Jones and Section M1B would be written (enrolls Tom_Jones M1B). The order of the arguments corresponds to the direction of the arrows: Tom_Jones is first, and M1B is second. Following is the KIF version of Figure 7.9:

```
(and (student Tom_Jones) (department Biology) (section M1B)
     (course Calculus_I) (major Tom_Jones Biology)
     (enrolls Tom_Jones M1B) (has Calculus_I M1B) )
```

In KIF, the operator "and" is used to combine all the information from the concepts and relations; its arguments may be listed in any order.

QUANTIFIERS.   To make general statements about instances, logic and natural languages use quantifiers. The following table compares the quantifiers in English, predicate calculus, conceptual graphs, and KIF:

English	PC	CG	KIF
some student	∃x:student	[Student]	(exists ((?x student)) . . .)
every student	∀x:student	[Student: ∀]	(forall ((?x student)) . . .)

Figure 7.10 shows a conceptual graph with four concepts, each of which is existentially quantified (blank referent). Surrounding the graph is a *context* box marked with a negation symbol ¬. The complete graph may be read *It is false that there exists a student who is enrolled in two different sections of the same course.* This

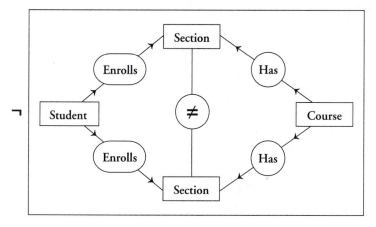

FIGURE 7.10 A constraint stated as a conceptual graph

constraint, which cannot be stated in E-R diagrams, requires the quantifiers of first-order logic.

In KIF, a variable is associated with each of the four concept boxes in Figure 7.10: ?x for the student, ?y for one section, ?z for another section, and ?w for the course. The question mark distinguishes a variable like ?x from a constant like M1B. The operator "exists" is used for the existential quantifier and "not" for the negation. Following is the KIF version of Figure 7.10:

```
(not (exists ((student ?x) (section ?y) (section ?z) (course ?w))
    (and (enrolls ?x ?y) (enrolls ?x ?z) (/= ?y ?z) (has ?w ?y) (has ?w ?z)) ))
```

This statement may be read, *It is false that there exist a student x, a section y, a section z, and a course w, where x is enrolled in y, x is enrolled in z, y is not equal to z, w has y, and w has z.* For readability, conceptual graphs may use special symbols like ≠ for *not equal,* but KIF uses /=, since it is restricted to a minimum number of special characters.

QUERY GRAPHS.   Besides representing tuples and constraints, conceptual graphs can also express any database query that can be expressed in SQL. Figure 7.11 shows a graph for the query *Which student is enrolled in two different sections of the same course?* That question might be used to search for students who violate the constraint in Figure 7.10.

The question mark in the concept [Student: ?] of Figure 7.11 characterizes the graph as a query. When used by itself, the question mark asks the question *Which student?* When the question mark is used with a variable, as in ?x, the combination corresponds to KIF variables like ?x or ?y. These two uses of the ? symbol correspond to the two uses of the word *which* in English: ? by itself corresponds to the interrogative *which* for asking questions; and ?x corresponds to the relative pronoun *which* used to make a reference to something else in the sentence. In the query language SQL, the question mark maps to the select verb, which designates the field

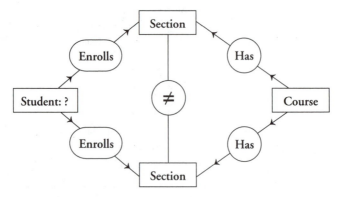

FIGURE 7.11 A query stated as a conceptual graph

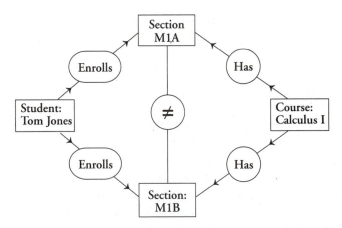

FIGURE 7.12 A constraint violation stated as a conceptual graph

of the database that contains the answer. In SQL, Figure 7.11 would be translated to the following query:

```
select a.student
  from enrolls a, enrolls b, has c, has d
    where a.student = b.student
      and a.section ^= b.section
      and a.section = c.section
      and b.section = d.section
      and c.course = d.course
```

Any or all of the four concepts in Figure 7.11 could contain a question mark in the referent field. If all four were marked with the ? symbol, the answer would be the constraint violation in Figure 7.12, which says *Student Tom Jones is enrolled in two different sections, M1A and M1B, of the course Calculus I.*

As these examples illustrate, logic can state constraints, queries, and answers to queries. But besides making statements, logic includes inference rules that can carry out computations. Chapter 4 showed how logical inferences can simulate any computation that can be performed by a digital computer. Chapter 5 showed how logic can represent distributed agents, encapsulated objects, and message passing between agents and objects. The next two sections of this chapter show how logic can represent various data structures of computer science.

7.3 Accommodating Multiple Paradigms

No single notation can ever be ideal for all purposes. Natural languages are good for asking questions and giving explanations, algebra is good for doing arithmetic, trees are good for representing hierarchies, and graphs are good for showing complex interconnections. In computer science, there is no end to the number of specialized notations. Besides the hundreds of programming languages, there are diagrams for circuits, flowcharts, parse trees, game trees, Petri nets, PERT charts, neural networks, design languages, and novel notations that are invented whenever two programmers work out ideas at the blackboard. Musical notation, which was discussed in Chapter 1, is an example of a complex language that is both precise and human factored. As long as the mapping rules are defined, all of these notations can be automatically translated to or from logic.

TREES.   Since a tree is a kind of graph, trees can be mapped directly to conceptual graphs and then to KIF or predicate calculus. Yet the highly specialized trees of computer science typically leave implicit many details a conceptual graph would make explicit. As an example, Figure 7.13 shows two common kinds of trees: a type hierarchy and a parse tree.

The two trees in Figure 7.13 have the same shape, but their arcs have different meanings. In the type hierarchy on the left, each arc represents a *subtype* relation: Plant, Mineral, and Animal are subtypes of Entity; Rabbit, Kangaroo, and Dog are subtypes of Animal. In the parse tree on the right, each arc represents the *part-of* relation: a variable, := operator, and expression are parts of an assignment statement; and a variable, + operator, and variable are parts of an expression. Another difference depends on the ordering of the branches. The type hierarchy is unordered: the branches for Plant, Mineral, and Animal could be listed in any order without changing the meaning. The parse tree, however, has a strict ordering: moving the branches around would create an ungrammatical statement.

A third difference is the distinction between *instances* and *types*. The parse tree relates instances: "+" is an instance of an operator, which is part of the expression "A+B," which is part of the assignment statement "X:=A+B." Every level of the parse tree says that the instances below are parts of the current instance, which in turn is part of the larger instance above. The type hierarchy, however, is a metastatement about types: the arc that shows Plant as a subtype of Entity includes vast

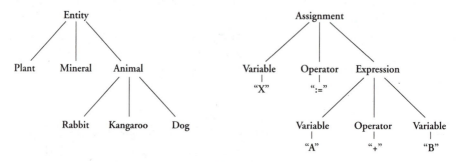

FIGURE 7.13 A type hierarchy and a parse tree

numbers of instances of plants within its scope. Logic can be used at either the instance level or the type level. Following are six pairs of formulas in logic that correspond to each of the six arcs in the type hierarchy:

Plant < Entity.	$(\forall x)(plant(x) \supset entity(x))$.
Mineral < Entity.	$(\forall x)(mineral(x) \supset entity(x))$.
Animal < Entity.	$(\forall x)(animal(x) \supset entity(x))$.
Rabbit < Animal.	$(\forall x)(rabbit(x) \supset animal(x))$.
Kangaroo < Animal.	$(\forall x)(kangaroo(x) \supset animal(x))$.
Dog < Animal.	$(\forall x)(dog(x) \supset animal(x))$.

Each formula on the left is a metalevel statement about types and subtypes; the corresponding formula on the right is a statement about instances of those types. The operator < represents the subtype relation: the type Plant is a subtype of Entity. The formula on the right relates the instances: for every x, if x is an instance of Plant, then x is an instance of Entity. For each of these formulas in predicate calculus notation, there is an exactly equivalent statement in CGs and KIF:

```
[Type: entity]→(Subt)→[Type: plant].    [Plant: ∀*x] [Entity: ?x].

(subtype entity plant)                   (forall (?x plant) (entity ?x))
```

The six arcs of the type hierarchy in Figure 7.13 represent six metalevel statements that could be represented in the conceptual graph of Figure 7.14.

PARSE TREE.   Figure 7.15 shows the parse tree represented as a conceptual graph. Instead of the Subt relation to link levels, it uses the Part relation. To show the ordering, the nodes are linked by the Next relation to their siblings. The referent fields of the concept nodes contain strings that represent the corresponding instances. For example, the string "X:=A+B" is the source code for the complete

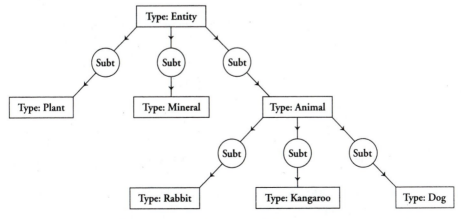

FIGURE 7.14 Type hierarchy of Figure 7.13 drawn as a conceptual graph

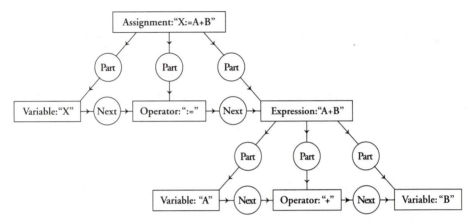

FIGURE 7.15 A parse tree expressed as a conceptual graph

assignment statement, and the lower-level concepts contain the corresponding parts of the statement.

The grammar rules that are used to derive a parse tree are usually stated in a linear notation, such as Backus-Naur form:

```
Assignment ::= Variable ":=" Expression
```

This grammar rule could also be expressed as a conceptual graph. Figure 7.16 says that every assignment has three parts: a variable, next an operator ":=", and next an expression. Figures 7.15 and 7.16 show the intimate relationship between grammar rules and parse trees: each grammar rule is a little triangle that can be joined with other grammar rules to build a parse tree. The rules of logic that allow the universal quantifier ∀ to be instantiated with particular instances determine the constraints on the way the triangles are assembled.

Figure 7.16 can also be translated to other systems of logic, such as KIF:

```
(forall (?x assignment)
    (exists ((?y variable) (?z operator) (?w expression))
        (and (part ?x ?y) (part ?x ?z) (part ?x ?w)
        (next ?y ?z) (next ?z ?w)
        (repr ?y ':=) )))
```

Although the KIF form is semantically equivalent to the conceptual graph, its syntax does not show the close correspondence between the parse tree and the grammar rule.

As these examples illustrate, tree diagrams can be mapped in a one-to-one fashion to conceptual graphs or KIF. But CGs and KIF are general-purpose notations that usually have more detail than the special-purpose trees that leave many

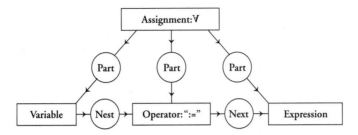

FIGURE 7.16 A grammar rule expressed as a conceptual graph

details implicit. If the detail is not important or is well understood, there is no reason to show it explicitly. People who are used to seeing parse trees and type hierarchies in the form of Figure 7.13 can continue to draw them in that style as long as they like. For a computer, however, no detail is implicitly "understood," and CGs provide a convenient way of showing the details explicitly. Graphics tools can offer users the option of seeing the details in CGs or suppressing them in more abbreviated notations.

MODELS AND METAMODELS. Computer systems are ideal modeling tools, but any model can itself be the subject of models, which are then called *metamodels*. The languages used to describe the models are metalanguages and metametalanguages: instead of talking about some aspect of the world, they talk about the programs and languages that talk about the world. Requirements, designs, specifications, explanations, evaluations, and help facilities use metalanguages for talking about the programs, languages, databases, and knowledge bases that directly address some aspect of the world. In their original paper on stored-program digital computers, Herbert Goldstine and John von Neumann introduced *flowcharts* as the metalanguage for describing the design of computer programs.

For database design, the *entity-relationship* (E-R) diagrams discussed in Section 7.2 are a popular metalanguage. Instead of describing external objects directly, an E-R diagram is a metalevel statement that describes the database that stores information about the objects. A sentence such as *Tom Jones is enrolled in section M1B of Calculus I* would be a statement about the objects Tom Jones, the section M1B, and the course in calculus. But a sentence about the *n*-to-*m* Enrolls relation is metalanguage about the language used to talk about the objects. Logic can be used to express language at any level: it can be used as a metalanguage to describe the relations or as a language that describes particular facts stored in those relations. Figure 7.17 shows a metalevel statement expressed as an E-R diagram followed by a collection of facts expressed as conceptual graphs. The diamond node in the E-R diagram represents the relation Has, which relates the types Course and Section. The labels 1 and *n* on the arcs are called *participation counts*. They express the constraint that each course may have some number n of sections, but each section is of exactly one course. Beneath the E-R diagram is a collection of conceptual graphs that represent instances. For a relational database, the E-R diagram represents a constraint on the relation and the entity types it relates. The conceptual graphs, however, represent the *tuples* or rows that contain the actual values stored in the database.

In Figure 7.17, the diamond node indicates that Has is a 1-to-n relation between courses and sections. The circles in the conceptual graphs show that course Calculus I has two sections M1A and M1B, course Calculus II has two sections M2A and M2B, and course Topology has one section M37. This example illustrates the point that E-R diagrams are a metalanguage for talking about types, and conceptual graphs are an object language for talking about instances. But since logic can be used at either level, the E-R diagram can be translated to an exactly equivalent statement in conceptual graphs or any other version of logic. Figure 7.18 shows the E-R diagram from Figure 7.17 translated to a metalevel conceptual graph.

The E-R diamond node becomes the concept [Relation: Has], whose type is Relation and whose referent names the relation Has. The E-R entity nodes become concepts of type Type, whose referents name the Course and Section types. The

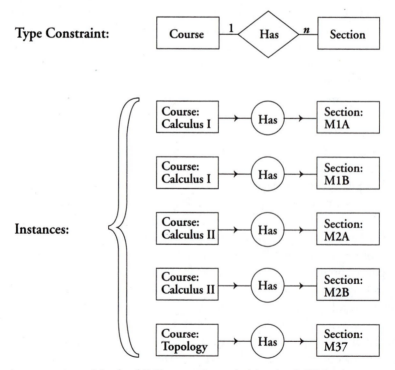

FIGURE 7.17 Metalevel E-R constraint and object-level CG instances

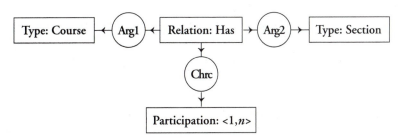

FIGURE 7.18 Metalevel E-R and CG constraint on the Has relation

links in the E-R diagram are represented by the conceptual relations Arg1 and Arg2, which indicate the first and second arguments of the relation. The 1-to-n constraint on the Has relation is shown by the *participation counts* 1 and n on the arcs of the E-R diagram. In the conceptual graph, the participation counts are specified by a separate concept [Participation: $<1,n>$], which is linked to the relation node by the characteristic relation Chrc.

Besides box and diamond nodes, E-R diagrams may have oval nodes for *attributes*, which can be linked to either entity or relation nodes. Figure 7.19 shows an E-R diagram and the corresponding conceptual graph for showing that the relation greaterThan has the attribute transitive.

As Figures 7.19 and 7.20 illustrate, when an E-R diagram is translated to a conceptual graph, the result usually has more nodes than the original. That kind of expansion is common when a specialized notation like E-R is translated to a more general notation like CGs or KIF. Following is the corresponding KIF formula for the CG in Figure 7.18:

```
(and (type course) (relation has) (type section) (participation '(1 n))
  (arg1 has student) (arg2 has section) (chrc has '(1 n)) )
```

Although the conceptual graph is more detailed than the E-R diagram, it has a more direct mapping to English. The CG in Figure 7.18 could be read as the following English sentence:

The Has relation has argument 1 of type Course, argument 2 of type Section, and a characteristic participation $<1,n>$.

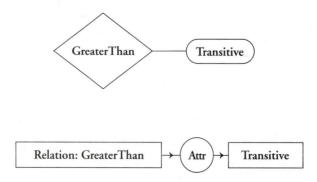

FIGURE 7.19 Metalevel E-R and CG showing that the greaterThan relation is transitive

Besides representing the metalevel information in an E-R diagram, CGs and KIF can also represent the rules for mapping from the metalevel to the instance level. As an example, Figure 7.20 shows a conceptual graph for an If-Then rule whose conclusion is another If-Then rule. The If-part of Figure 7.20 is the following conceptual graph, written in the linear notation:

```
[Relation: *r]→(Attr)→[Transitive].
```

This graph matches the CG in Figure 7.19, with the variable *r matching the name "greaterThan." The Then-part of Figure 7.20 is another If-Then rule, which

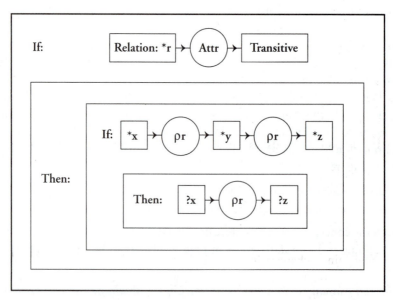

FIGURE 7.20 Metametalevel CG mapping from the metalevel to the object level

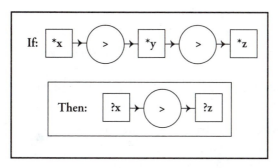

FIGURE 7.21 Object-level CG derived by applying the rule in Figure 7.20 to the CG in Figure 7.18

contains conceptual relations whose label is ρr. The Greek letter ρ represents an operator that maps a name like "greaterThan" to a label of a conceptual relation. The following statement defines the symbol $>$ as the value of ρ when applied to the name "greaterThan":

```
ρgreaterThan = '>'
```

With this definition, the If-Then rule in Figure 7.20 would generate the conclusion in Figure 7.21.

The If-Then rule in Figure 7.21 is the axiom that defines what it means for the greaterThan relation to be transitive. In English, Figure 7.21 may be read *If x is greater than y and y is greater than z, then x is greater than z.* The symbols *x, *y, and *z in the IF-part of Figure 7.21 represent the defining occurrences of the variables x, y, and z. The symbols ?x and ?z in the Then-part represent references back to the defining occurrences. KIF uses the same form ?x, ?y, and ?z for both the defining occurrences and the repeated references. Following is the KIF form of Figure 7.21:

```
(=> (and (> ?x ?y) (> ?y ?z))
    (> ?x ?z) )
```

As these examples illustrate, conceptual graphs and KIF can be used like E-R diagrams to represent metalevel information. But they can also state something that no E-R diagram ever could: the object-level axiom for transitivity in Figure 7.21. Furthermore, they can even state metametarules like Figure 7.20, which map from the metalevel to the object level. With such power, CGs and KIF can be used as the object language, the metalanguage, or even the metametalanguage. In fact, they can be used at a potentially infinite number of levels.

UNIFIED MODELING LANGUAGE. Many different design notations have been developed over the years, each with its own language, symbols, and graphics. All of them can be interpreted as variations or specializations of logic supplemented with an ontology of metalevel terms and a methodology for applying those terms to the design and description of computer systems and applications. Three authors who had developed competing notations, Grady Booch, Ivar Jacobson, and Jim Rumbaugh, pooled their resources to produce the *Unified Modeling Language (UML)*. The UML specifications, as described by the Rational Software Corporation (1997), are organized in four levels:

- *Metametamodel.* The starting level or metametamodel specifies a small number of entity types that are used to define the syntax and semantics of UML. The starting set includes high-order types such as MetaClass, MetaAttribute, and MetaOperation, as well as the general-purpose first-order types Integer, Real, String, and Boolean.

- *Metamodel.* The UML metamodels introduce more types such as Class, Attribute, Operation, Event, and Component as instances of the higher-order types of the metamodel.

- *Model.* For each application domain, a system analyst defines a model, whose types are instances of the types in a metamodel.

- *Application.* The working data of an application program consist of instances of the types specified in the model of the application domain.

The language used to define all the models and metamodels is a version of typed first-order logic called the *Object Constraint Language (OCL)*. As an example, the UML specifications include the following OCL statement, which says that all parameters of an entity have unique names:

```
self.parameter->forAll(p1, p2 |
  p1.name=p2.name implies p1=p2).
```

In OCL, *self* is an indexical that refers to the current entity being defined, and the names of functions are written after the entity to which they apply. In predicate calculus, the order would be interchanged: p1.name would be written $name(p_1)$. Following is a translation of the OCL statement to predicate calculus with the symbol #self representing the indexical:

$$(\forall p_1, p_2 \in parameter(\#self))$$
$$(name(p_1) = name(p_2) \supset p_1 = p_2).$$

This formula says that for every p_1 and p_2 in the set of parameters of the entity #self, if p_1 and p_2 have the same names, then they are equal.

As the example illustrates, OCL is about as readable as other variations of predicate calculus such as KIF or Z (Spivey 1992). For better readability, the UML metamodels define graphical notations as extensions of OCL. The graphics include many of the notations that have been described in this book: generalization and specialization hierarchies, entity-relationship diagrams, state-transition diagrams,

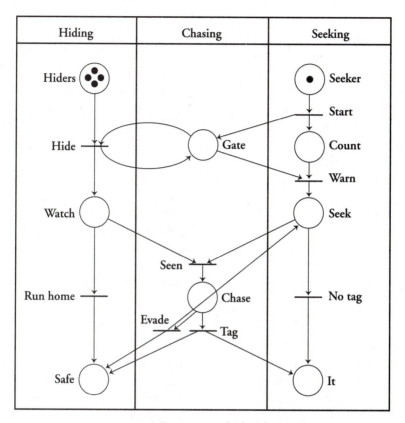

FIGURE 7.22 A Petri net overlaid with swimlanes

and Petri nets (which are called *activity diagrams* in UML). The logic-based OCL serves as the foundation for defining and relating these graphical notations. The design and development tools based on UML present the graphics to the programmers and systems analysts, but use OCL as the common internal representation.

Besides unifying many conventional notations, UML introduces some innovations, such as *swimlanes*, which partition the places and transitions of a Petri net, much like the partitions that separate competing racers in a swimming pool. In Figure 7.22, the Petri net of Figure 5.24 for the game of Hide and Seek has been overlaid with three swimlanes: the hiders proceed down the leftmost lane, which leads them to safety at the bottom; the seeker proceeds down the rightmost lane, but with the goal of avoiding the It place at the bottom; and the center lane shows the interactions between the seeker and the hiders.

The swimlanes have no effect on the procedure defined by the Petri net; instead, they serve as a metalevel commentary about its structure. In Figure 7.22, for example, they separate the actions performed by the hiders, the seeker, and the hider-seeker pairs. Such a separation can be useful for both explanation and implementation. It may divide a business organization into manageable units; it may partition a distributed system among different computers; or it may be the first step in decomposing a Petri net into a collection of finite-state machines, as in Section 5.7.

Swimlanes are an example of the open-ended number of notations that might be used to show different views of the same application. Each view is an abstraction from reality that highlights a different selection of objects, features, relationships, and behaviors. Yet ultimately, every view must be related to every other view in order to specify, develop, test, and deploy the system as an integrated whole. Logic is the universal language that can describe every feature represented in the more specialized notations and define the transformations from one to another. In his research, Guus Ramackers (1994) defined logical transformations for relating the different design notations of systems like UML. Hansen, Mühlbacher, and Neumann (1992) showed how logic in the CG form can be used to relate five different design notations: entity-relationship diagrams, NIAM, Remora, dataflow diagrams, and set-function segments. Their students implemented Prolog programs to translate each of the five notations to and from conceptual graphs.

7.4 Relating Different Knowledge Representations

Databases and knowledge bases created for different purposes by different people often represent the same information with a different choice of concept and relation types. Relational databases, for example, organize the data in tables, while object-oriented databases group the data by objects. To illustrate the differences, Figure 7.23 shows two structures of blocks and their representation in a relational database.

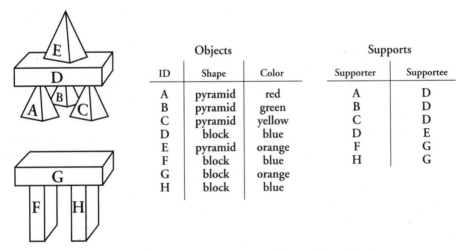

FIGURE 7.23 Two structures represented in a relational database

The two structures at the left of Figure 7.23 are composed of objects that support other objects. On the right are two database relations: the Objects relation lists each object's ID (identifier), its Shape, and its Color; the Supports relation lists the Supporter and the Supportee for each instance of one object supporting another. In English, the structure at the top left could be described *An orange pyramid E is supported by a blue block D, which is supported by a red pyramid A, a green pyramid B, and a yellow pyramid C.* That sentence could be represented by the CG in Figure 7.24.

The ontology of types and relations in Figure 7.24 does not correspond to the tables of the relational database in Figure 7.23. Figure 7.25 is another CG that uses the same ontology as the database.

REORGANIZING A DATABASE. The dyadic relations of Figure 7.24, which are based on the primitives of natural language, resemble the links in an object-oriented database. In a relational database, the data are often organized in tables with multiple columns, such as the Objects relation of Figure 7.23. To relate the two ontologies, their types and relations must be defined in terms of a common set of primitives, such as the sample ontology of Appendix B. Following is a definition of the type Block:

type `Block(*x)` **is** `[Object: ?x]→(Chrc)→[Shape: Block].`

This definition says that a block x is an object x with a characteristic (Chrc) shape of block. Next is a similar definition for the type Pyramid:

type `Pyramid(*x)` **is** `[Object: ?x]→(Chrc)→[Shape: Pyramid].`

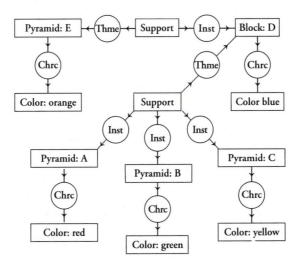

FIGURE 7.24 A conceptual graph that represents the top structure in Figure 7.23

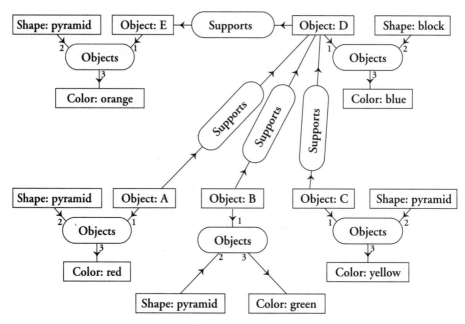

FIGURE 7.25 A conceptual graph generated directly from the relational database

Following is a definition of the dyadic relation Supports:

relation Supports(*x,*y) **is**   [Object: ?x]←(Thme)←[Support]→(Inst)→[Object: ?y].

This definition says that the Supports relation links an object x, which is the theme (Thme) of the concept [Support], to another object y, which is the instrument (Inst) of the same concept. The Objects relation is triadic:

> **relation** Objects(*x,*y,*z) **is**
> [Object: ?x]-
> (Chrc)→[Shape: ?y]
> (Chrc)→[Color: ?z].

This definition says that the Objects relation has three formal parameters: an object x, which has a characteristic shape y and a characteristic color z. In the relational database, the Supports relation has domains named Supporter and Supportee, which could also be related to Figure 7.24 by type definitions:

> **type** Supporter(*x) **is** [Object: ?x]←(Inst)←[Support].
> **type** Supportee(*x) **is** [Object: ?x]←(Thme)←[Support].

The first line says that Supporter is defined as a type of Object that is the instrument (Inst) of the concept [Support], and Supportee is a type of Object that is the theme (Thme) of [Support].

By expanding and contracting the definitions, conceptual graphs or the corresponding formulas in predicate calculus can be converted from one ontology to another. Unfortunately, the problems of mapping ontologies, which were illustrated in terms of natural languages in Section 7.1, also plague the mappings from one database or knowledge base to another. For most purposes, the French word *fleuve* can be translated to the English word *river*, but for technical accuracy, it may have to be translated by the clumsy phrase *river that flows into the sea*. For computer systems, the simple translations that may be adequate 99 percent of the time create annoying and potentially disastrous bugs when the unexpected conditions arise. See Exercise 7.10 for further discussion of this problem and various ways of solving it.

ANSWERING QUERIES. Restructuring a large database is a lengthy process that is sometimes necessary. But to answer a single question, it is usually faster to restructure the query graph than to restructure the entire database. To access a relational database such as Figure 7.23, the definitions can be used to translate the concept types in the query graph to concept types that match the domains of the database. As an example, the English question *Which pyramid is supported by a block?* would be translated to the following conceptual graph:

[Pyramid: ?]←(Thme)←[Support]→(Inst)→[Block].

The question mark in the referent field of the concept [Pyramid: ?] shows that this graph is a *query graph*. The identifier of the pyramid that makes this graph true would be the answer to the question. For Figure 7.24, the answer E could be derived by matching the query graph to the conceptual graph. But if the data are in a relational database, the query graph must be translated to SQL.

Figure 7.26 shows how the type and relation definitions are used to translate

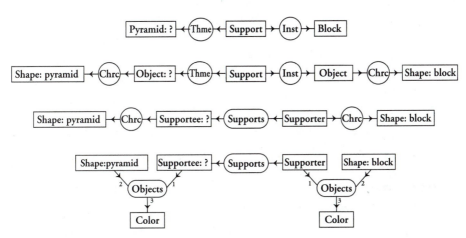

FIGURE 7.26 Translating a query graph to a form that maps directly to SQL

the English question to a CG that uses the same types and relations as the database. At the top is the original query graph. The second graph replaces the types Pyramid and Block with their definitions as object with shape pyramid or object with shape block. The third graph replaces the type Support and the relations Thme and Inst with the relation Supports, which links the supporter to the supportee. Finally, the bottom graph replaces the two occurrences of the Chrc relation with the Objects relation. Since the Objects relation has three arcs, two concepts of type Color are also introduced; they they are ignored in the mapping to SQL, however, since colors are irrelevant to this query.

By translating the bottom graph of Figure 7.26 to SQL, the system can generate the following SQL query for the original English question *Which pyramid is supported by a block?*

```
select supportee
  from supports, objects a, objects b
    where supportee = a.id
    and a.shape = 'pyramid'
    and supporter = b.id
    and b.shape = 'block'
```

The question mark in the concept [Supportee: ?] maps to the select verb in the first line of the SQL query. The three relations in the query graph are listed in the from-clause on line two. Since the Objects relation appears twice, it is listed twice on line two — once as Objects A and again as Objects B. Then the where-clause lists the conditions: the supportee must be equal to the identifier of object A; the shape of object A must be pyramid; the supporter must be equal to the identifier of object B; and the shape of object B must be block. Every feature of the SQL query is derived from some feature of the transformed query graph at the bottom of Figure 7.26.

MAPPING TO NATURAL LANGUAGE. Semantic representations for expert systems are often highly specialized for a particular application. One expert system for diagnosing cancer patients represented knowledge in a frame with the following format:

```
(defineType MedPatient
 (supertype Person)

 . . .

 (motherMelanoma (type Boolean)
           (question '(Has the patient's mother had melanoma?)) ))
```

This frame says that a medical patient, MedPatient, has a supertype Person. Then it lists several attributes, including one named motherMelanoma, which has two facets: one facet declares that the values of the attribute must be of type Boolean; the other specifies a character string called a question. Whenever the system needs the current value of the motherMelanoma attribute, it prints the character string on the display screen, and a person answers yes or no. Then the system converts the answer to a Boolean value (T or F), which becomes the value of the attribute.

Such frames are simple, but they omit important details. The words *mother* and *melanoma* appear in the character string that is printed as a question to some person at a computer display. Although the person may know the meaning of those words, the system cannot relate them to the attribute motherMelanoma, which by itself has no more meaning than the character string "MM". Whether the system can generate correct answers using values of that attribute depends on how the associated programs happen to process the character strings. To express those details in a form the computer can process, Figure 7.27 shows a conceptual graph for the sentence *The patient's mother suffered from melanoma.*

The concept [MedPatient: #] for the medical patient is linked via the child relation (Chld) to the concept [Mother]. The experiencer (Expr) and source (Srce) relations link the concept [Suffer] to the concepts [Mother] and [Melanoma]. The type hierarchy would show that a medical patient is a type of person; a mother is a woman, which is also a person; and melanoma is a type of cancer, which is also a disease:

MedPatient < Person
Mother < Woman < Person
Melanoma < Cancer < Disease

The type MedPatient could be introduced by the following definition:

type MedPatient(*x) **is**
    [Person: ?x]←(Ptnt)←[TreatMed]→(Agnt)→[Physician].

In this graph, the verb *treat* is represented by the type TreatMed to distinguish it from other word senses, such as giving the patient some candy. The definition may be read *The type MedPatient is defined as a person x who is treated by a physician.* Figure 7.28 defines MotherMelanoma as a dyadic relation that links a person *x* to a Boolean value *y*, where *y* is the mode of a proposition that *x* is the child of a mother who suffered from Melanoma.

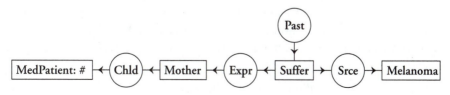

FIGURE 7.27 CG for the English sentence

type MotherMelanoma(*x, *y) is

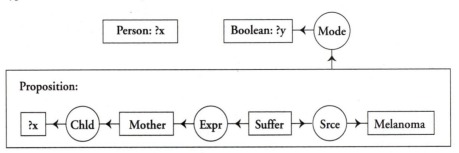

FIGURE 7.28 Definition of the MotherMelanoma relation

The amount of detail required for semantics shows why most expert systems do not have a natural language interface. A system that translated *The patient's mother had melanoma* to Figure 7.27 would be more complex than a typical expert system shell. Even then, it would still have to perform further inferences before it could deduce T or F for the motherMelanoma attribute. It is easier to print out a character string and let the user select *yes* or *no* from a menu. Yet that solution might make it harder to modify, extend, and link the system to other programs designed for other purposes. Consider some possible extensions:

- If the expert system were later linked to a database so that it could check the patient's records directly, the attributes stored in the database would probably not match those needed by the expert system. Instead of storing a mother-Melanoma attribute for each patient, the database would be more likely to list the person's mother. Before the system could determine the value of that attribute, someone would have to write a database query or view with the more detailed concepts of Mother, Disease, and Melanoma.

- Besides the prompts, many expert systems include additional character strings for explanations. Many of them are stored as canned phrases that are typed whenever a particular rule is executed. But better explanations would require some tailoring of the strings to insert context-dependent values. As the system becomes more complex, the help, prompts, and explanations could take more space than the rules, and they would have to be revised or rewritten whenever the rules were changed.

- Writing the help, prompt, and explanation messages and keeping them consistent with every modification to the rules is difficult enough with one language, but for a system used in different countries, they would all have to be written and revised for every language.

This example is another illustration of elaboration tolerance. McCarthy observed that a general-purpose representation in logic is usually the most flexible and the easiest to adapt to a wide range of applications. Experience with the Cyc system (Lenat & Guha 1990) confirms that point: Cyc began as a frame-based system augmented with constraints, but over the years the logic-based constraints evolved into the primary Cyc language (CycL), and the frames have been limited to simple data entry.

7.5 Language Patterns

Knowledge acquisition begins with natural language. The key words of a document or an interview with an expert express the concepts of an application. They map to predicates in logic, domains in a database, slots in frames, attributes in rules, or classes in O-O languages. But words and the concepts they express are not isolated symbols; they are interconnected in complex patterns of thought that cannot be understood in isolation. A person or computer with no background knowledge about the following subjects could not understand dictionary definitions of the terms they use:

- *Religion*: sin, kosher, taboo, karma
- *Automobiles*: ignition, transmission, differential
- *Finance*: tax shelter, depreciation, puts and calls

The entry for *sin*, for example, might define it as a transgression against God. But that introduces the concepts of transgression and God. A transgression is a violation of a law, but that raises questions about how God gives laws and how they differ from human laws or laws of physics. A few more steps lead to the concepts of heaven and hell and eventually all of theology. Understanding an automobile ignition requires knowledge about the electrical system, the fuel system, and even the operation of the engine itself. Puts and calls cannot be understood without detailed knowledge about the stock market and how it operates. In every field of human endeavor, from cooking and fashion to topology and quantum mechanics, concepts are only meaningful in relation to other concepts in tightly organized structures of thought. Knowledge acquisition begins with words, but it must find the connections that link those words in larger patterns.

CO-OCCURRENCE PATTERNS.   Words with the same semantic features tend to occur in the same kinds of expressions. Linguists take advantage of that tendency by looking for *co-occurrence patterns* — phrase or sentence patterns that systematically occur with words that have a certain feature. The co-occurrence patterns serve as an empirical test for the presence of that feature. As an example, consider the following pattern:

a *book*, three *books*
an *elephant*, three *elephants*
an *idea*, three *ideas*

Those phrases sound normal, but the following seem odd or incorrect:

a *water*, three *waters*

a *butter*, three *butters*

a *happiness*, three *happinesses*

A phrase like *three waters* may be used, but only to indicate three kinds, not three instances: *You have a choice of three waters: Perrier, Poland Spring, or New York City tap.* This co-occurrence pattern highlights a distinction between two kinds of nouns: *book, elephant,* and *idea* are *count nouns* that occur with the article *a* in the singular and can be used normally in the plural; *water, butter,* and *happiness* are *mass nouns* that do not occur with *a* in the singular and have different meanings in the plural. The distinction corresponds to a semantic difference that is important for knowledge representation: count nouns refer to things that can be counted, but mass nouns refer to substances that can only be measured. Although the distinction is usually quite sharp, some nouns, such as *cake*, may be used as both count nouns and mass nouns. As a count noun, *a cake* refers to an object; but as a mass noun, *cake* refers to the substance of which a cake is made. This is not an exception to the rule, but an example of a word with two different but related senses.

The presence or absence of an article in English signifies an important semantic distinction, but many languages, including Russian and Chinese, have no articles. Each language has its own syntactic ways of expressing semantic distinctions, and different languages emphasize different aspects. Although Russian and Chinese do not mark definite and indefinite noun phrases as clearly as English, they are more specific in indicating whether the action of a verb is complete (*perfective*) or incomplete (*imperfective*). English marks a different feature of verbs: the distinction between a simple verb form like *walks* and the *progressive* form *is walking.* That distinction, which is peculiar to English, is the basis for useful co-occurrence tests that cannot be translated directly to other languages. Co-occurrence patterns are used to detect language-independent semantic features, but they are always expressed in language-dependent syntax.

VERB PATTERNS.   Verbs have syntactic relations that are signaled by position in English and Chinese, but by case markers in Russian and Japanese. Those syntactic relations express different semantic information that can be distinguished by co-occurrence patterns. The verbs *eat* and *like*, for example, both occur in a pattern with a direct object:

I *ate* the doughnut.

I *liked* the doughnut.

This pattern can be used to group verbs in two major classes: the *transitive verbs*, which take a subject and an object, and the *intransitive verbs* like *sleep* or *walk*, which take only a subject. Those broad classes can be subdivided further with more distinctions. The following patterns sound natural or normal with the verb *eat*, but they sound odd with the verb *like*:

I am *eating* the doughnut.
I am *liking* the doughnut.
What I did was *eat* the doughnut.
What I did was *like* the doughnut.

These co-occurrence patterns distinguish actions from states: verbs in the *eat*-class express actions, while verbs in the *like*-class express states. Other verbs that can occur in the same patterns as *eat* include *mash, bake, dunk, discard,* and *explode.* Some verbs that occur in the same patterns as *like* include *own, admire,* and *know.*

In the classification of processes in Section 4.2, the end points are significant for distinguishing completed from continuing actions. But what determines completion depends on various factors, including the agent's intentions and the nature of the process itself. The philosopher Zeno Vendler (1967) developed co-occurrence tests to determine the nature of the processes expressed by the verbs. Following is a sample pattern:

John partially *wrecked* the house.
John partially *bought* the house.

The first sentence means that John did some damage, yet less than total destruction. But the second sentence is nonsense: buying is an indivisible action that cannot be done partially. Vendler used this pattern to distinguish *achievement verbs* like *buy,* which represent indivisible actions, from *accomplishment verbs* like *wreck,* which allow intermediate stages or degrees of completion. Other achievement verbs that cannot be done partially include *see, take, enter,* and *drop.* Some accomplishment verbs that can be done partially include *penetrate, cover, consume,* and *burn down.*

Each co-occurrence pattern divides the words in two classes: those that fit the pattern, and those that don't. Further tests may subdivide either or both of those classes. The transitive verbs that fit the pattern *I — — — the doughnut* are further classified as action verbs or state verbs by the pattern *What I did was — — — the doughnut.* With *n* patterns, up to 2^n co-occurrence classes may be distinguished; the actual number is often less than 2^n because some combinations may be mutually exclusive. Beth Levin (1993) presented a compendium of such patterns for classifying verbs and the processes they express. Appendix B summarizes the conceptual relations defined by such patterns.

SUBJECT PATTERNS. Different classes of verbs are characterized by different concept types, and those types may be linked to other concept types by different types of conceptual relations. The concepts of action verbs are subtypes of Action, and the subjects of the verbs are the agents that voluntarily perform the actions. The concepts of state verbs are subtypes of State, and the subjects of those verbs may have little or no choice about the experience. The next two conceptual graphs show the concept [Eat] with the agent relation (Agnt) and [Like] with the experiencer relation (Expr):

```
[Person: #I]←(Agnt)←[Eat]→(Ptnt)→[Doughnut: #].
[Person: #I]←(Expr)←[Like]→(Thme)→[Doughnut: #].
```

The symbol # marks indexicals. By itself, # represents the definite article *the*, and the symbol #I represents the speaker in the current context.

Not all verbs have animate subjects that can voluntarily perform an action, and they may have nonsentient subjects that cannot experience anything. In the sentence *John opened the door*, John is the agent who had some choice. But in the sentence *The key opened the door*, the key is not an animate being. To test for agents, the *on purpose* pattern may be used:

John opened the door on purpose.

The key opened the door on purpose.

Only agents can do things on purpose. Since the first sentence sounds normal, John is the agent of the concept Open. Since the second sentence sounds odd, the key cannot be an agent. Instead, it would be an instrument (Inst):

```
[Person: John]←(Agnt)←[Open]→(Thme)→[Door: #].
[Key: #]←(Inst)←[Open]→(Thme)→[Door: #].
```

If neither the agent nor the instrument is mentioned, some English verbs permit the direct object to be promoted to the subject position. In the sentence *The door opened*, the door cannot do anything on purpose, but its relationship to opening remains the same as in the previous sentences. It is the theme (Thme) of the action, which may be the subject when the other relations are omitted:

```
[Door: #]←(Thme)←[Open].
```

Sometimes a verb with multiple word senses may express different concept types in different syntactic patterns. In the following sentences, the verb *think* represents an action whose subject passes the tests for an agent:

I am thinking about the problem.

What I did was think about the problem.

I thought about the problem on purpose.

These sentences sound natural with the phrase *about the problem*, but they would sound strange with the phrase *that the sky is blue*. Therefore, *think* is an action verb in the pattern *think about*, but a state verb in the pattern *think that*. In the next two

CGs, the different word senses are distinguished by the concept type ThinkAbout with an agent and ThinkThat with an experiencer:

```
[Person: #I]←(Agnt)←[ThinkAbout]→(Thme)→[Problem: #].
[Person: #I]←(Expr)←[ThinkThat]-
   (Thme)→[Proposition: [Sky: #]→(Attr)→[Blue]].
```

In the second graph, the theme of Think is a proposition whose referent is a nested graph that says the sky has attribute blue.

OBJECT PATTERNS. All transitive verbs have direct objects, but the semantic relation depends on how the action or state of the verb affects the object. Something very different happens to the doughnut in each of the following sentences:

I *made* the doughnut.
I *liked* the doughnut.
I *ate* the doughnut.

Making causes the doughnut to come into existence, liking has no effect on it, and eating causes it to change or even disappear. The result relation (Rslt) is used for objects that are created by the action; theme (Thme) for objects that may be moved or experienced, but not changed internally; and patient (Ptnt) for objects that are structurally improved, damaged, or destroyed. Sometimes the same verb may be used to express creation or modification, as in the sentence *I baked the doughnut.* That sentence has two possible interpretations: *I created the doughnut by baking it,* which would use the result relation; or *I heated a pre-existing doughnut,* which would use the patient relation.

BUT TEST. Many co-occurrence patterns test for simple features like the distinction between states and events. But other patterns can detect complex structural relationships. As an example, Jerrold Katz (1966) used the following pattern:

The *razor blade* is good.
The *grain of sand* is good.

The first sentence is complete in itself and needs no further explanation. The second, however, immediately leads the reader to ask, *good for what?* Terms that fit in the same co-occurrence class as *razor blade* include *poker hand* and *lung.* These words refer to things that have implicit purposes: a razor blade is supposed to be good for shaving, a lung for breathing, and a poker hand for winning a game. Words that fit in the same class as *grain of sand* include *molecule, integer, liquid,* and *planet.* These words have no implicit relations that provide a scale of goodness. A grain of sand may be good for causing an oyster to grow a pearl, and a planet may be good as a target for space exploration, but those uses are not part of the meaning of *sand* or *planet*. As a test to determine the implicit relationships for a concept type, consider the next example:

> Here is a *razor blade*, but . . .
> Here is a *grain of sand*, but . . .

In the first sentence, one would expect a continuation that denies some typical relationship of a razor blade, such as *you can't shave with it* or *its blade is chipped*. In the second, however, there is no obvious continuation. In a discussion about cultured pearls, it might make sense to continue with *you can't grow a pearl with it*. Yet that continuation would be suggested by the previous context, not by any relationship intrinsic to the grain of sand itself. This example can be generalized to a co-occurrence pattern known as the *but*-test:

1. *Contradictory.* Macula is a dog, but she is not an animal.
2. *Normal.* Lucky is a pet, but he is not tame.
3. *Odd, but possible.* Muffy is a cat, but she is not black.
4. *Odd and nonsensical.* Yojo is a cat, but he is not a verb.

The first sentence is contradictory since the definition of dog implies animal. The second sounds normal since being tame is an expectation for a pet, but not a requirement. The third sounds odd with *but* since being black is not an expectation for a cat. That sentence, however, would sound normal with the conjunction *and* instead of *but*, since not being black is a possibility. The fourth is literally true, but it sounds odd, since there is no way that anything could ever be both a cat and a verb. In general, for any concept type t and predicate $p(x)$, the *but*-test has the following form:

> x is an instance of t, {but | and} not $p(x)$

A sentence of this form may be contradictory, natural, odd, or nonsensical with the conjunction *but* or *and*.

- If contradictory, then either $p(x)$ is part of the definition of t, or it is implied by the definition.
- If natural with *but* and odd with *and*, then $p(x)$ is implied by the expectations for t.
- If odd with *but* and natural with *and*, then $p(x)$ is possible for t, but it is not an expectation.
- If odd or nonsensical with both *but* and *and*, then $p(x)$ does not apply to instances of type t.

The expectations implied by a concept type are the defaults that can be used in nonmonotonic reasoning, as discussed in Sections 6.4 and 6.5.

BUSINESS RULES AND TYPES. The linguistic techniques of co-occurrence relations and the logical techniques of defining categories by distinctions with associated axioms apply to ontologies for every aspect of life. For families, they apply to kinship terms like *sister* and *grandfather*, which can all be defined by combinations of the dyadic relation parentOf and the binary distinction of male or female. For businesses, the techniques apply to *enterprise analysis*, which is the study of the information flow between various divisions, such as engineering, manufacturing, accounting, and sales. For example, Donald Burnstine (1977) developed the Business Information Analysis and Integration Technique (BIAIT) as a method of classifying the recordkeeping needs of business enterprises in terms of seven binary distinctions:

1. *Bill.* Does the supplier bill the customers, or do they pay cash?

2. *Future.* Does the supplier deliver the products at some time in the future, or do the customers take the products with them?

3. *Profile.* Does the supplier keep a profile of the customers, or is every transaction a surprise?

4. *Negotiate.* Is the price negotiated or fixed?

5. *Rent.* Is the product rented or purchased?

6. *Track.* Does the supplier keep track of the product after it is sold or not?

7. *Customize.* Is the product custom made or provided from stock?

These seven binary distinctions determine 2^7 or 128 types of businesses, distinguished by their recordkeeping needs. The first answer to each question implies more complex records. In the simplest case, a pushcart vendor does a cash-and-carry business with no records at all.

For each of the seven questions, the first answer implies one or more record types that must be prepared, processed, and saved for every sale. The question about billing, for example, implies that the business must do credit checks, bill preparation, accounts receivable, and debt collection. The question about future deliveries implies a need to remember addresses. Since packages may get lost or damaged in transit, it also implies a need to record the complete contents of each order in case one has to be duplicated or a client reimbursed. If a company does both billing and future deliveries, then it *inherits* all the recordkeeping requirements of both types of businesses. In general, the implications of each question are the rules or *axioms* of a certain type of business. Those axioms are inherited by every subtype. The complete axioms for a business constitute a *theory* of its record-handling and information-processing needs. Although business executives rarely use mathematical terms like *axiom* and *theory*, the record-handling and accounting procedures in their computers are just as mathematical as any program used in engineering or science. The only difference is that the theories that underlie the business programs haven't been analyzed as thoroughly as the theories of physics.

7.6 Tools for Knowledge Acquisition

Knowledge acquisition is the process of eliciting, analyzing, and formalizing the patterns of thought underlying some subject matter. In elicitation, the knowledge engineer must get the expert to articulate tacit knowledge in natural language. In formalization, the knowledge engineer must encode the knowledge elicited from the expert in the rules and facts of some AI language. Between those two stages lies *conceptual analysis*: the task of analyzing the concepts expressed in natural language and making their implicit relationships explicit. A deep understanding of logic, language, and philosophy is a prerequisite for conceptual analysis. Logic is essential, since every knowledge representation language is a thinly disguised version of logic; language is essential, since natural languages are the primary means of communication between the experts and the knowledge engineers; and philosophy is essential, as the discussion of ontology in Chapter 2 has shown. With such a large number of prerequisites, finding people who are qualified to do conceptual analysis can be challenging. One solution is to develop tools that can enable people with different specialties to collaborate.

CONCEPTUAL SCHEMA MODELING FACILITIES. Conceptual modeling is central to systems analysis, database modeling, and knowledge engineering. To support those tasks, the ISO SC32 project on Conceptual Schema Modeling Facilities (CSMF) is developing standards for appropriate languages and tools. Figure 7.29 shows how CSMF could be used to divide the task of knowledge acquisition into separate stages. At the upper left, logicians, linguists, and philosophers enter the ontological primitives of language and logic. Logicians could use CSMF to enter the definitions and axioms for logical operators, set theory, and basic mathematical concepts and relations. Linguists could use it to enter the grammar rules of natural languages and the kinds of semantic types and relations defined in Appendix B. Philosophers could use CSMF to collaborate with the linguists and logicians in analyzing and defining the fundamental ontologies of space, time, and causality common to all domains of application. Together they would provide the basic ontologies or starting definitions for the application developers and users.

In the center of Figure 7.29, application developers use CSMF to enter domain-dependent information about specific applications. Some of them would use CSMF to define generic ontologies for industries such as banking, agriculture,

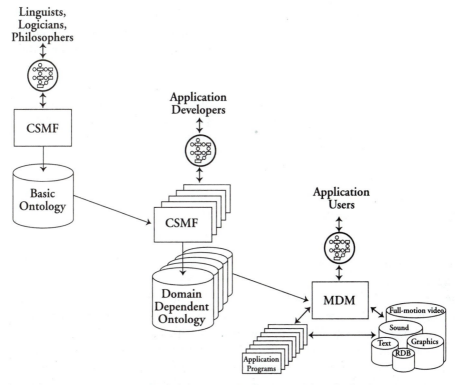

FIGURE 7.29 Using conceptual schema modeling facilities

mining, education, and manufacturing. Others would start with one or more generic ontologies and combine them or tailor them to a particular business, project, or application. The process of defining ontologies is an integral part of application development. The domain ontologies would actually be a byproduct of the implementation process: the same information that the developers use to define database formats, programming interfaces, and object declarations could be translated to natural language in the operational stage. The documentation could never be inconsistent with the implementation, since it would be generated automatically from the implementation.

At the bottom right of Figure 7.29 is a Multimedia Dialog Manager (MDM), which controls the interactions with the application users. Figure 7.29 shows conceptual graphs as the central knowledge representation for integrating the components of MDM and CSMF. The individual components, however, may use any appropriate language in their internal implementations. For communicating between components, any logic-based language with the same expressive power as CGs and KIF could be used. The ISO standards specify the abstract syntax and semantics for the CSMF, but they allow the implementers to choose any appropriate internal representation. Conceptual graphs may be used as a presentation language by the application developers who are writing and editing the domain-dependent knowledge. The application users would not see the CGs themselves, but the natural language messages generated from the CGs.

VARIETIES OF DOMAIN KNOWLEDGE. After the logicians, linguists, and philosophers have created the general-purpose dictionaries and ontologies, application developers can use CSMF to enter the domain knowledge in their area of specialization. As examples of the kinds of knowledge that must be entered, consider the following sentences:

1. *Wallets are used to carry money.*
2. *Charlie lost his wallet on the train.*
3. *Charlie lost all the money in his wallet.*

Sentence 1 is a general principle that might be found in a dictionary; it could be encoded in a rule that would apply to any instance of a wallet. Sentence 2 is a specific fact about a particular instance; it might be stored in a database, but it is not a general rule. Sentence 3 is an inference that an expert system might derive by combining the general principle (1) with the specific fact (2).

The general principles constitute the *semantic memory* of an expert system — its background knowledge about the world, including the ontology, axioms, and defaults. Specific facts constitute *episodic memory* about situations at particular times and places. It makes up the operational knowledge that is stored in a database, acquired from a user during a dialog, or derived by inference in answer to a question. Semantic memory includes five kinds of information:

- *Ontology.* A classification of the types and subtypes of concepts and relations necessary to describe everything in the application domain.
- *Definitions.* Necessary and sufficient conditions that define new types of concepts and relations in terms of more primitive types.
- *Constraints.* General principles or axioms that must be true of the instances of those concepts.
- *Defaults.* Information that is expected to be true of the instances of various concept types.
- *Behavior.* Rules that govern the actions by and upon each type of object and the interactions of collections of objects.

As an example, a definition of *automobile* would state the necessary and sufficient conditions that define the term: "a four-wheeled, self-propelled vehicle designed for transporting passengers." In that definition, *vehicle* is the genus or supertype, and the modifiers state the conditions that distinguish automobiles from other kinds of vehicles. Besides the defining constraints, there may be legal and practical constraints: on size, big enough to carry a human being, but small enough to travel on typical roads; on the engine, powerful enough to attain highway speeds, but with a limited amount of polluting fumes. Definitions and constraints must be true, but for different reasons: if the definition of automobile were false for some object, then it would not be called an automobile; if the other constraints were false, some law would be violated, or the thing could not be used for its normal purpose. Besides the requirements stated in the definitions and constraints, defaults state the expected background information: a typical automobile costs $20,000 when new; most families in the United States own one or two; they may be status symbols; teenagers covet them; they are essential for people living in Los Angeles, but not for those living in New York City.

MAPPING SPECIFICATIONS TO LOGIC.   The difficulty of translating specifications from English to any formal notation was discussed in Section 3.1. Although computers are not as good as people at resolving ambiguities, they are better than people at detecting ambiguities and finding statements where more precision or clarification is needed. Instead of automatic translation from specifications to programs, computer-aided tools can help a domain expert analyze informal specifications, clarify them, and rewrite them in more precise terms. By echoing its assumptions and asking for clarifications, the CSMF could work with a domain expert to develop precise specifications in logic, which it could then translate to natural language for the documentation and to programming languages for the implementation.

A CSMF that uses and reuses the same information in the design, implementation, and operation would ensure consistent definitions throughout all stages of software development and use. With such a CSMF, there would be no simpler or faster way to write a "quick-and-dirty" program than to enter its definition declaratively and let the CSMF tools compile it from the specification. The same source from which a program is generated should also be translated to its documentation and help messages. As an example of the mapping from language to logic, consider the following sentence, which might appear in a specification document:

Every employee is hired by some manager on some date.

The analysis starts with the *content words* in the sentence: *employee, hire, manager,* and *date.* In any database or knowledge base, these words would map to some significant feature. In conceptual graphs, they map to *type labels* for the associated concepts. The labels are written as upper-case character strings: Employee, Hire, Manager, and Date. Those labels must then be organized in a type hierarchy:

Manager is a subtype of Employee, which is a subtype of Person; Hire is a subtype of Act; and Date is a subtype of Time:

Manager < Employee < Person

Hire < Act

Date < Time

The other words in the sentence — *every, is, by, some,* and *on* — are usually called *function words.* Unlike the content words that map to concepts, function words map to conceptual relations or to quantifiers inside a concept node. The words *every* and *some* represent quantifiers; the auxiliary verb *is* and the ending *-ed* mark the passive voice, which indicates that [Hire] is linked to [Employee] by the Thme (patient) relation; and *by* indicates that [Hire] is linked to [Manager] by the Agnt (agent) relation. The preposition *on* maps to different relations in different contexts; in this example, the type Date, which is a subtype of Time, indicates that *on* represents the PTim (point in time) relation. Figure 7.30 shows a conceptual graph for that sentence.

In the concept [Employee: ∀], the type label is followed by a colon and a *referent field,* which contains the quantifier ∀ for *every.* The word *some* represents an existential quantifier. The ordinary existential ∃ is the default; the phrase *some manager* would be represented by the concept [Manager] with nothing in the referent field. That concept corresponds to the formula $(\exists x)$manager(x), which means that there exist one or more individuals x of type manager. If no further information were available, the default would be assumed for both *some manager* and *some date.* But whenever the word *some* is used, CSMF could ask questions to determine what kind of existential quantifier is intended:

Is each employee hired by exactly one manager?
Is it possible for an employee to be hired by several managers?

In predicate calculus, the quantifier ∃! is used to show exactly one; in conceptual graphs, the symbol @1 is used in the referent field: [Manager: @1].

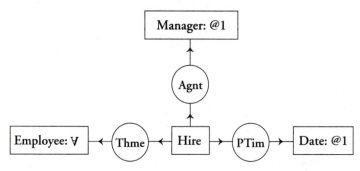

FIGURE 7.30 A CG specification generated from English

CONTROLLED NATURAL LANGUAGE. To support a readable notation for both people and computers, versions of *controlled* or *stylized* natural languages have been designed for special purposes. One of the first was COBOL, which uses an English-like syntax for common programming statements. Each verb in COBOL has a predefined template with options marked by special keywords. In the following statement, the verb *add* takes three operands; the first one follows the verb, and the other two follow the keywords *to* and *giving.*

```
Add Sales-Tax to Balance giving Amount-Due.
```

In C, the equivalent statement would be written

```
amountDue = salesTax + balance;
```

Although COBOL has been criticized for its verbosity, the amount of extra typing is less than a factor of two. The main limitation of COBOL is its fixed ontology of computer-oriented concepts and relations. The verb *add*, for example, is compiled to machine instructions, and the variables Sales-Tax and Amount-Due represent data in the computer rather than entities in the application domain. A computer-oriented ontology is necessary to make COBOL or C a programming language, but the inability to extend the ontology makes such languages inappropriate for any other purpose.

Pure logic, which has no built-in ontology, can be applied to any domain whatever. That flexibility is shared by any notation that can be compiled to logic. An example is Attempto Controlled English (ACE), which was designed by Norbert Fuchs and his students (Fuchs et al. 1998; Schwitter 1998). The only predefined terms in ACE are *function words*, which include the articles *the, a,* and *an,* the quantifiers *every* and *some,* the logical connectives *and, or, not, if* and *then,* the two verbs *is* and *has,* and a few prepositions. All *content words* (most nouns, verbs, adjectives, and adverbs) are defined implicitly by statements in ACE. Following are three ACE statements about employees and managers:

```
Every manager is an employee.
Every employee is a person.
For every employee, a manager hires the employee on a date.
```

From the syntactic form, the Attempto system assumes *manager, employee, person,* and *date* are nouns and *hires* is a verb. That information is sufficient to translate the first two statements to typed predicate calculus:

$$(\forall a{:}\text{Manager})(\exists b{:}\text{Employee})a = b.$$
$$(\forall a{:}\text{Employee})(\exists b{:}\text{Person})a = b.$$

The quantifier *every* maps to $\forall$, and the quantifier *some* or the indefinite article *a* maps to $\exists$. Nouns are translated to type labels in typed logic or to monadic predicates in untyped logic, and the verb *is* is translated to the $=$ operator. The third ACE statement requires more features:

$$(\forall a\text{:Employee})(\exists b\text{:Manager})(\exists c\text{:Event})(\exists d\text{:Date})$$
$$(\text{on}(c,d) \wedge \text{dscr}(c, \text{hire}(b,a))).$$

For verbs other than *is*, Attempto uses a context notation based on discourse representation structures (see Section 5.2). The DRS contexts are equivalent to CG contexts of type Event or State; in predicate calculus, they are represented by the description predicate. In this example, the event c is described by the nested proposition that manager b hires employee a. The definite article *the* marks a reference to some entity previously introduced by a quantifier. For further details about ACE and its translation to logic, see the example in Appendix C.2 and the subsequent discussion.

COBOL, Cyc, and ACE illustrate three approaches to the problem of defining and using ontologies for knowledge representation:

- COBOL is based on a predefined ontology for a single domain — the computer-oriented operations and datatypes used in a conventional programming language. That ontology, which is defined by an ISO standards committee, cannot be changed by the COBOL programmer.

- Cyc has an extensible logic-based language for defining knowledge of any kind and a predefined ontology with the scope of an encyclopedia. Knowledge engineers who use Cyc can adopt as much or as little of the predefined ontology as they find useful, but they can also redefine, extend, or modify the categories and definitions to tailor them to an application domain.

- Except for the assumption that verbs represent states or events, ACE is almost as ontologically neutral as first-order logic. Before it reads the statements about employees and managers, the Attempto system knows nothing about the domain. Afterward, it knows exactly what was entered and nothing more.

The COBOL approach is suitable for well-defined applications, but the lack of extensibility makes it difficult to adapt to new applications. The ACE language is the easiest one to implement, since it needs no built-in ontology, but it could be supplemented with ontologies defined in any logic-based language. A language like ACE could be used to enter and modify knowledge in Cyc, or it could be used to write programs. Exercises 7.17 through 7.20 illustrate the strengths and weaknesses of the ACE approach: it is general enough to specify a Turing machine, but predefined ontologies could make it easier to use by reducing the amount of detail that must be specified for each application.

DEVELOPING CSMF AND MDM. In Figure 7.29, the CSMF and MDM are hypothetical systems, but they include the features of many prototypes implemented by research and development groups around the world. Computer Aided Software Engineering (CASE) tools are being used to help programmers and system analysts with the middle stage of Figure 7.29. Most of them use notations like E-R diagrams, NIAM, and UML, which are close enough to logic that they could be translated automatically to and from CGs or KIF. Systems like Attempto support languages that can be read by people who have never studied logic, UML, or any other specialized notations. The developers of Cyc, WordNet, EDR, and other ontologies have been collaborating with ANSI and ISO standards organizations to design standard formats for defining and sharing ontologies for databases and knowledge bases. The ideal CSMF will not spring into existence as an overnight breakthrough. Instead, it is more likely to evolve through the integration of logic-based CASE tools with gradually improving systems for representing and using knowledge to assist in software development, documentation, and help facilities.

EXERCISES

1. Review the bilingual type hierarchies in Figures 7.2 and 7.3. Then draw a type hierarchy that includes types for the English terms *clock, watch, wristwatch,* and *pocket watch* and the Japanese word *tokei*, which means either clock or watch. Following are three sentences that have been partially translated from Japanese to English, leaving the word *tokei* untranslated.

   > *I took my tokei off.*
   > *I took my tokei out.*
   > *My tokei is slower than the tokei on the wall.*

   Which translation should be used for each occurrence of *tokei* in these sentences? What information would a computer system need to select those translations?

2. Study the representation of the missionaries and cannibals puzzle in the form of triples and constraints as described in Section 7.1. Write a program in a language of your choice that searches through the state space from the starting state <3,3,1> and finds a path to the goal state <0,0,0> that preserves the constraints.

3. Study the translation of the first MC sentence to the conceptual graph in Figure 7.5. Then translate the other sentences of that puzzle to conceptual graphs, predicate calculus, or any other knowledge representation language that you find convenient. Try to represent the details of the original English sentences as accurately as possible. Then analyze the issues that arise in translating this detailed representation to Amarel's triples and constraints.

4. Review the elaborations of the MC puzzle that were suggested by McCarthy. For each of them, show how the constraints would be modified and determine whether there exists a safe solution to the revised puzzle. Then modify the program you wrote for Exercise 7.1 to solve two different variations of the puzzle.

   As a result of your experience in revising the program to accommodate modifications, redesign the program to make it easier to modify. Then write programs to solve two more variations of the puzzle. As a class exercise, compare implementations in different languages to see how the choice of programming language affects the ease of modification.

5. After crossing the river, the missionaries and the cannibals decided to play a game of leapfrog, but with more complex constraints than the usual children's game. They agreed to the following rules:

   • Each state in the game consists of a line of people with one empty space, which may be somewhere inside the line or at either end.

   • The initial state has all the missionaries on the left, an empty space in the middle, and all the cannibals on the right. It could be represented by the character string mmm_ccc.

   • Missionaries are only permitted to move to an empty space on the right, either by stepping one space right or by leaping over one person, who may be either a missionary or a cannibal.

   • Cannibals are only permitted to move to an empty space on the left, either by stepping one space left or by leaping over one person, who may be either a missionary or a cannibal.

   • The goal state is ccc_mmm, which has all the missionaries on the right and all the cannibals on the left, with the empty space between them.

   Before choosing a programming representation, try playing a few games. If you can't find enough people to volunteer, use two different kinds of coins to represent the two kinds of people. Then answer the following questions:

   a. What would be a good representation if the primary purpose were to minimize the storage space for each state? Assume that the number of people might be arbitrarily large and millions of states had to be saved in long-term storage.

   b. Would a representation that minimizes storage space be convenient for a game-playing program that was designed to find an optimal strategy for the game in a minimum number of moves? If not, suggest a different representation that might simplify the programming and improve performance.

   c. Would the same representation improve efficiency and simplify programming, or might one representation be best for performance and another for ease of programming? Would the trade-offs between efficiency and ease of programming vary with different programming languages? If so, how?

d. If you wanted to display game positions in a way that would be easily readable by a person who was learning the game, what would be a convenient representation for the display? How would you translate to that representation from a representation designed to minimize storage or maximize performance?

e. Suppose you were given a program for generating English sentences from conceptual graphs and you wanted to use it for a tutorial that would explain positions and moves in the game. What choice of concept and relation types would be convenient for generating readable explanations? Try to avoid concepts that reflect aspects of the representation that were designed for ease of programming or machine efficiency.

f. Suppose that you wanted to use the same English generator to explain the internal states of the game to a programmer who wanted to know the details of the representation. What choice of concepts and relations might be convenient for representing the machine-oriented or programming aspects?

g. Using lambda expressions, define translations between the concept and relation types used to express the programming details and those used to explain the game to a nonprogrammer.

6. When played with coins, the game of leapfrog is easier to control than with people, who might get tired, bored, confused, injured, converted, or eaten during the game. Make a list of possible modifications of the rules to accommodate such possibilities. Represent the modified constraints in logic and show how each of them would affect the program for playing the game.

7. The ideas of elaboration tolerance apply to every application of computer systems. Select some working program or system that you are familiar with and study the effects of possible elaborations:

a. Start with a clear English description of the ideal or standard case that the system is required to handle.

b. Translate that description to a formalized representation in some version of logic or to a semiformal statement in stylized English, as in the trafficlight example of Section 3.1.

c. Make a list of the kinds of unexpected elaborations or modifications that might occur. By Murphy's law, the ones that can cause the system to fail are sure to occur.

d. Check to see what happens to the program or system when such cases occur.

e. Translate those elaborations to the same notation you used for part (b) and integrate them with that representation.

f. Translate the revised representation to a clear description that would be readable by a person who was not trained in logic.

8. Use the ideas discussed in this or earlier chapters to answer the following questions:

   a. Which of the following verbs represent actions, and which represent states?

      jump, want, love, eat, believe, kick, own

   b. Which of the following nouns represent entities according to their roles, and which represent entities according to some inherent characteristics?

      dog, brother, adult, employee, pet, tree, fastener

   c. Which of the following words represent mass nouns or count nouns?

      dog, butter, person, air, pencil, employee, happiness

   d. For each of the following transitive verbs, state which conceptual relation would be used for its direct object — result (Rslt), patient (Ptnt), or theme (Thme). Do any of them have different senses that might be used with different conceptual relations?

      cut, see, build, mash, carry, squash, take, decorate, bring, refurbish, love, hate, kill, want, paint, renovate, cook, construct, deconstruct, write, explode, fetch, carve

   e. Which of the following relationships can be represented by acyclic graphs or by graphs with possible cycles?

      part-whole, parent-child, homeowner-neighbor, lawyer-client, manager-employee, brother-sister, doctor-patient

9. In analyzing the problems of mapping language to logic, the logician Evert Beth (1939) discussed the following argument:

   John is a rascal.
   Peter is a rascal.
   Therefore, John and Peter are rascals.

   This conclusion is acceptable, but the following argument, which seems to have a similar structure, is dubious:

   John is a brother.
   Peter is a brother.
   Therefore, John and Peter are brothers.

This conclusion is syntactically unambiguous, but an axiom associated with the concept type Brother causes a semantic ambiguity. State that axiom in English and translate it to logic. Also consider the following argument:

> Mary is a mother.
> Susan is a mother.
> Therefore, Mary and Susan are mothers.

Is this conclusion acceptable? State an axiom associated with the concept type Mother and explain why it does not lead to the same kind of ambiguity as the axiom for Brother. While working on this exercise, review the discussion of conversational implicature in Section 5.2 and default reasoning in Section 6.4. Explain why those topics are relevant.

10. The phrases *half full* and *half empty* seem to be synonymous because they can be true of similar situations. Yet they may have different implications. Consider a cup of coffee that is described as half empty and one that is described as half full. Which one is likely to be hotter? What kind of knowledge would enable any reasoner — human or computer — to decide? Find other examples of phrases that may be true of similar situations but have different implications.

11. In English, the structure at the top left of Figure 7.23 could be described *An orange pyramid E is supported by a blue block D, which is supported collectively by three pyramids — a red one A, a green one B, and a yellow one C.* That sentence could be represented by the following conceptual graphs:

```
[Orange]←(Attr)←[Pyramid]←(Thme)←[Support]→(Inst)→[Block: D]-
   (Attr)→[Blue]
   (Thme)→[Support]→(Inst)→[Pyramid: Col{A,B,C}@3].
      [Pyramid: A]→(Attr)→[Red].
      [Pyramid: B]→(Attr)→[Green].
      [Pyramid: C]→(Attr)→[Yellow].
```

Show how the collective plural referent Col{A,B,C}@3 could be expanded in the same way as the graph for Alma's three husbands in Figure 4.2; then join the identical concepts to derive the CG in Figure 7.24. For the structure at the bottom left of Figure 7.23, state the English description, translate it to a CG with the collective plural Col{F,H}@2, and expand it to a CG similar to Figure 7.24. Then translate the question *Which block is supported by two blocks?* to a query graph with the plural referent Col{*}@2, expand the plural, and find the answer by matching graphs.

12. For the CG in Figure 7.25, replace the conceptual relations Objects and Supports with their definitions. Then replace the concepts of object with shape

pyramid and object with shape block with concepts of type Pyramid and Block. Is the resulting CG identical to Figure 7.24? If not, why not? Are the two CGs provably identical? If not, is one of them more general or more specialized than the other? State a constraint in English that adds information that could be used to convert the more general CG to make it identical to the more specialized one. Translate that English constraint to an if-then rule stated as a CG. Then apply that rule to the more general CG to derive the more specialized one. The issues illustrated by this exercise are the same kinds of issues that plague database and knowledge base conversions from one ontology to another. The use of constraints stated as if-then rules is a logic-based technique for ensuring compatibility between two different databases or knowledge bases.

13. The BIAIT technique discussed in Section 7.6 is based on seven questions that determine the information-processing needs of a business. The kinds of records implied by the first two questions were mentioned in that section. Study all seven questions and describe the records and procedures implied by the answers to each one. Consider the flow of records between different departments of a business; a custom-made product, for example, may impose requirements on the records used by sales, engineering, manufacturing, and accounting.

14. The oldest musical notations, like the oldest computer languages, were highly machine dependent. The family of notations called *tablature* specified the details of the strings, keys, frets, fingers, or feet used to produce the tones. Remnants of those notations are still used to specify fingering on the piano, bowing on the violin, or chords on the guitar. Before such notations can be translated to logic, an ontology must be defined that includes those parts of the musical instrument or the human body that correspond to the symbols of the notation. Analyze some musical score that includes such instrument-dependent notation, define an ontology for the notation, and show how the score could be translated to predicate calculus or conceptual graphs. Show how the result could be translated to the standard, machine-independent musical notation. Discuss some of the issues involved in translating from the machine-independent form to a machine-dependent form such as guitar chords or piano fingering. Can such translations be automated? If so, how? If not, why not?

15. The features of musical notation discussed in the previous exercise are typical of many languages and interfaces: instead of specifying a goal to be achieved (producing a melody), they specify the details of some technology used to achieve that goal (strings, keys, and fingers). A driver who wants to make an automobile stop, go, and turn must learn a great deal of detail about the wheels, the engine, the ignition system, the fuel system, and the various switches, levers, and pedals

used to control them. Automated systems help to reduce the amount of detail the users must learn, but that detail becomes annoyingly obtrusive when something goes wrong: the wheels are skidding, the battery is dead, there is moisture in the fuel tank, or a leak develops in the tires, the radiator, the transmission, the exhaust pipe, or the brake lines. Find similar examples in any field you may be familiar with. Show how the language or interface mixes an ontology about the desired goals with an ontology about the means of achieving those goals. How does that mixture affect the ease of learning and ease of use? How can either or both be simplified? Distinguish between ease of learning and ease of use. Do changes intended to improve one affect the other positively or negatively? Give examples.

16. Zachman's Information Systems Architecture (ISA), which was described in Section 3.6, has five design levels. Most of the development tools for object-oriented languages, however, are limited to entities at the technology level (row 4) and the component level (row 5). Design languages, such as UML, address the systems level (row 3). Very few notations represent the top two rows: the scope and enterprise levels. For the six ISA columns, most notations represent the data and function in the first two columns, and some represent the network, organization, and schedule. For his *strategic business models*, Ramackers (1994) represented the strategy column with E-R diagrams that show relationships between goals, problems, causes, critical success factors, and solutions; but E-R diagrams are inadequate to define and describe all the relationships and constraints. As a term project, review the design and development literature and determine which of the thirty boxes in the ISA framework are addressed by each notation and technique. Can any of them be adapted to represent information in other boxes of the ISA framework? Show how logic could be used to define the relations and transformations between the notations used for different rows and columns.

17. Study the ACE specification of the library database in Appendix C.2 and the methods of translating it to discourse representation structures, conceptual graphs, and typed predicate calculus. Then translate several of the LibDB rules to each of those three notations for logic.

18. Make a list of every verb used in the LibDB specification. Classify each verb as an expression of an action or a state. For several of the actions, draw a small Petri net that shows which states are preconditions and which states are postconditions; you may have to add some states that are not mentioned in the LibDB rules. Then translate the Petri nets to conceptual graphs according to the conventions of Chapter 4. For each concept that represents a state or event, write a short English sentence that describes the corresponding state

or event. Then translate the sentences to conceptual graphs nested inside the concept nodes.

19. Alan Turing (1936) defined a very simple, but general computing machine whose instructions have five parts: current state; current tape symbol; new state; new tape symbol; and a move (right, left, or stay in place). Because of their generality, Turing machines have become a standard for testing the generality of computing devices and specification languages: any language that can specify Turing machine instructions and their method of execution is in principle capable of specifying any program that can be executed on any digital computer. To show that the ACE language is general enough to specify a Turing machine, find some textbook on automata theory that describes Turing machines and their operation. Rewrite the definition of the Turing machine formats and method of execution in the syntactic forms permissible in ACE. Show that the specification is complete by translating the ACE statements to a program that can simulate any Turing machine described in the textbook you have been using as a reference.

20. Review the discussion of event variables and adverbial modifiers in Section 4.1. Then study the DRS notation used by Attempto in Section C.4. Why does DRS require special variables for events and states? Why doesn't the CG in Figure 7.30 require such variables? Show how the translation from ACE to predicate calculus can be simplified by using CGs instead of DRS as the intermediate notation.

21. Review the exercises concerning the hotel reservation problem in previous chapters and your analyses and solutions to them. Suggest possible tools and techniques that could be used to facilitate or automate some of that analysis and the subsequent design and implementation.

Summary of Notations

By relieving the brain of all unnecessary work, a good notation sets it free to concentrate on more advanced problems, and in effect increases the mental power of the race. Before the introduction of the Arabic notation, multiplication was difficult, and the division even of integers called into play the highest mathematical faculties. . . . Civilization advances by extending the number of important operations which we can perform without thinking about them.

ALFRED NORTH WHITEHEAD, *Introduction to Mathematics*

A.1 Predicate Calculus

Symbolic logic has two main branches: *propositional logic* and *predicate logic*. Propositional logic treats propositions as single units. The symbol *p*, for example, could represent the entire proposition *Trailer trucks have 18 wheels*. Predicate logic, however, makes finer distinctions. It analyzes propositions into combinations of predicates like trailerTruck(*x*) and wheel(*x*). Besides symbols for propositions, propositional logic also includes operator symbols for logical connectives like *and, or, not,* and *if-then*. Let *p* be the proposition *The sun is shining*, and let *q* be the proposition *It is raining*. Following are the most commonly used operators:

- *Conjunction* (and). $p \wedge q$ represents the proposition *The sun is shining, and it is raining.*

- *Disjunction* (or). $p \vee q$ represents *The sun is shining, or it is raining.*

- *Negation* (not). $\sim p$ represents *The sun is not shining.*

- *Material implication* (if-then). $p \supset q$ represents *If the sun is shining, then it is raining.*

- *Equivalence* (if-and-only-if). $p \equiv q$ represents *The sun is shining if and only if it is raining.*

The operators $\wedge$, $\vee$, $\sim$, $\supset$, and $\equiv$ are usually called *Boolean operators*.

Propositions may be true or false. The rules of propositional logic define the truth of a compound proposition in terms of the truth or falsity of the elementary propositions contained within it. The following truth table shows the truth values of compound propositions as functions of the truth values of their components. On the left are the four possible combinations of 1 and 0 for the truth or falsity of the simple propositions p and q. On the right are the resulting values for the compound propositions $p{\wedge}q$, $p{\vee}q$, $\sim p$, $p{\supset}q$, and $p{\equiv}q$. Such tables, which resemble the addition and multiplication tables of arithmetic, are known as *truth tables*.

p	q	$p{\wedge}q$	$p{\vee}q$	$\sim p$	$p{\supset}q$	$p{\equiv}q$
0	0	0	0	1	1	1
0	1	0	1	1	1	0
1	0	0	1	0	0	0
1	1	1	1	0	1	1

Boolean operators are called *truth functions* because they take truth values as input and generate truth values as output. There are sixteen possible truth functions of two arguments, but the five listed in the table are the most common. Another common operator is *exclusive or*, which is equivalent to p or q, but not both. Two operators used in computer circuit design are *nand* $\curlywedge$ and *nor* $\curlyvee$: ($p{\curlywedge}q$) is equivalent to $\sim(p{\wedge}q)$, and ($p{\curlyvee}q$) is equivalent to $\sim(p{\vee}q)$. One or two Boolean operators may be taken as primitives, with the others defined in terms of them. Following are the definitions of $\vee$ and $\supset$ in terms of $\sim$ and $\wedge$:

$$p{\vee}q \equiv \sim(\sim p \wedge \sim q).$$
$$p{\supset}q \equiv \sim(p \wedge \sim q).$$

Following are the definitions of $\wedge$ and $\supset$ in terms of $\sim$ and $\vee$:

$$p{\wedge}q \equiv \sim(\sim p \vee \sim q).$$
$$p{\supset}q \equiv \sim p \vee \sim q.$$

In fact, only one primitive operator, either $\curlywedge$ or $\curlyvee$, is necessary since $\sim$, $\wedge$, and $\vee$ can be defined in terms of either one of them.

PREDICATES.   A *predicate* or *relation* is a function that maps its arguments to the *truth values* 1 and 0 or T and F. One example is the predicate *less than*, represented by the symbol $<$. For the arguments 5 and 12, the value of $5{<}12$ is true, and the value of $12{<}5$ is false. Predicates may be written as infix operators with special symbols like $<$; they may be represented by single letters like $R(x,y)$ and $S(x,y,z)$; or they may be represented by longer names like $mother(x,y)$ and $between(x,y,z)$. Traditional mathematics uses only single letters or symbols, but programming languages and database systems permit longer names. The term *predicate* is a synonym for relation. Some authors say that relations must have two or more arguments; they would call a predicate with one argument a *property*. However, the terms *predicate* and *relation* are often used interchangeably.

Predicates may be defined either by *intension* or by *extension*. An intensional definition is a rule for computing a truth value for each possible input. An extensional definition is a list of all combinations of arguments for which the predicate is true; for all other combinations, it is false. In a database, a *stored relation* is one whose values are listed by extension, and a *virtual relation* is computed by some rule. In theory, implementation issues are irrelevant. In practice, the question of how a relation or a predicate is computed is of vital importance. The relation $x<y$, for example, is easy to compute, but it would require an infinite amount of space to store.

PREDICATE LOGIC.   In propositional logic, the proposition *Every peach is fuzzy* is represented by a single symbol p. In predicate logic, however, the structure of the proposition is shown in finer detail:

$$(\forall x)(\text{peach}(x) \supset \text{fuzzy}(x)).$$

The symbol $\forall$ is called the *universal quantifier*; the combination $(\forall x)$ may be read *for every x*. The predicate peach(x) may be read *x is a peach*, and fuzzy(x) may be read *x is fuzzy*. The entire formula, therefore, may be read *For every x, if x is a peach, then x is fuzzy*. Note that predicates are combined with the same Boolean operators used in the propositional logic. Predicate logic is not a replacement for propositional logic, but an extension or refinement of it.

Predicate logic has one other quantifier, the *existential quantifier* $\exists$. The combination $(\exists x)$ may be read *there exists an x such that*. The following formula uses an existential quantifier:

$$\sim(\exists x)(\text{peach}(x) \wedge \sim\text{fuzzy}(x)).$$

This may be read *It is false that there exists an x such that x is a peach and x is not fuzzy*. Formulas with more than one quantifier are possible. The English statement *For any integer x, there is a prime number greater than x* is represented as,

$$(\forall x)(\exists y)(\text{integer}(x) \supset (\text{prime}(y) \wedge x<y)).$$

Literally, this formula may be read *For every x, there exists a y such that if x is an integer, then y is prime and x is less than y*.

The order of quantifiers in symbolic logic makes a crucial difference, as it does in English. Consider the sentence *Every man in department B55 married a woman who came from Boston*, which may be represented by the formula

$$(\forall x)(\exists y)((\text{man}(x) \wedge \text{dept}(x,\text{B55})) \supset$$
$$(\text{woman}(y) \wedge \text{hometown}(y,\text{Boston}) \wedge \text{married}(x,y))).$$

This formula says that for every *x* there exists a *y* such that if *x* is a man and *x* is in department B55, then *y* is a woman, the hometown of *y* is Boston, and *x* married *y*. Since the two-place predicate married is symmetric, married(*x*,*y*) is equivalent to married(*y*,*x*). Interchanging the arguments of the predicate married makes no difference, but interchanging the two quantifiers makes a big difference:

$(\exists y)(\forall x)((\text{man}(x) \wedge \text{dept}(x,\text{B55})) \supset$
$\quad (\text{woman}(y) \wedge \text{hometown}(y,\text{Boston}) \wedge \text{married}(x,y))).$

This formula says that there exists a *y* such that for every *x*, if *x* is a man in department B55, then *y* is a woman, the hometown of *y* is Boston, and *x* married *y*. In ordinary English, that means, *A woman who came from Boston married every man in department B55*. If there is more than one man in department B55, the implications this sentence are very different from those of the preceding one.

FORMATION RULES.   The notation of propositional logic includes symbols for variables, parentheses, and Boolean operators. The notation of propositional logic includes those symbols plus symbols for quantifiers, functions, and predicates. These symbols are combined in formulas according to three *formation rules*:

- A *term* is either a *constant* such as 2, a *variable* such as *x*, or a function or an operator symbol applied to its arguments, each of which is itself a term.
- An *atom* is either a single letter such as *p* that represents a proposition or a predicate symbol applied to its arguments, each of which is a term.
- A *formula* is either an atom, a formula preceded by ~, any two formulas *A* and *B* together with any two-place Boolean operator **op** in the combination (*A* **op** *B*), or any formula *A* and any variable *x* in either of the combinations (∃*x*)*A* or (∀*x*)*A*.

The formation rules may be applied recursively to derive all possible formulas. If *f* is a one-place function and + is a two-place operator, then $f(x)$ and $2+2$ are terms. If P is a two-place predicate and Q is a one-place predicate, then P($f(x)$,$2+2$) and Q(7) are atoms. Since all atoms are formulas, these two formulas can be combined by the Boolean operator ⊃ to form a new formula:

$(\text{P}(f(x),2+2) \supset \text{Q}(7)).$

Since any formula may be preceded by ~ to form another formula, the following string is also a formula:

$\sim(\text{P}(f(x),2+2) \supset \text{Q}(7)).$

Putting the quantifier (∀*y*) in front of it produces,

$(\forall y)\sim(\text{P}(f(x),2+2) \supset \text{Q}(7)).$

Adding another quantifier (∃x) produces,

$$(\exists x)(\forall y)\sim(P(f(x),2+2) \supset Q(7)).$$

And preceding this formula with ~ produces,

$$\sim(\exists x)(\forall y)\sim(P(f(x),2+2) \supset Q(7)).$$

In this formula, the occurrence of x in $f(x)$ is *bound* by the quantifier (∃x). The quantifier (∀y) has no effect on the formula since y does not occur as an argument of any function or predicate in it.

RULES OF INFERENCE. Formation rules define the syntax of formulas, but they don't guarantee that the formulas are true. A *rule of inference* is a rule that preserves truth: if the starting formulas are true, the result of performing a rule of inference on them must also be true. In English, the following two sentences are equivalent: *Every peach is fuzzy* and *There is no peach that is not fuzzy*. To show the equivalence, first map both sentences into logic:

$(\forall x)(\text{peach}(x) \supset \text{fuzzy}(x))$
$\sim(\exists x)(\text{peach}(x) \wedge \sim\text{fuzzy}(x))$

If the first formula were represented by the single variable p and the second by q, there would be no way to prove that $p \equiv q$. The rules of predicate logic, however, can show the equivalence. The first rule relates the quantifiers ∀ and ∃. If A is any formula,

$(\exists x)A$ is equivalent to $\sim(\forall x)\sim A$
$(\forall x)A$ is equivalent to $\sim(\exists x)\sim A$

By replacing ∀ with ~∃~, the first of the peach formulas can be transformed to

$$\sim(\exists x)\sim(\text{peach}(x) \supset \text{fuzzy}(x)).$$

An implication of the form $p \supset q$ can be defined as $\sim(p \wedge \sim q)$. With this definition, the preceding formula becomes

$$\sim(\exists x)\sim\sim(\text{peach}(x) \wedge \sim\text{fuzzy}(x)).$$

Whenever a double negation (a sequence of two consecutive ~ symbols) occurs, both can be deleted. Then the formula becomes

$$\sim(\exists x)(\text{peach}(x) \wedge \sim\text{fuzzy}(x)),$$

which is the same as the second peach formula. This proof shows that the first formula implies the second. Another proof would use the inverses of these rules to show that the second implies the first. If each formula implies the other, then the two are equivalent.

Following are some rules of inference for propositional logic. The symbols p, q, and r represent any formulas whatever.

- *Modus ponens.* From p and $p{\supset}q$, derive q.
- *Modus tollens.* From $\sim q$ and $p{\supset}q$, derive $\sim p$.
- *Hypothetical syllogism.* From $p{\supset}q$ and $q{\supset}r$, derive $p{\supset}r$.
- *Disjunctive syllogism.* From $p{\vee}q$ and $\sim p$, derive q.
- *Conjunction.* From p and q, derive $p{\wedge}q$.
- *Addition.* From p, derive $p{\vee}q$. (Any formula whatever may be added to a disjunction.)
- *Subtraction.* From $p{\wedge}q$, derive p. (Extra conjuncts may be thrown away.)

Not all of these rules are primitive. In developing a theory of logic, logicians try to minimize the number of primitive rules. Then they show that other rules, called *derived rules of inference*, can be defined in terms of them.

Following are some common equivalences. Either of the formulas in an equivalence can be substituted for any occurrence of the other, either alone or as part of some larger formula:

- *Idempotency.* $p{\wedge}p$ is equivalent to p, and $p{\vee}p$ is also equivalent to p.
- *Commutativity.* $p{\wedge}q$ is equivalent to $q{\wedge}p$, and $p{\vee}q$ is equivalent to $q{\vee}p$.
- *Associativity.* $p{\wedge}(q{\wedge}r)$ is equivalent to $(p{\wedge}q){\wedge}r$, and $p{\vee}(q{\vee}r)$ is equivalent to $(p{\vee}q){\vee}r$.
- *Distributivity.* $p{\wedge}(q{\vee}r)$ is equivalent to $(p{\wedge}q){\vee}(p{\wedge}r)$, and $p{\vee}(q{\wedge}r)$ is equivalent to $(p{\vee}q){\wedge}(p{\vee}r)$.
- *Absorption.* $p{\wedge}(p{\vee}q)$ is equivalent to p, and $p{\vee}(p{\wedge}q)$ is equivalent to p.
- *Double negation.* p is equivalent to $\sim\sim p$.
- *De Morgan's laws.* $\sim(p{\wedge}q)$ is equivalent to $\sim p{\vee}\sim q$, and $\sim(p{\vee}q)$ is equivalent to $\sim p{\wedge}\sim q$.

RULES FOR QUANTIFIERS. In predicate logic, the rules of inference include all the rules of propositional logic together with rules for handling quantified variables. Before those rules can be stated, a distinction must be drawn between *free occurrences* and *bound occurrences* of a variable:

- If A is an atom, then all occurrences of a variable x in A are said to be free.
- If a formula C was derived from formulas A and B by combining them with Boolean operators, then all occurrences of variables that are free in A and B are also free in C.
- If a formula C was derived from a formula A by preceding A with either $(\forall x)$

or $(\exists x)$, then all free occurrences of x in A are said to be *bound* in C. All free occurrences of other variables in A remain free in C.

The rules for dealing with variables depend on which occurrences are free and bound and which variables must be renamed to avoid *name clashes* with other variables.

Let $\Phi(x)$ be a formula containing one or more free occurrences of a variable x. Then $\Phi(t)$ is the result of substituting a term t for every free occurrence of x in Φ. Following are permissible substitutions that preserve truth:

- *Universal instantiation.* From $(\forall x)\Phi(x)$, derive $\Phi(c)$, where c is any constant.
- *Existential generalization.* From $\Phi(c)$, where c is any constant, derive $(\exists x)\Phi(x)$, provided that every occurrence of x in $\Phi(x)$ is free.
- *Dropping quantifiers.* If the variable x does not occur free in Φ, then from $(\exists x)\Phi$ derive Φ, and from $(\forall x)\Phi$ derive Φ.
- *Adding quantifiers.* From Φ derive $(\forall x)\Phi$ or derive $(\exists x)\Phi$, where x is any variable whatever.
- *Substituting equals for equals.* For any terms s and t where $s=t$, derive $\Phi(t)$ from $\Phi(s)$, provided that all free occurrences of variables in t remain free in $\Phi(t)$.

Logically, there is never a need to assert a formula with free variables, but some rules of inference are stated in terms of subformulas with free variables.

TYPED PREDICATE LOGIC. The version of typed predicate logic used in this book is defined as a purely syntactic extension of untyped logic. The semantics of the typed and untyped versions are identical, and every theorem and proof in one version has an equivalent theorem and proof in the other. For knowledge representation, typed logic has the advantage of being more concise and readable. Further, it can support efficient rules of inference based on *inheritance*. These rules do not make the logic more expressive, since every theorem in typed logic has an equivalent in untyped logic, and vice versa. They can, however, shorten some proofs and help to support efficient implementations.

The only difference between typed and untyped logic is the addition of a *type label* after the quantifier. Every type label corresponds to a monadic predicate; in this book, the type labels are written with an initial capital letter, and the predicates are written with an initial lowercase letter. The spelling of the type label is identical to the spelling of the corresponding monadic predicate. Let L be any type label that corresponds to a monadic predicate $l(x)$, and let $\Phi(x)$ be any predicate or expression that contains a free variable x. Then the following typed and untyped formulas are defined to be equivalent:

- *Universal.* $(\forall x{:}L)\Phi(x) \equiv (\forall x)(l(x) \supset \Phi(x))$.
- *Existential.* $(\exists x{:}L)\Phi(x) \equiv (\exists x)(l(x) \wedge \Phi(x))$.

Note that the universal quantifier $\forall$ expands to a formula with an implication $\supset$, and the existential $\exists$ expands to a formula with a conjunction $\wedge$.

With a string of multiple quantifiers of the same kind (either $\forall$ or $\exists$) and with the same type label, it is permissible to factor out the common quantifier and type label. As an example, the axiom of transitivity for the $<$ operator on numbers may be stated in the following form:

$(\forall x,y,z{:}\text{Number})$
$\qquad((x < y \wedge y < z) \supset x < z).$

To expand this formula to the untyped form, replace the single quantifier with separate quantifiers and type labels for each variable:

$(\forall x{:}\text{Number})(\forall y{:}\text{Number})(\forall z{:}\text{Number})$
$\qquad((x < y \wedge y < z) \supset x < z).$

Then expand each quantifier separately:

$(\forall x)(\text{number}(x) \supset$
$\qquad(\forall y)(\text{number}(y) \supset$
$\qquad\qquad(\forall z)(\text{number}(z) \supset$
$\qquad\qquad\qquad((x < y \wedge y < z) \supset x < z)))).$

The rules of inference allow this formula to be simplified to the following:

$(\forall x)(\forall y)(\forall z)((\text{number}(x) \wedge \text{number}(y) \wedge$
$\qquad\text{number}(z) \wedge x < y \wedge y < z) \supset x < z).$

As this example illustrates, typed logic can often simplify the formulas and eliminate much of the tedious and error-prone bookkeeping. In Whitehead's terms, it advances civilization by reducing the need to think about the details.

An untyped formula can be considered a special case of a typed formula, where every variable has the *universal type label* $\top$. The type $\top$ can be expanded to a monadic predicate $\top(x)$, which is true for every possible value of x:

- *Universal.*

  $(\forall x{:}\top)\Phi(x)$
  $\quad\equiv (\forall x)(\top(x) \supset \Phi(x)$
  $\quad\equiv (\forall x)\Phi(x).$

- *Existential.*

  $(\exists x{:}\top)\Phi(x)$
  $\quad\equiv (\exists x)(\top(x) \wedge \Phi(x)$
  $\quad\equiv (\exists x)\Phi(x).$

EXTENDED QUANTIFIERS.   Many formulas can be simplified by introducing special operators or quantifiers. In the *Principia Mathematica*, Whitehead and

Russell defined two relational operators: E! for *exactly one* and E!! for *unique*. For each of those operators, there is a corresponding quantifier. Stephen Kleene defined the *exactly-one* quantifier $(\exists!x)$ by the following equivalence:

$(\exists!x)\Phi(x)$ is defined as
$$(\exists x)(\Phi(x) \land \sim(\exists y)(\Phi(y) \land y \neq x)).$$

The first line may be read *There exists exactly one x such that Φ is true of x*. The second may be read *There exists an x such that Φ is true of x and it is false that there exists any y for which Φ is true and y is different from x*.

Uniqueness is a more complicated notion that depends on two variables. Let $\Psi(x,y)$ be any dyadic predicate or expression. Then the *unique existential quantifier* $(\exists!!y)$ is defined by the following equivalence:

$(\forall x)(\exists!!y)\Psi(x,y)$ is defined as
$$(\forall x)(\exists!y)(\Psi(x,y) \land$$
$$\sim(\exists z)(\Psi(z,y) \land z \neq y)).$$

To illustrate the difference between exactly one and unique, consider the following two sentences and their translations into typed logic with the $\exists!$ and $\exists!!$ quantifiers:

- *Exactly one.* Every person has exactly one mother (but multiple people may have the same mother).

  $\forall x$:Person$)(\exists!y$:Mother$)$has(x,y).

- *Unique.* Every person has a unique social security number, (and no two people may have the same SSNo).

  $\forall x$:Person$)(\exists!!y$:SSNo$)$has(x,y).

When the unique existential quantifier with typed variables is expanded to the basic notation, there is usually an explosion of symbols. To expand the quantifiers, first expand the unique existential $\exists!!$ quantifier:

$$(\forall x\text{:Person})(\exists!y\text{:SSNo})(\text{has}(x,y) \land$$
$$\sim(\exists z\text{:Person})(\text{has}(z,y) \land z \neq y)).$$

Next expand the $\exists!$ quantifier:

$$(\forall x\text{:Person})(\exists y\text{:SSNo})(\text{has}(x,y) \land$$
$$\sim(\exists w\text{:SSNo})(\text{has}(x,w) \land x \neq w) \land$$
$$\sim(\exists z\text{:Person})(\text{has}(z,y) \land z \neq y)).$$

Then expand the type labels:

$$(\forall x)(\text{person}(x) \supset$$
$$(\exists y)(\text{ssno}(y) \land \text{has}(x,y) \land$$
$$\sim(\exists w)(\text{ssno}(w) \land \text{has}(x,w) \land x \neq w) \land$$
$$\sim(\exists z)(\text{person}(z) \land \text{has}(z,y) \land z \neq y))).$$

This formula may be read *For every x, if x is a person, then there exists a y where y is a social security number and x has y and it is false that there exists a w where w is a social security number and x has w and x is different from w and it is false that there exists a z where z is a person and z has y and z is different from y.* Examples like this illustrate Whitehead's point that a good notation can relieve the brain of unnecessary work.

To simplify formulas with sets, it is also convenient to use extended quantifiers with set qualifiers. *Restricted quantifiers* can be defined to limit the values of a variable to the elements of a set S:

- *Universal.*

  $(\forall x \in S)\Phi(x) \equiv (\forall x)(x \in S \supset \Phi(x)).$

- *Existential.*

  $(\exists x \in S)\Phi(x) \equiv (\exists x)(x \in S \wedge \Phi(x)).$

$(\forall x \in S)$ is read *for every x in S*, and $(\exists x \in S)$ is read *there exists an x in S*.

In classical first-order logic, quantification restricted to a particular type label t is equivalent to quantification restricted to the denotation of t: $(\forall x{:}t)$ is equivalent to $(\forall x \in \delta t)$ and $(\exists x{:}t)$ is equivalent to $(\exists x \in \delta t)$. This equivalence, however, does not hold for modal logic. As an example, the following formula is true in FOL:

  $(\forall x \in \delta \text{Unicorn})\text{cow}(x).$

This formula says that every element of the set of unicorns is a cow. That is only true because in the present world, no unicorns exist, and the set of all unicorns is empty. The following formula in modal logic is false:

  $\Box(\forall x{:}\text{Unicorn})\text{cow}(x).$

This formula says it is necessarily true that every unicorn is a cow. It is false because someone might genetically engineer a unicorn that is not a cow. For further discussion of the distinction between sets and types, see Section 2.6.

A.2 Conceptual Graphs

Conceptual graphs (CGs) are an extension of C. S. Peirce's *existential graphs* with features adopted from linguistics and AI. Besides Peirce's primitives, conceptual graphs provide means of representing *case relations, generalized quantifiers, indexicals,* and other aspects of natural languages. To illustrate the basics, Figure A.1 shows a conceptual graph for the sentence *A cat is on a mat.*

In a conceptual graph, the boxes are called *concepts*, and the circles are called *conceptual relations*. There is a *formula operator* φ, which translates conceptual graphs to formulas in predicate calculus. It maps circles to predicates with each arc

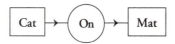

FIGURE A.I Conceptual graph for "A cat is on a mat

as one argument, and it maps concept nodes to typed variables, where the *type label* inside each concept box designates the type. If no other quantifier is specified inside a concept box, the default quantifier for the variable is the existential ∃. For Figure A.1, φ generates the following formula:

$(\exists x\!:\!\text{Cat})(\exists y\!:\!\text{Mat})\text{on}(x,y).$

This formula says that there exist an x of type Cat and a y of type Mat, and x is on y. To save space on the printed page, there is also a linear notation with square brackets instead of boxes and parentheses instead of circles:

`[Cat]→(On)→[Mat].`

The graph notation is usually more readable, and the linear notation takes less space. But both forms represent the same abstract graph, and they can be automatically translated to other versions of logic.

Informally, a conceptual graph is a structure of concepts and conceptual relations where every arc links some conceptual relation r to some concept c. Formally, the structure of the graphs is defined in a mathematical style that spells out the details with greater precision. The formal structure of conceptual graphs is defined by the following ten definitions, which are numbered A.2.1 to A.2.10.

DEFINITION A.2.I: CONCEPTUAL GRAPH.   A *conceptual graph g* is a bipartite graph that has two kinds of nodes called, *concepts* and *conceptual relations*.

- Every arc a of g must *link* a conceptual relation r in g to a concept c in g. The arc a is said to *belong* to the relation r; it is said to be *attached* to the concept c, but it does not belong to c.

- The conceptual graph g may have concepts that are not linked to any conceptual relation; but every arc that belongs to any conceptual relation in g must be attached to exactly one concept in g.

- Three kinds of conceptual graphs are given distinguished names:

  1. The *blank* is an empty conceptual graph with no concepts, conceptual relations, or arcs.

  2. A *singleton* is a conceptual graph that consists of a single concept, but no conceptual relations or arcs.

  3. A *star* is a conceptual graph that consists of a single conceptual relation and the concepts that are attached to its arcs.

To illustrate this definition, consider the following conceptual graph, which represents the sentence *John is going to Boston*:

```
[Person: John]←(Agnt)←[Go]→(Dest)→[City: Boston].
```

This graph contains three concepts: [Person: John], [Go], and [City: Boston]. It contains two conceptual relations: (Agnt) relates [Go] to the agent John, and (Dest) relates [Go] to the destination Boston. The term *bipartite* means that every arc of a conceptual graph links one concept and one conceptual relation; there are no arcs that link concepts to concepts or relations to relations. Two of the four arcs in the graph belong to (Agnt), and the other two belong to (Dest).

A conceptual graph g with n conceptual relations can be constructed from n star graphs, one for each conceptual relation in g. Since the sample CG above has two conceptual relations, it could be constructed from the following two star graphs:

```
[Person: John]←(Agnt)←[Go]   [Go]→(Dest)→[City: Boston].
```

If left as is, these two star graphs constitute a disconnected conceptual graph. To form a connected CG, they could be joined by overlaying the two identical concepts of type [Go] to form the graph above.

DEFINITION A.2.2: CONCEPT.   Every concept has a *type t* and a *referent r*.

In this abstract definition, the representations of the type and referent are not specified. In computer storage, they may be represented by a pair of pointers, one pointing to a specification of the type and the other pointing to a specification of the referent. On paper or a computer display, the type is usually written on the left side of a concept, the referent is written on the right, and the two fields are separated by a colon. In the concept [Bus], "Bus" is the type, and the referent is a blank, which represents an existential quantifier. In the concept [Person: John], "Person" is the type, and the referent "John" is the name of some person.

DEFINITION A.2.3: CONCEPTUAL RELATION.   Every conceptual relation r has a *relation type t* and a nonnegative integer n called its *valence*.

- The number of arcs that belong to r is equal to its valence n. A conceptual relation of valence n is said to be *n-adic*, and its arcs are numbered $1, 2, \ldots, n$.
- For every n-adic conceptual relation r, there is a sequence of n concept types $<t_1, \ldots, t_n>$, called the *signature* of r. A 0-adic conceptual relation has no arcs, and its signature is empty.
- All conceptual relations of the same relation type t have the same valence n and the same signature s.

- The term *monadic* is synonymous with 1-adic, *dyadic* with 2-adic, and *triadic* with 3-adic.

Certain conceptual relations, called *actors*, may have side effects that are not represented in the abstract syntax; formally, however, actors are treated like other conceptual relations.

In the examples, Agnt, Dest, and On are dyadic relation types. Examples of monadic relation types include Psbl for possibility and Past for the past tense. Figure A.2 shows the between relation (Betw) as an example of a triadic relation (valence 3), whose first two arcs are linked to two things that are on either side of a third. That graph may be read *A person is between a rock and a hard place.*

The signature of a relation represents a constraint on the types of concepts that may be linked to its arcs. For Agnt, the signature is <Act,Animate>, which indicates that the type of the concept linked to its first arc must be Act or some subtype, such as Go, and the type of the concept linked to its second arc must be Animate or some subtype, such as Person. For Betw, the signature is <Entity,Entity,Entity>, which shows that all three concepts must be of the general type Entity, which imposes no constraints whatever.

For a conceptual relation with n arcs, the first $n-1$ arcs have arrows that point toward the circle, and the n-th or last arc points away. In the linear notation, Figure A.2 may be represented in the following form:

```
[Person]←(Betw)-
       ←1-[Rock]
       ←2-[Place]→(Attr)→[Hard].
```

The hyphen after the relation indicates that its other arcs are continued on subsequent lines. The two arcs that point toward the relation are numbered 1 and 2. The arc that points away is the last or third arc; the number 3 may be omitted, since it is implied by the outward pointing arrow. For monadic relations, both the number 1 and the arrow pointing toward the circle are optional. For dyadic relations, either the arcs are numbered 1 and 2 or the first arc points toward the circle and the second arc points away.

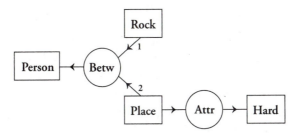

FIGURE A.2 A conceptual relation of valence 3

DEFINITION A.2.4: LAMBDA EXPRESSION.   For any integer *n*, an *n*-adic *lambda expression e* is a conceptual graph, called the *body* of *e*, in which *n* concepts have been designated as *formal parameters* of *e*.

- The formal parameters of *e* are numbered 1, . . ,*n*.
- There is a sequence $<t_1, . . , t_n>$ called the *signature* of *e*, where each t_i is the concept type of the *i*-th formal parameter of *e*. Since a 0-adic lambda expression has no formal parameters, its signature is the empty sequence $<>$.

This abstract definition does not specify how the formal parameters are designated. The traditional notation, which was introduced by the logician Alonzo Church, is to mark parameters with the Greek letter λ. If *n* is greater than 1, the parameters may be marked $\lambda1$, $\lambda2$, . . . , λn. As an example, the conceptual graph for the sentence *John is going to Boston* could be converted to the following dyadic lambda expression by replacing the name John with the symbol $\lambda1$ and the name Boston with $\lambda2$:

```
[Person: λ1]←(Agnt)←[Go]→(Dest)→[City: λ2].
```

Since this is a dyadic lambda expression, its signature is a list of the two types $<Person,City>$, which come from the type fields of the formal parameters. This lambda expression may be used to define a conceptual relation that relates a person to a city.

DEFINITION A.2.5: CONCEPT TYPE.   A *type hierarchy* is a partially ordered set T whose elements are called *type labels*. Each type label in T is specified as *primitive* or *defined*.

- For any concept *c*, the type of *c* is either a type label in T or a monadic lambda expression.
- The type hierarchy T contains two primitive type labels $\top$, called the *universal type*, and $\bot$, called the *absurd type*.
- For every defined type label, there is a monadic lambda expression, called its *definition*.
- A defined type label and its definition are interchangeable: in any position where one may occur, it may be replaced by the other.
- The partial ordering over T is determined by the *subtype* relation, with the symbols $\leq$ for *subtype*, $<$ for *proper subtype*, $\geq$ for *supertype*, and $>$ for *proper supertype*. If *t* is any type label, $\top \geq t$ and $t \geq \bot$; in particular, $\top > \bot$.
- The partial ordering of type labels must be consistent with the rules of inference defined over lambda expressions.

The type hierarchy starts with some set of primitive type labels, which includes at least ⊤ and ⊥. The definitional mechanisms introduce new type labels, whose place in the hierarchy is determined by their definitions. As an example, the following equation defines the type label MaineFarmer by a lambda expression for a farmer located (Loc) in Maine:

```
MaineFarmer = [Farmer: λ]→(Loc)→[State: Maine].
```

The symbol λ indicates that the concept [Farmer] is the formal parameter, and the sequence <Farmer> is the signature of the lambda expression. The type label of the formal parameter is always a supertype of the newly defined type: Farmer ≥ MaineFarmer. As an alternate notation, type labels can be defined with the keyword **type** and a variable:

```
type MaineFarmer(*x) is [Farmer: ?x]→(Loc)→[State: Maine].
```

Either the type label MaineFarmer or its defining lambda expression could be placed in the type field of a concept. The following two conceptual graphs are equivalent ways of saying *Every Maine farmer is laconic*:

```
[MaineFarmer: ∀]→(Attr)→[Laconic].
[ [Farmer: λ]→(Loc)→[State: Maine]: ∀]→(Attr)→[Laconic].
```

The second graph may be read *Every farmer who is located in the state of Maine is laconic*. Either graph could be converted to the other by interchanging the type label and its defining lambda expression.

DEFINITION A.2.6: RELATION TYPE.   A *relation hierarchy* is a partially ordered set R whose elements are called *relation labels*. Each relation label is specified as *primitive* or *defined*.

- For every relation label in R, there is a nonnegative integer n, called its *valence*.
- For every n-adic conceptual relation r, the type of r is either a relation label in R of valence n or an n-adic lambda expression.
- For every defined relation label of valence n, there is an n-adic lambda expression, called its *definition*.
- A defined relation label and its definition are interchangeable: in any position where one may occur, it may be replaced by the other.
- The partial ordering over R is determined by the *subtype* relation, with the symbols ≤ for *subtype*, < for *proper subtype*, ≥ for *supertype*, and > for *proper supertype*.

- The partial ordering of relation labels must be consistent with the rules of inference defined over lambda expressions.
- If r is an n-adic relation label, s is an m-adic relation label, and n is not equal to m, then none of the following is true: $r < s$, $r > s$, $r = s$.

As an example, the relation type GoingTo could be defined by an equation that makes GoingTo a synonym for a dyadic lambda expression:

```
GoingTo = [Person: λ1]←(Agnt)←[Go]→(Dest)→[City: λ2].
```

This definition says that the relation GoingTo relates a person (marked by $λ1$), who is the agent (Agnt) of the concept [Go], to a city (marked by $λ2$), which is the destination (Dest) of [Go]. With this relation, the graph for the sentence *John is going to Boston* could be represented by the following CG:

```
[Person: John]→(GoingTo)→[City: Boston].
```

This graph can be expanded to a more detailed graph by replacing the relation type label GoingTo with its definition:

```
[Person: John]→([Person: λ1]→(Agnt)→[Go]→(Dest)→[City: λ2])→[City: Boston].
```

The next step is to remove the lambda expression from inside the circle or parentheses, to join the first parameter [Person: $λ1$] with the concept connected to the first arc, and to join the second parameter [City: $λ2$] with the concept connected to the second arc:

```
[Person: John]←(Agnt)←[Go]→(Dest)→[City: Boston].
```

This graph says that the person John is the agent of going and that the city Boston is the destination of going. Each step of this derivation could be reversed to derive the original graph from the expanded graph.

Since the letter $λ$ is not present on most keyboards, it may be represented by the symbol @lambda. An alternative notation is to use the keyword **relation**, as in the following definition of GoingTo:

relation GoingTo(*x,*y) **is**
```
[Person: ?x]←(Agnt)←[Go]→(Dest)→[City: ?y].
```

A definition with the keyword **type** or **relation** cannot be written in the type field of a concept or relation; whenever it is used, however, labels like ?x and ?y can be rewritten as $λ1$ and $λ2$.

As in existential graphs, equality is not a primitive, since it can be defined in terms of coreference links. Following are definitions of the equal (Eq) and different (Dffr) relations:

relation Eq(*x,*y) **is** [⊤: ?x]- - -[⊤: ?y].
relation Dffr(*x,*y) **is** [⊤: ?x] ¬[[?x=?y]] [⊤: ?y].

The definition of Eq makes it a conceptual relation that is synonymous with a coreference link. It is defined for completeness, although there is no real need for it in conceptual graphs. The Dffr relation, however, is useful both to improve readability and to reduce the number of nested contexts.

DEFINITION A.2.7: REFERENT. The referent of a concept is specified by a *quantifier* and a *designator*.

- The quantifier is one of the following two kinds:
   1. *Existential.* An *existential* quantifier is represented either by the symbol ∃ or by the absence of any other quantifier symbol or expression.
   2. *Defined.* A *defined* quantifier is a symbol or expression in the extended syntax that may be translated to conceptual graphs that contain only existential quantifiers.

   A referent whose quantifier q is existential is called an *existential referent.*
- The designator is one of the following three kinds:
   1. *Literal.* A *literal* is a syntactic representation of the form of the referent. The three kinds of literals are numbers, character strings, and *encoded literals*, which are specified by a pair consisting of an identifier and a string.
   2. *Locator.* A *locator* is a symbol that determines how the referent may be found. The three kinds of locators differ in the way the referent is determined: an *individual marker* specifies a unique concept in the catalog of individuals of a knowledge base; an *indexical* is a symbol that determines the referent by an implementation-defined search, and a *name* is a symbol that determines the referent by some conventions that are independent of the current knowledge base.
   3. *Descriptor.* A *descriptor* is a conceptual graph that is said to *describe* the referent. A blank designator represents a blank conceptual graph as descriptor.

The referent of a concept determines the entity or set of entities the concept refers to. A designator specifies the referent by showing its form (literal), by pointing to it (locator), or by describing it (descriptor). An existential quantifier declares that at least one instance of the type exists; a defined quantifier may specify other quantities or amounts. Following are some examples:

- A literal shows the form of a referent, as in the concept [String: 'abcdefg']. For a multimedia system, a literal may encode a bit pattern that represents sound, graphics, or full-motion video.
- A locator is either a name like Boston or an implementation-dependent representation that begins with the symbol #. In the concept [Cake: #23846], the

locator #23846 is the serial number of some cake in a catalog of entities. Other examples include [Person: #you] and [Book: #ISBN-0-201-14472-7].

- A descriptor is represented by a conceptual graph nested in the referent field of a concept, as in the following example:

```
[Proposition: [Cat]←(Agnt)←[Chase]→(Thme)→[Mouse]].
```

This graph may be read *There exists a proposition, which states that a cat is chasing a mouse.* A concept with a completely blank referent, such as [Cat], has an implicit existential quantifier and a blank conceptual graph as descriptor. Since a blank graph does not say anything about the referent, the concept [Cat] by itself simply means *There exists a cat.*

In each of the above concepts, there is an implicit existential; the concept [String: 'abcdefg'], for example, may be read *There exists a string, whose form is represented by the literal* 'abcdefg'.

The defined quantifiers include the universal ∀, the quantity @1, and *collections,* such as {1, 2, 3} or {Tom, Dick, Harry}. To illustrate descriptors and literals in the referent field, Figure A.3 shows a concept [Situation] with a nested conceptual graph that may be read *A plumber is carrying a pipe.* In the nested graph, the agent relation (Agnt) indicates that the plumber is the one who is doing the action, and the theme relation (Thme) indicates that the pipe is the theme of the action. The situation box is linked via the image relation (Imag) to a concept of type Picture, whose referent field contains a literal that illustrates the situation. It is also linked via another Imag relation to a concept of type Sound, whose referent field contains another literal that encodes the associated sound. Internally, the encoded literals are represented by an identifier for the type of encoding such as WAV for sound or JPEG for a picture followed by a string that contains the encoded data.

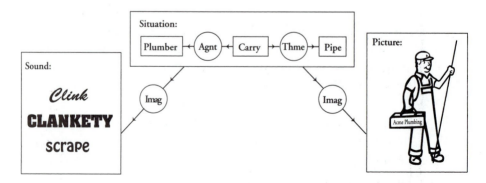

FIGURE A.3 A conceptual graph with a descriptor and two literal referents

DEFINITION A.2.8: CONTEXT.   A *context* $\mathscr{C}$ is a concept whose designator is a nonblank conceptual graph *g*.

- The graph *g* is said to be *immediately nested* in $\mathscr{C}$, and any concept *c* of *g* is also said to be immediately nested in $\mathscr{C}$.

- A concept *c* is said to be *nested in* $\mathscr{C}$ if either *c* is immediately nested in $\mathscr{C}$ or *c* is immediately nested in some context $\mathscr{D}$ that is nested in $\mathscr{C}$.

- Two concepts *c* and *d* are said to be *co-nested* if either *c*=*d* or there is some context $\mathscr{C}$ in which *c* and *d* are immediately nested.

- If a concept *c* is co-nested with a context $\mathscr{C}$, then any concept *d* nested in $\mathscr{C}$ is said to be *more deeply nested* than *c*.

- A concept *d* is said to be *within the scope* of a concept *c* if either *d* is co-nested with *c* or *d* is more deeply nested than *c*.

A context is a concept with a nested conceptual graph that describes the referent. In Figure A.3, the concept of type Situation is an example of a context; the nested graph describes the situation as one in which a plumber is carrying a pipe. Figure A.4 shows a CG with two contexts; it expresses the sentence *Tom believes that Mary wants to marry a sailor.*

In Figure A.4, Tom is the experiencer (Expr) of the concept [Believe], which is linked by the theme relation (Thme) to a proposition that Tom believes. The proposition box contains another conceptual graph, which says that Mary is the experiencer of [Want], which has as theme a situation that Mary hopes will come to pass. That situation is described by another nested graph, which says that Mary (represented by the concept [⊤]) marries a sailor. The dotted line, called a *corefer-*

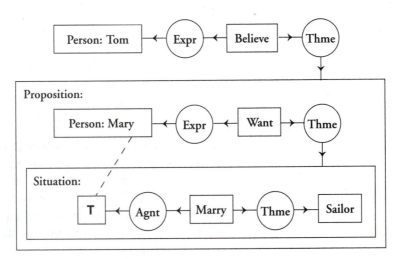

FIGURE A.4 A conceptual graph containing a nest of two contexts

ence link, shows that the concept [⊤] in the situation box refers to the same individual as the concept [Person: Mary] in the proposition box. Following is the linear form of Figure A.4:

```
[Person: Tom]←(Expr)←[Believe]→(Thme)-
   [Proposition: [Person: Mary *x]←(Expr)←[Want]→(Thme)-
      [Situation: [?x]←(Agnt)←[Marry]→(Thme)→[Sailor] ]].
```

Both the display form and the linear form follow the same rules for the scope of quantifiers. The outermost context contains three concepts: [Person: Tom], [Believe], and the proposition that Tom believes. Any graph in the outermost context has the effect of asserting that the corresponding proposition is true in the real world. Inside the proposition box are three more concepts: [Person: Mary], [Want], and the situation that Mary wants. Since those three are only asserted within the context of Tom's belief, the graph does not imply that they must exist in the real world. Since Mary is a named individual, one might give her the benefit of the doubt and assume that she also exists; but her desire and the situation she supposedly desires exist in the context of Tom's belief. If his belief is false, the referents of those concepts might not exist in the real world. Inside the context of the desired situation are the concepts [Marry] and [Sailor], whose referents exist within the scope of Mary's desire, which itself exists only within the scope of Tom's belief.

DEFINITION A.2.9: COREFERENCE SET. A *coreference set* C in a conceptual graph g is a set of concepts selected from g or from graphs nested in contexts of g.

- For any coreference set C, there must be one or more concepts in C, called the *dominant nodes* of C, which include all concepts in C within their scope. All dominant nodes of C must be co-nested.

- If a concept c is a dominant node of a coreference set C, it may not be a member of any other coreference set.

- A concept c may be member of more than one coreference set $\{C_1, C_2, . . .\}$ provided that c is not a dominant node of any C_i.

- A coreference set C may consist of a single concept c, which is then the dominant node of C.

In the graphic notation, the members of a coreference set C may be shown by connecting them with dotted lines, called *coreference links*. In Figure A.4, the dotted line connecting [Person: Mary] to [⊤] is an example of a coreference link. The concept [⊤] is within the scope of [Person: Mary], which is the dominant node. Since the two concepts represent the same individual, any information in the dominant node may be copied to the other node. The type label Person or the referent Mary, for example, could be copied from the dominant node to the concept [⊤].

In the linear notation, two concepts may be connected by a dotted line only when they are written next to each other on the same line. Otherwise, the coreference set must be marked by *coreference labels*, which follow the same conventions as the coreference labels used in existential graphs. One of the dominant nodes is marked with a *defining label*, prefixed with an asterisk; all the other nodes are marked with *bound labels*, prefixed with a question mark. In any coreference set, only one dominant node can be marked with the defining label; during a proof or computation, however, it is permissible to move the defining label from one dominant node to another.

DEFINITION A.2.10: KNOWLEDGE BASE. A *knowledge base* is a context of type KnowledgeBase whose designator is a conceptual graph consisting of four concepts:

1. *Type hierarchy.* A context of type TypeHierarchy whose designator is a CG T that specifies a partial ordering of type labels and the monadic lambda expressions for each defined type label.

1. *Relation hierarchy.* A context of type RelationHierarchy whose designator is a CG R that specifies a partial ordering of relation labels, the valences of the relation labels, and the lambda expressions for each defined relation label.

2. *Catalog of individuals.* A context of type CatalogOfIndividuals whose designator is a CG C that contains exactly one concept for each individual marker that appears in any concept in the knowledge base. The designator may also contain other concepts and relations that describe the individuals.

3. *Outermost context.* A context of type Assertion whose designator is a conceptual graph O.

The contents of the knowledge base must satisfy the following constraints:

- The type labels in any conceptual graph or lambda expression in : T, R, C, and O must be specified in T.
- The relation labels in any conceptual graph or lambda expression in : T, R, C, and O must be specified in R.
- The individual markers in any conceptual graph or lambda expression in : T, R, C, and O must be specified in C.

The type labels KnowledgeBase, TypeHierarchy, RelationHierarchy, CatalogOfIndividuals, and Assertion are metalevel labels that need not be specified in T. However, if a knowledge base contains information about a knowledge base, including knowledge bases that may be nested inside itself, then its type hierarchy must specify the metalevel labels.

This definition defines a knowledge base as a single concept, which may itself be nested inside another knowledge base. An entire knowledge base or any component of it, such as its type hierarchy, can be encoded in a concept that is transmitted across a network to another knowledge base. The outermost context of a knowledge base corresponds to what Peirce called the *sheet of assertion.* Every CG immediately nested in the outermost context states a proposition that is assumed to be true. The catalog of individuals lists all the named entities in the current universe of discourse.

Commercial databases and knowledge bases can be represented as special cases of a CG knowledge base:

- *Relational database.* The names of the SQL tables map to relation labels in the relational hierarchy R, and the names of the columns in the relations map to type labels in the type hierarchy T. The rows of the tables map to star graphs stored in the outermost context O. An SQL table with n rows and m columns is translated to n star graphs, each of which contains an m-adic conceptual relation whose label is the same as the label of the table; each of the n arcs of the relation is attached to a concept whose type label is the same as the name of the corresponding column and whose referent contains the data in the table element of the corresponding row and column. Integrity constraints on the database are translated to more general CGs that are also stored in the outermost context O.

- *Object-oriented database.* Since O-O databases may have more structure than relational databases, their representation in a CG knowledge base may have more complex graphs. The O-O class hierarchy determines the partial ordering of the type hierarchy T, and the O-O class definitions map to lambda expressions associated with the type labels in T. The data in an O-O DB map to CGs that may be larger than the star graphs that result from a relational database.

- *Expert system knowledge base.* Since there are many different kinds of expert system tools, the mapping to a CG knowledge base must be defined separately for each kind of tool. Frames, rules, and logic-based notations usually map directly to CGs in the outermost context. Procedures would be represented by logical assertions that define the preconditions and postconditions. The type hierarchy and relational hierarchy would be represented in the same way as the hierarchies of O-O databases.

Since CGs are a pure logic-based system, they represent logical structures directly. Procedural aspects can be defined in CGs by the same techniques used to specify procedures in other versions of logic.

TRANSFORMATION RULES. In analyzing the donkey sentences, the Scholastics defined transformations or conversion rules from one logical form to another. As an example, a sentence with the word *every* can be converted to an equivalent sentence with an implication. The sentence *Every farmer who owns a donkey beats it* is equivalent to the one represented in Figures 5.7, 5.9, and 5.10. In CGs, the word *every* maps to a universal quantifier in the referent of some concept:

```
[ [Farmer: λ]←(Expr)←[Own]→(Thme)→[Donkey]: ∀]-
(Agnt)←[Beat]→[Entity: #it].
```

In this graph, the quantifier ∀ does not range over the type Farmer, but over the subtype defined by the nested lambda expression: just those farmers who own a donkey. The symbol ∀ represents a *defined quantifier*, which can be expanded to the primitive CG form by a *macro definition*, which corresponds to a metalevel lambda definition:

```
&translate. ∀ precedence medium
  in [Typeμm1 :
    [Typeμm2 : ∀ ?CorefLabelμm3 ] CGμm4 ]
  &to.
    [&m1 :
      ¬[ [&m2 : *CorefLabelμm5 ]
        ¬[ [⊤: ?&m3 ?&m5] &m4 ] ] ].
```

This definition introduces the quantifier symbol ∀ with medium precedence. The **in**-clause states a *pattern*, which introduces *metavariables* marked by the symbol μ. The **is**-clause states the *expanded form*, whose metavariables are replaced with values obtained by pattern matching. When the ∀ symbol is found in the donkey CG, it triggers a pattern match, which expands the macro to produce the following CG:

```
¬[ [Farmer: λ]←(Expr)←[Own]→(Thme)→[Donkey]: *x]
  ¬[ [⊤: ?x]←(Agnt)←[Beat]→[Entity: #it] ].
```

The graphs in Figure 5.10 can be derived from this graph by expanding the lambda expression in the type field and resolving the indexical #it to a coreference label. This example shows how two sentences that have different surface structures are mapped to different conceptual graphs, which can be related by graph transformations.

A.3 Knowledge Interchange Format

Conceptual graphs are designed to have a direct mapping to and from natural languages; their graphic notation is designed for human readability. The Knowledge Interchange Format (KIF) has somewhat different design goals: it has been designed as a version of predicate calculus with a character set and syntax that simplify the mapping to and from computer systems. Human readability, although desirable, was a secondary consideration. Following are the predicate calculus and the KIF statement for the sentence *A cat is on a mat*:

$$(\exists x)(\exists y)(\text{cat}(x) \land \text{mat}(y) \land \text{on}(x,y)).$$

```
(exists (?x ?y) (and (cat ?x) (mat ?y) (on ?x ?y)))
```

Instead of special symbols and fonts, KIF uses a limited character set and a LISP-like syntax. The function or operator symbol comes at the beginning of a parenthesized list, followed by a string of operands. Instead of an italic font, variables are marked with a question mark, as ?x and ?y. Symbols like ∃, ∀, and ∧, which are not available in most character sets, are represented by alphanumeric strings like "exists", "forall", and "and". Although the basic form of KIF is an untyped version of logic, KIF also supports a typed form with the predicates that specify types written after the corresponding variables in the quantifier list. In typed form, the predicate calculus and the KIF statement become

$(\exists x{:}cat)(\exists y{:}mat)on(x,y).$

```
(exists ((?x cat) (?y mat)) (on ?x ?y))
```

The typed form is slightly shorter than the untyped form, and it maps more directly to and from conceptual graphs and other versions of typed or sorted logic. As examples, following are five conceptual graphs and their translations to the predicate calculus and KIF:

1. *Every cat is on a mat.*

   ```
   [Cat: ∀]→(On)→[Mat].
   ```

   $(\forall x{:}cat)(\exists y{:}mat)on(x,y).$

   ```
   (forall (?x cat) (exists (?y mat) (on ?x ?y)))
   ```

2. *It is false that every dog is on a mat.*

   ```
   ¬[[Dog: ∀]→(On)→[Mat]].
   ```

   $\sim(\forall x{:}dog)(\exists y{:}mat)on(x,y).$

   ```
   (not (forall (?x dog) (exists (?y mat) (on ?x ?y))))
   ```

3. *Some dog is not on a mat.*

   ```
   [Dog: *x] ¬[[?x]→(On)→[Mat]].
   ```

   $(\exists x{:}dog)\sim(\exists y{:}mat)on(x,y).$

   ```
   (exists (?x dog) (not (exists (?y mat) (on ?x ?y))))
   ```

4. *Either the cat Yojo is on a mat, or the dog Macula is running.*

   ```
   [[Cat: Yojo]→(On)→[Mat]]-(Or)-[[Dog: Macula]←(Agnt)←[Run]].
   ```

   $((\exists x{:}mat)(cat(Yojo) \wedge on(Yojo,x)) \vee$
   $((\exists y{:}run)(dog(Macula) \wedge agnt(y,Macula))).$

   ```
   (or (exists (?x mat) (and (cat Yojo) (on Yojo ?x)))
       (exists (?y run) (and (dog Macula) (agnt ?y Macula))))
   ```

5. *If a cat is on a mat, then it is happy.*

```
If:   [Cat: *x]→(On)→[Mat]
Then: [?x]→(Attr)→[Happy].
```

$(\forall x{:}\text{cat})(\forall y{:}\text{mat})(\text{on}(x,y) \supset (\exists z{:}\text{happy})\text{attr}(x,z))$.

```
(forall ((?x cat) (?y mat))
  (=> (on ?x ?y)
    (exists (?z happy) (attr ?x ?z))))
```

As these examples illustrate, KIF maps directly to the predicate calculus, but the mapping to and from conceptual graphs is more indirect. All three notations, however, have exactly the same semantics, and any statement in one can be translated to an equivalent statement in the others.

APPENDIX B

Sample Ontology

The art of ranking things in genera and species is of no small importance and very much assists our judgment as well as our memory. You know how much it matters in botany, not to mention animals and other substances, or again moral and notional entities as some call them. Order largely depends on it, and many good authors write in such a way that their whole account could be divided and subdivided according to a procedure related to genera and species. This helps one not merely to retain things, but also to find them. And those who have laid out all sorts of notions under certain headings or categories have done something very useful.

GOTTFRIED WILHELM LEIBNIZ, *New Essays on Human Understanding*

The task of classifying all the words of language, or what's the same thing, all the ideas that seek expression, is the most stupendous of logical tasks. Anybody but the most accomplished logician must break down in it utterly; and even for the strongest man, it is the severest possible tax on the logical equipment and faculty.

CHARLES SANDERS PEIRCE, *letter to editor B. E. Smith of the Century Dictionary*

B.1 Principles of Ontology

The subject of *ontology* is the study of the *categories* of things that exist or may exist in some domain. The product of such a study, called *an ontology*, is a catalog of the types of things that are assumed to exist in a domain of interest $\mathcal{D}$ from the perspective of a person who uses a language $\mathcal{L}$ for the purpose of talking about $\mathcal{D}$. The types in the ontology represent the *predicates, word senses,* or *concept and relation types* of the language $\mathcal{L}$ when used to discuss topics in the domain $\mathcal{D}$. An uninterpreted logic, such as predicate calculus, conceptual graphs, or KIF, is *ontologically neutral*. It imposes no constraints on the subject matter or the way the subject may be characterized. By itself, logic says nothing about anything, but the combination of logic with an ontology provides a language that can express relationships about the entities in the domain of interest.

An informal ontology may be specified by a catalog of types that are either undefined or defined only by statements in a natural language. A formal ontology is specified by a collection of names for concept and relation types organized in a partial ordering by the type-subtype relation. Formal ontologies are further distinguished by the way the subtypes are distinguished from their supertypes: an *axiomatized ontology* distinguishes subtypes by axioms and definitions stated in a formal language, such as logic or some computer-oriented notation that can be translated to logic; a *prototype-based ontology* distinguishes subtypes by a comparison with a typical member or *prototype* for each subtype. Large ontologies often use a mixture of definitional methods: formal axioms and definitions are used for the terms in mathematics, physics, and engineering; and prototypes are used for plants, animals, and common household items.

GLOSSARY. The following terms, which have been used in discussions of knowledge sharing, describe techniques for defining and merging ontologies:

alignment. A mapping of concepts and relations between two ontologies A and B that preserves the partial ordering by subtypes in both A and B. If an alignment maps a concept or relation *x* in ontology A to a concept or relation *y* in ontology B, then *x* and *y* are said to be *equivalent*. The mapping may be partial: there could be many concepts in A or B that have no equivalents in the other ontology. Before two ontologies A and B can be aligned, it may be necessary to introduce new subtypes or supertypes of concepts or relations in either A or B in order to provide suitable targets for alignment. No other changes to the axioms, definitions, proofs, or computations in either A or B are made during the process of alignment. Alignment does not depend on the choice of names in either ontology. For example, an alignment of a Japanese ontology to an English ontology might map the Japanese concept Go to the English concept Five. Meanwhile, the English concept for the verb *go* would not have any association with the Japanese concept Go.

axiomatized ontology. A terminological ontology whose categories are distinguished by axioms and definitions stated in logic or in some computer-oriented language that could be automatically translated to logic. There is no restriction on the complexity of the logic that may be used to state the axioms and definitions. The distinction between terminological and axiomatized ontologies is one of degree rather than kind. Axiomatized ontologies tend to be smaller than terminological ontologies, but their axioms and definitions can support more complex inferences and computations. Examples of axiomatized ontologies include formal theories in science and mathematics, the collections of rules and frames in an expert system, and specifications of conceptual schemas in languages like SQL.

differentiae. The properties or features that distinguish a type from other types that have a common supertype. The term comes from Aristotle's method of defining new types by stating the *genus* or supertype and stating the differentiae that distinguish the new type from its supertype. Aristotle's method of definition has become the de facto standard for natural language dictionaries, and it is also widely used for AI knowledge bases and object-oriented programming languages.

hierarchy. A partial ordering of entities according to some relation. A *type hierarchy* is a partial ordering of concept types by the type-subtype relation. In lexicography, the type-subtype relation is sometimes called the *hypernym-hyponym* relation. A *meronomy* is a partial ordering of concept types by the part-whole relation. Classification systems sometimes use a *broader-narrower hierarchy*, which mixes the type and part hierarchies: a type A is considered narrower than B if A is subtype of B or any instance of A is a part of some instance of B. For example, Cat and Tail are both narrower than Animal, since Cat is a subtype of Animal and a tail is a part of an animal. A broader-narrower hierarchy may be useful for information retrieval, but the two kinds of relations should be distinguished in a knowledge base because they have different implications.

identity conditions. The conditions that determine whether two different appearances of an object represent the same individual. Formally, if c is a subtype of Continuant, the identity conditions for c can be represented by a dyadic predicate Id_c. Two instances x and y of type c, which may appear at different times and places, are considered to be the same individual if the predicate $Id_c(x,y)$ is true. As an example, a predicate Id_{Human}, which determines the identity conditions for the type HumanBeing, might be defined by facial appearance, fingerprints, DNA, or some combination of all those features. At the atomic level, the laws of quantum mechanics make it difficult or impossible to define precise identity conditions for entities like electrons and photons. If a reliable identity predicate Id_t cannot be defined for some type t, then t would be considered a subtype of Occurrent rather than Continuant.

integration. The process of finding commonalities between two different ontologies A and B and deriving a new ontology C that facilitates interoperability between computer systems that are based on the A and B ontologies. The new ontology C may replace A or B, or it may be used only as an intermediary between a system based on A and a system based on B. Depending on the amount of change necessary to derive C from A and B, different levels of integration can be distinguished: alignment, partial compatibility, and unification. Alignment is the weakest form of integration: it requires minimal change, but it can only support limited kinds of interoperability. It is useful for classification and information retrieval, but it does not support deep inferences and computations. Partial compatibility requires more changes in order to support more extensive interoperability, even though there may be some concepts or relations in one system or the other that could create obstacles to full interoperability. Unification or total compatibility may require extensive changes or major reorganizations of A and B, but it can result in the most complete interoperability: everything that can be done with one can be done in an exactly equivalent way with the other.

knowledge base. An informal term for a collection of information that includes an ontology as one component. Besides an ontology, a knowledge base may contain information specified in a declarative language such as logic or expert-system rules, but it may also include unstructured or unformalized information expressed in natural language or procedural code.

lexicon. A knowledge base about some subset of words in the vocabulary of a natural language. One component of a lexicon is a terminological ontology whose concept types represent the word senses in the lexicon. The lexicon may also contain additional information about the syntax, spelling, pronunciation, and usage of the words. Besides conventional dictionaries, lexicons include large collections of words and word senses, such as WordNet from Princeton University and EDR from the Japan Electronic Dictionary Research Institute, Ltd. Other examples include classification schemes, such as the Library of Congress subject headings or the Medical Subject Headers (MeSH).

mixed ontology. An ontology in which some subtypes are distinguished by axioms and definitions, but other subtypes are distinguished by prototypes. The top levels of a mixed ontology would normally be distinguished by formal definitions, but some of the lower branches might be distinguished by prototypes.

partial compatibility. An alignment of two ontologies A and B that supports equivalent inferences and computations on all equivalent concepts and relations. If A and B are partially compatible, then any inference or computation that can be expressed in one ontology using only the aligned concepts and relations can be translated to an equivalent inference or computation in the other ontology.

primitive. A category of an ontology that cannot be defined in terms of other categories in the same ontology. An example of a primitive is the concept type Point in Euclid's geometry. The meaning of a primitive is not determined by a closed-form definition, but by axioms that specify how it is related to other primitives.

prototype-based ontology. A terminological ontology whose categories are distinguished by typical instances or *prototypes* rather than by axioms and definitions in logic. For every category c in a prototype-based ontology, there must be a prototype p and a measure of *semantic distance* $d(x,y,c)$, which computes the dissimilarity between two entities x and y when they are considered instances of c. Then an entity x can classified by the following recursive procedure:

- Suppose that x has already been classified as an instance of some category c, which has subcategories $s_1, . . ., s_n$.
- For each subcategory s_i with prototype p_i, measure the semantic distance $d(x, p_i, c)$.
- If $d(x, p_i, c)$ has a unique minimum value for some subcategory s_i, then classify x as an instance of s_i, and call the procedure recursively to determine whether x can be further classified by some subcategory of s_i.
- If c has no subcategories or if $d(x, p_i, c)$ has no unique minimum for any s_i, then the classification procedure stops with x as an instance of c, since no finer classification is possible with the given selection of prototypes.

As an example, a black cat and an orange cat would be considered very similar as instances of the category Animal, since their common catlike properties would be the most significant for distinguishing them from other kinds of animals. But in the category Cat, they would share their catlike properties with all the other kinds of cats, and the difference in color would be more significant. In the category BlackEntity, color would be the most relevant property, and the black cat would be closer to a crow or a lump of coal than to the orange cat. Since prototype-based ontologies depend on examples, it is often convenient to derive the semantic distance measure by a method that learns from examples, such as statistics, cluster analysis, or neural networks.

Quine's criterion. A test for determining the implicit ontology that underlies any language, natural or artificial. The philosopher Willard van Orman Quine proposed a criterion that has become famous: "To be is to be the value of a quantified variable." That criterion makes no assumptions about what actually exists in the world. Its purpose is to determine the implicit assumptions made by the people who use some language to talk about the world. As stated, Quine's criterion applies directly to languages like predicate calculus that have explicit variables and quantifiers. But Quine extended the criterion to languages of any form, including natural languages, in which the quantifiers and variables are not stated as explicitly as they are in predicate calculus. For English, Quine's criterion means that the implicit ontological categories are the concept types expressed by the basic content words in the language: nouns, verbs, adjectives, and adverbs.

refinement. An alignment of every category of an ontology A to some category of another ontology B, which is called a *refinement* of A. Every category in A must correspond to an equivalent category in B, but some primitives of A might be equivalent to nonprimitives in B. Refinement defines a partial ordering of ontologies: if B is a refinement of A, and C is a refinement of B, then C is a refinement of A; if two ontologies are refinements of each other, then they must be isomorphic.

semantic factoring. The process of analyzing some or all of the categories of an ontology into a collection of primitives. Conjunctions of those primitives generate a hierarchy, called a *lattice*, which includes the original categories plus additional ones that make it more symmetric. For the upper levels of an ontology, factoring can ensure that all possible combinations have been considered. For the more specialized concepts at lower levels, the resulting lattice may have many nodes that do not correspond to any naturally occurring concepts.

terminological ontology. An ontology whose categories need not be fully specified by axioms and definitions. An example of a terminological ontology is WordNet, whose categories are partially specified by relations such as subtype-supertype or part-whole, which determine the relative positions of the concepts with respect to one another but do not completely define them. Most fields of science, engineering, business, and law have evolved systems of terminology or nomenclature for naming, classifying, and standardizing their concepts. Axiomatizing all the concepts in any such field is a Herculean task, but subsets of the terminology can be used as starting points for formalization. Unfortunately, the axioms developed from different starting points are often incompatible with one another. Chapter 6 on Knowledge Soup discusses these issues.

unification. A one-to-one alignment of all concepts and relations in two ontologies that allows any inference or computation expressed in one to be mapped to an equivalent inference or computation in the other. The usual way of unifying two ontologies is to refine each of them to more detailed ontologies whose categories are one-to-one equivalent.

B.2 Top-Level Categories

The ontological categories discussed in this book are derived from ongoing research in philosophy, linguistics, and artificial intelligence. They provide a framework for organizing the more specialized concept types used in a knowledge base or natural language processor. This appendix summarizes those types as a starting set that may be used for representing word meanings in natural language or the basic types in a knowledge representation language. For further discussion of these types, see Chapter 2.

The following list summarizes the top-level types shown in Figure B.1 plus the types Entity and Absurdity, which are synonyms for $\top$ and $\bot$. Nine categories in this list have associated axioms: $\top$, $\bot$, Independent, Relative, Mediating, Physical, Abstract, Continuant, and Occurrent. Each of the other types is defined as the *infimum* (greatest common subtype, represented by the symbol $\cap$) of two supertypes, whose

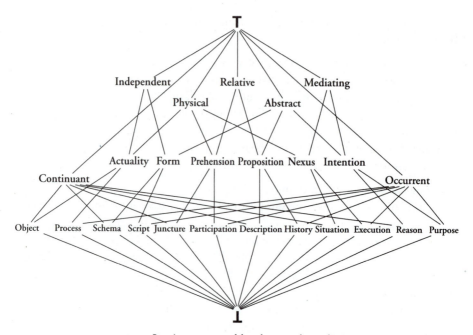

FIGURE B.I Lattice generated by the top three distinctions

axioms it inherits. For example, the type Form is defined as Independent ∩ Abstract; it therefore inherits the axioms of Independent and Abstract, and it is abbreviated IA to indicate its two supertypes.

⊤ ( ). The universal type, which has no differentiae. Formally, ⊤ is a primitive that satisfies the following axioms:

- There exists something: $(\exists x)\top(x)$.
- Everything is an instance of ⊤: $(\forall x)\top(x)$.
- Every type is a subtype of ⊤: $(\forall t{:}\text{Type})t{\leq}\top$.

⊥ (**IRMPACO**). The absurd type, which inherits all differentiae. Formally, ⊥ is a primitive that satisfies the following axioms:

- Nothing is an instance of ⊥: $\sim(\exists x)\bot(x)$.
- Every type is a supertype of ⊥: $(\forall t{:}\text{Type})\bot{\leq}t$.

Abstract (A). A pure information structure. Formally, Abstract is a primitive that satisfies the following axioms:

- No abstraction has a location in space: $\sim(\exists x{:}\text{Abstract})(\exists y{:}\text{Place})\text{loc}(x,y)$.
- No abstraction occurs at a point in time: $\sim(\exists x{:}\text{Abstract})(\exists t{:}\text{Time})\text{pTim}(x,t)$.

Absurdity (IRMPACO) = ⊥. A pronounceable synonym for ⊥. It cannot be the type of anything that exists.

Actuality (IP) = **Independent** ∩ **Physical.** A physical entity (P) whose existence is independent (I) of any other entity.

Continuant (C). An entity whose identity is preserved over some time interval. Formally, Continuant is a primitive that satisfies the following axioms:

- A continuant x has only spatial parts and no temporal parts. At any time t when x exists, all of x exists at the same time t.

- The identity conditions for a continuant are independent of time. If c is a subtype of Continuant, then the predicate $Id_c(x,y)$ for identifying two instances x and y of type c does not depend on time.

Description (RAC) = **Proposition** ∩ **Continuant.** A proposition (RA) about a continuant (C). A description expresses some aspect or configuration of the continuant by showing how it corresponds to the structure of some schema (IAC).

Entity () = ⊤. A pronounceable synonym for ⊤. It can be used as a default type label for anything of any type.

Form (IA) = **Abstract** ∩ **Independent.** Abstract information (A) independent (I) of any embodiment.

History (RAO) = **Proposition** ∩ **Occurrent.** A proposition (RA) about an occurrent (O). A history is a proposition (RA) that relates some script (IAO) to the stages of some occurrent (O). A computer program, for example, is a script (IAO); a computer executing the program is a process (IPO); and the abstract information (A) encoded in a trace of the instructions executed is a history (RAO). Like any proposition, a history need not be true, and it need not be predicated of the past: a myth is a history of an imaginary past; a prediction is a history of an expected future; and a scenario is a history of some hypothetical occurrent.

Independent (I). An entity distinguished by Firstness, independent of any other entity. Formally, Independent is a primitive to which the *has*-test of Section 2.4 need not apply:

- $(\forall x{:}\text{Independent}){\sim}\Box(\exists y)(\text{has}(x,y) \lor \text{has}(y,x))$.

If x is an independent entity, it is not necessary that there exists an entity y such that x has y or y has x.

Intention (MA) = **Abstract** ∩ **Mediating.** Abstraction (A) considered as mediating (M) other entities.

Juncture (RPC) = **Prehension** ∩ **Continuant.** A prehension (RP) considered as a continuant (C) during some time interval. The prehending entity is an object (IPC) in a stable relationship to some prehended entity during that interval.

Mediating (M). An entity that brings other entities into a relationship. Formally, Mediating is a primitive that satisfies the following axiom:

- $(\forall m{:}\text{Mediating})(\forall x,y{:}\text{Entity})((\text{has}(m,x) \wedge \text{has}(m,y))$
  $\supset \square(\text{has}(x,y) \vee \text{has}(y,x)).$

For any mediating entity m and any other entities x and y, if m has x and m has y, then it is necessary that x has y or y has x. An independent entity need not have any relationship to anything else, a relative entity must have some relationship to something else, and a mediating entity causes other entities to be related.

Nexus (MP) = Physical ∩ Mediating. A physical entity (P) mediating (M) two or more other entities. Examples include an action that relates an agent and a patient or a framework that relates the parts of a building. The entities mediated by a nexus may themselves be components of the nexus: the action consists of what the agent is doing to the patient, and the framework is composed of the parts of the building.

Object (IPC) = Actuality ∩ Continuant. Actuality (IP) considered as a continuant (C), which retains its identity over some interval of time. Although no physical entity is ever permanent, an object can be recognized by identity conditions that remain stable during its lifetime. The type Object includes ordinary physical objects as well as the instantiations of classes in object-oriented programming languages.

Occurrent (O). An entity that does not have a stable identity during any interval of time. Formally, Occurrent is a primitive that satisfies the following axioms:

- The parts of an occurrent, which are called *stages*, may exist at different times.
- There are no criteria that can be used to identify two occurrents that are observed in nonoverlapping space-time regions.

Participation (RPO) = Prehension ∩ Occurrent. A prehension (RP) considered as an occurrent (O) during the interval of interest. The prehending entity must be a process (IPO).

Physical (P). An entity that has a location in space-time. Formally, Physical is a primitive that satisfies the following axiom:

- Anything physical is located in some place: $(\forall x{:}\text{Physical})(\exists y{:}\text{Place})\text{loc}(x,y)$.
- Anything physical occurs at some point in time: $(\forall x{:}\text{Physical})(\exists t{:}\text{Time})$ $\text{pTim}(x,t)$.

More detailed axioms that relate physical entities to space, time, matter, and energy would involve a great deal physical theory, much of which is still incomplete.

Process (IPO) = Actuality ∩ Occurrent. Actuality (IP) considered as an occurrent (O) during the interval of interest. Depending on the time scale and level of detail, the same actual entity may be viewed as a stable object or a dynamic process. Even a diamond could be considered a process when viewed over a long time period or at the atomic level of vibrating particles.

Prehension (RP). A physical entity (P) relative (R) to some entity or entities.

Proposition (RA). An abstraction (A) relative (R) to some entity or entities. In logic, the assertion of a proposition is a claim that the abstraction corresponds to some aspect or configuration of the entity or entities involved.

Purpose (MAO) = Intention ∩ Occurrent. Intention (MA) that has the form of an occurrent (O). As an example, the words and notes of the song "Happy Birthday" constitute a script (IAO); a description of how people at a party sang the song is history (RAO); and the intention (MA) that explains the situation (MPO) is a purpose (MAO).

Reason (MAC) = Intention ∩ Continuant. Intention (MA) that has the form of a continuant (C). Unlike a simple description (Secondness), a reason explains an entity in terms of an intention (Thirdness). For a birthday party, a description might list the presents, but a reason would explain why the presents are relevant to the party.

Relative (R). An entity in a relationship to some other entity. Formally, Relative is a primitive for which the *has*-test of Section 2.4 must apply:

- $(\forall x{:}\text{Relative})\square(\exists y)(\text{has}(x,y) \lor \text{has}(y,x))$.

For any relative x, there must exist some y such that x has y or y has x.

Schema (IAC) = Form ∩ Continuant. A form (IA) that has the structure of a continuant (C). A schema is an abstract form (IA) whose structure does not specify time or timelike relationships. Examples include geometric forms, the syntactic structures of sentences in some language, or the encodings of pictures in a multimedia system.

Script (IAO) = Form ∩ Occurrent. A form (IA) that has the structure of an occurrent (O). A script is an abstract form (IA) that represents time sequences. Examples include computer programs, a recipe for baking a cake, a sheet of music to be played on a piano, or a differential equation that governs the evolution of a physical process. A movie can be described by several different kinds of scripts: the first is a specification of the actions and dialog to be acted out by humans; but the sequence of frames in a reel of film is also a script that determines a process carried out by a projector that generates flickering images on a screen.

Situation (MPO) = Nexus ∩ Occurrent. A nexus (MP) considered as an occurrent (O).

Structure (MPC) = **Nexus** ∩ **Continuant.** A nexus (MP) considered as a continuant (C).

The categories ⊤ and ⊥ are the only ones that are fully axiomatized. A prerequisite for formalizing the other seven primitives of Figure B.1 is a unified theory of physics and semiotics — a central part of Peirce's "stupendous logical task."

B.3   Role and Relation Types

Figure B.2 shows the type Actuality divided into three subtypes, Phenomenon, Role, and Sign. A phenomenal entity is an actual entity considered by itself; a role is considered in relation to something else; and a sign is considered as representing something to some agent. The trichotomy of Phenomenon, Role, and Sign in Figure B.2 and the trichotomy of Independent, Relative, and Mediating in Figure B.1 are both based on Peirce's distinction of Firstness, Secondness, and Thirdness, but they are applied to different aspects: the trichotomy in Figure B.1 is applied to the nature of the entities in themselves, but the trichotomy in Figure B.2 is applied to the way entities are viewed by some observer. For further discussion of these distinctions, see Sections 2.4 and 6.6.

As Figure B.2 shows, every role is involved in a prehension. In predicate calculus, roles are usually represented by dyadic predicates that relate a prehending entity to a prehended entity. In frames, they are usually represented by slots that are filled with an identifier of the prehended entity. In conceptual graphs, a lambda

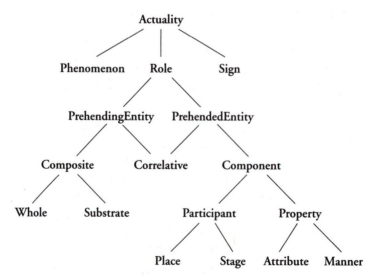

FIGURE B.2 Classification of entities according to the roles they play

expression can be used to define a dyadic relation type *r* in terms of a concept type R, which corresponds to the slot name of a frame:

$$r = [t: \lambda_1] \rightarrow (\text{Has}) \rightarrow [R: \lambda_2].$$

This definition uses the primitive relation type Has to relate the first parameter, which represents a prehending entity of type *t*, to the second parameter, which represents a prehended entity of the role type R.

In the following list, every role type is specified as a subtype of some type that is independent of an observer and of a role type shown in Figure B.2. Accompaniment, for example, is a subtype of Object in the role of Participant. The corresponding dyadic relation type is Accm, whose signature (Object,Object) indicates that it relates an object to an object. Most of the sample sentences can be paraphrased with the verb *has* and a syntactic construction that uses the name of the role.

Accompaniment < Object ∩ Participant; Accm(Object,Object). An object that participates with another object in some process.

Example: *Ronnie left with Nancy.*

```
(Past)→[Situation: [Leave]→(Agnt)→[Person: Ronnie]→(Accm)→[Person: Nancy]].
```

Paraphrase: *When leaving, Ronnie had Nancy as accompaniment.*

Amount < Quantity ∩ Measure; Amt(Characteristic,Quantity). A quantity used as a measure of some characteristic. The first argument of the Amt relation is a characteristic, which is usually expressed by a noun, such as *length, height, weight, age, speed,* or *temperature.*

Example: *The ski has a length of 167 cm.*

```
[Ski: #]→(Chrc)→[Length]→(Amt)→[Measure: <167,cm>].
```

By measure contraction, which is discussed in Section 1.4, this graph may be simplfied to

```
[Ski: #]→(Chrc)→[Length: @167cm].
```

Paraphrase: *The ski has a characteristic length whose amount is 167 cm.*

Argument < Data ∩ Role; Arg(Function,Data). Data in the role of input to a function. If the function takes more than one input, the arguments may be distinguished as Arg1, Arg2, and so on. This relation is used primarily for representing mathematical expressions.

Example: *Sqrt(16)=4.*

```
[Number: 16]←(Arg)←[Sqrt]→(Rslt)→[Number: 4].
```

Paraphrase: *The square root function has 16 as argument and 4 as result.*

Attribute < **Entity** ∩ **Property; Attr(Object,Entity).** An entity that is a property of some object. In English, attributes are usually expressed by adjectives, such as *circular, red, long,* and *heavy.*

Example: *The rose is red.*

```
[Rose: #]→(Attr)→[Red].
```

Paraphrase: *The rose has red as attribute.*

Base < **Type; Base(Attribute,Type).** A type of role that determines how an attribute is related to its object.

Example: *Sam is a good musician.*

```
[Person: Sam]→(Attr)→[Good]→(Base)→[Type: Musician].
```

Paraphrase: *Sam has the attribute good as musician.*

Because < **Situation** ∩ **Correlative; Bcas(Situation,Situation).** A situation in the role of causing another situation. A cause is correlative to an effect.

Example: *You are wet because it is raining.*

```
[Situation: [Person: #you]←(Attr)←[Wet]]→(Bcas)→[Situation:[Rain]].
```

Paraphrase: *Your being wet has rain as cause.*

Child < **HumanBeing** ∩ **Correlative; Chld(HumanBeing,HumanBeing).** A human being that is a child of some human being. A child is correlative to a parent.

Example: *Lillian is Katie's mother.*

```
[Mother: Lillian]→(Chld)→[Child: Katie].
```

Paraphrase: *Lillian has Katie as child.*

Comparand < **Object** ∩ **Correlative; Comp(Attribute,Object).** An object that serves as a standard of comparison for some attribute. An object being compared is correlative to another object.

Example: *Bob is taller than Mary.*

```
[Person: Bob]→(Attr)→[Tall]→(Comp)→[Comparand: Mary].
```

Paraphrase: *Bob is tall in comparison to Mary.*

Characteristic < **Type** ∩ **Property; Chrc(Entity,Entity).** A type whose instances are properties of entites. In English, characteristics are usually expressed by nouns, such as *shape, color, length,* and *weight.*

Example: *The rose's color is red.*

```
[Rose: #]→(Chrc)→[Color: Red].
```

Paraphrase: *The rose has a color red as characteristic.*

Role; Has(Entity,Entity). Has is a gneneral relation type used to define all roles. It represents the *has*-test of Section 2.4, which is used to determine the prehending entity and the prehended entity of a prehension. All relation types listed in Sections B.3 and B.4 are subtypes of Has.

Manner < Entity ∩ Property; Manr(Process,Entity). An entity that is a property of some process. In English, manners are usually expressed by adverbs, such as *quickly, boldly,* and *tentatively.*

Example: *The ambulance arrived quickly.*

```
[Ambulance:#]←(Thme)←[Arrive]→(Manr)→[Quick].
```

Paraphrase: *The arrival of the ambulance had a quick manner.*

Measure < Quantity ∩ Measure; Meas(Attribute,Quantity). A quantity used as a measure of some attribute. The first argument of the Meas relation is an attribute, which is usually expressed by an adjective, such as *long, high, heavy, old, fast,* or *hot.* The Meas relation links an attribute to a measure, and the Amt relation links the corresponding characteristic to the same measure.

Example: *The ski is 167 cm long.*

```
[Ski: #]→(Attr)→[Long]→(Meas)→[Measure: <167,cm>].
```

Paraphrase: *The ski has an attribute long, whose measure is 167 cm.*

Part < Object ∩ Component; Part(Object,Object). An object that is a component of some object. Unlike an attribute, a part is capable of existing independently.

Example: *A finger is a part of a hand.*

```
[Hand]→(Part)→[Finger].
```

Paraphrase: *A hand has a finger as part.*

Possession < Entity ∩ Correlative; Poss(Animate,Entity). An entity owned by some animate being. A possession is correlative to a possessor.

Example: *Niurka's watch stopped.*

```
[Person: Niurka]→(Poss)→[Watch]←(Thme)←[Stop].
```

Paraphrase: *Niurka had as possession a watch that stopped.*

Successor < Occurrent ∩ Correlative; Succ(Occurrent,Occurrent). An occurrent that occurs after some other occurrent. A successor is correlative to a predecessor.

Example: *After Billy ate the pretzel, he drank some beer.*

```
[Situation: [Person: Billy *x]←(Agnt)←[Eat]→(Ptnt)→[Pretzel: #]]-
   (Succ)→[Situation: [?x]←(Agnt)←[Drink]→(Ptnt)→[Beer]].
```

Paraphrase: *The situation of Billy's eating the pretzel had as successor the situation of his drinking some beer.*

B.4   Thematic Roles

The thematic roles are represented by conceptual relations that link the concept of a verb to the concepts of the participants in the occurrent expressed by the verb. Although they are all specializations of the roles and relations listed in Section B.3, they are listed separately because of their importance in representing natural language semantics.

Figure B.3 shows the subtypes of Participant in Figure B.2 further classified by two pairs of distinctions: *determinant* or *immanent* and *source* or *product*:

- A *determinant* participant controls the direction of the activity, either from the beginning as the initiator or from the end as the goal.
- An *immanent* participant is present throughout an event, but does not actively control what happens.
- A *source* must be present at the beginning of the event, but need not participate throughout the event.
- A *product* must be present at the end of the event but need not participate throughout the event.

As an example, consider the sentence *Sue sent the gift to Bob by Federal Express.* The gift and Federal Express are immanent participants, since the gift (essence) and Federal Express (resource) are present from beginning to end. Sue and Bob, however, are determinant participants, since they control the course of the process from the initiator (Sue) to the goal (Bob). Unlike the immanent participants, the determinant participants are involved primarily at the endpoints. If Sue happened to write the wrong address, the intended recipient, Bob, might not get involved at all.

After analyzing and summarizing various systems of case relations or thematic roles, Harold Somers (1987) organized them in a matrix with four kinds of

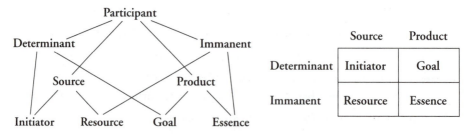

	Source	Product
Determinant	Initiator	Goal
Immanent	Resource	Essence

FIGURE B.3 Graph and matrix representation of the four participants

participants at the top and six categories of verbs along the side. In the twenty-four boxes of the matrix, Somers had some boxes with duplicate role names and some boxes with two roles that were distinguished by other properties: ±animate, ±physical, ±dynamic, or ±volitional. In using Somers's classification, Judith Dick (1991) applied the roles to conceptual graphs as a knowledge representation for legal arguments.

Sowa (1996) was stimulated by the work of Julius Moravcsik (1973) and James Pustejovsky (1995) to relate the four columns of the Somers-Dick matrix to Aristotle's four causes or *aitiai*, as described in the *Metaphysics*:

- *Initiator* corresponds to Aristotle's efficient cause, "whereby a change or a state is initiated" (1013b23).
- *Resource* corresponds to the material cause, which is "the matter or the substrate (*hypokeimenon*)" (983a30).
- *Goal* corresponds to the final cause, which is "the purpose or the benefit; for this is the goal (*telos*) of any generation or motion" (983a32).
- *Essence* corresponds to the formal cause, which is "the essence (*ousia*) or what it is (*to ti ēn einai*)" (983a27).

The four terms *intiator, resource, goal,* and *essence* better describe the participants of an action than the traditional translations for Aristotle's four causes.

In case of ambiguity, the hierarchy permits the more specialized types to be generalized to any supertype. In the sentence *Tom baked the pie*, the pie might be a result that is being created or a patient that is being warmed.

```
[Person: Tom]←(Agnt)←[Bake]→(Rslt)→[Pie: #].
[Person: Tom]←(Agnt)←[Bake]→(P tnt)→[Pie: #].
```

But according to the matrix in Figure B.4, Result < Goal < Product, and Patient < Essence < Product. Since Product is a common supertype, the initial interpretation could have the label Prod:

```
[Person: Tom]←(Agnt)←[Bake]→(Prod)→[Pie: #].
```

In the sentence *The dog broke the window*, the dog could be the agent or the instrument:

```
[Dog: #]←(Agnt)←[Break]→(Ptnt)→[Window: #].
[Dog: #]←(Inst)←[Break]→(Ptnt)→[Window: #].
```

But Agent < Initiator < Source, and Instrument < Resource < Source. Therefore, the initial interpretation could have the label Srce for Source. When further information becomes available, the general type can be restricted to the more specialized subtype.

| | Source | | Product | |
	Initiator	Resource	Goal	Essence
Action	Agent, Effector	Instrument	Result, Recipient	Patient, Theme
Process	Agent, Origin	Matter	Result, Recipient	Patient, Theme
Transfer	Agent, Origin	Instrument, Medium	Experiencer, Recipient	Theme
Spatial	Origin	Path	Destination	Location
Temporal	Start	Duration	Completion	Point in Time
Ambient	Origin	Instrument, Matter	Result	Theme

FIGURE B.4 Thematic roles as subtypes the four kinds of participants

The following list summarizes the thematic roles that appear in the boxes of Figure B.4.

Agent < Initiator; Agnt(Act,Animate). An active animate entity that voluntarily initiates an action.

Example: *Eve bit an apple.*

```
[Person: Eve]←(Agnt)←[Bite]→(Ptnt)→[Apple].
```

Beneficiary < Recipient; Benf(Act,Animate). A recipient that derives a benefit from the successful completion of the event.

Example: *Diamonds were given to Ruby.*

```
[Diamond: {*}]←(Thme)←[Give]→(Benf)→[Person: Ruby].
```

Completion < Goal; Cmpl(TemporalProcess,Physical). A goal of a temporal process.

Destination < Goal; Dest(SpatialProcess,Physical). A goal of a spatial process.

Example: *Bob went to Danbury.*

```
[Person: Bob]←(Agnt)←[Go]→(Dest)→[City: Danbury].
```

Duration < Resource; Dur(State,Interval). A resource of a temporal process.

Example: *The truck was serviced for 5 hours.*

```
[Truck: #]←(Thme)←[Service]→(Dur)→[Interval: @5hrs].
```

Effector < Initiator; Efct(Entity,Entity). An active determinant source, either animate or inanimate, that initiates an action, but without voluntary intention.

Example: *The tree produced new leaves.*

```
[Tree: #]←(Efct)←[Produce]→(Rslt)→[Leaf: {*}]→(Attr)→[New].
```

Experiencer < Goal; Expr(State,Animate). An active animate goal of an experience.

Example: *Yojo sees the fish.*

```
[Cat: Yojo]←(Expr)←[See]→(Thme)→[Fish: #].
```

Instrument < Resource; Inst(Act,Entity). A resource that is not changed by an event.

Example: *The key opened the door.*

```
[Key: #]←(Inst)←[Open]→(Thme)→[Door: #].
```

Location < Essence; Loc(Physical,Physical). An essential participant of a spatial nexus.

Example: *Vehicles arrive at a station.*

```
[Vehicle: {*}]←(Thme)←[Arrive]→(Loc)→[Station].
```

Matter < Resource; Matr(Act,Substance). A resource that is changed by the event.

Example: *The gun was carved out of soap.*

```
[Gun]←(Rslt)←[Carve]→(Matr)→[Soap].
```

Medium < Resource; Med(Process,Physical). A resource for transmitting information, such as the sound of speech or the electromagnetic signals that transmit data.

Origin < Initiator; Orgn(Process,Physical). A passive determinant source of a spatial or ambient nexus.

Example: *The chapter begins on page 20.*

```
[Chapter: #]←(Thme)←[Begin]→(Orgn)→[Page: 20].
```

Path < Resource; Path(Process,Place). A resource of a spatial nexus.

Example: *The pizza was shipped via Albany and Buffalo.*

```
[Pizza: #]←(Thme)←[ShipAct]→(Path)→[City: {Albany, Buffalo}].
```

Patient < Essence; Ptnt(Process,Physical). An essential participant that undergoes some structural change as a result of the event.

Example: *The cat swallowed the canary.*

```
[Cat: #]←(Agnt)←[Swallow]→(Ptnt)→[Canary: #].
```

PointInTime < Essence; PTim(Physical,Time). An essential participant of a temporal nexus.

Example: *At 5:25 PM, Erin left.*

```
[Time: 5:25pm]←(PTim)←[Situation: [Person: Erin]←(Agnt)←[Leave]].
```

Recipient < Goal; Rcpt(Act,Animate). An animate goal of an act.

Result < Goal; Rslt(Process,Entity). An inanimate goal of an act.

Example: *Eric built a house.*

```
[Person: Eric]←(Agnt)←[Build]→(Rslt)→[House].
```

Start < Initiator; Strt(Entity,Time). A determinant source of a temporal nexus.

Theme < Essence; Thme(Situation,Entity). An essential participant that may be moved, said, or experienced, but is not structurally changed.

Example: *Billy likes the Beer.*

```
[Person: Billy]←(Expr)←[Like]→(Thme)→[Beer: #].
```

B.5   Placement of the Thematic Roles

As subtypes of Participant, the thematic roles occupy an intermediate level in the ontology. Figure B.5 shows a path through the hierarchy from ⊤ to Participant and the graph of Figure B.3. Each of the thematic roles in Figure B.4 could then be arranged under the four categories of participants: Initiator, Resource, Goal, and Essence. At the bottom of Figure B.5 are sample branches of the ontology under Agent and Theme. Doer, for example, has a subtype Driver, which has more specific subtypes like BusDriver, TruckDriver, and TaxiDriver. In principle, any of the thematic roles could be subdivided further to show distinctions that might be significant in some culture or domain of interest. Other thematic roles listed in Section B.4 could also be subdivided further to represent the participants of specific concept types: Sayer < Agent; Senser < Agent; Addressee < Recipient; Experienced < Theme; Moved < Theme; Said < Theme. The incomplete lines in Figure B.5 suggest other branches of the ontology that have been omitted in order to keep the diagram from being cluttered.

Although the thematic roles represent a linguistically important class of onto-

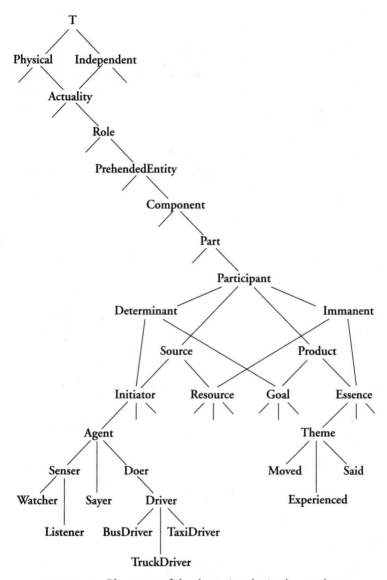

FIGURE B.5 Placement of the thematic roles in the ontology

logical categories, their common supertype Participant is several levels beneath the more general category Role. Therefore, Role would include many types that are not directly associated with verbs. As an example, the role Driver in Figure B.5 represents only a person who is actively driving a vehicle; that role would be incompatible with the role Pedestrian. The category LicensedDriver, however, includes people who are legally authorized to drive, whether or not they are, at the moment, driving. In New York City, licensed drivers probably spend more time as pedestrians than as actual drivers. As another example, a person might have a continuous period of employment as a chauffeur, but would not be an active driver continuously. Therefore, the type Chauffeur would be a subtype of Employee and Licensed-Driver, but not a subtype of Driver.

APPENDIX C

Extended Examples

Example is the school of mankind, and they will learn at no other.
EDMUND BURKE, *"Letters on a Regicide Peace"*

C.1 Hotel Reservation System

The following example, which describes a prototype reservation system for the National Park Service, is taken from a sample specification developed in the NCITS T2 Committee on Information Interchange and Interpretation. It illustrates the kind of informal specifications that a systems analyst or knowledge engineer must translate to a computable form.

The proposed system is being designed for the Old Faithful Inn Hotel in the Yellowstone National Park, the El Tovar Hotel in the Grand Canyon National Park, and the Ahwahnee Hotel in Yosemite National Park. The hotels can be uniquely identified by their names. The hotels have a normal address (line 1, line 2, city, state, zip code) and each one has a telephone number and a fax number. Each hotel has a rating from Mobil Travel Service of a certain number of diamonds (from one to five). Hotels may be open for only a certain period of a year. They may also have seasonal rates that reflect the change in demand for their rooms. Room rates are constant for different types of rooms during a season. Reservations are accepted up to thirteen months in advance (e.g., in January 1999 reservations can be made through January 2001). Reservations cannot be made in a hotel before it is open for business or after it is scheduled for permanent closure.

Rooms are of different types and are designated either smoking or nonsmoking. When making a reservation, the individual will select a room type and a smoking category. If a room is changed to a different type or smoking category, the change is effective on a certain date.

Reservations can be made by an individual or a travel agent. Reservations are confirmed for a specific time period, room type(s), smoking category(ies), and rate(s). An individual will give his or her name, address (see example above), phone, and possibly a fax number. A travel agent also gives this information, plus the agent's name and the travel agency identification number. This number will identify the specific travel agency making the reservation, its address, its telephone, and its fax number. Each reservation is made by a reservation clerk and is identified by a sequential number. When a reservation is complete, a timestamp is made for audit purposes.

If a reservation cannot be confirmed, the reservation clerk will ask if the guest would like to be waitlisted. The waitlist is for either a specific hotel or a category of hotels (number of diamonds) at a national park. The waitlist is for a certain period of days from the reservation date. If a room(s) matching the request on the reservation becomes available within the waitlist time period, a confirmation is automatically sent. On the day before the waitlist is to expire, the guest is contacted and asked if his or her place on the waitlist should be extended or if the room type(s) and smoking category(ies) could be changed to allow a reservation to be confirmed.

When a reservation is made, it must be either for a 16.00 hour arrival or guaranteed. A 16.00 hour arrival time allows a reservation to be made and at 16.00 hours on the date of arrival the reservation is automatically canceled without a penalty being assessed to the guest. To hold a reservation after 16.00 hours, the guest must guarantee the room. The guarantee is implemented through a credit card. A guest tells which type of credit card is to be used to guarantee the room and he or she must provide the credit card number and an expiration date.

If a guest with a guaranteed reservation does not show up and does not notify the hotel that he or she will not arrive, then the first night's rent for each reserved room will be charged against the credit card. Guests are encouraged to cancel their reservations if their travel plans change so that others on the waitlist can be accommodated. Guaranteed rooms can be canceled until 16.00 hours on the date of arrival and individuals then receive a cancellation number that insures that they will not be charged for the room. If a guaranteed reservation is canceled after 16.00 hours on the date of arrival then the hotel attempts to rent the room(s). If the room(s) are rented (this is decided based on the time of the cancellation and does not take into account the type or smoking category of the room), then a message is sent to the guest stating that he or she has not been charged for the room. If the room(s) are not rented, then the hotel management decides whether the guest will be charged and will be sent a notice that he or she has been charged or not charged.

A confirmation is sent to the guest when the reservation is confirmed. Each confirmation is time stamped for audit purposes. The confirmation includes all information pertinent to the reservation.

The cancellation notice is sent to the guest if a cancellation number is issued.

The notice identifies the reservation and the clerk who canceled the reservation. A time stamp validates that the reservation was canceled in time to avoid a penalty.

Check-in occurs upon the arrival of the guest at the hotel. The time of check-in is noted and the departure date is confirmed. Room number(s) are assigned and keys are given to the guests. If a credit card is to be used for payment, then the information previously noted is collected. A guest may use a different credit card for the stay than the one used to guarantee the reservation. The Park Service also has a policy that hotel bills above a certain limit must be cleared before the guest is allowed to remain in the hotel. The check-in process notifies the guest of the limit he or she must abide by. Because of the flexible reservation policy, walk-in guests without reservations are encouraged — especially right after 16.00 hours.

At the time of check-in a guest may designate one room as the primary room and specify the other room(s) that will have their charges appear directly on the primary room's invoice. This allows a family to have only one bill even though it is occupying several rooms. Invoices show which room made each charge so that guests can better audit their own bills. Guests who have regularly paid their bills when they reach their account balance limits normally check out on their departure date. All guests in rooms that charge a primary room must check out when the guests in the primary room check out. Check-out is required to occur by 12.00 hours, but can be extended to 14.00 hours on request. Guests will be charged for the room if they are not checked out by the cited check-out time. The actual check-out time is used to prevent any further charges from being invoiced to a room. At check-out, each guest is given a copy of the invoice showing all charges and how the balance was cleared. If a guest does not make a payment when his or her account balance reaches the predetermined limit, the guest is automatically checked out. Extensions to stays are routinely made if rooms are available.

C.2 Library Database

Norbert Fuchs and his students have designed a specification language called Attempto Controlled English (ACE), which looks like English, but has a formal syntax that can be translated automatically to logic and then to executable programs. The following ACE rules specify the operations for updating a library database named LibDB.

```
If a borrower asks for a copy of a book
    and the copy is available
    and LibDB calculates the book amount of the borrower
    and the book amount is smaller than the book limit
    and a staff member checks out the copy to the borrower
then the copy is checked out to the borrower.
```

If a copy of a book is checked out to a borrower
   and a staff member returns the copy
then the copy is available.

If a staff member adds a copy of a book to the library
   and no catalog entry of the book exists
then the staff member creates a catalog entry
      that contains the author name of the book
         and the title of the book
         and the subject area of the book
   and the staff member enters the id of the copy
   and the copy is available.

If a staff member adds a copy of a book to the library
   and a catalog entry of the book exists
then the staff member enters the id of the copy
   and the copy is available.

If a copy is available
   and the staff member removes the copy from the library
then LibDB deletes the id of the copy
   and the copy is not available.

If a user enters an author name
   and the user is a staff member or a borrower
then for every catalog entry that contains the author name
      LibDB lists the author name and the title.

If a user enters a subject area
   and the user is a staff member or a borrower
then for every catalog entry that contains the subject area
      LibDB lists the author name and the title.

If a user enters a name of a borrower
   and the user is a staff member
then for every copy that is checked out to the borrower
      LibDB lists the author name and the title.

If a user enters a name of a borrower
   and the user is a staff member
then for every copy that is checked out to the borrower
      LibDB lists the author name and the title.

If a user enters a name of a borrower
   and the user is the borrower
then for every copy that is checked out to the borrower
      LibDB lists the author name and the title.

```
If a staff member enters an id of a copy
   and the copy is checked out to a borrower
then LibDB displays the name of the borrower.
```

The data structures and constraints can also be specified by ACE statements that translate to logic. The following statement specifies a database constraint:

```
Every book has a title
   and an author name
   and a subject area.
```

This statement is true for all books, even those that are not in the library. For those in the library, a catalog entry represents the information in a computable form:

```
Every book in the library has a catalog entry
   that contains the title of the book, which is a character string,
      and the author name of the book, which is a character string,
      and the subject area of the book, which is a character string.
```

Following are some additional constraints:

```
Every copy of a book has an id.
Every borrower has a name and a book amount.
Every user is a borrower or a staff member.
There is a book limit, which is a positive integer.
```

Constraints stated in ACE have a direct mapping to logic, and they can be compiled to frames, SQL definitions, or Java declarations. UML or E-R diagrams can also be derived from the scope of quantifiers in the logical form.

The ACE rules are triggered by assertions that cause database updates and by questions that may ask for information in LibDB or metalevel information about LibDB. Following are some assertions represented in ACE:

```
There is a book that has an author name, which is John,
   and a title, which is Conceptual Structures,
   and a subject area, which is artificial intelligence.
Bill is a staff member who adds a copy of the book to the library.
Mary is a borrower. She asks for a copy of the book.
```

The Attempto system uses Kamp's rules of discourse representation to resolve the referents of pronouns and definite noun phrases, such as *the book*. To indicate how the references have been resolved, Attempto echoes its interpretation with the expanded referent enclosed in square brackets:

```
[Mary] asks for a copy of [the book that has an author name John].
```

C.3   ACE Vocabulary

Although ACE has a highly restricted grammar, the greatest obstacle to processing English is not grammar, but the enormous vocabulary. To reduce the complexity, the ACE vocabulary is divided in two broad classes: a small predefined set of *function words* and an open-ended set of *content words* that are never defined explicitly. The content words include most nouns, verbs, adjectives, and adverbs. The function words include prepositions, conjunctions, articles, pronouns, quantifiers, and the two special verbs *is* and *has*. For a particular application, a knowledge engineer who writes an ACE specification implicitly defines the content words used in that application by writing rules and constraints that use those words. In the LibDB example, the Attempto system knows that *borrower* is a noun, *enters* is a verb, and *available* is an adjective. For the purpose of the application, the meanings of those words are determined contextually by the rules and constraints in which they appear.

The primary difference between ACE and English is not in its syntax or choice of words, but in the presuppositions or *conversational implicatures* that are implicit in the normal use of natural languages. As an example, consider the next two sentences:

1. *Bob picked up the cup and drank the coffee.*
2. *Bob drank the coffee and picked up the cup.*

In English, the conjunction *and* between two actions often implies a time sequence; therefore, the two sentences would not be synonymous. In ACE, however, such implications are ignored, and both would be mapped to equivalent internal representations.

C.4   Translating ACE to Logic

The Attempto system translates ACE statements to an intermediate logical form based on discourse representation theory and then to an executable program in Prolog. A full description of the ACE syntax and semantics is given in a 258-page dissertation by Schwitter (1998), but for the purpose of this example, the translation rules can be summarized briefly. Following is the translation of first ACE rule in Section C.1 to a discourse representation structure (DRS):

```
[F]
named(F,'LibDB')
IF [A,B,C,D,E,G,H,I,J,K,L]
   borrower(A)  copy(B)  book(C)  bookAmount(G)
   bookLimit(I)  staffMember(K)  of(B,C)  of(G,A)
   event(D,  askFor(A,B))
```

```
state(E,  available(B))
event(H,  calculate(F,G))
state(J,  smallerThan(G,I)
event(L,  checkOutTo(K,B,A))
THEN [M]
   state(M,  checkedOutTo(B,A))
```

Kamp's original DRS notation, which is shown in Figure 5.7 on page xxx, uses a graphic representation for contexts. For the linear notation, the Attempo DRS uses the keywords IF and THEN instead of the DRS boxes and arrows. Brackets, such as [A,B,C], represent an existential quantifier, such as (∃a,b,c). Within a context, the conjunction ∧ is the default operator that connects the predicates.

Kamp's DRS notation is isomorphic to Peirce's existential graphs, and conceptual graphs are a typed version of EGs. Therefore, the corresponding CG is essentially a typed version of the DRS:

```
[Entity:  *f]→(Named)→[String:  "LibDB"].

[If: [Copy:  *b]→(Of)→[Book]
   [BookAmount:  *g]→(Of)→[Borrower:  *a]
   [BookLimit:  *i]  [StaffMember:  *k]
   [Event:  (AskFor ?a ?b)]
   [State:  (Available ?b)]
   [Event:  (Calculate ?f ?g)]
   [State:  (SmallerThan ?g ?i)]
   [Event:  (CheckOutTo ?k ?b ?a)]
   [Then:  [State:  (CheckedOutTo ?b ?a)]]].
```

DRS variables like A and B are mapped to CG coreference labels *a and *b at the point where the quantification occurs; they represent the noun phrases *a borrower* and *a book*, which are marked with an indefinite article. Subsequent references, which correspond to the definite noun phrases *the borrower* and *the book*, have an initial question mark, as in ?a and ?b. The DRS variables C, D, E, H, J, L, and M may be omitted in the CG since there is no subsequent reference to them. The CGs nested inside the concepts of type Event and State are represented in an abbreviated linear notation, which allows bound coreference labels to be represented inside the parentheses of a conceptual relation. The following representations are equivalent:

```
(AskFor  ?a ?b)  ≡  [?a]→(AskFor)→[?b].
(CheckOutTo  ?k ?b ?a)  ≡  (CheckOutTo)-
                           -1->[?k]
                           -2->[?b]
                           <-3-[?a].
```

As these examples illustrate, the abbreviated notation is especially convenient for conceptual relations with more than two arcs.

To emphasize the similarity between the DRS and the CG, the same ontology is used for both. The monadic predicates derived from nouns become type labels, but the predicate available(B), which was derived from an adjective, becomes a monadic conceptual relation. In the more common ontology used with CGs, the adjective *available* would be represented by the type label of a concept linked by the attribute relation (Attr):

```
[?b]→(Attr)→[Available].
```

The two different ontologies could be related by defining the DRS predicates in terms of the more detailed ontology given in Appendix B.

When the DRS or CG is translated to predicate calculus, the existential quantifiers in the if-context must be moved to the front of the formula, where they become universal quantifiers. Following is the typed predicate calculus for the first ACE rule:

$(\exists f)$named(f,'LibDB').
$(\forall a$:Borrower$)(\forall b$:Copy$)(\forall c$:Book$)(\forall g$:BookAmount$)(\forall i$:BookLimit$)$
$\quad(\forall k$:StaffMember$)(\forall d,h,l$:Event$)(\forall e,j$:State$)$
$\quad\quad((\text{of}(b,c) \wedge \text{dscr}(d, \text{askFor}(a,b)) \wedge \text{dscr}(e, \text{available}(b))$
$\quad\quad\quad \wedge \text{of}(g,a) \wedge \text{dscr}(h, \text{calculate}(f,g))$
$\quad\quad\quad \wedge \text{dscr}(j, \text{smallerThan}(g,i)) \wedge \text{dscr}(l, \text{checkOutTo}(k,b,a)))$
$\quad\quad \supset (\exists m$:State$)\text{dscr}(m, \text{checkedOutTo}(b,a))).$

As in Chapter 5, the concepts with nested CGs are represented by the description predicate dscr(x,p), which relates a state or event x to a proposition p that describes x. The character strings that identify the other predicates and types are constructed from the words that occur in the ACE statements. Following are the basic conventions:

- Proper names are represented by an existentially quantified variable linked to a character string, as in named(f,'LibDB').

- Common nouns and noun phrases map to type labels like Borrower or BookAmount.

- Adjectives and past participles map to predicates that represent states, such as available(b) or checkedOutTo(b,a).

- Verbs map to predicates that represent states or events: calculate(a,b) is an event, but contain(a,b) is a state.

- Indefinite noun phrases (marked with the article *a* or *an*) introduce new quantified variables, and definite noun phrases (marked with *the*) are assumed to be occurrences of a previously introduced variable of the corresponding type.

- Prepositions in noun phrases, such as *of*, map to dyadic predicates; but prepositions in verb or adjective phrases are combined with the verb or adjective to form predicates such as askFor(a,b) or checkedOutTo(a,b).
- The word *than* is combined with the comparative form of an adjective to form a dyadic predicate, such as smallerThan(g,i).

This brief summary is not sufficient to represent the full semantics of English, but it is sufficient to represent the semantics of ACE, an artificial language that looks like English. Despite its limitations, ACE is rich enough to specify programs and data structures that can simulate a Turing machine.

Answers to Selected Exercises

*Formulae have always frightened me. They frightened me, I remember, when
I was sixteen and had bought my books for the next year. I was particularly
alarmed by my new book on trigonometry, full of sines, cosines, and Greek
letters, and asked my mother — a gifted mathematician — whether
trigonometry was difficult. I gratefully acknowledge her wise answer:*

Oh, no. Know your formulae, and always remember that you
are on the wrong track when you need more than five lines.

*In retrospect, I think that no other advice has had such a profound
influence on my way of working.*
*And even now, my first reaction to formulae, written by someone else, is
one of repulsion — in particular when an unfamiliar notational
convention is used — and when reading an article, my natural reaction is
to skip the formulae.*
*At the same time, I have a warm appreciation for well-designed
formalisms that enable me to do things that I couldn't possibly
dowithout them.*
EDSGER W. DIJKSTRA, *"My Hopes for Computing Science"*

Chapter 1

1.4 The answer to the last question is highly domain dependent. For the representation by products of primes, the average amount of storage space depends
on the average number of differentiae needed to define each concept type. If
there is a large number of primitive differentiae, but each concept uses very few
of them, then the representation as products of primes might be more compact.

1.7 English: *There is no trailer truck that is composed of tractor #77 and trailer #238.*

~(∃x:TrailerTruck)(tractor(#77) ∧ trailer(#238) ∧ part(x,#77) ∧
part(x,#238)).
~(∃x)(trailerTruck(x) ∧ tractor(#77) ∧ trailer(#238) ∧ part(x,#77) ∧
part(x,#238)).

English: *It is false that there's a trailer truck with tractor #42 and not trailer #908.*

~(∃x:TrailerTruck)(tractor(#42) ∧ part(x,#42) ∧ ~(trailer(#908) ∧ part(x,#908))).

~(∃x)(trailerTruck(x) ∧ tractor(#42) ∧ part(x,#42) ∧ ~(trailer(#908) ∧ part(x,#908))).

1.8 To save space, all conceptual graphs presented as answers to exercises are written in the linear notation. As a further exercise, students should practice rewriting the linear forms as graphs.

English: *There is no trailer truck that is composed of tractor #77 and trailer #238.*

```
¬[ [TrailerTruck]-
   (PART)→[Tractor: #77]
   (PART)→[Trailer: #238] ].
```

English: *It is false that there's a trailer truck with tractor #42 and not trailer #908.*

```
¬[ [TrailerTruck: *x]→(PART)→[Tractor: #42]
   ¬[ [?x]→(PART)→[Trailer: #908] ]].
```

1.13 Proof that $p \supset \Diamond p$ is a theorem of System T:

1. Axiom:

   $\Box p \supset p$.

2. Since this is an axiom schema, which is true for any formula p, it is permissible to replace both occurrences of p with any other formula. Replace p with $\sim p$:

   $\Box \sim p \supset \sim p$.

3. Since $p \supset q$ is equivalent to $\sim p \lor q$,

   $\sim \Box \sim p \lor \sim p$.

4. Replace $\sim \Box \sim p$ with the equivalent $\Diamond p$:

   $\Diamond p \lor \sim p$.

5. Since $\lor$ is symmetric,

   $\sim p \lor \Diamond p$.

6. Replace $\sim p \lor q$ with $p \supset q$:

   $p \supset \Diamond p$.

   QED

1.19 English: *Sometimes, tractor #77 and trailer #238 are part of the same trailer truck.*

(∃t:Time)(∃x:TrailerTruck)(tractor(#77) ∧ trailer(#238) ∧ part(x,#77,t) ∧ part(x,#238,t)).

English: *Whenever tractor #42 is part of a trailer truck, the trailer is #908.*

$(\forall t{:}\text{Time})(\forall x{:}\text{TrailerTruck})((\text{tractor}(\#42) \wedge \text{part}(x,\#42,t))$
$\supset (\text{trailer}(\#908) \wedge \text{part}(x,\#908,t))).$

English: *No tractor is part of two different trailer trucks at the same time.*

$\sim(\exists x{:}\text{Tractor})(\exists y{:}\text{TrailerTruck})(\exists z{:}\text{TrailerTruck})(\exists t{:}\text{Time})$
$(\text{part}(y,x,t) \wedge \text{part}(z,x,t) \wedge \sim(y{=}z)).$

Sentence (d) can be paraphrased as *No tractor is ever part of two different trailer trucks*, which is equivalent to saying *It is false that sometimes there exists a tractor that is part of two different trailer trucks.* Sentence (e) could be paraphrased as *There exists a tractor, which is sometimes part of one trailer truck and sometimes part of a different trailer truck, and it is false that sometimes it is part of both trailer trucks.*

Sentences that represent arbitrary relationships between times can be expressed in FOL by adding new predicates, but they cannot be expressed in a temporal logic with just □ and ◊. Following is such a sentence: *Two hours after some tractor was part of one trailer truck, it was part of a different trailer truck.* To express this sentence in FOL with explicit reference to time, use a predicate such as $\text{sum}(t_1,i,t_2)$, which says that the sum of time t_1 plus an interval i is the time t_2.

1.20 English: *Sometimes, tractor #77 and trailer #238 are part of the same trailer truck.*

```
[TrailerTruck]-
  -1→(PART)-
    ←2-[Tractor: #77]
    →[Time: *t],
  -1→(PART)-
    ←2-[Trailer: #238]
    →[?t].
```

English: *Whenever tractor #42 is part of a trailer truck, the trailer is #908.*

```
[IF:  [TrailerTruck: *x]-1→(PART)-
                          ←2-[Tractor: #42]
                          →[Time: *t],
[THEN:  [?x]-1→(PART)-
                ←2-[Trailer: #908]
                →[?t] ]].
```

English: *No tractor is part of two different trailer trucks at the same time.*

```
¬[ [TrailerTruck]-
  -1→(PART)-
    ←2-[Tractor: *w]
```

```
    →[Time: *t],
 -(≠)-[TrailerTruck]-1→(PART)-
                    ←2-[?w]
                    →[?t]  ].
```

1.22 See Appendix A.1 for more discussion and a partial answer to this exercise.

1.29 Examples of characteristics: height, weight, hair color, attitude. The term *third-order type*, which represents the type ThirdOrderType, is fourth order because it has Rank, Characteristic, and SecondOrderType as instances. In general, the term *nth-order type* is $n+1$st order.

1.31

```
[Box]→(Chrc)→[Length]-
   (Chrc)→[Amount: <5,inch>]- - -[Amount: <12.7,centimeter>].
```

1.32

```
[Person: Bill]←(Agnt)←[Earn]→(Thme)→[Salary]-
   (Chrc)→[Amount]←(Twice)←[Amount]-
   (Chrc)←[Salary]←(Thme)←[Earn]→(Agnt)→[Person: Tom].
```

1.33 a. *Sue drank half a cup of coffee.*

```
(Past)→[ [Person: Sue]←(Agnt)←[Drink]-
   (Ptnt)→[Coffee: @ 1/2 cup]].
```

b. *Sue drank half as much coffee as there was in the cup.*

```
(Past)→[ [Person: Sue]←(Agnt)←[Drink]-
   (Ptnt)→[Coffee]→(Chrc)→[Amount]→(Half)→[Amount]-
   (Chrc)←[Coffee]→(In)→[Cup: #]].
```

Literally, this graph says that Sue drank some coffee of an amount that was half the amount of coffee in the cup.

c. *Sue drank half of the coffee in the cup.*

```
(Past)→[ [Person: Sue]←(Agnt)←[Drink]→(Ptnt)→[Coffee]-
   (Part)←[Coffee: *x]→(In)→[Cup: #]]
      (Chrc)→[Amount]→(Half)→[Amount]←(Chrc)←[?x].
```

This graph says that Sue drank some coffee that was part of the coffee *x* in the cup and whose amount was half the amount of *x*. Since the full graphic notation allows a cycle, the extra concept [?x] is not necessary; it shows more clearly that the only difference between graphs (b) and (c) is one additional Part relation.

1.34 Definition of the hasName predicate:

hasName = $(\lambda x, n)(\mathrm{chrc}(x,n) \wedge \mathrm{name}(n))$.

1.35 Representation of *The temperature of ninety is rising*:

```
[Temperature: # @ 90°]←(Thme)←[Rise].
```

Expansion of @ macro:

```
[Amount: <90, degree>]←(@)←[Temperature: #]←(Thme)←[Rise].
```

This graph may be read *The temperature, which has an amount of 90 degrees, is rising*. The concept [Rise] is directly linked only to the concept of the temperature, not to its current amount. After the temperature rises, its amount is different, but the original amount of 90 degrees remains unchanged. Note: the symbol # represents the definite article *the*; it is an example of an *indexical*, which is discussed further in Chapter 5.

The logician Richard Montague (1974) represented Partee's sentence in a more complex way that depended on a subtle distinction between intensions and extensions. The CG representation depends only on semantic features that are expressed in common English words.

1.36 Translation of the English sentence to typed predicate calculus:

$(\forall m, n{:}\mathrm{IndividualMarker})(\forall x, y{:}\mathrm{Entity})$
$((\mathrm{denote}(m,x) \wedge \mathrm{denote}(n,y) \wedge m \neq n) \supset x \neq y).$

1.37 Without the assumption about distinct surrogates or individual markers, a database with N distinct entities would require $N(N-1)/2$ inequalities of the form $x_i \mathrm{nex}_j$ to state that every possible pair represents two distinct entities. If $N=1000$, the single metalanguage statement would be equivalent to 499,500 inequalities of this form. In most computer languages, including SQL, there is no way to talk to any entities outside the computer system. In SQL, the entities stored in tables are numbers and character strings; any association between them and entities in the outside world is represented only in the comments (or in the programmer's head), but not in SQL itself. To ensure uniqueness, the programmer can use a statement of the following form:

```
create unique index X on Employee (SerialNo);
```

This is a metalevel statement that ensures that no two rows in the Employee table may have the same entry in the column called SerialNo. The programmer may assume that the values in the SerialNo column denote unique individuals in the outside world, but that assumption cannot be expressed in the SQL language.

Chapter 2

2.1 Lattice of the four elements:

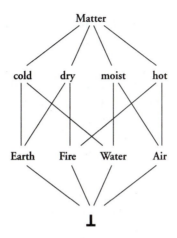

2.2 Elephant IPC. Number IAC. Storm IPO. RR crossing: RPC as a place, or RPO as an event. Photograph: IPC as an piece of paper, IAC as information, or RAC as information about something. Water IPC. Road map: IPC as a piece of paper, or RAC as a description. Computation: MPO as the process, or IAC as the computed result. Business: MPC as an organization, or MPO as an activity. Expectation: MAC for an object, or MAO for an occurrent. Pregnancy MPO. Motherhood MPO. Data structure IAC. Receipt RAO. Tetrahedron IAC. Task MPO. Imprisonment MPO. Traffic MPO. Schedule RAO. Weather report RAO. Dancing: IPO as an event, RPO when considered as participation by dancers, or MPO as a situation. Knot RPC. Hunger RPO. Plan MAO.

2.5 The replacement of a triadic Giving relation by the concept [Give] does not refute Peirce's claim because the Thirdness remains encapsulated in the undefined concept type Give. The three dyadic relations do not *define* the act of giving; they merely show the roles of the three participants in that act. To see the similarities, compare the following graph with the triadic relation Giving instead of the concept Give shown in Exercise 2.3:

```
(Giving)-
  1←[Animate]
  2←[Entity]
  3→[Animate].
```

Both graphs have exactly the same triadic structure, with the relation Giving or the concept Give at the center. The replacement of the labels Agnt, Thme, and Rcpt with the labels 1, 2, and 3 is a notational, not a structural change.

Peirce discussed the example of giving in one of his *Letters to Lady Welby*:

Analyze for instance the relation involved in "A gives B to C." Now what is giving? It does not consist in A's putting B away from him and C's subsequently taking B up. It is not necessary that any material transfer should take place. It consists in A's making C the possessor according to *Law*. (p. 8)

Intention (A3) is the essential mediation that distinguishes the concept types Give, Lend, Sell, Rent, and Lose. If A and C were passengers on a train, and A happened to rest a package B on the seat between them, C would not be entitled to take B unless A gave some verbal or nonverbal sign that B was intended as a gift. The sign of A's intention is necessary for a legal transfer of possession.

2.6 No definition of buildToPlan(x,y,z) could capture the causality between the studying and the method of construction or the causality between the construction and the correspondence. It is possible that x studied y, but completely forgot y while constructing z. In that case, any correspondence of y and z would be the result not of the plan, but of some random coincidence.

To express causality, add two more dyadic predicates, guide(s_1,s_2) and cause (s_2,s_3), which would relate the situations of studying s_1, construction s_2, and correspondence s_3:

buildToPlan(x,y,z) ≡
$(\exists s_1,s_2,s_3$:Situation)
(studies(s_1,x,y) ∧ constructs(s_2,x,z) ∧ corresponds(s_3,y,z)
∧ guide(s_1,s_2) ∧ cause(s_2,s_3)).

But note that this definition introduces triadic predicates *studies, constructs,* and *corresponds.* It also introduces the *guide* and *cause* predicates, whose arguments are situations, which themselves involve Thirdness, as shown in the lattice of Figure 2.7.

As another attempt to reduce the definition to dyads, introduce predicates for the thematic relations agent, theme, result, source, and goal:

buildToPlan(x,y,z) ≡
$(\exists s_1$:Study)($\exists s_2$:Construct)($\exists s_3$:Correspond)
(agnt(s_1,x) ∧ thme(s_1,y)
∧ agnt(s_2,x) ∧ rslt(s_2,z)
∧ srce(s_3,y) ∧ goal(s_3,z)
∧ guide(s_1,s_2) ∧ cause(s_2,s_3)).

This formula reifies the triadic predicates by variables s_i of type Study, Construct, and Correspond. In effect, the dyadic agnt, rslt, srce, and goal predicates relate x, y, and z to the Thirdness bundled into the variables s_i. Then the guide and cause predicates relate the s_i variables to one another. This construction has not eliminated the Thirdness; it has simply hidden it behind the s_i variables. See the answer to Exercise 2.3 for another discussion of the effect of the thematic relations.

2.7 The mediating entity is the plan, which appears in the antecedent of the implication, but not in the conclusion:

> buildToPlan $= (\lambda x{:}\text{Builder})(\lambda y{:}\text{Drawing})(\lambda z{:}\text{Building})$
> $((\exists{:}w{:}\text{Plan})$"Builder x interprets y as a plan w for a building z"
> $\supset$ "x constructs z to resemble y").

The quoted phrase in the antecedent represents a relation r, which relates the mediating entity w to x, y, and z. The quoted phrase in the consequent represents a relation s, which does not involve the plan w. In the usual syntax, the quoted phrases could be written interpretsDrawingAsPlanFor(x,y,w,z) and constructsTo Resemble(x,z,y). The implication operator $\supset$ represents the causal influence of the plan, which does not appear explicitly in the result.

2.8 a. A common property of all the items in the list is mass, which is the basis for sorting them in order of increasing mass. From an earth-centric viewpoint, weight could be considered an inherent property of an object, but technically, weight depends on Secondness, since it is the reaction of an object's mass with the gravitational attraction of another object.

   b. Items found in a bathroom: toothbrush, bar of soap, razor, roll of toilet paper, rubber ducky, towel. Items found in a book bag: eraser, pencil, pocket calculator, apple, sandwich, book, three-ring binder.

   c. Explanation: Items in the bathroom are used in water-based activities for personal hygiene. Items in the book bag are used during a student's day at school.

2.9 Pure mathematics is the study of form or Firstness. This theorem is a joke because the concept Interesting introduces a kind of Thirdness that is foreign to the practice of mathematics: some entity x is interesting to some person y for some reason z. The theorem as stated therefore depends implicitly on some unstated person y and reason z.

   It is possible to give a formal definition of the predicate interesting(n) by formalizing the metalanguage used to define reasons and defining a formal mapping between the integer n and the reason z. But unless the language for formalizing the reasons and the mappings allows infinitely long sentences, only a countable number of entities can be considered interesting. Since the real numbers are uncountable, only a countable subset of them can be interesting.

When formalized, proofs like this are closely related to proofs of computability and undecidability, which are serious subjects in logic and computer science. But words like *serious* and *useful* also involve Thirdness: some proof x is considered serious or useful by some person y for some reason z. Like the word *interesting*, the words *serious* and *useful* could be formalized, but then someone else might doubt (Thirdness) whether that formalization was serious, interesting, or useful.

Words like *interesting* or *useful*, which involve Thirdness, must relate three entities. A definition of such words by monadic predicates like interesting(x) must either ignore the person y and the reason z or treat y and z as fixed constants. But that approach is an oversimplification that could be challenged by any other person who happened to have different criteria for what is interesting or useful.

2.10 The word *funeral* describes a situation (Mediating Physical Occurrent) that relates all the participants mentioned in the rest of the story. The words *priest*, *pallbearer*, and *mourner* describe people by their roles (Secondness), not by any inherent characteristics. The word *coffin* describes an object by its function (Secondness), not by its structure or composition. The words *procession* and *follow* describe simpler occurrents (parts of the funeral) that determine how the people relate to one another as participants in the funeral.

2.13 Following is a direct translation of the second premise *For every person x, it is better for x to have a ham sandwich than for x to have nothing*:

```
(∀x:Person)betterThan(
   (∃y:HamSandwich)have(x,y),
   have(x,{})).
```

The {} symbol can be eliminated by expanding the last line:

```
(∀x:Person)betterThan(
   (∃y:HamSandwich)have(x,y),
   ~(∃y)have(x,y),
```

A direct translation of this version to stylized English would be *For every person x, it is better for x to have a ham sandwich y than for there not to exist any y such that x has y*. A more colloquial version is *You're better off having a ham sandwich than not having anything*.

2.17 Each of Tarski's five definitions involve two arbitrary spheres, x and y. Show that if Tarski's definitions were not equivalent to Euclid's, it would be possible to find two spheres that violated the constraints. For the definition of externally tangent and internally tanget, show that if a and b were not touching, it would be possible to find x and y that both contained a, but x contained only a part of y. For the definition of internally and externally diametrical, show that if a and b were not diametrically opposite, two very large spheres x and y would intersect on one side or the other. For concentric, show that if a and b did not have the same center, x and y would not have to be internally diametrical to b.

Chapter 3

3.5 Words like *absence* and *fail*, which have implicit negations, cannot be defined in pure EC logic. Representing the absence of something by failing to mention it requires the assumption of *negation as failure*. That assumption can only be stated in higher-order logic:

- If a proposition p cannot be proved from the current knowledge base, then assume its negation ~p.

This statement uses implication, negation, and metalanguage to talk about propositions. When added to EC logic, it not only provides a way of defining all the operators of first-order logic, it even supports versions of nonmonotonic logic.

3.6 Predicates for the ontology:

lakeWarmerThanAir(x)	A lake at x is warmer than the air at x.
eastOf(x,y)	Location x is east of y.
westWind(x)	The wind at x is blowing from the west.
air(x,y)	The air at x is y.

The second argument of the air predicate may be one of the following attributes: saturated, rising, cooler, precipitating, aboveFreezing, belowFreezing, raining, snowing. Following are the translations of the English sentences to predicate calculus:

($\forall x$:Location)(lakeWarmerThanAir(x) $\supset$ air(x,saturated)).

($\forall x$:Location)(air(x,saturated) $\supset$ air(x,rising)).

($\forall x$:Location)(air(x,rising) $\supset$ air(x,cooler)).

($\forall x$:Location)((air(x,precipitating) $\wedge$ air(x,aboveFreezing)) $\supset$ air(x,raining)).

($\forall x$:Location)((air(x,precipitating) $\wedge$ air(x,belowFreezing)) $\supset$ air(x,snowing)).

($\forall x$:Location)((air(x,saturated) $\wedge$ air(x,cooler)) $\supset$ air(x,precipitating)).

$$(\forall x,y{:}\text{Location})(\forall z{:}\text{Attribute})((\text{westWind}(x) \land$$
$$\text{eastOf}(x,y) \land \text{air}(x,z)) \supset \text{air}(y,z)).$$

3.7 Four English sentences translated to predicate calculus:

eastOf(Buffalo,LakeErie). lakeWarmerThanAir(LakeErie).
air(LakeErie,belowFreezing). westWind(LakeErie).

How to explain why it is snowing in Buffalo: Let $\sim p_1, \sim p_2, \ldots, \sim p_n$ be the chain of inferences where p_1 is the formula for the sentence *It is snowing in Buffalo* and p_n is the formula that was contradicted by the backward chain of inferences; the chain of formulas :f p sub i :ef. should include the original facts and rules, as well as the conclusions derived from them. Then let the English paragraph be the sequence of sentences 'E'(p_n), . . . , 'E'(p_1), where 'E'(p_i) represents the English reading of p_i.

3.15 The following if-then operation could be added to the action part of the updateEffectsOfPutOn:

```
(if (contains ? ?x)
  then (assert (deleteContainer ?x)) )
```

This retraction would have to be placed ahead of the assertion of the fact that ?y supports ?x; otherwise, it would also delete any facts about the new containing relationships. For case (a) in which ?x does not support anything else, the deleteContainer rule would retract all facts that asserted anything containing ?x:

```
(defrule updateEffectsOfPutOn
  ?dcontainer <- (deleteContainer ?x)
=>
  (retract ?dcontainer)
  (while ?dcon <- (contains ?y ?x)
    do (retract ?dcon) ))
```

For case (b) in which ?x might support other objects, the while loop would have to contain a nested while loop.

```
(while ?dcon <- (contains ?y ?x)
  do (retract ?dcon)
    (while (indSupports ?x ?z)
      (if ?dindcon <- (contains ?y ?z)
        do (retract ?dindcon) )))
```

This rule would also require the definition of another rule to define indSupports as the transitive closure of the supports relation.

Chapter 4

4.4 The data associated with a token may be an arbitrarily complex structure, one field of which could be used to save memory-bound data. Since each token in a Petri net has the effect of a separate task or thread, the memory of a task may be contained in the token for that task. To represent memory that is bound to a specific transition, add another place next to that transition with a single token in it. That place should have one arc as input to and another as output from the transition. The token in that place, which would go to the transition every time it fired, could contain any memory-bound data that may be needed by the transition. With these techniques, the transitions can be implemented in a purely functional language.

4.12 The unified Petri net represents all processes in one big simulation. It is convenient for showing a global view of all interactions simultaneously. Each finite-state machine focuses on just a single process while ignoring the details of other processes. It would be convenient for a programmer who wants to concentrate on one process at a time without worrying about the details of the others. See Section 5.7 for an application that decomposes a Petri net into separate finite-state machines that represent interacting agents.

4.13 On the producer loops:

- The P1 transition invokes InP with the pattern (Empty ?ptr).
- V2 invokes Out with the data tuple (Full PtrToBuffer).

On the consumer loop:

- P2 invokes InP with the pattern (Full ?ptr).
- V1 invokes Out with the data (Empty PtrToBuffer).

In Exercise 4.10, the decomposition of Figure 4.11 into seven finite-state machines treats the four buffers as equal in importance to the two producers and one consumer. In many applications, however, the buffers are passive objects, while the producers and the consumer may do a significant amount of computation. The decomposition into three machines would be simpler and more efficient for applications in which the buffers are passive. The decomposition into seven machines might be more convenient and modular for applications in which the buffer cycle does a significant amount of complex computation.

4.14 As Figure 4.8 shows, the number of processes in the Petri net of Figure 4.7 may increase without limit. Therefore, it cannot be decomposed into a fixed number of finite-state machines by the method of Exercise 4.10 or 4.11.

To decompose Figure 4.7, draw a finite-state machine for the loop consisting of place *a*, transition *b*, place *c*, and transition *f*. In transition *b*, make two calls to the Linda Eval operator to invoke two finite-state machines that start at places *d* and *e*, respectively. When the machine starting at *d* reaches place *i*, it would terminate with a result that the Eval operator would send in a tuple to BB. When the machine starting at *e* reaches transition *k*, it would use the Linda In operator to receive that message; then it would terminate in place *l*. The continuing threads shown in Figure 4.8 would be represented by an accumulation of tuples in BB for each machine that ended in place *l*.

4.15 Most Petri nets can be represented by finite-state machines that interact via Linda operators. However, there is one feature of Petri nets that cannot be adequately represented by Linda: the ability to delay firing a transition until tokens have been received in each of several input places. Since each Linda operator receives at most one tuple, some transitions must be represented by two or more Linda operators. If two or more transitions are competing for the same inputs, the representation in Linda might create a deadlock that would not occur in the Petri net. As Section 4.5 shows, all Linda operators can be represented by Petri nets, but not all Petri nets can be represented by combinations of Linda with finite-state machines.

4.17 To solve the problem in Prolog, first define a predicate choose(X,L,R), which selects an element X out of a list L and puts the remaining elements in R:

```
choose(X,L,R) ← L=[Head|Tail] &
  (X=Head & R=Tail | choose(X,Tail,R2) & R=[Head|R2]).
```

Following is an unoptimized Prolog predicate that solves the problem. For the goal solve(*,*,*), the Prolog system would return the answer solve([9,5,6,7], [1,0,8,5], [1,0,6,5,2]).

```
solve([S,E,N,D], [M,O,R,E], [M,O,N,E,Y]) ←
  choose(M,[0,1,2,3,4,5,6,7,8,9],R9) & choose(S,R9,R8)
  & choose(O,R8,R7) & choose(E,R7,R6) & choose(N,R6,R5)
  & choose(R,R5,R4) & choose(D,R4,R3) & choose(Y,R3,R2)
  & M>0 & (C4=0 | C4=1) & M=C4 & S>0
  & (C3=0 | C3=1)
  & O := S + M + C3 - 10 * C4
  & (C2=0 | C2=1)
  & N := E + O + C2 - 10 * C3
  & (C1=0 | C1=1)
  & R := 10 * C2 + E - N - C1
  & Y := D + E - 10 * C1.
```

This version can be optimized by reordering the generating and testing, as in the flowchart of Figure 4.15:

```
solve([S,E,N,D], [M,O,R,E], [M,O,N,E,Y]) ←
  M=1 & C4=1 & R9=[0,2,3,4,5,6,7,8,9]
  & choose(S,R9,R8)
  & S>0 & (C3=0 | C3=1)
  & O := S + M + C3 - 10 * C4
  & choose(O,R8,R7)
  & choose(E,R7,R6) & (C2=0 | C2=1)
  & N := E + O + C2 - 10 * C3
  & choose(N,R6,R5)
  & (C1=0 | C1=1)
  & R := 10 * C2 + E - N - C1
  & choose(R,R5,R4)
  & choose(D,R4,R3)
  & Y := D + E - 10 * C1
  & choose(Y,R3,R2).
```

On an IBM 3090 computer, the unoptimized version took 13 seconds of CPU time, but the optimized version took only 4 milliseconds — more than 3200 times faster.

NOTE: Various implementations of Prolog use different symbols. This example uses the notation of the book by Walker et al. (1990). In some versions of Prolog, the left implication is represented by the symbol :- instead of ←; the conjunction is represented by a comma instead of &; the don't-care symbol is represented by an underscore _ instead of an asterisk *; and the assignment := is represented by the keyword *is*. The vertical bar | represents a disjunction. On versions of Prolog without disjunction, it is possible to define a dyadic *or* operator by the following two rules:

```
or(P,Q) ← P.
or(P,Q) ← Q.
```

4.19 a. STRIPS had to face the same kinds of integrity problems that must be addressed in database systems when some relations depend on others. Since the NextTo relation depends on the At relation, an update to either relation may change the values in the other. The solution adopted for STRIPS is to allow updates only to the primitive relations such as At and to recompute the values of the dependent relations whenever the primitive relations change. In relational database systems, it is more common to store only the values of the primitive relations and to define the dependent relations as *views*, whose values are computed only when requested. The problem of preserving integrity if updates are made to dependent relations is unsolvable in general. For example, if the fact that A is next to B is added or deleted, there is no way of knowing whether A or B or both were moved.

b. The STRIPS world models are equivalent to the data stored in a relational database or a collection of ground-level clauses in Prolog. The problem of evaluating the truth of an arbitrary first-order statement in terms of such a model is routinely performed for SQL queries and Prolog goals. It can be solved in polynomial time.

4.22 A transition with two or more input arcs represents a conjunction, since it cannot fire unless all of its input places have a token. A place with two or more output arcs represents a disjunction, since a token in that place can only to go one or another of the output transitions. To simulate negation as failure, use a transition that can only fire if a particular place fails to have a token. In Figure 4.15, the Petri net for the InP operator has a transition labeled Null, which fires if there is no suitable token in the BB place. In Figure 4.20, the Misfire transition fires when there is no token in the Gun-loaded place; but unlike in Figure 4.15, there is no delay transition to prevent it from firing even when a token is present. Show how a delay transition could be added to Figure 4.20.

4.24 With single transitions for each action, the Petri net would require two transitions: the first one for the movement of Zayd's hand would enable the one for the movement of the key. For a series of partial movements, the Petri net would embed those two transitions in a loop where the output token from each movement of the key would enable another movement by Zayd's hand. The token that would start the loop would come from a transition for Zayd deciding to move his hand, and the token would be removed from the loop by another transition for Zayd deciding to stop. If the loop were cycled as rapidly as the frames of a movie, both movements would appear to be continuous.

4.27 Brief answer: The operational description of the way clocks measure time illustrates Whitehead's view of how time is "abstracted" from actual entities; it is also compatible with Peirce's pragmatism. According to Newton's view, space and time are independent physical entities (IP) with space as a continuant (IPC) and time as an occurrent (IPO). In modern physics, the structure of space and time depends critically on matter and energy, although the nature of that dependence is still an active research topic. According to Whitehead's view, which is consistent with modern physics, the spatial and temporal aspects of actual entities would be classified in categories IP, RP, and MP or their continuant and occurent subtypes. All measurements are abstractions that would be instances of the abstract categories of Figure 2.7. A map is a schema and a calendar is a script; their components — geographical coordinates and dates — would be monads of type Schema or Script. A date such as 28 January 1998 is an instance of Script; the proposition that 28 January 1998 is the beginning of a Chinese year is an instance of History; an explanation of why that date is considered the beginning of a year would be an instance of Reason. The processes that determine the temperature would be physical, and their measurements would be abstract. Generalizing the measuring techniques beyond the physical sciences raises many controversial issues. Whatever reality lies behind a stock market index or an IQ score would be physical; the measurements, meaningful or not, would be abstract.

4.28 Born's three postulates could be stated as constraints on the Petri nets that simulate physical processes:

- *Causality* postulates that for some combination of tokens in the places of a Petri net, the presence of a token in the place A is a prerequisite for the appearance of a token in the place B. A is called the cause, and B is called the the effect.

- *Antecedence* postulates that the appearance of a token in the cause must be prior to the appearance of a token in the effect.

- *Contiguity* postulates that cause and effect must be connected by a directed path of arcs leading from the cause to the effect.

The regions discussed in Section 2.7 could be could be represented by connected subgraphs of a history of firings of a Petri net. Map any such region $\Re$ to a timing diagram, such as Figure 4.9. If a time line exists for $\Re$, it would be a single thread through the timing diagram that starts before or simultaneous with any other thread in $\Re$ and ends after or simultaneous with any other thread in $\Re$. If the arrow at the bottom of Figure 4.9 is ignored, there are nine candidates for time lines; any of them could be adopted as a time line, but one with a large number of regularly spaced firings of transitions would provide the finest granularity for timing other processes. During the firing of any transition t on a time line, a snapshot would consist of a slice through all the threads above and below t. A continuant could be represented by single token that represents some object; its corresponding region would be a single thread that forms a time line of all the states and events that object performs or undergoes. A more detailed representation of a continuant could be represented by parallel threads that represent the parts of an object and the separate actions they perform during the life of the whole; an airplane, for example, has been described as three million parts flying in close formation. Any other region would represent an occurrent. A spatial form could be represented by a predicate $P(s)$ that is true of the token or configuration of tokens that flow along the threads of a region that represents a continuant.

Chapter 5

5.1 Since the go-moku board has 12 black stones and 11 white ones, White has the next move. Black is threatening to get 5 stones in a horizontal row on the next move; therefore, White's only chance to avoid an immediate loss is to place a stone to block that pattern. Following that move, Black will place a stone to form a diagonal row of 4 stones that is open at both ends. Since White cannot block both ends in a single move, Black will win on the following move.

Note that this go-moku game ends after 27 stones have been placed on the board; the go game did not end until 287 moves were made. In general, go-moku is a much simpler game than go. A typical go-moku game ends in a few minutes, but a go game may take hours or even days. At the 67th move of the go game illustrated in Chapter 4, the player with the black stones studied the board for three hours before making the move.

5.9 The basic superstition is that using the true name of something is the equivalent of calling it. By a variation of the superstition about fear, if you call a feared entity, then it is likely to appear. Since bears are fearsome animals that were more common in the northern areas where the Germanic and Slavic languages were spoken, the people in those areas would avoid using their true names.

5.12 Carnap's definition is equivalent to Montague's definition in any system of logic whose rules of inference are sound and complete. In such a case, all sentences that are provably equivalent would be true or false in exactly the same possible worlds. Therefore, they would generate the same equivalence classes for propositions. The definition in Section 5.3 allows more fine-grained distinctions that would generate more equivalence classes: provable equivalence is just one condition for a meaning-preserving function; the other conditions distinguish sentences that may be provably equivalent, but have different vocabulary or structure. Montague's definition cannot be computed because it is stated in terms of physical worlds or possibly fictitious worlds. Carnap's definition can be computed by a theorem prover, but in many cases the proof that two formulas are equivalent is undecidable, or it may take an exponential amount of time. The definition in Section 5.3, however, can be tested in at most polynomial time.

For examples, see Section 5.3. As another example, the statement $2+2=4$ and the statement of Fermat's last theorem are both true in every possible world in which Peano's axioms hold. Yet the proof of the first is trivial, but the best mathematicians in the world took several centuries to prove the second. By the definition of Section 5.3, however, there is no need to prove their logical equivalence, since they have a different structure and use different vocabulary.

5.13 Linguists have never formulated the rules for translating pairs of languages with enough precision to confirm or reject Quine's thesis. The definition of proposition in terms of meaning-preserving functions is compatible with Quine's thesis of indeterminacy, and it might be used to state that thesis in a more formal and testable way:

- Suppose that two manuals A and B define functions f.A' and f.B' for translating language $\mathcal{L}_1$ to language $\mathcal{L}_2$.
- It is possible that f_A and f_B meet the criteria for meaning-preserving functions stated in Section 5.3, but there exists at least one sentence s in $\mathcal{L}_1$ whose translations in $\mathcal{L}_2$ diverge according to the two manuals: i.e., the equivalence class in $\mathcal{L}_2$ of $f_A(s)$ is not the same as the class of $f_B(s)$.
- The possible existence of such divergent translation manuals in no way invalidates the definition of propositions according to 5.3. It simply means that there is no unique way of relating the propositions stated in $\mathcal{L}_1$ to those stated in $\mathcal{L}_2$.

For Quine's rabbit-gavagai example, one manual might translate the word *rabbit* to *gavagai*, and another manual might translate *undetached rabbit part* to *gavagai*. To confirm Quine's thesis, both translations and their inverses would have to be extended consistently to the entire languages $\mathcal{L}_1$ and $\mathcal{L}_2$ while preserving the criteria of Section 5.3 and without violating the usage of the native speakers of both $\mathcal{L}_1$ and $\mathcal{L}_2$. The ability to extend such translations for at least one pair of languages would confirm Quine's thesis; the inability to extend them consistently would count as evidence against it. Neither case would invalidate the definitions of Section 5.3.

The inability to give a satisfactory translation for the sentence about neutrinos from $\mathcal{L}_1$ to $\mathcal{L}_2$ would mean that the vocabulary of $\mathcal{L}_2$ is not rich enough to express sentences about that topic. If the topic is important, the vocabulary of $\mathcal{L}_2$ could be extended by borrowing or coining new words in the same way that English has been extended in the past 400 years. Whether the new language $\mathcal{L}_2$ is considered "the same" or "different" is another example of the identity puzzle illustrated in Figure 5.2. See Chapter 6 for more examples.

5.14 a. The second line follows from the first by two applications of GMP: from $p \supset r$ and p, the conclusion becomes $T \wedge r$; from $q \supset s$ and q, the conclusion becomes $T \wedge r \wedge s$; then "$T \wedge$" can be erased.

b. The conditions for GMP do not apply, since the context of $(m \wedge n)$ is negative (negation depth one). But since the context is negative, the second line can be derived from the first by the rule of insertion.

c. Yes, the conditions for GMP apply.

d. The conditions for GMP do not apply, since $(p \vee (q \supset r))$ is equivalent to $\sim(\sim p \wedge \sim(q \supset r))$. Therefore, the context of m does not lie inside the contexts of p and $q \supset r$. In case of doubt, draw the negations as ovals.

5.15 This theorem is easiest to prove when the contexts are shown explicitly, as in EGs, CGs, or DRSs. In the algebraic notation, the sequence of steps is exactly the same, but the test for nested contexts requires more careful checking. By the rule of double negation, start by drawing two negative contexts around the blank or T: $\sim(T \wedge \sim T)$. As an implication,

$$T \supset T.$$

By the rule of insertion in a negative context, the first T may be replaced with any specialization. In particular, it may be replaced with the entire left side of the formula to be proved:

$$((p \supset r) \wedge (q \supset s)) \supset ((p \wedge q) \supset T.$$

By the rule of double negation, draw two negative contexts around T to form $\sim(T \wedge \sim T)$, which may be written in the form of an implication:

$$((p \supset r) \wedge (q \supset s)) \supset ((p \wedge q) \supset (T \supset T).$$

By the rule of insertion in a negative context, the first T may be replaced by $(p \wedge q)$:

$$((p \supset r) \wedge (q \supset s)) \supset ((p \wedge q) \supset T).$$

This is the same as the first line in Exercise 5.14a. After two applications of GMP, the theorem is proved in a total of 6 steps. In the *Principia Mathematica*, which was published 13 years after Peirce discovered his rules, the proof of this theorem took 43 steps.

5.16 Parts (a) and (b) can be derived from the first formula in context $\mathcal{D}$ by one application of QE followed by deiteration to erase the extra copy of q. To prove (c), start with the formula

$$(u \wedge r) \equiv ((p \wedge \sim w) \equiv (\sim v \wedge s)).$$

Any identity of the form $p \equiv q$ can be written as a conjunction $(p \supset q) \wedge (q \supset p)$. Therefore, either implication is a generalization of the identity. By the rule of replacing a subformula with a generalization in a positive context, replace the first occurrence of $\equiv$ with $\supset$:

$$(u \wedge r) \supset ((p \wedge \sim w) \equiv (\sim v \wedge s)).$$

Since the consequence of an implication is also a positive context, replace the remaining occurrence of ≡ with ⊃, but in the reverse order:

$$(u \wedge r) \supset ((\sim v \wedge s) \supset (p \wedge \sim w)).$$

Applying QE,

$$(u \wedge r \wedge \sim v \wedge s) \supset p.$$

In the context $\mathcal{D}$, u and $\sim v$ occur outside any negations. Therefore, by two applications of deiteration, the copies of u and $\sim v$ may be erased to obtain

$$(r \wedge s) \supset p.$$

This proof takes five steps. Although the proof is short, heuristics or insight may be necessary to find the most promising steps to try. For parts (a), (b), and (c), the heuristic to use is easiest to state when the formulas are translated to EGs or CGs: if the conclusion of an implication occurs inside any nest of negated contexts, the implication can be derived in one step by an application of QE. For these proofs, the translation to EGs or CGs can be done in linear time, QE is also linear, and deiterations can be used to simplify the results.

Instead of heuristics, truth tables require brute-force computation that increases exponentially with the number of propositional variables. Since the context $\mathcal{D}$ contains 8 distinct variables, a truth table would have 2^8 or 256 rows. For each row, the three formulas in the context would have to be evaluated to 0 for false or 1 for true. Then for each row in which all three have the value 1, each formula to be proved would also have to have the value 1.

Heuristics can also be used to reduce the computation in truth tables. In this example, the formula $q \wedge u \wedge \sim v$ determines three values, $q=1$, $u=1$, and $v=0$, and allows the table to be reduced to 2^5 or 32 rows. Implications, which create dependencies between the rows, can be accommodated by further heuristics, which have the effect of replacing the rows of a truth table with a network of dependencies called a *truth-maintenance system* (TMS). In the worst cases, all of these methods — proofs, truth tables, and truth-maintenance systems — take exponential amounts of time; but the worst cases for each of them tend to occur on different kinds of problems. Unfortunately, many kinds of problems are computationally intractable (exponential) with all known methods.

5.17 Peirce observed that the symbols of any statement in any language, natural or artificial, must be linked to their domain of discourse by at least one indexical. Those indexicals could be contained within the statement itself, as they are in natural languages, or they could be contained in a metalanguage, as in the statements that determine the application of some formula in logic. The paradoxes of self-reference such as "This sentence is false" always involve some kind of indexical. The nonparadoxical sentence in Exercise 5.17 uses the indexical effect of tenses to distinguish the object language from the meta-language.

Words like *true* and *false* are metalevel terms that implicitly raise the meta-language by one level. Nonparadoxical statements can be mapped to a stratified semantics where each sentence can be assigned a unique level number that is at least one level above the level of the sentence to which the words *true* and *false* are applied. Paradoxical statements create cycles that cannot be mapped to the stratified levels.

5.18 The nature of the entity x and the laws logos(x) for each of Peirce's five kinds of modality:

- *Logical possibility.* x is { }, and the laws consist of all tautologies.
- *Subjective possibility.* x is some knowing agent, and the laws are everything x knows.
- *Objective possibility.* x is the universe, and the laws are the laws of nature.
- *Interrogative mood.* x is a community of enquirers or truth seekers, and the laws are the consensus of what is commonly known.
- *Freedom.* x is a community of animate beings seeking to live together harmoniously, and the laws are the norms of acceptable behavior.

To reconcile the personal and impersonal metaphysics, St. John the Evangelist identified the logos of the universe with God. He was probably influenced by the Jewish philosopher Philo of Alexandria, who was trying to harmonize the Torah with Greek philosophy.

5.22 In the Watch place, each hider would invoke a ReadP operator with the pattern tuple (see ?n). If the variable ?n contained the hider's own name, the hider would be required to enter the Seen transition; otherwise, the hider would be permitted to enter the Run-Home transition. During the Miss transition, the seeker would try to block further runs by invoking the In operator with the pattern (see *name*), where *name* is the name of the hider who just escaped. From the Seek place, the seeker might give up the search by entering the No-Tag transition; in that transition, the seeker uses the Out operator to send the message (all free). In the Watch place, hiders would periodically use the ReadP operator with a pattern (all free); when they found that pattern, they would enter the Run-Home transition.

5.25 Missing fact: Ronald Opus was the son of the old couple who lived on the ninth floor.

5.26 A definition that justifies the medical examiner's conclusion: A person x dies by *suicide* if x is guilty of mudering x. In this example, Ronald Opus intended to kill his mother. In the attempt, he performed an action that resulted in killing himself. By the conditions stated in Exercise 5.22, he is guilty of self-murder.

Another definition: A person x dies by *suicide* if x intends to kill x and in pursuing that intention, x performs an action that directly or indirectly causes the death of x. Although Ronald Opus intended to commit suicide, the action that caused his death was performed with the intention of killing someone else. Therefore, he is guilty of murdering himself, but not guilty of suicide.

Chapter 6

6.5 In the original design, the connectors for the upper walkway supported only the weight of the upper walkway, and the connectors for the lower walkway supported only the lower walkway. As built, however, the connectors for the upper walkway had to support the full weight of both upper and lower walkways. Therefore, they were the first to fail.

6.9 The possible outcomes can be represented by a truth-table with 16 rows. Evaluate each of the five statements in terms of that truth table to determine the Giants' opponent for each row. If the probability of any win or loss is 50%, the probability of each row is $(1/2)^4$ or 6.25%. Therefore, the probability that the Giants will play the Vikings is 37.5%; the Lions or Redskins, 25%; and the Buccaneers, 12.5%. With variables, the probability of each row is the product of the probability of each win w and each loss $(1-w)$.

NOTE: this exercise ignores ties, which have a low probability; if ties were considered, the statement of the problem would be more complicated, but the method of solving it would be the same.

6.11 Named default rules:

- Junk: $(\forall x{:}\text{Retailer})(\forall m{:}\text{Message})(\text{from}(m,x) \supset {\sim}\text{important}(m))$.
- Delivery: $(\forall x{:}\text{Retailer})(\forall m{:}\text{Message})((\text{from}(m,x) \wedge \text{awaitingDelivery }(\text{Karen},x)) \supset \text{important}(m))$.
- Favor: $(\forall m{:}\text{Message})(\text{from}(m,\text{fave.com}) \supset \text{important}(m))$.

Assertions of priority:

- overrides(Delivery,Junk). overrides(Favor,Junk).

Background knowledge:

- retailer(baby.com). retailer(paris.com). retailer(fave.com).

Messages:

- from(msg54,baby.com). from(msg81,paris.com). from(msg117,fave.com).

6.12 The classical first-order theory that determines that Molly the mollusc has a shell is the deductive closure of the following formulas:

- $(\forall x)(\text{nautilus}(x) \supset \text{cephalopod}(x))$.
- $(\forall x)(\text{cephalopod}(x) \supset \text{mollusc}(x))$.
- $(\forall x)(\text{mollusc}(x) \supset \text{shellBearer}(x))$.
- mollusc(Molly).

To derive the other two theories, replace the last two formulas with the appropriate formulas for Sophie or Natalie. For Karen's email agent, the FOL formulas for message #54 would be:

- retailer(baby.com). retailer(paris.com). retailer(fave.com).
- $(\forall x{:}\text{Retailer})(\forall m{:}\text{Message})(\text{from}(m,x) \supset \sim\text{important}(m))$.
- from(msg54,baby.com).

To derive the theories for the other two messages, replace the last two formulas. The effect of the default rules is to extract a different subset of classical formulas for each instance. In principle, the nonmonotonic reasoning is done by the metalevel rules, and the answer for each instance is derived by classical FOL. In practice, the inference steps at the two levels are intermixed, and the effective first-order theory is not shown explicitly.

6.15 There is no fixed order of the two axioms named Rep and Qua in Exercise 6.14 that can give the correct answers for both Nixon and Bob. One way to solve the problem is to change the object-level axioms to include conditions about political and religious activity. Another solution is replace the fixed ordering of defaults by metalevel axioms that determine which object-level rule takes priority:

$(\forall x)(\text{religious}(x) \supset \text{overrides}(\text{Qua,Rep}))$.
$(\forall x)(\text{politician}(x) \supset \text{overrides}(\text{Rep,Qua}))$.

Rules of this kind, which could also be used for theory revision, push the default reasoning into the metalevel. The same kinds of problems about default reasoning recur at the metalevel, and they might require metametalevel reasoning about the metalevel defaults. To stop an infinite regress in metalevels, some level should have no defaults or a fixed partial ordering of defaults. To reach a conclusion in any particular case, the reasoning at metalevel $i\mathcal{L}1$ must be completed before the reasoning at level i can proceed.

6.16 Fuzzy reasoning and default reasoning are being used in critical systems such as brakes. As computers become ubiquitous, software that might not seem critical could cause a failure that would propagate to other systems. To avoid a disaster, the engineers must analyze all the options that could occur and prove a metalevel theorem that guarantees safety: the reasoning methods must reach a safe conclusion in all cases, they must reach the conclusion within a fixed time limit, and no critical system may have dependencies on possibly unsafe systems. Even then, it is prudent to include backup systems and manual overrides.

6.18 Short answer: The three concept types Observation, Simulation, and Deduction are all examples of Thirdness, since they involve an agent (first) who extracts knowledge (second) from some source (third). They differ in the type of the source. For Observation, the source is Firstness: feelings or sensory inputs of some kind. For Simulation, the source is Secondness: the relation of the model to the entity that is being modeled. For Deduction, the source is Thirdness: a theory as explanation.

Chapter 7

7.2 For a solution in Prolog, see the depth_first predicate, which is described in the answer to Exercise 7.5. That predicate could be used without change to solve the MC puzzle. The move predicate for the leapfrog game, however, would have to be modified for the different formats and constraints. For other programming languages, a search program such as depth_first could also be written in a problem-independent way. All of the problem dependencies would be concentrated in the move program and the program that prints out the answers in a humanly readable form.

7.5 Following is a Prolog solution for the leapfrog game. It is invoked by typing the Prolog goal "leapfrog." This program represents one working version, which may be modified or used as a pattern for developing other versions as suggested in Exercise 7.6. Similar programs for breadth-first search, for heuristics to improve performance, and for applications to other problems are presented in Chapter 2 of the book by Walker et al. (1990). The nickel-and-dime game in that book is isomorphic to the leapfrog game.

The depth_first predicate searches the graph of all possible states in games such as the MC puzzle or leapfrog. It calls a predicate move(Current,Next) to make a move from the current state to a possible next state, and it keeps a history of all previous states that have been visited.

```
depth_first(Goal, Goal.*, Goal.nil).
depth_first(Goal, Current.Past, Current.Future) <- move(Current,Next)
  & ¬member(Next,Past)
  & depth_first(Goal, Next.Current.Past, Future).
```

The member predicate is used to avoid repeated states by checking whether a possible next state is a member of the history list.

```
member(Head,Head.Tail).
member(X,Head.Tail) <- member(X,Tail).
```

The move predicate, which is the only one called by depth_first that is specialized to the leapfrog game, makes one move from the current state to the next state. This version of move represents each state as a list of characters with "m" for missionaries, "c" for cannibals, and "_" for the empty space. The move predicate and the prtans predicate for printing the answer are the only two that need to be changed for different representations.

```
move(m."_".X, "_".m.X).
move("_".c.X, c."_".X).
move(m.X."_".Y, "_".X.m.Y).
move("_".X.c.Y, c.X."_".Y).
move(H.X, H.Y) <- move(X,Y).
```

The leapfrog predicate sets up the starting state, calls the depth_first predicate to play the game, and then prints out each state from start to finish.

```
leapfrog <-
 prst('Please enter the number of missionaries.') & nl & readat(M) & nl
& ((¬int(M) | lt(M,0)) -> (prst('Invalid input.') & nl & stop))
& prst('Please enter the number of cannibals.') & nl & readat(C) & nl
& ((¬int(C) | lt(C,0)) -> (prst('Invalid input.') & nl & stop))
& repeat(m,M,ML) & repeat(c,C,CL) & append(ML,"_".CL,Start)
& append(CL,"_".ML,Goal)
& depth_first(Goal, Start.nil, Answer)
& prst('Steps to the goal:') & nl
& prtans(Answer).
```

The repeat predicate creates a list of length N by repeating an element X.

```
repeat(X,0,nil).
repeat(X,N,X.L) <- diff(N,1,N1) & repeat(X,N1,L).
```

The append predicate appends two lists to form a third.

```
append(nil,L,L).
append(H.L1, L2, H.L) <- append(L1,L2,L).
```

The prtans predicate prints the steps of the game as character strings of the form "mmm_ccc." At the end, it prints the line "Finished."

```
prtans(nil) <- nl & prst('Finished.') & nl .
prtans(State.Tail) <-
    nl & write(State)
  & nl & prtans(Tail).
```

7.9 The concept types Rascal, Brother, and Mother are role types, since evidence of some relationship to external entities is necessary to classify a human being as any of those types. For the types Brother and Mother, the external entity is human, but the relationships are different. Following is an axiom associated with Brother:

> For every brother x, there is another person y who is a sibling of x.
> $(\forall x{:}\text{Brother})(\exists y{:}\text{Person})\text{siblingOf}(y,x)$.

Most, if not all of the ambiguities that arise in natural languages are caused by the conversational principle that people try to make their comments as brief as possible. In this case, the ambiguity arises because John's sibling may be Peter or it may be some other person y; similarly, Peter's sibling may be John or another person z. By the principles of conversational implicature, the default interpretation is the simplest one, which avoids introducing new individuals x and y. The ambiguity could be resolved by expanding the sentence:

> *John and Peter are brothers of other people.*

The axiom associated with Mother is similar to the one for Brother:

> For every mother x, there is another person y who is a child of x.
> $(\forall x{:}\text{Mother})(\exists y{:}\text{Person})\text{childOf}(y,x)$.

The crucial difference between this axiom and the one for Brother is that the childOf relation, unlike the siblingOf relation, must be asymmetric: Mary and Susan cannot be children of one another. Therefore, the semantic ambiguity that is possible with brothers does not arise with mothers.

7.11 When the CG from Figure 7.25 is translated to the same ontology as Figure 7.24, the result has three copies of the [Support] concept instead of one. It is more general because it is logically implied by the version with only one copy. To convert the more general CG to the same form as Figure 7.24, use the following constraint: "If an object x and an object y both support an object z, then the two instances of support are identical." That constraint can be represented by the following if-then rule:

```
[If: [Object: *x]←(Inst)←[Support: *w1]→(Thme)→[Object: *z]
    [Object: *y]←(Inst)←[Support: *w2]→(Thme)→[Object: ?z]
    [Then: [Support: ?w1]- - -[Support: ?w2] ]].
```

Two applications of this rule to the more general CG will introduce coreference links between the three copies of [Support], enabling them to be joined to form a single concept [Support]. As another exercise, translate all the CGs including this rule to predicate calculus, and show that the same inferences can be performed.

7.13 It is usually easier to delete unneeded information than to add new information. The translation of music to a machine-dependent form requires information about the instrument, the human body, and the performance techniques of a highly skilled musician. Such translation could be automated for many routine stylized musical passages, but the most challenging musical compositions have passages that are difficult even for professional musicians. The amount of human time and effort required to write the programs to automate such translations would be greater than the time to do the translations by hand. A more promising approach is to invent a device for recording which fingers a professional musician uses during an actual performance.

Bibliography

*The greatest part of a writer's time is spent in reading, in order to write:
a man will turn over half a library to make one book.*
SAMUEL JOHNSON, BOSWELL'S *Life of Johnson, 6 April 1775*

Albertazzi, Liliana, ed. (1999) *Shapes of Forms,* Kluwer Academic Publishers, Dordrecht.

Alchourrón, Carlos, Peter Gärdenfors, & David Makinson (1985) "On the logic of theory change: partial meet contraction and revision functions," *Journal of Symbolic Logic* **50:2**, 510–530.

Allen, James F. (1983) "Maintaining knowledge about temporal intervals," *Communications of the ACM* **26:11**, 832–843.

Allen, James F. (1984) "Towards a general theory of action and time," *Artificial Intelligence,* **23**, 123–154.

Allen, James F., & Patrick J. Hayes (1985) "A common-sense theory of time," *Proceedings AAAI-85,* 528–531.

Amarel, Saul (1968) "On representations of problems of reasoning about actions," in D. Michie, ed., *Machine Intelligence 3,* American Elsevier, New York, pp. 131–171.

Anderson, Alan Ross, & Nuel D. Belnap, Jr. (1975) *Entailment: The Logic of Relevance and Necessity,* Princeton University Press, Princeton.

Antonacci, F., M. Russo, M. T. Pazienza, and P. Velardi, (1989) "System for text analysis and lexical knowledge acquisition," *Data and Knowledge Engineering,* **4:1**, 1–20.

Apel, Karl-Otto (1975) *Der Denkweg von Charles S. Peirce,* translated by J. M. Krois as *Charles S. Peirce: from Pragmatism to Pragmaticism,* University of Massachusetts Press, Amherst, 1981.

Apt, Krzysztof R., Howard A. Blair, & Adrian Walker (1988) "Towards a theory of declarative knowledge," in Minker (1988), pp. 89–144.

Arens, Hans (1984) *Aristotle's Theory of Language and Its Tradition,* John Benjamins Publishing Co., Amsterdam.

Arieti, Silvano (1978) "The psychobiology of sadness," in S. Arieti & J. Bemporad, *Severe and Mild Depression*, Basic Books, New York, pp. 109–128.

Aristotle, *The Categories, On Interpretation, Prior Analytics*, Harvard University Press, Cambridge, MA.

Aristotle, *Metaphysics*, Harvard University Press, Cambridge, MA.

Aristotle, *Posterior Analytics, Topica*, Harvard University Press, Cambridge, MA.

Aristotle, *On the Soul*, Harvard University Press, Cambridge, MA.

Aronson, Jerrold L., Rom Harré, and Eileen C. Way (1994) *Realism Rescued: How Scientific Progress is Possible*, Duckworth Publishers, London.

Augustine, St., *Confessions*, Harvard University Press, Cambridge, MA.

Badler, Norman I., Barry D. Reich, & Bonnie L. Weber (1997) "Towards personalities for animated agents with reactive and planning behaviors," in Trappl & Petta (1997), pp. 43–57.

Bartlett, Frederic C. (1932) *Remembering*, Cambridge University Press, Cambridge.

Barwise, Jon, Jean Mark Gawron, Gordon Plotkin, & Syun Tutiya, eds. (1991) *Situation Theory and Its Applications*, CSLI, Stanford, CA.

Barwise, Jon, & John Perry (1983) *Situations and Attitudes*, MIT Press, Cambridge, MA.

Bateman, John A., Robert T. Kasper, Johanna D. Moore, & Richard A. Whitney (1990) "A general organization of knowledge for natural language processing: The Penman Upper Model," Technical report, USC Information Sciences Institute, Marina del Rey, CA.

Bergson, Henri (1889) *Essai sur les données immédiates de la conscience*, translated by F. L. Pogson as *Time and Free Will*, Harper & Brothers, New York.

Bernus, Peter, Kai Mertins, & Günter Schmidt, eds. (1998) *Handbook on Architectures of Information Systems*, Springer Verlag, New York.

Beth, Evert W. (1939) *Symbolic logic as a continuation of traditional formal logic*, reprinted in E. W. Beth, *Science a Road to Wisdom*, D. Reidel Publishing Co., Dordrecht, pp. 42–61.

Beth, Evert W. (1955) *Semantic Entailment and Formal Derivability*, North-Holland Publishing Co., Amsterdam.

Binnick, Robert I. (1991) *Time and the Verb*, Oxford University Press, Oxford.

Bläsius, K. H., U. Hedstück, & C-R. Rollinger, eds. (1989) *Sorts and Types in Artificial Intelligence*, Lecture Notes in AI 418, Springer-Verlag, Berlin.

Bledsoe, Woody W. (1977) "Non-resolution theorem proving," *Artificial Intelligence* **9**, 1–35.

Bobrow, Daniel, & Terry Winograd (1977) "An overview of KRL, a Knowledge Representation Language," *Cognitive Science* **1:1**, 3–46.

Bocheński, Innocenty M. (1970) *A History of Formal Logic*, 2nd edition, Chelsea Publishing Co., New York.

Bohr, Niels (1934) *Atomic Theory and the Description of Nature*, Cambridge University Press, Cambridge, UK.

Bohr, Niels (1958) *Atomic Physics and Human Knowledge*, Wiley, New York.

Boole, George (1854) *An Investigation into the Laws of Thought*, reprinted by Dover Publications, New York.

Borges, Jorge Luis (1941) "La biblioteca de Babel" translated as "The library of Babel" in *Ficciones*, Grove Press, New York.

Born, Max (1949) *Natural Philosophy of Cause and Chance*, Dover Publications, New York.

Bowen, Kenneth A., & Robert A. Kowalski (1982) "Amalgamating language and metalanguage in logic programming," in K. L. Clark & S.-A. Tärnlund, eds., *Logic Programming*, Academic Press, New York, pp. 153–172.

Brachman, Ronald J. (1979) "On the epistemological status of semantic networks," in Findler (1979), 3–50.

Brachman, Ronald J. (1985) "'I lied about the trees,' Or defaults and definitions in knowledge representation," *AI Magazine* **6:3**, 80–93.

Brachman, Ronald J., Richard E. Fikes, & Hector J. Levesque (1983) "KRYPTON: A functional approach to knowledge representation," *IEEE Computer*, **16:10**, 67–73.

Brachman, Ronald J., V. P. Gilbert, & H. J. Levesque (1985) "An essential hybrid reasoning system," *Proceedings IJCAI-85*, pp. 532–539.

Brachman, Ronald J., & Hector J. Levesque, eds. (1985) *Readings in Knowledge Representation*, Morgan Kaufmann Publishers, San Mateo, CA.

Brachman, Ronald J., D. L. McGuinness, P. F. Patel-Schneider, L. A. Resnick, & A. Borgida (1991) "Living with Classic: when and how to use a KL-ONE-like language," in Sowa (1991) pp. 401–456.

Bratman, Michael (1987) *Intentions, Plans, and Practical Reason*, Harvard University Press, Cambridge, MA.

Brennan, Andrew (1988) *Conditions of Identity*, Clarendon Press, Oxford.

Brentano, Franz (1862) *Von der mannigfachen Bedeutung des Seienden nach Aristoteles*, translated by Rolf George as *On the Several Senses of Being in Aristotle*, University of California Press, Berkeley, 1975.

Brentano, Franz (1933) *Kategorienlehre*, translated by R. M. Chisholm & N. Guterman as *The Theory of Categories*, Martinus Nijhoff Publishers, The Hague, 1980.

Brewka, Gerhard, ed. (1996) *Principles of Knowledge Representation*, CSLI, Stanford, CA.

Brewka, Gerhard, Christopher Habel, & Bernhard Nebel, eds. (1997) *KI-97: Advances in Artificial Intelligence*, Lecture Notes in AI 1303, Springer Verlag, New York.

Brooks, Rodney A. (1986) "A robust layered control system for a mobile robot," *IEEE Journal of Robotics and Automation*, **RA-2:1**, 14–23.

Brooks, Rodney A. (1991) "Intelligence without representation," *Artificial Intelligence* **47**, 139–159.

Brown, Frank M., ed. (1987) *The Frame Problem in Artificial Intelligence*, Morgan Kaufmann Publishers, San Mateo, CA.

Brownston, Lee, Robert Farrell, Elaine Kant, & Nancy Martin (1985) *Programming Expert Systems in OPS5: An Introduction to Rule-Based Programming*, Addison-Wesley, Reading, MA.

Bruin, Jos de, & Remko Scha (1988) "The interpretation of relational nouns," *Proceedings of the ACL*, Buffalo, NY.

Brunning, Jacqueline, & Paul Forster, eds. (1997) *The Rule of Reason: The Philosophy of Charles Sanders Peirce*, University of Toronto Press, Toronto.

Buchanan, Bruce G., & Edward H. Shortliffe, eds. (1984) *Rule-Based Expert Systems*, Addison-Wesley, Reading, MA.

Bunt, Harry (1985) *Mass Terms and Model-Theoretic Semantics*, Cambridge University Press, Cambridge, UK.

Burke, Edmund (1796) *Thoughts on the Prospect of a Regicide Peace, in a Series of Letters*, Printed for J. Owen, London.

Burke, Edmund (1796) *Two Letters on the Proposals for Peace with the Regicide Directory*, reprinted in *The Correspondence of Edmund Burke*, ed. by T. W. Copeland, University of Chicago Press, Chicago, 10 vols., 1958–1978.

Burke, Tom (1991) "Peirce on truth and partiality," in Barwise et al. (1991), pp. 115–146.

Burnstine, Donald C. (1977) *The Theory Behind BIAIT — Business Information Analysis and Integration Technique*, BIAIT International, Petersburg, NY.

Bylander, Tom, Dean Allemang, Michael C. Tanner, & John R. Josephson (1991) "The computational complexity of abduction," *Artificial Intelligence*, **49**, 25–60.

Carlson, W. M. (1979) "The new horizon in business information analysis," *Data Base* **10:4**, 3–9.

Carnap, Rudolf (1928) *Der logische Aufbau der Welt*, translated as *The Logical Structure of the World*, University of California Press, Berkeley, 1967.

Carnap, Rudolf (1947) *Meaning and Necessity*, 2nd ed., University of Chicago Press, Chicago, 1956.

Carnap, Rudolf (1958) *Introduction to Symbolic Logic and Its Applications*, English edition, Dover, New York.

Carnap, Rudolf (1966) *An Introduction to the Philosophy of Science*, Dover, New York.

Carpenter, Bob (1992) *The Logic of Typed Feature Structures*, Cambridge University Press, Cambridge.

Carriero, Nicholas, & David Gelernter (1990) *How to Write Parallel Programs*, MIT Press, Cambridge, MA.

Casati, Roberto, & Achille C. Varzi (1994) *Holes and Other Superficialities*, MIT Press, Cambridge, MA.

Cattell, R. G. G., & Douglas K. Barry, eds. (1997) *The Object Database Standard, ODMG 2.0*, Morgan Kaufmann, San Francisco, CA.

Ceccato, Silvio (1961) *Linguistic Analysis and Programming for Mechanical Translation*, Gordon and Breach, New York.

Chamberlin, Don (1996) *Using the New DB2*, Morgan Kaufmann Publishers, San Francisco, CA.

Chandrasekaran, B. (1994) "Broader issues at stake: a reply to Elkan," *IEEE Expert* **9:4**, 10–13.

Chapman, D. (1989) "Penguins can make cake," *AI Magazine* **10:4**, 45–50.

Charniak, Eugene (1993) *Statistical Language Learning*, MIT Press, Cambridge, MA.

Chomsky, Noam (1957) *Syntactic Structures*, Mouton, The Hague.

Chomsky, Noam (1959) "A review of B. F. Skinner's *Verbal Behavior*," *Language* **35**, 26–58. Reprinted in Fodor & Katz (1964) 547–578.

Chomsky, Noam (1968) *Language and Mind*, Harcourt, Brace, & World, New York. Extended edition 1972.

Chomsky, Noam (1982) *Some Concepts and Consequences of the Theory of Government and Binding*, MIT Press, Cambridge, MA.

Chomsky, Noam (1995) *The Minimalist Program*, MIT Press, Cambridge, MA.

Church, Alonzo (1941) *The Calculi of Lambda Conversion*, Princeton University Press, Princeton, NJ.

Church, Alonzo (1989) "Intensionality and the paradox of the name relation," in J. Almog, J. Perry, & H. Wettstein, eds., *Themes from Kaplan*, Oxford University Press, New York.

Codd, E. F. (1979) "Extending the relational model to capture more meaning," *ACM Transactions on Database Systems* **4:4**, 397–434.

Coffa, J. Alberto (1991) *The Semantic Tradition from Kant to Carnap to the Vienna Station*, Cambridge University Press, Cambridge, UK.

Cohen, Philip R., & Hector J. Levesque (1990) "Intention is choice with commitment," *Artificial Intelligence* **42:3**, 213–261.

Cohn, Anthony G. (1997) "Qualitative spatial representation and reasoning techniques," in Brewka et al. (1997), pp. 1–30.

Cook, Stephen A. (1971) "The complexity of theorem-proving procedures," *Proceedings of the Third ACM Symposium on Theory of Computing*, ACM, New York, pp. 151–158.

Cooper, Robin, & Hans Kamp (1991) "Negation in situation semantics and discourse representation theory," in Barwise et al. (1991), pp. 311–333.

Craik, K. J. W. (1952) *The Nature of Explanation*, Cambridge University Press, Cambridge, UK.

Cresswell, M. J. (1990) *Entities and Indices*, Kluwer Academic Publishers, Dordrecht.

Cyre, W. R., S. Balachandar, & A. Thakar (1994) "Knowledge visualization from conceptual structures," in Tepfenhart et al. (1994) pp. 275–292.

Davidson, Donald (1967) "The logical form of action sentences," reprinted in D. Davidson (1980) *Essays on Actions and Events*, Clarendon Press, Oxford, UK, pp. 105–148.

Davis, Ernest (1990) *Representations of Commonsense Knowledge*, Morgan Kaufmann Publishers, San Mateo, CA.

Davis, Randall, Howard Schrobe, & Peter Szolovits (1993) "What is a knowledge representation?" *AI Magazine*, **14:1**, 17–33.

Dennet, Daniel C. (1987) *The Intentional Stance*, MIT Press, Cambridge, MA.

Dennet, Daniel C. (1996) *Kinds of Minds*, Basic Books, New York.

Devlin, Keith (1991) "Situations as mathematical abstractions," in Barwise et al. (1991), pp. 25–39.

Devlin, Keith, & Duska Rosenberg (1996) *Language at Work*, CSLI Publications, Stanford, CA.

Dick, Judith P. (1991) *A Conceptual Case-Relation Representation of Text for Information Retrieval*, PhD dissertation, Report CSRI-265, Computer Systems Research Institute, University of Toronto.

Dijkstra, Edsger W. (1982) *Selected Writings On Computing: A Personal Perspective*, Springer-Verlag, New York.

Dinsmore, John (1992) "Thunder in the gap," in J. Dinsmore, ed., *The Symbolic and Connectionist Paradigms: Closing the Gap*, Lawrence Erlbaum Associates, Hillsdale, NJ.

Doyle, Jon (1979) "A truth-maintenance system," *Artificial Intelligence* **12**, 231–272.

Doyle, Jon, & Ramesh S. Patil (1991) "Two theses of knowledge representation: language restrictions, taxonomic classification, and the utility of representation services," *Artificial Intelligence* **48:3**, 261–297.

Dreyfus, Hubert L. (1992) *What Computers Still Can't Do: A Critique of Artificial Reason*, MIT Press, Cambridge, MA.

Dummett, Michael (1994) *Origins of Analytical Philosophy*, Harvard University Press, Cambridge, MA.

Dunn, J. Michael (1973) "A truth value semantics for modal logic," in H. Leblanc, ed., *Truth, Syntax and Modality*, North-Holland, Amsterdam, pp. 87–100.

Eco, Umberto (1979) *A Theory of Semiotics*, Indiana University Press, Bloomington.

Eco, Umberto (1986) *Semiotics and the Philosophy of Language*, Indiana University Press, Bloomington.

Eco, Umberto (1990) *The Limits of Interpretation*, Indiana University Press, Bloomington.

Eddington, Arthur Stanley (1928) *The Nature of the Physical World*, Cambridge University Press, Cambridge.

Eklund, Peter W., Gerard Ellis, & Graham Mann, eds. (1996) *Conceptual Structures: Knowledge Representation as Interlingua*, Lecture Notes in AI 1115, Springer-Verlag, New York.

Elkan, Charles (1994) "The paradoxical sucess of fuzzy logic," *IEEE Expert* **9:4**, pp. 3–8 and 47–49.

Ellis, Gerard (1992) "Compiled hierarchical retrieval," in T. Nagle, J. Nagle, L. Gerholz, and P. Eklund, eds., *Conceptual Structures: Current Research and Practice*, Ellis Horwood, New York, pp. 271–294.

Ellis, Gerard (1995) "Object-oriented conceptual graphs," in Ellis et al. (1995) pp. 144–157.

Ellis, Gerard, Robert A. Levinson, & Peter J. Robinson (1994) "Managing complex objects in Peirce," *International Journal of Human-Computer Studies*, **41**, 109–148.

Ellis, Gerard, Robert A. Levinson, William Rich, & John F. Sowa, eds. (1995), *Conceptual Structures: Applications, Implementation, and Theory*, Lecture Notes in AI 954, Springer-Verlag, Berlin.

Ellis, John M. (1993) *Language, Thought, and Logic*, Northwestern University Press, Evanston, IL.

Embley, David W. (1998) *Object Database Development*, Addison-Wesley, Reading, MA.

Ennis, R. L., J. H. Griesmer, S. J. Hong, M. Karnaugh, J. K. Kastner, D. A. Klein, K. R. Milliken, M. I. Schor, & H. M. Van Woerkom (1986) "A continuous real-time expert system for computer operations," *IBM Journal of Research and Development* **30:1**, 14–28.

Esch, John, & Robert Levinson (1995) "An implementation model for contexts and negation in conceptual graphs," in Ellis et al. (1995), pp. 247–262.

Etherington, David, & Ray Reiter (1983) "On inheritance hierarchies with exceptions," *Proc. AAAI'83*, pp. 104–108.

Euclid, *The Thirteen Books of the Elements*, translated by T. L. Heath, Dover Publications, New York.

Faggin, Federico, Marcian E. Hoff, Stanley Mazor, & Masatoshi Shima (1996) "The history of the 4004," *IEEE Micro* **16:6**, 10–20.

Fahlman, Scott E. (1979) *NETL: A System for Representing and Using Real-World Knowledge*, MIT Press, Cambridge, MA.

Fann, K. T. (1970) *Peirce's Theory of Abduction*, Martinus Nijhoff, The Hague.

Fargues, Jean, Marie Claude Landau, Anne Dugourd, & Laurent Catach (1986) "Conceptual graphs for semantics and knowledge processing," *IBM Journal of Research and Development* **30:1**, 70–79.

Faye, Jan, & Henry J. Folce, eds. (1994) *Niels Bohr and Contemporary Philosophy*, Kluwer Academic Publishers, Dordrecht.

Feigenbaum, Edward A., & Julian Feldman, eds. (1963) *Computers and Thought*, McGraw-Hill, New York.

Fellbaum, Christiane, ed. (1998) *WordNet: An Electronic Lexical Database*, MIT Press, Cambridge, MA.

Ferriani, Maurizio (1987) "Peirce's analysis of the proposition: grammatical and logical aspects," in D. Buzzetti & M. Ferriani, eds., *Speculative Grammar, Universal Grammar, and Philosophical Analysis of Language*, John Benjamins Publishing Co., Amsterdam, pp. 149–172.

Field, Hartry H. (1980) *Science Without Numbers: A Defense of Nominalism*, Princeton University Press, Princeton.

Fikes, Richard E., & Nils J. Nilsson (1971) "STRIPS: A new approach to the application of theorem proving to problem solving," *Artificial Intelligence* **2**, 189–208.

Fillmore, Charles J. (1968) "The case for case" in E. Bach & R. T. Harms, eds., *Universals in Linguistic Theory*, Holt, Rinehart and Winston, New York, pp. 1–88.

Fillmore, Charles J. (1973) "May we come in?" *Semiotica*, vol. 9, pp. 97–116.

Findler, Nicholas V., ed. (1979) *Associative Networks: Representation and Use of Knowledge by Computers*, Academic Press, New York.

Finke, Ronald A. (1989) *Principles of Mental Imagery*, MIT Press, Cambridge, MA.

Fodor, Jerry (1975) *The Language of Thought*, Harvard University Press, Cambridge, MA.

Fodor, Jerry (1981) *Representations*, MIT Press, Cambridge, MA.

Fodor, Jerry (1983) *The Modularity of Mind*, MIT Press, Cambridge, MA.

Foo, Norman (1995) "Ontology revision," in Ellis et. al (1995), pp. 16–31.

Ford, Kenneth M., & Patrick J. Hayes (1991) *Reasoning Agents in a Dynamic World: The Frame Problem*, JAI Press, Greenwich, CT.

Fowler, Martin (1997) *UML Distilled: Analyzing the Standard Object Modeling Language*, Addison Wesley, Reading, MA.

Frege, Gottlob (1879) *Begriffsschrift*, translated in Jean van Heijenoort, ed. (1967) *From Frege to Gödel*, Harvard University Press, Cambridge, MA, pp. 1–82.

Freuder, Eugene C., & Alan K. Mackworth (1994) *Constraint-Based Reasoning*, MIT Press, Cambridge, MA.

Frost, Robert (1963) *A Lover's Quarrel with the World* (film), WGBH Educational Foundation, Boston.

Fuchs, Norbert E., Uta Schwertel, Rolf Schwitter (1998) "Attempto Controlled English — not just another logic specification language," *Proceedings LOPSTR'98*, Manchester. Available from http://www.ifi.unizh.ch/~fuchs/.

Gabbay, Dov M. (1994) *What is a Logical System*, Clarendon Press, Oxford.

Gallaire, Hervé, & Jack Minker, eds. (1978) *Logic and Data Bases*, Plenum Press, New York.

Ganter, Bernhard, & Rudolf Wille (1996) *Formale Begriffsanalyze: Mathematische Grundlagen*, Springer-Verlag, Berlin.

Gärdenfors, Peter (1988) *Knowledge in Flux: Modeling the Dynamics of Epistemic States*, MIT Press, Cambridge, MA.

Gardner, Martin (1958) *Logic Machines and Diagrams*, McGraw-Hill, New York.

Garner, Brian J., & Eric Tsui, (1988) "General purpose inference engine for canonical graph models," *Knowledge Based Systems* **1:5**, 266–278.

Geertz, Clifford (1983) *Local Knowledge*, Basic Books, New York.

Gelernter, David (1985) "Generative communication in Linda," *ACM Transactions on Programming Languages and Systems*, pp. 80–112.

Gell-Mann, Murray (1994) *The Quark and the Jaguar*, W. H. Freeman & Co., New York.

Genesereth, Michael R., & Richard Fikes, eds. (1998) *Knowledge Interchange Format (KIF)*, draft proposed American National Standard, NCITS.T2/98–004. Available at http://logic.stanford.edu/kif/dpans.html.

Gentzen, Gerhard (1935) "Untersuchungen über das logische Schliessen I II," English version in *The Collected Papers of Gerhard Gentzen*, North-Holland Publishing Co., Amsterdam, pp. 68–131.

Gergely, Tamás, & László Úry (1991) *First-Order Programming Theories*, Springer-Verlag, New York.

Giarratano, Joseph, & Gary Riley (1994) *Expert Systems: Principles and Programming*, 2nd ed., PWS Publishing, Boston.

Ginsberg, Matthew L., ed. (1987) *Readings in Nonmonotonic Reasoning*, Morgan Kaufmann Publishers, San Mateo, CA.

Ginsberg, Matthew L. (1989a) "Universal planning: an (almost) universally bad idea," *AI Magazine* **10:4**, 40–44.

Ginsberg, Matthew L. (1989b) "Universal planning research: a good or bad idea?," *AI Magazine* **10:4**, 61–62.

Glasgow, Janice I. (1993) "The imagery debate revisited: A computational perspective," *Computational Intelligence*, **9:4**, 309–333.

Glasgow, Janice, N. Hari Narayanan, & B. Chandrasekaran, eds. (1995) *Diagrammatic Reasoning: Cognitive and Computational Perspectives*, MIT Press, Cambridge, MA.

Goldstein, I., & B. Roberts (1977) "NUDGE: A knowledge-based scheduling program," *Proceedings of the Fifth IJCAI*, pp. 257–263.

Goldstine, Herman H., & John von Neumann (1947) *Planning and Coding of Problems for an Electronic Computing Instrument*, Institute for Advanced Study, Princeton, NJ.

Goodman, Nelson (1951) *The Structure of Appearance*, Bobbs-Merrill Co., New York. Second edition 1966.

Goodman, Nelson (1956) "A world of individuals," reprinted in Goodman (1972), pp. 155– 172.

Goodman, Nelson (1963) "The significance of *Der logische Aufbau der Welt*," in P. A. Schilpp, ed., *The Philosophy of Rudolf Carnap*, Open Court, La Salle, IL, pp. 545–558.

Goodman, Nelson (1972) *Problems and Projects*, Bobbs-Merrill Co., New York.

Gray, J. Glenn (1977) "Heidegger on remembering and remembering Heidegger," *Man and World*, vol. 10, p. 77.

Grice, H. Paul (1975) "Logic and conversation," in P. Cole & J. Morgan, eds., *Syntax and Semantics 3: Speech Acts*, Academic Press, New York, pp. 41–58.

Grosof, Benjamin N. (1992) *Updating and Structure in Nonmonotonic Theories*, PhD Dissertation, Computer Science Department, Stanford University, Palo Alto, CA.

Grosof, Benjamin N. (1997) "Building commercial agents," *Proceedings PAAM'97*. For more information and copies of the software, see http://www.research.ibm.com/iagents/.

Grosof, Benjamin N. (1997) "Prioritized conflict handling for logic programs," *Proc. International Symposium on Logic Programming*. Extended version available as IBM Research Report RC 20836, http://www.research.ibm.com/people/g/grosof/.

Gruber, Thomas R. (1993) "A translation approach to portable ontology specifications," *Knowledge Acquisition*, **5**, 199–220.

Grünwald, Peter (1997) "Causation and nonmonotonic temporal reasoning," in Brewka et al. (1997), pp. 159–170. Extended presentation available in Technical Report INS-R9701, ftp://ftp.cwi.nl/pub/pdg/R9701.ps.Z.

Guarino, Nicola, ed. (1998) *Formal Ontology in Information Systems*, IOS Press, Amsterdam.

Guarino, Nicola, Stefano Borgo, & Claudio Masolo (1997) "Logical modeling of product knowledge: towards a well-founded semantics for STEP," in *Proceedings of the European Conference on Product Data Technology*, Sophia Antipolis, France.

Guha, R. V. (1991) *Contexts: A Formalization and Some Applications*, Technical Report ACT-CYC-423–91, MCC, Austin, TX.

Guha, R. V., & Douglas B. Lenat (1994) "Enabling agents to work together," *Communications of the ACM*, **37:7**, 127–142.

Haack, Susan (1978) *Philosophy of Logics*, Cambridge University Press, Cambridge, UK.

Haack, Susan (1996) *Deviant Logic, Fuzzy Logic*, University of Chicago Press, Chicago.

Hallaq, Wael B. (1993) *Ibn Taymiyya Against the Greek Logicians*, Clarendon Press, Oxford.

Hamlyn, D. W. (1968) "Translation, introduction, and notes to Aristotle's *De Anima*," Clarendon Press, Oxford. Second edition 1993.

Hamming, Richard (1962) *Numerical Methods for Scientists and Engineers*, McGraw-Hill, New York.

Hanks, Steven, & Drew McDermott (1987) "Nonmonotonic logic and temporal projection," *Artificial Intelligence* **33**, 379–412.

Hansen, Hans Robert, Robert Mühlbacher, & Gustaf Neumann (1992) *Begriffsbasierte Integration von Systemanalysemethoden*, Physica-Verlag, Heidelberg, Germany.

Hartley, Roger T., & Michael J. Coombs (1991) "Reasoning with graph operations," in J. F. Sowa, ed., *Principles of Semantic Networks: Explorations in the Representation of Knowledge*, Morgan Kaufmann Publishers, San Mateo, CA, pp. 487–505.

Hawkins, Benjamin S. (1981) "Peirce's and Frege's systems of notation," *Proceedings C. S. Peirce Bicentennial International Congress*, Texas Tech Press, Lubbock, TX.

Hayes, Patrick J. (1977) "In defense of logic," in *Proceedings of the Fifth IJCAI*, pp. 559–565.

Hayes, Patrick J. (1979) "The logic of frames," in D. Metzing, ed., *Frame Conceptions and*

Text Understanding, Walter de Gruyter & Co., Berlin. Reprinted in Brachman & Levesque (1985), pp. 287–295.

Hayes, Patrick J. (1985) "Naive physics I: Ontology for liquids," in Hobbs & Moore (1985), pp. 71–107.

Hays, David G. (1964) "Dependency theory: a formalism and some observations," *Language* **40**, pp. 511–525.

Hegel, Georg Wilhelm Friedrich (1831) *Wissenschaft der Logik*, translated by A. V. Miller as *Hegel's Science of Logic*, Humanities Press International, Atlantic Highlands, NJ.

Heidegger, Martin (1927) *Sein und Zeit* translated by J. Hofstadter & E. Robinson as *Being and Time*, HarperCollins, New York.

Heidegger, Martin (1975) *Die Grundprobleme der Phänomenologie*, translated by A. Hofstadter as *The Basic Problems of Phenomenology*, Indiana University Press, Bloomington.

Heidegger, Martin (1978) *Metaphysische Anfangsgründe der Logik im Ausgang von Leibniz*, translated by M. Heim as *The Metaphysical Foundations of Logic*, Indiana University Press, Bloomington.

Heraclitus, *Fragments*, in C. H. Kahn (1979), *The Art and Thought of Heraclitus*, Cambridge University Press, Cambridge, UK.

Hewitt, Carl (1971) *Description and Theoretical Analysis (Using Schemata) of PLANNER*, PhD dissertation, AI Memo 258, MIT, Cambridge, MA.

Hilbert, David (1899) *Grundlagen der Geometrie*, translated as *The Foundations of Geometry* (1971), Open Court Classics, La Salle, IL.

Hill, Patricia M., & John W. Lloyd (1994) *The Gödel Programming Language*, MIT Press, Cambridge, MA.

Hilpinen, Risto (1982) "On C. S. Peirce's theory of the proposition: Peirce as a precursor of game-theoretical semantics," *The Monist* **65**, pp. 182–188.

Hintikka, Jaakko (1961) "Modality and quantification," *Theoria* **27**, pp. 110–128.

Hintikka, Jaakko (1963) "The modes of modality," *Acta Philosophica Fennica, Modal and Many-valued Logics*, pp. 65–81.

Hintikka, Jaakko (1973) *Logic, Language Games, and Information*, Clarendon Press, Oxford.

Hintikka, Jaakko (1985) *The Game of Language*, D. Reidel Publishing Co., Dordrecht.

Hirota, K., ed. (1993) *Industrial Applications of Fuzzy Technology*, Springer-Verlag, New York.

Hoare, C. A. R. (1969) "An axiomatic basis for computer programming," *Communications of the ACM* **12:10**, pp. 567–580, 583.

Hobbs, Jerry R. (1995) "Sketch of an ontology underlying the way we talk about the world," *International Journal of Human-Computer Studies* **43**, pp. 819–830.

Hobbs, Jerry R., & Robert C. Moore, eds. (1985) *Formal Theories of the Commonsense World*, Ablex Publishing Co., Norwood, NJ.

Hobbs, J. R., M. E. Stickel, D. E. Appelt, & P. Martin (1993) "Interpretation as abduction," *Artificial Intelligence*, **63:1–2**, 69–142.

Hoopes, James, ed. (1991) *Peirce on Signs*, University of North Carolina Press, Chapel Hill.

Houser, N., D. D. Robers, & J. Van Evra, eds. (1997) *Studies in the Logic of Charles Sanders Peirce*, Indiana University Press, Bloomington.

Hume, David (1748) *An Inquiry Concerning Human Understanding*, Liberal Arts Press, New York.

Husserl, Edmund (1900–01) *Logische Untersuchungen*, 2nd ed., translated by J. N. Findlay as *Logical Investigations*, Routledge & Kegan Paul, London, 1973.

Husserl, Edmund (1913) *Ideen auf einer reinen Phänomenologie und phänomenologischen Philosophie*, translated by F. Kersten as *Ideas Pertaining to a Pure Phenomenology and to a Phenomenological Philosophy*, Kluwer, Dordrecht, 1982.

Jakobson, Roman (1978) *Six Lectures on Sound and Meaning*, MIT Press, Cambridge, MA.

Jakobson, Roman (1980) *The Framework of Language*, Rackham School of Graduate Studies, Ann Arbor, MI.

James, William (1897) *The Will to Believe and Other Essays*, Longmans, Green & Co.

Jensen, Karen, George E. Heidorn, & Stephen D. Richardson, eds. (1993) *Natural Language Processing: The PLNLP Approach*, Kluwer, Boston, 1993.

Jensen, Kurt (1992) *Coloured Petri Nets*, vol. 1, Springer-Verlag, New York.

Johnson, Mark (1987) *The Body in the Mind*, University of Chicago Press, Chicago.

Kamp, Hans (1981a) "Events, discourse representations, and temporal references," *Languages* **64**, 39–64.

Kamp, Hans (1981b) "A theory of truth and semantic representation," in *Formal Methods in the Study of Language*, J. A. G. Groenendijk, T. M. V. Janssen, & M. B. J. Stokhof, eds., Mathematical Centre Tracts, Amsterdam, 277–322.

Kamp, Hans, & Uwe Reyle (1993) *From Discourse to Logic*, Kluwer, Dordrecht.

Kanazawa, Makoto, & Christopher J. Piñón, eds. (1994) *Dynamics, Polarity, and Quantification*, CSLI Publications, Stanford, CA.

Kant, Immanuel (circa 1780) *Wiener Logik*, in *Kants gesammelte Schriften*, vol. 24, De Gruyter & Reimer, Berlin, 1910–1983.

Kant, Immanuel (1787) *Kritik der reinen Vernunft*, translated by N. Kemp Smith as *Critique of Pure Reason*, St. Martin's Press, New York.

Kant, Immanuel (1800) *Logik: Ein Handbuch zu Vorlesungen*, translated by R. S. Hartmann & W. Schwarz as *Logic*, Dover Publications, New York, 1988; also translated as *Lectures on Logic* by J. M. Young, Cambridge University Press, Cambridge, 1992.

Karp, Peter D. (1992) "The design space of frame knowledge representation systems," Technical Note No. 520, SRI International, Menlo Park, CA.

Karttunen, Lauri (1976) "Discourse referents," in J. McCawley, ed., *Syntax and Semantics* vol. 7, Academic Press, New York, pp. 363–385.

Kasper, Robert T. (1993) "Typed feature constraint systems," in H. Trost, ed., *Feature Formalisms and Linguitic Ambiguity*, Ellis Horwood, New York, pp. 1–19.

Katz, Jerrold J. (1966) *The Philosophy of Language*, Harper & Row, New York.

Kayser, Daniel (1988) "What kind of thing is a concept?" *Computational Intelligence* **4:2**, 158–165.

Ketner, Kenneth Laine, ed. (1995) *Peirce and Contemporary Thought*, Fordham University Press, New York.

Kluge, Werner (1992) *The Organization of Reduction, Data Flow, and Control Flow Systems*, MIT Press, Cambridge, MA.

Kolodner, Janet L. (1993) *Case-Based Reasoning*, Morgan Kaufmann Publishers, San Mateo, CA.

Konolige, Kurt (1997) "COLBERT: A language for adaptive control in SAPHIRA," in Brewka et al. (1997), pp. 31–52.

Kowalski, Robert A. (1979) *Logic for Problem Solving*, North Holland, New York.

Kowalski, Robert A. (1994) "Logic without model theory," in Dov M. Gabbay, ed., *What is a Logical System?*, Clarendon Press, Oxford, pp. 35–71.

Kowalski, Robert A. (1995) "Using metalogic to reconcile reactive with rational agents," in K. R. Apt & F. Turini, eds. (1995) *Metalogics and Logic Programming*, MIT Press, Cambridge, MA, pp. 227–242.

Krantz, Luce, Suppes, & Tversky (1971) *Foundations of Measurement*, vol. I, Academic Press, New York.

Kretzmann, Norman, & Eleonore Stump, eds. (1988) *The Cambridge Translations of Medieval Philosophical Texts, Volume One: Logic and the Philosophy of Language*, Cambridge University Press, Cambridge, UK.

Kripke, Saul A. (1963a) "Semantical considerations on modal logic," *Acta Philosophica Fennica, Modal and Many-valued Logics*, 83–94.

Kripke, Saul A. (1963b) "Semantical analysis of modal logic I," *Zeitschrift für mathematische Logik und Grundlagen der Mathematik* **9**, 67–96.

Kuipers, Benjamin J. (1984) "Commonsense reasoning about causality: deriving behavior from structure," *Artificial Intelligence* **24**, 169–203.

Kuipers, Benjamin (1994) *Qualitative Reasoning: Modeling and Simulation with Incomplete Knowledge*, MIT Press, Cambridge, MA. For related information, see http://www.cs.utexas.edu/users/qr.

Lakoff, George (1987) *Women, Fire, and Dangerous Things*, University of Chicago Press, Chicago.

Lakoff, George, & Mark Johnson (1999) *Philosophy in the Flesh*, Basic Books, New York.

Lambert, Karel (1967) "Free logic and the concept of existence," *Notre Dame Journal of Formal Logic*, vol. 8, pp. 133–144.

Lambert, Karel, ed. (1991) *Philosophical Applications of Free Logic*, Oxford University Press, New York.

Lao-Tzu, *Te Tao Ching*, translated by R. G. Henricks, Ballantine Books, New York, 1989.

Lehmann, Fritz, ed. (1992) *Semantic Networks in Artificial Intelligence*, Pergamon Press, Oxford.

Lehmann, Fritz, & Anthony G. Cohn (1994) "The egg-yolk reliability hierarchy: Semantic data integration using sorts with prototypes," *Proceedings of the Conference on Information and Knowledge Management, CIKM-94*, ACM Press, New York.

Leibniz, Gottfried Wilhelm, *Selections*, P. P. Wiener, ed., Charles Scribner's Sons, New York.

Leibniz, Gottfried Wilhelm (1705) *Nouveaux Essais concernant l'Entendement humain*, translated as *New Essays on Human Understanding*, P. Remnant & J. Bennet, Cambridge University Press, Cambridge, 1981.

Lenat, Douglas B. (1995) "CYC: A large-scale investment in knowledge infrastructure," *Communications of the ACM* **38:11**, 33–38. For further information, see http://www.cyc.com.

Lenat, Douglas B., & R. V. Guha (1990) *Building Large Knowledge-Based Systems*, Addison-Wesley, Reading, MA.

Lenat, D. B., G. A. Miller, & T. Yokoi (1995) "CYC, WordNet, and EDR: Critiques and Responses," *Communications of the ACM* **38:11**, 45–48.

Leonard, H. S., & N. Goodman (1940) "The calculus of individuals and its uses," *Journal of Symbolic Logic* **5**, 45–55.

Leśniewski, Stanisław (1992) *Collected Works*, S. J. Surma, J. T. Srzednicki, D. J. Barnett, & V. F. Rickey, eds., Martinus Nijhoff, The Hague.

Levesque, Hector J. (1986) "Making believers out of computers," *Artificial Intelligence*, vol. 30, pp. 81–108.

Levesque, Hector J. (1989) "A knowledge-level account of abduction," *Proceedings IJCAI-89*, 1061–1067.

Levesque, H. J., R. Reiter, Y. Lespérance, F. Lin, & R. Scherl (1996) "GOLOG: A logic-programming language for dynamic domains," *Journal of Logic Programming*.

Levi, Isaac (1980) *The Enterprise of Knowledge*, MIT Press, Cambridge, MA.

Levi, Isaac (1991) *The Fixation of Belief and its Undoing*, Cambridge University Press, New York.

Levi, Isaac (1996) *For the Sake of Argument*, Cambridge University Press, New York.

Levin, Beth (1993) *English Verb Classes and Alternations*, University of Chicago Press, Chicago.

Levinson, Robert A. (1989) "A self-learning, pattern-oriented chess program," *International Computer Chess Association Journal*, **12:4**, 207–215.

Levinson, Robert A. (1992) "Pattern associativity and the retrieval of semantic networks," *Computers and Mathematics with Applications*, **23:6–9**, 573–600. Reprinted in Lehmann (1992).

Levinson, Robert A., & Gerard Ellis (1992) "Multilevel hierarchical retrieval," *Knowledge Based Systems*, **5:3**, 233–244.

Levinson, Robert A. (1993) "Towards domain-independent machine intelligence," in Mineau et al. (1993), pp. 254–273.

Levinson, Robert A., Brian Beach, Richard Snyder, Tal Dayan, & Kirack Sohn (1992) "Adaptive-predictive game-playing programs," *JETAI*, **4**, 315–337.

Lewis, Clarence Irving (1918) *Survey of Symbolic Logic*, University of California Press, Berkeley.

Lewis, Clarence Irving, & C. H. Langford (1932) *Symbolic Logic*, Dover, New York.

Lewis, David (1991) *Parts of Classes*, Basil Blackwell, Oxford.

Lewis, Frank A. (1991) *Substance and Predication in Aristotle*, Cambridge University Press, Cambridge.

Łukasiewicz, Jan (1930) "Many-valued systems of propositional logic," reprinted in S. McCall, ed., *Polish Logic*, Oxford University Press, Oxford, 1967.

Lukose, Dickson, Harry Delugach, Mary Keeler, Leroy Searle, & John Sowa, eds. (1997) *Conceptual Structures: Fulfilling Peirce's Dream*, Lecture Notes in AI #1257, Springer-Verlag, New York.

Lull, Ramon (1303) *De nova Logica*, reprinted in *Raimondi Lulli Opera Latina*, ed. by Walter Euler, Brepols, Turnhold, Belgium, 1998.

Lull, Ramon (1308) *Ars brevis*, translated in *Doctor Illuminatus: A Ramon Lull Reader*, ed. by A. Bonner, Princeton University Press, Princeton, 1993.

Luschei, E. C. (1962) *The Logical Systems of Leśniewski*, North-Holland, Amsterdam, 1962.

MacGregor, Robert M. (1994) "A description classifier for the predicate calculus," *Proceedings of AAAI 94*, pp. 213–220.

Maida, Anthony S., & Stuart C. Shapiro (1982) "Intensional concepts in propositional semantic networks," *Cognitive Science*, vol. 6, no. 4, pp. 291–330.

Malcolm, Norman (1977) *Thought and Knowledge*, Cornell University Press, Ithaca, NY.

Manzano, María (1996) *Extensions of First-Order Logic*, Cambridge University Press, Cambridge, UK.

Marek, V. W., & M. Truszczyński (1993) *Nonmonotonic Logic: Context-Dependent Reasoning*, Springer-Verlag, New York.

McCammon, R. B. (1990) "Maintaining Prospector II as a full-sized knowledge based system," *AISIG '90 Research Workshop on Full-Sized Knowledge Base Systems Working Papers*, IEEE Computer Society, pp. 1-14–1-32.

McCarthy, John (1960) "Recursive functions of symbolic expressions and their computation by machine," *Communications of the ACM*, **3:4**, 184–195.

McCarthy, John (1963) "Situations, actions, and causal laws," Stanford AI Project Memo No. 2. Reprinted in Minsky (1968), pp. 410–418.

McCarthy, John (1977) "Epistemological problems of artificial intelligence," *Proceedings of IJCAI-77*. Reprinted in McCarthy (1990).

McCarthy, John (1979) "First-order theories of individual concepts and propositions," in J. E. Hayes & D. Michie, eds., *Machine Intelligence*, vol. 6, Wiley, New York, pp. 129–147.

McCarthy, John (1980) "Circumscription — a form of nonmonotonic reasoning," *Artificial Intelligence* **13**, 27–39, 171–172.

McCarthy, John (1981) "History of LISP," in R. L. Wexelblat, ed., *History of Programming Languages*, Academic Press, New York, pp. 173–197.

McCarthy, John (1990) *Formalizing Common Sense*, Ablex, Norwood, NJ.

McCarthy, John (1993) "Notes on formalizing context," *Proceedings of IJCAI-93*, Chambéry, France, pp. 555–560.

McCarthy, John (1997) "Elaboration tolerance," available at http://www-formal.stanford.edu/jmc/elaboration.html.

McCarthy, John, & Saša Buvač (1994) *Formalizing Context*, Technical Note STAN-CS-TN-94–13, Stanford University. Available at http://sail.stanford.edu.

McCarthy, John, & Patrick Hayes (1969) "Some philosophical problems from the standpoint of artificial intelligence," in B. Meltzer & D. Michie, eds., *Machine Learning 4*, Edinburgh University Press.

McCarthy, John, & Patrick J. Hayes (1969) "Some philosophical problems from the standpoint of artificial intelligence," in D. Michie & B. Meltzer, eds., *Machine Intelligence* vol. 4, Wiley, New York, pp. 463–502.

McDermott, Drew V. (1976) "Artificial intelligence meets natural stupidity," *SIGART Newsletter*, no. 57, ACM.

McDermott, Drew V. (1987) "A critique of pure reason," *Computational Intelligence* **3**, 151–160.

McDermott, Drew V. (1987) "AI, logic, and the frame problem," in Brown (1987), pp. 105–118.

Meinke, K., & J. V. Tucker (1993) *Many-Sorted Logic and Its Applications*, Wiley, New York.

Mich, L. (1996) "NL-OOPS: from natural language to object-oriented requirements using the natural language processing system LOLITA," *Natural Language Engineering* **2:2**, 161–187.

Mill, John Stuart (1865) *A System of Logic*, Longmans, London.

Mill, John Stuart (1867) "Inaugural Address at St. Andrews University," reprinted in J. M. Robson, ed., *John Stuart Mill, A Selection of His Works*, The Odyssey Press, New York, pp. 379–420.

Miller, George A. (1995) "WordNet: a lexical database for English," *Communications of the ACM* **38:11**, 39–41. For copies of the database and associated software, see http://www. cogsci.princeton.edu/~wn/.

Miller, G. A., R. Beckwith, C. Fellbaum, D. Gross, & K. J. Miller (1990) "WordNet: an on-line lexical database," *International Journal of Lexicography*, **3:4**, 235–312.

Mineau, Guy W., Bernard Moulin, & John F. Sowa, eds. (1993) *Conceptual Graphs for Knowledge Representation*, Lecture Notes in AI 699, Springer-Verlag, New York.

Minker, Jack, ed. (1988) *Foundations of Deductive Databases and Logic Programming*, Morgan Kaufmann Publishers, San Mateo, CA.

Minsky, Marvin (1965) "Matter, mind and models," *Proceedings of IFIP Congress 65*, pp. 45–49.

Minsky, Marvin, ed. (1968) *Semantic Information Processing*, MIT Press, Cambridge, MA.

Minsky, Marvin (1975) "A framework for representing knowledge," in P. Winston, ed., *The Psychology of Computer Vision*, McGraw-Hill, New York, pp. 211–280.

Minsky, Marvin (1987) *The Society of Mind*, Simon & Schuster, New York.

Minsky, Marvin (1991) "Logical versus analogical or symbolic versus connectionist or neat versus scruffy," *AI Magazine* **12:2**, summer 1991, 34–51.

Moffat, David, & Nico H. Frijda (1995) "Where there's a *Will* there's an agent," in Wooldridge & Jennings (1995b), pp. 245 ff.

Montague, Richard (1970) "English as a formal language," reprinted in Montague (1974), pp. 188–221.

Montague, Richard (1973) "The proper treatment of quantification in English," reprinted in Montague (1974), pp. 247–270.

Montague, Richard (1974) *Formal Philosophy*, Yale University Press, New Haven, CT.

Moore, Robert C. (1985) "Semantic considerations on nonmonotonic logic," *Artificial Intelligence* **25:1**.

Moore, Robert C. (1995) *Logic and Representation*, CSLI, Stanford, CA.

Moravcsik, Julius M. (1991) "What makes reality intelligible? Reflections on Aristotle's theory of *aitia*," in L. Judson, ed., *Aristotle's Physics: A Collection of Essays*, Clarendon Press, pp. 31–47.

Morris, Charles (1946) *Signs, Language, and Behavior*, Braziller, New York.

Moulin, Bernard (1995) "Discourse spaces: a pragmatic interpretation of contexts," in Ellis et al. (1995), pp. 89–104.

Mugnier, Marie-Laure, & Michel Chein, eds. (1998) *Conceptual Structures: Theory, Tools, and Applications*, Lecture Notes in AI 1453, Springer-Verlag, Berlin.

Nagle, T. E., J. A. Nagle, L. L. Gerholz, & P. W. Eklund, eds. (1992) *Conceptual Structures: Current Research and Practice*, Ellis Horwood, New York.

NCITS T2 (1998) *Conceptual Graphs, A Presentation Language for Knowledge in Conceptual Schemas*, Working draft of proposed American national standard, Document No. X3T2/96–008.

NCITS T2 (1998) *Knowledge Interchange Format*, Working draft of proposed American national standard, document.

Newell, Allen, J. C. Shaw, & Herbert A. Simon (1959) "A general problem-solving program for a computer," *Computers and Automation* **8**:7, 10–16.

Newell, Allen, & Herbert A. Simon (1961) "GPS, a program that simulates human thought," reprinted in Feigenbaum & Feldman (1963), pp. 279–293.

Newell, Allen, & Herbert A. Simon (1972) *Human Problem Solving*, Prentice-Hall, Englewood Cliffs, NJ.

Newton, Isaac (1687) *Philosophiae Naturalis Principia*, translated by Andrew Motte as *The Principia*, Prometheus Books, Amherst, NY.

Nijssen, G. M., & T. A. Halpin (1989) *Conceptual Schema and Relational Database Design*, Prentice-Hall, New York.

Nilsson, Nils (1986) *"Probabilistic logic,"* *Artificial Intelligence* **28**, 71–87.

Nussbaum, Martha C., & Hilary Putnam (1992) "Changing Aristotle's mind," in M. C. Nussbaum & A. O. Rorty, eds., *Essays on Aristotle's De Anima*, Oxford University Press, Oxford. Reprinted in H. Putnam, *Words and Life*, Harvard University Press, Cambridge, MA, pp. 22–61.

Ockham, William (1323) *Summa Logicae*, Part II, translated as *Ockham's Theory of Propositions* (1980) by A. J. Freddoso & H. Schuurman, University of Notre Dame Press, Notre Dame, IN.

Ogden, C. K., & I. A. Richards (1923) *The Meaning of Meaning*, Harcourt, Brace, and World, New York, 8th ed., 1946.

Øhrstrøm, Peter, & Per F. V. Hasle (1995) *Temporal Logic: From Ancient Ideas to Artificial Intelligence*, Kluwer, Dordrecht.

Ortony, Andrew, ed. (1993) *Metaphor and Thought*, 2nd ed., Cambridge University Press, Cambridge., UK.

Parsons, Terence (1990) *Events in the Semantics of English*, MIT Press, Cambridge, MA.

Pearl, Judea (1986) "Fusion, propagation, and structuring in belief networks," *Artificial Intelligence* **29**, 241–288. Reprinted in Shafer & Pearl (1990).

Pearl, Judea (1988) *Probabilistic Reasoning in Intelligent Systems*, Morgan Kaufmann Publishers, San Mateo, CA.

Pearl, Judea (1988) "Embracing causality in default reasoning," *Artificial Intelligence* **35**, 259–271. Reprinted in Shafer & Pearl (1990).

Pearl, Judea (1996) "Causation, explanation, and nonmonotonic temporal reasoning," *Proceedings of TARK-VI*, Morgan Kaufmann, San Mateo, CA, pp. 51–73.

Peirce, Charles Sanders (1885) "On the algebra of logic," *American Journal of Mathematics*, vol. 7, pp. 180–202. Reprinted in Peirce (W) vol. 5, pp..

Peirce, Charles Sanders (1887) "Logical machines," *American Journal of Psychology*, **1**, Nov. 1887, 165–170.

Peirce, Charles Sanders (1891) "Review of *Principles of Psychology* by William James," *Nation*, **53**, 32.

Peirce, Charles Sanders (1897–1906) Manuscripts on existential graphs. Some are reprinted in CP 4.320–410; others are summarized by Roberts (1973).

Peirce, Charles Sanders (1898) *Reasoning and the Logic of Things*, The Cambridge Conferences Lectures of 1898, K. L. Ketner, ed., Harvard University Press, Cambridge, MA, 1992.

Peirce, Charles Sanders (1903) *Pragmatism as a Principle and Method of Right Thinking*, The 1903 Lectures on Pragmatism, by P. A. Turrisi, ed., SUNY Press, Albany, 1997.

Peirce, Charles Sanders (1905) "What Pragmatism Is," *The Monist*, reprinted in CP 5.411–36.

Peirce, Charles Sanders (1906) "Prolegomena to an apology for pragmaticism," *The Monist*, **16**, 492–497.

Peirce, Charles Sanders (1931–1958) *Collected Papers of C. S. Peirce* (CP), C. Hartshorne, P. Weiss, & A. Burks, eds., 8 vols., Harvard University Press, Cambridge, MA.

Peirce, Charles Sanders (1953) *Letters to Lady Welby*, I. C. Leib, ed., Whitlock's Press, New Haven, CT.

Peirce, Charles Sanders (1955) *Philosophical Writings of Peirce*, J. Buchler, ed., Dover, New York.

Peirce, Charles Sanders (1966) *Selected Writings: Values in a Universe of Chance*, P. P. Weiner, ed., Dover, New York.

Peirce, Charles Sanders (1982–1993) *Writings of Charles S. Peirce* (W), vols. 1–5, Indiana University Press, Bloomington, 1982–1993.

Peirce, Charles Sanders (1991) *The Essential Peirce*, vol. 1, N. Houser & C. Kloesel, eds., Indiana University Press, Bloomington.

Pelletier, Francis Jeffry (1990) *Parmenides, Plato, and the Semantics of Not-Being*, University of Chicago Press, Chicago.

Peng, Yun, & James A. Reggia (1990) *Abductive Inference Models for Diagnostic Problem Solving*, Springer-Verlag, New York.

Perez, Sandra, & Anthony Sarris, eds. (1995) *IRDS Conceptual Schema*, Technical Report X3H4/92–003, American National Standards Institute, New York.

Perry, John (1979) "The problem of the essential indexical," *Nous*, **13**, 3–21.

Peterson, Brian J., William A. Andersen, & Joshua Engel (1998) "Knowledge bus: generating application-focused databases from large ontologies," *Proc. 5th KRDB Workshop*, Seattle, WA. Available from http://sunsite.informatik.rwth-aachen.de/Publications/CEUR-WS/Vol-10/.

Peter of Spain or Petrus Hispanus (circa 1239) *Summulae Logicales*, I. M. Bocheński, ed., Marietti, Turin, 1947. Selections translated in Kretzmann & Stump (1988).

Petri, Carl Adam (1962) *Kommunikation mit Automaten*, Ph.D. dissertation, University of Bonn. English translation in technical report RADC-TR-65–377, Griffiss Air Force Base, 1966.

Petrie, Charles J., Jr., ed. (1992) *Enterprise Integration Modeling*, MIT Press, Cambridge, MA.

Petroski, Henry (1985) *To Engineer Is Human*, St. Martin's Press, New York.

Pfeiffer, Heather D., & Timothy E. Nagle, eds. (1993) *Conceptual Structures: Theory and Implementation*, Lecture Notes in AI 754, Springer-Verlag, New York.

Pierce, Benjamin C. (1991) *Basic Category Theory for Computer Scientists*, MIT Press, Cambridge, MA.

Plato, *Theatetus, Sophist*, Harvard University Press, Cambridge, MA.

Poole, D. (1989) "Normality and faults in logic-based diagnosis," *Proceedings of IJCAI-89*, pp. 1304– 1310.

Pople, H. E. (1977) "The formation of composite hypotheses in diagnostic problem solving," *Proceedings of IJCAI '77*, pp. 1030–1037.

Pople, H. (1982) "Heuristic methods for imposing structure on ill-structured problems," in P. Szolovits, ed., *Artificial Intelligence in Medicine*, Westview Press, Boulder, 119–190.

Pople, H. E., J. D. Myers, & R. A. Miller (1975) "DIALOG: a model of diagnostic logic for internal medicine," *Proceedings IJCAI-75*, pp. 848–855.

Porphyry, *On Aristotle's Categories*, translated by S. K. Strange (1992), Cornell University Press, Ithaca, NY, 1992.

Potter, Vincent G. (1997) *Charles S. Peirce on Norms and Ideals*, Fordham University Press, New York.

Przymusinski, Teodor (1991) "Three-valued nonmonotonic formalisms and semantics of logic programs," *Artificial Intelligence* **49:1–3**, 309–343.

Pustejovsky, James (1996) *The Generative Lexicon*, MIT Press, Cambridge, MA.

Putnam, Hilary (1990) *Realism with a Human Face*, Harvard University Press, Cambridge, MA.

Quillian, M. Ross (1966) *Semantic Memory*, PhD Dissertation, Carnegie-Mellon University. Abridged version in Minsky (1968) 227–270.

Quine, Willard Van Orman (1937) "New foundations for mathematical logic," reprinted in Quine (1953), pp. 80–101.

Quine, Willard Van Orman (1948) "On what there is," reprinted in Quine (1953) pp. 1–19.

Quine, Willard Van Orman (1953) *From a Logical Point of View*, 2nd ed., Harvard University Press, Cambridge, MA, 1961.

Quine, Willard Van Orman (1954) "Reduction to a dyadic predicate," *Journal of Symbolic Logic*, **19**. Reprinted in Quine (1995), pp. 224–226.

Quine, Willard Van Orman (1960) *Word and Object*, MIT Press, Cambridge, MA.

Quine, Willard Van Orman (1963) *Set Theory and Its Logic*, rev. ed., Harvard University Press, Cambridge, MA, 1969.

Quine, Willard Van Orman (1972) "Responding to Saul Kripke," reprinted in Quine (1981), pp. 173–174.

Quine, Willard Van Orman (1981) *Theories and Things*, Harvard University Press, Cambridge, MA.

Quine, Willard Van Orman (1992) *Pursuit of Truth*, rev. ed., Harvard University Press, Cambridge, MA.

Quine, Willard Van Orman (1995) *Selected Logic Papers*, enlarged ed., Harvard University Press, Cambridge, MA.

Ramackers, Guus J. (1994) *Integrated Object Modeling*, Thesis Publishers, Amsterdam.

Rao, Anand S., & Norman Y. Foo (1989a) "Formal theories of belief revision," *Proceedings of the First International Conference on Principles of Knowledge Representation and Reasoning*, Morgan Kaufmann Publishers, San Mateo, CA, pp. 369–380.

Rao, Anand S., & Norman Y. Foo (1989b) "Minimal change and maximal coherence: a basis for belief revision and reasoning about actions," *Proceedings of IJCAI-89*.

Rao Anand S., & Michael P. Georgeff (1991) "Modeling rational agents within a BDI architecture," in *Proceedings of the Second International Conference on Principles of Knowledge Representation and Reasoning*, Morgan Kaufmann Publishers, San Mateo, CA, pp. 473–484.

Rao, Anand S., & Michael P. Georgeff (1993) "A model-theoretic approach to the verification of situated reasoning systems," in *Proceedings IJCAI-93*, Chambéry, France.

Rassinoux, Anne-Marie (1994) *Extraction et Représentation de la Connaissance tirée de Textes médicaux*, Thesis no. 2684, Éditions Systèmes et Information, Geneva.

Rational Software Corp. (1997) *UML Semantics*, available at http://www.rational.com/uml.

Reggia, J. A., D. S. Nau, & P. Y. Wang (1983) "Diagnostic expert systems based on a set covering model," *International Journal of Man-Machine Studies* **19:5**, 437–460.

Regoczei, Stephen, & Graeme Hirst (1990) "The meaning triangle as a tool for the acquisition of abstract, conceptual knowledge," *International Journal of Man-Machine Studies* **33**, 505–520.

Reichenbach, Hans (1927) *Philosophie der Raum-Zeit-Lehre*, translated as *The Philosophy of Space and Time* (1957) by M. Reichenbach & J. Freund, Dover Publications, New York.

Reichenbach, Hans (1947) *Elements of Symbolic Logic*, Macmillan, London.

Reiter, Ray (1978) "On closed world data bases," in H. Gallaire & J. Minker, eds., *Logic and Data Bases*, Plenum Press, New York, pp. 55–76.

Reiter, Ray (1980) "A logic for default reasoning," *Artificial Intelligence* **13**, 81–132.

Rescher, Nicholas (1967) *Temporal Modalities in Arabic Logic*, D. Reidel, Dordrecht.

Rescher, Nicholas (1991) *G. W. Leibniz's Monadology*, University of Pittsburgh Press, Pittsburgh.

Rieger, Chuck (1976) "An organization of knowledge for problem solving and language comprehension," *Artificial Intelligence* **7:2**, 89–127.

Rieger, Chuck (1977) "The declarative representation and procedural simulation of causality in physical mechanisms," *Proceedings of IJCAI-77*, pp. 250–256.

Riesbeck, Christopher, & Roger C. Schank (1989) *Inside Case-Based Reasoning*, Lawrence Erlbaum Associates, Hillsdale, NJ.

Roberts, Don D. (1973) *The Existential Graphs of Charles S. Peirce*, Mouton, The Hague.

Robinson, J. Alan (1965a) "A machine oriented logic based on the resolution principle," *Journal of the ACM* **12**, 23–41.

Robinson, J. Alan (1965b) "Automatic deduction with hyperresolution," *International Journal of Computational Mathematics* **1**, 227–234.

Ruspini, Enrique H. (1987) "Epistemic logics, probability, and the calculus of evidence," *Proceedings of IJCAI-87*, pp. 924–931.

Ruspini, Enrique H. (1996) "The semantics of approximate reasoning," in C. H. Chen, ed., *Fuzzy Logic and Neural Network Handbook*, McGraw-Hill, New York, pp. 5.1–5.27.

Russell, Bertrand (1918) "The philosophy of logical atomism," reprinted in B. Russell (1985) *The Philosophy of Logical Atomism*, D. Pears, ed., Open Court, La Salle, IL, pp. 35–155.

Russell, Bertrand (1945) *A History of Western Philosophy*, Simon & Schuster, New York.

Saint-Exupéry, Antoine de (1943) *Le petit prince*, translated by K. Woods as *The Little Prince*, Harcourt Brace Jovanovich, New York.

Sandewall, Erik (1990) "Towards a logic of dynamic frames," Reprinted in Ford & Hayes (1991), pp. 201–217.

Sandewall, Erik (1994) *Features and Fluents*, Clarendon Press, Oxford.

Saussure, Ferdinand de (1916) *Cours de linguistique générale*, translated by W. Baskin (1959) as *Course in General Linguistics*, Philosophical Library, New York.

Scha, Remko (1980) "Distributive, collective, and cumulative quantification," in J. Groenendijk, T. Janssen, & M. Stokhof, eds., *Truth, Interpretation, and Information*, Foris Publications, Dordrecht, pp. 483–512.

Schank, Roger C., ed. (1975) *Conceptual Information Processing*, North-Holland Publishing Co., Amsterdam.

Schank, Roger C. (1982) *Dynamic Memory*, Cambridge University Press, Cambridge, UK.

Schank, Roger C., & Robert P. Abelson (1977) *Scripts, Plans, Goals and Understanding*, Lawrence Erlbaum Associates, Hillsdale, NJ.

Schank, Roger C., Alex Kass, & Christopher K. Riesbeck (1994) *Inside Case-Based Explanation*, Lawrence Erlbaum Associates, Hillsdale, NJ.

Schank, Roger C., Michael Lebowitz, & Lawrence Birnbaum (1980) "An integrated understander," *American Journal of Computational Linguistics* **6**, 13–30.

Schank, Roger C., & Lawrence G. Tesler (1969) "A conceptual parser for natural language," *Proceedings of IJCAI-69*, pp. 569–578.

Schenk, Douglas A., & Peter R. Wilson (1994) *Information Modeling the EXPRESS Way*, Oxford University Press, New York.

Schoppers, Marcel J. (1987) "Universal plans for reactive robots in unpredictable environments," *Proceedings of IJCAI-87*, pp. 852–859.

Schoppers, Marcel J. (1989) "In defense of reaction plans as caches," *AI Magazine* **10:4**, 51–60.

Schröder, Ernst (1890–1895) *Vorlesungen über die Algebra der Logik*, 3 vols., Teubner, Leipzig. Reprinted by Chelsea Publishing Co., Bronx, NY, 1966.

Schröder, Martin (1994) *Erwartungsgestützte Analyse medizinischer Befundungstexte: Ein wissensbasiertes Modell zur Sprachverarbeitung*, Infix Verlag, Sankt Augustin.

Schwitter, Rolf (1998) *Kontrolliertes Englisch für Anforderungsspezifikationen*, Studentdruckerei, Zurich. Available from http://www.ifi.unizh.ch/~schwitter/.

Scott, Dana S. (1970) "Advice on modal logic," in K. Lambert, ed., *Philosophical Problems in Logic*, D. Reidel, Dordrecht.

Scott, Dana S. (1980) "Relating theories of the λ-calculus," in J. P. Seldin & J. R. Hindley, eds., *To H. B. Curry: Essays on Combinatory Logic, Lambda Calculus and Formalism*, Academic Press, New York, pp. 403–450.

Searle, John R. (1980) "Minds, brains, and programs," *Behavioral and Brain Sciences*, **3**, 417–424.

Searle, John R. (1983) *Intentionality*, Cambridge University Press, Cambridge, UK.

Seligman, Jerry, & Lawrence S. Moss (1997) "Situation Theory," in van Bentham & ter Meulen (1997), pp. 239–309.

Selz, Otto (1913) *Über die Gesetze des geordneten Denkverlaufs*, Spemann, Stuttgart.

Selz, Otto (1922) *Zur Psychologie des produktiven Denkens und des Irrtums*, Friedrich Cohen, Bonn.

Sextus Empiricus (1933) *Against the Logicians*, Harvard University Press, Cambridge, MA.

Shafer, Glenn, & Judea Pearl, eds. (1990) *Readings in Uncertain Reasoning*, Morgan Kaufmann Publishers, San Mateo, CA.

Shannon, Claude E. (1948) "The mathematical theory of communication," *Bell System Technical Journal*. Reprinted in C. E. Shannon & W. Weaver, *The Mathematical Theory of Information*, University of Illinois Press, Urbana.

Shapiro, Stuart C. (1979) "The SNePS semantic network processing system," in Findler (1979) pp. 263–315.

Shapiro, Stuart C., & William J. Rapaport (1992) "The SNePS family," in Lehmann (1992) pp. 243–275.

Shortliffe, Edward H. (1976) *Computer-Based Medical Consultations: MYCIN*, American Elsevier, New York.

Simon, Herbert A. (1981) "Otto Selz and information-processing psychology," in N. Frijda & A. D. de Groot, eds., *Otto Selz: His Contribution to Psychology*, Mouton, The Hague.

Simon, Herbert A. (1989) "Human experts and knowledge-based systems," in M. Tokoro, Y. Anzai, & A. Yonezawa, eds., *Concepts and Characteristics of Knowledge-Based Systems*, North-Holland Publishing Co., Amsterdam, pp. 1–21.

Simons, Peter (1987) *Parts: A Study in Ontology*, Clarendon Press, Oxford.

Simons, Peter (1992) *Philosophy and Logic in Central Europe from Bolzano to Tarski*, Kluwer Academic Publishers, Dordrecht.

Slagle, J. R., Gardiner, D. A. and Han, K. (1990) Knowledge specification of an expert system, *IEEE Expert* **5:4**, 29–38.

Smith, Barry, & David Woodruff Smith, eds. (1995) *The Cambridge Companion to Husserl*, Cambridge University Press, Cambridge, UK.

Smith, Brian Cantwell (1982) "Prolog to *Reflections and Semantics in a Procedural Language*," reprinted in Brachman & Levesque (1985) pp. 31–39.

Smith, Brian Cantwell (1996) *On the Origin of Objects*, MIT Press, Cambridge, MA.

Somers, Harold L. (1987) *Valency and Case in Computational Linguistics*, Edinburgh University Press, Edinburgh.

Sowa, John F. (1976) "Conceptual graphs for a database interface," *IBM Journal of Research and Development* **20:4**, 336–357.

Sowa, John F. (1979) "Definitional mechanisms for conceptual graphs," in *Graph Grammars and their Application to Computer Science and Biology*, V. Claus, H. Ehrig, & G. Rozenberg, eds., Springer-Verlag, New York, pp. 426–439.

Sowa, John F. (1984) *Conceptual Structures: Information Processing in Mind and Machine*, Addison-Wesley, Reading, MA.

Sowa, John F. (1988) "Using a lexicon of canonical graphs in a semantic interpreter," in M. Evens, ed., *Relational Models of the Lexicon*, Cambridge University Press, Cambridge, UK, pp. 73–97.

Sowa, John F. (1989) "Knowledge Acquisition by Teachable Systems," in J.P. Martins and E.M. Morgado, eds., *EPIA 89*, Lecture Notes in Artificial Intelligence 390, Springer-Verlag, New York, pp. 381–396.

Sowa, John F. (1990a) "Definitional mechanisms for restructuring knowledge bases," in Z. W. Ras, M. Zemankova, & M. L. Emrich, eds., *Methodologies for Intelligent Systems, 5*, North-Holland Publishing Co., New York, pp. 194–211.

Sowa, John F. (1990b) "Crystallizing theories out of knowledge soup," in Z. W. Ras & M. Zemankova, eds., *Intelligent Systems: State of the Art and Future Directions*, Ellis Horwood, New York, pp. 456–487.

Sowa, John F. (1990c) "Knowledge representation in databases, expert systems, and natural language," in R. A. Meersman, Z. Shi, & C-H. Kung, eds., *Artificial Intelligence in Databases and Information Systems (DS-3)*, North-Holland Publishing Co., Amsterdam, pp. 17–50.

Sowa, John F., ed. (1991a) *Principles of Semantic Networks: Explorations in the Representation of Knowledge*, Morgan Kaufmann Publishers, San Mateo, CA.

Sowa, John F. (1991b) "Towards the expressive power of natural language," in Sowa (1991a), pp. 157–189.

Sowa, John F. (1992a) "Semantic networks," in S. C. Shapiro, ed., *Encyclopedia of Artificial Intelligence*, 2nd ed., Wiley, New York, pp. 1011–1024.

Sowa, John F. (1992a) "Logical structures in the lexicon," in J. Pustejovsky & S. Bergler, eds., *Lexical Semantics and Knowledge Representation*, Lecture Notes in Artificial Intelligence 627, Springer-Verlag, New York, pp. 39–60.

Sowa, John F. (1992b) "Conceptual graphs summary," in Nagle et al. (1992) pp. 3–51.

Sowa, John F. (1993a) "Logical foundations for representing object-oriented systems," *Journal of Experimental and Theoretical AI*, **5:2&3**, 237–261.

Sowa, John F. (1993b) "Lexical structures and conceptual structures," in J. Pustejovsky, ed., *Semantics and the Lexicon*, Kluwer Academic Publishers, Dordrecht, pp. 223–262.

Sowa, John F. (1993c) "Logic-based standards for the conceptual schema," in J. Cuena, ed., *Knowledge Oriented Software Design*, North-Holland Publishing Co., Amsterdam, pp. 251–280.

Sowa, John F. (1995a) "Syntax, semantics, and pragmatics of contexts," in Ellis et al. (1995), pp. 1–15.

Sowa, John F. (1995b) "Top-level ontological categories," *International Journal of Human-Computer Studies*, **43:5/6**, 669–686.

Sowa, John F. (1996) "Processes and Participants," in Eklund et al. (1996), pp. 1–22.

Sowa, John F. (1997a) "Peircean foundations for a theory of context," in Lukose et al. (1997), pp. 41–64.

Sowa, John F. (1997b) "Matching logical structure to linguisierten structure," in N. Houser, D. D. Roberts, & J. Van Evra, eds., *Studies in the Logic of Charles Sanders Peirce*, Indiana University Press, Bloomington.

Sowa, John F. (forthcoming) *Logic: Graphical and Algebraic.*

Sowa, John F., & Eileen C. Way (1986) "Implementing a semantic interpreter for conceptual graphs," *IBM Journal of Research and Development* **30:1**, 57–69.

Sowa, John F., & John A. Zachman (1992a) "A logic-based approach to enterprise integration," in C. J. Petrie, ed., *Enterprise Integration Modeling*, MIT Press, Cambridge, MA, pp. 152–163.

Sowa, John F., & John A. Zachman (1992b) "Extending and formalizing the Framework for Information Systems Architecture," *IBM Systems Journal* **31:3**, 590–616.

Sperber, Dan, & Deirdre Wilson (1986) *Relevance: Communication and Cognition*, Harvard University Press, Cambridge, MA.

Spivey, J. (1992) *The Z Notation: A Reference Manual*, Prentice-Hall International.

Stansifer, Ryan (1992) *ML Primer*, Prentice-Hall, Englewood Cliffs, NJ.

Steele, Thomas B., Jr. (1975) "Data base standardization: a status report," in *Data Base Description*, B. C. M. Douquè & G. M. Nijssen, eds., North-Holland Publishing Co., New York, pp. 183–198.

Stein, Lynn Andrea (1990) "An atemporal frame problem," reprinted in Ford & Hayes (1991), pp. 219–230.

Straub, Pablo A., & Carlos A. Hurtado (1997) "Control in Multi-threaded information systems," in M. V. Zelkowitz, ed., *Advances in Computers*, vol. 45, Academic Press, New York, pp. 1–52.

Sussman, Gerald J., & Drew V. McDermott (1972) *Why Conniving Is Better than Planning*, AI Memo 255A, MIT, Cambridge, MA.

Sussman, Gerald J., Terry Winograd, & Eugene Charniak (1970) "Microplanner Reference Manual," AI Memo 203, MIT, Cambridge, MA.

Talmy, Leonard (1983) "How languages structure space," in H. Pick & L. Acredolo, eds, *Spatial Orientation: Theory, Research, and Application*, New York, Plenum Press, pp. 225–282.

Talmy, Leonard (1996) "The windowing of attention in language," in M. Shibatani & S. Thompson, eds., *Grammatical Constructions: Their Forms and Meaning*, Oxford University Press, Oxford, pp. 235–287.

Tarski, Alfred (1929) "Foundations of the geometry of solids," reprinted in Tarski (1982), pp. 24–29.

Tarski, Alfred (1935) "Der Wahrheitsbegriff in den formalisierten Sprachen," translated as "The concept of truth in formalized languages," in Tarski (1982), pp. 152–278.

Tarski, Alfred (1982) *Logic, Semantics, Metamathematics*, 2nd ed., Hackett Publishing Co., Indianapolis, IN.

Taylor, John R. (1995) *Linguistic Categorization: Prototypes in Linguistic Theory*, Clarendon Press, Oxford.

Tepfenhart, William M., Judith P. Dick, & John F. Sowa, eds. (1994) *Conceptual Structures: Current Practices*, Lecture Notes in AI 835, Springer-Verlag, New York.

Thomason, Richmond H., & David S. Touretzky (1991) "Inheritance theory and relational networks," in Sowa (1991a), pp. 231–266.

Thoreau, Henry David (1854) *Walden, or Life in the Woods*, Beacon Press, Boston, 1997.

Toulmin, Stephen (1958) *The Uses of Argument*, Cambridge University Press, Cambridge, UK.

Trappl, Robert, & Paolo Petta, eds. (1997) *Creating Personalities for Synthetic Actors*, Springer Verlag, New York.

Troelstra, Anne Sjerp (1992) *Lectures on Linear Logic*, CSLI, Stanford, CA.

Turing, Alan (1936) "On computable numbers with an application to the Entscheidungsproblem," reprinted in M. Davis, ed., *The Undecidable*, Raven Press, Hewlett, NY.

van Bentham, Johan, & Alice ter Meulen (1997) *Handbook of Logic and Language*, Elsevier, Amsterdam.

van Eijck, Jan, & Hans Kamp (1997) "Representing discourse in context," in van Bentham & ter Meulen (1997), pp. 179–237.

van Emden, Maarten, & Robert A. Kowalski (1976) "The semantics of predicate logic as a programming language," *Journal of the ACM* **23**, 733–742.

Van Gelder, Allen (1988) *Negation as failure using tight derivations for general logic programs*, in Minker (1988), pp. 149–176.

Velardi, Paola, Maria Teresa Pazienza, & Mario De Giovanetti (1988) "Conceptual graphs for the analysis and generation of sentences," *IBM Journal of Research & Development* **32:2**, 251–267.

Vendler, Zeno (1967) *Linguistics in Philosophy*, Cornell University Press, Ithaca, NY.

Waismann, F. (1952) "Verifiability," in A. Flew, ed., *Logic and Language*, first series, Basil Blackwell, Oxford.

Walker, Adrian, Michael McCord, John F. Sowa, & Walter Wilson (1990) *Knowledge Systems and Prolog*, 2nd ed., Addison-Wesley, Reading, MA.

Warren, David H. D., & Fernando C. N. Pereira (1982) "An efficient easily adaptable system for interpreting natural language queries," *Computational Linguistics* **8:3–4**, 110–122.

Way, Eileen C. (1991) *Knowledge Representation and Metaphor*, Kluwer Academic Publishers, Dordrecht.

Whewell, William (1858) *History of Scientific Ideas*, J. W. Parker & Son, London.

Whitehead, Alfred North (1911) *An Introduction to Mathematics*, H. Holt & Co., New York.

Whitehead, Alfred North (1919) *An Enquiry Concerning the Principles of Natural Knowledge*, Cambridge University Press, Cambridge, UK.

Whitehead, Alfred North (1920) *The Concept of Nature*, Cambridge University Press, Cambridge, UK.

Whitehead, Alfred North (1929) *Process and Reality: An Essay in Cosmology*, corrected edition, D. R. Griffin & D. W. Sherburne, eds., (1978),Free Press, New York 1978.

Whitehead, Alfred North (1937) "Analysis of Meaning," *Philosophical Review*, reprinted in A. N. Whitehead, *Essays in Science and Philosophy*, Philosophical Library, New York, pp. 122–131.

Whitehead, Alfred North (1938) *Modes of Thought*, Macmillan, New York.

Whitehead, Alfred North, & Bertrand Russell (1910) *Principia Mathematica*, 2nd ed., Cambridge University Press, Cambridge, UK, 1925.

Wielinga, Bob, Guus Schreiber, Wouter Jansweijer, Anjo Anewierden, & Frank van Harmelen (1994) "Framework and formalism for representing ontologies," Report DO1b.1-Framework-1.1-UvA-BW+GS+WJ+AA, University of Amsterdam.

Wierzbicka, Anna (1996) *Semantics: Primes and Universals*, Oxford University Press, Oxford.

Wille, Rudolf (1992) "Concept lattices and conceptual knowledge systems," *Computers and Mathematics with Applications*, **23**, 493–515.

Williamson, Timothy (1994) *Vagueness*, Routledge, London.

Winograd, Terry (1972) *Understanding Natural Language*, Academic Press, New York.

Winograd, Terry, & Fernando Flores (1986) *Understanding Computers and Cognition*, Ablex, Norwood, NJ.

Wintraecken, J. J. (1990) *The NIAM Information Analysis Method: Theory & Practice*, Kluwer Academic Publishers, Dordrecht.

Wittgenstein, Ludwig (1922) *Tractatus Logico-Philosophicus*, Routledge & Kegan Paul, London.

Wittgenstein, Ludwig (1953) *Philosophical Investigations*, Basil Blackwell, Oxford.

Woods, William A. (1975) "What's in a link: foundations for semantic networks," in D. G. Bobrow & A. Collins, eds. (1975) *Representation and Understanding*, Academic Press, New York, pp. 35–82.

Woods, William A., & James G. Schmolze (1992) "The KL-ONE Family," *Computers and Mathematics with Applications* **23:2–5**, 133–177. Reprinted in Lehmann (1992).

Wooldridge, Michael J., & Nicholas R. Jennings (1995a) "Agent theories, architectures, and languages: A survey," in Wooldridge & Jennings (1995b), pp. 1 ff.

Wooldridge, Michael J., & Nicholas R. Jennings, eds. (1995b) *Intelligent Agents*, Lecture Notes in AI 890, Springer-Verlag, New York.

Wright, J. R., E. S. Wexelbaum, G. T. Vesonder, K. E. Brown, S. R. Palmer, J. I. Berman, & H. H. Moore (1993) "A knowledge-based configurator that supports sales, engineering, and manufacturing at AT&T Network Systems," *AI Magazine* **14:3**, 69–80.

Yates, Frances A. (1982) *Lull and Bruno*, Routledge & Kegan Paul, London.

Yokoi, Toshio (1995) "The EDR electronic dictionary," *Communications of the ACM* **38:11**, 42–44. For further information, see http://www.iijnet.or.jp/edr/.

Zachman, John A. (1987) "A framework for information systems architecture," *IBM Systems Journal* **26:3**, 276–292.

Zadeh, Lotfi A. (1965) "Fuzzy sets," *Information and Control*, **8**, 338–353.

Zadeh, Lotfi A. (1975) "Fuzzy logic and approximate reasoning," *Synthése*, **30**, 407–428.

Zadeh, Lotfi A. (1986) "A simple view of the Dempster-Shafer theory of evidence and its implication for the rule of combination," *AI Magazine* **7:2**, summer 1986, 85–90.

Name Index

Subject Index

Special Symbols